175
65.7/148

Vladimir Jankélévitch

Series Board

James Bernauer

Drucilla Cornell

Thomas R. Flynn

Kevin Hart

Richard Kearney

Jean-Luc Marion

Adriaan Peperzak

Thomas Sheehan

Hent de Vries

Merold Westphal

Michael Zimmerman

John D. Caputo, *series editor*

Perspectives in
Continental
Philosophy

AARON T. LOONEY

Vladimir Jankélévitch
The Time of Forgiveness

FORDHAM UNIVERSITY PRESS
New York ▪ 2015

Copyright © 2015 Fordham University Press

All rights reserved. No part of this publication may be reproduced, stored in a retrieval system, or transmitted in any form or by any means—electronic, mechanical, photocopy, recording, or any other—except for brief quotations in printed reviews, without the prior permission of the publisher.

Fordham University Press has no responsibility for the persistence or accuracy of URLs for external or third-party Internet websites referred to in this publication and does not guarantee that any content on such websites is, or will remain, accurate or appropriate.

Fordham University Press also publishes its books in a variety of electronic formats. Some content that appears in print may not be available in electronic books.

Visit us online at www.fordhampress.com.

Library of Congress Cataloging-in-Publication Data

Looney, Aaron T.
 Vladimir Jankélévitch : the time of forgiveness / Aaron T. Looney.
  pages cm. — (Perspectives in continental philosophy)
 Summary: "Discusses the moral and metaphysical philosophy of Vladimir Jankélévitch, his reflections on the conditions for forgiveness, especially in light of the Shoah, and the temporality of forgiveness in its relation to creation, history, and memory"— Provided by publisher.
 Includes bibliographical references and index.
 ISBN 978-0-8232-6296-0 (hardback)
 1. Jankélévitch, Vladimir. 2. Forgiveness. I. Title.
 B2430.J34L65 2015
 194—dc23
                                                                    2014016468

Printed in the United States of America

17 16 15   5 4 3 2 1

First edition

In Loving Memory of J. J. Looney,
P.-G. Schwesig, and G. G. Olsen

Contents

Acknowledgments   *xi*

    Introduction: In the Margins   *1*

1   **First Philosophy**   *12*
    Wholly Other: Creation   13
    Intervals and Instants   28
    Intuition   30
    Two Sources of Morality   34
    Good Will: The Future of Duty   39

2   **Apophatic Approaches**   *44*
    The Decay of Time and Forgetfulness   45
    Ataraxia and Apathy   51
    Megalopsychia   52
    The Excuse   55
    Total or Intellective Excuse   56
    Sungnômê (Understanding)   59
    Partitive Excuse: Between Indulgence and Severity   66
    Pardon and Mercy   70

3   **The Temporality of Human Existence and Action**   *77*
    Irreversibility   78
    Irrevocability   84
    Imprescriptibility: Axiology versus Chronology   89

4   Translating Resentment   **93**
      Aristotle's Nemesis   94
      Butler's Sermons   97
      Nietzsche's Doubling   102
      Scheler's Deferral   109
      Jankélévitch's Protest and Fidelity   119
      The Duration of Justice: Values and Singularities   122
      Missing Humanity   129

5   The Inexcusable and the Unforgivable   **136**
      Freedom and Wickedness   137
      The Correlation of Punishment and Forgiveness   155
      The Organ-Obstacle   164
      More Stupid Than Wicked, More Wicked Than Stupid   164
      Penultimate Acts: Love Is as Strong as Evil   168

6   Love and Justice   **171**
      Two Absolutes   171
      Origins, Ends, and Interruptions   176
      Im/pure Gifts   187
      Gratitude and Benevolence   193
      Dissonances of Love   197
      Normative Ideal or Impossibility?   202

7   Repentance: Concerning Unconditionality   **208**
      Philosophical Conversions   211
      Theological Returns: Levinas's Talmud Readings   215
      The Coming of the Messiah   216
      Motivations for Changing the Past   219
      In My Hands?   223
      Becoming Other: The Paradox of Repentance   227
      Hartmann, Sartre, and Kierkegaard   229
      A Self-Healing of the Soul: Max Scheler   232
      Jankélévitch's Remorse   238
      Asymmetrical Reciprocity   248
      Negotiations   256

8   What Remains   **261**
      Biblical Metaphors   262
      As If . . .   266
      Coincidentia Oppositorum   269

Notes   **281**

Bibliography   **357**

Index   **373**

Acknowledgments

One does not have to write a book about forgiveness to acknowledge a need to be forgiven. The process of research and writing, regardless of topic, is reason enough. It is a solitary, time-consuming endeavor. It is simultaneously an endeavor that leads to many others, to thinkers of different times, languages, and places within the rich and multifaceted intellectual history we have inherited. The publication of this work extends the contact with others in ways that will involve and surpass me. I thank the people at Fordham University Press, especially the late Helen Tartar, Thomas Lay, Eric Newman, and Teresa Jesionowski, for helping me realize this project. This publication represents a revision of my Doktorarbeit submitted to the Philosophy Faculty at Eberhard Karls University, Tübingen, Germany, in the summer of 2011. Johannes Brachtendorf and Reiner Wimmer have accompanied and guided me from the very beginning, and I am grateful to them for their conversations and critiques. I have learned from many people, both academic and otherwise, friends and relative strangers, and to all of my teachers I extend a word of gratitude. Without my family, this book would not have been able to take its present form: Special thanks to my mother, Dr. Sandra Looney, a model of teaching and giving; to my aunt, Florence Olsen and my uncle Dr. Rodney Olsen, who not only helped shaped my writing but also provided the sketch of Jankélévitch for the jacket; and finally, to my wife, Judith, in particular, and our two daughters, Hilda and Ellinor, for their unconditional love and the gift of time.

Introduction: In the Margins

There is a time of forgiveness. Such a time may arise when the acuteness of the pain stemming from a personal or moral injury has abated, when a relationship that is dear outweighs the hurt of an offense, or when a decision is made to put an end to the cycles of violence and revenge. In a grammatical analogy, forgiveness may be said to be like a period, marking an end—an end to feelings of rancor and resentment toward another. This pointed end gives way to a new beginning, and ideally, this new beginning allows for the parties involved in strife to renew their relationship under the sign of reconciliation. The renewal of relationships may entail the restoration of a previous relation fractured by betrayal, or it may entail a new relationship that does not restoratively return to a previous condition but rather establishes open possibilities in positive directions. In a moral framework, the time of forgiveness asks about the time *for* forgiveness. It asks if the time to forgive is now; it asks whether I *should* forgive the other person and whether I *can* forgive the other person.

Through an equivocation of the genitives, the time of forgiveness equally inquires into the temporal structure of the act of forgiveness. If forgiveness potentially ends embitterment and embattlement and opens onto new possibilities, it is fundamentally positioned between the past and the future. In fact, it marks the qualitative transition from the one to the other. As a rupture of what has been, it allows something new to emerge. It breaks with the past and brings forth the future, announcing a fresh start for both the one who forgives and the one who is forgiven. It thus releases one from the burden of the past and lets the past pass, opening onto something new, potentially even a wholly other order not contingent on the past. Yet forgiveness relates to the past insofar as it is a response to a personal injury or moral offense. But it severs the chain of violence because it represents a free response of simultaneous condemnation and liberation that is undetermined by the offense. It therefore allows one to leave the past behind or perhaps even transform its meaning in the light of forgiveness.

The French Jewish philosopher Vladimir Jankélévitch (1903–1985) has addressed these questions at the heart of forgiveness with exceptional subtlety and profundity. He has been called "one of the most singular voices of twentieth-century French philosophy," whose writings exhibit "originality, breadth, and beauty."[1] And yet in the history of twentieth-century philosophy he has remained a relatively marginal figure whose name and works are largely unknown in the English-speaking world. Jankélévitch's inimitable style, predilection for neologisms, penchant for irony, and the rhythm of his prose undoubtedly resist the efforts of translation. His style is poetic and sinuous. His prose, like his speech, as Emmanuel Levinas remembered it, is sporadic and spontaneous: "In the perfect clarity of the statement, each word sprang up new, as if unforeseeable in that which preceded it. As if, here, thought never left the flowing waters of its spontaneity, mistrusting the facile aspects of language, its verbal habits and its rhetoric."[2] His originality therefore consists in the art of re-creation. His texts read like works of art, even musical pieces, which exude inspiration, alacrity, joy, and a pure elegance that he combines with the diligent and patient labor of close textual interpretation. From one work to the next, Jankélévitch interweaves topics and themes, reviving previous texts, rewriting, repeating, and complementing what he has written before as if one book overflowed the closures of its borders into the next—simultaneously saturated and incomplete.[3]

One of Jankélévitch's achievements is the correlation of his style to his subject matter. Against its scientific self-understanding, philosophy, for Jankélévitch, is preeminently poetic. It is an act and a way of life more than a discourse. His poetics thus enacts a *poiesis*, a making or doing, which is always a remaking and a redoing, and the poetic grace with which he writes points to the moment of poetic grace itself. In this respect, his philosophy of music serves as more than an illustration of the thought of this talented pianist and philosopher of music. For music, Jankélévitch claims, moves us beyond explanation, and, like love and the good, it is an act that is to be done, even in the form of attentive listening. Music is ineffable and efficacious. Its character is transitive. Its message is not something inside of it to be uncovered or decoded; rather, its uncontainable movement moves us in body and soul.[4] Jankélévitch thus interprets efforts to explain music through technical analysis or hermeneutics, for example, as flights from this lived experience. Yet he does not therefore advocate a mystical silence with respect to the sublime. Although that which we intimate in its manner and occasion cannot be made into a content or subject of discourse, it inspires our understanding to discursively comprehend what it merely glimpses in a moment. In other words, the lived experience of the moment that escapes our understanding engenders in us a desire to understand what we cannot grasp but only intimate (*entrevision*). Jankélévitch's revisitation of themes, his interruptions, circumlocutions, repetitions, and the dynamic spiraling of his voice can be seen as performances. His writings are performative and material acts that interact with the intentionality of his reader to position and inspire him or her to glimpse the ineffable. In a dual sense, then, Jankélévitch's philosophy is a philosophy of desire and inspiration.

As Arnold Davidson comments, "Anyone who could entitle one of his books *Le Je-ne-sais-quoi et le presque-rien* [*The I-know-not-what and the almost-nothing*] is not your everyday academic philosopher." But this title is also surprisingly precise and conceptually rich. The "I-know-not-what" does not mean that one simply does not know something. Rather, it expresses a minimal knowledge, or, more precisely, a knowledge of facticity, that-ness, what Jankélévitch calls *quoddity*. Jankélévitch uses words to dance around a point without extension, an instant without interval, a tangency without touch. Whether in his analyses of charm (*charme*), genius, charity (*charité*), love, or forgiveness, Jankélévitch's philosophy focuses not on the extension of being but on emergent effectivity. Each of these ideas, which are difficult to locate and thus identify, represents "an animating and mobilizing principle." They are poetic, creative, or effective principles.[5] They do not have an essence, are not phenomena, or potential objects of cognition. They move us; they awaken, quicken, and enlighten concrete human life. In other words, they are almost nothing, but they are not nothing. They are in between being and nothingness. Like Plotinus, one of his main influences, Jankélévitch establishes a kind of immanent transcendence in which humans have something in them that is greater than themselves even if they do not know what it is. It is something in them but also something that is radically other than them, which remains irreducible to them.[6] In a glancing point of contact, it comes to them as an appearing and disappearing spark of grace that makes a qualitative difference.

Discursively, this point without extension can be approached only apophatically and asymptotically. Jankélévitch's philosophy thus demonstrates a proximity to the early church fathers and especially to mysticism. He understands the *via negativa* as the sole systematic way to handle what is so simple, so other, so otherwise, and transcendent that it is incomprehensible. But unlike both the church fathers and the mystics, he does not operate on a theological premise. His apophaticism does not defer at the end of the road to an ontological positing of God, nor does he suggest that the finite human individual can enjoy a fusion or identity with the absolute.[7] Instead, the eternal and absolute remain inaccessible. The finite limits of human corporeality and human cognition constrict the experience of the absolute to a given instant as an intimation or intuition that does not yield any substantive knowledge.

Robert Maggiori thus characterizes Jankélévitch's agnostic philosophy as the sole representative of an "existentialistic spiritualism" whose forefathers include Schelling, Kierkegaard, and Bergson.[8] Indeed, Jankélévitch wrote his doctoral thesis on Schelling's later philosophy, and his first publication was on Henri Bergson, an acclaimed work that remains a standard in the field.[9] But the characterization of Jankélévitch as an existentialistic spiritualist is not without qualification. For he resists the "caricature" of Bergson as an "eminent spiritualist" and insists that Bergsonism is an avant-garde philosophy. As Davidson points out, Jankélévitch adopts from Bergson, rather than any specific doctrine, "a certain attitude and conception of philosophy."[10] As Jankélévitch explains in an interview:

> The philosophy of Bergson . . . is a conception of life that demands an inner reform; a thoroughly new method, such is its exacting philosophical intuition. It demands a new form of thought and cannot be approached like the others. Bergson always said that philosophy was not an arrangement of concepts but an original intuition. It is the function of the philosophical deed that is in question. To the extent that Bergsonism demands an inner renewal, it is a kind of wisdom, a conception of life. Intuition is not only a new mode of knowledge, but a new mode of being and of essential union with other beings. It brings responses to questions posed in life.[11]

This concentration on questions posed in life corresponds to Jankélévitch's emphasis on the individual person, his or her action and commitment, as well as his conception of philosophy as irreducible to a constructed system of concepts. In his brief essay reflecting on a phrase that Bergson repeatedly invokes, "Do Not Listen to What They Say, Look at What They Do," Jankélévitch claims that "only the person who acts—hero, saint, or poet—makes us want to resemble him." In the place of a conception of freedom as a freedom of choice in thought and speech, Jankélévitch associates freedom with the act and commitment. "That's it," he writes, "to be committed, and nothing else . . . to commit oneself by an immediate and primary act, by an effective and drastic act, by a serious act of the whole person; not to adhere halfheartedly but to convert passionately to the truth, that is to say, with one's entire soul, like Plato's liberated captives." Such is the mark, he states, of the "simple soul, that is to say, the serious and sincere soul."[12]

Jankélévitch's philosophy is a philosophy of concrete life. In this sense, it is an ethical philosophy. He is not interested in uncovering the rational foundations of moral norms and values, for the establishment of universal norms remains too abstract, too rule-based, and too removed from concrete, situated subjective existence. Wiard Raveling explains that morality for Jankélévitch is autonomous and does not require the legitimating blessing of analytical reason. Jankélévitch claims instead that ethical demands and attitudes are prerational. The instance of morality is not rational thought but conscience. Consequently, the task of morality arises ever anew, and this task is always directed at "me."[13] For the good, as Jankélévitch reiterates, always remains to do. In this sense, his ethics is less of a moral philosophy than an explication of the call of conscience to love the other and to will the well-being of the other.[14]

In many respects, Jankélévitch's life can be seen as a living testament to the call of conscience and the call to commitment and action. In 1939 he was mobilized in the war against Germany and was injured in 1940. Upon the Nazi occupation of France, his citizenship, along with that of all naturalized French Jews, was revoked. He subsequently fled to Toulouse, where he took up a teaching position at the university and joined the Resistance, writing for an anti-Nazi, anti-Vichy organization called the Mouvement nationale contre le racisme. Even after he no longer could officially teach at the university, he organized secret lectures, and his writings were circulated by students underground. He lamented that because of hesitation, egoism, and cowardice the majority of intellectuals did not join the Resistance, and he resented the fact that those who deliberated and reflected on the situations incurred by the war both outnumbered and overshadowed those who actively resisted the reign of racist regimes.[15]

In 1951, Jankélévitch returned to normal academic life, having been appointed to the chair of moral philosophy at the Sorbonne. He entered the public debates in 1964–65 surrounding the question of statutory limits with regard to crimes against humanity. He argued that crimes against humanity are not only irreversible but also irrevocable and that the moral axiological plane is heterogeneous to chronology or the simple passing of time. In both written and spoken word, he defended the imprescriptibility of such crimes and rejected the notion that they could be subject to statutory limits. His engagement was also manifest in his support of the student revolution of 1968. He was one of the few professors whom the students listened to; he sympathized with their efforts to change things in the world.[16] Moreover, he explored the margins within the academic setting, holding lectures in moral philosophy that were attended not only by philosophy students but also by students of other disciplines and interested persons outside of academia. For more than twenty-five years, his Monday lectures were broadcast over Radio-Sorbonne. He was less concerned with the acknowledgment of his philosophical peers—though the general lack of acknowledgment invariably pained him—and more concerned with those people in the margins or outside of academic philosophy who cultivated a speculative curiosity and were interested in ideas, analysis, and discussion.[17] Jankélévitch's focus on the philosophical deed and on concrete existence thus oriented his teaching and led him to take on the responsibility of a public intellectual.

Beyond the fact that his target audience was outside of the strictly academic purview, beyond his dedication to unfashionable topics of civic morality such as fidelity, love, forgiveness, and bad conscience—even beyond his enchanting and ecstatic style and his affinity for invoking opera works and such marginal figures within the history of philosophy as Baltasar Gracián, François Fénelon, and Lev Shestov—the repercussions of the war were largely responsible for the subsequent marginalization of Jankélévitch's philosophy. Postwar French philosophy was and still is dominated by the German philosophies of Friedrich Nietzsche and Martin Heidegger. In the wake of the rise to prominence of these philosophies, Bergson's philosophy fell into disrepute. But even though Jankélévitch was heavily influenced by Bergson, he did not share Bergson's optimism or his emphasis on continuity and unity. More important, however, because of his experiences during the war and the horrendous crimes of the Nazis, Jankélévitch made the conscious effort to purge his life and his work of German language, culture, and philosophy. This purging was no superficial matter for the man who had not only learned German but who had become very knowledgeable about German culture and could even be considered a pioneer in the convergence between French and German cultures. His father, Samuel, was the primary translator of Freud's works into French, and he also translated works by Hegel and Schelling. Jankélévitch himself was a great admirer of Novalis, Schelling, and Schumann. But his refusal to engage in recent German philosophy alienated him from mainstream postwar French thought. And since he made his refusal into "a philosophical and existential dogma," the discrepancy between Jankélévitch and the changing zeitgeist became ever greater.[18] This remove from mainstream intellectual tendencies undoubtedly had to do with his individual style and his approach to philosophy, which made him suspicious of groups and rigid schools of thought at a time in France when, as he maintains, "there [was] room only for herds: Marxists, Catholics, existentialists." But it was Jankélévitch's unreconciled and irreconcilable resentment toward Germany and German culture that first and foremost led him to become a relatively isolated figure on the French intellectual scene.[19]

In the light of this discrepancy between his work and the zeitgeist, Jankélévitch, like another thinker of the margins, Jacques Derrida, held two equal and opposing convictions concerning the future of his writings. In the summer before his death, Derrida spoke in an interview of a "double-feeling" or a dual conviction of contradictory hypotheses. He claimed that perhaps readers have yet to truly read his works, which will first have their chance at a later time; or, on the contrary, perhaps nothing of his will remain and that he will soon be forgotten.[20] Similarly, in a letter to the German Wiard Raveling at the end of his life, Jankélévitch wrote that he would speak for the last time in his book *Le Paradoxe de la morale*, for why should he insist on speaking when the world was largely deaf to his words and to his voice.[21] To this resignation is opposed a comment he once made to his friend Louis Beauduc: Jankélévitch claimed, "I am writing for the twenty-first century."[22] Although Derrida was more well known during their lives, Jankélévitch and Derrida share this joint pessimism and hope for surviving themselves in their works. Jankélévitch's positive vision seems to be coming true as the numerous recent translations of his works into English and German as well as the prominence of his writings on forgiveness in the books of Derrida and Paul Ricoeur, for example, testify.

It is my intention to bring to light the introspective power and verbal brilliance of this thinker of our times and thus to contribute to a future that should not come without an awareness of the insights and manner of his philosophy. Although I focus on his understanding of forgiveness, I attempt to embed this understanding in the contours of his general philosophy derived from works that have not yet been translated into English. Since it is his own words and his unique speech that should be heard, I have frequently quoted Jankélévitch at length. Simultaneously, I do not shy away from subjecting his philosophy to a systematization required for explication. Thus, I attempt to remain faithful to Jankélévitch's intentions and his style while risking a certain infidelity that, as he claims, is an intrinsic aspect of fidelity. Beyond the central place of his analysis of forgiveness in his philosophy, I engage Jankélévitch's reflections on forgiveness with other thinkers both contemporary and historical and from both continental philosophy and moral analytical philosophy. Inspired by what

Jankélévitch opens in the idea of forgiveness, I endeavor to outline what forgiveness gives us to think.

Shaped by the Shoah and his experiences n the French Resistance, Jankélévitch approaches forgiveness in its historical, political, and moral complexity. After the Shoah, the concept of forgiveness must be treated anew, for its possibility and its moral validity have become problematized by the concrete events of history. In the shadow of the crimes of the twentieth century, it is, first of all, necessary that philosophy shoulder the task of reevaluating the idea of forgiveness.[23] Writing both as a Jew and as a philosopher but not as a Jewish philosopher, Jankélévitch takes up this task with an integrity and earnestness both compelling and realistic. I explicate the philosophical basis of Jankélévitch's understanding of forgiveness, showing particularly how it is grounded in his conceptions of time and paradox.

The centrality of time in the works of Jankélévitch illuminates, on the one hand, the temporal character of forgiveness that is usually overlooked. Influenced by the Jewish and especially the Christian traditions, forgiveness in his meditations constitutes what Paul Ricoeur calls "the horizon common to memory, history, and forgetting."[24] This common horizon drawn by the idea of forgiveness offers the platform for analyzing the relationship between history and freedom. Forgiveness decides the problematic of liberation, informing the human relation to time and to the past.[25] Thus, through forgiveness, Jankélévitch ventures a rethinking of such fundamental issues as memory, freedom, history, and time.

On the other hand, the time of forgiveness implies the question whether there can be a moral or a social-political compulsion for forgiving, which brings to a close the searing wound of a history of war and terror. As Jankélévitch personally and provocatively asks, "Has the time come to forgive, or at least to forget?"[26] Working from the atrocities of the Shoah, his study of forgiveness is not limited to the historical question of whether to forgive after Auschwitz. As a metonym for the unforgivable, Auschwitz constitutes the limit-experience of forgiveness. Jankélévitch paradoxically suggests that although nothing is impossible for forgiveness, forgiveness may not be able to overcome some crimes. He states that although there is no unforgivable act or person, there are acts that are inexcusable, and it is precisely those acts that are inexcusable that call for forgiveness. With his notion of the *organ-obstacle*, however, he shows how the inexcusable that forgiveness is called to overcome may indeed become the obstacle to forgiveness.

I examine, therefore, his two works on forgiveness, "Pardonner?" ("Should We Pardon Them?") and *Le Pardon* (*Forgiveness*) to demonstrate their argumentative unity. He describes *Forgiveness* as a "book of philosophy" and

"Should We Pardon Them?" as "simple, very aggressive, [and] very polemical." In *Le Pardon* (published in 1967), Jankélévitch draws out an ethics that he claims "could be qualified as hyperbolical, for which forgiveness is the highest commandment."[27] In "Pardonner?" (published in 1971 but originally based on an essay titled "L'Imprescriptible" from 1965, which itself has its origins in a letter to the newspaper *Le Monde*, published on January 3, 1965), he makes a seemingly contrary assertion.[28] Addressing proposals that statutory limits be placed on Nazi war crimes, he observes that the history of forgiveness came to a close at Auschwitz.[29] "Forgiveness," he writes in that essay, "died in the concentration camps."[30] As Arnold Davidson contends, Jankélévitch's formulations in this essay, "with all of their starkness, still constitute one of the most morally powerful texts ever written about Nazi atrocities, a permanent contribution, the equal of unequaled works like Primo Levi's *The Drowned and the Saved*. Its philosophical force, and the questions one confronts in reading it, are no less vivid today than they were when it was first published."[31] Consequently, it is not as if he wrote his essay as an actor, a Jew victimized by the atrocities of Nazi Germany, and his philosophical book as a spectator, distanced from actual events. For he philosophically disavows such a separation.

One of Jankélévitch's main points of contention at the time of composing his essay "Should We Pardon Them?" is the lack of remorse, the absence of gestures of repentance, offers of reparations, or requests for forgiveness on the side of the perpetrators. In demanding that forgiveness be requested and thus subsequent to some form of repentance, Jankélévitch follows a logic that is not merely a "logic of circumstance" because, as Derrida remarks, "it picks up on the strongest, the most strongly traditional, logic of the religious and spiritualist semantics of forgiveness, which grants it when there is repentance, confession, a request for forgiveness, a capacity to expiate, to redeem oneself, and so forth." The hyperbolical ethics inspired by the Jewish-Christian tradition, therefore, is at odds with the primary logic of this tradition, and the hyperbolical ethics of Jankélévitch's *Forgiveness* "*both* lies in the wake of this tradition *and* is incompatible with it."[32] The tension between unconditional or pure forgiveness and conditional forgiveness, however, does not trace the difference between Jankélévitch's two works as Derrida and others suggest. Rather, even in his exposition of pure forgiveness, Jankélévitch remains insistent on the condition that forgiveness be requested. This tension between unconditional forgiveness and conditional forgiveness thus marks the tension inherent in the Abrahamic traditions and in Jankélévitch's treatment of forgiveness. Can pure forgiveness be conditioned by the petition and by repentance?

In his book *Forgiveness*, Jankélévitch portrays the purity of the idea of forgiveness, proceeding negatively in the manner of an apophatic method. Through this method, he examines what he calls forms of "simili-forgiveness" or "apocryphal forgiveness": replacement acts that often can serve as forgiveness because they, too, put an end to a situation that is critical, tense, or abnormal.[33] Jankélévitch's method is negative because forgiveness is not only difficult to ask for and grant; it is also difficult, if not impossible, to conceptually grasp. The negative foil of these apocryphal forms points to a suprarational forgiveness, free from hidden motivations, rewarding returns to the self, or remnant reservations or ressentiments. As in negative theology, the *via negativa* paves the way both theoretically and practically for the *via eminentiae*, which indicates the eminence or height of forgiveness. Jankélévitch concedes, however, that pure forgiveness has perhaps never been granted in the concrete acts of forgiveness.[34] He demonstrates how the purity of the instant is corrupted by its extension in time and consciousness and thus how human forgiveness is always laden with traces of impurity. The idea of pure forgiveness therefore serves Jankélévitch as a normative ideal. But beyond the immanent critique of acts of forgiveness, the idea of pure forgiveness also allows for critique when forgetting, acceptance, excuse, or even reconciliation are invoked under the guise of forgiveness. To a large degree, the seeming contradictions between his polemical essay on the public handling of Nazi war crimes and his philosophical treatise on forgiveness can be resolved by distinguishing between what he sees commended or performed in the name of forgiveness and the idea of pure forgiveness itself.

For Jankélévitch, pure forgiveness is an event that is tied to the rupture of the instant of creation. He claims that it is a limit-experience (*expérience-limite*), indicating the "almost-nothing" character of the instant in its very occurrence.[35] But this limit-experience also indicates that forgiveness is at the limits of human power. At this limit, forgiveness is both beyond human power and at the outer reaches of human power. It constitutes the almost divine response to the human capacity for evil, for humans, Jankélévitch maintains, are capable of extraordinary wickedness, and, like forgiveness, the freedom to commit evil acts cannot be understood but rather marks the limits of our understanding. Confronted with evil, humans are thus faced, according to Jankélévitch, with the moral dilemma of a choice between justice and love. Although Jankélévitch elucidates a conception of forgiveness that highlights its extralegal and extrajudicial character, he simultaneously recognizes that at times humans must make a decision between the absolute imperatives to either forgive evil or to actively and even violently resist it and seek its prosecution in the name of justice. More broadly conceived, Jankélévitch understands this aporia as the moral choice between the hyperbolic love of the other and the accordance of justice to him or her along the lines of universality and reciprocity.

But Jankélévitch uncovers a further aporia between the power of forgiveness and the power of evil. Echoing the psalmist of the Song of Songs (8:6) for whom "love is as strong as death," he insists that forgiveness is as strong as evil, but evil is conversely as strong as forgiveness. So although the imperative of love informs the response of forgiveness in the face of evil, Jankélévitch undermines any unwavering certainty of love's victory. The overcoming of evil through love always represents a fragile finality. As Jankélévitch writes, "Between the absolute of the law of love and the absolute of vicious liberty there is a tear that cannot be entirely undone." And for this tear, he finds no closing or reconciling suture. Instead, he confesses that "I have not attempted to reconcile the irrationality of evil with the omnipotence of love. Forgiveness is as strong as evil, but evil is as strong as forgiveness."[36] Consequently, Jankélévitch situates human existence in its moral complexity, dissonance, and temporal openness. His philosophy on forgiveness is therefore not a philosophy of forgiveness. His philosophy is rather taut in the oscillating tension between two equal philosophical beliefs: "I believe in the immensity of forgiveness, in its supernaturality, and I believe in wickedness [*mechanité*]."[37] In Jankélévitch's philosophy, this tear between absolutes remains unsewn and leaves us without a final word.

Jankélévitch treats forgiveness as an exceptional act. In his moral philosophy, forgiveness constitutes an exception to the rule of law and the rules of justice and morality. Rather than attenuating the paradoxes involved in forgiveness, he exposes the aporias and emphasizes the need for negotiations between the spontaneity of forgiveness and reason in the form of moral and legal systems. While unfolding the idea of forgiveness, Jankélévitch never loses sight of the difficulty of forgiveness within the human condition.

1

First Philosophy

The title of Vladimir Jankélévitch's first major work is *Philosophie première*. Traditionally, a first philosophy provides the cornerstone on which the rest of a thinker's philosophy is constructed either upward in the architectonics of systematic structures or outward in concentric circles extending from the initial pulse of inspiration at the epicenter. Jankélévitch is fond of citing Henri Bergson, who wrote that a philosopher of value has said only one thing and the rest of his life and work is dedicated to that single point.[1] Or more poignantly, Jankélévitch's philosophy follows Bergson's insight that there is "something simple, infinitely simple, so extraordinarily simple that the philosopher has never succeeded in saying it. And that is why he has spoken his entire life."[2] Jankélévitch's first philosophy is an introduction to a philosophy of the "almost [*presque*]" and is dedicated to the idea of creation. The "almost" forms a third category between being and nothingness. It is, therefore, not ontology that constitutes first philosophy or epistemology, because that which is almost is almost-not. As Jankélévitch observes, it is almost something and almost nothing; it is not a datum or an object of consciousness. Instead, it puts the primacy of consciousness into question because the "almost" cannot be thoroughly grasped and, consequently, is not conducive to the order, definitions, conceptual constructions, and categories of systems. All of these depend on being.

In this sense, Jankélévitch exhibits a parallel to Heidegger. Both criticize the history of philosophy as a history of metaphysics or ontotheology, and both seek to explicate the origin of being that ontologically differs from all beings.³ But whereas Heidegger believes that the history of philosophy has neglected the question of being, Jankélévitch believes that philosophy has lost sight of the notion of creation. As his friend and student Lucien Jerphagnon comments, Jankélévitch is one of the few philosophers who has observed the Jewish contribution to metaphysics, namely *Beresit bara Elohim* (In the beginning God created) (Gen. 1:1).⁴ First philosophy, according to Jankélévitch, is thus metaphysics, but it is a philosophy of effectivity, of setting (*poser*), of action, and of doing. It is a philosophy of creation and re-creation. It is also, therefore, a metaphysics that serves as a guide for morals, not in the sense of a mimesis of the ideas inscribed ideally in the nature of reality but in the sense of a mimesis of decision and action itself. And since it is difficult—even impossible—to adequately comprehend and speak about that which is pure act and not substance and which, moreover, provides the condition of comprehension and speech, Jankélévitch's first philosophy is largely a negative philosophy—a philosophy that speaks of one thing only but in many ways and from various approaches because it is that which cannot be wholly said.

Wholly Other: Creation

Jankélévitch divides his metaphysics into the metaempirical and metalogical. He is critical of Aristotle's metaphysics not because it follows physics but because it represents a discourse of definition, which, in Jankélévitch's eyes, testifies to its inherently secondary character: It simply announces and explicates the essence of what already is. Aristotle's metaphysics exemplarily represents a hypothetical metaphysics in Jankélévitch's eyes because Aristotle does not deal with the *fact* of being but proceeds from being. His unconcern with the *einai* allows him to focus on the universal predicate of the *on* and the *ousia* of this being, the essential being (*ens*) of this being.⁵ Although Aristotle establishes the unmoved mover as the source and beginning of all movement, Jankélévitch detects in this originary being the same characteristics as the attributes of a triangle, for example. There is not an absolute beginning or an absolute end but grounds of reason, which are eternal: eternal grounds of reason. One arrives through such hypothetical metaphysics at the order of rationality and intellection—the order of the universal, eternal, and necessary. Although Jankélévitch recognizes the distinction between the intellectual order and the empirical order of individual existents, he misses a metaphysical earnestness that posits a wholly other order to the intellectual order. Moreover, he refuses to reduce the wholly other to a mere difference in degree to the already known order or the order of knowability itself. In this respect, his language of a "wholly other order" is misleading, first of all, because it insinuates an "order" that as such is always already an order of intelligibility and, second, because its wholly otherness seems to indicate what Hegel would call "bad infinity" or a contingent reversal of what is finite, knowable, and so on. What Jankélévitch misses in the history of metaphysics and what he intends to express in the wholly other is a notion of radical transcendence and the beyond (*epekeina*).

Jankélévitch witnesses certain traces of transcendence within the philosophical tradition, however, particularly in Plato's good beyond being and beyond essences pronounced in the sixth book of the *Republic*. Like Levinas, Jankélévitch takes this passage to be decisive for an ethics that is not ontologically grounded but is oriented by the desire for the good.[6] Jankélévitch, however, is much more inclined than Levinas to embrace the suprarationality and even irrationality of this move. Both of them sketch an ethics that can be described as hyperbolic. The good beyond being is hyperbole! Indeed, on hearing Socrates tell of the good beyond being and beyond essence, his dialogue partner Glaucon exclaims that it is *daimonic hyperbole*—an exaggeration, a supernatural excess.[7] It is toward the wonderful and supernatural that Jankélévitch looks to orient his ethical vision, but it is a vision that for this very reason is filled with absence. It is composed of desire (*Eros*) and could be said to be daimonic in the sense of the daimonic conscience of Socrates, on the one hand, and, the daimon herself of the *Symposium*, Diotima, on the other hand. The former allows Socrates to sacrifice himself, and the latter narrates the restless, godlike, daimonic character of love. It is consequently no wonder that Jankélévitch takes as the hallmark of his ethics a pure love that is willing to sacrifice itself for the other—an ethics that is hyperbolic and inexhaustible.

Jankélévitch doubts, however, that the idea of the good according to Plato is really of a wholly other order. Plato takes a much more guarded stance toward daimonic hyperbole and does not seem convinced of such hyperontic majesty or the infinite transcendence of the *epekeina*. Already in book 7 of the *Republic*, Socrates says that the good is the brightest and best of being.[8] And even in the context of the good beyond being, Socrates identifies the absolute good and the absolute beautiful with the idea of essence and as that which is.[9] For Plato that which most truly is is the idea of all of the things that can be subsumed under it. The single idea of the many things that are considered beautiful or good is the essence of those things, and the essence is that which most truly is. The world of the many participates in that of ideas and essences. Therefore, Plato's doctrine of participation entails that the philosopher, the lover of wisdom, is distinguished from the philodoxer, the lover of opinion, only by degree, just as the appearances in the world of images and shadows are less real and have less being than the ideas.[10] Platonism, according to Jankélévitch, is, therefore, too wary and simultaneously too optimistic. It is too wary of appearance because it does not allow for a trustworthy appearance, and it is too optimistic because the appearance only requires essentialization. It acts as if the intelligible is somehow written with invisible ink onto the sensible, which then only requires the dialectic to read through it. It is clear that appearance is not the essence, but, for Plato, it is partitively something of the essence; there is the essential in it. It is known that the appearance does not appear without deforming essence, or inversely, that it does not deform without allusion to the essence of which it is the appearance, which, through a manner of irony, leads us on the path of truth. In short, Plato holds to the truth in appearance although it is not the truth.[11] For the image refers to the idea and the sensible to the intelligible as two absolutely different orders, but these two orders read like the same text in two different languages—the one apparent and the other hidden.[12]

Instead of then turning to the pre-Socratic philosophers as Heidegger does, Jankélévitch finds in Plotinus, in Neoplatonism in general, and in the mystics advocates of radical transcendence. Plotinus degrades the *ousia*, the essence, to the level of the second hypostasis, thereby positing the One, the first hypostasis, as an absolute beyond—beyond knowledge, beyond the intelligible, beyond essences and being.[13] In fact, Plotinus claims that the good does not even have the predicate of being good. It is beyond being identical with itself in the idea of the good and beyond the reification of adjectives and predication. The good, for Plotinus, is more than good, more than beautiful: "hyperontological, hypernoetic . . . , hyper down the whole line!" Jankélévitch exclaims.[14] He thus contends that Alexandrian philosophy was the first to integrally exhibit the metaphysical earnestness of positing a wholly other order. Its refusal to reduce the wholly other to a mere difference in degree to the known order bestows the *epekeina* its true eschatological sense.[15]

But how, if at all, can it be known that there is such a transcendence as the wholly other? Jankélévitch recognizes three different forms of knowledge: perception, intellection, and intuition.[16] Perception corresponds to the empirical and pertains to appearance; intellection corresponds to the metaempirical and pertains to essences and necessary principles; and intuition corresponds to the metalogical and pertains to position or creation. Each order is separated qualitatively and categorically, not gradually, and yet each is in relation to the others. The metaempirical plane, he claims, is wholly other than the empirical, and the wholly other order of the metalogical is heterogeneous to both the empirical and the metaempirical. He posits, in other words, two different kinds of transcendence or two forms of *epekeina*.[17] Against Platonic and Neoplatonic tendencies, Jankélévitch makes it clear that since these three orders are distinct, the finite empirical being does not and cannot ascend to the eternal, the necessary, or the universal or, what is more, arrive at the wholly other order through reason. Whoever proceeds from the *hic et nunc,* or the here and now, of empirical existence does not by mere extension arrive at the other order of essences, and whoever remains in the realm of the intellect never attains to the wholly other order of creation.[18] The metaempirical plane begins with itself; it is self-evident to thought, Jankélévitch claims, and the metalogical cannot be thought.

For Jankélévitch, the objective is thus not to ascend out of the cave of appearances into the intelligible world of ideas and essences because there is no other world than the concrete world we live in. Consequently, he does not doubt that Kant has cured us of all transcendental illusions, for experience, he states, is always finite and perception necessarily partial and partitive. Perception is composed of differentiation; it is a mixture of negative and positive. The difference is that which one can perceive.[19] The empirical does not thus lead to the beyond; it leads only to other relations, relativity, and finitude. At the same time, he claims that that which is given to the senses does not signify something other than what it is. Against the allegorical readings of the essential in and from the sensible, Jankélévitch demonstrates the tautological positivity of appearances. This rehabilitation of appearances should not be confused with the optimistic stance that the appearance is always that which it appears to be as if appearance announced immediately and incorruptibly its being, but it does put a stop to making of nature a system of ciphers. The empirical world is not a shadowy double of the more real intelligible world. Jankélévitch consequently deems the potential illusion of appearances a scientific problem, for it is a matter of interpreting precisely that which one perceives, not of deciphering its hidden meaning.[20]

Jankélévitch's distinction between the metaempirical and the metalogical planes can be understood in part through Kant's distinction between the *transcendental (a priori)* and the *transcendent*.[21] Whereas the transcendental concerns that which enables us to experience objects and which plays a role in the way our mind constitutes objects as the conditions of the possibility of knowledge in general, the transcendent is that which is beyond the categories of reason. The metaempirical, according to Jankélévitch, involves the plane of essences, ideas, and ideals—the plane of the logos. It includes eternal truths, the principle of identity, and the ideas of universality and necessity. This intelligible plane renders understandable and knowable the empirical. The empirical world as underintelligible is thus made intelligible.[22] Although the intelligible gives meaning to that which alone as mere inchoate sense experience cannot have meaning, it does not give being to existents. The intelligible plane has to do with thought only, not being. Jankélévitch thus establishes two planes of truth: the truth of perception and essential truth. In accordance with tradition, he maintains that these two orders of truth relate to each other hierarchically: The essential order corrects, verifies, or sometimes contradicts the order of perception. As a result, the order of reason is "truer" than that of perception because it honors rational principles and axioms the negation of which would make thought impossible. The a priori condition, in short, functions to govern thought. It does not stand in a synthetic and natural relation but is the analytic condition sine qua non, the general condition without which thought is impossible and through which every thought is possible, but only possible. This means that it does not determine that something here and now is thought. It is formal and inefficient but not ineffective.[23] The relation between the steps of truth corresponds to the relation of experience and the principles of reason. It is the double truth, Jankélévitch states, of humans as sensible and thinking creatures.[24]

This a priori formal and enabling condition becomes clearer when the plane of the intellect and reason is considered as the plane of values, moral law, and the truth. One cannot kill or destroy eternal truths, according to Jankélévitch, for the simple fact that they do not exist. For example, the truth remains the truth whether or not Peter or Jacob thinks it *hic et nunc*. The transcendence from the empirical domain to the metaempirical thus occurs through a sudden and global disinterest with respect to the questions where? and when?[25] The possibility of thought is, therefore, not simply inexistent but infinitely applicable as possibility. Similarly, when the moral law is transgressed by a bad action, the truth or the essence of morality remains unimpaired. The purity of the condition remains untainted because it is untaintable. The ideality of the necessary principles remains untouched. Jankélévitch distinguishes between the value irrespective of the contingencies of time and the consciousness of that value, which is a historical and psychological phenomenon situated in time.[26] As a line extending from Socrates to Augustine and Malebranche maintains, even an insincerity or a trespass, which is deaf to the evidence, hears the silent accusation and the mute protest of the inner word.[27] Jankélévitch thus characterizes the a priori as self-evident and eternal, or, rather, timeless: It is what is always already there.

Beyond perception and intellection, the third form of knowledge is intuition. Following Plotinus and, in Kant's wake, Schelling, Jankélévitch claims that we have an intuition of the second transcendence, the *epekeina* beyond both existence and essence. Whereas Hegel's critique of Kant's limitation on metaphysical speculation assumed that to know a boundary is also to know that which is beyond the boundary, Jankélévitch assumes that intuition offers a glimpse of that which one cannot know. Intuition, in other words, does not yield any substantive knowledge of the essence of the *epekeina*. It does not ascend into the heavens or to God; it does not render objective the *quid* (the essence, or the what) of the beyond but only the *quod* (the *that*, or the facticity). What is more, this *quoddity*, he claims, is revealed only by the withdrawal of the *quid*. Jankélévitch calls this intuition "almost-nothing" (*presque-rien*), for it is given in the instant as the instant—given and taken, born and died in an instant.

The intuition of the wholly other is the subject of Jankélévitch's first philosophy. It is the order of creation and position and is concerned with the problem of the beginning and the end. Jankélévitch suggests that the necessity of eternal essences served the Greeks to neglect the question of origin and end—that is, the great mystery of quoddity—whether represented in the being of Parmenides' notion of a universe of *Plenum* without interruption of continuity or in the becoming of his counterpart Heraclitus, who says of the world, defined as transformable fire, that it is uncreated and sempiternal.[28] Even Leibniz, who asks the metaphysical question par excellence, "Why is there something rather than nothing?" quickly defers to the eternal necessity of rational principles and the necessary being of the creator God who creates the best possible world according to the divinity of logic and the law of sufficient reason. These propositions render the radical question of origin a semblance of a problem. Schopenhauer provides an exception to the acquiescence to and the justification of the already-thereness of being, when, in response to Leibniz, he poses the moral question whether there *should* be something rather than nothing. In fact, he suggests that it would be perhaps better if there was not something.[29] Such a moral interrogation of being does not have its place in Jankélévitch's metaphysics. Jankélévitch merely highlights the fact that Schopenhauer addresses the unsettling thought of the contingency of being. Jankélévitch's first philosophy is, therefore, metaphysical because, like Schelling and Heidegger, he takes up Leibniz's question about the origin of all things. It is the fact that there is something rather than nothing that constitutes in his eyes the great mysterium. He consequently dedicates his first philosophy to the absolute contingency of all that is and to the absolute contingency even of that which is eternal and necessary.

As Leibniz points out in his treatise "The Principles of Nature and Grace," the metaphysical question is actually twofold. First, why is there something and not nothing, and second, why is it thus and not otherwise.[30] The relations of the three types of knowledge—perception, intellection, and intuition—apply to this twofold question and demonstrate what Jankélévitch means by the wholly other that he sees in and as creation. The intelligible order makes the empirical order understandable and can be verified in the world of things, but the enabling condition of comprehension and orientation does not cause, create, or position that which it conditions. Just as existence does not lead to essences in a continuum, essences do not lead to existence. Thought and being remain categorically separated, although in relation. Moreover, the act of creation is not simply a manifestation of the idea. Creation is not to be understood in terms of generation or even in the Neoplatonic terms of emanation.

This point is not radical. In his creation myth, *Timaeus*, Plato does not have the world of existents rise from the world of ideas; rather the intermediate instance, a demiurge, creates the world as a technician following pregiven eternal forms. Similarly, Leibniz stipulates that although God created the existence of the good, the beautiful, and all that is, God did not create the essence of the good, the beautiful, and all that is. The radicality of Jankélévitch's first philosophy, however, maintains that the a priori, too, was posited by an act of creation. He focuses on the very fact of the essences, the fact of the a priori, and the fact of necessity, claiming that although the truth is so and so, necessity the way it is, and the conditions for intelligibility such as they are, the very fact of their "existence" as well as the composition of their internal constitution is contingent. For Jankélévitch, the point is fairly simple: The facticity of the world in its totality constitutes the metaphysical problem of all problems. So, for instance, although necessity, insofar as it is immanent, is absolutely necessary, the fact of necessity is contingent.[31] Or, in other terms, the condition of the a priori condition is not itself a priori or ideal (which does not entail that it is ipso facto a posteriori and empirical).[32] Or, more concretely, whereas life may be represented as involving the self-understanding of mundane consciousness, the fact of life is a mysterium.[33]

This first order is the order that gives existence and posits the a priori and ideal. It is otherwise than both existence and essence and is not truly an order like the others; it is rather pure act, effectivity . . . creation. Jankélévitch represents the relations of empirical existence to the preexistent essences and both of these to the metalogical act of position as undergirding their qualitative differences:

> If the intermittent empirical exists without consisting or subsisting and if the essential metaempirical consists and subsists without existing,

one could say that the metalogic is that which makes the inexistent consistence of essentiality exist just as the metaempirical is the consistence itself of inconsistent existence; but not that the metampirie *makes* [*fasse*] whatever subsists or consists in the creative sense of the auxiliary verb "make [*faire*]," essence being precisely eternal *inexistent preexistence to existence*, anew and always preexistence to infinity, uncreated already-there, atemporal, completely realized, without beginning and end. . . . The wholly other who makes the subsisting essence does not itself exist . . . nor does it a fortiori subsist. Literally that which confers existence does not exist; because if that which confers existence would itself be an existent, it would presuppose, in turn, another giver of existence. And yet the giver of existence makes exist [*fait exister*] at once the essence, being in general, and the contingent empirical beings; it is therefore just as inexistent as inconsistent and insubsistent.[34]

Beyond existence and beyond essence, the wholly other is also beyond truth (*la survérité*). This beyond-truth accords that which metalogically—but not logically or metaempirically—could be otherwise the fact of being as it is. Jankélévitch calls this positing act an immemorial fact from which that which is otherwise is eternally excluded. Necessity and truth are installed as eternally already there and as unengendered self-evidence (*cela-va-de-soi*).[35] But that which posits truth is not itself truth; that which makes the truth the truth is prior to and beyond the dichotomy of true and false. The *survérité* that effectuates that the truth is true and that establishes the truth and all values arbitrarily is not itself a value or a truth, nor is it value itself or truth itself.[36] Jankélévitch sharply distinguishes this beyond-truth from a deeper truth. It is not a more profound truth but that which founds truth; it does not serve as the foundation of truth like an ontological platform on which the many truths may be constructed but is rather solely the founding (*fondatrice*) of truth itself.[37] This act of founding is prior to the binaries that it establishes in a past that was never present.

It is significant, however, that, for Jankélévitch, this act of founding does not serve to justify and make normative the essential order that it founds. It does not abide like a holy presence in the essences as the substantial guarantee of their validity. In contrast, the intuition of the first order, according to Jankélévitch, does not substantiate the immutable, immemorial truths but raises doubt about their sacrosanct value by exposing the ultimate arbitrariness and the radical contingency of the essential a priori order. He writes:

> If, therefore, the intelligible order is that which makes the sensible disorder understandable and renders it significant, the in-intelligible

over-order [*le surordre inintelligible*] does not have in view to make comprehensible the completely transparent and truly maximal intelligibility of the axioms and eternal principles, but it founds this intelligibility and, in founding, reveals the non-sense of its sense, the contingence and relativity of its necessity, finally the night from which its light issues.[38]

And in another passage, he explains:

> Unlike identity, pure position is not an unthinkable that renders thinkable, an unknowable that makes knowable, an incomprehensible that makes comprehensible: it is much more that which makes the principles of reason absurd or at least spurious and contingent; the pure position is the unfathomable mystery that renders . . . precarious the eternal truths as well as all of the evidences that are most firmly established.[39]

For Jankélévitch, the pure act of pure position problematizes that which is self-evident, necessary, and eternal—a problem the Greeks and the whole of occidental philosophy in their wake attempted to conjure away by dismissing the question of a radical beginning.

Jankélévitch's determination of the relation of the metaempirical to the metalogical is, therefore, complex. The metalogical "order" of creation establishes both of the lower orders. But, at the same time, the paralogical or metalogical paradox scandalizes the logos. This scandal constitutes, however, a fruitful aporia. The glimpse of the thetic act of creation in intuition mobilizes the vital circulation of thought and potentially sets alight the intelligent idea in the ashes of memorized concepts.[40] The knowledge we can have, however, prevents us from inquiring into or seeking the beyond-truth. We have no need of the beyond, but intuition awakens us to the beyond in the form of inquietude, inspiration, desire, and eros. Jankélévitch writes:

> The reasonable human finds in his intermediarity as creature everything that there is to know, and it conforms to metaempirical wisdom and to vital earnestness not to search beyond. . . . Nothing is missing . . . and yet something is missing,—a something that is nothing. What is missing from this complete and incomplete truth? It is missing an I-know-not-what of the inexplicable, unjustifiable, and impalpable that is the principle itself of metaphysical inquietude: the metalogical human burns madly to achieve that which is nonetheless self-sufficient onto itself and that appears incomplete to him whatever he does; therefore this infinite desire for something other has

some similarity with the profane Eros of the *Symposium* and with the sacred Eros of John of the Cross.[41]

The desire is infinite because the object of desire is that which is absolutely and necessarily missing—the wholly other. The metalogic wholly other is neither being nor nothing—it is almost-nothing; it will never be rendered an object of knowledge; it will only be glimpsed in the insubstantial I-know-not-what of the instant of intuition. This pure position is similar to eros because it is, on the one hand, infinitely poor and naked: Without being, it is a gift without having. And it is, on the other hand, simultaneously infinitely rich because it gives value and existence to everything that is, which is sufficient onto itself.[42] The thetic act cannot be included in the totality of a system, although the self-sufficient construction of the system depends on the exclusion of this radical origin. Through the principle of metaphysical inquietude, Jankélévitch links eros and the act of creation.

He draws a subsequent parallel between the relation of the metalogical thetic act of pure position to that which has been posited or created and the relation between the mystery of intuition to intellection. Although intuition does not found intellection, it is not only qualitatively distinguished from intellection; it is also contrary to it and the limit of it. It calls the established orders into question, not merely superficially but in their very foundations. But, according to Jankélévitch, this calling into question does not primarily aim at destruction but at re-creation. Intuition provides the loosening, opening, and revitalization of these structures. It is the moment of desire opened by that which qualitatively and infinitely exceeds the parameters of totality. The intuition of the metalogical interrupts the closure of the circular system and invigorates that within it which becomes static and reified. This interruption is not autopoetic: It is not from within but comes from the intuition of the wholly other as the radical calling into question of established orders. Intuition, in other words, does not provide access to an alternative world, neither parallel to, outside, nor after our world. It does not offer escape; it rather inscribes itself as the opening of what is that escapes its own inscription.

Beyond empirical being and essence, the *survérité* is pure position and active operation, radical origin, creative primacy. For Jankélévitch, the key word is the verb *faire*—to act or to do. If Hamlet had not been so obsessed with "things," Jankélévitch asserts, he might have discovered the principle of action between being and nonbeing. Action, he claims, is neither of being nor of nonbeing; it is instead an excluded third principle between the contradictories, not logically, for such a third is necessarily excluded, but "irrationally" and "drastically." The instant that is almost-nothing is itself the suspension of the principle of contradiction and its consequence, the principle of disjunction.[43] Our thought capacity is impotent to think of a reality that is not "res [a thing or an object]," much less an irreal reality or a real irrationality of pure operation. With our categories of discursive reason, we inevitably incline toward hypostasization and substantialization, making something of nothing, an object of God, a personification of evil.[44]

The opening passage of the book of Genesis, however, testifies to this pure position of the *survérité*: "Fiat lux!" the creator says; "Let there be light," from which follows the divide of day and night.[45] This primordial position is illuminative: Its light does not shine on a preexisting day, nor is it created from the possibility or the preexistent essence of light. The uniqueness of the creator of Genesis can best be illustrated by comparing it to Plato's creation myth, *Timaeus*. Whereas *Timaeus* has an intermediate being, a demiurge, execute the creation of the world by looking to the eternal forms as models, the God of Genesis creates ex nihilo before all distinctions. The demiurge of *Timaeus* is a technician, and the God of Genesis is pure poetic genius. Jankélévitch explains:

> Plato's attachment to the world of "models" proves that, according to him, there is no being that a pre-being does not preexist, no creation that does not presuppose prescheme, prefigure, prenotion or preconception.... Now, it is *Genesis*, not *Timaios* or *Theogony*, that begins at the beginning and that truly confronts the mystery of inchoation! The creator of *Genesis* does not extract the real light from possible light, does not bring to act a potential light, does not fill out the preexisting essences or flesh out already given virtualities; but he creates the effective light of lights and the possibility of light with one and the same blow and in one sole act; in the same instant, he created physical light . . . and he invented the very idea of light. . . . This creation is genial and supergenial position, thetic overflowing, simultaneous improvisation of effectivity and of the possibility of this effectivity.[46]

True creation, according to Jankélévitch, is simultaneously ontic and ousic, existential and essential. It is absolute. Such an absolute, however, cannot even be conceived as a categorical subject of being, not even as the subject of action. It is pure act. The wholly other, Jankélévitch states, is act-without-being (*faire-sans-être*).[47]

For "expedience's sake," he calls this pure act of creation *God*.[48] Yet Jankélévitch distances himself from theology. In fact, he deems a science of God impossible not only because discourse is infinitely inadequate and reason ultimately impotent but also because language and grammar stand in the service of a metaphysics of being with its quidditative nomination.[49] For the same reason, his metaphysics is not really a metaphysics in the strict sense because it does not entail a knowledge of the absolute or transcendent. Even the mystics, he thinks, are ultimately garrulous because they, too, speak, speaking in terms of being as if abiding in a house where there is, in fact, no dwelling.[50] As he explains, "Divine ipseity has no other definition than the opening itself, the infinite opening that is precisely the impossibility to define, to circumscribe or to 'comprehend.'"[51] In Jankélévitch's moral philosophy, *God* has a functional value, namely as the possibility of thinking the absolute.[52] This absolute, God, is pure subject. Accordingly, it is not that God acts as if God were a preexistent subject of a substantive attribute; rather, God is extraverted in the operative verb—pure operation before every ontic reification.[53] Action is thus not God's nature or essence; rather God acts in the sense that God is the action that neither is nor is not but is the excluded third between being and nonbeing. Jankélévitch also calls this wholly other *lui-même* (he-himself) in order to express a pure subject without relation. Beyond the principle of identity and not bound to the spatiotemporal coordinates of being, this he-himself is himself and always other than himself—*ipse* and *alius* together. As Plotinus would say, God is more than God; God is otherwise than Godself.[54]

Following Plotinus, Jankélévitch believes that *innocence* is perhaps the true name of the creator who acts out of a grace without reflection, an *autos* without *philautie* (literally self-love).[55] It is this innocence that Jankélévitch associates with the good and with love. Jankélévitch recognizes in love the power of creation and in creation the power of love, for to create is to make be and to establish value, and love creates the value of the beloved in and through loving. Jankélévitch points out that in our relationships, love is all the more selfless and all the more gratuitous the less it is tied down to being, the less it is aware of itself, and the less it is laden by the weight of egoism. Jankélévitch thus reverses the relation of love and the distinction "worthy-to-be-loved." Love makes the other worthy as opposed to one's being drawn only to that which is lovable, good, or worthy of being loved. The very value of value—its effectivity and normativity—is posited in the act of creation.

Jankélévitch's outline of the positing of love echoes the so-called *Euthyphro* dilemma posed in Plato's early dialogue on the nature of piety. It is asked whether "the pious is loved by the gods because it is pious? Or is it pious because it is loved by the gods?"[56] Thus it is a rephrasing of the question of the good. With so much at stake, Socrates quickly makes it clear that the priority is piety itself. The good draws the gods to it; it is not their love that makes it good. Jankélévitch takes the opposite stance. He criticizes as dogmatisms the intertwined philosophical beliefs that because being *is* it *acts* and that preferability in itself magnetizes the preference. Instead, he reverses the *Because*. It is the prevenient preference alone, he suggests, that founds preferability. Being is heterogeneous to action, and the act is the beginning and the end, the alpha and the omega of everything.[57] Jankélévitch explains, therefore, that although "the norm sanctifies force . . . the norm itself germinates in the prevenient effectivity of the prime decision."[58] For Jankélévitch, God is this prevenient creational fiat: Or, more simply, as the Gospel of John says, God is love.[59] This love is without being and without self-consciousness. It is pure position, the simple act, beyond being and reason. So why does God create? Both Genesis and *Timaeus* respond, because God is good.[60] Love, Jankélévitch observes, is the operation of goodness itself and is, therefore, a sufficient answer.[61] And as Pascal suggests, reasons come only later—after the fact, the fact of position.

Jankélévitch, therefore, outlines three major paradoxical metalogisms that constitute the mystery of creation. These metalogisms revolve around the very paradoxes of the absolute gift positing existence and essence. They constitute what he calls "the triple grace of making-be without being" (*la triple grâce du faire-être sans être*).[62] First, he states, that which makes is not that which it makes (*ce qui fait n'est pas ce qu'il fait*). The principle, in other words, is not that which it is a principle of; posited being can only have something as a principle which is not of being, just as the source of light is illuminative but not therefore luminous.

Second, that which gives gives that which it is not (*ce qui donne donne ce qu'il n'est pas*), to which Jankélévitch adds, all the more does it give what it does not have.[63] The distinction between the gift of creation and all other gifts, he asserts, is that gifts are always partitive; one gives something of that which one has, which means, first, that giving presupposes having and, second, that one gives from a standpoint of wealth or excess. In contrast, and underlining the first paradox, Jankélévitch describes the creator as pure doing without having or being. He is pure gift and wholly this gift, not as a gift given or as a giver of a gift but as the pure act of giving (*dondatio*; *dosis*). Creation is the movement of giving itself, which creates the gift at the same time as it is made a giver. In sum, the gift, the given, and the giver are given in the position of one and the same act of giving.

Third, although that which gives does not have what it gives, it is also inversely the case, according to Jankélévitch, that that which gives still has what it gave (*ce qui donne a encore ce qu'il a donné*). Particularly in the light of the other two, this paradox is undoubtedly the strangest. How can that which has nothing and which is not still have what it gives? Jankélévitch adopts here a paradox of Plotinian Emanatism: The One that moves out of itself remains within itself, its powers extended yet undiminished. This last metalogism, therefore, entails that the absolute does not become less absolute through creation, that the creator is not exhausted by the act of creation as if the creator's potentiality or latent possibility had been fulfilled or realized. Theologically speaking, God's kenosis in creation does not entail that God is only immanent in the world.

More significantly, however, Jankélévitch highlights with this third paradox the literally unjust arithmetic of grace, charity, and love. He demonstrates that his metaphysics is deeply concerned with concrete human existence. It is the mystery of grace, love, and charity that challenges the alternative of the conservation principle or the various forms of commutative or distributive justice in which the wealth of one comes at the cost of another. Against this balancing act of a logic of equivalence and zero-sum physics, Jankélévitch witnesses in the order of grace that one can give and be enriched, that expenditure can yield great returns. "Is this not the case with love?" Jankélévitch seems to ask. The more you give, the more you receive, not automatically or as a matter of course or calculation, but as the movement of love itself.

Humans are called, in the manner of a vocation, to this order of grace—called to love, to create, and to act. Love for Jankélévitch, as Jeffrey Bloechel observes, is a call to kenosis.[64] Echoing Nicholas of Cusa's mystical notion that the human is a "contraction" of God's creative nature, Jankélévitch describes the human person as God dipped in discourse, God of a thousand-millionth of a second.[65] The human task is thus nothing less than to be second creators and continue creation beyond the seventh day. But as creatures, Jankélévitch realizes, we are immersed in being and in time, and the most we can do is re-create what has been created. This restriction does not preclude real ingenuity. In fact, Jankélévitch's own reflections are inspired by the romantic obsession with genius. But human creation is grounded in being. Whatever humans create, being is presupposed; humans have to be in order to create. The human present always has a past, whereas divine creation marks a past that was never present. For Jankélévitch, the difference between the divine and the human comes down to the fact that human immersion in time and being or the time of being renders of creation a re-creation, of position re-position, of original pure and spontaneous act the whole contradiction of "initial iteration or iterative initiative."[66] This distinction does not only refer to the pastness of being but to being's extension and alterity, or its temporality, altogether.

The seventh day, the Sabbath, is one way Jankélévitch expresses this fundamental temporal difference between human and divine creation. He detects an anthropomorphism in the representation of the Sabbath because in it the creator who is pure act becomes the spectator of his own work. The good conscience, the sacralization of deposition, or the delight Plato describes that the demiurge finds in having created an image of the eternal—all point to a self-indulgent repose in the ontic sedimentation of idolatry. Or, more simply, the difference consists in the emergence of reification, hypostasization, and substantiation, on the one hand, and, contemplation and self-reflection, on the other. For Jankélévitch, these two belong integrally together to form what he identifies as the culprit in both aesthetics and ethics, namely complacency.[67] Whereas contemplation is seen as the highest form of philosophical life by Plato and Aristotle, Jankélévitch situates it as the downfall of the first philosophy of action. By beginning with vision, humans tend to imitate instead of re-create. Creation, he insists, is not to be imitated in the mimetic sense of copying the copies of archetypes; rather the prevenient initiative of creation is to be imitated in the mimetic sense of decision and of the act—the taking of initiative and performative re-position.[68]

In re-position and re-creation, Jankélévitch discovers both limitation and chance. Humans are responsible for continued creation, and this re-creation is open to human freedom. This opening or this openness itself marks, for Jankélévitch, the similarity between God and the human. The transcendence or self-transcendence of human temporality, he claims, makes it impossible to reduce the human to a concept or an essence. The ipseity of the relative subject remains infinitely beyond the sum of the predicates one can attach to it. Although the human may be a rational being, or a being capable of language, or a social animal, none of these alone defines the human nor does a mosaic of the totality of such predications constitute the truth of the human. For Jankélévitch, the human is neither this nor that: The human, he writes, "is that which is not and he is not that which he is . . . and is constantly another as himself."[69] In other words, divine creation created creators.[70] The continued continuation is a new beginning ever anew. The relative beginning or the small beginning that is inaugurated with each moment in the decisions of the will refers to the immemorial beginning of beginnings. Jankélévitch thus acknowledges the radical transformative capacity of freedom, for the freedom to re-create makes of mere extensive continuity intensive continuity.[71] But this remains a vocation, and Jankélévitch recognizes that humans are ambiguous, ambivalent, even amphibian by nature, taut between what he calls vocation and nostalgia—that is, between acting-without-being (*faire-sans-être*) and the complacency of being-without-acting (*l'être-sans-faire*).

Intervals and Instants

The human creature as creator is taut between being and act. Jankélévitch conceives of this difference in the temporal terms of the *interval* and the *instant*. Following Bergson, the interval implies for Jankélévitch the duration of time, which he understands as the duration of lived experience. The instant is that which disrupts the continuity of the interval, interrupting the static air of being and inaugurating becoming. The interval mixed with the instant composes the nature of becoming. Neither is completely isolable from the other, although they remain qualitatively distinct. But the instant is simultaneously the moment of creation encompassed on both sides by the omnipresence and sempiternity of being. In the flash of an instant, Jankélévitch claims, the paradox of the relative-absolute occurs. Only for an instant does the relative finite human being coincide with the absolute. To borrow a phrase from the medieval mystic Nicholas of Cusa, this *coincidentia oppositorum* constitutes the paradox of intuition and highlights the paradox of forgiveness.

Underlying Jankélévitch's concept of forgiveness are his reflections on time. Jankélévitch begins to define time by drawing from Aristotle, who says that time has no *ousia*, no essence, or substance.[72] Whenever one tries to grasp the "now" (*nunc*), one comes up with either the no-longer-of-the-past or the not-yet-of-the-future. That means, Jankélévitch asserts, that "I can never determine the punctual point of the now."[73] Jankélévitch "names" this punctual point the instant and says that it is "almost-nothing [*presque-rien*]." Yet even the naming, he observes, betrays the almost-nothing character of the instant, for names use language, which belongs to being—that is, to the ontology of the interval.[74] Because of the insufficiency or overdeterminacy of language, discursive or conceptual thought is incapable of grasping the instant. There is nothing to think in the "almost-nothing" because "there is by definition not the time to think it."[75] The instant is not nothing and yet is not something, not even the shortest possible duration; it is in between nonbeing and being, including and excluding both. To represent this third term between nonbeing and being, Jankélévitch, therefore, turns to the verbal expression of the *event*. He thereby links the excluded third position of the instant to the third position of action. The event's way of being is to happen (*advenir*). As he explains, "One says '*advenit*' of that which is never a thing and which nonetheless is not nothing, as it indeed happens or occurs."[76] If it did not happen, Jankélévitch admits, it would be absolutely nothing.[77]

With their categories of being, philosophy and discursive thought always come too late to the event. In the suddenness of the instant, Jankélévitch observes, alpha and omega coincide, leaving the logos without the time to unfold the discursive succession of its concepts. Although the event involves the negation of everything except its facticity, its occurrence, or its coming to pass, the instant is not completely obscure. Although the event has no quiddity—that is, what-ness or essence known through cognition—it is experienced, Jankélévitch claims, in its quoddity (*quoddité*), in its that-ness. The minimal knowledge of facticity constitutes what he calls the "I-know-not-what [*je-ne-sais-quoi*]" of a lived intuition. I-know-not-what, in other words, is the sense of the event's coming to pass. Rather than using the static categories of being and of essence, Jankélévitch seeks a new way of thinking and speaking that expresses this I-know-not-what.[78] By doing so, he attempts to bring forth the very timeliness of time.

Whereas most philosophers prioritize the indissolubility of continuity epitomized in being and essence, Jankélévitch prioritizes the qualitative difference inherent in the event and therefore in temporality. His focus on discontinuity coincides with his emphasis on singularity: the singular moment in time, the singular human life sealed by a singular death—death being not merely a great equalizer but also the great individualizer. Plato's depiction of the death of Socrates in *Phaidon* negatively illustrates his point.[79] Socrates is conversing with friends as he drinks the poisonous hemlock. He dies, and the scene is picked up again as Socrates is on the island of the holy, calling other friends to the conversation that has been merely briefly interrupted by his death. Discontinuity is whisked away in underlying continuity. The essential and eternal prevail over the finite and mortal—despite all appearances.

This prioritization of ontology is present in moral philosophies as well. Morality for Platonists of all kinds supposes the priority of essence over existence and of the idea of the good before action. Subsisting ideas are embodied and transcendent values are realized in time.[80] In a variation of this same theme, Aristotle's ethics, for example, employ a scale of gradations on which principles such as good and evil are located on opposite ends. Qualitative distinctions are obscured, if not expelled. Successive approximations of more-or-less do not allow for the possibility of something new or something different. Similarly, Leibniz's discovery of the *infinitesimal* represents such a repudiation of qualitative differences. Jankélévitch fears that as soon as good and evil are placed on the same line, separated only by insignificant degrees, good and evil will inevitably be confounded, and as soon as life and death are put in a continuum, their differences diminish and disappear in the dull hum of being.[81]

Against this tide, Jankélévitch emphasizes radical discontinuity and singularity. The instant, he claims, is epoch-making; it introduces the disjunction between being and nonbeing without itself constituting a mediating third principle. Born in the instant, the event is characterized by fissure and rupture, an unmarked transition from one being exposed to nothingness to another being exposed to nothingness. It is, according to Jankélévitch, a spark or a flash. Not surprisingly, Jankélévitch finds expression for the instant and event in the language of the mystics. In Meister Eckhart's "Fuenklein," Jankélévitch recognizes the instant as "a fugitive spark, a spark *brévissime* that alights as it goes out and that appears in disappearing."[82] In coming to pass, the almost-nothing has no tomorrow and no next moment that would make it empirically measurable. Instead, Jankélévitch suggests that the instant commences a new beginning; it is the very opening of time, an imperceptible threshold at which a change comes to pass.[83]

Jankélévitch describes the instant accordingly as "an inner airing" constitutive of becoming. The instant is (only) an instant because, on the one hand, the mass of the interval flattens it out, compresses and constricts it until it is reduced to quasi inexistence, to almost nothing; on the other hand, the interval moves, is structured and articulated by the instant. Vivified by the instant, the interval becomes continuation instead of mere prolongation.[84] To imagine that the interval and the instant are two sides of a coin, therefore, is too static and spatial an image for Jankélévitch. He instead asserts that the one is only thanks to the other.[85] Requiring both duration and interruption—interval and instant—becoming is the being or essence of human existence, for the only possible manner of being for humans is that of becoming.[86] Jankélévitch thus understands humans as a mixture of instant and interval. The instant and interval themselves are mixtures that have meaning only through their reciprocal relation in lived experience.[87] Therefore, one can apprehend the instant enfolded in the interval only in a living act of thought, a lived response, an intuition of the moment. Jankélévitch's notion of intuition reflects the mystics when he calls intuition "the wisdom of the instantaneous fracture," an arising-fading wisdom of the spark, suspending reflexive thought in the flash of a searing act.[88]

Intuition

The concept of intuition has a long tradition in the history of philosophy. And although Jankélévitch's conception of intuition has primarily three inspirations, namely, Plotinus and Neoplatonism in general, Schelling, and Bergson, it would be amiss to merely look for that which is of Plotinus, taken from Schelling, or adapted from Bergson when reading Jankélévitch.[89] For Jankélévitch intuition involves the breakthrough of the absolute into human life, which does not yield any substantial knowledge of the absolute but which potentially transforms individual human existence. In explaining this kind of intuition, Jankélévitch follows Schelling's discussion of the "*nicht Nichts* [not nothing]," except Jankélévitch prefers to call the instant of intuition "almost nothing [*presque rien*]." The breakthrough of transcendence into the encompassing context of immanence proves to be an extremely unstable contact because the human person does not overcome his or her finitude in the instant of intuition. To speak of contact is already too much, as Jankélévitch characterizes the instant of intuition as an imperceptible wink of the absolute. A wink promises neither rest nor domicile.[90] It is a contact with the absolute that he describes as tangential, not nothing but on the threshold to nothing as on the threshold to being—almost nothing.

Jankélévitch aligns intuition with the event. It makes itself suddenly contemporary with the ever-fleeting "delicate tangency" of the instant. Intuition is the mode of consciousness of the instant. It requires the greatest subtlety, he maintains, to become conscious of a mutation without thickness or of the pulsation of the interval that renders being porous. Since intuition corresponds to the instant without duration, it, too, is fleeting to the point that it is a thought that dies in arising: Without even flickering it alights and is extinguished. This spark leaves no time for its apprehension. In poetic terms, he explains that "the intuition is a becoming conscious that is loss of consciousness, an awakening that is blacking out, a flash tearing the night; consciousness awakens in the same instant that it blacks out, is resurrected in the instant it dies. The instant is dying rebirth, a death that is a life."[91] Jankélévitch uses poetic terms because the instant of intuition cannot be accessed by ordinary or philosophical discourse. But his poetic circumscription underlines two important aspects of intuition. First of all, the *poesis* of poetry signals that the instant of intuition is a matter of an act, of doing and creating; it is an event that resembles or, more precisely, re-acts, re-positions, and re-creates the absolute creation that as an act precedes both existence and essence. Second, this re-creation occurring in the instant of death and rebirth simultaneously invokes the key notion of conversion.

As a relative and finite being, the human has no privileged access to the metaempirical except in the mystery of the instant. At this finest and most subtle of points there is a coincidence of the absolute and the relative, the infinite and the finite, the divine and the human.⁹² This *coincidentia oppositorum*, according to Jankélévitch, is the instant of intuition. He writes that "in the tangency of the instant a wholly drastic evidence is revealed: the coincidence of creaturely reposition with creative position."⁹³ The instant of intuition is at the limits of human strength. Jankélévitch recognizes the paradox of the limit: Human consciousness, on the one hand, is irreconcilable with the unconditional and the absolute, and yet, on the other hand, the human is most truly human in the instant of tangency with the principle of creation. The instant of the coincidence of opposites simultaneously demonstrates the self-transcendence of the individual and the establishment of finite human boundaries. For Jankélévitch, this coincidence is characterized by a simplicity of three kinds: The simplicity of the object and the simplicity of the subject coincide in the simplicity of the instant without interval. It cannot endure: There is no abiding, no habitus; there is no transversal to the beyond or the taking up of an elevated state on the way toward identification or fusion. It is rather a disappearing identity of three almost-nothings—punctual and tangential. Jankélévitch calls it the *instant of grace*: the instant of a life that conforms to the gratuity of positional efference.⁹⁴

So although Jankélévitch asserts that "the human is the God of the instant," he is also aware that this divinity is solely of an instant.⁹⁵ The difference is categorical. The difference is being. The human being exists, and his or her being is posited in the act of creation by a creator without being. Humans, according to Jankélévitch, are amphibious beings, belonging to both the interval and the instant—that is, to an instant that is inseparable from the interval. This "intermediateness," "middleness" (Pascal), "metaxy" (Plato), or "Mittelstellung" (Simmel) is of ontological significance for Jankélévitch.⁹⁶ Although the instant marks the third position between being and nonbeing, it cannot become a state; it cannot be. Being thus hinders creative subjectivity, but it also enables it to take on form. The radical freedom of the instant materializes only in the world of being. Only here does it have the opportunity to make history, even if there is nothing outside of the context of history, as Derrida might say. The intuition of the instant imitates the original creation through creative repetition. It is the little yes that echoes and responds to the positivity of the primordial position.⁹⁷ Interrupting posited being to reshape being, human creation is consequently re-creation, and human position is always already re-position. The stage has been set. In contrast to the creator God, the finite creature already is before it acts—always and necessarily.

The instant of intuition, according to Jankélévitch, is thus the human vocation. On both the grand stage of history and in small acts of morality, the best of humanity lies in its ability to create. It is the time and the manner in which the human is the *imago Dei*. In intuition, position coincides in the point of an instant with conversion. It is the identity of position and conversion. The individual converts to the positing or creation of being: He or she converts to making-being or to a being who makes, creates, or acts (*faire-être*).[98] The act par excellence, Jankélévitch explains, is the act that posits a *plus*, a more. It creates, edifies, or enriches.[99] Amphibious beings straddling being and doing, humans, he claims, are called to act, do, and create, and yet the enclosing and complacent structures of being often prevent humans from their vocation. Humans "make themselves" from time to time, Jankélévitch observes, and the rest of the time, they are made. In privileged instants of willful decision they make themselves; otherwise they change intransitively like a passive mutation, like the ripening of apples. For at every moment and with every turn, becoming tends toward being and toward a state. In a different metaphor, that which is to come is rendered an extension of today. Jankélévitch calls this inclination a gravitation: It is the decadent digestion of initiative.

The creature, he asserts, is a mixture of supernatural operation and of constituted reality. The coincidence of opposites is the coincidence of divine *facere* (act, making, creating) and human *fieri* (becoming). It is the coincidence of pure creative operation and the impure creaturely process.[100] There are thus two inverse tendencies depending on whether consciousness accents the *semper* (always) or the *positio* (position). Whereas the latter tends toward creation and is the subject of conversion, the former dissolves the singular decision or act in iterative being, pulling the pneumatic and ephemeral down and out with a force of gravitation, degradation, and decadence.

Jankélévitch is, moreover, unequivocal that the always already nature of being is predominant over creation. Everything keeps us away from converting to doing, as if it sufficed just to be. The pneumatic tends toward thing-ness as vocation turns to stuttering:

> Indeed, the law of exercise and the law of economy, custom, adaption, tradition, and imitation that rule the periodic of our life, memory, and the association that assimilates the new into the old, thought itself that adopts so easily the reproductive rhythms of our naturalness, everything and even the spatial installation of the body and of the sensorium in the intermediate existence—everything conspires

to make the necessary effort to coincide with the focal point of position violent for us.[101]

Bergson even identifies the "counter to nature torsion" of conversion as the distinguishing feature of intuition, for it violently tears us from the garments of being. As Plato, Plotinus, and the whole philosophical tradition attest, conversion is difficult. Comparable to Heidegger's analysis of inauthentic fallen existence in the light of *das Man*, Jankélévitch protests against the fact that humans let things and others decide for us, as opposed to grasping freedom and responsibility for making oneself and shaping the world.[102]

For Jankélévitch, humans are called to decision to counter the complacency of being without action. They are called to action without being, which entails both the rupture of being and its reestablishment. Human becoming can thus be a passive state that tends toward the iteration of the past and the reification of the status quo, which involves the reduction of the to-come to what-already-is. Or human becoming may take the form of successive continuation and re-creation—that is, intensive continuity or continued creation.[103] Jankélévitch remarks that such re-creation has the nature of decision.[104] It does not follow rules subscribed in the heavens or on stone tablets. The orders of being, in other words, do not culminate in an act that executes their hidden inscription. The act of decision—the decision as act par excellence—always entails rather a leap, as Kierkegaard claims. As creatures of discursive reason, as beings of the interval, we may try to flee from the rupture of the moment, seeking to rid ourselves of impending decisions. But human existence commands a constant responsibility for the affirmation, reformation, or destructive-creative revolution of existing forms. Following the vitalist tradition, Jankélévitch sees life as a continual destruction of forms.[105] By sacrificing positive freedom in passive consent to what has been or to what others do, one abandons this responsibility. In both the realization and the evasion of responsibility, human freedom is opened up by the instant, by the interruption inherent in time, as the propulsive element in becoming. Freedom is in the opening; it is the opening itself, that which is most uniquely human.

Two Sources of Morality

Jankélévitch's priority of the instant excludes a conception of morality as a system of rules or principles. For Jankélévitch, morality carries the task of constant re-creation through action and choice. Morality does not consist of theoretical knowledge that allows one to know the good in order to subsequently do the good on the basis of that knowledge. Rather, one must continually choose the good in the rupture of the moment. Offering no laurels or plateaus, moral choice is ever upon us. The moral task is to be endlessly begun again in vigilance and responsibility. "As soon as one wants to seize virtue," Jankélévitch explains, "it becomes a caricature." "Virtue," he concludes, "exists only in escaping us."[106] Far from allowing a moral relativism in which the good is whatever one does, Jankélévitch rejects the idea that any formula or system can substitute for the moral responsibility demanded by the instant. In the instant, one is compelled to respond immediately but without assurance to the question, "What is the good?"

With its emphasis on creativity and the continual process of rupture and re-definition, Jankélévitch's philosophy consequently conveys an eschatological tone. This eschatological rupture of time, conceived not at the end of time but as the very condition of becoming, is equivocal, however, as Keiji Nishitani explains this "double meaning":

> The constant origination of new things, on the one hand, has the positive significance of genesis or creation. In that sense, time is a field of unlimited possibility in creative freedom, or, rather, it is that very possibility itself.... It enunciates the character of indefiniteness maintained by the possibilities we have within our nature as time-being (or being-time). On the other hand, this same constant origination is not something we could put a stop to even if we wanted to. It gives us no rest.... This obligation to unceasing newness makes our existence an infinite burden to us.[107]

An infinite inquietude characterizes Jankélévitch's philosophy. The task of morality is always future. It is always to come. Even the good that is done remains yet to do, Jankélévitch suggests, for the good is never done; it never is; it is beyond being—a vocation, a desire, a source of bad conscience.

Jankélévitch insists, however, that life is constituted in the dialectic of the instant and the interval. Both the interval and the instant are integral parts of his moral philosophy. He focuses on classical philosophy's concern for character and virtues and correlates particular sets of virtues to the instant and to the interval, respectively. He counts forgiveness, courage, love, charity, and humility among the virtues of the instant, and he includes friendship, fidelity, and justice among the virtues of the interval.[108] This relation between a moral order of the interval and an order in touch with the wholly other in the instant of intuition resembles Bergson's claim in his main moral treatise of the same name, *The Two Sources of Morality and Religion*.

Bergson identifies two constitutional sources of morality that form a creative tension. This principled duality or duality of two complementary principles at the foundation of morality reflects the mixture of forces inherent in life itself. Bergson identifies, on the one hand, a closed morality whose aim is social cohesion. This morality is need-based and characterized by a rigidity of rules. Obedience and duty are its key words, and its scope is particular and limited. These societies are closed and particularistic, delimited by the erection of walls that strictly separate those who belong to that society and the others who are necessarily excluded. Determined by the polarities of inclusion and exclusion, inside and outside, us and them, these societies inevitably enter into conflicts with each other and thus into war. They have their correspondence in the doctrine-laden, dogma-heavy, daily-life governing prescriptions of static religions.

On the other hand, Bergson identifies a morality that is open. This openness hinges on its creativity. Whereas intelligence is the source of knowledge for closed societies, intuition (or "creative emotions") provides the impulse for open societies. Such societies seek to overcome the particularism of the rules, which simultaneously delimit societies, in the name of greater universalism. Because they are creative, they induce disequilibrium into the parameters of social cohesion. They open what is closed and shake the balance that has been struck within closed morality. The static religion of the closed society gives way to the largely mystical experiences of dynamic religions. Although Bergson recognizes both the open and the closed within the Judeo-Christian tradition, he witnesses in the prophets, saints, and mystics the profound opening experience to all of humanity that manifests the possibility of lasting peace. He associates this opening with the upsurge of the works of love. Although he emphasizes the vitality of reform and renewal toward universalism and peace, Bergson maintains the duality of these two principles at the heart of social life and at the heart of morality. Every society, he claims, is a mixture of the open and the closed, and every religion is a mixture of the priestly and the prophetic, just as all of life is composed of the alternation and codependency of equilibrium and disequilibrium, stability and creation.

For Bergson, individual and contingent genius raises the bar of a closed society, opening it onto new and unexplored avenues—that is, opening it to the otherness of the future. The creative work of individual genius, he believes, paves the way not only for others but also for the understanding of itself. The innovative artistic work, for example, may at first stir mere consternation, but its appearance may gradually shape the interpretation of art and the atmosphere for making it. Retrospectively, the innovative artist may be called a genius, but this understanding is arrived at only through the work itself.[109] As Kierkegaard says, life may be understood by looking back but it must be lived forward.[110] Jankélévitch shares Bergson's skepticism of definition and concepts precisely for this reason. Definitions and concepts are valid for the past, but rarely can they orient decisions for the future.[111] The very definiteness of definition gathers the future into itself, rendering the event already comprehensible, whereas if one emphasizes the event as that which is to come, as creation, innovation, or genius, it renders the concept ultimately indeterminate and exposes the violent reduction of conceptualization. With both Bergson and Jankélévitch, the focus on creation and genius underlies the parallel between art and ethics. A closed society resists what calls it into question even if only by extension. True transition is rarely organic and smooth, stemming immanently from the society itself. It is rather rupture, revolution, and radical reformation on the part of individuals who, in an instant of intuition, introduce the new and the other—the new idea, the new form, the other person, or all others.

This duality at the heart of morality is also at the heart of Jankélévitch's ethics. It is in the mixture of the instant and the interval. On the one hand, the contact the finite creature has with the absolute is always only for an instant, whether it is in the creative inspiration of genius, the arousal of charity, the decisive fiat of courage, or the heroic élan of sacrifice.[112] These are all only of an instant and a quasi-incomprehensible existence. These virtues of the instant are almost nothing. Jankélévitch is well aware, on the other hand, that because the intuition does not survive the instant, every initiative carries with itself its own burgeoning decadence. Ingeniousness is always on the verge of iteration. Immediately in the wake of creation follows its normalization.[113] Initiative gives rise to imitation. Jankélévitch recognizes that this thetic grace of beginning is always the source of a scandal, but it simultaneously founds a new interval and a new legalism.[114] The innocence of creation is replaced by—or rather, gathered in and by—reflective consciousness. This gathering is at first perhaps the critical conscience of crisis, but it also yields to the consciousness of mundane self-assurance.

It is the tale of the decadence of the initial flash of lightning (*initiative-éclair*). What Georg Simmel developed under the name of the "tragedy of culture," Jankélévitch calls "metaphysical irony." The innovative spirit leads to works that dement it, deny the original intention, and ungratefully—even if unconsciously—turn away from it; creative thought becomes unrecognizable in its progenitors, and the revolution petrifies in bureaucracy. Such decomposition may take the form of worship, repetitious reproduction, or museum-like preservation. Decadence, in other words, is inevitable, just as a permanent revolution would be exhausting and a continued intuition contradictory. In short, the metaempirical cannot live in the empirical world, or it can be only otherwise, namely as repercussion or impact. Outside of a miracle, the initial gesture cannot be sustained in the world. But for Jankélévitch, the sinking (*enlisement*) of the instant represents only one side of the relapse into naturality that is decadence. An obsession with the instant can also lead to frenzy (*frénésie*), a "morbid swelling" that, no longer an affirmative plenitude, reveals the violent outbreak of making life a series of escalating instants. The metaphysical irony of which Jankélévitch speaks is thus twofold. It entails the instant that takes the detour of dissimulation into its contrary, glowing like cinders in the dull flame of the interval, awaiting and incessantly demanding rekindling.[115] And as intermediate beings, humans straddle the alternative of an absolute without duration and an interval of pure relativity.[116]

The language of mixture, therefore, obfuscates Jankélévitch's meaning. He describes the absolute metaempirical as qualitatively distinct from the relationality governing the empirical and the instant as heterogeneous to the interval. At the same time, he wants to emphasize their inseparability. Derrida has impressed this conjunction of heterogeneity and inseparability in his analyses of forgiveness and hospitality, among others.[117] He thus expresses Jankélévitch's meaning more clearly than Jankélévitch himself does in his usage of Bergson's term *mixture*. Jankélévitch's writings treat the instant and interval as distinct and yet held together. It is, therefore, appropriate to say that the instant and the interval, the absolute and the relative, the unconditional and the conditional are respectively heterogeneous to each other yet inseparable—irreconcilable and indissociable.

The question for forgiveness is thus the same as the question of conversion: How can this tangency with the wholly other, this fine and delicate point mark the threshold to a new life, especially if this infinitesimal interruption of the course of the interval excludes continuation, constancy, and established and enduring order? How, in other words, can it be the foundation of a new era? Or how can it be the source of sustenance for a new Adam when the instant of intuition begins and ends simultaneously and all that is is of the interval? It would seem that the instant that cannot be made permanent or even extended is ultimately impotent and necessarily without future. Jankélévitch argues, however, that the intervals ruptured in the instant differ from each other qualitatively. Conversion thus entails the conversion from one interval to another. With an ascending élan struggling against the gravitational pull of being, the instant potentially inaugurates another plane, another calendar—a new interval. He explains that even if it is without consequences that can be measured, predicted, or experimentally repeated, the tangency with the wholly other generates a certain pneumatic, invisible, and inexpressible transfiguration of being. After the tangential, the person is not the carrier of a secret message; he or she cannot discursively communicate what happened, for it is incommunicable and unverifiable.[118] Rather, he or she is this message, this message of an I-know-not-what that is nothing and simultaneously and contradictorily the surprised regard with which he or she views the world. Everything has changed for this person, but the transformation and the giving of new eyes does not necessarily exteriorly order or organize anything around it.[119] For Jankélévitch, the advent of the future is experienced intuitively in the moment of change, but the fact that the instantaneous advent is capable of inaugurating a future, of founding a new life, of instituting new relations is a miracle and a mystery.[120]

Jankélévitch weaves these two aspects of time, the instant and the interval, into the fabric of forgiveness. As the spontaneous, fleeting threshold, the instant is the present that never presents itself but comes to pass. This threshold presents an abrupt change from one quality to another.[121] Since humans are unable to stay on the "vertiginous peak" or "tapered summit" of the instant or of the instant of forgiveness, the miracle consists in that "the instantaneous advent is capable of inaugurating a future, of founding a new life, of instituting new relations among men; the miracle is that an era of peace could outlive the joyous instant."[122] Thus, the future is the openness of this possibility for the interval. Peace is not an inevitability or a logical consequence. It is presented as an eschatological hope whose possibility is engraved in the time of birth.

Good Will: The Future of Duty

The entire human structure suggests to Jankélévitch the idea of a natural and moral sense that is always going forward. The advent of the future seems to him a human vocation that can be identified with moral life itself. "The future," he writes, "is above all an appeal, a solicitation of the will."[123] Jankélévitch understands that this does not mean that what is future is necessarily moral. There is a natural course of time as well as a morally neglected time, for example, in the implicit decision of indecision or in the passive allowance of being made instead of making. The future-oriented character of morality, however, applies to Jankélévitch's central notions of *intention* and *duty*.

Ethics is first philosophy for Jankélévitch because it comes before ontology and metaphysics and before epistemology and questions of self-consciousness. The moral question, "What should I do?" he claims, precedes the question "Who am I?"[124] Coupling the substantivist and constructivist positions, Nietzsche famously proclaims, "Werde, was du bist [become what you are]."[125] Similarly, Jankélévitch emphasizes that although human being enables human willing, human willing transforms human being. Self-consciousness is preceded by the moral question regarding what I should do because being is dialectically defined through action such that my being awaits me in the future.[126] Since the human is an open and indeterminate being, a problematic entity, a question to and for itself, the question "What should I do?" is of vital interest and underlines the fact that morality is impossible to circumvent. It is not a matter that is resolved through contemplation but is determined by action. The moral question of human action is thus future-oriented, according to Jankélévitch, because it is the determinant factor of what will be. Three constitutive factors should be highlighted: the decision, duty, and the intention. From these three, we should acquire a better grasp of Jankélévitch's conception of what Kant says is the only thing that is good, namely a good will.[127]

The essence of morality, for Jankélévitch, is not ontological or metaphysical in the traditional or strict sense. Moral obligation, he claims, is grounded solely in itself and in the consciousness of the one who perceives it. Whereas in metaphysics the good is primary and the obligation grounded in the good is secondary, in ethics, the good is the good because one must do it. Although Jankélévitch believes that religion inclines toward metaphysics and mediation, he observes in ethics and religion a shared ideal of groundlessness according to which the good "is nothing outside of the imperative of the imperative."[128] This groundlessness is epitomized in the decision. In the instant of decision one does not have the rules or prescriptions inscribed into the order of things; rather it, requires, as Kierkegaard says, a leap. Jankélévitch maintains that the decision is indistinguishable from an irrational gesture—it is blind and groundless. Whereas Jankélévitch tends to relish in his reappraisal of the irrational, his point can be made less provocatively but, for that, no less drastically. As Derrida argues, one should inform oneself, gather reasons, weigh the plurality of sides, deliberate the pros and cons, but action will not automatically emerge from deliberation. The act of decision is heterogeneous to thought and contemplation. Under the exigency of the moral situation and the compulsion of the moral imperative, one cannot wait. One must decide. Jankélévitch recognizes in the alternative of infinite consultation either a potentially Machiavellian or cowardly solution in order to not have to decide.[129]

The intention is, for Jankélévitch, the soul of the decision.[130] There obtains a fundamental difference between the imperative and the indicative.

The imperative has a meaning only through the presence of an absence or, more precisely, a hesitation between the indicative and the imperative.[131] The intention closes that gap and resolves hesitation. It has a projective nature, and its domain is that of urgency. Beyond the passivity of expectation and hope for what may come, it demonstrates the initiative toward the outside world: It has an aim. The intention, Jankélévitch writes, "implies a moral organization and a temporal construction beyond the stillborn present."[132] The intentional soul, he concludes, is of the immediate future, but this future of intentionality constitutes the interiority of the present time. The time of action is thus an imminent future, a future-present, or, following a line from Augustine to Husserl, this imminent future is the projective future of the present, a present in becoming.

The immediate future is, however, only one aspect of the moral future. Jankélévitch portrays the more distant future beyond the prospective future-present as the domain of duty. He detects in the auxiliary verb *devoir*—and one could say the same, for example, of the English word *should* or the German words *sollen* or *müssen*—the coincidence of a temporal meaning and a meaning of obligation.[133] The good there is to do should be done immediately, not later as a silent and impassive wish for an aesthetic utopia. But Jankélévitch's notion of duty implies that the good that there is to do is continually to be done. What is more, the good that has been done is yet to be done. In other words, duty mandates that the good is always (yet) to be done; it is continually to do. There is no such thing as an accomplished or fulfilled duty.[134] The good is antithetical to goods: It cannot be accrued; there is no capitalization or credit, Jankélévitch suggests, except among hypocrites and holy rollers. Nor is there progress in matters of morality, for the illusion of progress is actually a regress if one is content with progress. Duty remains. It remains future; even if it has been done, it remains to do again and to do anew.[135] It is the vigilance of duty that renders the future moral.

Moreover, intention and duty, according to Jankélévitch, are bound by love. The good will, he claims, is literally *bene-volent*. It is the will of love that wills the good for the other, wills his or her happiness, or, one could say, is responsible for the life of the other. The object of my task is thus a concrete though incomprehensible and pneumatic demand: That which I should do is love the other. The moral of duty and the moral of love coincide because love is the good will toward the second person for his or her own sake.[136] Jankélévitch represents this love as both sacrifice and freedom. It is, in fact, the freedom to sacrifice, for humans affirm their freedom in renouncing pleasure (which is not equivalent to the negation of pleasure) and in renouncing their own will (which is not equivalent to the negation of will).[137] Jankélévitch thus speaks of an "ecstatic will" that allows us to contradict our pleasures and ourselves.[138] Such ecstatic freedom, he observes, is more supernatural than counternatural.

One loves the other innocently, Jankélévitch claims, when one forgets oneself. Francis de Sales and Fénelon capture this notion succinctly in their emphasis that one must love for the beloved and not in order to love.[139] Innocence and selflessness characterize the movement toward the other, and, contrary to a moral elitism of philosophers or saints, Jankélévitch insists that this unconditional love is universal. Everybody, at one time in his or her life, has been at least momentarily and approximately innocent and selfless. Everyone has glimpsed the love that forgets itself for the sake of the beloved. The universality does not make it any less exceptional, though. Such love is only of the instant. There comes a time when one returns to oneself, self-reflexively and self-assertingly, at the very least in the pleasure of loving or in the demand for love in return.

This time, Jankélévitch elucidates, is not just any time; it is the presence of the present. Whereas the future is other-oriented, egoism is always bound to the present. The egoist makes of the future a pseudofuture, a future that is for himself, a horizontal extension of the present, a part of the self's personal existence.[140] The egoist closes the gap between the imperative and the indicative by eliding their difference, rendering the imperative indicative. In contrast, Jankélévitch asserts that the other is *always future*. The other cannot be grasped or comprehended; rather, an ontological and metaphysical distance separates the I from the You. This does not mean that the other is an abstraction. An abstraction like humanity does not ultimately exhibit distance because it is an often empty intellection on the part of the self. The infinity of the other is, however, concrete, as concrete as one's neighbor. The good will wills the happiness of the other. He or she composes the immediate future that is the object of the imperative. In other words, the immediate future of the intention of good will is the immediate future of the other, the You, the neighbor, the second person of love. And yet this intention for the other will never be complete.[141]

The other thus does not only represent, for Jankélévitch, the immediate future of the moral intention but also the distant future of duty. His or her happiness will never be obtained or fulfilled; responsibility for him or her does not end such that one may say "up to here but no further and no more." No, according to Jankélévitch, responsibility is never finished. The perception of duty arises out of an inevitable insufficiency. Or, inversely, it arises as the desire for the other—the concrete other whose well-being I immediately will and who yet forever and repeatedly demonstrates his or her poverty. From this perspective, I will not ever have been moral; I will never be even with the other, never have been done with her or him or done with being responsible for her or him, She or he will not be reduced to my present or my horizon, and yet she or he is not a distant chimerical dream. She or he is before me, concrete and always future.

Jankélévitch's morality is thus inspired. Morality is not about success or accomplishment. It is intentional, invisible, future. Jankélévitch adopts the focus on the good will that unifies both the Gospel and Kant's morality. The disposition of the heart is more important than the realized goal. Jankélévitch greets this break with the Greek unity of moral life and success, for he senses the disparateness between the inner and outer life. The good is not measured in and cannot be measured by success. In fact, Jankélévitch believes that morality is more aligned to futile protest and unrequited love. And like Socrates, Rousseau, and Kant, Jankélévitch upholds that every human maintains a moral spark no matter how great the sin.[142] Since he links morality with the future, the good is always to do. Whether one has done good or bad, the openness of the future and the compulsion of duty demonstrate that it is never too late to do the good.

Apophatic Approaches

Forgiveness, for Vladimir Jankélévitch, is simple. It is almost nothing (*presque rien*). For this reason, he approaches the topic of forgiveness apophatically. As he writes, "The élan of forgiveness is so impalpable, so debatable, that it discourages all attempts at analysis." He sees no points of contact or solid ground "in this fleeting shock, in this imperceptible flickering of charity" that would make a philosophical discourse possible. The negative method he adopts, therefore, primarily takes account of the "empirical substitutes for metaempirical forgiveness [or] the natural forms of supernatural forgiveness." About these he has a vast amount to say.[1] To begin, Jankélévitch lays out three criteria by which he distinguishes substitutive forms from pure forgiveness. Pure "metaempirical"—or "metalogical"—forgiveness is (1) an event, (2) a relation with another person, and (3) miraculous and ineffable, a "gracious gift" that exceeds the order of systems, whether moral, legal, or juridical.

Forgiveness designates a foundational freedom, according to Jankélévitch, in its ability to respond to an offense without the provocation's determining the response. It frees the offender and the offended from the consequences of past actions, and it opens up a qualitatively different future. He recognizes, however, that the end of inner resentment and moral hatred—that is, the end of revenge and the desire for retribution—does not have to be metaempirical or supernatural. Jankélévitch admits that such an end can be achieved, sometimes even more realistically, in *forgetting*, by allowing the decay through time to heal all wounds; or in *excusing*, by offering reasons for understanding the wrongdoing or, especially, the wrongdoer; or in *renouncing,* by denying the need for forgiveness or justice. Jankélévitch concedes that these phenomena and other social, psychological, moral, and political phenomena have something in common with authentic forgiveness, for they can put an end to a hostile, critical situation, and unravel the vicious knot of anger.[2] But they all differ from forgiveness in significant ways, and ultimately they are also distinguished from each other. Although Jankélévitch demonstrates that certain forms of simili-forgiveness have validity in their own right, whether practical or moral, he maintains that they tend to obscure the nature of forgiveness. The apophatic approach, he believes, is the way to understand forgiveness. The idea of forgiveness requires sorting through the forms of simili-forgiveness in order to develop, *via negativa,* a clearer understanding of forgiveness.

The Decay of Time and Forgetfulness

Becoming is, for Jankélévitch, "essentially *futurition.*"[3] The term indicates the single-directedness of time as the constant positing of a future. This positing of a future, Jankélévitch observes, simultaneously entails a depositing of the past. The opening onto the future builds up the past. "Becoming qua advent of the future," Jankélévitch says, "is secondarily a factory of memories."[4] These memories created by the present made past in the movement toward the future do not have a value in and of themselves. They acquire significance only insofar as they enrich experience by providing a horizon of experience, an interest and passion for the arising present, and an élan for the "to come." This assertion echoes Nietzsche's contention in his *Untimely Meditations* that the past must be left behind or be made to serve life.[5] Otherwise its weight inhibits the capacity to make decisions and to move onward. If the past is looked at purely for itself, then it is dead and has the bone-dry quality of pale objectivity. If it is appropriated, used to inform decisions, then it is essential to human existence. Since life is becoming, Jankélévitch says, the future predominates over the past; it obtains a higher value than the past. This point merely underscores that, morally, the good always remains to do.

Jankélévitch outlines three ways in which the process of becoming functionally resembles forgiveness. He demonstrates, first of all, how the decay of time exhibits certain qualities found in the idea of forgiveness. The decay of time, first and foremost, offers the expediency of forgetfulness. For if an excess of history lames human engagement, action, and decision, then a history primarily determined by guilt for past crimes and offenses would paralyze the present and cast a shadow over the future.

Whereas the phrase "let bygones be bygones" certainly represents a similitude between the passing of time and forgiveness, the conjunction in the phrase "to forgive *and* forget" raises the question of a qualitative difference between forgetting and forgiving.[6] Moreover, Jankélévitch concedes the possibility that the decay of time dictates the eventual defeat of memory, whether individual or cultural. With the fading of memory comes the fading of rancor, suffering, and mourning. Time, in this view, is the great consoler that leaves no one uncomforted.

Second, the equation of time and forgiveness rests on the idea that the totality of history offers a perspective that makes all crimes and offenses appear minuscule. Whether in the Stoic bowing to the course of time and its necessity or a Hegelian reconciliation with the course of history, becoming places offenses into an oceanic perspective in which the exigency of forgiveness is washed away.

Third, the relation of time and forgiveness stresses the change naturally involved in becoming: "Have not I, the offender, become another, especially after many years? And he, the offended, has he not naturally undergone a change of heart?" In the light of these three arguments, the effects of forgiveness appear to have been achieved through the simple lapse of time, either substituting for forgiveness or rendering it useless.

The decay of time is a natural process and a product of becoming. As Jankélévitch observes, "qualitative and irreversible entropy" is essential to becoming.[7] Aristotle recognized early that time is the originator of decay (*phthoras*).[8] Time works on existing forms, decaying the past. Jankélévitch explains that time does not entail the eradication of the past for the sake of ever-new arising forms, for otherwise there would be no passage of time, no decaying, but only the perpetual present. Instead, he understands becoming as "relative renewal." It involves a fragile dialectic of memory and forgetting. Without forgetting, there would be no passage; without memory, future, present, and past would be permanently severed.[9] Jankélévitch therefore describes "a present that is always other because it is always the same, a present continually different from the past and yet similar to this past, a present slowly transformed over the course of one thousand imperceptible modifications—this is what can be called evolution."[10] What Jankélévitch, following Bergson, understands as evolution is the unavoidability and irreversibility of a forward movement that is always in relation to the past. In ethical and religious terms, Kierkegaard calls this "repetition." In his critique of the Platonic-Hegelian idea of "recollection," Kierkegaard writes that life must be lived forward.[11] The priority, even in the making of the past, is thus the future.

From the priority of the future Jankélévitch extrapolates the decay of our emotions and sentiments. "Our sentiments," he says, "demonstrate this: if the futurism of the project and of hope is retarded by backward-looking attachment, then attachment to the past by rancor and by remorse, by fidelity, or by regret and by gratitude disintegrates little by little with the effect of futurition."[12] The glance of futurition abides in the hope that the present has a future, that there will be a tomorrow, however modified, of what is today. The reverse of this hope is despair, a sense that the present has no future.[13] Forgiveness, for Jankélévitch, entails the overcoming of rancor or resentment. Thus, insofar as time washes "pebbles on the beach smooth," it appears to be "the infallible comforter and the irresistible pacifier."[14] The erosion of rancor under the compelling motion of futurition appears to always have the last word, regardless of the depth of the sentiments. The last word of futurition equates to the assured victory of forgetting. Jankélévitch writes, "No matter what happens, forgetting will be the strongest, forgetting will have the last word in all cases. One day, sooner or later, the ocean of forgetting will submerge all, and our powerless despair will itself finish by giving in to the irresistible tidal wave of indifference or the rise of new interests and of new preoccupations. . . . This is the pressure of each minute."[15]

Nevertheless, as a response to the catastrophes of history, Jankélévitch believes one should will to remember; one should face what has happened and hold on to what is valuable. Even to forgive, one must remember. "This is how one pictures the angel of history," Walter Benjamin writes. "His face is turned toward the past. Where we perceive a chain of events, he sees one single catastrophe which keeps piling wreckage and hurls it in front of his feet." Inspired by Klee's picture *Angelus Novus,* Benjamin expresses in visual terms Jankélévitch's resistance to the simple and inevitable procession of time:

> The angel would like to stay, awaken the dead, and make whole what has been smashed. But a storm is blowing in from Paradise; it has got caught in his wings with such a violence that the angel can no longer close them. The storm irresistibly propels him into the future to which his back is turned, while the pile of debris before him grows skyward. This storm is what we call progress.[16]

Personal loss or the inexplicable horrors of humanity confound the suggestion that time heals all wounds, alleviates all conflicts, and provides succor. Time is a "double-edged sword," Jankélévitch observes; it is "*natura anceps* [dubious nature]."[17] He explains that time

> discolors all the colors and tarnishes the flash of emotions, time amortizes joy just as it consoles pain, time puts gratitude to sleep just as

it disarms rancor, the one and the other indistinctly. It dries our tears, but it also puts out the flame of passion. Love loses itself in the sands; enthusiasm is destined for ossification, for mineralization, for fossilization.[18]

In this sense, the last word of futurition or forgetting is that of death and dissolution. Decay disregards the contours of human existence; it progresses irrespective of whether tears are of suffering or joy. Like pebbles on the water's edge of a beach, their accumulation is simultaneously a washing away. Jankélévitch, therefore, separates this natural process underneath notions of progress from the ethical question of forgiveness. "If we admit that this immediate forgiveness, that this instantaneous and continued forgetting merits being called 'forgiveness,'" he writes, we will have consequently conflated nature with morality.[19]

Despite its unmerited name, this "immediate forgiveness" has often been invoked in the name of political, social, and economical expediency. Was it not this "forgiveness," Derrida inquires, that was solicited by ministers in France who, after the first rounds of purging, "decided on the great amnesty of 1951 for the crimes committed under the occupation?" In the light of what was at that time perceived as the present and future crisis of Communism, they proclaimed, "It is necessary to know how to forget."[20] Although it has been stated that there is no future without forgiveness, a motive for encouraging and ordaining forgiveness is the enablement of a future by means of forgetting: Without forgetting, there would be no future; and reciprocally, without a future, there would be no forgetting.[21] In such cases, one forgives in order to forget. Or one forgets in the name of forgiveness—that is, in the place of forgiveness. Under these circumstances lightly veiled, immediate forgiveness is equivalent to forgetting. John Caputo establishes such a correlation of forgiving and forgetting. He writes, "Forgiving is just forgetting . . . just forging ahead and forgetting."[22] As Jankélévitch realizes, forgiveness that is synonymous with immediate forgetting "helps becoming to become, while becoming helps forgiveness to forgive."[23]

Forgiveness can thus be used as an effective political strategy to initiate the reconciliatory process of healing in order to reconstruct unity and enable a hopeful future. To a great extent, political and social futures are dependent on forgetting, on moving on, on accepting that "what is done is done," and on the willful confrontation of the new constellations of problems at hand, which demand new dispositions, new alliances, and, most importantly, new unity. But merely turning one's attention elsewhere and ahead does not remove the problems of past conflict, at least not at their source. Moreover, a recommendation to forgive in the sense of to forget often comes from those who can benefit from the moving-on process, from those indifferent to the sufferings of the past, or from those weary of hearing the cries of victims. "Thus," Jankélévitch protests, "there is an imprudent manner of recommending forgiveness to us that rather is a means for making us disgusted with it." He, therefore, concludes that "time, far from justifying forgiveness, renders it suspect."[24]

The portrayal of forgiveness as forgetting also misses the intentional relation to the other. Jankélévitch persists in saying that "forgiveness is an intention, and this intention is quite naturally directed at the Other, since it addresses itself to a sinner, and its raison d'être is to absolve, since it looks him in the eyes."[25] Through the apophatic method of working against the foil of forgetting, Jankélévitch makes the criteria for what constitutes forgiveness clearer and more concrete. He states that forgetting is not an intention. Nietzsche recommended an active forgetting, but this active forgetting does not represent an intentional relation with the other person. The forgetful person, as Jankélévitch writes, ceases "to have something against the offender, breaks off any relation with him. Not only does the negativity of forgetting not imply this relation, but it rather excludes it."[26] Time is not naturally oriented toward the other; its orientation is simply its vacant, forward glance.

Just as the time of forgetting does not engage with the other, it is not an event but only a gradation. Although forgetting fulfills Jankélévitch's requirement that resentment be overcome in forgiveness, forgetting overcomes passion only little by little, while memory and rancor become less and less, and indifference greater and greater. Jankélévitch consequently asks, "At what moment has the event come to pass?"[27] No event occurs; no decision is made; no gratuitous gift is given in the evolution of continuous and immanent time.[28] Jankélévitch insists that forgiveness is a "first movement like undeliberated charity." It is "always a fiat, an event, an act . . . that comes to pass in the suddenness of an instant."[29] This instant has a supernatural, transformative capacity. Mere forgetfulness in the decay of time, he writes, "does not at all possess the conversionary and transfiguring power of forgiveness. . . . The man in mourning, consoled by the very ancientness of his old sorrow, has not metamorphosed his sadness into joy, nor found positive reasons to be happy."[30]

Since Jankélévitch locates forgiveness in the instant as the radical possibility of something new, it follows that forgiveness obeys an either-or structure, the structure of decision. In contrast, time is "the natural dimension of mediation, for mediation is essentially temporal."[31] Temporality can be seen as that which is constantly mediating, while ensuring, in its forward march, that there is always something to mediate. Organic metaphors of integration demonstrate the priority of the present and especially the future over the past. Just as an organism adapts to a foreign body, the offended person discovers a modus vivendi with the offense.[32] Dissimulation, deference, and digestion, on the one side, and compromise, concession, and conciliation, on the other side, mark the paths of synthesis and mediation. With forgiveness, it is rather that one either asks for forgiveness or not, according to Jankélévitch, and forgiveness is either granted or not—in the suddenness of a decision. As a relation of one to the other, forgiveness refuses the mediation of the third—the attempted synthesis between contraries. Jankélévitch explains that "synthesis integrates through fusion the innuendos and understated rancors within a totality." It is consequently "not so much the goal of a moral life as it is the masterwork of a learned chemistry."[33] Even the "total mixture" still contains traces of rancor and injury like a drop of wine in water, even if it is a single drop in an ocean.

In the *Corpus Hippocraticum*, it is said that "healing happens at times through *chronos*, other times through *kairos*."[34] Although forgiveness represents the healing though *kairos*, Jankélévitch does not doubt that the flow of time, the unidirectionality of becoming, also contains potential healing. He calls forgetfulness a pseudoforgiveness because of this very capacity to put an end to the cycles of violence, heal the wounds of the past, and open renewed relations. He questions, however, whether "the long road of becoming [is] the straightest and most sincere path for arriving at peace."[35] The problem with mere forgetting, Jankélévitch observes, is that it "does not at all solve the problem once and for all or does not put a final end to the hostilities. . . . Let us rather fear that the hostilities will spring back to life!"[36]

For Jankélévitch, as long as there is no justice, as long as justice remains unfulfilled and laws and actions remain yet unjust, the societal attempts at quiet and security will be plagued by falsity and frail illusions. Crimes and offenses create unease and disorder in a society, but as soon as the public consciousness loses the memory of the offense, the unease subsides, disappearing into the black of night that is already broken by the dawn of a new day.[37] Jankélévitch thus acknowledges the manner in which society often seeks its own security and generally ignores damaged lives; it looks at the overall picture and not at the individual lives that constitute its fabric; it looks ahead. At best, this look ahead is meant to ensure that nothing like the Shoah recurs. But such recurrence may come in a form deferred. The return of the repressed in a destructive and perverse way, as Freud taught, equally applies to the mass of forgotten individuals who accompany us like silent *golem*.[38] Their return is the return of the impossible, the impossible coming back of what has been done and of those who have been within the seeming docility of becoming.

Jankélévitch claims that forgetting and the flow of time, therefore, remain incapable of inaugurating a new era. The decay of time and forgetting exert only a negative positivity. Raw time might alleviate sorrow; it might console in the sense that one loses touch with the passion that made one inconsolable, but this negativity, resembling the Hegelian negation of negation, does not obey the code of formal logic and, at the end, produce a positive. Or, more precisely, the positive that forgetting introduces is the simple negation of the negation that was the source of suffering in the first place. Consequently, forgetting alone cannot found a new order or introduce the advent of positive relations, for underneath the negative positivity (the negation of negation) may still smolder the resentments that lie latent in memory and await but a spark to catch fire.[39] The equation of forgiving and forgetting targets exactly such smolders in the belief that what is remembered is still a vital force harbored in the psyche the dismissal of which achieves the intention of forgiveness. Jankélévitch, on the contrary, brings out the dark corners of forgetting. First of all, forgetting would always have to entail the forgetting of forgetting, for otherwise that which is forgotten has not disappeared or has not been entirely "blotted out." Rather, it is marked by consciousness and perhaps by the trial or pain of forgetting the offense. Even the forgetting of forgetting, therefore, can become a dialectical game of consciousness ad infinitum between memory and the condition of memory, forgetting. If the passive forgetting removes the traces of conscious decision, the doubling of a forgetting of forgetting would mark perhaps less the doubled distance to the phenomenon or event forgotten and much more the doubling back. Active forgetting is a schism consciously chosen, and the forgetting of this tear allows that which is severed not necessarily or only to disappear in doubled distance but also to haunt or lurk in the mind's recesses.[40] Jankélévitch doubts, in short, that forgetting alone heals yesterday's wounds, much less that it opens onto a transformed tomorrow.

Ataraxia and Apathy

Jankélévitch's arguments against a "temporal forgiveness" (forgetting, futurition, and concomitant decay) apply equally well to the notion that wrongs might be lost in the vastness or totality of history or being. According to Plato, philosophy has the task of leading the contemplative life. In the contemplative life, he states, the philosophical mind has a view toward the totality of time and being, which renders human affairs insignificant and even contemptible.⁴¹ Similarly, as Pierre Hadot has demonstrated, the Stoics practiced "spiritual exercises" meditating on the infinity of history, a perspective from which present concerns appear minute and the bloated ego is instilled with humility. Seneca, for example, writes, "Place before your mind's eye the vast spread of time's abyss and embrace the universe; and then compare what we call human life with infinity."⁴² And Marcus Aurelius reminds himself:

> Reflect often on the speed with which all things in being, or coming into being, are carried past and swept away. Existence is like a river in ceaseless flow, its actions a constant succession of change, its causes innumerable in their variety: scarcely anything stands still, even what is most immediate. Reflect too on the yawning gulf of past and future time, in which all things vanish.⁴³

From the view on high circumscribing the infinite and meditating on the nature of fate, individual life is but an insignificant speck. *Volens nolens* (whether willing or not) time runs its course, and fate stakes its claim. Wisdom, then, for the Stoics, entails the alignment of the will with the fate of time and, what is more, the love of it (*amor fati*). For it is better to assume one's destiny and avoid suffering than to protest against it.⁴⁴ As the subjection to universal nature or universal reason, the goal of apathy or indifference dismisses offenses by relativizing what has happened in the larger scheme of things. Although the contemplative life and cosmological contextualization may offer a perspective on personal offenses, little harms, and the concerns of ordinary human life, the embedment of injury into a cosmological vision should not be confused with an act of forgiveness. No one, Jankélévitch rather bluntly claims, opens Epictetus's *Discourses* to find insight into the nature of forgiveness. "Hardened by ataraxia, analgesia, and apathy," the Stoic makes of injuries mere scratches and disregards insults as misjudgments, making offenses null, the offended untouched, and forgiveness useless.⁴⁵ Therefore, the eagle's-eye view cast by Marcus Aurelius on the infinite span of history has nothing to do with pure forgiveness, according to Jankélévitch.⁴⁶ Like the decay of time, reflections on the infinity of time and being do not involve the transformative instant, the intentional act, the gratuitous gift, or the relation to the other.

Megalopsychia

The Stoic notions of ataraxia and apathy represent certain characteristics of the Greek ideal of the sage in general. The sage is one who does not require forgiveness because he acts wisely or in accordance with universal reason. A unique form of the sage is portrayed by Aristotle in the ideal of *megalopyschia*—the ideal of the magnanimous person. The reason for Aristotle's exclusion of forgiveness from the virtues, according to Charles Griswold, "lies in the character of his perfectionist ethical scheme, for it is one that seeks to articulate and recommend the character of the man of complete virtue."[47] The person possessing perfect moral virtue—the *megalopsuchos*—certainly has no need for being forgiven because by definition he is morally perfect, and for two main reasons he would also seem unforgiving of others. First, the situations and faults of nonvirtuous persons are of little account to him. The magnanimous person is largely dismissive of "inferior people." Aristotle's hierarchical value scheme stipulates that nonmagnanimous victims of wrongdoing do not have any standing to be treated better, or at least their being wronged is of no concern to the virtuous person. In short, the inherent dignity of persons seems missing from this perfectionist or "aristocratic" scheme.[48] Second, the completely virtuous person would judge himself immune to being injured by others morally. He would be above resenting the actions of the *hoi polloi,* and by definition another person of perfect moral virtue would not injure him, his equal and friend, or any other for that matter. Aristotle states that the magnanimous person

> cannot let anyone else, except a friend, determine his life. For that would be slavish; and this is why all flatterers are servile and inferior people are flatterers. He is not prone to marvel, since he finds nothing great; or to remember evils, since it is proper to a magnanimous person not to nurse memories, especially not of evils, but to overlook them.... He does not speak evil even of his enemies, except [when he responds to their] wanton aggression. He especially avoids laments or entreaties about necessities or small matters, since these attitudes are proper to someone who takes these things seriously.[49]

The person of complete virtue is "self-sufficient" (*autarkos* [1125a12]); he has no need of others and is not affected by others. This self-sufficiency is precisely the condition for the contemplative life. The sage removes himself from human affairs in order to focus on the theoretical life abstracted from involvement with other human beings. Whereas the sage is the finite exemplum of the contemplative life, god is the eternal representative of the equation of the moral and theoretical life. Griswold comments that "the perfect theorizer is god, and Aristotle's god manifests no concern whatever for anything or anybody but himself qua thinking about himself. Strictly speaking he (or, it) can neither be said to act nor to have emotions; god neither forgives nor requires forgiveness. For Aristotle, god leads the life of the mind, and is therefore the paradigm of perfection."[50]

The Nietzschean noble man represents the modern revision of this ancient ideal. He swells with the power to shape, recuperate, and forget. He merely shrugs off the offenses of his enemies as pesky little vermin.[51] Nietzsche's example from the modern world of such a person is Mirabeau, who, he claims, had no memory for insults or baseness and couldn't forgive only because he forgot. For Nietzsche, if the love of one's enemies is at all possible on earth, then it is in this manner alone. This "forgetful love" derives its power from the immunity of self-strength to being touched or moved by others.

In contrast to this character of what he calls "clemency," Jankélévitch believes forgiveness is neither a humble exercise in acceptance nor a haughty assertion of the will. Such reactions concern the self but dismiss the other. They mock the biblical admonition to turn the other cheek. Jankélévitch explains that "the one who turns the other cheek, not out of love of man as Jesus demanded, but in order to exercise his will and resistance to vindictive temptation is not a generous man."[52] Thus the magnanimous person with "greatness of soul" (literally *megalopsychia*), according to Jankélévitch, excludes "every truly transitive or intentional relation with the next person." The relation to the dismissed and often contemptible other represents a solipsism, as the other is not a "true partner of flesh and bones." Jankélévitch even compares the indiscriminate magnanimity of the noble person to nature, which does not love anyone in particular and is "unaware of the alterity of the other, [and] a fortiori it is unaware of the relation to the other."[53] Others concern the magnanimous solely as recipients of and witnesses to their greatness. Aristotle observes that "magnanimous people seem to remember the good they do, but not what they receive, since the recipient is inferior to the giver."[54] In contrast, Jankélévitch presupposes a condition of human finitude that is fallible and vulnerable.[55] He emphasizes the vulnerable exposure of one to the other that makes possible a relation with the other, admitting of both intimacy and a vulnerability to violence.

Moreover, Jankélévitch elevates human dignity to a universal category and upholds the fundamental moral value of all persons. The universality of human value, for him, is grounded in the uniqueness and irreplaceability of each and every person. He applies the linguistic term *hapax legomenon*, meaning that a word is used only once in a work or corpus, to individuality. In its incomparable haecceity, the individual as hapax will have been only once in all of history. In contradistinction to the view of the totality of being and time, the facts that the individual did live and that a misdeed was done are not subject to the decay of time or the erosion of forgetting.

The Excuse

Jankélévitch further outlines several necessary, albeit insufficient, conditions for forgiveness. Forgiveness, first of all, obviously presupposes a misdeed or an offense and thus an offender and an offended. Second, it requires time between the misdeed and forgiveness; this indeterminate length of time is the time in which the claim of justice arises: It is the time of memory and moral resentment. Third, as an intentional relation of one to the other, only the offended can forgive the offender for the offense committed. Alongside the characteristics of forgiveness as belonging to the instant, involving a relation with the other, and constituting a gratuitous gift, these necessary conditions provide a composite against which Jankélévitch examines the excuse.

Jankélévitch distinguishes forgiveness from the excuse because the excuse, he claims, is neither an event nor a relation with the other nor a gratuitous gift. He maintains that the excuse remains in the realm of justice—that is, in the sphere of reciprocity and rationality. Just as he goes to great lengths to demonstrate that to forgive is not simply to forget, he demonstrates that understanding and forgiveness are neither synonymous nor even analogous. For him, the relation of the excuse to forgiveness is the relation of reason to superrationality. Although what is not understandable is inexcusable, what is inexcusable is still forgivable. Jankélévitch associates what is inexcusable with wickedness or evil. Since wickedness is not understandable, he claims, it is thus inexcusable. But Jankélévitch speaks of that which is inexcusable to demarcate a forgiveness for which there is nothing that is unforgivable. It is imperative, therefore, to research the limits of the excuse, as he sees it, for the inexcusable marks the limits of understanding itself. To be able to excuse, one must be able to understand—that is, to be able to explain not *that* something happened but *how* it came to happen. The excuse thus searches out the rationality, motivations, even the history or genealogy of a misdeed. The excuse seeks to understand, but Jankélévitch rejects the conclusion that "to understand is to forgive," or, as the French expression indicates, that *tout comprendre c'est tout pardonner*. Instead, it is precisely the inexcusable, according to Jankélévitch, that calls for forgiveness. His understanding of forgiveness can thus be illuminated in contrast to the Greek notion of *sungnômê* (understanding), which, particularly in Aristotle, illustrates the equation of the excuse with understanding. Jankélévitch's systematic examination of the excuse focuses, first of all, on the intellective excuse or total excuse and, second, on the partitive excuse disclosed exemplarily in "mitigating circumstances."

Total or Intellective Excuse

The total excuse, according to Jankélévitch, entails the metaphysical negation of evil, of wickedness, and of sin.[56] More precisely, it excuses human action and inaction by denying positive will and responsibility. Whereas forgetting does not claim that there is no wickedness, the "intellective excuse" implicates a moral appreciation of the act that it excuses.[57] Rooted in a metaphysical vision of the nature of reality, the intellectualist, as Jankélévitch describes him, sees transparently through the single acts of purported evil and misdeeds, rendering them illusions or misapprehensions, and making of them naught.

Jankélévitch uncovers three types of intellective excuse. First of all, one might posit an eternal principle of evil in which the principle or the personification of the principle—the devil, for instance—carries culpability in the place of this or that individual. Such a principle inoculates the will against culpability. No one is culpable, in this metaphysical recourse, for the devil's shoulders are broad.[58]

Second, Jankélévitch declares that in the "contemplationist" vision of someone like Leibniz, it is not that sin does not exist per se, but only that it is subsumed into the general plan of the universe. Another term for this view is *theodicy*—a term invented by Leibniz in order to justify God, bestow meaning on suffering and evil, and make the case that the real world is as it is supposed to be. For Leibniz, it is the best of all possible worlds; we just need to realize it.[59] Although all forms of determinism uncover the root of a necessity underlying every action, the embedment of human action in a cosmological scheme, as we saw with the Stoics, or in God's providence, overlooks the puniness of finite particulars in order to focus on the infinite order of universal reason and necessity according to nature or God. In his *Introduction to the Lectures on the Philosophy of World History*, Hegel, for instance, claims that "the aim of philosophy is to defend reality against its detractors . . . . [and] to *eliminate the contingent*."[60] Philosophical inquiry, for him, is nothing less than theodicy.[61] In the speculative enterprises of Leibniz, Spinoza, and Hegel, Jankélévitch recognizes an effort "to reintegrate the misdeed into a universal necessity where it becomes intelligible, to dissipate the areas of shadow and the opacities that the mirage of wicked liberty projects into the world."[62] In the revelatory light of his metaphysical vision, they can assuredly assert that evil is "implicitly null" and eventually overpowered by the spirit of light and consciousness.

Third, Jankélévitch addresses the Greek theme, ranging from Plato's Socrates to the Stoics, in which ignorance or *amatheia* is cast as the root of all sin. For "no one," claims Plato's Socrates in *Apology*, "goes willingly toward the bad or what he believes to be the bad."[63] Although people do commit misdeeds, according to this view, they do not do so with the intention that it is bad. In the *Meno*, Socrates leadingly asks, "Do you think, Meno, that anyone, knowing that bad things are bad, nevertheless desires them?"[64] Jankélévitch sees what he calls the Greek excuse embodied in the intellectual optimism of Socrates, who negated the possibility of ill will.[65]

The intellective excuse does approximate forgiveness, Jankélévitch explains, in that it eliminates sin and aims at universal absolution. It eliminates sin, however, in advance. It denies the reality of sin, and it is moved by good reasons into the nature of reality, whereas forgiveness is unmotivated by such insight.[66] "Intellectualism," he explains, "is the negation of all irrational supernaturality, be this supernaturality that of evil or that of love."[67] He therefore concludes that since forgiveness is the rationally unmotivated, ungrounded gracious gift given in the instant of creative decision, it has as its prerequisite the positivity of sin and the irrationality of evil. Sin, evil, and suffering may not be sacrificed at the altar of universal reason.

The intellective excuse is consequently not an event, a relation with others, or a gratuitous gift. It is not an event because, as an understanding or a comprehension, it is linked to the laborious discovery of the truth in the interval. Like value, truth, according to Jankélévitch, is atemporal; it exists whether or not it is recognized. Truth is, therefore, discovered, not invented. Jankélévitch concedes that discovery may take place on a certain date, but that date marks the advent of the eternal in time, the atemporal in the temporal. The truth discovered was also true before the discovery; it did not become true; it became known, recognized, and acknowledged after the discursive labor of intellectual intuition. It is not time, Jankélévitch observes, that makes us understand the truth; time simply measures the duration of the intellectual effort.[68] If and when something is comprehended, it does not possess the event-character of the creative instant; it is much more the nature of the intellect "to read within" what is always already there.[69]

The intellective excuse does not imply a relation with the other, because it entails more immediately the relation to "impersonal and anonymous truth."[70] Jankélévitch contends that to encompass misdeeds in the horizon of a general truth is to overlook the specificity of the persons involved and to dull or even extinguish the offense. The intellectual abstracts from circumstantial aspects, subordinating them to essential knowledge. The offense is handled with pure negativity. According to this logic, the perception of the situation that dictates action is extrapolated from the truth in general. Indifference and a lack of intention thus characterize the similiforgiveness of the intellective excuse. "Such forgiveness," Jankélévitch explains, "does not have a second person; it concerns the anonymous universality of 'third' persons; it does not address itself to *you*. It is not engaged like true forgiveness in an immediate relation with the person opposite from it, but it is impartial."[71] In contrast, pure forgiveness is personal, directive, and intentional.

As opposed to being directed to the other as a you, this third person perspective is the perspective of "omnilaterality," the encompassing perspective of reason and justice. As such, the law of reciprocity requires that one consider things not only from the perspective of self-love, or "philauty"—to follow Jankélévitch's etymological coinage—but also from the perspective of the other person. This perspective does not simply entail seeing things from the other side; it also, and primarily, involves the view of the third person, which is always at least potentially the third person plural—the other "multiplied infinitely . . . *alterity* par excellence."[72] While differentiating understanding from forgiveness, Jankélévitch draws the positive consequences stemming from the valid domain of understanding. Falling under the law of universality, reason, and justice, this viewpoint distinguishes the moral misdeed from the merely personal offense. Often that which is deemed necessary to be forgiven, or at least be subject to forgiveness, is to the offended merely a blow to his or her own ego, an act or harsh word that deflates his or her self-esteem. In this manner, the perspective of the distant neighbor, the manifold third of universality, invites the one who claims offense to dismiss every pettiness and acknowledge the truth. For knowledge, too, Jankélévitch observes, has the capacity to soothe the wells of rancor and resentment. Understanding implies an interior transformation of the one who understands, resolving through comprehension the misunderstandings born of miscomprehension.[73]

But to recognize the nothingness of sin—that is, to understand that everything can be understood—cannot be equated with the giving of a gift to the other. Jankélévitch says there is nothing gratuitous or gracious about understanding the understandable or about excusing the excusable. To excuse a person because he or she is ignorant or sick or otherwise not accountable is not to be gracious toward him or her. It is purely to give him or her justice.[74] "To excuse is simply to pay one's debt, to render to the guilty person who is recognized as innocent what is due to him, and to give it to him outside of all graciousness."[75] In one sense, then, to understand is to excuse, but, Jankélévitch qualifies, for that reason, it is only to excuse.[76] It has its limits in the inexcusable and incomprehensible. And this limit is not only theoretical. Rather, even accounting for the tiresome effort of comprehension and the deflation of egos, intellection costs little and is relatively without pain. But forgiveness, according to Jankélévitch, involves an agonizing sacrifice, and only comes into question in pain. The pain Jankélévitch refers to is that "irrational effectivity" and "lived affectivity" inherent in the relations with violent people, wicked people, and torturers.[77]

Therefore, to understand is not to forgive. And in another sense, to understand is not even to excuse. For Jankélévitch acknowledges that the excuse does not flow automatically and in every case from comprehension. Like forgiveness, it, too, is "synthetic" with the act of understanding and thus requires a "supplement of élan." Without this supplementary élan or "gratuitous impetus," he claims, one stays a witness and an indifferent spectator to the reasons for excusing, instead of *oneself* actually excusing.[78] The personal act or decision-character of excusing, in other words, while bound to understanding remains distinct from deliberation. One still has to do it. Neither forgiveness nor the excuse simply flows out of intellection like a logical conclusion.

The difference between the excuse and forgiveness, for Jankélévitch, comes down to their relation to motives and reasons as well as to the gift-relation with the other. The excuse is motivated by the understanding, whereas forgiveness is unmotivated, or, what is for him the same, it is motivated by love. One must be able to understand in order to excuse; and in a sense, one should morally excuse what one understands because it is excusable. The excuse moves in the arena of reciprocity, reason, and justice; it maintains and demands symmetry through reflection on universals. Forgiveness, in contrast, incites hyperbole and asymmetry. It is spontaneous, a singular grace or charity that aims at the inexcusable.

Sungnômê (Understanding)

Whereas the Greek terms from *megalopsychia* to *ataraxia* can readily be distinguished from forgiveness, the Greek poets and philosophers also seem to invoke the vocabulary of forgiveness. It is, therefore, important to acknowledge, as Griswold states, that "contrary to common wisdom," views about forgiveness "did circulate in pre-Christian pagan thought and culture."[79] While recognizing a family resemblance, it is, however, even more important to emphasize the basic differences between a Greek (and also Roman) understanding of forgiveness and a modern, Judaic-Christian-inspired understanding.[80] From Herodotus to Sophocles, Euripides, and Aristophanes to Plato, Xenophon, and Aristotle, the word often translated as forgiveness is *sungnômê,* or a cognate thereof, which has a broad range of meanings depending on context. It can mean acknowledgment, consent, agreement, compassion, or fellow feeling with another, as well as excuse, pardon, and forgiveness. The cognitive connotations of the term revolve around the notion of "understanding."

At the beginning of Plato's dialogue *Critias,* for example, Critias requests *forbearance* of what he is about to discuss. Although Timaeus, too, asked for *indulgence* for his discourse on the "high matters" of creation, Critias believes that he is in still greater need of indulgence, for "to speak well of gods to men is far easier than to speak well of men to men." He consequently pleads to be *excused* for his inability to express his meaning on this difficult subject. As an intent and polite listener, Socrates grants him his request and even extends "by anticipation" the same *indulgence* to the next speaker, Hermocrates.[81] Granted, this situation of discourse is far removed from the moral situations of conflict often represented in Greek drama, involving offense and retributive anger, and one of a set of reconciliatory responses from pity to excuse. But Plato's dialogue does demonstrate that the term *sungnômê* is much closer to what we would translate as "having understanding" for someone in the light of their situation, "being lenient or indulgent" with him, or "excusing" that person. Jacqueline de Romilly summarizes these attitudes under one word, *douceur* (gentleness, mildness), and Karin Metzler reconstructs their core as the capacity to place oneself in the position of another.[82] Jankélévitch treats the Greek "understanding" under the rubric of the excuse. Although he acknowledges that, in its gentleness and leniency, the Greek excuse tended toward forgiveness, he upholds the qualitative distinction between the two.[83]

In contrast to the moral hierarchy of megalopsychia, sungnômê is accorded to equals. As Danièle Aubriot explains, the excuses put forth to diminish responsibility are of diverse orders, ranging from external constraint or compulsion to the unreflective acts of youth to anger and other passions and even appetites to which humans naturally succumb. In sum, the excuse requests the recognition of attenuating circumstances, alleging that one was not in the full possession of one's judgment at the moment of committing an offense. The notion of voluntary action, therefore, plays a prominent role in the determination of whether something may be excused or not. If, for example, one voluntarily falls into error or commits an offense, there is no excuse. It may be said, then, that excusable acts, whether for lack of experience or knowledge, entail an action that takes place "despite oneself." Such actions are deemed involuntary (*akousios*). Mitigating circumstances can thus disengage the responsibility of the agent altogether, showing him to be not guilty in the sense that his action was indeliberate and without express intent. They can thus render an act of injustice or a crime a mere imprudence, an accident, or a matter of negligence.[84] But it is also possible that attenuating circumstances do not totally excuse a harm done but merely lessen the responsibility of the offender and, as a consequence, lessen the punishment.

Aristotle's usage of the term *sungnômê* in his *Nicomachean Ethics* clearly demonstrates this understanding. The term first appears in the context of Aristotle's distinction between voluntary and involuntary actions. Since virtue, according to Aristotle, "is about feeling and actions," they receive either "praise or blame if they are voluntary, but pardon, sometimes even pity, if they are involuntary."[85] It is therefore only involuntary acts that deserve understanding, leniency, or pity—that is, acts that do not reflect the moral quality of one's character.

Aristotle divides involuntary acts into those done under compulsion and those done out of ignorance.[86] If the principle (*arche*) of an act is outside of oneself, as in cases of external compulsion, then one cannot be made responsible for them. Such acts are involuntary in a strict sense. If, however, the compulsion is of an internal kind, then one possesses in oneself the principle of action and is responsible. Taking into account the situational complexity of human actions, Aristotle therefore adds a third category to the voluntary and involuntary, namely "mixed actions." For instance, he explains, if a tyrant has control over one's parents or children and threatens their lives unless one does something that is shameful, or if a boat is sinking and one is faced with the choice of unloading cargo into the sea or saving oneself and others, one can legitimately claim that the act is voluntary because the actor "has within him the principle of moving the limbs that are the instruments" of the action and, moreover, "it is up to him to do them or not to do them." At the same time, Aristotle concedes that no one would do them willingly and that they are thus to be considered involuntary. The virtue of such actions is dependent on the situation, the good for which one endures shame, and the result. Some may be praised; others are blamed. Those actions that neither deserve praise nor incur blame, however, may prove to be understandable or pardonable, for, he explains, "There is pardon, whenever someone does a wrong action because of conditions of a sort that overstrain human nature, and that no one would endure."[87]

Among the acts out of ignorance (*agnoia*), Aristotle distinguishes between the involuntary and the "nonwilling." As he explains,

> Everything caused by ignorance is nonvoluntary, but what is involuntary also involves pain and regret. For if someone's action was caused by ignorance, but he now has no objection to the action, he has done it neither willingly, since he did not know what it was, nor unwillingly, since he now feels no pain. Hence, among those who act because of ignorance, the agent who now regrets his action seems to be unwilling, but the agent with no regrets may be called nonwilling, since he is another case—for, since he is different, it is better if he has his own special name.[88]

Aristotle first separates an ignorance of particulars from an ignorance of universals, and he secondly associates the former with involuntary actions and the latter with moral decision and thus with vice. Those actions he calls involuntary imply an ignorance of particulars. He specifies these as regarding (1) the agent, (2) the act, (3) the occasion or circumstances of the act, and, sometimes, (4) the instrument or tool, (5) the object (e.g., safety), and (6) the manner of doing an act (e.g. gently or hard).[89] For instance, a person may be said to have acted involuntarily if he is ignorant of what he is doing as when a secret slips from one's lips in speaking; or if he deploys a weapon when he only wanted to demonstrate it; or if in battle, he confuses his son with an enemy; or if he gives someone a drink to save her life that turns out to be a poison that might kill her; or if in sparring, he wounds another when he merely intended to prick. An agent who acts out of such ignorance, he maintains, feels pain and regret for his action because it is now clear to him what he did. It is not his general character that is in question. *Involuntary* here takes on the sense of the *unintentional*, which is determined in specific circumstances. In book 5 on justice, Aristotle states that an action rooted in one or more of the criteria for involuntary action is to be considered an "error" or, if the result exceeds reasonable expectation, as would be the case in the death of the other, a "misfortune."[90] In both cases, no harm was intended, and intention is what matters.

Such ignorance at the basis of involuntary action is not to be confused with the ignorance of the unjust. Aristotle insists that the "ignorance of what is beneficial is not taken to make action involuntary. For the cause of involuntary action is not [this] ignorance in the decision, which causes vice; it is not [in other words] ignorance of the universal, since that is a cause for blame."[91] As a cause for blame, such actions would not be subject to pardon or excuse.[92] A person of bad character, according to

Aristotle, does not feel the pain of regret because he or she does not recognize the wickedness of his or her act. The act coheres with the character, and the person's ignorance pertains to the prudential good (*agathon*) and the moral good (*kalon*). Due to his false disposition of character, he holds the bad (*kakia*) for the good and thus is ignorant of his true interest. For Aristotle, we are responsible for our character, for the habits we cultivate, and the decisions we make.[93] Ignorance of the good cannot, in other words, be excused.

With a view to human frailty and weakness, however, Aristotle extends what may be deemed involuntary and thus potentially excusable, to the passions and, to a lesser degree, to the appetites that motivate human action. As an example, he considers an action caused by anger. Although he admits that, if the infliction of harm is done in knowledge but without previous deliberation, it is an act of injustice, he also maintains that this person is neither unjust nor wicked since it is not vice that causes him to inflict the harm.[94] For Aristotle, the person who acts out of anger does not do so as a deliberate moral choice; he rather acts out of the passion of anger. He concludes that "whenever his decision is the cause, he is unjust and vicious."[95] Although the act may be an act of injustice, succumbing to the passion of anger does not make the person unjust.[96] In other words, the isolated act is not necessarily reflective of a person's moral character. Being angered is an exceptional though thoroughly natural and human passion.

Passion in general and anger specifically, according to Aristotle, entail a partial listening to reason. He compares the passion of anger to hasty servants who hear an order but do not hear the order out. Acting out of passion, he says in another analogy, is like a dog who barks without waiting to see if it is a friend. Reason registers that an injury or injustice has taken place, and passion rushes through the door. Since reason is at least partially present, however, Aristotle assumes that moral conscience will invoke pain and regret at having acted out of anger. Juxtaposing acts of anger that are elicited by a foregoing injustice to wanton aggression, he claims, "no one feels pain when he commits wanton aggression; but whatever someone does from anger, he feels pain when he does it, whereas the wanton aggressor does what he does with pleasure."[97]

Aristotle is less understanding of acts that are motivated by appetites. In book 7 on incontinence (*akrasia*), he argues that incontinence due to passion or emotion (*thumia*) is less shameful than incontinence due to appetite (*epithumia*). He states: "It is more pardonable to follow natural desires, since it is also more pardonable to follow those natural appetites that are common to everyone and to the extent that they are common."[98]

Although both are excusable, he insists that the passions of anger and irritability are more natural than excessive and unnecessary appetites.[99] Being more natural, they are more common and may thus be met with greater understanding.

Moreover, Aristotle associates incontinence more closely with appetites because of its immediate correlation to the seeking of pleasure, and he is unhesitant in his qualification of incontinence as a kind of vice. But in contrast to the person of bad character and to the licentious person, the incontinent person has in general the *prohairesis* (the deliberate decision) to seek the pleasant in an appropriate measure and acts accordingly, even against weaker appetites. He merely strays from this intention in the case of intense appetites.[100] Aristotle recognizes that, in specific situations under the pressure of desires, we humans sometimes do violate our better knowledge, beliefs, or moral judgment.[101] He explains that "it is not surprising if someone is overcome by strong and excessive pleasures or pains; indeed, this is pardonable, provided he struggles against them. . . . But it is surprising if someone is overcome by what most people can resist."[102] The incontinent person is thus situated between the intemperate person who has a false general orientation and the weak-willed, self-indulgent person who readily gives in at the first sign of pleasure. It is a most human and natural situation to fail the good at some times and in small degree. He concludes:

> Some involuntary actions are to be pardoned, and some are not. For if someone's error is not only committed in ignorance, but also caused by ignorance, it is to be pardoned. But if, though committed in ignorance, it is caused not by ignorance but by some feeling that is neither natural nor human, it is not to be pardoned.[103]

In his view, blameworthy acts, viciousness, or bestiality remain inexcusable. But human fallibility and the exceptional human susceptibility to error constitute grounds for excuse and should be taken into consideration in the evaluation of moral life.

To take human fallibility into consideration is to move within the realm of justice. It belongs to the justice of the virtue of what Aristotle calls *decency* (*epieikeia*). In book 6 on the intellectual virtues, Aristotle describes *sungnômê*, which Terence Irwin exceptionally translates in terms of "consideration," as a virtue of taking particulars into account. He writes that "considerateness is the correct consideration that judges what is decent; and correct consideration judges what is true."[104] He thus associates considerateness with the decent person, and decency with the category of justice. Aristotle estimates decency as superior to what is just, however, because it does not strictly follow the letter of universal law but judges in accordance with the spirit of the law. Since the law is universal but human action is situated in contexts, decency functions as a "rectification" of legal justice.[105] Aristotle recognizes that the law cannot always be correct when it is dealing with particulars and that it commits errors when it is applied inflexibly. It, therefore, requires individuation and interpretation—the consideration of particulars—in order to justly handle particular cases. Decency is, however, not confined to the legislator or judge. The decent person can generously yield to another even though the law is on his side. According to Aristotle, the decent person abides in the mean. He is mild. Although he is aware of a "slavish" willingness to excuse out of weakness, the mild person, Aristotle claims, "seems to err more in the direction of [this] deficiency, since the mild person is ready to pardon, not eager to exact a penalty."[106]

Sungnômê is, therefore, indulgent, apparently self-reflective in its determination of what is human and natural, and even generous, but it differs in three significant respects from forgiveness. First of all, whereas the excuse excludes voluntary offenses, offenses done out of viciousness, and all that is blameworthy, forgiveness is graciously given to the deliberate offense. There are no types of offenses that may not be forgiven, and, in fact, it is, according to Jankélévitch, precisely the inexcusable acts that require forgiveness. Second, the excuse is limited to the realm of justice and reason. It is just to excuse; or better, it is the decency of justice that allows there to be excuses. Although a person may "justly" refuse to be understanding of the circumstances of another's action, it is decent and thus just to be understanding for things that are common and natural, and that constitute a mere exceptional lapse from good character.

Aristotle thus establishes conditions for permissible excusing. One has moral grounds to excuse, and for that which falls outside of these legitimate and legitimating grounds there is no excuse. In contrast, if forgiveness is of the order of grace, it is not bound to moral reasons; it does not seek to find permission or be justified.[107] Third, a result of the Greek link between reason, justice, and the excuse in *sungnômê* is that the excuse may be tendered by anyone. Someone outside of those involved in an infraction—whether a judge, a witness, or one who simply hears the story—may extend excuse. Perhaps it is best if the other immediately affected does so, but the excuse at least leaves open whether it is morally possible even to excuse oneself (a none too seldom affair). Either way, if it is proper for someone who was not the injured party to be able to understand and thus extend excuse for the behavior in question, then we are unequivocally in the presence of the excuse, not forgiveness.[108]

Partitive Excuse: Between Indulgence and Severity

Aristotle's conception of *sungnômê* involves a first reflection on what Jankélévitch calls the partitive excuse. Both address the more problematic and immediate form of excuse embedded in the murky ambiguity of human action far removed from the clarity of metaphysical visions and the comfortable distance they afford. Whereas the total excuse is exculpatory, the partitive excuse circles around the phenomenon of mitigating circumstances. In the context of blameworthy offenses, the term *mitigating* indicates solely the lightening of the responsibility of the offender without, however, eliminating the *commissio peccati*—that is, the fact of having committed an offense. Far from excluding the principle of responsibility, mitigating circumstances presuppose such responsibility.[109] "In fact," Jankélévitch explicates, "the partitive excuse excuses the guilty person not because evil is nonexistent in general, but because every intention is complex."[110] Among other reasons, he claims, like Kant, that we can never be completely assured of what the maxim or the intention of an action is. The externality of the action itself does not allow for a reconfiguration of the motives.[111] Motives remain nontransparent to both the actor and the spectator. In contrast to the equivalence of understanding and excuse in *sungnômê*, however, Jankélévitch focuses on acts that are blameworthy and even considered wicked. So while he is mindful of the merits of understanding, his portrayal of the partitive excuse demonstrates its limits by juxtaposing it to forgiveness.[112]

The partitive excuse, according to Jankélévitch, refuses the all or nothing and either-or of either good or evil, either innocent or guilty; the parititve excuse concentrates instead on the more or less of degrees. The complexity of human action often demands nuanced evaluations that do not take into consideration just the individual person in relation to the isolated misdeed but also society, heredity, and psychology. Jankélévitch observes, therefore, that nuanced assessments of action consider "at the same time, the past, the organism, and the milieu."[113] The partitive excuse is thus discriminating and involves a "progressive focusing"; it requires time to be able to regard the person up close and take all things into consideration. Yet at the end of this process, it excuses only what is excusable.[114]

The partitive excuse thus shows itself to be full of gradations; it takes on the ambiguity of actions and sorts through how an action happened and how it came to be. It therefore ranges through all sorts of degrees from indulgence to severity. On the one extreme, the indulgent believe that the offenders who are responsible but might be excused or partially excused are "more stupid than wicked." Severity takes the opposite extreme stance: "No, humans are more wicked than stupid." "Stupid," as Jankélévitch understands it, involves ignorance, deprivation, and potentially even seeing the perpetrators themselves as victims. In this view, humans are only, primarily, victims, not perpetrators. This view asserts that "all in all, [the offender] merits pity."[115] The indulgent could be, moreover, the optimist, who does not pin the person to the isolated misdeed but believes in the future of the person and how the openness of the future holds open his or her future chances of amendment.[116] The lenient or indulgent person tends, according to Jankélévitch, to be more willing to examine the manifold elements that lead up to and surround a crime, whereas, for the severe person, circumstances are loopholes for avoiding the responsibility for and the ineradicable quoddity or facticity of the crime, which admits neither gradation nor mitigation.[117] In short, whereas attenuating details excuse, condemning details spark the fire of rigor. And every excuse, insofar as it is discriminating, is itself a mixture of severity and indulgence.

For Jankélévitch, however, forgiveness is neither indulgent nor severe, although he claims that in one respect it is "quite severe,"[118] for only the condemned crime can be forgiven. He writes:

> To forgive is neither to change one's mind on the score of the guilty person, nor to rally around the thesis of innocence. . . . Quite the contrary! The supernaturality of forgiveness consists in this, that my opinion on the subject of the guilty person precisely has not changed; but against this immutable background it is the whole lighting of my relations with the guilty person that is modified, it is the whole orientation of our relations that finds itself inverted, overturned, and overwhelmed! The judgment of condemnation has stayed the same, but an arbitrary and gratuitous change has intervened, a diametrical and radical inversion, *peristophē*, which transfigures hatred into love. To pardon is to turn one's back on the direction that justice indicates to us. . . . For forgiveness is not simply a relative conversion of contrary to contrary, but a meta-empirical conversion of contradictory to contradictory.[119]

Forgiveness looks the offense in the eye for what it is, inexcusable, and while condemning it, moves with love toward the other person. Jankélévitch is wary of the manner in which forgiveness may fall into condonation of the offense, whether out of weakness or out of self-love.[120] But he is equally adamant that forgiveness is precisely invoked when there are no grounds to excuse the other person or when the grounds for excuse remain insufficient. In the case of the latter, forgiveness forgives what remains beyond what the consideration of mitigating circumstances excuses, namely what remains inexcusable. He explains that "it is forgiveness that takes charge of the inexcusable, for the inexcusable can be forgivable even though it is not excusable. The excusable is, a fortiori, forgivable, but it does not need for us to forgive it since the rational excuse suffices to demonstrate its innocence."[121] The excuse is tied to a rationale, to rationality, and to an understanding for the offender and the offense that consequently merits his or her release. That which is excusable, therefore, should be excused; the reasons explain why. The excuse observes criteria according to which the unbinding of the person from the misdeed is justified. It operates along the lines of the deliberating scales of justice, weighing for and against.[122]

In contrast to the excuse, Jankélévitch asserts that forgiveness has something scandalous about it. As in the folly of love, the person who is the object of forgiveness does not merit it. Moreover, forgiveness does not forgive because of this or that reason. It pays no attention to justifying itself, for, as a gratuitous act and a spontaneous act of charity, it has no reasons and remains foreign to the criterion of any "according to."[123] Ungrounded, unjustified, and unmotivated, forgiveness has the character of that which is in and of itself. Jankélévitch even accords forgiveness the title of *aseity*. It is *causa sui*—that which is "from itself." Although forgiveness is occasioned by the misdeed, it remains heterogeneous to any empirical causality in relation to the misdeed. The order of charity in which one loves one's enemies is the order of forgiveness, which forgives the guilty and those who do not merit excuse. For Jankélévitch, forgiveness does not discriminate by character or other justifying criteria: "It forgives man insofar as he is a man, and not with regard to this or that."[124] The indiscrimination of forgiveness dictates that it does not have a limit to its forgiving. The gradations integral to the accounting and measured excuse thus yield to the abundance and infinitude of forgiveness.[125]

Moreover, in both forms of excuse—the total and the partitive—Jankélévitch detects an inability to initiate a new order. At best, if the excuse is total and the reprieve entire, the excuse can reestablish the status quo ante—that is, the condition of things before the misdeed. Its capacity, however, is as such purely negative. Jankélévitch claims it cannot inaugurate a new era, resuscitate existence, and celebrate a second birth.[126] Whereas understanding *discovers* that the misdeed can be declared naught, whether totally or partially, forgiveness "*decides* to consider the event as null and as not having come to pass, even though it certainly did. . . . In spite of everything, forgiveness decrees generously, heroically, despite the absurdity, and against all evidence, that what took place did not take place."[127] Partaking in the character of the decision, forgiveness cannot have any external or internal compulsions that sufficiently cause it or explain it. No path leads immediately to forgiveness. It is a leap!

Jankélévitch therefore breaks with the Greek tradition's similitudes of forgiveness, and in doing so he highlights the diametrical opposition of Christian thinking on forgiveness to this tradition. Even though he phrases it in terms of ignorance, Augustine makes this distinction decisive. Far from involving an insight or the taking up of the perspective of another, he connects forgiveness precisely with a lack of recognition or acknowledgment and with nonknowledge or nescience. Adopting a prevalent biblical metaphor of God turning his back on sin, Augustine asks, "What is the same as being unobservant, but not knowing? What is, not to know? Not to take notice."[128] Forgiveness, in a Christian sense, does not, therefore, entail insight or understanding but has rather a lack of understanding as its presupposition. Georg Simmel, in a work with which Jankélévitch was undoubtedly familiar, expresses this notion succinctly: "It is not because one understands that one forgives but despite the fact that one does not understand."[129]

Since Jankélévitch insists on taking earnest note of sin, however, he does not merely follow a Christian demarcation of forgiveness; he surpasses it and describes interpersonal forgiveness as "mad," both in its groundlessness and in its superabundance. This does not mean that its spirit is foreign to the mundane, even in its exceptionality. The spirit of forgiveness can be witnessed in ungrounded acts of generosity and kindness. But beyond its overarching spirit, the concrete act of forgiveness is much more difficult. In forgiveness, the one who forgives does so in the face of the condemnation of the act of the other person and in the light of the indignation at the misdeed's injustice and the hurt of the injury. The "madness" of a generous act that is transitive or intentional and not anonymous or given out of great bounty or the wellspring of self-sufficient happiness places the victim before a daunting task. Biblically expressed, acts of generosity involve the welcoming of the stranger. But how much more is involved in the love of one's enemies?

For Jankélévitch, it is precisely this "how much more" that marks the quality of forgiveness as an excess that breaks the logic of returns, the economies of selfhood, and the perpetuity of cycles of violence and retribution. He explains that "the counter-to-nature gesture of forgiveness inhibits the natural and long-anticipated reaction that makes us respond to the same with the same and that is the servile echo and stupid counterpunch to sin."[130] His description of the "more" of forgiveness finds its source of expression in religious vocabulary. The excess is not within rationality but rather calls the economy of rationality into question. Linking forgiveness to the order of grace, Jankélévitch invokes a passage from Paul's epistle to the Romans: "Law came in, to increase the trespass; but where sin increased, grace abounded *all the more*."[131] And he uses the Greek term, *perissos*, found, for example, in the Gospel of Matthew (meaning surplus, excess, the extraordinary, or superabundant) to illustrate the hyperbolic nature of forgiveness.[132]

Pardon and Mercy

What Jankélévitch calls the madness or scandalous character of forgiveness appears, at least potentially, as well in the notions of pardon and mercy. The Greeks acknowledged the existence of a "royal virtue" of pardon fit for princes and kings. But pardon was hardly considered a virtue by the Greeks, and the royal virtue of pardon, considered a mark of superiority, was primarily depicted as a royal virtue for foreign princes. In fact, from a Greek point of view, pardon was considered less a mark of nobility than a threat to justice. Pardon can readily degenerate into a permissive license that threatens egalitarian law. According to Aubriot, the Greeks were skeptical of pardon because it could ruin the authority of law in two ways: It could give potential criminals the impression that they might escape their punishment, and, with the power to grant pardon or amnesty, an authority would be placed above the binding power of the law.[133]

The danger to justice and to the rule of law by someone beyond the law is hardly a Greek concern alone, however. Kant, for example, advocates "the majestic right" of the sovereign to pardon. In fact, he insists that this right demonstrates the radiance of the sovereign's majestic dignity and is thus the only one that deserves the name of majestic right. This identification of pardon with majesty is perhaps best expressed by Shakespeare in *Measure for Measure* in terms of mercy:

> No ceremony that to great ones 'longs,
> Not the king's crown, nor the deputed sword,
> The marshall's truncheon, nor the judge's robe,
> Become them with one half so good a grace
> As mercy does.[134]
>
> Isabella in *Measure for Measure*, 2.2

Or as Portia claims in *The Merchant of Venice*, mercy "'Tis mightiest in the mightiest; it becomes / The throned monarch better than his crown (4.1.184)." But Kant is equally well aware that the right to pardon (*Begna-*

digungsrecht, which contains the word *grace, Gnade*) constitutes "the most slippery [*das schlüpfrigste*]" right because it bestows the sovereign great latitude to do injustice.[135] This capacity of the sovereign to act beyond the law in a suspension of the law was made the definition of the sovereign himself by the legal theorist and National Socialist Carl Schmitt, who defined the sovereign as the one who decides over the state of exception.[136] Thus the right to pardon held, for example, by state governors and the president of the United States—that is, the right to decide over life and death—is in close proximity to, if not of one accord with, the presidential authority to declare a state of exception in which the rule of law is suspended. Pardon, therefore, touches on the foundation of the relation of sovereignty and law itself.

The question then is: How does forgiveness differ from mercy and pardon? Although Jankélévitch does not explicitly address the distinctions between forgiveness and mercy or pardon in his apophatic approaches, we can use his criteria to briefly illustrate important differences between them. Several of the distinguishing features are common to both mercy and pardon, but they cannot be treated with one broad stroke. In short, however, it may be claimed that, whereas pardon and mercy share with forgiveness a seemingly arbitrary and morally equivocal openness to "unjust" usage, they do not represent a gift from one to another in an instant of selflessness directed toward the other.

One of the reasons Jankélévitch largely excludes a reflection on mercy and pardon in his apophatic approach is that they both, but pardon in particular, belong to the sphere of laws and politics. This situated difference also reflects a difference in the will, power, and decision of pardon, on the one hand, and forgiveness, on the other hand. Forgiveness, according to Jankélévitch, does not consist in the arbitrary assertion of the power of the will or the will to power. He distinguishes the decision to forgive from a sovereign decision that resembles a victory over temptation. Forgiveness, he claims, is *like* the decision in that it is an event that is initial, sudden, and spontaneous.[137] But the decision of forgiveness or the decision to forgive resembles more the decision of faith than that of pardon. It is our own, but it is granted us in an instant at the limits of human strength.[138]

Whereas pardon may be conceived as a gift given to the other, it is executed by an authority above the person receiving it.[139] The person who pardons does so in the position of a political office, not as a private person or as the person who was immediately affected by the offense. This difference marks the separation between the moral and the political domains. Although an asymmetry of power is always involved in forgiveness, forgiveness proceeds from an equality of the persons implicated in the offense. The relation is interpersonal and moral, whereas the relation implied in pardon is official and political. In fact, pardon does not entail a personal relation with the other at all in most cases. And even though Jankélévitch insists that only the offended has the right to forgive, this "right" is a moral, not a political, right.

As a political tool, pardon is often exercised for political reasons of utility, whereas the interpersonal relation is, according to Jankélévitch, nonstrategic and nonteleological. It gives to the other for the other, unmotivated either by self-concern or by the merits of the other. And in the cases where pardon is not extended for ulterior purposes, it may be said to be just, as, for example, when an offender's record is wiped clean after he has demonstrated that he is not only no longer a threat to society but also, by changing his ways, even a positive contributor to it. In this extension of decency beyond the strict obligation of the pardoner and the right of the pardoned, the reasons of justice taken into consideration determine the act of pardon to be in accordance with justice and the law rather than outside of it or against it. Regardless of whether the motivation of pardon is "political" or just, however, pardon is to be distinguished from forgiveness due to its political-juridical character, which entails a qualitative difference in position and power as well as the intervention of a third and outside party.

As intimated in the quotations from Shakespeare, mercy is often used synonymously with pardon. For example, one of the definitions of *mercy* offered in Webster's dictionary states that mercy is "the discretionary power of a judge to pardon someone or to mitigate punishment, especially to send to prison rather than invoke the death penalty." By this definition, mercy is distinguished from forgiveness for mostly the same reasons as was the case with pardon. Shakespeare, however, provides more subtle and poignant distinctions. Therefore, in order to determine what mercy is, its relation to justice and, finally, to forgiveness, we will compare Isabella's previously quoted statements about mercy with those contained in Portia's climactic speech on the nature of mercy and its relation to justice:

> The quality of mercy is not strain'd;
> It droppeth as the gentle rain from heaven
> Upon the place beneath: it is twice blessed;
> It blesseth him that gives and him that takes:
> 'Tis mightiest in the mightiest; it becomes
> The throned monarch better than his crown;
> His scepter shows the force of temporal power,
> The attribute to awe and majesty,
> Wherein doth sit the dread and fear of kings;

> But mercy is above this scepter'd sway,—
> It is enthroned in the heart of kings,
> It is an attribute to God himself;
> And earthly power doth then show likest God's
> When mercy seasons justice.
> *The Merchant of Venice*, 4.1.184–97

The philosopher of law Jeffrie Murphy outlines some of the widely held views expressed in Portia's commendation of mercy. He writes,

> (1) It is an autonomous moral virtue (i.e., not reducible to some other virtue—especially justice). (2) It is a virtue that tempers or "seasons" justice—something one adds to justice (the primary virtue) to dilute it and perhaps, if one takes the metallurgical metaphor of tempering seriously, to make it stronger. (3) It is never owed to anyone as a right or a matter of desert or justice. It always therefore transcends the realm of strict moral obligation and is best viewed as a free gift—an act of grace, love, or compassion that is beyond the claims of right, duty, and obligation. ("The quality of mercy is not [con]strained.") (4) As a moral virtue, it derives its value at least in part from the fact that it flows from a certain kind of character—a character disposed to perform merciful acts from love or compassion while not losing sight of the importance of justice. (5) It requires a generally retributive outlook on punishment and responsibility.[140]

With such terms as "a free gift," "an act of grace or love" beyond obligation, right, and duty, we seem to be approaching the nature of forgiveness. Moreover, in religious terminology, one speaks of a merciful God as basically equivalent to a forgiving God. So are mercy and forgiveness interchangeable? I believe there are important reasons to think they are not.

It is helpful, first of all, to establish the contexts of the passages from Shakespeare's two "comedies of mercy." In *Measure for Measure*, Isabella is pleading with a judge in a criminal case to show her brother mercy. In *The Merchant of Venice*, Portia acts as a judge of a civil case involving a contract dispute. The former operates under what Murphy calls a "criminal law paradigm," whereas the latter constitutes a "private law paradigm." The context in *Measure for Measure* consequently demonstrates, as does the invocation of God in many cases, that it is not necessary to be the injured party in order to show mercy. Whether in the legal situation of a judge in a courtroom or as an appeal to God as the supreme and final judge, mercy, like pardon, is not always a matter between the parties immediately involved in an offense.

Remaining within this context of the criminal law paradigm, the argument is often made that a good judge is one who "seasons" justice with mercy. But this view is problematic for two reasons, or, rather, it is problematic on both sides. If, on the one hand, mercy is conceived of as a virtue distinct from justice, then a judge who acts according to mercy or even tempered by mercy may thereby act unjustly. As Murphy explains, "A judge in a criminal case has an *obligation* to do justice—which means, at a minimum, an obligation to uphold the rule of law. Thus if he is moved, even by love or compassion, to act contrary to the rule of law—to the rules of justice—he acts wrongly (because he violates an obligation) and manifests a vice rather than a virtue."[141] This obligation to the rule of law is simultaneously and by that fact an obligation to all the others under the law. Angelo, the judge in *Measure for Measure*, acknowledges this obligation when he responds to Isabella's petition:

> I show [pity] most of all when I show justice,
> For then I pity those I do not know,
> Which a dismissed offense would after gall;
> And do him right that, answering one foul wrong,
> Lives not to act another.
> *Measure for Measure,* 2.2.100–104

On the other hand, insofar as the counterclaim of the advocates of seasoning justice with mercy aims at greater individualization and the consideration of circumstances, it may be said, along with Aristotle, that this individualization and consideration—or decency, as Aristotle depicts it—is the task of justice itself.[142] As Murphy explicates:

> Basic demands of justice are that like cases be treated alike, that morally relevant differences between persons be noticed, and that our treatment of those persons be affected by those differences.... The legal rules, if they are just, will base required penal treatment on morally relevant differences, or they will give judges the discretion to do so; ... Judges or lawmakers who are unmindful of the importance of individuational response are not lacking in mercy; they lack a sense of justice.[143]

Individuation and the consideration of morally relevant differences are thus owed to persons as a right and as a measure of justice itself; they do not constitute an optional free gift or act of grace.

A shift to the civil law paradigm refocuses on the immediate relation of the two parties involved. Whereas Shylock, according to the law, has a right to seek harsh treatment for the violation of his contract with Antonio, he does not have an antecedent obligation required by the rules of justice. If he chooses, therefore, to show mercy, he is merely waiving a right but not infringing on an obligation.[144] In the light of the demands of justice, he is free to free Antonio from the binds of the defaulted bond but is not required to do so. Similarly, a knight who vanquishes another in chivalric combat has the right or, more appropriately, the power to take the life of the other, but if the fallen knight begs for mercy, the victor may be moved by compassion or pity to spare the vanquished's life.

Each of these two examples demonstrates distinct differences between mercy and forgiveness. First, on arriving at the scene of the courtroom, Portia immediately asks whether Antonio is able to pay back the sum of money owed to Shylock according to the bond. Antonio's friend, Bassanio, who just happens to also be Portia's husband, even offers twice—if need be, even ten times—the sum owed (4.1.210–11). In the role of mediator and judge, Portia requests of Shylock, "Be merciful:/Take thrice thy money; bid me tear the bond" (4.1.233–34). She does not ask him to drop his claim and waive his right absolutely; she merely requests of him to show mercy by taking reparations in the place of the demanded pound of flesh. Money represents here the substitute of human life and thus a humanization of vindictive or, at least, retributive justice. In this scenario, mercy allows for degrees and substitutes, whereas forgiveness, according to Jankélévitch, entails an all-or-nothing decision. Mercy can mean to take less than what one by right could take, or, since for Shylock the sum he would receive is more than the bond was worth, to take something else in place of what one by right is owed (the pound of flesh as stated in the contract). Forgiveness, as Jankélévitch portrays it, does not follow such a schema of gradations or substitutes.

The second example of the embattled knights does, however, exhibit this absoluteness, this all-or-nothing decision. Although it obeys the same structure as forgiveness in this respect, it differs from forgiveness in the sense that mercy often does not and does not necessarily presuppose a moral offense, whereas without an offense, there is no question of forgiveness. Moreover, mercy does not represent an act but rather the withholding or forbearance of an act. As such, another definition of *mercy* as "compassionate or kindly forbearance shown toward an offender, an enemy, or other person in one's power" appropriately applies to this situation. Whereas interpersonal forgiveness may be said to exude a certain moral power in the sense that the offender is in the hands of the victim who decides to forgive or not to forgive, it does not command the authority to decide over life and death. Equally important, however, showing mercy means to refrain, desist, or abstain from acting from the position of power. In contrast, forgiveness is a decision and an act; it is not negative in the sense of refrainment from doing what the other is due or what one has the power to do to the other; it is a positive act directed intentionally toward the other for the other.

Moreover, the term *forbearance* indicates that mercy takes place on the background of "a generally retributive outlook on punishment and responsibility," whereas forgiveness is not dependent on the framework of retribution. In the immediacy of the private law paradigm, one who forgives does indeed forgo exercising the right he or she has against the other and thus does not demand either retribution or reparations. Within the criminal law paradigm, however, forgiveness can be viewed outside of the retributive framework by means of a shift in perspective between the person offended and a third instance as judge. Insofar as forgiveness is a moral category heterogeneous to that of law and politics, it focuses on the personal relation with the other. As a free gift to the other for the sake of the other, forgiveness can thus coexist with punishment, though not with revenge. One can forgive the other, in short, even if he is punished.[145] But in both paradigms, forgiveness suggests a positivity that exceeds the framework of retribution and mercy. The positive act of forgiveness entails the consideration of the offense as null and void and the possible inauguration of a new era. It does not merely suspend punishment out of pity or compassion; it represents a radical conversion to love, which orients the whole relation to the other. The image of a merciful God, for example, depends on the notion that God has not only the power but the right to exact a punishment on humans for their sin. But a God who is not only merciful but also forgiving is not merely moved not to exact punishment; God moves in an act of love to annul human sin: God moves toward humans and toward reconciliation with them. The potentially transformative capacity of forgiveness allows the other self-distance to himself as the agent of an offense, which constitutes both the opening of the self to moral rebirth and the opening unto a new era of new relations.

3

The Temporality of Human Existence and Action

Irreversibility, irrevocability, and imprescriptibility relate to each other as the natural to the ethical to the legal. In a sense, these terms represent a progression of an idea, moving from one category to another, sharpening and narrowing its scope in the procession from nature to ethics to the legal and juridical domains. The idea driving these notions is that of time or, more precisely, the temporal constitution of human affairs. Temporality forms the core of each of these terms individually and in their interrelation. Time is irreversible and subjects all things to its one-way directedness; free will and action take place on this one-way street and inscribe themselves indelibly into the history of humankind, making their acts not only irreversible but also, and more poignantly, irrevocable; and the irrevocability of certain crimes, designated as crimes against humanity, calls into existence and serves to justify the law of imprescriptibility—that is, the law stating that crimes against humanity are not subject to statutory limits. In the interrelation of irreversibility, irrevocability, and imprescriptibility, Vladimir Jankélévitch explores the role of memory and the interconnections of the new and the old, the future and the past, and transcendence and immanence. This interconnection results in a tension between human impotence and the human capacity for re-creation. Jankélévitch views this tension between impossibility and the work of reconstruction as inherent in human morality.

Irreversibility

Jankélévitch emphasizes the irreversibility of time—that is, its inherent unidirectionality. In fact, he states that time *is* only to the extent that it is irreversible. Another time is not imaginable. As Aristotle observes, time has no *ousia,* no essence or substance.[1] Put simply, time *is* not; it becomes. It *is* only insofar as it is becoming—that is its only modality. Irreversibility thus constitutes the very temporality of time itself. Correspondingly, the human temporal constitution, Jankélévitch argues, is also of the order of becoming. Becoming, therefore, is not merely one modality of our being or of our substance. Instead, it is our only way of being. We are becoming through and through; we exist, in other words, only insofar as we are in the process of becoming. For Jankélévitch, this movement extends from the past to the future and implies the natural movement from the self to the other in the sense that one becomes relatively other than oneself through the process of aging. Since nothing is impervious to aging or to the movement of time, the temporal a priori is an absolute precondition of all existents. Jankélévitch conceives of this temporal a priori in terms of *je-ne-sais-quoi* (I-know-not-what), for it is imperceptible and beyond the grasp of thought. It is neither a dimension nor a form nor a category. In short, he states, it does not exist but is nonetheless indispensable, for everything on earth is conditioned by time.[2] Nothing is outside of it. Jankélévitch therefore follows ancient thinkers such as Aristotle, Plotinus, and Augustine in describing time in terms of an omnipresent milieu that both envelops and conditions all things.[3]

Jankélévitch is, moreover, persistent in distinguishing time from a static notion of space. The Odysseus who leaves his beloved homeland and Penelope only to return after many adventures is not the same person as when he departed. In an important sense, his journey stands in stark contradistinction to the nomad wanderer Abraham sent forth by God from his homeland toward the unknown Promised Land, because it symbolizes the circle of life and a knowledge that always implies a return to self. But Jankélévitch maintains that there are no returns, no possibility of coming or going back; there are only further stations on the way of an outward journey. The fact of having gone, of having experienced other things and places cannot be denied or undone. Although the arrival home may soon make it seem as if one had never left, it remains, he insists, only *as if.* The prodigal son, to take up a favorite metaphor of Jankélévitch's, will always differ somehow in some way from the son who stayed home. His before is not the same as his after. A trace will remain—inextinguishably—even if it is the difference only of je-ne-sais-quoi.

For Jankélévitch, irreversibility thus vividly expresses what he calls the "hapax" character of existence, referring to the Greek *hapax legomenon* (a word that is used only once in a work or corpus): It is an event that comes to pass only once. All of life is thus constituted as a farewell, he claims, for each moment of becoming separates the human from a hapax, which would appear invaluable to him if he were only aware of its singularity.[4] Time passes and with the passing of time, all of lived experience is fleeting. The moments shared—this very moment—will never be again. The shift from what is no longer to that which will never be again consequently underlines the preciousness of persons and events in our lives. They are, Jankélévitch suggests, of infinite value. Experiences—and indeed existence itself—are priceless, not despite their fleeting character but rather because of it. Each experience, according to Jankélévitch, is unexchangeable and nonrefundable, and each life is unique and infinitely valuable because it cannot be replaced or compensated.[5] Becoming, therefore, marks, for Jankélévitch, the tragic beauty of finite existence.

In a similar vein, Jankélévitch rules out the possibility of repetition in the strict sense of a repetition of the same. Kierkegaard's pseudonym Constantin Constantius, for example, attempts to "recollect forward" and repeat a memorable trip to Berlin but instead finds that "time passed" and that "there is no repetition at all. . . . The only repetition was the impossibility of a repetition."[6] Kierkegaard concludes in a draft of his book *Johannes Climacus* that "even if everything in the world were completely identical, there would be no repetition because reality is only in the moment."[7] The second time, Jankélévitch explains, already has a tradition behind it. Even if the second time arrived after passing through the currents of the Lethe and, by a miracle, conformed to the first time to a T, it would occur in another context and in relation to other circumstances. The second time, he observes, is therefore another first time. It carries with it the seal of newness.

Jankélévitch thus contradicts the preacher Solomon's claim that there is nothing new under the sun. He contends, on the contrary, that everything is constantly new under the sun. In the place of the monosyllabic recurrence of repetition that Solomon despairs of, Jankélévitch emphasizes irreversibility. The ennui expressed in the resignation that everything has already been said, seen, and heard misses the renewal not just of content but of the how, expressed in the manner, the perspective, the light. Consequently, Jankélévitch argues that, although recurring things may grammatically be the same, the manner in which they pneumatically appear is perpetually otherwise. The "same" things seen again are seen differently. With Heraclitus, Jankélévitch proclaims one cannot bathe in the same river twice. For neither the one bathing nor the river will be the same. At the same time, he dismisses the attitude captured in the life-dictum "see Venice and die" because it attempts to preempt the tediousness or disappointment of repetition. Jankélévitch observes that death, in such a case, is completely superfluous because one will never see again the Venice one has seen before.[8] The city will have changed and the person visiting, too. Kierkegaard's pseudonym captures this notion in short and more philosophical terms: "The dialectic of repetition is easy, for that which is repeated has been—otherwise it could not be repeated—but the very fact that it has been makes the repetition into something new."[9]

For Jankélévitch, the irreversibility of time constitutes its objectivity; it is what Aristotle called *ametapeiston*, the inexorable.[10] It constrains and is unable to be persuaded by our will. Although Goethe's Faust petitions the moment to linger, time moves on nonetheless, objectively like a fate or a fact of unyielding contours, *volens nolens*. Irreversibility highlights the mobility of time, which is to say, the impossibility of immobility.[11] What remains for human action is the mode of progression. In other words, how we live within this temporal a priori is decisive. As Jankélévitch writes, "Indeed, the human changes the modes of daily time without annulling the quoddity or temporality of time, without overcoming, as Leibniz would have said, the irreversibility of the Styx; thus our freedom over against time is purely adjectival and superficial."[12] This freedom of action mirrors, too, the freedom of thought in relation to time. Jankélévitch claims that time defeats the thought that sends itself to think it; it cannot be made an accusative object of the verb "to think." Rather, thought itself is always temporal.[13]

Yet it is precisely modes of thought, on his account, that make irreversibility relative, not absolute. Jankélévitch calls the constant movement of becoming *futurition,* and for every step into the future, he observes, there is a composition of the past, which he calls *preterition*. Through preterition's unceasing compensation of futurition, becoming, he suggests, proves to be as conservational as it is innovative. In other words, the newness of the future is retarded by the preformation of an already present future through possibility, on the one hand, and, by the endurance of a still actual past through memory, on the other hand. Thanks to these extensive dimensions of immanence, the future of futurition, according to Jankélévitch, does not constitute radical transcendence. He argues that humans can err either in the direction of too much transcendence or too much immanence. Accordingly, he diagnoses two potential sicknesses resulting from either a lack of openness to the new (transcendence) or a lack of continuity (immanence), namely *boredom* and *fear*. The monotony of

Solomon portrayed at the beginning of Ecclesiastes expresses this boredom. In boredom, Jankélévitch observes, one fails to see renewal. The flip side is fear. Fear arises, he suggests, when the approaching future overwhelms action because it arrives outside of every possibility of repetition.[14]

Jankélévitch therefore admits that there is indeed repetition. In fact, repetition is another name for the dialectic of futurition and preterition. Everything is repetition. Becoming is neither a source of effervescent novelties nor mere parrot-like imitation.[15] Nothing is absolutely new or absolutely old. Becoming itself is dependent on the interplay between the new and the old, originality and banality, because the oscillating tension of pure endurance and perpetual innovation provides the composition of duration. Duration thus depicts the extension of experience from the already to the not yet.

Within duration, Jankélévitch recognizes memory as the primary mode of thought for preterition. Memory, he claims, is both impotent and capable of relative impossibility. He thus stresses, on the one hand, both the impossibility of swimming against the inexorable tide of time and the impossibility of joining the present and the past, and yet, on the other hand, he allows memory to weaken this double impossibility. The return of memory to the past, he says, can symbolically or ideally compensate for the fact of irreversibility. The mind has access to the past but not in its lived vitality and reality. It retains and accesses an image of the past, a semblance of itself, a simulacrum of what has been. "Memory," Jankélévitch writes, "is certainly a metaphorical and ghostlike manner of recurrence," but it nevertheless delays futurition.[16] It also provides the condition for action. If futurition is the condition by which the new can enter history through the will, preterition is the condition for granting continuity to action. As Françoise Schwab explains, a moral intention requires at least a minimum of futurition in order to act and a minimum of preterition in order to maintain engagement.[17] The repetition of the past will always be new and otherwise, but the past orients the present and future. Another way of expressing this notion is that memory spans both the commitment to the future and the fidelity to the past.[18] Although the past serves the future as the material—the *res*—of which it is made, a commitment to the past must be continually recommitted in the future.

Jankélévitch thus portrays two alternative approaches to memory in the light of irreversibility: (1) nostalgia and (2) reconstruction and fidelity. Nostalgia, Jankélévitch claims, is indeed an *algos*—a pain or sorrow, for in every memory there is a deficit and an absence: the deficit between the reality and its image, the absence of the vitality of the past. Jankélévitch observes that the Greek word for regret, *pothos,* is the same word used by Plato in the *Phaedrus* for desire. The Latin word for regret, *desiderium,* also literally contains the term *desire.*[19] Nostalgia is, then, a primarily aesthetic form of memory expressed in the desire to really relive the past that one recalls symbolically in memory. According to Jankélévitch, it is precisely the impossibility and the dreamy irreality of the "longing memory" that makes nostalgia so enticing.[20] He describes its "groundless pain" simultaneously as an "earnest enjoyment" and discovers in this earnestness an ethical element in addition to its aesthetic character. It refers to the semelfactive or the irreplaceable—the incomparable singularity of what has been. Nostalgia consequently serves as a reminder of the tragic in life. The definitiveness of that which will not return and to which one can only symbolically return transfigures the "no longer" into the "never again." But as a "feeling of infinite incompletion," nostalgia reflects the ambivalence between the earnestness of the impossibility of a retrospective possibility and a vague hope of a return of the past or a return to the past.[21] The pain of nostalgia stems from its impossible desire, and in its earnestness, it recognizes that it is now too late. In contrast to the open horizon of the "not-yet" or "too early," the form of inopportunity or of nonbeing characteristic of the "too late" is left no hope for a future; it knows no remedy or consolation—no longer, no more.[22] Jankélévitch concludes that in this mode, Mnemosyne confirms and deepens irreversibility more than it mollifies it.[23]

But memory, for Jankélévitch, also enacts the positive possibility of repetition. One cannot collect the past, for it is not something one can have like a possession. First, what one has of the past is its memory, not the thing itself. But the ideal or symbolic character of the remembered past also provides the condition for appropriating it and making it one's own, one's history, freed in memory of the strangeness of what has been lived.[24]

Second, in this mode of having (as a memory), the existence of the past also depends on its being carried forth—that is, on having a future or being possible again. Jankélévitch therefore celebrates the shift from having to being and from being to acting. His conception of memory thus differs fundamentally from the notion of memory, originating with Augustine, as "a container." Memory, he says, is not a container of recollections but the possibility of actualizing them or of creating them anew.[25] Jankélévitch draws an example from Greek mythology: While returning from the underworld, Orpheus turns around to make sure his beloved Eurydice is behind him. In doing so, he fails to realize that Eurydice was his future life and that she is to be sought before him, not behind him.[26] Whereas nostalgia entails the longing glance backward and is therefore primarily reduced to an aesthetics of simultaneous pain and enjoyment, the repetition of memory moved forward becomes a task for action and is therefore ethical.

The dual edge of this simultaneously faithful and reconstructive memory can be conceptually divided into two moral responses: protest and repetition. Out of the impotence to change the past is born the moral attitude of protest.[27] Before the things one can no longer change or effect, the moral attitude of protest asserts that what happened should not have happened, thereby underscoring its essential contingency. In its negativity, this protest also is the primary factor in retarding futurition, which is paced by the ability and need to forget. This protest thus forms the cry of "no" to the having-been or the having-done, disallowing the past to be put to rest. It ultimately proves to be a vain gesture, or rather, it is merely retarding, Jankélévitch concedes, because it is impotent to halt completely the all-pervasive onward march of becoming. Second, the reconstructive attitude assumes more positive contours by repeating in the symbolic form of memory that which has happened, recollecting it forward. For Jankélévitch, this reconstruction is not merely a rejuvenating complement to fidelity. Rather, he claims that fidelity is a sustained creation that runs the risk of infidelity at every moment.[28] A truly creative fidelity will always be unfaithful, but it is unfaithful out of faithfulness.[29] This tension precisely represents the moral vocation of repetition.

The paradoxical formulation of a fidelity that is faithful by being unfaithful is illuminated by the connection between memory and salvation. In a line that is reminiscent of Walter Benjamin, Jankélévitch explains that to remember is an act, and the act memory performs is that of rescue: resuscitating the past back to life, resurrecting it from the forgotten banks of the Lethe, while breathing life into its limp remains.[30] In concert with Jankélévitch's understanding of repetition, this resuscitation will always be something new. Beyond antiquarianism and monumentalization, the renewal is the very rescue of the past.[31] It is in fact the rescue of the past from itself—both from its nonbeing and the unreality of being past and from the static finality or definitive identity of that which has been lived and has been done. In memory lies salvation—not because it holds steadfast that which is slipping into the stream of time but because it paradoxically gives the past a future. It does not rest on the indicative of archives but is relived in the imperative that carries it on, though always otherwise.

Memory, according to Jankélévitch, is therefore both impotent to change the past and charged with its resuscitation. It both entails the retardation of futurition and provides the basis for the infusion of moral commitment toward a future respectful of, and even faithful to, the past.

To cast a permanent eye backward is indeed to lose reality but to remember the past is to repeat it otherwise—whether as renewal of the positive or as improvement of the negative. What remains of the past is not itself but its future. In the tension between the work of memory and its impotence, to repeat is, for Jankélévitch, a duty.

Irrevocability

If the irreversible signifies that a person cannot go back into the past or reverse that past, irrevocability means that the "having-been" and the "having-done" of the past cannot be extinguished.[32] The having-done (*fecisse*), Jankélévitch states, is just as irreparable as the having-been (*fuisse*) is irreversible. The fact that the individual did live and the fact that a misdeed was done is not subject to the decay of time or the erosion of forgetting. The words on the wall of Jankélévitch's apartment near Notre Dame in the Quai aux Fleurs in Paris indicate the importance to him of the ineradicable, irrevocable "having been" of individual existence: "He who has been cannot ever not have been: From now on, this mysterious and profoundly obscure fact of having lived is his sustenance for eternity."[33]

With this absolute irrevocability of the facticity or quoddity of the past, Jankélévitch links the existence of the unique individual to the event. Its hapax-character cannot be repeated or replaced. Every past moment, every past life consequently has an "ineluctable discreteness," through which time occurs and the finitude of existence comes to the fore.[34] Irrevocable, not just irreversible, finite existence is grasped in its essence as that which has been; it may no longer be, but it cannot not have been. The loss of the individual existence is irretrievable, and yet in the fact of having-been, it obtains the vestment of immutability. Jankélévitch thus understands irrevocability as the fact of having-been or as the fact raised to the second power: The fact of the fact of having been is irrevocable.

This understanding is not merely a facile consolation, a play of words to cover the death of the irreplaceable. Rather the irrevocability of the having-been and the having-done introduces, according to him, an ethical category. Thus having-been and particularly having-done cannot be exterminated by forgetting. Time, Jankélévitch claims, is morally neutral—that is, without normative value. Therefore, the flow of time cannot truly have an effect on the event itself.[35] Jankélévitch observes that the loss of someone "is no better compensated twenty years after his disappearance than the day itself when it happened."[36] Even provided that one will find others to love, the loss of that one remains irrevocable. Chronology has no common measure with axiology.[37]

Although irreversibility is undoubtedly the condition for irrevocability, the formative character of human action inscribes upon chronology the artifices of its own creation, condensing and amplifying the roadblocks to all returns. To the natural irreversibility of time for human action thus comes the additional complication concomitant with history. For human decisions determine the course of history. Irrevocability thus doubles the impossibility of returning. What is more, the human attitude toward irrevocability tends to be less concerned with the nostalgic return to the positiveness of what has been or with having this past return in the resuscitation of repetition. Instead, it often seeks the destruction of this past. Whereas, with irreversibility, the nostalgic feeling quickens the longing to live again what has been or to be anew what one once was, the despair over the irreparable makes the annihilation of the preterit desirable. In this sense, the vector of human desire is inverted. It is not a matter of a desire to make an irreversible absence become present but rather of a desire to undo the facticity of the past. Instead of longing to return to the past, one seeks to revoke it. The inscription of freedom into history, however, cannot be erased. The having-done, Jankélévitch maintains, always remains.[38]

Besides the value of each individual human existence, freedom is thus the condition that marks the accentuation of irrevocability over irreversibility. Whereas the irreversibility of an action has its source in the fact of succession, irrevocability hinges on the scandalous contingency of freedom. Whereas irreversibility can be seen as a natural procession, irrevocability is a matter of human agency. Whereas all occurrences in life are irreversible, only those occurrences that depend on human freedom are irrevocable. Within the rubric of irrevocability, nostalgic regret is expressed in the statement, "I could have done otherwise." But, as Jankélévitch reminds us, it is impossible not to experience what one has experienced, and it is impossible not to have done what one has done.[39]

Jankélévitch further specifies and sharpens this notion of agency, focusing not only on what is or has been done but also, and originally, on volition. Like Jesus, who situates the fact of having sinned in the thought, the desire, or the intention as opposed to merely in the act itself, Jankélévitch claims that the mere fact of having-willed is irrevocable. This shift in the problematic of morality symbolizes the suspension of the difference between the sinful thought and the sinful action. Instead of the moral question consisting in not acting on sinful thoughts, the thought itself is already indicting. Equally significant is the transition from an outward and tangible sign to the unobservable interiority of intention. Consequently, the history of the inscription of human freedom is not equivalent to the recordable history of chronicles or even of diaries. For Jankélévitch, the heart of morality is a matter of volition and intention. His emphasis on interiority, moreover, reflects the invisibility of so much of the violence inscribed in the history of both the offender and the victim. Jankélévitch is attuned to the fact that, even when injuries are compensated for and healed, even when further repercussions do not appear, they inscribe themselves indelibly in a person's history of development. And even the sin that has disappeared and from which the penitent offender has freed himself has become an inalienable and eternal part of his moral experience.

Although freedom can lead to fate through the indelibility of inscription, the openness of the future relativizes what otherwise seems absolute. Jankélévitch contends that, just as the *fuisse* (having-been) is simultaneously irreversible and relatively reversible in memory, the *fecisse* (having-done) is both irreparable and relatively reparable. There is an opening of the irrevocable toward transformation and revision. "There is no human disaster," he writes, "that cannot be humanly mended. Everything that has been done can be undone again; everything that has been undone can be done anew. And one can consequently do better, do something else."[40] This opening toward future action that makes right of the wrong remains, however, adjacent to what has been done, as in a series. The future allows for things to be done otherwise. The misdeeds may be followed by good deeds; in a future similar situation, one can do good instead of perpetuating a wrong. With this possibility of revision, Jankélévitch exhibits his refusal to fix a character absolutely or reduce the agent to a specific and singular action. The future opens onto the possibilities of acting otherwise and not out of the blindness of a forgetfulness of the past but with a commitment in the light of this past to do better and to handle oneself and things differently.

Nonetheless, future deeds do not affect the fact of having done something. A future action cannot make the fact of having-done disappear. As Jankélévitch phrases it, future action cannot make an *infectum* (an undone) out of a *factum*. The having-done, Jankélévitch unequivocally asserts, is utterly ineffaceable:

> With time, all that has been done can be undone; all that has been undone can be redone. But the fact-of-having-done [*fecisse*] is indefeasible. We can undo the thing done, but we cannot make it so that the thing that was done never happened, we cannot, as Cicero says, following Aristotle, make an *infectum* from a *factum*. . . . To commit a crime is an act that happens once in the chronicle, but the fact of having committed it will always last! Such is the paradox of *atemporal semelfactivity*. Thus, the fact of having-taken place, which is the

misdeed reduced to the pure advent of the event, is in itself eternal. Eternal or rather imperishable—for it is not atemporal at both ends. Culpability has indeed begun, although it does not have to finish. The commission of the misdeed happens in a history that previously knew nothing of it. Does not this temporal initiative that decides in favor of the atemporal, and that is infinitely surpassed by its own consequences, in itself sum up all the asymmetry of our freedom? . . . The thing done appears to disappear progressively by the effect of becoming, but the fact of having done makes itself eternal as a disappearing appearance. Little by little, the inert time of continuation erases *that which* has been done, but it has no hold over the *fact-that*.[41]

The intention, in a case of a bad or evil intention, however fleeting, triggers an action that falls under the senses and into the course of history and time, but it itself is of the creative instant, "impalpable and pneumatic." All the good intentions that may follow the bad intention remain heterogeneous to and incompatible with it. They do not balance out, nor does the assuagement of time erase the fact that a moral misdeed was committed. For liberty is the source of having-done, Jankélévitch observes, and responsibility is its consequence.[42]

With three analogies, Jankélévitch illustrates the relation of deeds past and future. In the first analogy, he describes the irreparable-irrevocable as if it were coated by a kind of cohesive agent, representing the soft assimilable part of fate, that renders the bitter and hard core of the irreparable imperceptible. In his second analogy, the mystery of the irreparable is surrounded by an expansive development site for repairs, which represents the workshop of transformative and active work. Jankélévitch lastly compares the irrevocable to death, writing that, like death, the irrevocable is inexorable, though melioristic therapies are available to remedy sicknesses. Although therapies are important, they can serve to mask the reality of death. He thus asks whether the despair over the invincibility of death is not veiled by the boundless hope for healing the suffering and extending life.[43]

Jankélévitch is aware that the act and its consequences are finite, so he concentrates on the facticity of that which has been done. Although the consequences of sin can be removed from the world and perhaps even all memory can be erased, the fact that the sin took place, Jankélévitch argues, is indestructible. In other words, the blood from Macbeth's hands can be washed away, but the invisible spot cannot be washed clean: "What's done is done."[44] Between power and impotence, humans can do and undo and do again; they can modify and mold the modalities of being, but they cannot annihilate the quodditas—neither that of time nor that of freedom.[45]

Time, according to Jankélévitch, is taut with a tension inherent in being both the condition for possibility and the condition for impossibility. It both allows for contradiction and is the reason the quoddity cannot be removed. The flow of time, on the one hand, liquefies the contradiction of the evil and the good deed. The synthetic function of time places them in a series, allowing both to stand next to each other in succession: first the one and then the other. But the two of them cannot be done simultaneously or co-obtain simultaneously. As Jankélévitch explains, the principle of identity forbids that what has been done has not been done.[46] The facilitating role of time, as we saw with irreversibility, makes a return to the status quo forever impossible. Jankélévitch thus distances himself from the nostalgia of a restoration to a previous time or state of existence. Instead, forgiveness, for him, must entail something different from restoration or a return to Eden. Redemption, if there is any, must lie ahead, for there is no turning back. But his hope for a different and better future is also deflated by the indestructible tautology of the having-done. The creative creature Jankélévitch holds humans to be is incapable of rendering that which he has done that which he has not done. Jankélévitch's moral thought abides in this essentially temporal tension. On the one hand, duty, according to Jankélévitch, is always future-oriented: What is done is never done but remains to do and endlessly to do again. But, on the other hand, the irrevocability of what has been done will forever remain a stain or a "damned spot," like an invisible and haunting ghost we often, though ultimately futilely, attempt to be rid of, for it is immune to the having-passed of time.[47]

There is thus a temporally conditioned asymmetry between the good and the bad or evil in Jankélévitch's morality. Picking up on what Max Horkheimer proposes as a possibility, Jankélévitch asymmetrically assesses the good and the bad acts in relation to time. He suggests that, whereas the good always remains yet to do and to do again, the misdeed of having-done inscribes itself indelibly and infinitely.[48] The good is open-ended and cannot content itself with a good conscience or rest on its laurels as if moral acts were capital. Instead, morality, for Jankélévitch, is impoverished and creatively striving like Eros himself. The good is no one's possession and therefore knows neither a moral elite nor accumulation. Regardless of whether one has done a good deed or the most heinous crime, the good remains to do. But the irrevocability of having-done, which Jankélévitch casts purely as the irrevocability of the misdeed, will have remained regardless of what has been done since then and what is left to do and do again, namely the good.

Because of the temporal-ethical category of irrevocability, then, there will always be an indissoluble remnant of that which has been done despite future good acts, compensation, and reparations. In forgetting the *rest* of this inscription, Jankélévitch concedes, the repentant sinner can resemble the innocent person, and the restored conscience can become almost interchangeable with the conscience before the fall. But only almost! One can act *as if* that which has been done has not been done, but only as if. Whether out of convention, weariness, or as a consequence of approximate estimation, it is possible for humans to act as if their free act, their decision, or the event of having-willed (*voluisse*) was not. Jankélévitch is adamant, however, that this behavior *as if not* is qualitatively different from the quoddity of having-done. The fate established in the wake of a decision is absolute in its quoddity. The facticity of having-done wrong—or even having-willed it—forms the irreparable, which, according to Jankélévitch, "cannot be repaired in any case, in any form, in no measure and at no instant."[49] To will as if what has been done has not been done does not replace the having-done. To act "as if not" superficially compensates for the having-done. Although it may express a change in the mode of moral existence, it does not annul the quodditas of the having-done.

Moreover, the "as if" or "as if not" potentially denies the temporality of time and the irretrievable remnant of having-lived between one act and another. This disparity between the "as if" and "the fact that" is illuminated by an example Jankélévitch offers from the history of jurisprudence. In 1944, he explains, the provisory government of Libération in France declared all of the laws, edicts, and sanctions of the four previous years null and void. With one single decree, he writes, one brushed a pile of injustices from the table. By creating a new starting point, one acted *as if* nothing during those four nightmarish years had happened, but one did not and could not bring it about that nothing in that time had happened. Jankélévitch concludes that "no human justice can restore the past to a person. The compensated citizen will always remain a damaged man."[50] Therefore, it is not merely the fact-that something was done that is irrevocable; it is also a matter of the time lived in the wake of what was done that cannot be reversed or revoked or made naught.

Imprescriptibility: Axiology versus Chronology

Jankélévitch constructs his defense of the law of imprescriptibility on the basis of irrevocability. In the 1960s, Jankélévitch voiced his opposition to efforts in France to establish statutory limits for the prosecution of Nazi war crimes. Jankélévitch's arguments first appeared in his essay "L'Imprescriptible," which originally appeared in *Le Monde* on January 3, 1965, and later became part of the English translation "Should We Pardon Them?" In *Forgiveness*, he extends the logic of his argument through an explication of fidelity. He insists that crimes against values, in particular crimes against humanity, stand morally outside the confines of time.[51] The duty to atemporal values compels from beyond time. In this sense, he suggests, morality is beyond the law:

> The French Parliament proclaims that crimes against humanity are a priori imprescriptible, that is, are not allowed to be prescribed. Granting the fact that it is a question of an absolute principle, temporary prorogation of the prescriptive delay has to be considered as a miserably empirical measure; the moral dilemma would be just as acute thirty years after the expiration date as in the twentieth year. Strictly speaking and theoretically, every misdeed is imprescriptible, since every having-taken-place, from the moment in which it takes place onward, becomes eternal. . . . The attack against the humanness of man has something inexpiable where the quoddity lays itself bare. . . . The prescription of a colossal crime is a monstrous caricature of ordinary prescription and in fact makes manifest the absurdity of it.[52]

Jankélévitch principally recognizes that not every offense is an offense against the humanity of the person. He acknowledges a wide spectrum, ranging from personal snubs and moral offenses to crimes that aim at personhood. In this passage, he treats all of these as if in a continuum solely with regard to their irrevocability or inexpiability. Nonetheless, Jankélévitch conflates irrevocability with imprescriptibility and thus morality with law. Every misdeed may be irrevocable, but not every misdeed is therefore necessarily imprescriptible. Although imprescriptibility is founded on the moral order of the irrevocable—indeed, it is, according to Jankélévitch, the inscription of this moral order into law—it is reserved for particular crimes, crimes against humanity.

What Jankélévitch emphasizes, though, is that empirical measure is of a qualitatively different order than moral principles. A crime against humanity will never not be a crime against humanity. Jankélévitch makes clear that any limit set on the claim of justice for such crimes can only be an arbitrary one established by social and political exigencies. Such limits cannot be justified on the principled grounds of justice but fall under the course of utilitarian means. Prescription sets a definitive end to all procedures of justice. The prescriptibility of crimes revolves around the assumption that time somehow affects duties that by their character presuppose validity throughout time. Taking irreversibility, not irrevocability, as its point of origin and primary axis, the law of prescription, as Paul Ricoeur points out, denies any return to the criminal act or its traces and effects after an arbitrarily established period of time. After that time, it forbids the pursuit of prosecution of acts that oblige the right and even the duty to prosecute.[53] The traces and the effects of an action of wrongdoing are not removed, but the judicial path of calling them into question is extinguished. Jankélévitch is wary of such a juridical notion of "extinguishment" because he detects in it not only the phenomena of social passivity, inertia, negligence, and inactivity but also the active endeavor to inhibit the execution of justice in the name of social advantage.[54]

For Jankélévitch, social expediency highlights the link between forgetting and prescription. Prescription, he observes, simply makes forgetting normative and official.[55] The doctrine assumes that there needs to be a proximate time-correlation between a crime and its punishment in order for the prosecuted and the public to see the reason in punishment. Appealing to the educative quality of punishment during the debate on imprescription, the attorney Maurice Garçon invoked the image of a child who, disciplined for an act long after its occurrence, protests, "But that was a long time ago!"[56] The notion of prescription is based on a similar logic of the potential assuagement of time: "We have moved on: Can't we just move on?" or "We are not the ones we were then! You are looking to prosecute people who are not there anymore!" Jankélévitch unveils in such substitutions for repentance the "commercial repentance for business purposes" and "diplomatic repentance for reasons of state."[57] Prescription, as a replacement for remorse and authentic contrition, leaves a host of questions unanswered, especially when prescription is equated with forgiveness. Jankélévitch wonders, "Why are they in such hurry to turn the page and to say . . . '*Schluss damit*?'" In what name, he inquires, may indulgent judges "forgive"? "On what grounds would they dare offer pardons in our name?" With which right may they "forgive" the offenses committed against others? In whose name? According to which principles? Under the obligation of which interests? And with which goals?[58]

Any forgiveness that is "finalized," that is, subjugated to an "in order to" or an "in order that" is, according to Jankélévitch, instrumental and utilitarian. Such empirical substitutes for forgiveness miss its metaempirical essence. In his apophatic approach to forgiveness, Jankélévitch seeks to uncover what Derrida calls "the confusions which reduce forgiveness to amnesty or to amnesia, to acquittal or prescription, to the work of mourning or some political therapy of reconciliation, in short to some historical ecology."[59] The law of imprescriptibility resists these pragmatic strategies and upholds the virtue of a justice that, in the words of Derrida, "signals toward the transcendent order of the unconditional . . . toward a sort of ahistoricity, even eternity and the Final Judgement . . . [that] goes beyond history and the finite time of the law: for ever, 'eternally,' everywhere and always, a crime against humanity will always be subject to judgment, and it will never be effaced from the judicial archive."[60] Beyond all statutes of limitations, the law of imprescriptibility thus invokes the eternal—or better, the imperishable—claim of justice.

4

Translating Resentment

For Vladimir Jankélévitch, the protest against forgetting that which is irrevocable is not merely an intellectual endeavor. It entails the emotive and passionate task of justice itself. Consequently, at the limits of passion, he conceives this protest as a duty to both values and to the individuals. Values, according to Jankélévitch, are not simply to be conceded with the cold eye of rationality; they rather form the lifeblood of ethical-emotional life. His assessment of ressentiment therefore shows that the ethical life is not dispassionate. To the contrary, justice, he explains, must be a love of justice and must include a resentment of injustice; it must be impassioned in order to transform things, especially since it is passion alone that has a hold on passion.[1] Jankélévitch thus intimately links the passion of ressentiment to the emotive force of moral anger or rancor. Both positively and negatively, it indicates an inability or unwillingness to let go. Although he is aware that purely subjectively or psychologically, ressentiment and rancor can be frivolous, egoistical, and even destructive passions, he focuses on the charge of ressentiment that is responsible to justice.

The role of retributive emotions in moral theory is one part of a growing field dedicated to the relation between emotions and rationality and between emotions and ethical life and ethical theory.[2] Although many moral philosophies implicitly accept that emotions are linked to morality, justice, and rationality, most do not delve into the murky waters surrounding their conceptualization. Resentment therefore remains "a rather unfashionable subject in moral philosophy."[3] Some thinkers, such as Jeffrie Murphy, have bucked this trend, even offering "two cheers for vindictiveness." This positive estimation maintains the commonsense belief that it is both natural and appropriate to feel resentment in response to cruelty. From this perspective, perhaps the burden of proof should be inverted and placed on those who claim the illegitimacy of retributive emotions on account of their supposed immorality or irrationality.

The problem with vindictive passions, however, concerns less their principled rationality than the risks and dangers they engender in their excess. Whereas they might be said to uphold order, they equally can be seen as destructive of social and moral order in their tendency to consume and act as a contagion of violence. In the final play of Aeschylus's *Oresteia* trilogy, Athena contends that these passions are neither irrational nor evil but represent "legitimate emotional indicators of self-respect, self-defense, and allegiance to the moral and social order."[4] Thus the Furies who represent these passions are not banished from Athens but sheltered in the city. These literary and mythological themes are further embodied in the figure of Nemesis, who regulates a cosmic law of compensation. This Greek goddess personifies the indignation against and retribution for evil deeds and undeserved good fortune. Nemesis combats apparent impunity and levels Fortune (*Tykhe*). A predecessor and model for the Roman lady of justice, she is the goddess of equivalence and equilibrium. In short, Nemesis represents an avenging, punishing divinity. Her conjunction with justice is, therefore, somewhat ambiguous. Indicative of this ambiguity is the fact that among the Latin translations of the Roman appropriation of her cult are the names *Rivalitas* (jealousy/rivalry) and *Invidia* (envy). As "the dispenser of dues" (*nemesis, nemein*), her justice is shrouded in ambiguity—the ambiguity of the gift, the human and the divine, the friend and the foe.[5]

Aristotle's Nemesis

In his explication of the doctrine of the mean, Aristotle invokes *nemesis*, which can be translated as *resentment* or *indignation*.[6] He associates it even with good moral character. Juxtaposed to pity (*eleos*), indignation signifies, for Aristotle, the pain at unmerited good fortune in others, whereas pity signifies pain at unmerited bad fortune. They are inverse sides of the same moral quality. Aristotle thus claims that "it is our duty both to feel sympathy and pity for unmerited distress, and to feel indignation at unmerited prosperity; for whatever is undeserved is unjust, and that is why we ascribe indignation even to the gods."[7] He is acutely aware of the effects of such a mythological gift to philosophy. He therefore takes pains to distinguish indignation from envy. In the *Rhetoric*, he observes that it might indeed be thought that envy is similarly opposed to pity, on the ground that envy is closely akin to indignation, or even the same thing. But it is not the same. It is true that it also is a disturbing pain excited by the prosperity of others. But it is excited not by the prosperity of the undeserving but by that of people who are like us or equal with us.[8]

The difference between indignation and envy is that "righteous indignation" is a mean state between the extremes of envy and malice. The envious person goes further than indignation at the prosperity of the undeserving, being pained by those who deserve prosperity. In contrast, the malicious person is so far removed from being pained that he actually rejoices at misfortunes. However, envy and malice are not diametrically opposed. Instead, Aristotle bears out their intimate correlation, locating both in the same person: "The man who is delighted by others' misfortunes is identical with the man who envies others' prosperity."[9] This type of moral character is contrary to the moral character compelled by the duty to pity and indignation.

For Aristotle, indignation is primarily an aristocratic passion limited to those of noble birth who deserve good, either on account of their morality or in their alignment with "nature." "Hence," he explains, "servile, worthless, unambitious persons are not inclined to indignation, since there is nothing they can believe themselves to deserve." Although to be indignant is to "loathe any kind of injustice," the injustices Aristotle has in mind are less malicious crimes than the undue dispensation of wealth and power. "Indignation," he writes, "is pain caused by the sight of undeserved good fortune. . . . It is roused by the sight of wealth, power, and the like—by all those things, roughly speaking, which are deserved by good men and by those who possess the goods of nature—noble birth, beauty, and so on."[10] His question, therefore, is not how the wicked can prosper while the good suffer. The object of indignation is not bad fortune or moral wrongdoing but good fortune—that is, good fortune for those undeserving by nature, birth, or a traditionally established place in the hierarchies of society.

Accordingly, Aristotle focuses on temporal goods and precludes matters of virtue from the chiasm of pity and indignation.[11] The sight of virtue, he is certain, should not cause indignation in any person: "Thus a man may be just or brave, or acquire moral goodness: but we shall not be indignant with him for that reason, any more than we shall pity him for the contrary reason." Under the ideal of *kalokagathos* (the beautiful and the good), success, beauty, and prosperity are the natural crown jewels of virtue.[12] He therefore believes that there are real goods that can accrue justly and unjustly to the worthy and unworthy alike, whereas the goods of the soul cannot accrue to the unworthy. One may be deemed unworthy, however, either with respect to virtue or with respect to social standing. Indignation is thus, first and foremost, the just passion reinforcing the social and economic inequality requisite for social stability in an aristocratic society.

Both pity and indignation, according to Aristotle, are regulated by the notion of "to each his due," and they both share a spectator's view. But pity, in contrast to indignation, involves empathetic reflexivity. Pity invokes the requisite "condition of remembering that similar misfortunes have happened to us or ours, or expecting them to happen in the future."[13] In order to feel pity, one must be able to identify with the other, whether through one's past in memory or through a projection of the future, and whether it immediately concerns oneself, one's family, friends, or one's possessions.[14] Aristotle concludes that the people we pity are those whom we know, though they cannot be very closely related to us or else we would feel about them as if we were in danger ourselves.[15] Pity balances between indifference and fear.[16] The noble mean applies here equally to the balance between distance and proximity. This balance between the near and the far resembles that of the spectator and the actor, or the crisis and security, in the process of catharsis Aristotle associates with tragedy.[17] The person close enough for there to emerge a sense of identification but distant enough to quell the anxiety concomitant with crisis is the neighbor. He is neither friend nor foe; he is likely an equal and shares in the same qualities. He is temporally and spatially in proximity but is not family. "What we fear for ourselves," Aristotle explains, "excites our pity when it happens to others."[18] The pain of pity, however, does not excite action. It is a nonpractical emotion attached to the scene of the theater.

Aristotle's distinction between fear felt in the first person and sorrow felt in witnessing injustice from a second or third person perspective may be applied to nemesis as well. As a sorrow that straddles proximity and distance, *nemesis* is best translated as *indignation*, not *resentment*. It is directed toward what is happening to our neighbor. This distinction is helpful. Whereas resentment represents the pain at the injustice aimed at "me" or those with whom I immediately identify, the pain invoked by the injustice that is not directed at me or mine but is felt in the name of some greater generality like class or morality, in the case of Aristotle, or even humanity represents indignation.[19] At the very least, the notion of indignation describes the moral pain experienced in witnessing injustice suffered by those beyond the extensions of immediate identification. The difference between the inside and the outside of the circle demarcates the difference between resentment and indignation, and whereas injustice within the circle perhaps naturally raises resentment, injustice without it should raise indignation.

For Aristotle, indignation is, however, a mere pain or a sorrow, which does not have any inherent practical quality. Insofar as it is interpreted solely in terms of the sorrow felt by the unworthy accruement of a putative good, it fails to account for the feeling of indignation as a just, practical response to wrongdoing. Although Aristotle recognizes a certain closeness between indignation and envy, possibly even a conflation of the two—which is key for Nietzsche's portrayal of this passion—he siphons it off from the more dynamic emotion of anger. Anger, he claims, is praiseworthy in the mild person—that is, the just person—who is angry at the right things, toward the right people, in the right way, for the right length of time, as prescribed by reason.[20]

Jankélévitch's understanding of resentment invokes both Aristotle's conception of indignation as pain and his conception of moral anger, which moves us to exact a penalty from the offender. When indignation is also aligned with moral anger and when it extends to the injustice suffered by others as opposed to merely the natural passion of anger raised by the wrong done to oneself, as Aristotle implies, then it can serve the demand for justice in its capacity as an emotive force. As Jeffrie Murphy explains, "True allegiance to morality and law is not merely intellectual but also must be revealed in passionate commitment; and indignation and resentment represent such commitment."[21] Bishop Joseph Butler takes up moral injury as the appropriate object of the passion of resentment and links it to the pursuit of justice.

Butler's Sermons

In two sermons, 8 and 9, the Bishop Joseph Butler (1692–1752) addresses first the naturalness and appropriateness of resentment and then the relation of resentment to forgiveness. Butler adopts the task of representing the social and moral value of resentment as a response of resistance and as a possible corrective to injury. He therefore understands resentment as a counterbalance to benevolence. In a critique of Thomas Hobbes's philosophy of pervasive egoism, Butler holds benevolence to be as intrinsic to human nature as self-love. So whereas resentment counterbalances benevolence, benevolence is required to balance resentment, to maintain it in its mean and thus keep it measured and just.

Since Butler sees religion and morality grounded in the natural world order, he frames the question of theodicy pragmatically. He opens Sermon 8 by asserting that God is perfect goodness and the creator and preserver of the world and that "general benevolence is the great law of the whole moral creation." Proceeding from this hypothesis, Butler inquires why humans have a principle implanted in them like resentment, which appears directly contrary to the law of the moral universe, namely benevolence. Any other line of inquiry into the reasons of God, he warns, would run the risk of being mere "impertinent curiosity." Butler's goal is to grasp and explicate "why, or for what end, such a passion was given us: And this chiefly in order to show, what are the abuses of it."[22]

According to Butler, resentment has "moral evil" as its object. He distinguishes injury from harm, pain, and loss; it alone is a result of wickedness, "the only deformity in creation."[23] As a response to moral evil, resentment is a good pain, even "a generous movement of mind" of which there are two kinds, one "hasty and sudden," the other "settled and deliberate." Butler associates the former with "mere instinct" and locates it in infants, in lower species of animals, and in the people he believes are inclined toward the animal and the infantile. The lack of reason in the sudden eruption of anger consists, for Butler, in its blindness and impulsiveness; its naturalness is not moral or reflective but the mere response of counterforce to force. In contradistinction, Butler connects the deliberate anger of resentment with a sense of virtue and vice, moral good and evil. It is raised by cruelty and injustice along with the desire to have cruelty and injustice punished. He suggests that, since it is also felt by persons unconcerned and without malice, it provides "one of the common bonds, by which society is held together." Whereas sudden anger stands for "self-defense," settled anger is concerned with "the administration of justice."[24]

Within its proper bounds of degree and duration, resentment provides the necessary gravity to pursue the course of justice. Butler thus views resentment as a compensation for the meekness of the benevolent forms of compassion and pity. So much, he concedes, may "justly be allowed to resentment, in the strictest way of moral consideration."[25] But he concedes no more! For Butler, resentment is purely a necessary evil, "a painful remedy" against injustice.[26] Considered in itself, he deems it very undesirable and what society must very much wish to be without.[27]

Butler understands forgiveness as the way to prevent the slide of resentment into malice, hate, and revenge. Contrary to Murphy's reading, forgiveness does not entail for Butler "the foreswearing of resentment—the resolute overcoming of the anger and hatred that are naturally directed toward a person who has done one an unjustified and non-excused moral injury."[28] In fact, Butler states quite explicitly that resentment is not inconsistent with love or forgiveness. He argues that, though the passions of resentment and love may mutually have the effect of lessening the other, they do not necessarily destroy each other. It is consequently possible, even commendable, Butler tells us, to love our enemy yet harbor resentment against him for his injurious behavior. According to Butler, it is only when this resentment entirely destroys our natural benevolence toward the offender that resentment becomes malice or revenge.

Butler intuitively points to the distinction between the private and the public realms, their division allowing for their conjunction—within the private realm one can personally forgive and still within the public realm have the wrongdoer judicially punished.[29] But this separation of spheres is not absolute. The duty to love may not be abandoned in the prosecution of the guilty, and benevolence is not heterogeneous to punishment. He observes, for example, that capital punishment may not be executed out of malice or in the spirit of revenge. Rather it should be a measured but negative, necessary consequence of the fallibility of humanity, which is to be executed in the spirit of respect.[30]

He also recognizes, however, that it is a slippery slope between just resentment and the malice, revenge, and hatred from which he wants to distinguish it. Since God cannot have implanted in us a passion that is evil, he reasons, it must be the way and the degree in which humans indulge in this passion that cause it to deviate from its original purpose. Although Butler attempts to carefully distinguish the beneficial violence of resentment from harmful and injurious violence, he simultaneously demonstrates that evil and the violent measures taken to combat evil are essentially the same.[31] He portrays this contagion of violence inherent in resentment in two steps. Resentment inclines toward mistaking the whole person for the individual action. He acutely observes the propensity of resentment to move from the singular misdeed to a generalization and totalization of the agent's entire personality and being.[32] In this manner, resentment loses all proportionality to the crime and with it all justification for its "rational" uprising. Butler therefore warns that, in resentment,

> the whole character and behaviour is considered with an eye to that particular part which has offended us, and the whole man appears *monstrous*, without any thing *right* or *human* in him; whereas the resentment should surely, at least, be confined to that particular part of the behaviour which gave offence, since the other parts of a man's life and character stand just the same as they did before.[33]

An isolated act or acts may not be taken for the whole of the person. From action one cannot deduce being. The problem Butler sees with resentment is that it makes monsters of humans, but humans are not monsters.

Spreading from the act to the person, the contagion of resentment spreads to the resented person. No longer heeding his own distinction between the beneficial and necessary evil of resentment and the plain evil of malice, Butler preaches that "malice or resentment towards any man hath plainly a tendency to beget the same passion in him who is the object of it, and this again increases it in the other."[34] The feeling grows like a circulating disease feeding off of itself and becoming stronger, penetrating and permeating more and more members of the social body. Butler states:

> It is of the very nature of this vice to propagate itself, not only by way of example, which it does in common with other vices, but in a peculiar way of its own; for resentment itself, as well as what is done in consequence of it, is the object of resentment. Hence it comes to pass, that the first offence, even when so slight as presently to be dropt and forgotten, becomes the occasion of entering into a long intercourse of ill offices. Neither is [it] at all uncommon to see persons, in this progress of strife and variance, change parts; and him, who was at first the injured person, become more injurious and blameable than the aggressor.... There is no going on to represent this scene of rage and madness: it is manifest there would be no bounds, nor any end.[35]

The end of this dissemination of resentment, malice, and the cycles of revenge is such, he claims, "so as almost to lay waste the world."[36] Making matters worse, the violence stemming from resentment is more heinous than malice because it hides under the aegis of moral justification for retaliation, which "knows no end and can have no end."[37]

It is precisely "the end" of malice and revenge, however, which conjoins these stages of contagion.[38] The end of malice or the gratification of resentment, according to Butler, is self-destructive and self-defeating. The purpose of resentment—indeed, the reason Butler thinks it was implanted in us—is either to prevent or to remedy "disorder," "irregularity," or "injury." The problem is that the gratification of resentment, as Butler observes, "consists in producing misery; i.e. in contradicting the end for which it was implanted in our nature." Whereas other passions or principles may cause misery, none of them, according to Butler, has as its end the production of misery in other humans, except malice and revenge, and these do nothing less than mediate evil itself. Although malice and revenge, on the one hand, and resentment, on the other hand, may differ in degree, they are, in their aim, all too much the same. For resentment designs "to do mischief, to be the author of misery," and this alone is what gratifies the passion of resentment.[39]

Butler therefore concludes that resentment may not know any gratification. It must be interrupted and the chain of contagion broken. As Charles Griswold explains, "Unchecked, resentment consumes everything and everyone."[40] The intervention of forgiveness or the love of one's enemies provides this check and this interruption. Following the exhortation of Paul, "Be ye angry and sin not" (Eph. 4:26), Butler maintains that resentment has to remain a passion, not lead to action.[41] Of its own accord, resentment leads to excesses and perversions, to revenge, malice, sickness, and destruction . . . unless forgiveness intervenes—not to overcome resentment, but rather to forswear the act, forswear revenge, and forswear the cycles of violence that resentment otherwise propagates.

As a gift from God to human nature, resentment does have a place in the moral order. For Butler, it serves to balance the weakness of our natural pity and compassion. Without it, he confesses "the execution of justice" would prove "exceedingly painful and difficult." Indeed pity and compassion may "quite prevent it." Without this passion, in other words, a world of compassion, a world of love, might prove to be too meek to execute justice. Such a world, according to Jankélévitch, would accordingly risk the reign of the unjust, even potentially a reign of hangmen.[42] Resentment is thus a necessary evil, Butler argues, because "it is necessary" that "injustice and cruelty" should be punished, and benevolence would perhaps prove impotent.[43] It is, however, "manifest" to him in its logic of theodicy that "resentment is to be considered as a *secondary passion*, placed in us upon supposition, upon account of, and with regard to injury."[44] Resentment exists, he concludes, only on account of moral evil as a supplement to our benevolent nature for our weakness. This is its ambiguity—useful and destructive, necessary but evil, a practical good that is such only in appropriate measure. It exhibits the ambiguity of God's gift that is *Gift* (German for poison). Resentment is a kind of *pharmakon*, both remedy and poison, depending on the dose.[45] Love, for Butler, is charged with counterbalancing resentment. With the weight of a first principle, benevolence must establish the measure. The health of the social body depends on it. Forgiveness, according to Butler, prevents the abuse of resentment by maintaining the balance between love and resentment, first and second order principles, benevolence and bloated self-love.[46] Although Butler admits that it would be preferable to act from the "better principle" of "reason and cool-reflection," he recognizes that reason does not move us like passion, while the natural passion of resentment only leads to justice if tempered by the natural passion of love.[47]

Nietzsche's Doubling

Whereas Butler has experienced a revival in contemporary works on the relationship between retributive emotions and forgiveness, no other modern philosopher or thinker has shaped the conception of resentment like Nietzsche. His imprint already comes to the fore in his appropriation of the French term, *ressentiment,* a re-feeling of something or the feeling again of a feeling. Although the English word *resentment* translates the French term *ressentiment* almost exactly, it has a different connotation. Whereas resentment for Butler resembles Aristotle's notion of deliberate anger insofar as it is an emotion of the first order, a reactive feeling to a wrong done, ressentiment is clearly a second-order emotion whose object is less the external act than the internal response to the act. Since Nietzsche, ressentiment has become a *terminus technicus* for this doubling, and it is "one of the key conceptions of Nietzsche's psychology and the clue to many of his philosophical contentions."[48]

In the first essay of *On the Genealogy of Morals,* Nietzsche's most concentrated study on this passion, Nietzsche declares that the birth of morality stems from the spirit of ressentiment—that is, the spirit of ideal and imaginary revenge. As Richard Bernstein observes, Nietzsche's method of genealogy takes up the task of the "genuine historian" outlined in his essay "On the Uses and Disadvantages of History for Life." He proceeds as one who is "both a knower and a creator." Blending critical, monumental, and antiquarian history in an imaginative manner, Nietzsche seeks to unmask what underlies our morality, and his construction of the past and the future possibility serve the purposes of his critique of the present.[49] What underlies morality, he claims, is ressentiment. Contrary to Kantian belief, morality is not self-sufficient or self-justifying. Nietzsche's genealogy discovers both a historical origin and a foreign source of morality: It begins with the Judeo-Christian tradition and is rooted in a nonmoral, psychosomatic phenomenon.

According to Nietzsche's redescription, the birth of morality overthrew the Greek opposition of the good and the bad, replacing it with the opposition of good and evil. The aristocratic equivalence of values between the good, the noble, the strong, the happy, the beautiful, and those loved by the gods was maintained by inversion on the part of the weak and the ugly. He accuses the meek of having identified noble values as evil and predatory, and through the method of genealogy, Nietzsche seeks to bring to light the will to power that the weak have wielded in the shadows in order to covertly erect a moral structure suited to subdue the strong and condemn their nature and, in the same stroke, nature itself.

Nietzsche problematizes the propagation of a morality that prioritizes the other, whether in love, pity, benevolence, or compassion. The idea of altruism, that the other should concern me more than myself, he argues, is unnatural. Concretely altruistic acts, moreover, prove often to be condescending and degrading. They help neither the beneficiary nor the benefactor. The former is not respected because, as Nietzsche would say, it is the feeble creature not the creator in him that is pitied; and the latter flees from himself. Love of the other, he observes, frequently becomes an escape from oneself, a welcome distraction.[50]

In contrast, Nietzsche esteems the morality of antiquity for its focus on self-perfection and self-mastery, where the moral relation is not that of love of neighbor but rather that of friendship, in which the goal is to assist the other, often by being hard, toward his own perfection and mastery. Nietzsche does not necessarily exclude love of neighbor. He merely stipulates that the prerequisite for neighbor-love is self-love.[51] Nietzsche thus pronounces the warning that graciousness, benevolence, and indeed forgiveness are often offered out of weakness or fear. He therefore criticizes a morality established on humility, shame, and meekness as illusory. To be moral, Nietzsche insists, one must have teeth; one must be capable of violence but choose the good, whereas to uphold impotence as a virtue of intrinsic good is nothing less than a perverse morality—a slave's morality. Zarathustra therefore proclaims to his disciples, "I know you [are] capable of all evil—therefore from you I want the good. Indeed, I often laughed at the weaklings who believe themselves good because their paws are lame."[52]

Nietzsche attributes the introduction of this slave's morality to the Jewish-Christian tradition. The slave's revolution in morality begins when ressentiment becomes creative and starts to bear values. In a profound way, this creation is negative, however, because it comes to fruition neither in the act nor in affirmation. Instead, it forms a negative foil in denying the values of the noble and the values of life, taking the negation of noble Hellene morality as its point of reference and its point of departure:[53]

> The slave revolt in morality begins when the *ressentiment* itself becomes creative and gives birth to values: the ressentiment of natures that are denied the true reaction, that of deeds, and compensate themselves with an imaginary revenge. While every noble morality develops from a triumphant affirmation of itself, slave morality from the outset says No to what is "outside," what is "different," what is "not itself"; and *this* No is its creative deed. This inversion of the value-positing eye—this *need* to direct one's view outward instead of back to oneself—is of the essence of *ressentiment*: in order to exist,

slave morality always first needs a hostile external world; it needs, physiologically speaking, external stimuli in order to act at all—its action is fundamentally reaction.[54]

The aristocratic moral order is thus preserved through inversion. The reaction of those intimidated by the threat of natural power is to deny that such power is good. The terms, however, have significantly, changed. What was once an opposition of the good, noble, and strong, on the one hand, and the "low," "the common," and the "bad," on the other, is transformed into an opposition of good and evil. The battle of morality therefore revolves around the power of naming and ascription. It was the weak, Nietzsche states, who named the strong evil; they feigned humility, love, and forgiveness, remaining harmless while exercising revenge imaginarily in the establishment of morality. Their victory was sealed as soon as the strong and noble acquiesced to this imaginary morality and subjected themselves to the definition and judgment of the weak until finally they, too, judged themselves in accordance with this moral grammar.[55] Whereas indignation (*nemesis*), for Aristotle, was a social instrument for maintaining the social order and protecting the aristocratic class against the low and the common, Nietzsche conceives ressentiment as a source of moral revolution on the part of the low and the common. Its subversive power is necessarily indirect and deceptive. He thus understands himself as a link in the lineage of the greatest philosophers since Socrates who have "shown how much hypocrisy and . . . how many lies are hidden beneath the most highly honored type of their present-day morality."[56]

The ideals of present-day morality have been fabricated in the inner factories of ressentiment. Its creative capacity has created nothing less than the ideals on which morality has been erected, but these ideals themselves are nothing more than "counterfeits" and "lies." Nietzsche writes:

> Weakness is being lied into something *meritorious*. . . . And impotence which does not requite into "goodness of heart"; anxious lowliness into "humility"; subjection to those one hates into "obedience" . . . The inoffensiveness of the weak man, even the cowardice of which he has so much, his lingering at the door, his being ineluctably compelled to wait, here acquire flattering names, such as "patience," and are even called virtue itself; his inability for revenge is called unwillingness to revenge, perhaps even forgiveness ("for *they* know not what they do—we alone know what *they* do!"). They also speak of "loving one's enemies"—and sweat as they do so.[57]

Morality appears to him as composed of inverted images, which are deflected and distorted. Indeed, Nietzsche discovers in slave morality a will to power made up of smoke and mirrors. These moralists resemble "black magicians, who make whiteness, milk, and innocence every blackness," and who, through projection, are even capable of making of others monsters (*Scheusal*).[58] Nietzsche accuses these magicians of having cast a spell on history.

One of ressentiment-laden morality's most potent spells, according to Nietzsche, is the creation of the subject, the production of the soul, and the origin of bad conscience. Anticipating Freud, he traces them back to the mechanisms of internalization and repression.

> All instincts that do not discharge themselves outwardly turn inward—this is what I call the *internalization* of man: thus it was that man first developed what was later called his "soul." The entire inner world, originally as thin as if it were stretched between two membranes, expanded and extended itself, acquired depth, breadth, and height, in the same measure as outward discharge was *inhibited*.... Hostility, cruelty, joy in persecuting, in attacking, in change, in destruction—all this turned against the possessors of such instincts: *that* is the origin of the "bad conscience."[59]

Separate from what it does, as well as from its impulses and drives, the subject henceforth represents something hypothetically free to be against its own nature and is therefore guilty for what it is. "The subject (or, to use a more popular expression, the *soul*)," Nietzsche explains, "has perhaps been believed in hitherto more firmly than anything else on earth because it makes possible to the majority of mortals, the weak and oppressed of every kind, the sublime self-deception that interprets weakness as freedom, and their being thus-and-thus as a *merit*."[60] Since such merit does not immediately manifest itself, if at all, past and present misery may feed the hope for future reward, fortifying the supposed unconditionality of love and humility. Morally compensating for its impotence with a transcendental omnipotence, the gift of love becomes *giftig*, or noxious, poisoning both those filled with ressentiment because they retain their hatred and vengeance in the cellars of their existence and, through its contagion effect or spell, all those around them.

For Nietzsche, the contrast to the noble person could not be greater. Whereas the person of ressentiment holds his peace in a deadly and poisonous silence, walks secretive ways, and uses backdoors, always seeking a certain hiddenness from the light, Nietzsche associates the noble person with a certain innocence and naïveté, with a strength that is genuine, upright, natural, carefree, even careless, and manifest. Even on the rare case that a noble person is suddenly overcome with ressentiment, he will not become infected by it but will discharge it in an immediate and exhaustive reaction. In his parallel sermon on the mount, Zarathustra thus recommends "a small revenge" because it "is more humane than no revenge at all. . . . It is more noble to pronounce oneself wrong than to remain right, especially if one is right. Only one has to be rich enough for that."[61] In general, the noble person has no need of revenge or forgiveness, however, as his carefree manner allows him to forget the bad deeds, the mistakes, and even his enemies, thus remaining unencumbered and free. Nietzsche explains that this "is the sign of strong, full natures in whom there is an excess of the power to form, to mold, to recuperate and to forget. . . . Such a man," he adds, "shakes off with a *single* shrug many vermin that eat deep into others; here alone genuine 'love of one's enemies' is possible—supposing it to be possible at all on earth."[62] In order to give freely, he contends, one must remain unburdened by the malicious acts of others, unfettered by past wrongs, utterly divested of memory.

The value of values is therefore at stake. Ressentiment is more than a purely psychological phenomenon. As the root morality, it decides the relationship between morality and nature and the definition of culture and the human. In Nietzsche's view, ressentiment has been instrumental in the taming and domestication of the human beast of prey. It has become an adopted instinct and an essential instrument of culture that has disgraced and overpowered the noble races.[63] He thus characterizes this adopted instinct as one of oppression, and the bearers of it—these barkers of a revenge disguised as justice (sometimes even in the name of love)—as antagonists to the values of nature and life.

As in Heine's description of two types of characters, the Hellene and the Nazarene, Nietzsche equates the struggle between two value systems—that of good and bad, on the one hand, and that of good and evil, on the other hand—to the symbolic battle between Rome and Judea. He portrays this battle as literally for the ages. At stake are the rights of culture and nature; on both sides, it is a battle for humanity and against monstrosity.

> There has hitherto been no greater event than *this* struggle, *this* question, *this* deadly contradiction. Rome felt the Jew to be something like anti-nature itself, its antipodal monstrosity as it were: in Rome the Jew stood "*convicted* of hatred for the whole human race"; and rightly, provided one has a right to link the salvation and future of the human race with the unconditional dominance of aristocratic values, Roman values.[64]

Albeit in already corrupted terms, Nietzsche recognizes this battle again in the politico-religious wars surrounding the Reformation and later in the French Revolution—in the leveling effects of Martin Luther's idea of the universal priesthood, Rousseau's contract making unequals equal, and the French Revolution's democratic uprising of the common people in fraternity and equality.[65]

Nietzsche's critique of morality is, therefore, a critique of modernity's society of the masses. In contrast to Aristotle, for whom indignation served to protect the aristocratic social order and its differences in class, power, and wealth, Nietzsche describes the effectiveness of ressentiment in demolishing these differences through a construction of sociality based on equality. The movement of ressentiment, which Nietzsche depicts as the "antipodal monstrosity" to nature, represents, for him, "the decline and twilight of mankind." His diagnosis of the times culminates in the statement that man suffers of man.[66] Nietzsche, therefore, ironically vitiates the pervasive belief in "progress" and in the notion that humanity is getting "better" all the time. What is called betterment is, from his perspective, more akin to weariness—that is, becoming "more good-natured, more prudent, more comfortable, more mediocre, more indifferent, more Chinese, more Christian."[67] Humanity, he believes, has lost its Eros. Humans have sacrificed admiration to abate their fear; they misunderstand themselves when they feel they are the pinnacle and the meaning of history despite having sacrificed excellence and vigor for mediocrity. The "settling for" mentality of mediocrity has settled down with a complacent superiority, having replaced all striving for greatness and perfection. Mediocrity suffices for excellence when it stands in stark contrast to the surrounding stench of the languid, sick, dull, and the spent, which he identifies as the "last man."[68]

Although scathing in his indictment of the morality rooted in ressentiment, Nietzsche nevertheless recognizes its constructive role in the development of the human animal. Ressentiment and bad conscience constitute a danger (*Gefahr*) or a double-edgedness: They bear both threat and opportunity.[69] On the one hand, he depicts ressentiment as "the gravest and uncanniest illness, from which humanity has not yet recovered," and, on the other hand, he diagnoses this illness as an illness that is "pregnant with a future."[70] It constitutes "an illness as pregnancy is an illness."[71] This illness has borne fruit for centuries, and Nietzsche's genealogical work acknowledges the necessity of understanding it in order to understand ourselves.

The particular achievement of this historically creative force of ideals, in Nietzsche's eyes, consists in providing human suffering with meaning. As he describes it,

> Apart from the ascetic ideal, man, the human *animal*, had no meaning so far. His existence on earth contained no goal: "Why man at all?" was a question without an answer. . . . *This* is precisely what the ascetic ideal means: that something was *lacking*, that man was surrounded by a fearful *void*—he did not know how to justify, to account for, to affirm himself, he suffered from the problem of his meaning. . . . His problem was *not* suffering itself, but that there was no answer to the crying question, "*why* do I suffer?"[72]

Ascetic ideals bestowed suffering with meaning, making suffering itself bearable because it is no longer meaningless. But the erection of ideals on earth has come at a tremendous cost, according to Nietzsche.[73] Although humans were saved from the void, from nihilism, the interpretive structure of the transvaluation of values inherent in slave morality is a self-destructive one. The historical emergence of the Judeo-Christian God "saved" the will from senselessness, but because it offered meaning only in the will against itself, against life, it harbored a will to nothingness and the potential dissolution of the will Nietzsche recognizes in the modern nihilism of the last man.

The ascetic ideal of the priestly aristocrats in the morality of good and evil is therefore to be deemed a will to power. The aim of this will is itself. It is a will turned against itself, a "hatred of the human, and even more of the animal, and more still of the material, this horror of the senses . . . longing to get away from all appearance, change, becoming death." In willing an ascetic ideal, a transcendence beyond time and behind appearance, this will amounts to "a will to nothingness, an aversion to life, a rebellion against the most fundamental presupposition of life." "But," he quite significantly adds, "it is and remain a will. . . . Man would rather will *nothingness* than *not* will" (Lieber will noch der Mensch das Nichts wollen, als nicht wollen).[74] So although the moral person wills what is not, what is only an ideal, the last man has stopped willing altogether.

The nihilism Nietzsche bears witness to is encapsulated in the lost faith in humanity; humans become weary of themselves. He thus concludes that the health and future of humankind depends on overcoming the self-hate and envy of ressentiment. From the perspective of the last man, however, when one comes "who justifies humanity" and "for whose sake we can hang onto a faith in humanity," he will necessarily be seen as a "synthesis of the inhuman and the superhuman."[75] Nietzsche therefore proclaims the advent of a god-beast and the overcoming of the human in the name of the human.

This synthesis establishes a new ideal, realigning the distinctions of what is human or all-too-human and introducing the *Übermensch* and the

Untermensch. But it does so through the dissolution of all distinctions as they are presently conceived in the wake of morality: between man and beast, between man and god, and between man and human, and man and woman. Such a collapse of distinctions entails the collapse of the social and cultural order.[76] Everything, Nietzsche suggests, depends on the perspective and on who has the power to determine the lines of definitions and form their contours, borders, and oppositions. Nietzsche himself is thus the embracer and agent provocateur of nihilism as well as the torchbearing creator for its overcoming.

With the figure of Zarathustra, Nietzsche invokes the danger of the superman who will overcome the nihilism of the last man, who has emerged from the ascetic ideal. This "redeeming man of great love and contempt," "strong enough" to reverse the inseparability of natural inclinations and bad conscience, would not signal a return to the Greeks and the difference between good and bad.[77] He would bring about a reversal of the slave morality, wedding bad conscience "to all the *unnatural* inclinations, all those aspirations to the beyond, to that which runs counter to sense, instinct, nature, animal, in short all ideals hitherto, which are one and all hostile to life and ideals that slander the world."[78] He would establish an ethic *beyond good and evil.* Zarathustra's doctrine of the "eternal return of the same [ewige Wiederkehr des Gleichen]" marks Nietzsche's hope for a value system beyond good and evil. It is his response to what may come, to what he believes must come: The Übermensch, "this Antichrist and antinihilst; this victor over God and nothingness," he prays and prophesies, "*must come one day.*"[79]

Scheler's Deferral

Max Scheler can be read as a rereading of Nietzsche. He defers to Nietzsche, adopting and deepening his critique of the doubling of ressentiment. Ressentiment, he claims, indicates a repeated reliving of a particular emotional reaction to another person or person's action that sinks deeper and deeper into the center of one's personality, while becoming further and further removed from a person's capacity for expression and action. In contrast to the memory of an event in which one establishes a distance from it and enables a response to it, ressentiment consists in a reliving and a refeeling of what was felt. Its character of impotence makes of it a negative emotion, which, according to Scheler, contains "a movement of hostility."[80] Echoing Nietzsche, Scheler offers a brief phenomenological description of ressentiment in the place of a simple definition:

> Ressentiment is a self-poisoning of the mind which has quite definite causes and consequences. It is a lasting mental attitude, caused by the systematic repression of certain emotions and affects which, as such, are normal components of human nature. Their repression leads to the constant tendency to indulge in certain kinds of value delusions and corresponding value judgments. The emotions and affects primarily concerned are revenge, hatred, malice, envy, the impulse to detract, and spite.[81]

Like Nietzsche, Scheler interprets the impulse for revenge as the primary point of departure for the formation of ressentiment.

Scheler discovers in revenge two essential characteristics. There must be at least a momentary inhibition and restraint of the immediately arising impulse of reaction. The temporary delay of revenge distinguishes it from anger and rage. Instead of immediately and instinctively reacting to the blow with a counterblow, revenge requires a postponement of this reaction to another time and a more appropriate situation. This inherent delay allows for consciousness and the advantage of projective deliberation, but it also opens up the possibility of repression and increasing impotence.[82] Whereas the person who is filled with revenge is motivated to action, the resentful person becomes filled with repressed forces that produce impotence.[83]

Without discharge, affectation enters the psychical dynamic of ressentiment. Whereas the feeling of revenge is linked to a particular object, the deferment of action out of ressentiment increases one's impotence and displaces the object occasioning its feeling. Just as the acquisition of the good that one envies of another annuls the feeling of envy, successful revenge in the form of punishment, for example, nullifies the feeling of revenge. This same nullification occurs, according to Scheler, in the act of true forgiveness. The formation of ressentiment, in contrast, occurs where there is neither moral overcoming of the negativity, as in forgiveness, nor a compensatory action or expression of one's inner disposition, as in cursing or shaking one's fist. Such a person is paralyzed whether out of physical or intellectual weakness or out of fear either of the other person or the consequences of one's actions. The desire of revenge and envy are thus necessary but insufficient conditions for ressentiment. The character of impotence and the inability to let go, overcome, or annul the feeling gnaws its way into the core of a person and shades everything that comes from it like a contagion of psychical poison.[84]

Accordingly, the more the forces of repression become effective, the less the person concerned can specify what he is afraid of or what he is incapable of doing. Scheler thus associates ressentiment with angst as opposed to fear: Fear has an object, whereas angst expresses a deep inhibition of one's life feeling. Inhibiting expression and laming the capacity for action, the forces of repression lead to a type of interiorization that does not lead to self-discovery but to delusion. Inner cognition is repressed, occluding consciousness of the affect. The contagion effect of ressentiment consequently eases and accelerates the process of repression for each successive repression after the first. Although I might be well aware of the person toward whom I have an impulse of revenge as well as of what he did to me, the repression of this impulse increasingly displaces it from its ground, the person, and the deed. This contagion of ressentiment, according to Scheler, spreads from the original ground first to attributes, actions, and expressions and then to other people, relations, things, situations, and even the appearance of values associated with that person or event. Filtered through ressentiment, the impulse for revenge, Scheler writes, "radiates in all directions."[85]

A life compromised by angst and impotence, he claims, engenders inferiority complexes and a mechanism of value compensation or what he calls ressentiment's specific delusion of values. The person filled with ressentiment either suppresses valuable attributes or becomes blind to them. As Nietzsche claims, ressentiment typically leads to the fabrication of values itself.[86] In contrast to Nietzsche's contention that ressentiment is the source of all ideal values, however, Scheler believes the hierarchy of values is a priori "objective and clearly 'evident' as mathematical truths."[87] Scheler thus argues against the theory that the value of good and bad is synonymous with "what is desired or strived for," on the one hand, and "the content of repulsion," on the other hand. Against this position that he associates with Spinoza and the contemporary propagation of moral relativism, he insists that striving is secondary to and founded on a consciousness of the value of something. The delusion of values in ressentiment cannot, therefore, consist in the absence of the experience of positive values as such. Instead, Scheler maintains that the positive values are covered over by the delusional values.

He thus considers ressentiment a means of removing the tension in consciousness between striving for the good and the inability to reach it. If, for example, we futilely seek love and acknowledgment from someone, then we readily begin to find negative attributes in him and discover reasons to "unmotivate" our striving: "He is not worthy of my love—not so honest, courageous, beautiful, or smart as I originally thought." This devaluation of a person or object lessens the pain attached to the object desired when the desire remains unfilled. It is the object or person that is devalued in this context, however, not the value. The values of beauty and courage, for example, remain; they are simply disassociated from that object or person.[88]

This discrepancy between striving and power can lead to the transvaluation of values of which Nietzsche speaks. Since the person of ressentiment cannot identify with or understand his life in terms of the positive value judgments such as independence, freedom, health, beauty, and power because he does not share these attributes and lacks the power to appropriate the objects or bearers of these attributes, he psychically annihilates them, saying implicitly to himself that they are nothing. Usurping their place are their negative correlates. All of the characteristics Nietzsche draws from the master-slave dialectic reappear. The binary of moral values remains but is inverted. Poverty, sickness, impotence, and death are represented as redemptive of human life, instead of wealth, health, power, and life; and those who possess the positive values are consequently no longer to be envied or considered "worthy of revenge." They are instead to be pitied.

Although Scheler's analysis of ressentiment adopts and refines Nietzsche's conception of ressentiment, it diverges radically from Nietzsche with respect to the role of ressentiment in the formation of morality. This difference is foundational. It constitutes a reversal. For morality, according to Scheler, is not founded on ressentiment, as Nietzsche believes; rather "ressentiment helps to subvert this eternal order [of moral values] in man's consciousness."[89] Although Scheler acknowledges Nietzsche's genealogical "discovery" of ressentiment as the source of value judgments, he rejects Nietzsche's moral skepticism and relativism, and, in particular, his specific claim that Christian morality, especially Christian love, is the finest flower of ressentiment. It is this claim he sets out to discredit.[90]

Maintaining Nietzsche's juxtaposition of Greek and Roman ethics and Christian morality, Scheler claims that the Greek/Roman tradition diametrically diverges from the Christian tradition in its interpretation of the direction of the movement of love. The Greeks, according to Scheler, emphasize law and justice over love or—in other words—the rational in morality, which is concerned with measure and equality, over the exceptional singularity of love. Within this framework, the movement of Eros is always from the lower to the higher, from appearance to essence, from nonbeing to being, and from ignorance to knowledge and wisdom. Eros, then, always remains bound to the sensible realm in its association with need, desire, and imperfection. The sage has no real need of love, and, as Plato intimates, "If we were gods, we would not love."[91] Scheler therefore emphasizes how in the Greek tradition all things strive toward the Nous, which moves the world as the beloved moves the lover while the beloved remains unmoved. Plato's ideas and Aristotle's "unmoved mover" are paradigmatic in this regard. Although movement involves change, and change implies imperfection, the highest being is perfectly rational, balanced, and complete—that is, beyond love.

Scheler witnesses the emergence of a radically different paradigm in the Christian tradition. "Christian love," he writes, "is a spiritual intentionality which transcends the natural sphere, defeating and superseding the psychological mechanism of the natural instincts (such as hatred against one's enemies, revenge, and desire for retaliation). It can place a man in a completely new state of life." Whereas the conception of love from antiquity portrays the lover as below the beloved, who represents the model of being, willing, and acting for the lover, Christian love enacts what Scheler calls "a reversal of the movement of love." Love is demonstrated in the movement from the noble to the base, the rich to the poor, the beautiful to the ugly, the good and holy to the bad and cruel, the Messiah to the tax-collectors and sinners—and all this without the fear of contamination that pervades antique culture. From this reversal of the movement of love, Scheler draws a significant consequence concerning the idea of God and the good. Christianity's God is not an eternal, restive goal that moves the world as the beloved does the lover. God is rather essentially love, and, according to Scheler, it is from this essence of love that creating, willing, and acting follow.[92]

Could it really be, Scheler asks, that ressentiment is the moving force of this love? Although he concedes that there is no value that is more easily feigned by latent ressentiment than love, he is equally clear that the root of Christian love is totally free of ressentiment. He consequently clarifies the downward movement of love as a spiritual act, separating it from a mere state of feeling or pathology. He claims that it is a "spontaneous overflow of force" before all teleology, calculation, deliberation, or understanding.[93] Such love, he explains, is unselfconscious and unreflective because of a latent and grounding trust in the power of life itself. The nature of love, according to Scheler, is to be filled, to be overflowing with life-fullness. It is, he proclaims, "a blissful ability to stoop, born from an abundance of force and nobility!"[94] Love thus grows as it is dispensed, and its height increases the further downward it extends. For Scheler, the requirement to love both the good and the bad, the just and the unjust follows from the idea of a God who is love and of a creation out of love. The love of the unjust simply manifests love's true, supernatural character.

He therefore distinguishes this love from a love antithetical to life's forces. Scheler qualifies that, in Christian love, one is not called on to love the sick, poor, ugly, and unjust because they are poor, sick, ugly, and unjust, for this would be a perversion of value. One rather loves them because of the positive values hidden in them. As Scheler repeatedly states, it loves what is behind them and helps bring the good, the beautiful, and the just out of them. The hierarchy of values, for Scheler, therefore remains fully intact. In sum, love does not love because of the negative moments but despite them. The intention of love is always directed at the positive higher values masked by or repressed by the manifest lower qualities. Its assistance in sparking the positive values in others and cultivating in them a resistance to the evils of sickness and poverty is an expression and result of inner firmness and fullness of life. But even beyond its vision of the underlying positive and vital values, love, as a spiritual act, aims at the spiritual value of the person in his or her very personhood, which, Scheler claims, is completely independent of outward appearance, status, or condition.[95]

Scheler thus understands love as a sovereign power. He recognizes in the freedom of the one who loves a similarity to Nietzsche's vision of the noble man, if not the Übermensch. Drawing from the waters of love's spontaneous abundance of power, the one who loves is willing to sacrifice his life for higher ideals. Scheler describes him as happy, light, bold, and as having a knightly indifference toward life's conditions since he is free from natural inclination, egoism, the fear of death, and other signs of a crumbling, sick, and broken life.[96] For both Nietzsche and Scheler, the creative is a sovereign vital force, but whereas Nietzsche sees creativity as arising from the amoral will to power's creative and destructive overcoming of nature that culminates in the Übermensch, Scheler witnesses in the spontaneously overflowing formative powers an expression and symbol of love. He therefore interprets Jesus' command to turn the other cheek as undermining reactive actions altogether and actions measured by base rules and norms.[97] As an expression of love, turning the other cheek defuses a situation by disengaging from any exchange and acting independently from the conditions and common expectations of the situation and times.

The sovereignty of love also appears in its self-referentiality, or what Jankélévitch calls its aseity. Scheler claims that the value of love cannot be found in its works; it cannot be measured in what it achieves or produces or in what way it is useful. It is an "act-value." The value of love is circularly itself: love. For example, the parable about how a poor widow who gave mere pennies gives more than the luxurious gifts of a rich man does not value poverty above wealth; it does not exalt the base. Instead, her gift, on Scheler's interpretation, is worth more before God because she gave it with more love. Her gift symbolizes her love and demonstrates its being in her person. Human blessedness thus consists in loving and giving.[98] Like

Jankélévitch, Scheler claims that the act of love is the summum bonum; the summum bonum does not have a content beyond or independent of the act of love itself. This act is detached from its object and the value of its object and flows out of itself toward the other.[99] In the act of love, the lover loses himself and gains himself eternally, not in the beyond of the kingdom of God but in the immediate return of love to itself.[100] This dialectic of love in Christian morality, Scheler writes, has a profound individualistic character with the redemption and being of the individual soul at its heart.[101]

Scheler distinguishes such love from the weak and degenerate love contained in the morality of his time, especially in the doctrines of socialism and altruism. He focuses Nietzsche's polemic on these. They contain a flight from oneself or, what Sartre later will call, in accordance with a type of ressentiment, "bad faith." They do not commend love of the other for the positive value on which the movement of love finds its ground, nor do they recognize the flashing of the positive value in love itself but instead turn away from the self to the other on account of the mere otherness of the other. What they propagate as love, he insists, is a form of self-hate, and their moral position of love for the little ones, the poor, the weak, and the oppressed is the outward inverted sign of their repressed envy of wealth, strength, and power.[102] Whereas these social and political forms intend to weaken the wealthy and powerful by the coercive means of law and policy, Christian love depends on the positivity of the individual's free act.

Scheler thus maintains that Nietzsche makes the error of conflating modernity with Christianity. The modern political forms of socialism and communism and the social ethical propulsion of abstract humanitarianism and altruism, he claims, have nothing to do with Christianity. Nietzsche's great error in his profound hypothesis on the origin of Christian morality, according to Scheler, consists in his misrecognition and misrepresentation of the essence of Christian morality. For Scheler, Christian morality does not laud poverty but upholds wealth as a positive good, while praising the independent and personal act of renouncing wealth. The goods of wealth, power, and all earthly fulfillments are esteemed but also possibly overcome in love.[103]

Scheler understands forgiveness precisely within this framework. It entails the suspension of both the natural impulse and the ethical demand of justice in the free act of the spirit. Forgiveness, then, does not degrade, much less deny, the impulse for revenge, which he sees as inherent in the social measure of punishment. On the contrary, he claims that whoever does not feel the compulsion of revenge cannot forgive. The value of forgiveness does not consist in the cessation, abatement, or subjugation of the impulse of revenge but rather in the free sacrifice of it.[104] It marks, in other words, the overcoming of the natural in the name of the spiritual and the suspension of the social for the sake of the eminent possibility of love. The impulse of retribution for a moral offense upholds the order of values, both metaphysical and social, and forgiveness freely forfeits the right to retribution in the positivity of love.

Scheler thus acknowledges that Nietzsche is right in associating forgiveness with sacrifice, but this sacrifice is not out of impotence or need; it rather symbolizes precisely the sovereignty of the one offering it. This positivity presupposes the impulse to revenge and the rights of law; it does not avoid them out of fear. Forgiveness is, therefore, not a sign of weakness or timidity, according to Scheler, but an act of radical sovereignty. It is God-like.[105] It does not come from below but from above; it is not biological or psychological but spiritual, not social but individual. The commandment of love, Scheler explains in a way similar to the way Jankélévitch explains it, is directed at the spiritual core of humans—that is, at the individual personality itself, by which the individual participates as a member of the kingdom of God.[106] Scheler extends Nietzsche's horizon of what constitutes the real and life. Following Augustine, he upholds a fundamental ontological order of spiritual community, independent of the political and the social realm, in which humans find the ultimate meaning and value of their existence.

Scheler's attempt to integrate Nietzsche's insights while disassociating Christianity from the brunt of his attacks leads, however, to difficulties in his conception of forgiveness that should be briefly addressed. They pertain to the spiritualization and sovereignty of forgiveness in his understanding. The forgiveness he portrays remains ineffectual, self-centered, and rational.

Since the kingdom of God is of another ontological, spiritual order, it has little to no external effect on the structures of the status quo. As the order in which human individuals find their ultimate meaning and value, the kingdom of love serves merely to relativize the goals sought in human strife. The order of the religious command of love does not, however, call them or their underlying structures into question but rather presupposes and consequently substantiates their existence. Scheler writes that

> the forces and laws which rule the evolution of life and the formation and development of political and social communities, even wars between nations, class struggle, and the passions they entail—all those are taken for granted by Jesus as permanent factors of existence. He does not want to replace them by love or anything else. Such de-

mands as universal peace or the termination of the social power struggle are entirely foreign to his religious and moral sermon. The "peace on earth" for which he asks is a profound state of blissful quietude which is to permeate, as from above, the historical process of struggle and conflict which governs the evolution of life and of human associations. It is a sacred region of peace, love, and forgiveness, existing in the depth of man's soul in the midst of all struggle and preventing him from believing that the goals of the conflict are ultimate and definitive. Jesus does not mean that the struggle should cease and that the instincts which cause it should wither away. Therefore the paradoxical precept that one should love one's enemy is by no means equivalent to the modern shunning of all conflict. Nor is it meant as a praise of those whose instincts are too weak for enmity (Nietzsche speaks of the "tamed modern gregarious animal")! On the contrary: the precept of loving one's enemy presupposes the existence of hostility, it accepts the fact that there are constitutive forces in human nature which sometimes necessarily lead to hostile relations and cannot be historically modified. It only demands that even the true and genuine enemy—he whom I know to be my enemy and whom I am justified in combating with all means at my disposal— should be my "brother in the kingdom of God." In the midst of the struggle, *hatred* should be absent, especially that *ultimate* hatred which is directed against the salvation of his soul.[107]

Presupposing an underlying ontological community, Scheler doubles human interaction, separating and simultaneously stipulating hostility and inner love. His position thus resembles Butler's and even more poignantly, in anticipation, Carl Schmitt's.

In *The Concept of the Political*, Schmitt famously distinguishes between the Greek terms *polémios* and *ekhthrós* and their Latin parallels *hostis* and *inimicus*, and he identifies the political enemy solely with *polémios* or *hostis*. For Schmitt, the line of distinction corresponds to the line between the public or political and the private. I may be hostile toward a public enemy, but this same person may be my friend in private. In other words, "The enemy in the political sense need not be hated personally, and in the private sphere only does it make sense to love one's enemy, that is, one's adversary."[108] Although Scheler's distinction is not between the public and private per se, he demarcates the outward action from the inner attitude of love and divides the physical world from the underlying ontological unity of a community of persons in the kingdom of God. For both Schmitt and Scheler, love and hate (at least a hate that goes soul deep) are incompatible, but love, fraternity, and friendship may coincide with enmity and war.

Scheler, moreover, presupposes the historical necessity of conflict and war. Even Jesus, in his interpretation, acquiesces to something like what Hegel calls the "cunning of reason." In this teleological view, human history is driven by underlying propulsion beyond the intentions of individual or group agents. Conflict and war are seen as necessary for the constructive forces of this dynamic, whether it is called life, nature, providence, or reason. Jesus' religious and moral sermon, according to Scheler, is thus confined to a spiritual sphere within this inherent dynamic. But how is the reign of peace, love, and forgiveness to be thought in the middle of conflict, if forgiveness is, as Scheler claims, the positive act of the free forfeit of the forces that lead to the extension and escalation of violence? The spiritual value of love, which simultaneously accepts and relativizes the lower life values, contradicts the act-value of love.

This contradiction is connected to Scheler's association of love and forgiveness with subjective sovereign power. In Scheler's spiritualization, forgiveness is not, as Jankélévitch contends, a gift given to the other for the other. His understanding of forgiveness incorporates a spiritualized psychology: Forgiveness only really concerns the forgiver. As Scheler asserts, the growth of the value of love is originally and always on the side of the lover, not on the side of the one who is loved.[109] The other primarily serves as an occasion for the growth of the value of love in and for the individual who loves, and the works of love merely symbolize and demonstrate the being of love in the person who loves.[110]

The order of grace, which Jankélévitch connects with the instant that as quickly as it is given to the giver dispossesses itself from him, becomes, for Scheler, a resource and well of power located within the spiritual core of the individual person. Forgiveness can be seen as the power of freedom par excellence. It is a power that renders an individual free from the vulnerability of being affected by others. The individual is thus God-like, according to Scheler's vision, because he is not subject to others but is above them. The downward movement inherent in love is to be taken quite literally. Love flows downward from its height and outward from its life power, stability, and security.[111] In sum, Scheler does not adequately acknowledge the vulnerability of human existence or the sociality of love and forgiveness.

Finally, Scheler's conception of love vacillates between a rationalization of love and what Jankélévitch calls the aseity of love. On the one hand, Scheler claims that one loves what is hidden behind the other. In that case, one only loves what is lovable or worthy of love, whether that be the character of the person beyond the offense or the spiritual core of the other as a member of the kingdom of God. Such a love preserves the a priori hierarchical order of values and is just insofar as it is measured by the value or worthiness of the object that is loved. In this respect, Scheler's conception does not differ as much as he thinks from the Greek love that takes its measure in the beloved. On the other hand, he speaks of a positive value of a love that begins with itself. Such a value-positing act does not require the rational justification of a love that loves only that which is worthy of love. As Scheler observes, this kind of love does not love justly according to external criteria. Instead, the worth of the other is determined in the act of love itself and by love itself.[112] Such a love is not just but is unmeasured and overflowing in abundance. Scheler's reflections on love and forgiveness within the Christian tradition contain both: the conception of overflowing love beyond rationality and justification, and the conditional logic of love as stipulated by the independent positive value of the other individual.

This tension is not particular to Scheler's interpretation, however. As Derrida argues, it is indicative of the whole Jewish-Christian tradition, which abides in the tension between a logic of rationality and conditionality, on the one hand, and the logic of suprarationality and unconditionality, on the other hand. This ambivalence is also present in Jankélévitch. Although he emphasizes the value-positing act of love and suggests that the forgivability of an offense has its cause alone in the initiative of forgiveness itself, he simultaneously maintains that, beyond distinctions and discrimination, forgiveness aims at "the universally human," at the humanity of the individual person, or at the ipseity of the individual human person.[113] The "human" thus seems to constitute for Jankélévitch a value underneath, within, behind, or congruent with each individual that forms the basis of forgiveness. In this sense, the minimal "reason" of forgiveness consists for him in the minimal condition of a common humanity.

Jankélévitch's Protest and Fidelity

Jankélévitch is an heir to the conceptions of ressentiment set forth by Nietzsche and elaborated by Scheler. Like that of Jean Améry, his own understanding is one of indebted difference.[114] Having inherited the tenor and direction of ressentiment from these two German philosophers of existence, Jankélévitch nonetheless submits a reevaluation of ressentiment that highlights both its negativity and its possible contribution to morality. It is particularly this second aspect that requires attention. Like Nietzsche, Jankélévitch interprets ressentiment as inhibiting life and the human dimension of the future.¹¹⁵ He realizes that forgetting is necessary for life, its movement forward, and its vitality. Yet he is reluctant to acquiesce to a morality that strictly follows this course. He thus casts ressentiment as conditioning and impelling memory. Through this connection, ressentiment becomes morally imperative and intimately linked to justice. Moreover, since it is necessary for there to have been an offense that is remembered in order to forgive, Jankélévitch stipulates ressentiment as a prerequisite for forgiveness, while forgiveness remains irreducible to the mere overcoming of ressentiment.

In line with Joseph Butler, Jankélévitch distinguishes between the buildup of ressentiment due to a moral offense and that due to a personal offense. With regard to personal offenses, he is clear that the corrosive rancor of ressentiment should indeed be abandoned. He explains that "when rancor is a simple spite and a wholly negative stubbornness, then forgiveness is a duty of charity."¹¹⁶ Consequently, he concedes that there exists a ressentiment that is psychologically and moral damaging because it is born out of egoism and fosters a shameful desire for vengeance. Such personal ressentiment, he observes, leads to a confusion of one's perceived rights with real rights and one's personal cause with a just cause. This confusion culminates in accusing adversaries of injustice while invoking principles in order to simultaneously veil and sanctify one's own passions.¹¹⁷ Ressentiment does not create values in this scenario, but it is delusional in its attempt to disguise vengeance and spite in the name of justice and rights. Jankélévitch claims that personal ressentiment rarely, if ever, appears uncloaked from the deceptive form of these displacements and false pretenses. When personal offenses are at stake, ressentiment maintains the bitter and poisonous aftertaste that Nietzsche and Scheler polemically decry.¹¹⁸ But as the reaction to moral wrongdoing, ressentiment proves to be not merely an emotion but also a moral stance of protest against a wrong that has occurred.¹¹⁹ So although he acknowledges the ever-lurking danger of feigned principles for resenting an offense, he also recognizes the distinctions between rationalizations and reasons and justifications and justice.

Jankélévitch thus focuses on the moral affront or sin that produces ressentiment. Like Butler, Jankélévitch believes that the natural reactions to crimes against human dignity are horror and anger. Martha Nussbaum recounts a story Elie Wiesel told about a soldier who was part of the liberation of the camp he was in as a child that powerfully underscores this sentiment:

> Walking into the camp and seeing what was there to be seen, this man began to curse, shouting at the top of his voice. As the child Wiesel watched, he went on shouting and cursing for a very long

time. And the child Wiesel thought, watching him, now humanity has come back. Now with that anger, humanity has come back.[120]

Nussbaum comments that the soldier's "anger was an acknowledgement of the importance of the wrong, and therefore of the human values against which it had offended. . . . His outrage expressed the judgment that things not be this way, that one must expect better of human beings."[121] Faced with such atrocities, Jankélévitch insists, the natural movement of the heart is passionate outrage, which resists forgetfulness and promises, like the judges of Nuremberg, to hunt the criminals until the end of the world, for as Elie Wiesel himself comments, "Forgetfulness leads to indifference; [and] indifference to complicity."[122]

What Jankélévitch encounters not long after the war, however, is what he calls "a perversity" of this most natural sentiment in the heart and understanding among his contemporaries.[123] The reaction of horror to crimes is often at best momentary, but without the rigor of fidelity it is missing the earnestness of moral commitment. The feeling of outrage passes and is abandoned for future concerns. The call for justice is often replaced by an optimism for a better tomorrow already signaled by the resumption of normalcy today.

In contrast, Jankélévitch defines ressentiment as the moral feeling accompanying and sustaining the demand for justice. As a just emotion, ressentiment combines outrage with protest against the act and its agents. It protests, too, against those preachers of easy or strategic reconciliation. Especially in "Should We Pardon Them?" Jankélévitch expresses "the insurmountable horror over what happened, horror of the fanatics who perpetrated this thing, of the passive who accepted it, and the indifferent who have already forgotten it."[124] The naturalness of outrage, he suggests, gives way all too naturally to other things, to time and forgetting. His protest issues forth in the interjection of ethics whose "function is not at all to ratify nature but rather to contradict it, to refute it, and to protest against it."[125] This protest directs itself against a compulsion toward futurition and against a "moral amnesty that is nothing but shameful amnesia."[126]

Upon the blow of the Shoah, according to Jankélévitch, followed the blow of a society and a world that pressed onward in reconciliation, demanded and already bestowed forgiveness, and degraded the protests of those who resisted reconciliation with urges to get with the program. Such forgiveness, he laments, becomes a "glorious pretext" to forget.[127] It has nothing to do with morality. It is business, indifference, cowardice. As he writes:

It is not so much love for one's neighbors that inspires the apostles of reconciliation, it is rather practical commodities; this is the perspective of attractive relations. Charity has nothing to do with it. They present as duty simply that which they wish to do and which they do out of egoism, cowardice, and frivolity.[128]

These attempts to circumvent the reality of what happened make Jankélévitch "disgusted with forgiving." They render forgiveness "suspect" because none of these "reasons" contains a moral attitude.[129]

In this context, morality for him is first and foremost a protest against the currencies of time, money, and politics, and at the heart of this morality is the anachronism of ressentiment, which refuses to go with the times.[130] Ressentiment prohibits the second victory of the enemy, the obliteration of the traces of the crimes.[131] As the literal "re-feeling of a feeling," ressentiment can be a renewed and intensively experienced passion for that which is unreconciled, he claims; it upholds the flame of disquiet, the flame of conscience and justice, while maintaining the vow to the disappeared and absent.[132] Ressentiment thus has the character of fidelity because it does not lose sight of virtue, regardless of the opinion of the day or the rise of indifference toward what has already been done. "Fidelity," he writes, "is always, in one form or another, fidelity-despite becoming and the disaffection that this becoming encourages." He, therefore, describes the moral task at hand as primarily "to maintain fidelity, to stay intransigent among caprices, to keep one's faith among renegades, such are the forms under which the constancy of virtue-despite is affirmed."[133]

Against the unreflective prioritization of the future, the individual of ressentiment upholds the moral domain, demanding even, in the words of Jean Améry, the moralization of history.[134] This individual's sense of time is "turned around [*verdreht*]," "mad" or "displaced [*verrückt*]."[135] As Jankélévitch summarizes, for the respect of human dignity ressentiment stands rigorously in opposition to the indulgence that is injurious to values. In the name of a more stringent justice, ressentiment represents the willingness "to prolong the regime of enmity." Its "heart is committed" to the difficult and uncomfortable path of justice.[136]

The Duration of Justice: Values and Singularities

Ressentiment is more than a marginal phenomenon in Jankélévitch's ethics; it is an outgrowth of his conception of justice. He claims that justice indeed does function as a "compensatory mechanism," an "allopathic remedy that neutralizes the contrary with its contrary." Jankélévitch's distributive justice moderates the favors and inflations of history and nature; it is compensating and counterfactual: "It takes the opposite course to the superiorities of the fact."[137] Adopting the emphasis of the Hebrew Bible on the "widow, the orphan, and the stranger," Jankélévitch writes that justice "goes to the aid of the weak, helping the widow and the orphan, defending the humiliated and the offended, assisting the oppressed and the exploited, and arming the unarmed." His conception of justice is thus essentially tied to action, for justice involves the effort to stop the "proliferation of abuses" through rectifying compensation.[138] It seeks to balance the scales and is willing to be militant for equality and equivalence.

The more literal than proverbial widow, orphan, and stranger represent those without an immediate network. They represent those without rights. Justice works toward the establishment of the rights of those who do not have rights, the defense of those rights once established, and the realization of the substantial claim in those rights. Since some have the wealth, the education, and the political and economic power and others have been systemically excluded, the first expression of justice, Jankélévitch claims, is protest and contradiction. He sees the acquiescence in and ratification of the natural as synonymous with the confirmation of violence and the reinforcement of force, even potentially the force of the law.[139] The "antireal" or, more precisely, the counterfactual character of his conception of justice protests against and contradicts the powerful. It refuses to allow the law to justify and bless those who already have everything else. Justice, according to Jankélévitch, is not neutral. It calls to action, and it takes sides.

The balancing act of justice cannot signify a mere inversion of power, however. Jankélévitch is wary of the potential perversion of power that would accompany a victory of the weak. He maintains that the weak instead have to fight on two fronts: against the oppressors and against themselves. With a radical vigilance the oppressed must guard against the consequences of their empowerment and the reification of their righteousness. Jankélévitch claims that continuous mindfulness is necessary to prevent the tortured from becoming the torturer. The struggle must be "to ensure the power of justice and not the justice of power." The goal must be to act so that there are neither firsts nor lasts, neither strong nor weak, rich nor poor—or, in other words, so that the whole world is rich.[140]

Justice, then, requires rigorous engagement or fidelity. Fidelity is an act over time; it belongs, according to Jankélévitch, to the virtues of duration. The direction forward follows the path of facility and desire, but it does not necessarily mark the path of normativity and duty. Jankélévitch sees great merit in Kant's practical philosophy for its disjunction of desire and duty. Both Kant and Jankélévitch break with the optimism of eudaemonism or the eudaemonism of the optimism that the natural human tendency coincides with morality.[141] Morality is not congruent with nature. It is furthermore not advantageous or necessarily useful to be moral or just. Jankélévitch accepts that moral fidelity may be "anachronistic," even "useless," and possibly "absurd." Fidelity to the past bears witness to the "invisible things" and the "innumerable things that have disappeared," and the voice of justice reminds us "that the real is not only made of things that are palpable and obvious."[142] Such fidelity to things unseen can be understood in two ways: as fidelity to values or as fidelity to what he problematically calls "martyrs."[143] For Jankélévitch, it means both.

Jankélévitch's use of the language of *martyrdom* is highly problematic because it implies that the murdered died willingly or on behalf of some greater cause, principle, or belief. Although he normally avoids terms such as *martyr* or even overemphasis on the status of *victim*, the occurrence of these terms reveals his tendency to heroicize the weak and the oppressed. In such cases, he runs the risk, which is latent in ressentiment, of morally ontologizing the weak, oppressed, or victims so that they make up a category intimately associated with the good, the righteous, and the just—a view that has catastrophic ideological ramifications. Although he commends vigilance in the struggle for equality, such that the weak must struggle both against the strong and self-critically against themselves, their power, and their righteousness, he is not always mindful of the necessary self-critique that helps avert a merely one-sided and extreme position. Jankélévitch's use of the term *martyrs* is, finally, unnecessary, because he has already established the uniqueness and irreplaceability—that is, the hapax-character—of each individual. In the place of martyrs, it is the incomparable haecceity or, more significantly for Jankélévitch, the ipseity of each person that should be emphasized, especially when individuals are treated as a mass, a number, or left in the shadows or ash.[144]

Jankélévitch's foregrounding of the widow, the orphan, and the stranger demonstrates his concrete moral commitment to the value of individuality. The unique turn in his thinking, however, revolves around his closer qualification of the widow, the orphan, and the stranger. He claims that it is the absent ones of the past who are first and foremost in need of aid. He writes that "the past will not defend itself all alone! As the past is inactual, it is indeed necessary that we spontaneously take the initiative to go to it."[145] Those lost in the past, those no longer actual, the invisible, inaudible ones compose, in their absence, our social and historical reality but require that the living hold them in memory and seek them out in the pursuit of justice. A child can cry, the needy can beg, and the widow can pester the judge in order to direct attention to themselves, assert themselves, and make themselves somebody to contend with, but there is, as Kierkegaard observes, "no one who inconveniences the living less than one who is dead, and there is no one easier for the living to avoid than one who is dead."[146]

Consequently, the past and the wrongs of the past do not serve Jankélévitch simply as lessons for the future in some instrumental sense. The dignity of the human life, as a value pure and simple, must extend to those who have been, not just to those contingently now present. Jankélévitch thus turns the vector of justice toward the dignity due to the absent ones who may not function merely as building blocks for those to come. In doing so, he upholds the atemporality of the sense of justice and dignity. He contends that, if the murdered are neglected, ignored, and dishonorably condemned to being "an anonymous force of history," then the terms *dignity*, *value*, and *justice* surrender their seriousness when applied to the living and those to come.

With the irrevocable trace of the having-done on the one side of the temporal line and the "inevitable triumph of forgetting" on the other side, the moral person, according to Jankélévitch, is reduced to a defensive stance of protest. He interprets this both "Platonic" and "impotent" protest as a form of "moral sublimity."[147] He describes the protest of fidelity as Platonic because it adheres to the suprahistorical order of values. But values as such, he explains, have no need of our rancor. Being atemporal, no infamy touches them, nor can abuses make us doubt their perpetuity. Chronology remains without any relation to axiology. The good, the true, and the just find themselves intact after the attack.[148] Jankélévitch juxtaposes this atemporaliy of values to the finitude and vulnerability of humans and human action. He sees the innumerable lives lost and exterminated as in need of our rigor.[149] He does not ground this rigor in individual subjectivity, however, but in the atemporality or eternity of values. This loyalty to values imbues the sense of duty that cuts across the grain of capricious human feeling and nature. He therefore concludes that the "loyalty to values, unfailing attachment to justice, and respect for the truth" are not mere "memories" but are "duties."[150]

Jankélévitch conjoins the fidelity to values to the fidelity to human singularity. "Values," he explains, "are wronged only in the measure in which an attack against the I can be an attack against human dignity."[151] Linking the ipseity of the individual to the atemporality of values, Jankélévitch connects existence with eternity. In the singularity of each human life, Jankélévitch sees an eternal truth that has a beginning and that will one day die (an *immortalis moritura*).[152] For him, the fact that each individual is singular and unique, which is what he understands by ipseity or selfhood, is a fact that not only will not but also cannot be repeated.[153] Each ipseity has the character of a hapax, and the singularity of the ipseity of each individual is sealed with irrevocability: The fact of once having been who one is makes it such that one will never not have been. The having-been and the having-done constitute what he calls an eternal event *a parte post*. Although demonstrating a beginning in time, the individual person and the sin both remain thereafter irrevocable in their bare facticity. He thus concludes that the moral problem is situated "outside of time."[154] Moral fidelity to the past in the name of justice is consequently good, not just because it is rigorous and against the natural flow of time; it is resistant to the pressures to forget because the value in the name of which memory is sustained as a duty is itself eternal.

For Jankélévitch, therefore, the moral motivation of ressentiment coincides with indignation. The ressentiment that is a result of a personal offense is nourished by the first-person perspective, which allows for a confusion of rights with the right. But, as Jankélévitch points out, "A crime against humanity is not my personal affair. To forgive is not to renounce one's rights but to betray *the* right." He thus contends that "the person who harbors rancor against the criminals of such a crime literally *has the right*: the right and, what's more, the duty."[155] The protest expressed by ressentiment is, in his interpretation, not a psychological state that needs to be overcome. It is and is not my own, for it runs counter to inclination and is compelled by the voice of conscience, the voice of the other, who commands remembrance.

Ressentiment consequently should be felt not only as an initial reaction to the horrors of humanity; it commands the duration of moral abhorrence. It requires the conjunction of duty because, as a mere feeling or re-feeling, it is apt to fade, succumbing to the psychological and social pressures induced by futurition. So although personal ressentiment can be expressed as holding a grudge, Jankélévitch asks whether in cases concerning crimes against human dignity it truly can be considered "holding a grudge."[156] He represents ressentiment in such cases as moral indignation relentlessly protesting against the fact that wrong has occurred and calling for accountability. Concerning crimes against human dignity, which are always perpetrated against concrete, historical persons, there should be no difference, according to Jankélévitch, between me and the others or between the present and the past. For it concerns "me" as a human being in "my" very being as a human and in the singularity of my existence.

As a duty, ressentiment not only sets passion alight and sustains the fires of fidelity; it also precipitates action. Drawing on Jankélévitch's own efforts to balance the scales of justice before and during the war, in the

Resistance, and after the war, in publications and lectures, Françoise Schwab concludes that the courage required to protest and resist is itself a result of the force of moral indignation.[157] Jankélévitch describes moral indignation as a "more" not inherent in conceptual frameworks of justice and rights. Directly contradicting Nietzsche and Scheler, he calls it "the sole motor" behind the shift from the Platonic contemplation of social, political, and economic disparities to effectivity.[158] Spurred by "legitimate ressentiments and the most sacred memories," such action is primarily resistance and defense. It resists the forces that seek to destroy or forget the value of humanity, and it defends human rights, especially the rights of those who can no longer defend themselves: it works both in their name and, to the extent possible, with them—the oppressed, disadvantaged, overlooked, and forgotten.[159]

Jankélévitch concedes, however, that ressentiment has finite limits in retaining the past. "The man of time, a finite creature," he observes, is not made "for an undying rancor; for such an eternity is really the hell of the damned; for such an inconceivable eternity would actually be unbearable despair for us." Nonetheless, he asserts, the duty to remember "proves at least that the past does not allow itself to be abolished without protesting."[160] In his Nobel lecture, Elie Wiesel offers a similar sentiment: "Because I remember, I despair. Because I remember, I have the duty to reject despair. . . . There may be times when we are powerless to prevent injustice, but there must never be a time when we fail to protest."[161] Jankélévitch says that, even when ressentiment does not lead to action, it constitutes the bare minimum of a moral response. He pleads that where nothing can be done, one can remember and protest.

Unquestionably, for many survivors of moral atrocities, memory is traumatic such that it cannot be gotten rid of. As Jankélévitch himself confesses, "Sleep does not return. We think about it during the day; we dream about it at night."[162] There is also, however, a will to remember that links the present to the past and the past to the future. Both Jankélévitch and Wiesel are aware that such memory is the source of suffering.[163] But in solidarity with those who suffered wounds that imperceptibly still bleed, Jankélévitch willingly and dutifully extends the pain that was spared him.[164] Memory and the willed and unwilled re-feeling of things absent and abused carry the promise that prohibits the second deathblow to the victims, namely that of forgetfulness. Nietzsche calls this a "memory of the will." It represents for him what one does not want to rid oneself of.[165] And since, according to Jankélévitch, the having-been and the having-done leave an invisible but irrevocable trace into eternity, the memory of the will constitutes the acknowledgment of that which one cannot be rid of—neither the incorruptibility of the irrevocable nor the duty.¹⁶⁶

Beyond my fidelity, beyond my intentionality, beyond my power to retain or resuscitate in memory, Jankélévitch recognizes, however, the claim of values and the claim of others on me. With respect to the latter, he approaches an aspect of Levinas's notion of an ethical anteriority of responsibility. The past, Levinas claims, concerns me not only beyond the limits of what could be my fault or my deed but also beyond what has been within my freedom and my power, and beyond what is now within my freedom and the power of memory. The responsibility for the other person, he states, comes "in the heteronomy of an order" that is "outside of all reminiscence, re-tention, re-presentation, or reference to a remembered present. . . . Such is my nonintentional participation in the history of humanity, in the past of others, who 'regard me.'"¹⁶⁷ The others past and gone regard me, place their demand on me, and press upon me their plea before deliberation, before I choose to go to them, and before my engagement.

Jankélévitch concedes that the forward march of futurition limits the possibilities of human subjectivity. He portrays fidelity as a "mad protest" against overwhelming tides. But his protest and fidelity also indicate a modal category between those of possibility and impossibility and necessity and contingency, the modal category of exigency. "Exigency," Giorgio Agamben explains, "does not forget, nor does it try to exorcise contingency. On the contrary, it says: even though this life has been completely forgotten, there is an exigency that it remain unforgettable."¹⁶⁸ Agamben himself understands the category of exigency as a kind of fidelity. As he explains:

> The alternatives at this juncture are therefore not to forget or remember, to be unaware or become conscious, but rather, the determining factor is the capacity to remain faithful to that which having perpetually been forgotten, must remain unforgettable. It demands [*esige*] to remain with us and be possible for us in some manner.¹⁶⁹

At the limits of the feeling of ressentiment and the will to remember, exigency demands a response and historical responsibility to the unique lives that have been and for the inexorable crimes that have been done. Against the indifferent consumption of time, there remains the duty to protest against its passing and the duty of fidelity despite its having passed. It is perhaps what remains from a past in ashes.

Missing Humanity

Jankélévitch repeatedly reminds us of the simple fact that we must first remember in order to forgive. Rancor and ressentiment against moral injury are thus prerequisites to forgiveness.[170] This precondition further distinguishes forgiveness from mere forgetfulness. It makes forgiveness a matter of earnestness. Jankélévitch writes that ressentiment implies "seriousness and profundity," and this is why it is a "prelude to cordial forgiveness."[171] Even for the personal offenses that do not invoke a violation of values, there must be a lapse of time so that the offense is registered as an offense and so that, in the case of sins, the claim of justice can assert itself. Otherwise, Jankélévitch unequivocally states, there is nothing to forgive:

> The immediate and instantaneous forgetting of the offense intervening "in the innocence of each new minute" constitutes a *mens momentanea*—a mind without memory—and reduces futurition to an *aeternum nunc* and a perpetual present. So, there is no longer even forgiveness, for forgiveness requires that a minimal delay open up between the offense and the absolution, that we have had the time . . . to hold a grudge against the sinner; it requires that infinitesimal rancor at least have the time to form; for *ressentiment*, a sentiment on top of a sentiment, does not exist without temporalization. Without this temporalization, without this interval that perpetuates the injury, where would forgiveness find something to forgive?[172]

Forgiveness must go through memory; it must address the offender as offender and cannot bypass the claim of justice. Through the establishment of this precondition for forgiveness, Jankélévitch underscores the intertwinement of memory and therefore fidelity with justice and ressentiment.

The ambiguity of ressentiment, however, consists in its incapacity to function as a reliable moral indicator. Although resentment is an emotion that serves, in the terms of Martha Nussbaum, as "a judgment of value" and is thus aligned with morality and justice, it is simultaneously an unreliable moral indicator because the personal feelings of ressentiment are not equivalent to moral indignation.[173] The equivocalness of ressentiment extends deeper than that of the distinction between personal offenses and moral misdeeds and deeper than Jankélévitch acknowledges. Ressentiment revolves around the question of humanity and, simultaneously and ineluctably, the question concerning the existence of moral monsters.

With regard to the correlation of ressentiment and humanity, I will trace whether ressentiment is directed at an act or an agent and, further, whether ressentiment nails the offender to the past misdeed such that his or her being is equated with this act. A reductionist identification and ontological fixation of the offender precludes the openness to the future so critical to Jankélévitch's morality and with it the possibility for revision, correction, and compensation. I will then explicate the manner in which ressentiment seems to presuppose humanity. It appears to presume that the offender belongs to the moral community in order to raise a claim against him or her. In the light of the horrendous crimes of the twentieth century Jankélévitch resents the missing humanity of the perpetrators, but perhaps due to ressentiment, he, too, misses the humanity he misses in others.

Despite their differences, Butler, Nietzsche, and Scheler all acknowledge the tendency of ressentiment to equate the sinner with the sin. It thereby locks the present and future into an encompassing past. Jankélévitch is equally aware of the capacity of ressentiment and rancor to imprison a person in his or her deed:

> The refusal to forgive immobilizes the guilty person in his misdeed, identifies the agent with the act, and reduces the being of this agent to the having-done. But the misunderstood person protests against this simplification: one lie does not yet make a liar. The person infinitely exceeds the sin in which our rancor wants to imprison him.[174]

The counterpart to an unyielding ressentiment is thus a forgiveness that draws on the Augustinian dictum "to hate the sin but love the sinner"—that is, a forgiveness that separates the sin from the sinner, the act from the agent.[175] Forgiveness, on this view, is commendable because it does not reduce being to an isolated act or personhood to a single decision. Already the contextualization of the misdeed in the catalogue of a person's other actions, those past and those possible in the future, allows for a more differentiated perception of the agent. But, as Trudy Govier argues, it is also the very being of the person or her personhood that demands a broader vision. "No person," she claims, "should be labeled as irretrievably and irredeemably bad."[176]

A reductionist ressentiment thus engenders debate about whether there are so-called moral monsters and, concomitantly, whether there is something or someone who cannot be forgiven. Is there something inextinguishable about the humanity of humans that nothing they do can remove? Or is there some act that would potentially exclude a human from the human community and therefore the moral community? Archbishop Desmond Tutu concretely confronts the tension between inhumane acts and the being of the person who committed them. In an article in the *Cape Times*, from 1997, he writes:

> There are people in South Africa who have committed the most unbelievable atrocities and I am willing for their deeds to be labeled with the harshest of epithets: monstrous, diabolical, even devilish. However, monstrous deeds do not turn the perpetrators into monsters. A human person does not ultimately lose his or her humanity, which is characterised by the divine image in which every individual is created.... The premise underlying this ... is that it is possible for people to change, insofar as perpetrators can come to realise the evil of their actions and even be able to plead for the forgiveness of those they have wronged.[177]

His argument is grounded in the notion of humans as *imago dei*. This theological supposition simply undergirds the fact that the humanity of a person cannot be gained or lost.

Kant similarly dismisses the notion of moral monsters, or what he calls "devilish" beings, on account of the inseparability of the idea of the moral law from personality, "understood as the idea of humanity considered intellectually."[178] Besides asserting a predisposition to animality and to humanity, he describes the predisposition to personality as "the capacity for respect for the moral law as *in itself a sufficient incentive of the will*." These predispositions, for Kant, are original, not contingent.[179] They cannot be extirpated because they necessarily constitute the being of the human being. This inextirpable presence of the moral law in reason dictates that no one, not "even the most wicked," repudiates the moral law in the manner of a rebel (renouncing obedience to it). "The law, rather, forces itself upon him irresistibly by virtue of his moral predisposition."[180] "Even the most wicked scoundrel," Kant concludes, can adopt "the standpoint of a member of the world of understanding," and even he actually wishes to be disposed to the good once he understands himself as a member of the intelligible world, as a *homo noumenon* and not merely a *homo phainomenon*.[181]

This inextirpable presence of the moral law in the very being of humans forever leaves open the possibility of betterment. Kant argues, in a manner that Tutu follows, that no matter how much evil someone has done in the past, the duty still remains to better himself, and, what is more, the duty to do so "must be within his power."[182] Tutu's argument from the *imago dei* similarly focuses on this possibility of the good on the basis of the being of the person. It is not mere change that Kant and Tutu refer to; it is rather the specific axiological, not chronological, change of moral reformation or moral revolution. Tutu's understanding of change entails that of conversion, remorse, and repentance. It consists in acknowledging the wrongs done, approaching the victims as well as moving forward otherwise. Govier addresses this type of possibility in terms of the unforgivable itself. She states:

> To regard people as absolutely unforgivable on the grounds that what they have done is atrocious is to extend attitudes, unwarrantedly, from acts to person, to argue from acts to character in such a way as to mark an irrecoverable stain on the agents. The line of reasoning is mistaken: logically, metaphysically, and psychologically, the act is not the agent. To claim that because he has committed terrible deeds a moral agent is reducible to those deeds and is thus absolutely unforgivable is to ignore the human capacity for remorse, choice, and moral transformation.[183]

Following Tutu, Govier depicts forgiveness as future-oriented and therefore frames the question of the unforgivable as the refusal of possibility or the refusal of a future that can stand in stark contradistinction to the past. According to this logic, to not forgive would be to give up on that person and perhaps people in general.

Legitimate ressentiment, however, does not conflate the singular act with being and does not denigrate the possibility of moral change. Although maintaining the irrevocability of all offenses, Jankélévitch explicitly recognizes the human potential to redress the past, to wipe away the consequences of sin, and to begin again to pursue and to do the good. Legitimate or reality-based ressentiment, therefore, has a different objective, namely that the singular act not be forgotten or repressed but be acknowledged and confessed.[184] It is the passionate holding upright of the claim of justice through which all forgiveness must go. In this sense, it can lead to action, not only on the part of the offended and those whose moral outrage is not readily quelled but also on the part of the offender himself. For Jankélévitch, ressentiment involves the turn to the past that awaits and provokes the return of offenders to their having-done and to their victims. Ressentiment can thus be characterized as an active instigation of a return that may precipitate repentance.[185] Although this act entails a precarious endeavor that can potentially engender ressentiment in turn, the steadfast claim of justice demands an acknowledgment of truth. Améry captures this possibility that Jankélévitch advocates when he writes, "My ressentiments are there so that the offense receives moral reality for the offender, so that he is pulled into the truth of his misdeed."[186] The past misdeed must be confronted, not effaced. The legitimacy of ressentiment maintains its focus on the act, the having-done, without ontological extrapolations about the core of the person.[187]

Is this openness for future reformation unlimited or itself even imprescriptible? And does the distinction between act and agent persist even if it is the core of the person that is aimed at in a crime? Jankélévitch addresses the first question with Job's own question, "How long yet?" At the time of writing his essay on forgiveness, Jankélévitch had waited over twenty years for a renunciation, a plea for forgiveness, a symbolic gesture of repentance from those who are responsible, from those who represent that in the name of which the atrocities were committed, and from the intellectuals who either justified or acquiesced in this wave of violence.[188] "We have waited for a word for a long time, a single word of understanding and sympathy. We have wished for it, this fraternal word!"[189] His nonhateful ressentiment, like that of Améry and others, waxes in the waiting, especially when forgiveness is already presented as a fait accompli.[190]

Contrary to Kant, Jankélévitch does seem to think, however, that those who have denied the humanness of humans and sought to extinguish it have denied themselves their own humanity. Jankélévitch explicitly depicts such crimes as "metaphysical," and he is not hesitant to call its perpetrators "monsters." He subsequently distinguishes them from "simple fanatics," "blind doctrinaires," and "abominable dogmaticians."[191] It is the monstrous that presses the question of the unforgivable. Those deprived of humanity no longer could be forgiven, for monsters, like animals, cannot be forgiven—that is, unless one forgives the human for making himself a monster. The vicious circularity of this reasoning ultimately only highlights Tutu's distinction between monstrous deeds and monsters. Monstrous, even metaphysical, crimes are committed by humans capable of and responsible for a diabolical wickedness that Kant deems impossible. The conditions of remorse, repentance, or gestures of contrition involve, then, the acknowledgment of one's own humanity and with it one's participation in the moral community of humanity. Jankélévitch seems to have something like this in mind when he stipulates that "before there can even be a question of forgiveness, it is first necessary that the guilty person, instead of protesting, recognize himself as guilty without pleas or mitigating circumstances."[192]

Jankélévitch claims, contrary to Govier and in line with Kant, however, that in regard to crimes against humanity, it is not the innate human possibility of moral transformation that may provide the enabling condition for forgiveness; it is rather actual moral transformation, or at least a sign of its beginnings. In gestures of repentance, however symbolic or simple, the offenders demonstrate that they belong to the human community and are subject to the moral order. In short, through a word of fraternity, an act of repentance, or a demonstrated commitment to betterment, those who perpetrated heinous deeds demonstrate their humanity and open therewith the possibility of forgiveness.

Unfortunately, though understandably, Jankélévitch's essay "Should We Pardon Them?" is full of overgeneralizations and totalizations. It may even be that his ressentiment causes him to dismiss the humanity he seeks to uphold. Derrida criticizes, for example, his indiscriminate and vehement rhetorical use of "us" and "them."[193] And in invoking "them," Jankélévitch moves fluidly between *Nazis*, *Germans*, *torturers*, and *sadists*, among other designations. The "we" and "us" seems to refer to the Jewish victims. But how broadly or narrowly should these circles be drawn? With regard to the question of forgiveness, Jankélévitch maintains that only the specific victims can forgive, but he simultaneously or alternatively appears to include and exclude himself as the one or one of the ones who should be asked and hasn't been asked for forgiveness. In short, Jankélévitch's provocative tone and polemic blur the distinctions that are otherwise so crucial to his analysis.

Even more problematic, though indicative of these troubling generalizations and distortions, Jankélévitch repeatedly equates the abstract "them" with beasts and animals.[194] "Forgiveness," he writes in both his polemical essay and in his philosophical treatise, "is not made for swine and their sows."[195] In another passage, he asks how it came to be that such "good-natured people" became like "rabid dogs." With the entire weight of his rhetorical vehemence, he closes this comparison with a bitter concession: "One will reproach us for comparing these evildoers with dogs? I confess it indeed: the comparison is insulting to the dogs. Dogs would not have discovered the incinerators or conceived of applying phenol shots into the hearts of small children." His words of condemnation are to be taken seriously. He is no doubt right in assuming that wickedness does not apply to animals, that only humans are capable of wickedness. This is the crisis of morality. But it is disconcerting that Jankélévitch would deny the humanity of the offenders, identifying them with the "less than human" since the Nazi ideology propagated the Übermensch and justified the oppression and finally the extermination of the Jews, Gypsies, homosexuals, and others by identifying them with the Untermensch. Nietzsche himself was aware of how ressentiment-laden the Aryan ideology of the blond beast was, and Jankélévitch, as if by contagion, perpetuates the division of the human and the less than human.[196] Whereas the Nazis missed humanity on both sides—above and below—Jankélévitch condemns the one to the other, the self-proclaimed Übermensch to the less than human: the swine, the sows, the dogs, the monsters.

Beyond mere rhetorical provocation, Jankélévitch's language undermines one of the key elements of ressentiment, namely that it arises because of the discrepancy between an expectation or a demand and an action of an agent subject to that demand. Its claim is contingent on viewing the other as belonging to the moral community. As Peter Strawson points out, ressentiment and other reactive attitudes entail continuing to perceive the offender as a member of the moral community, now only as one who has offended its demands.[197] In other words, it is possible to feel ressentiment only against someone on whom one can place and continues to place a moral demand upon. Animals and monsters are necessarily excluded. The claim of justice held steadfast and upright against the tides of time as well as against socioeconomic, political, and psychological pressures is exactly that, a claim—a claim of contingency that the other could have done otherwise; a claim compelling responsibility for a wrong done; a claim on the other that demands better of him, that waits and hopes for signs acknowledging that claim and the wrong. The legitimate ressentiment that Jankélévitch accentuates thus presupposes the humanity of the other, which, in his language of beasts and monsters, he implicitly denies.

Jankélévitch's moral philosophy commands this presupposition precisely in its characterization of human freedom as being radical to the extent of wickedness. Although Kant may be right in suggesting that there are no moral monsters, he does not conceive evil radically enough. Acts of wickedness and cruelty—acts nearly unimaginable and unspeakable—are acts of human freedom. The Roman playwright Terence wrote that "I am human, nothing human is alien to me." Jankélévitch qualifies this phrase to read "nothing is human that is not moral."[198] He surely does not believe that humans are essentially moral in the common sense of "morally good." For that he takes freedom all too seriously, so seriously that he offers powerful exposés on the capacity of human freedom for wickedness. Such a capacity can be neither dispelled nor expelled to another realm of being. It is not a matter of higher or lower, above or below; it is a matter of better (but always only better, never good) and worse (to the point of the unspeakable); or, more precisely, it is a matter of the humanity of humans juxtaposed to the inhumanity of humans. This is the stuff of undying hope and utter despair. It is the reason of indignation and the need for fidelity and protest. It also constitutes the dilemma of forgiveness.

5

The Inexcusable and the Unforgivable

What can be excused need not be forgiven. The excuse excuses the excusable because the excuse, according to Vladimir Jankélévitch, is of the order of reason and understanding. What can be excused has grounds for excuse. Conversely, what is inexcusable exceeds the parameters of understanding and surpasses the contextualization of the misdeed. As Jankélévitch claims, sometimes a misdeed is performed as a cry for help, a cry to be understood, or even as a cry to be loved. He therefore encourages us to try to understand as much as we can understand, but he is also insistent that there are some acts by some persons that cannot be understood. For Jankélévitch, the acts that exceed the reasons that would render them understandable are acts of wickedness. The fact that humans are capable of the radical evil Jankélévitch calls wickedness is due to the radical character of human freedom. But the human freedom for evil implies an equally radical human capacity for the good. We are thus at the limits of human action. Forgiveness forgives the inexcusable, Jankélévitch claims; but is there an unforgivable that is beyond the category of the inexcusable? In other words, is there an act that is so heinous that it exceeds the human capacity to forgive, whether in principle or in practice? Jankélévitch maintains that there is nothing that cannot be forgiven, but this claim does not diminish his belief that there is also the unforgivable.

Freedom and Wickedness

For Jankélévitch, the idea of forgiveness oscillates between two equal philosophical beliefs: "I believe in the immensity of forgiveness, in its supernaturality . . . and on the other hand, I believe in wickedness [*mechanité*]."[1] Both of these beliefs revolve around his understanding of what is human. Crimes against humanity, he claims, aim at the essence of what is human, at the ipseity of the person. In "Should We Pardon Them?," for example, he writes that the Jews were persecuted not because of religious or political ideological differences but plain and simply because they were "them." The persecutors, he claims, aimed precisely at the "beingness of the being, that is, at the human of every human being." It was "the very being of humanity, *esse*," that the genocide attempted to annihilate.[2] Jankélévitch also understands forgiveness as an act directed at the humanity of the human and the ipseity of the person. Forgiveness and wickedness, love and evil, according to Jankélévitch, have as their object the essence of the other, his or her personhood, his or her humanity. This antithetical correspondence of forgiveness and wickedness constitutes on both sides the limits of human freedom, and it is within this irresolvable tension that Jankélévitch presses the question of the unforgivable.

Jankélévitch's conception of evil stands in stark contradistinction to the two predominant theories of evil in Western thought, namely that evil is rooted in ignorance and that evil is a privation of being. The view that evil has its roots in ignorance is first and foremost associated with Plato. He represents this view throughout several of his dialogues, particularly the *Meno*, *Gorgias*, and *Protagoras*. In the *Meno*, Socrates tells Meno that no one wills evil.[3] Plato does not appear, however, to advocate the strong interpretation that no one commits misdeeds deliberately or consciously. The thief steals intentionally, and the murderer kills with purpose. What he claims is, first, that the thief, for example, steals not with theft as his goal. It is not the act—in this case, stealing—that he wills; it is rather the desired good—in this case, riches—that he wills. In the *Gorgias*, Socrates explains that "we do not will simply to kill a man or to exile him or to despoil him of his goods, but we will to do that which conduces to our good, and if the act is not conducive to our good we do not will it; for we will, as you say, that which is our good, but that which is neither good nor evil, or simply evil, we do not will." According to Plato, we do not ever will evil for evil's sake. Humans are always and always believe themselves to be pursuing a good. The agent of an action, therefore, does not understand himself to be doing evil or, more important, to be evil. His self-understanding may even be that he is a good person.[4] But the person who wills a good such as wealth, health, justice, or wisdom, may err in understanding either what the good is or in what is actually good for him.[5] Of course, he consciously pursues what he does. That is not the question. Socrates' point is that he subjectively errs in what is objectively good or errs in his means of pursuing this good. He does what appears to him to be good, but he is mistaken: The appearance deludes him. No human, Plato concludes, "voluntarily pursues evil, or that which he thinks to be evil," for "to prefer evil to good is not in human nature." What he sees as common to human nature, however, is ignorance, which consists in having "a false opinion and being deceived about important matters." It is ignorance, not malice, that constitutes, for Plato and the Greeks following him, the root and stem of evil.[6]

The notion of evil as privation also demonstrates a certain indebtedness to Plato. The argument that evil is a privation of good has a long history in Christian theology. Augustine was an early advocate of this conception, which portrays evil as a derived or secondary principle. Augustine establishes this perspective in contrast to the dualistic teachings of Manichaeism and Zoroastrianism. After converting from Manichaeism to Christianity, Augustine became a staunch defender of Christianity's monotheism against the teachings of Manichaeism that there are two fundamental principles or two gods, one good and one evil. Although the dualistic doctrines were able to give meaning to suffering and reflected the human experience of a mixture of happiness and suffering, vice and virtue, Augustine held steadfast to the idea, which became standard among the Scholastics, that being is interchangeable with the good (*ens et bonum convertuntur*).[7] Like Plato, Augustine draws an analogy between evil and sickness, using the metaphor of the body to illustrate the ill of the soul. He explains, that just as sickness is understood as the absence of the normal condition of health, evil is the absence of good. "What are called vices in the soul," Augustine writes, "are nothing but privations of a natural good. And when they are cured, they are not transferred elsewhere: when they cease to exist in the healthy soul, they cannot exist anywhere else."[8] This last point is decisive for his line of argumentation: Evil has no ontological reality; it is not a substance, and it has no essence or actuality.

Aquinas deepens this insight into the nature of evil as privation in both his *Summa contra gentiles* (bk. 3, chaps. 7–13) and *Summa theologiae* (1.48, 49). "Privation," he elucidates, "is not an essence; it is rather, a negation in substance. Therefore, evil is not an essence in things."[9] And in another passage he explicates that "something is called evil due to the fact that it causes injury. But this is only because it injures the good, for to injure evil is a good thing, since the corruption of evil is good. . . . So evil must be in the good."¹⁰ What Aquinas means is that evil requires a subject, a being, and it is the lack in that being of what should be and normally is a part of it that is evil. This conception relies on the theological idea of the inherent goodness of God's creation. In Genesis it is written that God created the world and called it good. Therefore, the being of the world cannot be evil. As Aquinas states, "Every being, as being, is good. For all being, as being, has actuality and is in some way perfect."¹¹ Finite, creaturely existence, however, is not perfect like God is perfect. Whereas God is incorruptible, humans, like all finite goods, are corruptible. They share in God's perfection but demonstrate various degrees of perfection. This idea is what Leibniz, in his *Theodicy*, gives the name *metaphysical evil*: the privation of reality inherent in finite, created things.¹²

Evil, then, "exists" as the negation of the positivity of being in finite existence. The Anglican theologian John Milbank criticizes Jankélévitch's insistence on the resistance of the past having-done precisely on the basis of the juxtaposition of the creator who is perfect Being, eternal or infinite, on the one hand, and the creatures of finitude, consisting of the commingling of being and nonbeing, perfection and corruption, on the other hand. He claims that, "since evil is only of the finite, not of the infinite, which as infinite and enduring is without rupture or impairment of power, it can indeed absolutely fall away, because finitude in its own right is nothing whatsoever and only receives being as participation in the infinite. Hence time, which was first the time of gift, becomes, after the intrusion of evil, the time of mercy."¹³ Milbank invokes Augustine's account of the inseparability of time and memory to justify this vision, and his interpretation of an Augustinian theory of time as memory shows a clear connection between forgiveness and evil as privation. He explains that "evil can only pass away, be forgiven and forgotten, if not only the past can be revised, but also what is deficient in the past can be revised out of existence. This means that what really and fully occurs and has the capacity to recur in memory is the good and positive."¹⁴ In this manner, Milbank interprets Augustine as an optimistic Nietzschean because eternally "only the positive returns." One can see at this point how the Platonic heritage's understanding of evil as ignorance and this theological vision of evil as privation are connected. What *is* is alone the good and the truth (*ens et verum convertuntur*). The negative is rooted in deficient knowledge in what is good, insufficient or delusional self-knowledge, and a privation in being.

In Milbank's interpretation of Augustine, time is conjoined with being. It is not morally neutral; it is rather always remembered time, which reconstitutes the past solely in its ontological positivity. Milbank thus concludes that a victim who harbors hatred against his or her perpetrator mistakes hate for love:

> The victim comes to remember and revise his past hatred more objectively as a correct refusal of the negative and of the impairment of his own power; but at the same time through re-narration he is able to situate and qualify this hatred in relation to a renewed understanding of the deluded motives of his violator. . . . Eventually, at the heart of his hatred, he re-discovers the love for his own and others' good, which essentially motivated it, and sees indeed that this love is the entire, real, actual content of hatred, since what was really hated was the negative impairment of love and the good. What was hated was nothing, and in consequence, hatred actually falls away from the positively remembered reconstituted past which is the real past.[15]

Milbank makes abundantly clear that this is "necessarily a theological vision." He explains that "time as remembered in its ontological positivity is only real because it participates in the divine, infinite eternal memory. Otherwise it would be destined to pass away, like the original merely past past, into pure oblivion, thereby rendering the good and actual ontologically as nugatory as the privative and deficient."[16] Forgiveness simply negates the negation that is evil to uncover the underlying ontological and metaphysical priority of the good. As Aquinas states, "The corruption of evil is good," or, formulated dialectically, as Hegel does, the negation of the negation that negates the good is itself good.

Following the tradition from Augustine and Aquinas, Milbank is concerned with the consequences of ontologizing evil. If evil is considered an ontological reality, a substance or an essence, it would potentially introduce a duality in which evil is equal to God or the good and is as strong as God or the good. In contrast, the theological vision begins and ends with the one God, in the good creation of the world and humans, and in the unnecessary though inevitable victory of good over evil. Milbank is skeptical of the modern talk of radical evil and of crimes so horrendous that they remain incomprehensible, inexpressible, and ultimately unforgivable, and he accuses thinkers like Jankélévitch of reifying and ultimately deifying evil. He explains:

> Talk of radical evil, an absolutely corrupted will, a motiveless crime that can never be atoned, and so forth, falsely *glamorizes* this (perhaps) most terrible of events, by rendering it outside all comprehension whatsoever, and absolutizes it, granting it a demonic state equivalent to divinity, and finally perpetuates its terror, since what is

unredeemed remains in force. The argument which runs "This evil was so terrible that we belittle its horror if we describe it as negative" effectively means that this evil was really so impressive that we had better accord it a status in being equivalent to the good.[17]

It remains a question, however, what the alternative is outside of a theological vision. Even theologically, it is questionable whether Milbank's representation takes sufficient consideration of human responsibility, on the one hand, and human suffering, on the other hand. If the past runs into oblivion without the infinite memory of God, does the good that is not safeguarded by the creation and redemption of God become less sure of its victory and more dependent on a human freedom capable of both radical evil and love?

The idea of radical evil itself is inextricably connected with Immanuel Kant, who caused quite a stir among his Enlightenment contemporaries by speaking of what was considered a vestige of mythology and religion. In a time of unshakable faith in human freedom and progress, Kant's anthropological focus on evil at the heart of human will broke a taboo. He claims that all humans have a propensity to evil that is interwoven into their nature. This radical innate evil in the entire species is nonetheless to be understood as having been brought upon us by ourselves.[18] Man himself, Kant unequivocally states, is the "author" of evil.[19]

In order to explain the fact that humans are responsible for their nature, Kant develops an Augustinian line of thinking. Although Augustine maintains that evil (*malum*) is to be understood as a *privatio boni*, he introduces something foreign to Greek philosophy: the will. He interprets evil as a perversion of the will.[20] In his *Confessions*, Augustine consciously parallels the story of the Fall to sin in the Garden of Eden, telling how in his youth he stole some pears. He concludes that it was not so much the pears that he desired but the sublimity of God's freedom. He wanted what the snake in Genesis promises (Gen. 3:5): to be like God.[21] Human pride (*superbia*), the forgetting of one's own creatureliness in the desire to ground oneself in oneself, is thus, according to Augustine, the root of all evil: the estrangement from God and the estrangement from one's true self. In his own secular reinterpretation of the Fall, Kant, too, claims that evil is a matter of the will. Just as there is nothing "in the world, or indeed anything at all outside it, that can be held to be good without limitation, excepting only a *good will*," so there is no evil in the world except for an evil will.[22] The only evil possible, according to Kant, is moral evil, which is dependent on the self-determination of the will. But in contrast to Augustine, Kant claims that it is our unwillingness to be godlike in our creative capacity to be the moral-legislators that is at the root of this evil.[23] Both agree that the free and originary choice comes down to a preference for self-love over the love of God, but for Kant, this choice amounts to the subordination of ourselves as universal lawgivers to ourselves as sensuous and rational beings.

Augustine and Kant agree that everything is made good. Our bodies (animality) and our rationality (humanity), according to Kant, have predispositions to good, but instead of the moral law conditioning sensuous nature, which is essentially good, and putting it in the service of the good, its "proper function," self-love conditions the moral law, obeying it conditionally when it serves one's own subjective interests. Kant makes clear that it is not our sensuous nature that causes evil, however. It is rather our free will (*Willkür*). We choose to obey our sensuous nature, taking its laws and incentives as the ground for our action as opposed to obeying the moral law within us. All three of the sources Kant identifies as sources of moral evil— human frailty or weakness, impurity or the mixtures of our motivations (from duty or in accordance with duty), and wickedness (*vitiositas, pravitas, corruptio*)—are found "in what, according to laws of freedom, touches the ultimate ground of the adoption or the observance of our maxims, and not in what touches sensibility."[24] Therefore, Kant concludes, "Nothing is morally evil (*i.e.*, capable of being imputed) but that which is our own *act*."[25] The individual who freely adopts a heteronomous maxim, John Silber explains, "freely renounces his power as a free being to act independently of desires. He freely chooses to act just the way he would act if he had no such freedom at all."[26] In other words, we are utterly responsible for all of our individual decisions, actions as well as for the characters we have become.

Why humans make this originary choice is incomprehensible. The origin of evil, according to Kant, is "inscrutable" to us because freedom is inscrutable.[27] As Richard Bernstein concludes, "Not only is this inscrutable; it *must* be inscrutable, because this is what it means to be a free and responsible being."[28] But this fundamental choice determining the self for good or evil is a choice between laws: the law of self-love or the moral law, heteronomy or autonomy; it is a choice between maxims or principles that will provide the basis of all further decisions. For Kant, this fundamental decision for evil (*peccatum orinarium*) is, therefore, qualitatively different from the subsequent ones (*peccatum derivatum*). Over the abyss of inexplicability Kant constructs principles that render all actions understandable. The decisions subsequent to the first one between good and evil have their reasons and follow certain laws and principles, even if neither an observer nor the agent has absolute access to or transparency of the inner moral motivations.

At the same time, the fact that Kant locates the origin of this original decision "in reason" not "in time" has two important interconnected consequences. As Kant stipulates, every evil act "must be regarded as though the individual had fallen into it directly from a state of innocence." That means that we perpetually remake the original decision for moral evil, or, as Kant writes, that, independent of cultivated character and outside causes, our action "must always be judged as an *original* use of will."[29] We are not held responsible for what some originary ancestor decided or for what we once decided and are now determined by. For Kant, we are responsible for every decision and every act because in each of them we repeat the originary decision for self-love over the moral law. This responsibility simultaneously means that we have the power to resist the propensity to evil at every turn.[30] Although Kant interprets the propensity to evil as a universal characteristic of humans, he also insists that the moral law in us is inextirpable and thus never ceases demanding of us to be better. Because it demands this of us as a duty, it is something that is always within our power.[31]

By radical evil Kant does not, consequently, indicate a certain extremity of evil. Rather the "radical" he speaks of indicates quite literally the root, the stem, "the ultimate subjective ground" of the concrete acts of evil. Kant thus refuses to call the "depravity [*Bösartigkeit*] of human nature wickedness [*Bosheit*]." For wickedness, he claims, would be the adoption of "evil as evil" into human maxims. Such an incentive for action would constitute what he calls the "diabolical." He instead prefers to designate the human propensity to evil as a "perversity of the heart."[32] Contrary to Augustine, however, who recognizes in the prideful rebellion against God's law the heart of evil, Kant rejects even the notion that humans "repudiate the moral law in the manner of a rebel (renouncing obedience to it)." Without implying that humans as a species are diabolical, without even contesting the fact that humans must acknowledge the authority of the moral law, it seems, on account of Kant's conception of free will or radical free choice (*Willkür*), that it must be possible that an individual can deliberately defy the moral law.[33] As Bernstein explains, "Of course, our respect for the law *may be* a sufficient incentive to act morally. But our *Willkür* may choose to defy the moral law. If recognition of the moral law can serve as an incentive to act morally, there can always be a counter-incentive. We can choose to be perverse, we can choose to be devilish, we can choose to defy the moral law."[34] There is thus a certain type of evil that is more radical than Kant's conception of radical evil suggests.

Jankélévitch follows this line from Augustine to Kant in determining the will as the source of moral good and evil, and, like Kant, he focuses on the intention of the will for judging morality. But confronted with the atrocities of the twentieth century, he considers evil precisely on the basis of the human capacity for wickedness. He believes that humans are not only free not to do good but are also free to do evil. Freedom, he qualifies however, is not the source of evil; rather, malevolent freedom is "the only conceivable evil or evil itself," he claims, "for there is no other evil than the willing of evil."[35] In Kant's terms, Jankélévitch bears witness to the original freedom of choice as a decision that needs to be made again and again, but, for him, this decision is not only between self-love and respect for the moral law. It also entails the opening for the possibility of wickedness.

What Kant calls the inscrutability of freedom, Jankélévitch, inspired by Schelling's late philosophy, expresses in terms of quoddity, the "thatness," or the free act, which cannot be completely reconstructed rationally or established in a system. Jankélévitch's philosophy is a practical philosophy in which the concept cannot completely catch up to or subsume the free act that precedes and exceeds it. It is the quoddity of freedom that marks the quoddity of evil. It is a minimal knowledge without content or substance, which Jankélévitch expresses by the phrase "I-know-not-what." One can understand *that* without knowing *what*, understand that there is freedom without being able to objectify it for consciousness. Although Jankélévitch should not be interpreted as claiming that we can have no knowledge of evil, he insists that our efforts at total comprehension will ultimately fail. The free will that intends wickedness is, according to Jankélévitch, beyond our comprehension: "We can no longer understand; there is no longer anything to understand. For the chasms of pure wickedness are incomprehensible."[36] Jean-Luc Nancy explains that "wickedness is the infinite tenacity that tears apart the mere promise of the good . . . without signification or consistency."[37] He therefore concludes that the mystery of freedom is that of "a spontaneity of wickedness" and that "in the final analysis nothing else is incomprehensible about freedom except the possibility of wickedness."[38] As Jankélévitch writes, "There is nothing indeed to understand in the *mystery of gratuitous wickedness*."[39]

In a religious language paralleling revelation, he distinguishes between a "mystery" and a "secret." A secret has something hidden, something behind it in the night of the phenomenon that perhaps appeals or fascinates; a secret has something that can be discovered. A mystery, however, is transparent; it is in the fact itself of existence or in the fact of occurrence; there is nothing in it to be discovered, for in the bright of day, it reveals itself in its nakedness.[40] Mystery consists, then, in the facticity or, to utilize Jankélévitch's preferred term, in the quoddity. Wickedness is a quoddity that cannot be explained or gotten behind. Wicked freedom defies the "becauses," "despites," and "even thoughs" because freedom is irreducible. It "always begins with itself." Jankélévitch consequently describes freedom as a *causa sui* because "the effect is explained by itself, founds itself, and itself is its own cause." He even speaks of the "aseity of freedom" in which "there is nothing indeed to understand in the mystery of gratuitous wickedness except that the wicked person is wicked." "Here," he explains "the circular 'because' would . . . express the scandal of a freedom that is absolutely unjust and absolutely malevolent and incredibly wicked, of a freedom that is free to the point of sacrilege, of a freedom that is the only radical evil here below."[41] The hurricane of malevolence destroys being and the future in its annihilating movement toward nothingness.[42]

Evil is accordingly experienced as a transcendence or an excess that overwhelms the categories of understanding. In his essay "Transcendence and Evil," Emmanuel Levinas describes how the experience of evil surpasses the parameters Kant establishes for experience itself.

> In its malignancy as evil, evil is an excess. . . . Evil is not only the nonintegratable; it is also the nonintegratability of the nonintegratable. It is as though to synthesis, even the purely formal synthesis of the Kantian "I think," capable of uniting the data however heterogeneous they may be, there would be opposed in the form of evil, the nonsynthesizable, still more heterogeneous than all heterogeneity subject to being grasped by the formal, which exposes heterogeneity in its very malignancy. . . . In the appearing of evil, in its original phenomenality, in its *quality*, is announced a *modality*, a manner: not finding a place, the refusal of all accommodation with—a counternature, a monstrosity, what is disturbing and foreign of itself. *And in this sense transcendence!*[43]

For Jankélévitch, as for Levinas, this excess resists the temptation of theodicy, that is, the effort, whether in its religious or secular form, to integrate evil into a coherent economy of reason and morality. The why or the what of wickedness will not adequately explain it or explain it away. It has no place. Instead, its "essence" is that of transcendence, or, in Jankélévitch's terms, it has no quiddity but only a quoddity.[44]

Jean Nabert touches on another aspect of the excess-character of evil in his *Essai sur le mal*.[45] In the chapter titled "The Unjustifiable" (*L'Injustifiable*), he describes the unjustifiable as an excess that goes beyond the inadmissibility of offenses against norms or postulated laws. As Paul Ricoeur explains, evil extends beyond the contradiction between the admissible and the inadmissible, prescriptions and prohibitions.[46] Similarly, Jankélévitch says that the excess of evil exceeds the possibility of compensation or proportionality between the crime and the punishment, which is essential to any form of retributive justice.[47] In short, evil defies in surpassing penal logic. As Nabert comments, evil implies a tearing of the inner being, a suffering without any conceivable alleviation.[48] The excess of evil that Nabert calls "the unjustifiable" corresponds to what Jankélévitch calls "the inexcusable." The evil of inexcusable crimes demonstrates itself, for example, when those who have suffered from the acts of evil cannot even name what they have suffered.[49] And in the wake of the Shoah, Jankélévitch addresses the question of forgiveness for that which is "unspeakable," for a crime "without name" that is "beyond all measure" and "inexplicable."[50]

For Jankélévitch, crimes against humanity, which surpass all measure and defy the limitations of language, constitute the inexcusable par excellence. What he means by crimes that aim at the humanity of the person or the being of the human in his or her human being can be demonstrated in a comparison with Levinas and Arendt. All three of these thinkers highlight the singularity of each individual, a singularity, as Bernstein states, "that resists reduction to a common essence."[51] The deeds that qualify as wicked, according to Jankélévitch, are those that attempt to annihilate what Levinas calls the face of the other, the other whose otherness I cannot "neutralize." In *Totality and Infinity*, Levinas states that "to kill is not to dominate but to annihilate, it is to renounce comprehension absolutely. . . . The Other is the sole being I can wish to kill."[52] Nazi crimes thus could be said to aim at the "face of the other." Such violence, Jankélévitch suggests, seeks the annihilation of the inner self.[53]

Arendt's deep reflections on evil and crimes against humanity exhibit several parallels to Jankélévitch's concerns as well. After completing *The Origins of Totalitarianism*, Arendt sent a copy to her mentor Karl Jaspers. In a letter from 1951, she responds to his immediate response to her work, writing:

> Evil has proved to be more radical than expected. In objective terms modern crimes are not provided for in the Ten Commandments. Or: the Western tradition is suffering from the preconception that the most evil things human beings can do arise from the vice of selfishness. Yet we know that the greatest evils or radical evil has nothing to do anymore with such humanly understandable, sinful motives. What radical evil really is I don't know, but it seems to me it somehow has to do with the following phenomenon: making human beings as human beings superfluous (not using them as means to an end, which leaves their essence as humans untouched and impinges only on their human dignity; rather, making them superfluous as human beings). This happens as soon as all unpredictability—which,

in human beings, is the equivalent of spontaneity—is eliminated. And all this in turn arises from—or better, goes along with—the delusion of the omnipotence (not simply the lust for power) of an individual man. If an individual man qua man were omnipotent, then there is in fact no reason why men in the plural should exist at all—just as in monotheism it is only God's omnipotence that makes him ONE. So, in this same way, the omnipotence of an individual man would make men superfluous.[54]

Although Arendt concedes that "none of this is thought through at all," she touches on several of the aspects that are important to her own and to Jankélévitch's understanding of evil.

First, she addresses the inability to speak about evil and the impossibility of developing a concept of evil, particularly because "the horror itself in its naked monstrosity" transcends moral categories and explodes all juridical standards. Such evil cannot be understood as a simple violation of norms, symbolized by the tablets of the Ten Commandments. It is not even reducible to a preference for self or particularity over universality, as Kant's doctrine of radical evil maintains. Instead, like Jankélévitch, Arendt sees that the mystery of evil lays itself bare in its facticity, constituting that with which "we shall not be able to become reconciled." In its excess, she states, it presents itself as that which has no place, as a past event that cannot be mastered by anybody, that resists the healing power of time, and that should make us doubtful of any sudden return to "normality," however much it is complacently assumed.[55]

Second, the radical evil of which Arendt speaks goes beyond "humanly understandable, sinful motives," "making human beings as human beings superfluous." Jankélévitch claims that the Jews were sought to be exterminated, not because of this or that, not because they embodied a religious or political opposition or because they were followers of an antithetical ideology. He admonishes that they were reproached for *being*. To the Nazis, Jankélévitch observes, a Jew "does not have the right to be; his sin is to exist.... The crime of being a Jew is inexpiable."[56] Jankélévitch concludes that it was their being itself—what he calls the hominity (*hominité*), or the very humanness of humanity, the essence of the human—which was aimed at. The violence "grounded" in the intent to annihilate the very existence of the other does not have political, religious, or ideological reasons, but rather this violence exhibits the groundless abyss of evil. "The extermination of the Jews," he writes, "is the product of a pure wickedness, of *ontological* wickedness, of the most diabolical and gratuitous wickedness that history has ever known. This crime is not motivated, even by 'villainous' motives."⁵⁷ Jankélévitch thus maintains that the crimes were not motivated by anything a person or people had done or even stood for. Instead, they were reproached simply for existing. He calls this act ontological wickedness precisely because it aims at the being of the other and seeks to annihilate the ipseity of the individual and the *who* of the person beyond this or that.⁵⁸ It denies not only the dignity of being human but also the very right to be.⁵⁹

By connecting this superfluity, on the one side, with omnipotence, on the other, Arendt invokes something similar to the sovereign man of the Marquis de Sade.⁶⁰ In his essay on Sade, Maurice Blanchot asks, "Is it not eminently clear that those who perish in these gigantic butcheries no longer possess the slightest reality, and if they disappear with such ludicrous ease it is because they have previously been annihilated by a total, absolute act of destruction, because they are present and die only to bear witness to this kind of original cataclysm, this destruction applicable not only to themselves but to everyone else as well?" The perpetration of genocide depends on a combination of the intention of annihilation and a magnitude of quantification in which the being of the individual counts for nothing. Blanchot explains that "to consider human beings from the viewpoint of quantity kills them more completely than does the physical act of violence which annihilates them. . . . The victim does not of itself exist, he is not a distinct individual but a mere sign, which is indefinitely replaceable. . . . All are interchangeable, each is only a unit, a cipher in an infinite progression."⁶¹ The annihilation of the face of the other thus amounts to his defacing such that the other is not an individual human being but an infinitely quantifiable cipher. The annihilation of the human being, according to this logic, is simultaneously an annihilation of humanity.⁶²

Third, for Arendt, the making superfluous of human beings as human beings is predicated on the elimination of "unpredictability," or "spontaneity." In her reconstruction of the stages toward total domination, she explains that "the first essential step on the road to total domination is to kill the juridical person in man." He is placed outside the law, outside the belongingness to community, and exposed to "the calamity of the rightless" in which he remains perfectly "superfluous" because nobody can be found to "claim" him.⁶³ After killing the juridical person, according to Arendt, "the next decisive step in the preparation of living corpses is the murder of the moral person in man. This is done in the main by making martyrdom, for the first time in history, impossible."⁶⁴ Martyrdom, she explains, becomes impossible when one no longer has a legitimate moral choice:

> When a man is faced with the alternative of betraying and thus murdering his friends or of sending his wife and children, for whom he is in every sense responsible, to their death; and when even suicide would mean the immediate murder of his own family—how is he to decide? The alternative is no longer between good and evil, but between murder and murder.[65]

As Sade knew well, the worst form of evil makes the victims into accomplices to the crime.[66] To this point, Susan Neiman observes that "the Nazi regime's capacity to implicate victims . . . suggests that not the *Musselmann* but the *Sonderkommando* is its most terrible product." She concludes that "condemning the victim to participate in the mechanics of murder was one way of obliterating morality itself."[67]

Beyond rendering moral choice impossible and enveloping the individual in the insidious snares of evil, Arendt recognizes a destruction of freedom, a freedom that she interprets in terms of natality, the ability to begin something new, something unpredictable. Like Jankélévitch, she suggests that this capacity to begin something new belongs essentially to the very being of human beings. Augustine formulates this idea in *The City of God* as follows: *Inititium ut esset homo creatur est*, "that this beginning might be, man was created."[68] Arendt closes her book *The Origins of Totalitarianism* with this beginning: "This beginning is guaranteed by each new birth; it is indeed every man."[69] She claims that after "the murder of the moral person and annihilation of the juridical person," this spontaneity or natality is extinguished:

> The camps are meant not only to exterminate people and degrade human beings, but also to serve the ghastly experiment of eliminating, under scientifically controlled conditions, spontaneity itself as an expression of human behavior and transforming the human personality into a mere thing, into something that even animals are not.[70]

The evil of totalitarian regimes, according to Arendt, transforms humans into less than humans, into mere things, because it extirpates moral freedom and sterilizes natality. This sterilization of natality is a principal reason why Arendt believes that such crimes against humanity are unforgivable. The excess of evil surpasses the human capacity to adequately respond.[71]

Fourth, Arendt witnesses in the crimes of the twentieth century the loss of plurality. Linking universality and singularity, equality and distinction, in a manner similar to that of Jankélévitch, she claims that plurality "is the condition of human action because we are all the same, that is human, in such a way that nobody is ever the same as anyone else who ever lived, lives, or will live."[72] Action, for her, is dependent on natality and plurality, the possibility of introducing something new into the world shared by others, who view and judge it from different perspectives. Because it is the basis for communicative action and language, "this plurality," she writes, "is specifically the condition—not only the *conditio sine qua non*, but the *conditio per quam*—of all political life."[73] The Nazi regime eliminated this plurality by encompassing every individual singularity into a totality, by eradicating the freedom of the individual, and by subsuming each ipseity into the interchangeable neutrality of the species. She explains that "total domination, which strives to organize the infinite plurality and differentiation of human beings as if all of humanity were just one individual, is possible only if each and every person can be reduced to a never-changing identity of reactions, so that each of these bundles of reaction can be exchanged at random for any other."[74] Such regimes not only misrecognize "that men, not Man, live on the earth and inhabit the world," they "eradicate the concept of the human being" by eradicating freedom and singularity.[75]

Arendt, Jankélévitch, and Levinas all take the Shoah as their point of departure for their analyses of evil, and their respective theories can be interpreted as responses to the evil of the twentieth century.[76] Several significant differences, however, between Arendt and Jankélévitch should be highlighted. Although Arendt and Jankélévitch primarily handle the question of evil and the question of crimes against humanity with regard to the extermination of the Jews, Arendt is particularly clear that even her report on the Eichmann trial is not limited in scope. In a letter written in 1960 to Jaspers, she emphasizes this point: "The crucial point is that although the crime at issue was committed primarily against the Jews, it is in no way limited to the Jews or the Jewish Question."[77] Jankélévitch is not as clear. In fact, his claim that the persecutors aimed precisely at the ipseity of being or the humanness of the humans and that it was the being of humans itself that the genocide attempted to annihilate is difficult to reconcile with what he recognizes as its inherently "racist" character.[78] He tends to universalize the Jewish people and in their exceptionalism make of anti-Semitism a grave mortification of the human in general. Although Jankélévitch undoubtedly believes that Jews embody or at least reveal something essential of humanity, the power of his claim has a broader validity.[79] It revolves around the fact that the Nazis' "work of hatred" did not intend this or that quality or attribute of a particular human or group—whether communist, freemason, or ideological adversary—but aimed at the extinguishment of the elementary and vital right to exist and to be respected simply for the fact of one's humanness.

Due to the monstrosity of these crimes, Jankélévitch suggests that they have something "sacred" and "supernatural" about them.[80] With his equally pronounced penchant for provocation, Jankélévitch would likely agree with the statement from Theodor Adorno and Max Horkheimer that "only exaggeration is true."[81] As is the case with his ascription of moral monsters, Jankélévitch's language underscores the unmotivated, gratuitous character of wickedness, the infinitude of the malevolence aimed at the infinitude of the face of the other, and the magnitude of the crimes against humanity. His language, however, portends a certain mythologization of the crimes and the criminals, tending to demonize the perpetrators, even treading the line of an ontological dualism between good and evil that undermines his overarching claim.

Arendt, in contrast, was more than wary of "the impulse to mythologize the horrible" or to demonize the agents even before writing her work on totalitarianism. This reluctance to mythologize constitutes a motivating factor for developing the notion of the *banality of evil*. In doing so, she ultimately follows Jaspers's advice on regarding the atrocities of the Nazi regime "in their total banality [*in ihrer ganzen Banalität*], in their prosaic triviality, because that's what truly characterizes them."[82] During the trial of Eichmann, Arendt observes that both the prosecution and the defense proceeded under the assumption that Eichmann's responsibility depended on his intentions. Both philosophy and jurisprudence have their foundation in this correlation of intent and responsibility. Kant is the principal witness. Accordingly, the prosecution tried to demonstrate Eichmann's high position in the Third Reich, his anti-Semitism, and his at least latent malevolence, while the defense attempted to portray him as having relatively good intentions.[83] Arendt decisively departs from Kant, to whom she is otherwise largely indebted, on this point, stating that responsibility and guilt do not depend on malice and forethought. Eichmann, in her view, was not evil-minded or ill-willed. He was rather small-minded, with petty, private, bourgeois goals like performing his job well and pleasing his superiors. He was, she claims, simply thoughtless: "He *merely* . . . never realized what he was doing."[84] Evil, she concludes, may be "extreme," but it is not "radical." It has no depth. In a letter to Gershom Scholem, she compares it to a "fungus," which though only on the surface, "can overgrow and lay waste the whole world."[85]

As Bernstein points out, the phenomenon Arendt identifies as the banality of evil presupposes her understanding of radical evil because even the act of making human beings superfluous does not yet answer questions regarding the intentions and motivations of the individuals responsible for it.[86] But Arendt does change her mind on the issue of the motivation behind these crimes. Radical evil, she had claimed, could not be deduced from humanly comprehensible motives, whereas in the banality of evil she describes how monstrous deeds were not motivated by evil intentions.[87] Arendt shifts her analysis of evil from the incomprehensible to the comprehensible. What she offers is consequently nothing less than a theodicy. Neiman explains that "to call evil banal is to offer not a definition of it but a theodicy. For it implies that the sources of evil are not mysterious or profound but fully within our grasp."[88] Evil, Arendt suggests, may be overcome only if we recognize how it subtly overwhelms us, that is, if we acknowledge the appalling fact that "the most unprecedented crimes can be committed by the most ordinary people."[89] Arendt's portrait of Eichmann reveals him to be *human, all too human*.[90] He is thoughtless, unable especially "to think from the standpoint of someone else" or appropriately gauge the consequences of his actions.[91] He is evil, not because of his deeply seated malice but because he was thoughtlessly engrossed in his own petty world. According to Arendt, his harmless intentions do not mitigate his responsibility, but he did give her occasion to rethink the concept of responsibility itself.[92]

Jankélévitch, on the contrary, follows the line from Augustine to Kant, which associates accountability with intention and evil with the will. Like the church fathers and Kant, he insists that the will is the sole source of evil. His belief in wickedness is not a belief in a principle of wickedness but rather a belief in the capacity of human free will to freely and incomprehensibly will evil. In the language of the Cappadocian, Gregory of Nyssa, Jankélévitch sees man as "a demiurge of evil."[93] This creator of evil in the world is not some other being or a mythologization of the human. It is rather the human who is a demiurge of evil. The difference Jankélévitch establishes in contradistinction to this church tradition is that the human is not simply ignorant of the highest good (*ignorantia*) and too weak to pursue it, even if he or she does recognize it (*difficultas*). The will does not will the nothingness of that which, in the cosmological hierarchy of values, is not real or less real as the argument of *privatio boni* suggests. Contrary to Augustine, moreover, Jankélévitch rejects theodicy's imputation of human responsibility for the correlation of moral evil and natural evil, vice and suffering. Evil, he contends, remains inexplicable. And even though Kant recognizes the inscrutability of freedom, it is, for him, a freedom that is always aligned with practical reason (*Wille*), which is the moral law. Freedom, Kant states, is the *ratio essendi* of the moral law, and the moral law is the *ratio cognoscendi* of freedom.[94] Jankélévitch severs this tie between freedom and reason, however, and claims that humans can defy and have defied the moral law, making themselves diabolical or demiurges of evil.

The evil quality of intention, he admits along with Kant, is impossible to locate in the action committed. Jankélévitch thus shares with Kant the dilemma regarding the detectability of intentionality in experience: We do not have an experience of the intention itself but only of the act. He nevertheless maintains that the evil intention comes to pass in the misdeed that can be experienced.[95] Levinas describes something similar when, commenting on the excess of evil, he writes that evil is experienced as an "intention," as "aiming at me."[96] Jankélévitch takes this notion a step further, claiming that it is not merely that I experience evil as an intentionality but also that I can glimpse or intuit, but not know, the intentionality of the other. Although the banality of evil and radical evil may coincide in accounting for the various forms of evil represented in the complexities of the Nazi reign, Jankélévitch is adamant that, though there undoubtedly was much thoughtlessness, there also was much deliberation and much malevolence.

In its excess and intentionality, wickedness shows itself precisely in its incomprehensibility. Jankélévitch observes that evil confronts us as an irreconcilable facticity. History cannot absorb the event into its patterns of narration. Explanations, whether historical, cultural, political, economic, or genealogical remain heterogeneous, or, at best, ex post facto. The reasons come after the happening of the event in reconstructions and categories of thought. As Jean Améry writes, "What happened, happened. But *that* it happened is not so easy to accept."[97] In the words of Jankélévitch, the "fact that"—the quoddity of its occurrence—remains a mystery. It is a stumbling stone that reveals the limits of reason. Evil, the wickedness of human freedom, is evil in its very arbitrariness and irrationality. It is not merely the freely chosen inversion of reason and the passions, as Augustine and Kant suggest. It is diabolical because the will is free to will the annihilation of what is and the face that is beyond being. Jankélévitch insists that we will never be finished in our efforts to fathom this mystery of arbitrary malevolence; its horror grows the more we examine it.[98]

Levinas, too, recognizes the "horror of evil." He writes that "evil strikes me in my horror of evil. . . . The excess of evil by which it is a surplus in the world is also our impossibility of accepting it." This final characteristic of evil amounts to a "hatred of evil," on the one hand, and a "waiting on the good," on the other hand. Evil, Levinas suggests, opens up one's being and invites a response to that which neither can be synthesized into experience or categories of meaning nor can be accepted.

In his reading of Philippe Nemo's book *Job et l'excès du mal*, Levinas writes that "in the evil that pursues me, the evil suffered by the other man afflicts me. . . . It touches me, as though from the first the other was calling to me, putting into question my resting on myself and my *conatus essendi*, as though before lamenting over my evil here below, I had to answer for the other." In *Otherwise Than Being*, Levinas expresses this idea in terms of "substitution" and "hostage": The persecuted one for whom I am responsible to the point of being a hostage for him.[99] It is precisely in the condition of being hostage that Levinas witnesses the possibility of pity, compassion, and pardon.[100] The other's claim on me calls into question my spontaneity and will to be because it precedes them. According to Levinas, this claim of the other allows me to transcend my being precisely when suffering seems to isolate me most in my being. This self-transcendence in the hostage situation constitutes "a breakthrough of the Good in the 'intention' of which I am in my woe so exclusively aimed at."[101]

Levinas's reflections on evil constitute both a critique of Heidegger's ontology and Arendt's idea of spontaneity. He criticizes Heidegger for subsuming humans in the "law of being," which he associates with the *conatus essendi*. Human beings, he emphasizes, are indeed beings, but ethics entails the breach of being. Levinas shares with Jankélévitch the view that, although human beings are beings, we are not exclusively beings.[102] Moreover, Levinas does not understand the human subject in terms of spontaneity but in terms of ethics. Ethical subjectivity arises in and through the claim of the other upon me. This primordial and privileged heteronomy antecedent to Kantian autonomy "does not clash with freedom," however, "but *invests* it."[103] Whereas Arendt maintains that the camps extinguished human spontaneity and the ability to respond and to initiate, Levinas upholds a responsibility that is not contingent on the originary power of the "I can." The horror of evil cannot be simply accepted; it must be responded to because of my responsibility for the other. It must be responded to out of the ability to respond that emerges in the responsibility for the other. My freedom to respond to evil arises as a response to the claim of the other upon me. I must answer for the other, Levinas suggests; no one else can in my place.

Against the temptation of theodicy, Levinas explains that "the breakthrough of the Good . . . is not a simple inversion of Evil" in the economy of symmetrical relations. The discovery of the good in the horror of evil means that the good, for Levinas, cannot be conceived as a "repayment for evil," an "equivalent return," or a "reciprocal appeal of terms that negate one another." Instead, he describes it as an "elevation," as that which "commands and prescribes" but "does not please."[104] The breakthrough of the good thus entails a nonindifference to the double expression of the other:

his or her weakness and suffering and his or her urgent requirement of me.[105] As Bernstein comments, "The excess of evil solicits a transcendence that shines forth in the face of the other."[106]

This other to whom and for whom I am responsible could be, according to Levinas, either the persecutor or the persecuted. When Levinas writes that "the horror of the evil that aims at me becomes horror over the evil in the other man," he leaves open whether the evil in the other means the one suffering evil or the one freely committing evil.[107] It is one or the other, for Levinas, but it could be either one because my nonsubstitutable responsibility extends to a responsibility for the freedom of others.[108] Even when the other commits a crime, he claims, I am responsible.[109] With the metaphor *maternity*, he signifies an asymmetrical responsibility to the point of substitution that "bears even the responsibility for the persecution by the persecutor."[110] I may be infinitely responsible, therefore, for the evil in the other who is a persecutor, and I may be infinitely responsible for the one who is persecuted. My responsibility to the one does not, however, relieve me of all obligation to the other. This tension in Levinas's thinking coincides with the tension between ethics and politics or ethics and justice, that is, between the infinite claim of the other and the claims of the other(s) of the other.[111]

For Jankélévitch, this tension is between love or forgiveness and justice. Evil elicits a response, but how we respond presents us with a moral dilemma. The response of justice, however, does not invoke the good beyond being of which Levinas speaks. Instead, it represents the counterbalance within the opposition of good and evil, a compensating dialectical negation of the negation of the crime. Evil, both Levinas and Jankélévitch claim, is not merely a negation. It signifies excess.[112] For Jankélévitch, the asymmetrical response to evil that implies no recompense and is indifferent to remuneration and reciprocity is that of love, and the love that loves one's own persecutor is forgiveness. As a response to the claim of the other upon me, forgiveness thus could be interpreted as an act of taking responsibility for the responsibility of the other. For Jankélévitch sees in love not a return of good for evil but a radical good aiming at the infinity of the other ipseity that transcends evil. His criticism of Kant focuses on this point: Just as Kant does not conceive of wickedness, that is, evil outside of the moral law and irreducible to a place within morality, he is also unable to conceive of the radical good that is the love of forgiveness.[113]

The Correlation of Punishment and Forgiveness

If wickedness surpasses the understanding, then it represents what constitutes for Jankélévitch the outer limits of the inexcusable. At the very limits of the inexcusable is a crime that is so monstrous that it is deemed unforgivable. Such a crime would be unforgivable not only in practice but also in principle. In ordinary parlance, it is often said that what someone else has done is "unforgivable." This claim usually means that the offended cannot overcome the offense to be able to forgive the other or that the trust and relation with the other is damaged to the degree that one no longer sees fit to forgive the other. This practical unforgivability is a matter of moral negotiation on the part of the offended, but there is a still stronger version of practical unforgivability, namely in situations where forgiveness becomes impossible in practice. As long as one maintains that only the direct victims of a crime may forgive the perpetrator, their death by murder or their severe incapacitation would entail a practical unforgivability. The same applies to cases in which the perpetrator is no longer there to be potentially forgiven. In the latter, one may still forgive the other, but it is no longer a gift to the other, and it can mark only a one-sided personal new beginning. In this sense, it is more of a psychological act than a moral one. An unforgivability out of principle, however, assumes that the crime exceeds the human power or the human right to forgive. It is this form of unforgivability that dictates the discourses of Jankélévitch, Arendt, and Derrida.

In order to measure and delimit the order of the humanly possible, Jankélévitch conceives of a correlation between punishment and forgiveness, a view that connects him to Arendt. She claims that although punishment is by no means the opposite of forgiveness, it is the alternative to forgiveness.[114] Both have in common the attempt to put an end to the cycles of violence that, without definitive interruption, could go on endlessly. Like Arendt, Jankélévitch assumes that the person wronged must decide between the right to punish and forgiveness. Principally, he claims, forgiveness can forgive only that for which there has been no expiation, compensation, or atonement:

> An impurity purified according to the rigors of justice no longer has need of gifts from anyone. . . . Forgiveness finds a raison d'etre when the moral debtor is still a debtor: hurry up and forgive before the debtor is cleared! Forgive in haste while there still is a punishment to shorten and more generally in order still to dispose of a penalty for which you can give grace to the guilty person. If you wait too long forgiveness will be nothing more than a bad joke. To forgive is to release the guilty one from his punishment or from a part of his punishment, or to liberate him before the completion of his punishment, and all this for nothing and in exchange for nothing, gratuitously, from beyond the marketplace! But for that, it is still necessary

> that there be a punishment or a bit of punishment to remit. . . . The material for forgiveness, then, is the unexpiated offense or the unexpiated portion of the offense; in other words, it is the offense that is unexpiated or partially unredeemed that is the object of gracious remission. . . . Without being obliged, the offended person renounces any claim to what is due to him and any exercise of his right; he freely interrupts his pursuits and decides not to take into account the wrong that he has suffered.[115]

Forgiveness, Jankélévitch claims, involves the abandonment of all rights on the side of the forgiver. The offended person has a right to prosecute, but he or she does not; he or she has a right to compensation and reparations, but he or she declines. For Jankélévitch, it constitutes a contradiction when one wants to forgive and simultaneously to seek retribution. In fact, he claims that any insistence on one's own rights invalidates the possibility of forgiveness.

A forgiveness that is the alternative to punishment is not to be confused, however, with a condonation of the crime. Rather, according to Jankélévitch, "The judgment of the condemnation has stayed the same, but an arbitrary and gratuitous change has intervened, a diametrical and radical inversion, *peristophē*, which transfigures hatred into love."[116] This change takes place outside the world of reasons, grounds, and rational motivations. The decision for forgiveness stems from the disinterestedness that forgives *for* the other. So if there is a change of mind about the culpability of the offender, then he or she cannot be forgiven. There would be no need because if he or she is found inculpable, he or she may be excused. Forgiveness, Jankélévitch succinctly states, "accuses in order to absolve."[117] Neither vindictive nor blind, it looks at the misdeed squarely without making excuses or concessions for the guilty person.

Like Hannah Arendt, Jankélévitch asserts that punishment is the alternative to forgiveness. Beyond Arendt, he casts forgiveness in opposition to justice. Forgiveness, he claims, "renounces justice."[118] That is why it "poses the true moral dilemma" and "provokes the acute scandal."[119] It doubles the scandal of the offense:

> Far from leveling the injustice that sticks out, it doubles the scandal scandalously. In opposition to justice, forgiveness claims neither to neutralize the disequilibrium of pleonexy, nor to compensate the asymmetry of the sin. But, on the contrary, it aggravates this asymmetry and this disequilibrium, and in aggravating them, it cures them. In its way, forgiveness annuls sin, not literally and by inverting the direction of evil through punishment, and by returning violence

to the violent person, like a player who sends the ball back to his partner, but rather by inverting and converting at the same time the intentional quality of the act and the direction. The generous person gives back the good that he did not receive in place of the evil that he received. He exchanges an offering of love for the bad behavior of malevolence; he thus makes himself capable not only of neutralizing the evil act but of reforming, of transfiguring, of converting the malevolent intention.[120]

Whereas justice "neutralizes" tit for tat and "compensates" with penal or financial compensation, the one who forgives "doubles the scandal" by offering her shirt to the one who stole her coat.[121] Jankélévitch maintains that due to its transformative intention, forgiveness can usher in a new era of peace by breaking with the "game" and by refusing to return the act of violence with violence, whether personal or institutional. Thus, the conversion inspired by forgiveness is not a relative conversion of reform or the reestablishment of equilibrium. It is a metaempirical conversion of "contradictory to contradictory."[122] Nevertheless, the wrongdoer must still owe in order to be forgiven. According to Jankélévitch's logic, the expiation of punishment annuls the possibility of forgiveness. Inversely, forgiveness annuls punishment. Just as the Hebrew Bible understands forgiveness as a "turning of one's back," forgiveness, for Jankélévitch, turns its back "on the direction that justice indicates to us."[123]

This scandalous character of forgiveness is absent in Arendt. The alternative between forgiveness and punishment is not an opposition for her because both are predicated on human power. But both Jankélévitch and Arendt recognize the limits of human power to adequately respond to the heinous crimes of the Shoah. For Arendt, the limits of the human capacity to forgive coincide with the human capacity to punish. As a consequence, she claims that what transcends the boundaries of human capacity should be rendered over to God on Judgment Day, which is not characterized by forgiveness but by just retribution.[124] She argues as follows:

> It is therefore quite significant, a structural element in the realm of human affairs, that men are unable to forgive what they cannot punish and that they are unable to punish what has turned out to be unforgivable. This is the true hallmark of those offenses which, since Kant, we call "radical evil" and about whose nature so little is known, even to us who have been exposed to one of their rare outbursts on the public scene. All we know is that we can neither punish nor forgive such offenses and that they therefore transcend the realm of human affairs and the potentialities of human power, both of which

they radically destroy wherever they make their appearance. Here, where the deed itself dispossesses us of all power, we can indeed only repeat with Jesus: "It were better for him that a millstone were hanged about his neck, and he cast into the sea."[125]

Radical evil turns out to be unforgivable in Arendt's view because it is that which destroys the human possibility of responding to it by dispossessing us of the power to adequately respond to it. At this limit of power, she claims that what reveals itself to be unforgivable is unpunishable. The unforgivable coincides with the unpunishable. It is unforgivable in the practical sense but also, and eminently, unforgivable in principle because it is beyond human measure.

Jankélévitch, too, contends that there is an unforgivable and that the "metaphysical crime" of Auschwitz constitutes the unforgivable. This crime, he explains, "is incommensurable with anything else whatsoever. . . . It is a metaphysical abomination."[126] According to Alain Gouhier, Jankélévitch outlines three circumstances that push the inexcusable into the unforgivable: First, the absence of the dead victims as the only ones capable of forgiving the authors, coauthors, and accomplices of the crimes leading to their deaths renders a crime unforgivable; second, the absence of the request or petition to be forgiven, that is, the absence of repentance or a confession of guilt, a remorse for having committed an irremediable crime, or even the distress of being plagued by the irrevocable; finally, the intervention of a malevolence so radical that it surpasses the measure of punishment.[127] The first two criteria invoke an unforgivable that is impossible in practice. The third, however, is a question of principle. From the perspective of this last criterion, one cannot forgive what is immeasurable, what exceeds human power as represented in the power to punish. The Shoah, Jankélévitch claims, is *not* a crime in human measure. One cannot punish the criminal with a punishment that is adequate or even proportionate to the crime. In the light of infinity, he writes, all finite measurements tend toward equality, making the degree of punishment almost a matter of indifference.[128]

This anthropological feature that forgiveness must rest on a human possibility decides everything, Derrida comments, because it is a question of human power, of the sovereign "I can." Derrida assumes that, like Arendt, Jankélévitch takes the correlation of forgiveness and punishment as delimiting human power. Although he detects a fundamental difference in Jankélévitch's two works on forgiveness, the polemical essay "Pardonner?" ("Should We Pardon Them?") and the book *Le Pardon* (*Forgiveness*), he interprets Jankélévitch's logic as proceeding from the singularity of the

Shoah to the inexpiable for which there is no possible forgiveness. He writes:

> For Jankélévitch, as soon as one can no longer punish the criminal with a "punishment proportionate to his crime" it is a matter of the "inexpiable,". . . . From the inexpiable or the irreparable, Jankélévitch concludes the unforgivable. And one does not forgive, according to him, the unforgivable. . . . This logic continues to imply that forgiveness remains the correlate to a judgement and the counterpart to a possible punishment, to a possible expiation, to the "expiable."[129]

According to Derrida, however, it is only in the essay "Should We Pardon Them?" and not in *Forgiveness*, that Jankélévitch "places himself in that exchange, in that symmetry between punishing and forgiving."[130]

Derrida reads Jankélévitch's argumentation in "Should We Pardon Them?" as implementing a certain causal progression of concepts. The immeasurability of the crime renders all forms of retribution relative to each other and disproportionate to the magnitude of the crime itself. The inexpiability of the crime is thus derived by a certain logic from this immeasurability or infinity, which, in turn, leads to the notion of the unforgivable. On Derrida's reading, Jankélévitch apprehends the idea of the unforgivable as the negative limit to the human possibility of forgiving: What is beyond the human capacity to proportionately punish must be beyond the human capacity to forgive.

Jankélévitch does not argue that the crime that is inexpiable is for that reason unforgivable, however. In fact, he claims that ultimately all offenses are inexpiable by the fact that the having-done is irreparable and irrevocable. In his defense of the imprescriptibility of crimes against humanity, Jankélévitch makes this point abundantly clear. Insofar as the having-done has been done, there is no difference between personal offenses and offenses against values, between venial offenses and monstrous ones.[131] Jankélévitch explains that "the sole fact of having at one time willed evil, that is, the sole fact of having had a bad intention . . . is what is inexpiable, strictly speaking."[132]

"Strictly speaking," regardless of the magnitude or the seriousness of the offense, the having-done, according to Jankélévitch, is implacable and in this sense inexpiable. Because of his assertion of the universal category of the irreversible and irrevocable Jankélévitch cannot qualitatively distinguish between venial offenses and atrocious crimes with regard to their inexpiability. The latter merely reveal the structure of the inexpiable in general and in revealing it demonstrate the absurdity of the proposition that time, or even later actions, can attenuate the moral dilemma.[133] The having once willed and the having-done are, according to Jankélévitch, indestructible. He writes that "the impossibility of destroying has the impotence of man as its verso," but "considered from its positive side, it is nothing other than the necessity of the quoddity. The notion of the Imprescriptible, in general, refers us to this diptych of an impossibility and a necessity."[134]

Derrida, too, recognizes this impotence and necessity of the pastness of the offense. He recognizes that many "related and different notions" refer to it: "*the irreversible, the unforgettable, the ineffaceable, the irreparable, the irremediable, the irrevocable, the inexpiable.*" Echoing Jankélévitch, he writes:

> All of these notions, in spite of the decisive differences that separate them, have in common a negativity, a "[do] not," the "[do] not" of an im-possible which sometimes, or at the same time, signifies "impossible because one cannot," "impossible because one should not." But in all cases one should not and/or cannot go back over a past. The past is past, the event took place, the wrong took place, and this past, the memory of this past, remains irreducible, uncompromising. . . . One will never have treated forgiveness if one does not take account of this being-past, a being-past that never lets itself be reduced, modified, modalized in a present past or a presentable or re-presentable past. It is a being past that does not pass, so to speak. It is this impassableness, this impassivity of the past as well, and of the past event that takes on different forms, which we would have to analyze relentlessly and which are those of the irreversible, the unforgettable, the ineffaceable, the irreparable, the irremediable, the irrevocable, the inexpiable, and so forth. Without this stubborn privileging of the past in the constitution of temporalization, there is no original problematic of forgiveness.[135]

Derrida's point of contention with Jankélévitch is that the irreparable, the inexpiable, and the imprescriptible are not synonymous with the unforgivable.[136]

Derrida affirms that there is the unforgivable and that Auschwitz constitutes an unforgivable, but he does not believe that "forgiveness died in the death camps," as Jankélévitch pronounces.[137] He instead begins from "the fact that, yes, there is the unforgivable," and it is, for him, the only thing to forgive, the only thing that calls for forgiveness. In proclaiming the death of forgiveness, Jankélévitch himself commits what for Hegel would be the unforgivable, namely the denial of the power of the spirit to forgive.[138] For the victims who were killed in the concentration camps and for their murderers, forgiveness is impossible in practice, according to

Jankélévitch, because it is the prerogative of the victims to forgive or at least to be asked for forgiveness.[139] But does Jankélévitch declare the end of the idea and practice of forgiveness with the death camps of Auschwitz? Does he maintain, like Derrida, that there is an unforgivable, but, in contrast to Derrida, that the unforgivable is not that which calls for forgiveness but that which marks the limits, the end, even the death of forgiveness?

Contradicting the interpretations of Derrida, Gouhier, and Verena Lemcke, Jankélévitch answers no.[140] In Jankélévitch's thought, inexplicable, ineffable, and incomprehensible forgiveness parallels the misdeed, which is incomprehensible, inexplicable, and inexcusable. Forgiveness is thus called on to forgive that which is without excuse and without attenuating circumstances. It is called on to forgive even what is called unforgivable. "To the infinite unforgivable [*l'impardonnable infini*]," Jankélévitch exclaims, "infinite forgiveness!"[141] Those misdeeds for which no understanding, no mitigating circumstances, indeed, no excuse can be found, Jankélévitch asserts, are precisely those that call out for forgiveness. He suggests that, for crimes involving a "freedom of ill will" or "an evil of malevolence," all there remains to do is forgive.[142] And in the conclusion of *Forgiveness*, he writes, "In spirit, if not in letter, all offenses are 'venial,' even the inexpiable ones. For if there are crimes that are so awful that the criminal who commits them cannot atone for them, then the possibility of forgiving them still remains, forgiveness being made precisely for such hopeless or incurable cases.... Which amounts to saying: there is an inexcusable, but there is not an unforgivable."[143]

Jankélévitch hyperbolically claims that forgiveness forgives absurdly, supernaturally, and unjustly the inexcusable and the unforgivable, for if the misdeed were excusable, then indulgence, understanding, or leniency would suffice.[144] Jankélévitch, therefore, understands forgiveness as a gesture at the extremity of an unconditional love, a love that loves those who normally engender hate. Such is the nature of the supernatural exertion that is demanded of one by a moral calling that demonstrates its veracity in tangency with despair. He confesses that the forgiveness of the Nazi executioners would exhibit precisely this tangent as it is a matter of forgiving those who have never asked for forgiveness, who do not even understand the meaning of the word, and who have never shown remorse for the horrendous deeds. He thus concludes that "it is the most difficult test of all ... the impossibility par excellence: to forgive absolute wickedness."[145]

Pure, unconditional forgiveness, therefore, has its calling as the response to pure wickedness because, for Jankélévitch, "the more that wickedness is unforgivable, the more that forgiveness will be sublime."[146] To the infinity of wickedness he responds with the infinity of forgiveness. It the only possible response that is as radical as wickedness, responding in its height to evil's abyss. A love that loves and forgives those who hate, according to Jankélévitch, is infinite, irrational, gratuitous, and excessive: It is without measure. Against inexcusable crimes there can be no just, that is, proportionate, punishment. Instead, in a chasm of love responding to evil, it is immeasurable to immeasurable, infinite to infinite, gratuitous freedom to gratuitous freedom. Evil provides the material for forgiveness, and wickedness alone solicits forgiveness.[147]

Jankélévitch is thus much closer to Derrida than Derrida realizes or at least admits. Although Jankélévitch and Derrida share the interpretation that forgiveness has its meaning in its transcendence of the contexts and economies of meaning, enclosure, and return, their terminologies differ. Derrida states that the monstrous crimes of the twentieth century are indeed unforgivable but that the unforgivable is, according to the idea of forgiveness, "the only thing to forgive."[148] Jankélévitch maintains that these atrocities are inexcusable and unjustifiable due to the excess of evil, and it is in the inexcusable that forgiveness receives its "daily bread." Although Jankélévitch does at times invoke the paradoxical formulation of the unforgivable, his category of the inexcusable extends to mark the wickedness that beckons forgiveness. Nonetheless, like Derrida, Jankélévitch embraces the paradox and aporia of forgiveness, namely that forgiveness forgives wickedness, which is inexcusable and which, at the outer limits of the inexcusable, can also be called unforgivable.[149]

Derrida acknowledges the logic of a hyperbolical ethics in Jankélévitch's thought. He reads him, however, as representing a conditional polemical logic of forgiveness in his essay "Pardonner?" and a hyperbolic ethics in his book *Le Pardon*. The latter proposes an ethics, in Derrida's view, "that would command precisely that forgiveness be granted where it is neither asked for nor deserved, and even for the worst radical evil."[150] But there is no contradiction in principle between these two works. Although there are undoubtedly disparities, incongruities, and tensions, one cannot divide the two into a conditional and unconditional treatment of the topic of forgiveness.

Jankélévitch's practical, polemical essay, first and foremost, rejects the simili-forms of forgiveness propagated in the name of pure forgiveness. It highlights, moreover, the scandal and even the absurdity of forgiveness when precisely those whom one is concretely called to forgive are unrepentant torturers who now enjoy prosperity and the support of a world that ultimately, to a certain but horrific degree, allowed them to commit crimes of atrocity and now takes up their defense, the defense of normalcy, amnesty, and amnesia. Jankélévitch does not attenuate this absurdity or the nearly humanly impossible dilemma of forgiving one's torturers. With this extremity he underlines the difficulty of forgiveness pressed to its limits and, simultaneously, its vocation.

The Organ-Obstacle

On the one hand, Jankélévitch holds that "there is an inexcusable, but there is not an unforgivable."[151] On the other hand, he suggests that there is an unforgivable.[152] Although he states that "no misdeed is so grave that we cannot in the last recourse forgive it," he also suggests that "if all is not excusable for the excuse, everything is forgivable for forgiveness, all save, of course, the unforgivable, admitting that an unforgivable exists, that is, a crime that is meta-empirically impossible to forgive."[153] This apparent contradiction in his writing rests on the aporetic structure of forgiveness, which Jankélévitch calls the "organ-obstacle." Wickedness serves as the organ that facilitates, enables, and is the precondition for forgiveness, but it can serve as an obstacle that forgiveness cannot surmount. According to Jankélévitch, the ambiguous character of evil as an organ-obstacle initiates an oscillation in the human mind and in human values. This oscillation symbolizes the irresolvable tension between wickedness and forgiveness, a tension that is not static but dynamic. One side alternately gives way to the other in this conjunction that is also a collision.

More Stupid Than Wicked, More Wicked Than Stupid

Jankélévitch captures the oscillations within the organ-obstacle of evil in the phrase "more stupid than wicked, more wicked than stupid." With this phrase, Jankélévitch platitudinously ironizes the Greek tracing of evil to ignorance: People who do evil things are more stupid than wicked. But he simultaneously remarks that people can also be more wicked than stupid. The former involves the sin of ignorance, the latter the sin of malevolence.[154] When Jesus in the Gospel of Luke says, "Father, forgive them, for they know not what they do" (23:34), he is not asking for forgiveness for the crucifiers because they are not cognizant of having nailed a man on a cross or aware that this action would lead to his death. He seems to be petitioning for their forgiveness because they do not recognize that they are crucifying the messiah, the Son of God. The argument for ignorance maintains that they would not have crucified Jesus had they recognized him as the promised one. If they had known, they surely would not have nailed him to the cross. This perspective is found in the Acts of the Apostles in which Peter says to the Jews, "And now, brethren, I know that through ignorance ye did it, as did your rulers" (3:17). Jankélévitch discovers a "Socratic" turn in this interpretation. Divine forgiveness, he surmises, "would not be necessary. . . . It would be better to teach them."[155] In a similar vein, Jeffrie Murphy adds that it would be more "correct" had Jesus said, "Father *excuse* them, for they know not what they do."[156] The ignorant require a lesson, a teaching about the good, and they are excused for not doing the good because they simply did not know any better under those circumstances.

From the statement "for they know not what they do" Hannah Arendt derives the duty to forgive. She attributes to Jesus of Nazareth the discovery of the role of forgiveness for the human realm, and she examines in a secular sense what took place in a religious context and was articulated in religious language as an explication of a fundamental social and political bond.[157] In her interpretation of the New Testament, forgiveness "does not apply to the extremity of crime and willed evil." It aims solely at the release or dismissal (*aphienai*) of trespasses (*harmartanein*), which obtain through failure, by missing the mark or the point, or by going astray. Trespasses, she insists, are everyday occurrences, and they are inherent in the concept of action so central to her thought.[158] She highlights the fact that forgiveness entails a "mutual release" from the consequences of action that implicate us in webs of relations whose bonds may become so established and restricting as to jeopardize life and the freedom of human agency. In human action, she argues, consequences go beyond intentions and therefore a constant release from the responsibility of human consequences caused unknowingly is required to allow agency to begin again, and begin anew.

Whereas Arendt's example strays from the cross to the polis, Jankélévitch focuses on the history of the interpretation of the crucifixion, which he deems exemplary for the ambiguity of the phrase "more wicked than stupid, more stupid than wicked." Christian theologians have insisted that it was out of blindness, even stubbornness, that the followers of the old faith did not recognize Jesus as the messiah. In this regard, Jankélévitch writes, "They were thus guilty of puerility and frivolity more than perfidy."[159] But at the same time that one may understand and excuse the Jews for not having recognized the messiah, there arises the reproach "of not having wanted to recognize him." This accusation sets forth that "in reality they recognized him, but on purpose made out to misjudge him": "out of wickedness" and "from ill will."[160] This perspective, as Jankélévitch observes, forms the other, dark side of the historical relation of Christians and Jews: Not simply ignorance but the idea that there was malevolence behind their ignorance impelled the Christian charge of deicide against the Jewish people and set off waves of anti-Semitism and persecution. The question of wickedness thus revolves around the will to know and the will to take responsibility. What, Jankélévitch asks, is the relation between blindness and the will to be blind, between inexcusable responsibility and excusable irresponsibility?[161] In the wake of the National Socialist crimes against humanity the matter is clearer to Jankélévitch. He consequently turns Jesus' "petition on its head": "Lord, do not forgive them, for they know precisely what they do."[162] From the executioners to the *Mitläufer* (the followers and nominal members) and those who looked the other way—they all knew what they were doing, according to Jankélévitch, or they willed not to know. For them, there is no excuse; there was and remains responsibility.

Although Jankélévitch posits that there is wickedness, he maintains that there is an unceasing ambiguity between the voluntary and attentive power of freedom and the very possibility of that power or the pregiven, preexistent fact of freedom that is common to all humans. Jankélévitch states that, in one look, the inexcusable sometimes says to us "understand me." Forgiveness, he concludes, must therefore "understand many things before finally forgiving without understanding." One should attempt to understand as much as one can. Still, the instant of decision, the tangent of intuition, is not of the order of knowledge; it cannot be encompassed in a system. Instead, forgiveness, according to Jankélévitch, understands that there is an incomprehensible: "It understands that there is in the end nothing to understand! It *understands that*, but it does not know how to say *what* it understands; it understands without knowing *what*."[163] Forgiveness consequently must at least understand or presuppose that there is such a thing as wicked freedom. What forgiveness understands, Jankélévitch asserts, is exactly the quoddity of wicked freedom, that is, the fact that there is wicked freedom. What this is, forgiveness does not know (*Je ne sais quoi*); the aseity of freedom denies the possibility of its becoming a quid, a what. Thus, for Jankélévitch, forgiveness "does not understand what it understands and understands what it does not understand. This empty intellection of the incomprehensible is forgiveness itself."[164]

On the one hand, the one who has to forgive must be careful not to expel from herself all resemblance or community with the wicked person in the name of an innocence or victimhood that sets her on a different and higher plane. Jankélévitch recognizes in absolute claims of innocence a principle of pride and a ruthless rigor. A person putting forth such a claim behaves as if she were of another, elevated essence than the guilty person, above sin, above humanity, and definitely above responsibility for possibly playing a part in the cycles of violence, maltreatment, and ressentiment. In contrast, Jankélévitch writes that forgiveness "whispers in a quiet voice: *Et ego!* Me, too. . . . *De vestris fuimus.* You are sinners, well, I am another one of them too. I, as well, I sinned or will sin. I could have done as you did; maybe I will do as you did. I am like you, weak, fallible, and miserable."[165] Jankélévitch draws here on a Platonic and Augustinian tradition: The one who does unjust or evil deeds is not a happy or fortunate person; rather misery and misfortune accompany him like shadows do his feet. In the conclusion of *Forgiveness,* Jankélévitch thus shifts the emphasis of the phrase "more stupid than wicked," to state that sinners are more misfortunate or miserable than wicked.

On the other hand, the fact also remains that the attentive power of the perpetrator's will willed evil. No crime is excusable on account of the notion that others, including oneself, could potentially have committed it as well.[166] Although Jankélévitch readily admits that there is much to understand and much to pity in the circumstances, the ignorance, or the misfortune of the offender, there is a point where the freedom of the bad intention and the wicked act is irreducible. At that point, "There is nothing indeed to understand in the mystery of gratuitous wickedness except that the wicked person is wicked."[167] For Jankélévitch, the scandal of freedom is that it is free to the point of sacrilege, absolutely unjust and malevolent. In such cases, he explains, "It is their wickedness itself that is a misfortune, the infinite misfortune of being evil."[168]

The two sides—the sympathetic optimism and the rigorous condemnation—constitute an either-or, but, according to Jankélévitch, they also stand in conjunction with each other. They collide as antimonies concerning the nature of humanity and the nature of evil. As Kant's situating of radical evil in human nature between the animal and the diabolical demonstrates, the question of the human is always at stake in the determination of evil. Jankélévitch claims that, while contradictory, the two sides of the phrase are both equally true. One cannot stand absolutely or solely on one side or the other of the either-or dichotomy of wickedness or misfortune. Indulgence, leniency, understanding, sympathy, excuse, even the acknowledgment of coresponsibility are right and good, he claims; they are even required . . . but there is still wickedness. "It comes to pass," Jankélévitch writes, "like an intuitive and sudden glimpse that reveals to us, in the instant, the irreducible, qualitative simplicity of the bad intention and the indivisible mystery of freedom."[169]

In the presence of this naked mystery, the two positions on wickedness and ignorance or misery confront each other as "two pieces of evidence, contradictory and yet each as evident as the other in a collision from which there is no escape." According to Jankélévitch, we cannot maintain both of these contradictory positions simultaneously, so our minds are sent incessantly from one to the other, such that "the collision changes for us into an oscillation."[170] He thus situates human existence in the moral ambiguity of the conjunction and collision of and oscillation between excuse and evil. Humans, he concludes, are more stupid than wicked, more wicked than stupid.

Penultimate Acts: Love Is as Strong as Evil

This oscillation between sympathy, optimism, understanding, on the one hand, and the testimony to wickedness and evil, on the other, is a prelude to the oscillation between love and evil. Because it is part and parcel of the human condition, Jankélévitch does not see that there is any reason for the oscillation to stop. It even seems to gain momentum and metaphysical weight in his thinking, like a pendulum swinging madly between poles as the line of tension is increasingly tightened and pulled. On the one hand, evil constitutes the organ of forgiveness. On the other hand, evil or wickedness may prove to be too much for forgiveness. The hyperbolic height of forgiveness is pronounced in its response to the motiveless depths of wicked freedom, but wicked freedom perhaps can also introduce a hyperbolic unforgivable. As Jankélévitch states, "The misfortune of this radical wickedness can, in turn, be the object of an exponential forgiveness; and the wickedness of this misfortune becomes a hyperbolic Unforgivable."[171] Even the commentators who recognize the absoluteness of Jankélévitch's idea of forgiveness as forgiving precisely what is inexcusable or unforgivable miss this aspect of his morality, despite his constant emphasis on the infinitely equivocal.

Jankélévitch does not simply reintroduce through the conceptual back door a reason or a ground for forgiveness. He does not argue, for instance, on the basis of a common humanity, a shared sinfulness, or a coimplication of responsibility for all the histories and cycles of violence that forgiveness is indeed rational and universally justifiable, and conceivably even universally commendable. Rather, he argues that malevolent freedom "is infinitely the organ-obstacle. Or, better yet, the organ-obstacle is, infinitely and in its own right, sometimes organ and sometimes obstacle."[172] At times, and at the limits of human strength, forgiveness forgives the evil willed by the other, but at other times, something holds one back, even precisely at the moment of forgiving. In his discussions with Béatrice Berlowitz in *Quelque part dans l'inachevé*, Jankélévitch describes that which holds one back as a "metaphysical tragedy."[173] What holds one back is the bare existence, the intensity, and immeasurability of evil itself, which one cannot forgive. It is the breaking point of forgiveness for the one who has to forgive. Not only does he or she not will to forgive, he or she cannot forgive. The ill-intention is too much to respond to with love. The metaphysical tragedy, then, reflects the never-ending oscillation between the power of forgiveness and the power of evil, which is to say, between the omnipotence of forgiveness and its impotence, and inversely, the omnipotence of evil and its impotence.

Evil, according to Jankélévitch, is the precondition or *organ* of forgiveness, and simultaneously it is that which is the *obstacle* to forgiveness. As Jankélévitch confesses, he is caught between two equal beliefs: the belief in love and the belief in wickedness. In the Song of Songs, it is written that "love is strong as death" (8:6). For Jankélévitch, this equivalence is decisive: "It does not say that love is stronger than death, and indeed it cannot say this, since the lover has to die one day. Love is strong like death, but death is strong like love. In truth, love is simultaneously stronger than and weaker than death, and it is thus just as strong." Transposing the Psalmist's terms of love and death to love and evil, Jankélévitch concludes that "love is stronger than evil and evil is stronger than love; each is stronger than the other! . . . This extreme and almost heartrending tension is that of the mad forgiveness that is accorded to the wicked person. . . . The mystery of irreducible and inconceivable wickedness is, at the same time, stronger and weaker, weaker and stronger than love. Likewise, forgiveness is strong like wickedness; but it is not stronger than it."[174]

Forgiveness overcomes evil, yet there is always the "rest" of evil, the residue of the oscillation between an infinite love and an infinite evil. Evil is thus sometimes overcome by forgiveness, and sometimes it overcomes forgiveness. It is both the organ facilitating forgiveness and its insurmountable impediment. If evil would have the last word or if the unforgivable would become petrified and thus remain ultimate and definitive, the result, Jankélévitch unequivocally acknowledges, would be nothing other than hell. Hell is where wickedness has finally triumphed over love, banishing it along with the dynamic of all of life. Fortunately, evil does not have the last word. Inversely, if love would triumph over evil, then we would have arrived at the great feast of the kingdom of God. Unfortunately, evil is not absolutely vanquished by the act of selfless love or by forgiveness. Nothing, neither in good nor in evil, will ever congeal and solidify.[175] Fortunately and unfortunately, "the last word is always the penultimate word . . . so that the debate between forgiveness and the unforgivable will never have an end."[176]

The unforgivable in Jankélévitch's understanding is thus twofold. First, it is the evil that has become a limit and an absolute impediment for the one who has to forgive. In the call to forgive what is inexcusable and, paradoxically, unforgivable, the immeasurability of the evil that one is called to forgive prevents one's ability to forgive, both in practice and in principle. Second, the unforgivable is the residue of the infinite oscillation between love and evil. Since love will never finally and ultimately triumph over evil, according to Jankélévitch, there remains an "irreducible residue of an infinite and always unfinished reduction."[177] As the "residue" of two responding infinities, the abyss of evil and the height of forgiveness, the unforgivable, in this respect, consists in the fact that it is never finished: "To infinite evil, infinite grace, and reciprocally. Always reciprocally." Jankélévitch does not understand this reciprocity as an economy of returns between equivalents, however. Evil and love stand rather in a relation of mutual asymmetry to each other. Each is characterized by an excess, a transcendence, which surpasses the other in its response. Thus, to Paul's words, "where sin increased, grace abounded all the more," Jankélévitch adds, "where grace overflows, evil overflows in response and submerges this overflowing itself, with an infinite and mysterious outbidding."[178]

These two sides cannot be suspended in a synthesis or an *Aufhebung* of reconciliation. Auschwitz indeed ends the history conceived as the history of forgiveness or reconciliation in the Hegelian sense, for the good, the spirit, even the spirit of forgiveness, is not assured of its victory.[179] "The human spirit," Jankélévitch explains, "does not know how to go beyond," beyond the conjunction and collision of love and evil.[180] Jankélévitch therefore establishes a critique of reason that cannot smooth out the paradoxes of moral existence. Morality cannot be reduced purely to a system of normative ethics because humans are forced, in the language of Derrida, to negotiate the nonnegotiable and decide the undecidable. For Jankélévitch, there is no ultimate, no ending but only the penultimate and abiding responsibility. The eschatological reservation expressed in his statement that "it is never finished" suggests an infinity of human responsibility.[181]

6

Love and Justice

For Vladimir Jankélévitch, forgiveness presents a moral dilemma. The oscillation between the unfortunate and the wicked and the oscillation between love and evil imply a dilemma that Jankélévitch maintains is insoluble. This dilemma contains within it the tension between justice and forgiveness and forces a decision within morality itself, for forgiveness and love, according to Jankélévitch, introduce an asymmetry that is at odds with the symmetry implicit in ethics and in law. This moral dilemma consequently appears as the conflict between two moralities, or, as Jankélévitch says, as the paradox of morality itself: on the one hand, the system of ethics and justice; on the other hand, the hyperbolic ethics of love and forgiveness.[1] The transcendence of forgiveness, in other words, conflicts with the demands of justice while going beyond it.

Two Absolutes

Jankélévitch believes that, when encountering evil, we have three options in what he describes as a situation of "finitude and irrationality." The first option, he claims, condemns us to impotence. Faced with having to make a decision that is not rationally decidable, one may suspend moral judgment. In other words, moral judgment will "hesitate indefinitely before the equivocation of an intention that is both malevolent and unfortunate, before this equivocation of the wicked-miserable." Jankélévitch quickly rejects this possibility as a viable option. Morality demands a Kierkegaardian leap in decision, a judgment without the security of being on stable, rational grounds. This lack of foundation entails, however, that the other two "solutions" are "unilateral and shaky." As Jankélévitch portrays this decision,

> [Either] we will choose to forgive the miserable person although it may mean the establishment of the reign of the hangmen for one thousand years; or, in order that the future be saved and that essential values survive, we will agree to prefer violence and force without love over a love without force.[2]

These two options are not mere options, according to Jankélévitch; they are equally duties. Both propositions address the question of how we can and how we should respond to evil. Although they place us before a decision, Jankélévitch asserts that both sides of the either-or represent duties. In short, we are called to and claimed by the duty to justice *and* the duty to love. Jankélévitch explains:

> For if the imperative of love is unconditional and does not have any restrictions, then the obligation to annihilate evil, and if not to hate it (for it is never necessary to hate anyone), at least to reject its negating force, to put it out of action or to damage its destructive rage, such an obligation is no less imperious than the duty to love; of all the values, love for humans is the most sacred, but indifference to crimes against humanity, but indifference to crimes against the essence and hominity of the person is the most sacrilegious of all misdeeds. And we have no means either for choosing one of these superlatives over the other, or for honoring them together: the choice of one Absolute necessarily leaves the "other Absolute" outside, the combination and conciliation of the *two Absolutes* is impossible; the sacrifice of one Absolute gives birth to misgivings and remorse in us; the synthesis of the two Absolutes would be a miracle: for the Absolute is plural and irremediably torn apart.[3]

Jankélévitch thus presents moral life as cast in the double bind of the double imperative. We are called to love *and* to be just. But this calling is impossible. The two are at odds with each other. As Andrew Kelley comments, "The moral human condition, for Jankélévitch, is the constant struggle between spontaneity—love, forgiveness, grace—and reason in the guise of following moral and legal systems."[4] This "between" demonstrates, on another level, the limitation of moral systems, justice systems, and reason. According to Jankélévitch, there is no reason, means, or rule for deciding for one over the other, for love or for justice. It is, therefore, this decision made from "between" that exemplifies the moral condition of humanity. The difficulty of moral indecidability without criteria that offer assurance characterizes the nature of responsibility. Both justice and love are respectively uncompromising and noncontingent. Jankélévitch accordingly calls them absolutes that preclude each other through the choice with which we are continually confronted. Consequently, whereas Plato esteemed the harmony of the world of ideas and values, Jankélévitch raises the chord of dissonance. Like the temple veil, the world of values, he claims, is "irremediably torn apart."[5]

This decision, therefore, implies a contradiction, or what Derrida calls a perjury, a sacrifice of love for justice or vice versa. Jankélévitch nonetheless prioritizes the duty to combat and negate evil with the violence of retributive justice. Since we live in a world of violence, he argues, it is better to take up arms and combat evil with a lesser evil.[6] Under the heading of justice, Jankélévitch encompasses the necessity and right to resist, fight, and punish evil. From his own choice and in the light of the Shoah, he writes, "Such was, as we know, the heroic choice of the Resistance. Is not the fight against fanatics the least of all evils by far? It is better to disavow oneself in punishing than to contradict oneself in forgiving!"[7] This thought allows not only for justified resistance but also for wars and invasions in the name of human rights and in the name of justice and civil society.

Jankélévitch's account of the double bind of the absolute imperatives to love thy neighbor and to defend the rights of humanity can be analyzed in terms of the relation between the second person and the third person and the relation of both to the first person. Jankélévitch makes a distinction similar to that of Levinas between ethics as the relation to the other and the order of justice as the relation to the third. The relation to the other involves the asymmetry of infinite responsibility (Levinas) or the asymmetry involved in the duty to love (Jankélévitch), epitomized in the hyperbolic love of one's enemies.[8] Levinas's explications, therefore, elucidate Jankélévitch's paradox. It is not only the ineradicable nature of evil that paradoxically limits this infinite love or responsibility toward the other but also the entrance of the third party as the interruption of the exclusivity of the obligation to the other. Levinas claims that this interruption "is of itself the limit of responsibility and the birth of the question: What do I have to do with justice? . . . Justice is necessary, that is comparison, coexistence, contemporaneousness, assembling, order, thematization, the visibility of faces and thus . . . the intelligibility of a system."[9] With the entrance of the third party, the demand for justice arises. Importantly, Levinas situates the third as contemporaneous with the other; he is the neighbor of the other; by raising the question of justice, he places distance between "me" and the other for whom I am (otherwise) infinitely responsible.

Without the duty to be just, no borders would delimit my responsibility or my duty to love the other person. This third party does not wait. Rather, he or she comes at the origin of the face and of the face to face.[10] The third announces the demand for justice, law, and systems simultaneously and equal to the relation with the other. If forgiveness is, for Jankélévitch, a possible impossibility at the limit of human strength (simultaneously including the capacity to forgive and demarcating its limit), then it can be said with Levinas that "what is truly human is beyond human strength. Society according to man's strength is merely the limitation of this right and this obligation toward [the other]."[11] Societal practice formalizes the logic of correspondence inherent in the Golden Rule. This formalization of the logic of equivalence, the logic of reciprocity, or of equal obligation is visible, for example, in the precept *audi alteram partem* (hear the other side too) and in the egalitarian demand of juridical practice to handle the same cases in the same fashion.[12] By introducing the order of reciprocity or the order of symmetry, society and justice mark the return to the human but also the return to the all-too-human, that is, to what is merely within human strength.

Forgiveness, therefore, cannot become a law for society; it remains and must remain exceptional, beyond the law. Because it engages absolute singularities, forgiveness may not be extended by a third party, not only because that would be a violation of the victim's rights but also because forgiveness itself goes beyond the stringency of any system of ethics. The third party, whether an institution or a survivor, is bound by the perspective of justice, whereas forgiveness implies the immediate relation of the one to the other. "As soon as the third party intervenes," Derrida comments, "one can again speak of amnesty, reconciliation, reparation, etc. but certainly not of pure forgiveness in the strict sense."[13] Thus, only in the immediacy of love, in the face-to-face relation, can there be forgiveness.

The dilemma of forgiveness consequently reaches its peak in the contrast between the logic of equivalence, reciprocity, and neutralization that orders society, on the one side, and the logic of superabundance, asymmetrical love, and exceptional forgiveness, on the other. It is to be between the duty to love the other and the duty to respect the other(s) of the other; between the obligation to return good for evil in the act of forgiveness and the obligation to resist the order that threatens the human in general; that is, between the duty to the singular other and the duty to the perspective of universality and justice.

Nonetheless, Jankélévitch's comments about the paradox of justice and love require qualification. His presentation of the either-or between forgiveness and resistance or punishment conflates the difference between the forgiveness of moral guilt and the disavowal of legal prosecution. The two remain independent of each other. An alternative between punishment and forgiveness does not obtain, as Jankélévitch and Hannah Arendt claim, because what is punishable is punishable by a state that cannot forgive but should punish. This mandate of prosecution does not rule out, however, that one forgives the prosecuted criminal. One may personally forgive while justice is enacted. I personally may forgive, but insofar as the offense is a crime against the social order represented by the law, I do not have the right to forgive in the name of all the others constituting society, much less humanity. The second-person perspective of morality and the third-person perspective of law are, therefore, compatible because the orders are heterogeneous. On the one hand, the relation with the other is personal: It is the order of the face to face. On the other hand, the relation with the other is determined from the third person perspective, the order of law and justice. One cannot suspend the moral or judiciary law by means of the interpersonal act of forgiveness. Rather, the two orders run separately from and parallel to each other. Derrida clearly distinguishes between these two orders. He explains that "the notion of forgiveness remains foreign to the order of the juridical and the political. In the course of a trial, one can very well condemn someone to death inflexibly and without amnesty and on the other hand, outside the trial, forgive, forgive him his crime. These are different orders."[14]

But Jankélévitch's paradox between the duty to love and the duty to justice is, in another respect, enduring. In the relation with the other, I can be just or loving; I can allow my relation to the singular other to be commanded by the second-person perspective of the duty to love or by the third-person perspective of the duty to be just. In other words, in the face of the other I can maintain the position of justice and the ressentiment felt at the injustice suffered. With regard to personal offenses or offenses against values that are not also crimes, one is indeed faced with the decision of demanding punishment and retribution or forgiving. One is faced with this decision, too, not only in civil court but also in criminal court, insofar as one may decide to press charges or not. Derrida is therefore right to assume that forgiveness and punishment are simultaneously possible, but only through a shift in perspective. It is through this separation of responsible agents that justice and love may be conjoined, but the institutional right to punish does not mean that the person is relieved of the decision between justice and forgiveness. Before it is a question of punishment, one still must choose between resisting evil with violence and encountering an aggressor with nonresistant love. And beyond or outside of the administration of the law, one can still either cultivate ressentiment or forgive interpersonally and morally.

Derrida recognizes that, in *Forgiveness*, Jankélévitch proposes an idea of forgiveness that "defies penal logic" and thus remains foreign to and exceeds the juridical space.[15] Although the main thrust of Jankélévitch's argument is that, in forgiving the inexcusable, forgiveness exceeds or surpasses the juridical space, he also intends *defiance* to mean the abrogation and sacrifice of the claims of justice. Jankélévitch writes that "it does not matter how paradoxical the love that is addressed to the wicked person is—it loves the wicked person after all! Forgiveness, in the moment in which it forgives, has to make a violent effort over itself in order to absolve the guilty person instead of condemning him. Absurd forgiveness of sin is a defiance of penal logic."[16] Andrew Kelley explains this defiance in opposition to, and not merely in excess of, the order of justice as follows: "Justice would require that the person be held accountable and make restituition for his or her actions. Insofar as forgiveness abolishes the fact that one holds the crime against the person and abolishes one's demands for reparation or restitution, it goes against justice or a system of legalistic ethics."[17]

The perseverance in the realm of justice may justify a lack of love. Faced with the other, I can remain just in the universal but am thereby not generous, charitable, or loving, and I do not fulfill my duty to (love) the other. Placed before the double injunction, I cannot justify why I allow my relation to the other to be defined by the duty of justice that I can fulfill, giving only so much as I (ethically) owe the other, which is the same as I owe to anyone else. By giving what I (ethically) owe, I am justified before the world precisely by not going beyond and by not giving more in love "beyond human strength." In the immediacy of the face to face, I can hide my face or the face of the other behind the anonymous mask of universality, or I can welcome the other, come what may or in light of whatever has been. This position embodies the duty that is beyond the debt of symmetrical duty, beyond reciprocity and expectation. For Jankélévitch, it is the duty of love, charity, and forgiveness. The double imperative, therefore, can be expressed as follows: The order of justice entails giving what is due; the order of forgiveness entails giving not what is due, which is not just to give or to give justly but to give abundantly and superlatively.

Origins, Ends, and Interruptions

Jankélévitch ends his treatise on forgiveness with a double paradox: the paradox of forgiveness and wickedness and the paradox of love and justice. His determination of the relation between the order of grace and the order of justice, however, is more complex. In Jankélévitch's understanding, justice and grace are intertwined in a repetition of the temporal relation between the interval and the instant. Three features of this relation deserve highlighting.

First, the order of grace, according to Jankélévitch, fulfills the order of law both in the act and in its end. Like Kant, Jankélévitch distinguishes between morality and legality. Although the good may be done in accordance with morality, it is not always done in the spirit of morality. In contrast to an act that is simply in accordance with duty, love, he maintains, is an act that fulfills duty with intentionality and with heart. Love wills the good, in other words, for its own sake. Similarly, the order of grace fulfills the end of justice, insofar as the end of justice is peace, as Jankélévitch contends. Closer to Derrida than Kant, Jankélévitch believes that peace ultimately remains unattainable by laws and rights. Peace, especially perpetual peace, he claims, is only possible through the interpersonal act of love.

Second, just as justice cannot achieve its end of peace without love, it cannot justify its own existence either as an ideal or value or in the actual formation and structure of laws. In short, justice does not have its beginning and principle—its *arché*—in itself but receives it from the other. The intellectual ideal of justice, Jankélévitch claims, is posited in the original creative act of a past that was never present. The laws of justice can only rationalize and justify what is immanent in them, but they cannot provide the grounds for their own foundation or the fact that they are what and how they are. This foundation is posited in the decision of creation, in God's creation out of grace. Grace, then, represents the upsurge of justice that justice cannot completely appropriate.

Third, in linking the instant of the order of grace to the interval of the order of justice, Jankélévitch states that the élan, the spirit, or the innovative movement within justice is due to the interspersal of instants that air out what tends toward conservation and even petrification. The temporal relation of the instant to the interval, as the interruption and the opening disruption of the interval, is therefore constitutive of his conception of the relation between grace and justice.

Whether burned by the vigilant fires of memory or as the resistance to and punishment of violence and injustice, Jankélévitch maintains a notion of justice that is distributive and based on the ideal of equilibrium or fairness. In its best form, it moves toward the needy and the powerless: the widow, the orphan, the stranger. In its worst form, it legalistically serves the order established in the status quo. Jankélévitch's conception of justice is thus largely informed by Aristotle's distributive justice. Consequently, his critique of justice is aimed at Aristotle's determination of justice in terms of proportionality, reciprocity, the just mean, and his intimate association of justice with the law.[18] For Aristotle, the just is the mean between excess and defect, and justice is the greatest of virtues, or even the complete virtue itself. In contrast, Jankélévitch maintains the primacy of hyperbolic love over the proportionality of justice. As a critique of both Aristotelian ethics and politics, Jankélévitch juxtaposes a temperate justice of the mean with the extremity of love.

This juxtaposition parallels Jankélévitch's juxtaposition of being and creation. The foundations of the order of justice are to be found, he claims, in the creative grace of love. Creation is the excluded act that initiates and establishes the order of justice itself. The creative initiative of the instant, according to Jankélévitch, both grounds the order of justice and law and calls its grounds into question.[19] Justice, he says, belongs to the interval and the order of being. Parmenides, the philosopher of ontological fullness par excellence, believes, for example, that justice does not allow for generation or loss but is redistributive, compensating for every appearance and disappearance. A balancing act of preservation, justice is inherently or tendentially a conservative principle or a principle of conservation. This is the always potential stagnancy of which Jankélévitch speaks. He links this sterile contentment to be or this contentment of being with a satisfaction or a good conscience that prevents the initiative of something new in order to preserve the status quo and invest it with normative value. In other words, justice tends to make of the ontic horizon an ontological given or an ideal.

"Being," Jankélévitch writes, "is this decided, cooled down, deposited decision."[20] The creative act is declined into the metaempirical plane of idealization and deported into the empirical plane where the creative fervor of the decision is reified into essences and things. This unmotivated and spontaneous grace is the carrier of justice, which, in turn, denies it.[21] The instant of grace is not of the order of reason, and reason cannot explain or justify, rationalize or appropriate it, which means that it cannot justify the establishment or the fact of its own order. The ideal of justice, according to Jankélévitch, thus denies the foundational gift of its own ideal existence, as it in fact denies that it has a beginning or an origin at all. The originary act of creation is then repeated in human acts of creation. As in the contingent act of creation that founds the realm of essences and existents and that makes it such that there is something rather than nothing, the creative act of the instant reenacts the creative positing of originary creation. However, since the ideal of justice as well as positive law always already obtains for humans situated in historical time and place, this reenactment of originary creation is always only a re-creation or a repositioning of what already is. Hence, although the grace of the original creative decision founds the order of justice and law, love is always already in relation to the order of justice and to the law. This relation is not only an oppositional alternative to justice but also an opening—an extending and transcending more (*plus*) or in addition (*perisson*)—that invokes the justice of justice. In other words, each act of love, as an innocent and spontaneous movement of genius, recommences anew, and to a small degree, the grand cosmological improvisation.[22]

In this mimesis of the act of creation, Jankélévitch's exposition resembles Bergson's distinction between the creative and the conservative. It is also analogous to Walter Benjamin's distinction between law-making (*rechtsetzende*) and law-preserving (*rechtserhaltende*) violence.[23] This proximity to Benjamin reveals a lacuna in Jankélévitch's reflection. He does not reflect on the possibility that this creative act of founding, which precedes and escapes the rational and legal order that it founds, could also be an act of violence. But it is precisely the structural parallel of love to the freedom of wickedness that suggests this connection. Benjamin lays bare that the concrete and historical founding act of an order is not and cannot be accounted for by that order, though that order in turn serves to justify its unjustified "mythic" origin, as Benjamin phrases it. As Jankélévitch claims, the instant is codified in the interval. Revolutionary discourses, on both the left and the right, justify recourse to violence in this vein by alleging that the law will retrospectively justify the original violence. As Derrida observes, the violence that inaugurates a new law, a new state, or a new era, to use Jankélévitch's term, is already seen as justified by the future anterior.[24] Although Jankélévitch aligns this founding act with grace and determines it to be love, he does not adequately account for the real possibility that the founding, exceptional, decisional act might be an act of power, force, or violence (*Gewalt*). He instead concentrates on another aspect that Benjamin and especially Bergson highlight, namely the capacity of the creative act to transform the relations of law.

One of Jankélévitch's ultimate concerns is the manner in which justice is conceived of as an extension of economics or mathematical calculation. Such calculation functions as a depersonalization in two important respects: The other person is rendered an abstraction, and the good is made into an economics of self-restricting equivalence. Therefore, he propagates an opposition between the metrics of justice and the maximal passion of love, between the just mean and the charitable extreme. Whereas justice seeks to give to each his own and not more to one than to another, love creates disequilibrium through an unjust preference rooted in the lover's preference for the other to himself or herself. It is not love but the just person, Jankélévitch claims, who says enough! or nothing more! and responds to the question how much? Love, in contrast, recognizes a single law, the illegal law of the frenzy of excess, inflation, and hyperbole.[25] In short, Jankélévitch decries the fact that, to be just, is only to be just. He makes the analogy that such economic justice is like the functionary who does not stay thirty seconds beyond what he is paid for. One is just, indeed one is only just and not more than just, in giving solely what one owes or only what the other is due. He explains that, although justice aspires not to owe anything to anyone and expires in the acquitted charge, charity represents the waxing of infinite duty beyond any finished debt; it is a duty that does not count or measure and believes to have never done enough for his brother, his sister, or the neighbor; it is a duty that never considers itself quits toward those who suffer.[26] To Jankélévitch, then, economic justice reeks of a "dogmatism of 'Satis,'" for, he writes, "that which suffices is insufficient; just enough is not enough, it is too little." In other words, it is necessary to give more in order to have given enough, "because the surplus for this paradoxical arithmetic is just the strictly necessary!"[27]

In Jankélévitch's framework, justice is primarily in charge of abstract and administrative generalities; it aims at anonymous equality, whereas love is for concrete face-to-face situations. Without limits, measure, or self-interest, love attends to the second person, a You, who is favored to the point of imbalance and disequilibrium, that is, to the point of injustice. This other does not entail a vague love of the often empty abstraction called humanity; love is directed at a face; it gazes toward the beloved himself or herself. According to Jankélévitch, the other has a face for us only if it is loved as ipseity,[28] for, he explains, "persons are in effect comparable not by their ipseity, which is incomparable, but by their dentition, their talents, or the angle of their nose."[29] In short, love loves the person for her person and in her person, independent of her appearance, character, or merit. So although justice sees the rights and the works of the other, love loves the personal being of the other. Each side has its risks: Love tends to lose itself and all others in its dedication and responsibility for the second person, the beloved; and justice tends to lose the concrete bodiliness and face of the persons who are represented merely by their rights. Jankélévitch consequently criticizes a justice that lets the neighbor become others (*autrui*), everybody and nobody.[30]

Moreover, the potential blindness of justice to the human, which is always the human singularity of the individual self, according to Jankélévitch, is not incidental to justice because justice is based not on human singularity but on the rational principle of the logos. With her eyes covered and her balancing scales, justice, he asserts, is logos.[31] As Aristotle writes, "We allow only reason [*logos*], not a human being, to be ruler."[32] Justice requires the third-person perspective of objective reason. Jankélévitch recognizes in this conjunction of positive law and reason a concomitant disjunction from the personal relation to the other:

> [Justice] does not address itself to *you*. It is not engaged like true forgiveness in an immediate relation with the person opposite from it, but it is impartial in the manner of the transcendental instance that Aristotle calls *dikaion empsuchon* [for Aristotle, the judge is justice personified, the embodiment of the identification of the king-law, *Ethics* 5.1132a22]. For in order to *decide between* antagonistic truths, it is necessary not *to participate in* any one of them.— However, intellection, like forgiveness, can imply a real communication with the offender and a real transfiguration of the offended person. First, an equitable form of forgiving, a form of forgiving that entails renouncing the optic privilege of the first person, the autistic point of view of philauty [literally, "self-love"], and in a word the egocentrism of the me-for-myself, lacks neither warmth nor generosity. Indeed, the interlocutor of the allocution is no longer called the Other [*L'Autre*], *Alter*, the partner in the immediate tête-à-tête, but the Other [*Autrui*], the Other who is a legion, the Other multiplied infinitely. In spite of his anonymity, this Other of a thousand heads, this hydra of the not-I in the plural, indeed represents, around the I, alterity par excellence. In spite of its indetermination, the Neighbor who is so far away is for the offended and hurt ego a permanent invitation to deflate the tumor of self-esteem and the hypertrophy of passionate susceptibility. . . . In his lucidity, he [the intellectual] draws on courage to treat the other as himself, in treating himself as another. The law of reciprocity, which asks us not to be unilaterally in one single party, and in the case at hand, in the camp of the me, but to be at the same time in one's own camp and that of the other and by surveying the two truths, this law is called Justice. Justice and also Reason. For justice is reasonable as reason is just.[33]

Reason, according to Jankélévitch, ensures that this reciprocity is universal and thus just. He emphasizes the ethical significance of shifting perspectives as far and as much as possible from oneself to that of the other and to others. He is critical, however, of the manner in which the concrete other is abstracted to become one of the others or any other, and of how potentially the blindness of justice does not make one blind to this or that about the person, whether race, creed, wealth, or status, but makes one blind instead to the person himself or herself. He underlines, therefore, that reason and justice constitute one side and one type of morality that is counterbalanced by the asymmetrical and hyperbolic obligation to the other in love.

As is the case in both his treatment of the excuse and his rehabilitation of ressentiment, Jankélévitch is skeptical about whether the reliance on reason ever moves us to act. He inquires, therefore, whether the connection between positive existing laws and justice is set to function as a resolution to the practical dilemma of action. Out of reason alone action is not necessarily compelled. The law, according to Jankélévitch, primarily obligates through its interdictions, that is, through external coercion. Action, he claims, is heterogeneous to the logos and of a wholly other order than deliberative reason. Either one is compelled to act by authority and by law, willingly or not, or one is moved to act by love. Of its own accord, Jankélévitch contends, justice is inoperative and impotent. It requires either power or goodness (*bonté*). Whereas the force of law often merely serves to preserve the existing law and conserve the power dynamic of the status quo, the grace of love and charity is what illuminates the good in justice. And whereas the order of justice tends toward "sterile stagnation," love acts as the "mobility of justice." Being of the instant, love, according to Jankélévitch, represents the principle of movement altogether. Consequently, justice only moves, he writes, because it is already a little loving.[34] Jankélévitch thus detects even in the conservatory capacity of law a trace of creation. It is the trace of originary creation in the ideal being, and it is the infinitesimal creation of the conserving force itself.[35] The instant of love, charity, graciousness, therefore, airs out the stifling interval of justice as the oxygen of equity.[36]

Jankélévitch explains that, like love and charity, forgiveness "is an opening in a closed morality, a type of halo around a strict law."[37] He claims that the supramorality or the logic of superabundance implicit in forgiveness causes the rigorous contours of the law "to become hazy, diffuse, and atmospheric."[38] For the law attempts to appropriate what is superfluous and gratuitous into the order of system and calculation. "The law," Jankélévitch writes, "endeavors to impose its delays and limits on generous illegality. This is how a 'tip' seems to lose its optional, spontaneous character and becomes part of the bill, how little by little gifts become taxes."[39] But this appropriation of law and normative ethics, which regulates giving and the gift, does not entail simply a reduction of grace to the law, for pure forgiveness, as Jankélévitch claims, "infinitely reconstitutes itself outside of contract and beyond the service for which one pays. Unceasingly, law codifies and encompasses the gracious movement of forgiveness. Unceasingly forgiveness escapes beyond the limits where a massive codex claims to contain it."⁴⁰ The infinitude of forgiveness does not merely escape the laws; it continually reconstitutes its heterogeneity to the law.

This hyperethical quality of forgiveness resembles Kierkegaard's "teleological suspension of the ethical," but, for Jankélévitch, this suspension is neither teleological nor so antithetical to the order of law. It is more so, as Paul Ricoeur explains, that the imperative to love or to forgive suspends the ethical and the law, disorienting the laws and parameters of a system of ethics so that they may reoriented.⁴¹ Since forgiveness is of the order of grace, according to Jankélévitch, it is "a principle of mobility and fluidity for the law," which ensures that the law remains pneumatic and approximate.⁴² This ever-renewed reorientation marks the opening of the economy of law that perpetually potentially degenerates into the closed economy of the status quo, self-interest, or self-limitation. Jankélévitch's concern focuses on the potential reduction of justice to the law and the law to formal legality; on missing the relation to the concrete other in the name of all others; and on the complacency of an ethics of good conscience that corrupts inexhaustible duty. It is in this sense that Jankélévitch rhetorically asks, "Is not love more true than the truth and more just than justice?"⁴³

He recognizes, of course, that love, too, is not immune to degeneration, ossification, and sterilization. Love always runs the risk of becoming ontologized or essentialized, like the instant becoming appropriated into and by the interval. Love and forgiveness may, on the one hand, cover latent forms of self-interest; or they may, on the other hand, become all too just and all too reasonable, codified, and legislated. With reference to the Gospels of Luke and Matthew on the love of enemies, Jankélévitch writes,

> There where we were expecting disinterestedness, we suspect an ulterior motive of exchange. To love those who love us, *agapān tous agapōntas,* to detest those who detest us, *misein ton echthron,* to repay each person in kind, as much as he merits it, to give to each person an eye for an eye and a tooth for tooth, or to give each person the same thing back again, this is within reach of those with souls of iron and lead. This is not to go beyond talion justice; it is to give in order to receive, *ina apolabōsin ta isa perisson,* and consequently to lend so that the gift is given back to us.⁴⁴

The gift of love, too, may be regulated by justice, but such just love, Jankélévitch insists, is soulless. One may pursue in the gift of love the utilitarian maxim of exchange: "I give so that you will give" ("*do, ut des*").⁴⁵ Such giving, Jankélévitch interjects, simply transfers the gift like a good, a commodity. Instead, he stipulates that whereas justice asks the question of merit and desert, love is radically indiscriminate in its overflowing exuberance.

Whereas justice maintains the self in its equilibrium of fairness at least as an other of the others, to speak with Levinas, love and forgiveness invoke a selflessness that amounts to a self-forgetfulness. The love of one's enemies is love par excellence, or, as Jankélévitch phrases it, "When love is asymmetrical there is an additional chance that we are dealing with a disinterested lover."[46] Therefore, the love that is least suspect and most pure is "unmotivated love, unmerited love, immutual love."[47] The reciprocity implicit in systems of ethics, societal structures, and justice is thus not simply overruled or canceled out in the spirit of forgiveness and love, nor can love or forgiveness provide the basis of society or law in the sense of becoming the order by which society abides. The order of forgiveness instead challenges reason to think what it cannot appropriate: the spontaneous gift of love, the inversion and conversion beyond calculation, and the unconditioned, undeserved response of one to the other.

Reason can grasp neither the excess of unjustifiable evil nor the grace of forgiveness. In other words, it cannot grasp the event. The order of forgiveness is thus, on the one hand, against reason, against justice, and against ethics, so long as these rest on the view of what one can morally expect from others, make into general or universal rules, or set in stone. As an event that surpasses and surprises the horizon of expectancy, the gift of forgiveness is that which singularly and abundantly gives without hope of return. The order of forgiveness is not, on the other hand, against reason or justice insofar as these can be reoriented toward a more just, more reasonable world and insofar as the economies that tend to curve in on themselves and close the circle can be opened and extended. Beyond all restrictions, the idea of forgiveness enjoins us to think beyond what is expected of us and beyond what we might receive in return(s). It beckons us to think not only beyond ourselves (justice does that too) but also toward the other, for the other.

Jankélévitch interprets the interruption of the interval of justice by the instant of grace as not only the opening of justice but also its fulfillment. For "love itself is the good [*le Bien*]."[48] Love, therefore, represents the intentional fulfillment of justice. Mere correspondence to the law does not distinguish between a justice without conviction and a sincere will of justice.[49] Jankélévitch argues that, although it is possible to unwillingly be just, "love is the will of justice."[50] Consequently, he claims that an act of pure justice would be indiscernible from love.[51] Such an act would be oriented by the good toward the good. Whereas justice is often primarily concerned with the continuation of order, love is the heart of justice. In short, grace constitutes the principle of justice, according to Jankélévitch, which of its own accord demands mere legality. In the name of justice, the order of law is accountable to the moral order of love.

The will that love does so absolutely, without egoism and without hesitation or reservation. The will, Jankélévitch claims, does not will the good as if the good willed would by contagion render good the will itself, which is otherwise neutral and indifferent. It is the manner of willing that makes what is willed good or loved. The adverb, he explains, is much more decisive than the direct object because the intention sanctifies and justifies and purifies conduct. Since he understands love as the intention of benevolence (*bienveillance*), he does not differentiate between the good will and the will of the good.[52] Jankélévitch's association of love with aseity or with the notion of *causa sui* highlights that he is speaking of a practical, not a pathological, love.[53] Pure moral love is not an emotion or a product of subjective affection or appetite; it is not generated by the object, neither by attraction nor by merit; instead, it begins with itself and has its criterion and principle in itself alone.[54]

Love not only fills justice with intentionality and will, according to Jankélévitch, it fulfills the goal of justice, which is peace. Jankélévitch is skeptical that peace may be attained through law or rights, or more precisely, he is skeptical that lasting, much less perpetual, peace may be attained through the systems of law and rights. Such peace, he counters, can result only from a living inspiration or from an intimate conversion to peace and to truth. Social reform remains precarious and fumbling without the reform (Kant would say revolution) of the will, and this conversion of the will is created by love. Whereas systemic transformation may yield an armistice and intermittence to war, the peace created by love is unwavering because it entails a disarmament of the heart which alone is capable of transforming the truce into a perpetual concord and the provisory into the definitive. Love alone, he states, is sufficiently disinterested to guarantee permanent peace. Drawing on the myths of Schelling, Jankélévitch claims that the relation of the grace of love to justice is analogous to the relation of the sacrifice of Christ to Dionysian sacrifices. The latter in each of these pairs must be repeatedly commenced indefinitely, like a therapy, whereas the former in the pair is definitive, one time for all and for all humans.[55] Although the peace afforded by the efforts of justice may be more or less extensive, love alone assumes an intensive duration. For justice, according to Jankélévitch, is largely reactive and negative. It annuls the encroachments, neutralizes trespasses, and levels the distinctions. It reacts against disequilibrium and returns to latency when equilibrium has been reestablished.[56] But in doing so, justice treats only the manifestations of injustice but not its causes. Love and forgiveness, in contrast, extirpate the roots of evil by creating the will to peace.[57] Therefore, it is Jankélévitch's firm belief that justice can only truly declare peace in the face of violence if love is in it.[58]

The will to peace nevertheless remains the will to peace, the will of the absolute, the eternal. It is enough to will it in a moment, Jankélévitch insists, but this will does not entail realization. As belonging to the instant, love consists in the joyous announcing of the advent of peace. Jankélévitch writes, "The miracle is that the instantaneous advent is capable of inaugurating a future, of founding a new life, of instituting new relations among men; the miracle is that an era of peace could outlive the joyous instant."[59] Love, as rebirth and re-creation, "is capable" of founding a new life, and an era of peace "could" outlive the instant. It is the only real possibility for a new age and lasting peace, but it is also without guarantee because it requires the miracle of the instant extending through the interval. Love promises peace, but it must survive its own demise, and even then peace remains dependent on others whom love does not seek to control.

The relation between love and justice in Jankélévitch's thought is manifold. Grace is the founding and the transcending of justice; it is juxtaposed with justice, and it is the critique of justice; it acts to interrupt and rupture the order of law, and it gives life breath to justice, even in the name of justice. This relation is a repetition of the relation between the instant and the interval and exhibits its temporal structure. It also helps clarify Jankélévitch's understanding of the instant and the interval. Following Bergson, Jankélévitch frequently describes their relation as a mixture.[60] The interval, he states, is what makes of the instant the almost-nothing of an instant, whereas the interval is dramatized by the instant. But he also treats these two "orders" as distinct, each as irreducible to the other: the interval as the order of being, the instant as the event of creation. In this respect, Derrida's designation of the relation between the unconditional and the conditional as "heterogeneous and indissociable" seems more appropriate than calling it a mixture. Grace, love, and forgiveness give us to think what both Jankélévitch and Derrida say we cannot know, namely purity and unconditionality. Both purity and unconditionality refer to the idea of the absolute, unconditional, and transcendent. Jankélévitch claims that the exclusive way of approaching the absolute for humans is in the instant.[61] Yet as finite creatures, humans do not abide alone in the intensive coincidence of the absolute and the instant but are bound to the extensive interval of temporality and consciousness. If love, charity, and forgiveness are connected to the instant, the question then arises whether there exists at all a pure love, an unconditional gift, or unconditional forgiveness beyond the flicker of an instant? In other words, is love always and inherently impossible? Or only possible as impure, corrupt, and mixed?

Im/pure Gifts

Jankélévitch's treatise on forgiveness is dedicated to pure forgiveness. But since Nietzsche and Freud, skeptics doubt the possibility of such purity or unconditionality, whether in forgiveness, in love, or in the gift. It is first and foremost with another moral philosopher of purity, however, that Jankélévitch shares an epistemological skepticism, namely Immanuel Kant. Kant maintains that, if a duty is done out of duty but *with* pleasure, then there can be no certainty that the duty has not been fulfilled *for* pleasure. Similarly, Jankélévitch introduces the concept of complacency (*complaisance*), which is the secondary pleasure that one takes in one's own action or feeling. Applied to the intention directed at the other in the act of forgiveness, complacency represents the latent egoism lurking in the selfless gift. Jankélévitch suggests that the primary dimensions of complacency involve the reflection of consciousness and chronological succession.[62] Time and consciousness invoke, without being named, the specters of Bergson and Husserl: time and consciousness and the consciousness of time, that is, consciousness as time or as innately temporal. Although Jankélévitch deals with time and consciousness separately, he is always aware of their intimate connection.

Circumscribing what Jankélévitch calls the "innocence" of the instant of giving are a "foretaste" and an "aftertaste," each marking the assumption of the instant into the interval, that is, into the duration of temporality and consciousness. The foretaste represents the anticipation or prospective and thus parallels Husserl's notion of *protention*. As soon as the intention to give arises, Derrida explains, a symbolic acknowledgment begins that congratulates and gratifies the giver in a self-approval that already entails a payback.[63] Through pleasure in the act of giving, the ego becomes aware of the gift given and aware of itself as the giver of the gift. The pleasure is already the reflective consciousness aware of itself in its immediacy. Even the blink of an eye, Jankélévitch observes, will always have a certain duration, and with a mere breath of consciousness all innocence is lost. For example, the virtuoso pianist who becomes aware of his genius while playing turns into a boor merely mimicking genius and playing himself.[64] In and through duration, Jankélévitch explains, "Consciousness reconstitutes a perimeter of egoism around the point of charity, so a temporality that is retrospective and prospective reintegrates a continuation on both sides of the instant."[65] The gift of forgiveness thus appears on the horizon of consciousness, losing its unexpectedness and its event-character. By taking a place in time, it is or can be expected, anticipated, and recalled. The point or peak of forgiveness, therefore, is always reconstituted into a "state."

Jankélévitch claims, however, that in pure forgiveness, "there is a point, but there is exactly no state."[66] Pure love or pure forgiveness exists only in the flash of an instant, and the giver is unaware of himself in giving. Jankélévitch focuses in particular on the consciousness of one's own goodness or the goodness of one's intention, for in giving the gift or in forgiving, the self cannot be aware of itself doing good; it cannot be conscious of itself as good with the enjoyment and complacency of good conscience that accompanies such self-consciousness. To ensure that the instant of giving is a flashpoint, not a state or even a "peak state," the gift and the giving should be forgotten in the very giving. The one who forgives must forget herself in order to give purely, out of disinterestedness. Such a forgetting has nothing to do with repression or denial; it would have to be an absolute forgetting that absolves, absolutely releases, and unbinds the giving of the gift from the giver.[67] As Jankélévitch explains, as soon as it is a matter of (self-) consciousness, forgiveness is plagued by reservations, afterthoughts, ulterior motives, vanity, self-interest, or an at least infinitesimal amount of remnant ressentiment.[68]

The coincidence of the gift with consciousness is the coincidence of the gift with presence. Jankélévitch thus has the gift disappear in the name of the gift. In order to be a present, the present cannot become present. The possibility of the gift binding the other leads both Jankélévitch and Derrida to posit the disappearing appearance of the gift, such that the gift self-destructs, becomes invisible, or nonexistent. Far from inserting a world between the giver and the given like the child between lovers, as Arendt suggests, the pure gift must tend toward diminished objectivity of the object given, eviscerated sovereignty on the part of the giver, and an absence of binding obligation for the receiver of the gift. Derrida formulates the tension concerning the appearance of the gift as perhaps the "most artful" of the aporias of forgiveness:

> On the one hand, when someone forgives someone else (for example, the worst possible wound, or, still more simply, what may repeat it even perversely, the recall of a wound), well then, one must above all not tell the latter. The other must not hear [*il ne faut pas que l'autre entende*], one must not say, that one forgives, not only in order not to recall the (double) fault but also not to recall or to manifest that something was given (forgiven, given as forgiveness), something was given back again, that deserves some gratitude or risks obligating the one who is forgiven. At bottom, nothing is more vulgar and impolite, even wounding, than to obligate someone by telling them "I forgive you," which implies an "I give you" and already opens a scene of ac-

knowledgment [*reconnaissance*], a transaction of gratitude, a commerce of thanking that destroys the gift. . . . One must therefore say nothing [*il faut donc se taire*], one must say nothing of forgiveness [*il faut taire le pardon*] where it takes place, if it takes place. . . .

But, on the other hand, and inversely, what would a silent forgiveness be, an unperceived forgiveness, an unknown forgiveness, granted unbeknownst to the one receiving it? What would be a forgiveness of which the forgiven one would know nothing? It would no longer be forgiveness. Such silence, in forgiveness, would be as disastrous [*néfaste*] as what silence would have wanted to avoid.[69]

The problem Derrida sharply outlines is the problem of communication. In order that the message of forgiveness "successfully arrives" at the one it is spoken to, there must be a common understanding of the words spoken and/or of the conventions the message presupposes and enacts. There must be, in other words, a shared world, and since there must be some common ground, language seems to be the most common and the most direct.

It is precisely this use of language that makes it tempting to analyze the "performative utterance" of "I forgive you" as a "speech act." John Austin explains that to issue a performative utterance "*is* to perform an action—an action, perhaps, which one could scarcely perform, at least with so much precision, in any other way."[70] This locution belongs to the class of what Austin calls "behabitives," which, he explains, "include the notion of reaction to other people's behavior and fortunes and of attitudes and expressions of attitudes to someone else's past conduct or imminent conduct." In other words, the saying of "I forgive you" to the person who has morally harmed me expresses forgiveness itself. The saying of it does it: With the words, the act takes place. The illocutionary act of performance is in the performed locutionary act, as is the perlocutionary act of communicating to the listener that he is forgiven.[71] There are two advantages to this approach. First, by focusing less on the normative meanings of the concepts invoked, it shows that forgiveness is what it does. Second, spoken words have little materiality. They express an intention with a minimum of objectivity and are perhaps the least distorted and most direct means of communicating something from one presence to another presence. The apparatus of the medium of language is, however, a historically and socially structured complexity. Besides the implicit assumptions that set the stage for forgiveness, namely that (a) a wrong has been done, (b) S is responsible for that wrong, and (c) T was hurt by the wrong done, Austin outlines six general conditions for performative utterances that apply to forgiveness: (1) there must exist an accepted conventional procedure having a certain conventional effect; (2) the particular persons and circumstances in a given case must be appropriate for the invocation of the particular procedure invoked; (3) the procedure must be executed by all participants correctly and (4) completely; (5) sincerity: the person participating in and invoking the procedure must in fact have these thoughts or feelings, and the participant must intend so to conduct himself or herself; and (6) consistency: the participant must actually so conduct himself or herself subsequently.[72] An offense against any of the first four conditions results, according to Austin, in the failure or "misfiring" of the act in question, which means the act is not achieved. If, however, one of the last two conditions is offended, then, although the specific act is achieved, the formula is "abused," and the act is rendered "hollow," "empty," and does not characteristically "take effect."[73] The first four conditions are thus conditions of principle, whereas the latter two are contingent.

Applied specifically to the act of forgiveness, the latter two conditions, especially that of sincerity, are key. The structure of a promise serves Austin as an example of how a speech act can fail regarding these contingent conditions: A promise can be made but not fulfilled due to later developments. With reference to forgiveness, then, the consistency on the part of the one who forgives entails not changing his mind or behaving toward the other as if he still harbored resentment and did not forgive. But the example of a promise, which is more than an example, reveals several drawbacks to the conception of forgiveness solely on the basis of the speech-act theory. The performative utterance of the promise differs from that of forgiveness because forgiveness more essentially involves another person. A promise is made regardless of whether one keeps it and regardless even of whether one intends to keep it; but is a forgiveness that is without heart or sincerity really forgiveness? And is a word of forgiveness really given when it does not reach the other? In this theory, the interpersonal relation is superseded by a conventional effect. The immediate success of forgiveness in this scenario is not dependent on the intention of the one who gives the gift of forgiveness to the other. Rather, the appropriate and correct use of conventional procedure performs the act. But the intention to forgive the other is indispensable to forgiveness, and if missing, it should not be considered a mere abuse of the conventional formula. Despite the right words, the illocutionary act does not constitute forgiveness. In this sense, the utterance's emptiness entails a failure equal to that of a performative misfiring, and the contingent conditions become indistinguishable from or on a par with the principled ones.

This point is related to another one: The speech-act theory of forgiveness is wrapped up with securing a certainty of forgiveness and measuring its success. The conventional regulation of the speech act of forgiveness belies an effort to secure its achievement. But forgiveness is a risk, and its achievement is less than certain and in no way guaranteed by the power of words, as if they performed magic by ritual. In other words, the act of forgiveness is not reducible to the saying of words or to the invocation of a conventional formula. As Thomas Macho states, the instant or the kairos of forgiveness is not disposable; it cannot be codified.[74] To conflate a conventional rule with a spontaneous event is, therefore, to substitute the pneuma of forgiveness with a grammar of forgiveness.

Moreover, this model overlooks the potential abrasiveness of speech in the context of forgiveness. It underestimates the power dynamics and the question of authority. Forgiveness is unlike the performative "I dos" in a marriage ceremony, which receive their binding authority from their reciprocity but also, and more importantly, from the setting in which they are uttered: the presence of an authority, being before a judge or a pastor. As Derrida points out, the assumption of the sovereignty of the "I" which is in position to, or which has been bestowed the right and the power to bestow, to give, and to rescind what "you" have done demonstrates a power over the other that may wound the hearer or incite revolt. Among many innuendoes and implicit messages or misunderstandings, the words of forgiveness may say that, in giving, I take away from you what is yours because it is bad but I am good, so good that I will even do this for someone like you who did something like that. The thematization inherent in the articulation calls to mind for both parties what has transpired. This reminder may be helpful; it may be important, but it can also be harmful and used as a means of causing pain and wielding power.

Sometimes forgiveness is perhaps most aptly and least obtrusively communicated in silence or in an embrace, a wink, or a kiss. Jankélévitch invokes Dostoyevsky's account of the Nazarene responding to the Grand Inquisitor with a kiss. Jankélévitch writes, "The word of grace is often pronounced in silence and has no other commentary than the paradoxical kiss, the unjust and incomprehensible kiss, the scandalous kiss given to the persecutor. But the kiss is not a word, any more than tears are a 'language.' The accolade is much more of a gesture."[75] Whereas Austin maintains that the rules obtain under normal circumstances, Jankélévitch makes clear that the circumstances of forgiveness are always exceptional. The exceptionality of forgiveness makes it an event dependent on the situation and the person. His linking of forgiveness with the event allows for its manifold concrete expression in human life. He recognizes, however, that the more subtle, pointedly poignant, discretely discreet forgiveness is, the more it approaches the almost-nothing character of the instant.

It is on the basis of this almost-nothing character of forgiveness that Jankélévitch claims that forgiveness is both more and less than the gift.[76] It is evidently less than the gift, for, as far as "giving" is concerned, it "gives" nothing. Despite the structural homology between the *gift* and *forgiveness* (or between *don* and *pardon* and *geben* and *vergeben*), there are important distinctions. First of all, forgiveness always has to do with the past, with what has occurred and with what failed to be done.[77] As Jankélévitch reminds us, it is necessary to remember in order to forgive.[78] Second, according to Jankélévitch, forgiveness involves greater "intensity and fervor" on both parts than the gift. This passion entails the sacrifice implied in forgiveness. Although the giver may give generously and not solely from an overabundance, the gift generally concerns only the sacrifice of possessions of the one giving. The gift is typically partitive: One gives part of the whole that one possesses. For Jankélévitch, this difference in passion and sacrifice separates the total gift of forgiving from the partitive gift of offering. As he elucidates:

> The one forgiving has need of all his courage in order to sacrifice not a part of his possessions but his being itself, and even more to brave social taboos, to challenge the duty to punish, and to support himself in so-called moral dilemmas. We will see how the decision to forgive opposes the hyperbolic paradox of a *total gift* to the partitive gesture of giving, otherwise referred to as offering this or that. Aristotle, himself, knew the gift: but only the Bible truly knew forgiveness.[79]

In Jankélévitch's reading, biblical forgiveness invokes the absolute gift, the absoluteness of the gift, the gift of oneself to the other for the other. What he means is that forgiveness gives without being or beyond being, selflessly, literally disinterested. Such unconditionality makes of forgiveness the gift par excellence, the total gift. For it "is a gift without something being given, a *datio* without *donum*." It gives absolutely because it does not give any thing. In fact, it gives by taking, taking away the moral stain of having committed an offense.[80] Stated differently, what forgiveness gives is liberation. As Jankélévitch explains, "It does not confer this or that, does not do this or that, it gives the gift of liberty, that is, itself, to others. Liberty is all deliverance and only deliverance."[81] In other words, forgiveness gives absolutely because it does not give something but is a pure giving, a re-creation.

Since the instant of forgiveness, according to Jankélévitch, cannot be completely isolated from the interval, however, human consciousness envelops the gift of forgiveness, rendering it impure. Since impurity is human, inevitable in the light of the finite temporal structure of human existence, human individuals have the obligation to examine their own intentions for these impurities. Inner consciousness, he observes, should be attentive to the impurity of our love or our gift.[82] As the instant is extended in time, one will always find impurities. This self-critical aspect entails the work of refinement, refining one's own intention and acknowledging that the good remains to do. Having forgiven, the good is not done, and one has not by consequence become good. Such self-critique is a defense against the complacency of good conscience. This work, however, takes place in the interval, but the good itself arises in an indisposable instant when we ourselves do not notice it and naïvely, innocently, know nothing about it.[83] As a result, the work of refinement will never be done, and the good will always escape us.

Following Fénelon and many of the mystics and mystical poets, Jankélévitch claims that whoever loves without thinking about being loved will have recognized the composition of the divinity of love: It is a love on behalf of the other and not a love in order to be loved; it is a unilateral passion: self-forgetful, selfless, and unconditional.[84] To have love or the gift return, in another form at another time, which are essential characteristics of the sociality of gift giving, is to negate the essence of giving and to render it an exchange. The condition of self-forgetting expresses the absence of a sense of obliging the other. The mundane verbal expressions "*de rien*," "*de nada*," "*da nicht für*," "it was nothing," for example, are attempts, once consciousness arises, to deny the presence of the gift, its actuality, and its bindingness. Although they may sometimes be formulated to repress the gift and to avoid the acknowledgment of the receiver, such expressions also de-emphasize one's sacrifice and the impending obligation on the other. Without the hold of memory, the gift disappears and, with it, every obligation: There is nothing that has been given, and no one who has given. But what about the one who receives? What has thus far been outlined has focused on the giver, the lover, and the forgiver, but love, giving, and forgiving all fundamentally involve a relation to the other.

Gratitude and Benevolence

Paul Ricoeur argues both against a commercial form of giving that is motivated by latent interests and against the asymmetry of a gift without any return. He proposes that we must learn how to receive, for it entails the virtue of humility. This reciprocity between giving and receiving, Ricoeur claims, puts an end to the asymmetry of giving without any return.[85] Ricoeur's critique of the overemphasis on the asymmetry of giving serves as an important reminder of how the concentration on the giver and the giving (forgiver and forgiving) tends to overlook the relation, especially the positive relation, of the gift to the one who receives it. Gift giving always involves three: the giver, the gift, and the recipient. With regard to the third term of this triad, Jankélévitch focuses on a response to having been given that exceeds the gift and its spectral compulsion to return, as Marcel Mauss formulates it.[86] Jankélévitch is interested in the way the response of the recipient is occasioned but not compelled or coerced by the gift. Although he emphasizes the virtue of giving and loving without return, he understands that both the gift and love are ultimately fulfilled by a benevolent response: to the gift, gracious gratitude and to love, love.

In *On Benefits*, the Stoic Roman philosopher Seneca offers a double rule for the relation of memory and the gift. "The rule for the giver and receiver of a benefit is, that the one should straightway forget that he has given, the other should never forget that he has received it."[87] These two sides conjoined are also symbolically represented by the divided waters of Mount Purgatory and the portals of Dante's heavenly paradise. According to Dante, the waters of Lethe and the waters of Eunoe share the same source. In other words, forgetting and positive remembrance have a common origin and reciprocally feed each other. Drawing on this image of Dante's, J. E. Erdmann, a student of Hegel's, remarks that, in forgiveness, the forgetting of the misdeed is simultaneously the forgetting of one's self. The one who forgives forgets herself in forgiving and the guilt or indebtedness of the other toward her. This forgetting brings forth and encounters the remembrance of the offender. Thus the forgetting does not wipe out all traces of the misdeed or the trace of forgiveness. Instead, the forgetting of the forgiver quickens the memory of the one forgiven.[88] Klaus Kodalle comments that, in the spirit of forgiveness, forgetting leaves a trace that engrains itself in the complex of the *conditio humana* insofar as the perpetrator is mindful of the forgiver's forgetting.[89]

Far from a simple reversal of the asymmetrical and power positions, forgiveness creates through such a dialectic a new bond of love that opens up the paths of communication and ways to encounter each other. Granted, this forgiveness always implies an indebtedness of the one to the other, but it is ideally a debt without weight, a debt conjoined with a freedom in both the self-relation and in the relation to the other. Erdmann explains:

> Where the one speaks: since you have forgiven me of this and forgotten, I will eternally remember you, and the other is continually brought to new forgiveness on account of the fact that the friend or beloved remembers what he had already long forgotten. At this point,

remembrance is ignited by the forgetting, the forgetting by the remembrance, and one has the experience that in human contact, there are moments in which the letting oneself be forgiven (to be absolved) is the highest enjoyment, and thus one's own debt becomes the means to the sweetest and holiest pleasure.[90]

In this *felix culpa*, the sweetest and holiest pleasure accompanies being forgiven because the memory is of having been forgiven, and the present is lived as one forgiven. Forgiveness is here infinitely repetitive, not because of the impotence of the one who forgives but because it is repeatedly occasioned by the memory of the one forgiven. The remission of debt potentially creates a new relation to the one who releases the debtor of the servitude and oppression of his debt.

Jankélévitch, too, tells that "joy is in liberation more than in liberty, in the passage from pain to health more than in health itself."[91] Joy, in other words, belongs for Jankélévitch to the instant: It is the joy of the *felix culpa*. This thought echoes the New Testament emphasis on the greater joy in heaven over a repentant tax collector than over ninety-nine just persons.[92] It states that the one who owed much and whose debt is remitted is the one who loves the most.[93] Conversion turns debt into love. The biblical verse does not say that the woman of disrepute who anointed Jesus feels the most indebted but rather that she is the one who loves most. Jankélévitch takes as his paradigm the story of the prodigal son: "But the model son, having known neither perdition, nor temptations, nor the Wily Women [Prokofiev], will not know joy either, joy reserved for those who have rebounded from nonbeing into being. . . . Forgiveness announces a rebirth or, better yet, a new birth. . . . An inalienable richness forever distinguishes the prodigal son from the stay-at-home son."[94]

The response of memory on the part of the one forgiven is a form of gratitude. Gratitude is, in this sense, the act of remembrance that one has been given or forgiven. Jankélévitch distinguishes, however, between a gratitude for the gift and a gratitude to the person. This distinction contains, for him, the difference between the simple remission or repayment of debt and graciousness. "Gracious gratitude," he writes, "is addressed to the benefactor beyond the beneficence; if it simply said thank you for the gift, then it would be nothing more than a symbolic and conventional manner of being debt-free and a way of repaying the debt, not by giving back the sum itself, but by pronouncing a ritual, magic word. Gratitude would then be a simple appendix to justice."[95] As long as the saying of "thank you" refers to the gift, he considers it an equivalent good: The giving, the gift, and the return of thanks constitute links in an economic exchange. If one person pays for dinner or drinks of another, for example, the one who has been treated might say in German or French, "Ich möchte mich gerne bei Dir revangieren," or "je te revaudrai ça," which means that one would like to "repay the favor in kind" or, more literally, to "take revenge" for what one has been given in order to "even the score." In English, one might make the promise of future returns by saying, "I'll get you later" or "I'll pay you back next time," which, like the other phrases, can be used as a form of threat or as a word of thanks, depending on the person and situation. This game of equivalence and linguistic equivocalness gives Nietzsche occasion to claim that gratitude is indeed a form of revenge.[96]

In contrast, Jankélévitch suggests that gratitude can also manifest graciousness, which does not merely entail a symmetrical relation of equivalence or justice. He claims that it involves rather an intensification. In returning good for good, "it is gracious justice or just grace, just charity."[97] Accordingly, gracious recognition of the other is not oriented by the object received; it does not repay in kind, return what is merited, or seek to equalize the debt. Instead, it exhibits the *perisson* or unmerited "in addition" toward the other: It demonstrates the character of grace. The grace of gratitude does not consist in giving what is owed but of giving precisely that which one is not and cannot be required to give in accordance with the given gift.

Just as forgiveness requires the misdeed, gratitude requires the good deed, and like forgiveness, gratitude moves from the act that occasions it to the ipseity of the agent. As Jankélévitch explains:

> Gratitude aims at the being of the person beyond the having, at the ipseity of the donor beyond the given thing. Open to an infinite horizon, gratitude is the equal not only of a benefit, nor only of a beneficence, but of a benevolence for which there exists no quietus; for the beneficiary of a kindness that nothing exhausts or compensates, such a beneficiary is an eternal debtor.[98]

The equality of gratitude and benevolence can consequently be only a matter of the will or the intention. As Seneca wrote long before Jankélévitch, "Neither gold, nor silver, nor any of those things which are most highly esteemed, are benefits, but the benefit lies in the goodwill of him who gives them."[99] Gratitude, Jankélévitch claims, is infinite because the good will of the benefactor in the instant of giving is infinite and because gratitude aims at the other who is both the direct object of its intention and the one who remains future as the figure of duty. It is, therefore, not a measured equality that obtains between benevolence and gratitude but an equality of immeasurables, not bounded by causality or social norms and beyond the logos of equivalence, measure, and reason. The good will of the giver is responded to by the good will of the recipient. The free response of forgiveness to the misdeed is freely responded to in gracious gratitude. Both represent, for Jankélévitch, the infinity and inexhaustibility of the good will directed at the other; both, therefore, represent the duty to love the other. In the light of the misdeed, forgiveness then is the concrete, historical response of love, and gratitude is the manner of love to respond to this response of love that responds to ill will. It is alone this will that is good: The will that is giving, that is gracious, that is benevolent, that is love.

Dissonances of Love

Jankélévitch's focus on benevolence, whether in forgiveness or gratitude, underscores three correlated aspects of his idea of forgiveness: its directedness at the personhood of the other, its superrationality, and its noneconomic character. Since he describes forgiveness as a gift that gives without something being given, a *datio* without *donum*, it is nothing less and nothing more than the liberating good will extended from the one to the other.[100] The object that calls for equivalence or even for a greater gift in return does not mediate the relation of the one to the other. Forgiveness represents a greater transcendence of the logic of likeness and desert than gratitude because, instead of returning good for good, it renders, in a chiastic crossing, good for evil. In both of these senses, forgiveness is the purest gift. In giving nothing but liberation, nothing but love, forgiveness illustrates a threshold of overcoming that is absent in the return of good for good or love for love.

For Jankélévitch, forgiveness is foreign to the logic of rationality. The love for the person who is most difficult to love cannot be a love *because* or a love *despite*. Jankélévitch observes that forgiveness is often conjoined to the preposition *despite*, as in the sense that one forgives despite the other's wickedness. Since forgiveness is attached to the creative instant of intuition and the instant carries over into and is absorbed by the interval of duration and reason, it inevitably happens that reasons are found and given for forgiveness. Jankélévitch depicts this relation between the instant and the interval and between forgiveness and reason as follows: "Love, solicited to say why it loves (as if it were necessary that there be a why!), looks into itself and naturally finds for itself, right away, some becauses.... And likewise, impulsive forgiveness ... finds reasons for excusing what it was wholly disposed to forgive without reason." One's willingness to give reasons demonstrates how rationality attempts to reappropriate for itself the event that supersedes it. "For no thinking being," Jankélévitch explains, "either willingly admits to an unmotivated and undeliberated decision or renounces the exercise of reasoning." These "good reasons" for having acted with generosity beyond the justificatory bounds of reason, however, are "more or less retrospective."[101] The reasons come after. They legitimate before the tribunal of reason the free act that precedes them. And "who knows," Jankélévitch asks, "if such and such an unknown circumstance will not justify a forgiveness which, for the instant, is unjustified, illegitimate, and unreasonable, but which tomorrow will be reasonable, legitimate, and justified?"[102] He thus introduces the dialectic of the instant and the interval into the dialectic between the groundlessness of forgiveness and the ground of reason. For forgiveness does not take up, on Jankélévitch's account, a rebellious, spiteful attitude toward reason, proclaiming "all the less reason, all the more reason." Such an inversion of reason constitutes a counterreason, which simply follows the reverse logic of reason. As the mere inversion of rationality, the irrationalism of a "philosophy of *reason without reasons*" does not reflect the suprarationalism of forgiveness.[103] In other words, the negative aspect of reasonlessness cannot account for the positivity of forgiveness. The grace of forgiveness is beyond reason.

Because forgiveness extends beyond reason, Jankélévitch denies that the guilty person has any claim on the offended to be forgiven. He insists that the "right to forgiveness" is a contradiction, hardly less absurd than a "right to grace."[104] Since forgiveness engages precisely the inexcusable misdeed, it loves that which one should morally resent. Therefore, it is not *because* of the innocence or lovableness of the ill-willed neighbor that he or she is forgiven. Nor can the *because* be a *because* of his or her guilt, for loving because of guilt would be a perverse love, a love that loves the detestable because it is detestable, a sadism that sections off wickedness in order to love it.[105] Although forgiveness does not shy away from scandal, and Jankélévitch at times overeagerly embraces that fact, he is aware that forgiveness is not scandalous in order to be scandalous. Like Paul, Pascal, and Kierkegaard, who emphasize the profundity of faith in its very folly and absurdity, Jankélévitch claims that to forgive is not to forgive *because* it is absurd, but that does not necessarily mean that forgiveness forgives *despite* the wickedness of the other.

In the "even if" of every "despite," Jankélévitch uncovers the structure of symmetry and justice. To forgive "notwithstanding the obstacle" tacitly implies the structure of *because*. Jankélévitch discloses that "to plead for a forgiveness-despite is tacitly to suppose that a forgiveness that is granted to the innocent person is alone normal and natural and alone goes without saying."[106] He adds that "when we profess love for someone, *even if* it is someone detestable, *even if* he is odious, *despite* his stupidity and wickedness, we indirectly suggest this: the detestable person is normally worthy of hatred, and consequently, by right, the lovable person alone deserves to inspire love."[107] Thus, the latent structure of "even if—because" underlying the unmerited love of the "despite" validates a hierarchical order of values as well as the order of symmetry and reciprocity. As such, it is merely a "homage to common sense."[108] Although the forgiveness-despite upholds the unlovableness of the other, it makes a concession to forgive the other. In its defiance and commitment to the other person, it resembles an unshakable fidelity, but Jankélévitch exposes that such love is full of reproaches for its obstacles and is consequently strained. It too easily tends to love reluctantly, begrudgingly, and unwillingly. He even calls it a "bad grace" for the contorted and sullen violence it does to itself.[109] Therefore, the heart Jankélévitch found lacking in the counterfeit forms of similiforgiveness is also missing from a forgiveness-despite. A forgiveness-despite would signify forgiving ill will against one's better judgment and with a heavy heart.

Although Arendt conceives of forgiveness on the basis of respect and not of love, she recognizes in love what Jankélévitch means by the *causa sui* that transcends reasons and aims at the personhood of the other. She writes:

> For love possesses an unequaled power of self-revelation and an unequaled clarity of vision for the disclosure of *who*, precisely because it is unconcerned to the point of total unworldliness with what the loved person may be, with his qualities and shortcomings no less than with his achievements, failings, and transgressions. Love, by reason of its passion destroys the in-between which relates us to and separates us from others.[110]

Neither love nor forgiveness is thus a matter of desert. "One may deserve an excuse," Derrida acknowledges, "but ought not forgiveness be accorded without regard to worthiness?"[111]

Beginning with itself and having its ground in its own act, pure love, according to Jankélévitch, is infinite, other-oriented, and self-forgetful. Without a reason to love, pure love establishes the value of the beloved by loving. It is not the worthiness of the other that attracts love, but rather love that makes the other worthy of love. Such pure love finds its necessary and sufficient ground in its absurdity, which is simultaneously its absoluteness, or what Jankélévitch calls its aseity. The person who loves hyperbolically demonstrates the purity of his love by loving those who hate him. This love for the one who hates is the test of the asymmetrical, unilateral character of a love that does not seek a reward, compensation, or even a cup of love in return. It is not strategic or teleological; rather it loves the other for the other, on his behalf, and for his sake, not for anything that it might receive from the beloved or by loving.

At the same time, Jankélévitch does not hesitate to claim that there is no true love without reciprocity. He believes that something is missing from such one-sided love, namely the response of the other, the revealing flow of the back and forth and the possibility of growth through this movement. It is thus *reciprocal love* or the justice in love, not *possessive love*, that he contrasts with *ecstatic love* in which the one loses oneself in the other. In mutual love, one loves and is loved; one is thrown back on oneself by the other when the looks cross and one is seen in seeing, seeing while being seen.[112] Jankélévitch describes how the passive and active sides of love amplify and inspire each other and how their doubled current creates a flowing exchange so that the one cannot lose himself in infinity but is braced by the embrace of the other and by the movement of his opposite love.[113] It is in this mutual love that the I receives itself back from the other. This reciprocity is consequently not a matter of rights. In the words of Theodor Adorno, "The mystery of justice in love" consists in the claiming *and* suspending of the right to be loved that does and does not belong to me.[114]

Jankélévitch acknowledges how ecstatic love challenges the comfort of reciprocity and symmetry. He therefore concludes that the one-sidedness of unrequited love and the reciprocity of loving and being loved form two constitutive poles of love. The one is not more truly love than the other. Both are true; both belong to love, which is torn between a pure love without return and a mutual love of reciprocity. It is one and the same love, he claims, taut in the oscillation between two sides:

> Why wouldn't the groundless love not warm itself on reciprocity, be carried along and illuminated by it since it did not expressly demand this reciprocity as a reward? Every one of us feels in his or her heart this oscillation between the poles of mutual love and of unrequited love; but this does not mean that one has to decide absolutely between the one and the other love, the one that holds us back in the stillness without promise and in the expectation without recompense and the one that lets us laugh and sing out of love: love does not claim to be coherent; coherence has no more meaning in love than in music! Love itself is torn, the logic of passion therefore accepts ambivalence. What am I saying? The contradiction is often more of a paradoxical nourishment of love than an obstacle to love . . . for

these two sides of love, between which we do not cease to oscillate, are like systole and diastole; it is their alternation that regulates the vital pulsation, and it is its rhythm that our heart beats.[115]

This oscillation characterizes the lifeblood of love. It does not allow love to become static or calculating, on the one hand, or feverish and sacrificial, on the other hand. The ambivalence of love combines stability and creativity, a dynamic that nurtures love, like life, as opposed to hindering it. It renders love human, removed from the pure giving, selflessness, and unilaterality of divine creative love. Love need not be unconditional, though that remains an ideal within it. At the same time, it cannot be reduced to the conditions of *do, ut des* (I give in order that you may give). What Seneca wrote about the giver of benefits thus applies to Jankélévitch's conception of a love torn between asymmetry and reciprocity: "The best man is he who gives readily, never asks for any return, and is delighted when the return is made, because, having really and truly forgotten what he gave, he receives it as though it were a present."[116] In this scenario, the lover loves not to be loved, *and* love finds its calling in the echo of love by the other. This echo is not a copy or reflection of one's own love, as if it were the cause or origin of it; rather, it is the initiative response of the other to which one's own love is also a response. Being loved and loving are, therefore, both original acts of the self and responses to the other.

Even here, though, Jankélévitch reserves a primacy for the instant over the interval. Love does not exist per se; it does not have its place in being. Jankélévitch states that one cannot both love and be; one must choose between the hard winter of being without love and the death in spring of love without being. He claims that love is simultaneously nothing and everything. Like freedom and God and the I-know-not-what of creation sensed in intuition, love is a mystery, an almost-nothing. Jankélévitch admits that love, like music, philosophy, and moments of joy, may not be necessary and one can live without it, but, he adds, not so well. As the falling together of the subject and object in the instant of positing the beloved in the reposition of creation, love is not extended from the instant to the interval but must continually be repeated, reiterated, recharged, and renewed, that is, rediscovered, or re-created. One does not have love or have lovers or beloved. Love is not a belonging or a thing or a feeling. Though frequently claimed, one is not even ever really *in* love as if love were a residence, a resting place, a Taj Mahal. Even beyond having, love is not a state of being. As a creature, in contrast to the creator, one *is* not love, and one's being is not filled with love. Jankélévitch claims that it is quite the opposite: The more there is love, the less there is being; the more being, the less love.[117] Love is therefore not a self-sufficient and, once inaugurated, automated condition. Rather, love is an act, an act that, according to Jankélévitch, always has at least a trace of purity as a pure act beyond having and beyond being. Consequently, love cannot be proved; it cannot be demonstrated either by goods or by gifts; it cannot be possessed or sure of itself; it is not self-evident like being. One loves, and, if one is so fortunate, one is loved.

Throughout his treatises on love, forgiveness, and justice, the notions of tension, paradox, and oscillation appear as recurring themes: The relation of love, he contends, is torn; between love and justice there exists a dissonance that confronts us with a choice between absolutes or between two goods; between love and wickedness there is an oscillation of two truths that infinitely contradict each other. Jankélévitch is torn between these two contradictory beliefs: He believes "in the immensity of forgiveness, in its supernaturality," on the one hand, and "in wickedness," on the other hand. It is not only a matter of belief, or of his personal belief. These separate but intertwined themes circumscribe Jankélévitch's anthropology. He grasps the *conditio humana,* especially in modernity, as dissonance itself. He does not deem it possible to hold in a single mind, a single position, or under a single flag what one loves and what one respects. No, he claims, the heaven of values itself is torn.[118] Dissonance has replaced the vision of harmony from Plato to Leibniz. The world is at odds with itself. Time, as Hamlet proclaims, "is out of joint," and existence is beset with insoluble paradoxes and aporias.[119] Jankélévitch conceives of human morality and existence in the tension between poles of duty and within contradictions. Instead of covering up or attempting to synthesize or harmonize these dissonances in morality, he accepts the ambiguities, paradoxes, and aporias of morality and therewith the singular and ceaseless responsibility of negotiating among them.

Normative Ideal or Impossibility?

Jankélévitch concedes that "it is very possible that a forgiveness free from any ulterior motive has never been granted here below."[120] From the opening sentence of his treatise on forgiveness, he, therefore, accords forgiveness the status of duty. Precisely because forgiveness is not rightly in the indicative, he explains, it is only in the imperative.[121] This duty to forgive forms the normative ideal of forgiveness, the counter-to-nature gesture that responds to violence with grace.

When Jankélévitch declares that, as an event, pure forgiveness has perhaps never occurred in the history of humanity, he indicates that pure forgiveness is not a phenomenon in the world; it does not exist, nor does it appear. It is an event linked to the instant that is always absorbed by the duration in both directions: from consciousness of the past to a consciousness of the future. Does this mean that pure forgiveness has not occurred in history because it *cannot* occur or because of some practical, circumstantial, or semistructural reason?

Since Jankélévitch conceives of forgiveness on the basis of the will, his understanding of the will implies possibility, an "I can," for to will is to be able to. Consequently, to will forgiveness is to will what is possible, what one theoretically can do. "If our will is infinite," Jankélévitch observes, "then our ability in this sense is no less." From this perspective, he draws a Kantian conclusion important for morality. "If the good will wills what is good," Jankélévitch declares, "it can do it; and, consequently, the good is something that everyone can do on the condition of willing it. For the good is precisely something that it is necessary to do! From this we conclude that one can always do that which one should do if one sincerely wills it." Thus our ability to do something depends on our will, and "in order to will," he explains, "it suffices to will." Freedom is therefore intimately bound to responsibility because "the will to will, infinitely, depends only on our liberty, and it rests on an instant."[122]

Jankélévitch thus situates his conception of pure forgiveness in the realm of human possibility, and he frowns on the alternative adherence to an impossible purism. He is aware of the way such moral rigor ultimately furnishes all kinds of excuses, pretexts, or perversions and ends up, in its extremism, leading to demoralization.[123] He feels that talk of a forgiveness that is structurally impossible and beyond human strength would mimic an empty, and potentially derisory, chatter that does not present the agent with a truly serious option and cannot truly represent moral integrity.

This, however, is just one side. Although Jankélévitch acknowledges that our capacities are limited and finite, he suggests we "ignore this and act as if we were capable of doing all that we will."[124] Still, why should we hold steadfast to what is possibly an illusion? While underlining the temporal quality of the instant, Jankélévitch reconstructs Kant's "regulative idea." He explains:

> It suffices that the possibility of pure forgiveness is conceivable; even if it has never been attained in fact, the limit of pure forgiveness would still designate our duty for us, would determine and orient our efforts, would furnish a criterion for permitting us to distinguish the pure and the impure, and would give a standard of measure to evaluation and a direction to charity. The one who never attains the ideal

(the ideal being made precisely for never being attained) can get infinitely nearer to it.... To say that the forgiveness-limit is the horizon of an infinite quest or that immediate proximity is the ideal of an asymptotic approximation or of an endless approximation comes back to admitting implicitly the possibility of a quick-as-lightning encounter with pure innocence.... Forgiveness is not a tangible thing, but it is not an unreachable ideal either.[125]

Outside of and beyond empirical and conceptual categories, the idea of forgiveness constitutes, for Jankélévitch, a normative ideal. It gives us to think what pure forgiveness is, but the ideal is an idea based on the tangential, asymptotic character of intuition, not a concept of knowledge. The criterion or a measure is the unconditional itself or purity. This purity can be approached only negatively: There is no objective, positive, or linear "progress" toward the ideal.[126] As he explains, "The unapproachable excludes all approximation."[127] Since the constitution of intuition is the appearing-disappearing spark of the instant, it is nondiscursive and leaves no time for extensive, temporal consciousness to acquire knowledge of the inspired intuition in which forgiveness is given. Consciousness always comes too late.

Moreover, the intuitive instants, as Jankélévitch conceives of them, are drastic and incisive, that is, discontinuous renewals of each other. Intuitions cannot be accumulated, neither in a treasure chest of mystical experience nor as a series on a continuous, progressive line. As a consequence, Jankélévitch suggests that one cannot successively get better and better at forgiving or build up a store of forgiveness until one finally and ultimately reaches pure forgiveness. Although each act of forgiveness does the same, each differs from the last and differs from the other acts by other people in different contexts as distinct instances of intuitive inspiration.[128] The negatives of negative philosophy, however, may serve to dispose the mind to the state of grace, or to conversion, which alone allows access to the wholly other of creation, to the pure act or innocence. Jankélévitch explains that "after the gradual cleansing, there comes gracious purification which alone is the true catharsis and the sole effective conversion of the entire soul. This conversion is the intuition."[129]

Between absolute unreachability and the extensive contact requisite for comprehension, Jankélévitch posits "instantaneous tangency.... Tangency but not touch!"[130] He depicts the limit of forgiveness as a horizon, which, on our approach, incessantly recedes. Although it orients us, it is not made to be realized.[131] It is thus with neither a pessimistic nor an optimistic emphasis that Jankélévitch defines pure forgiveness as an "ideal limit" or an "inaccessible horizon," possible only because the instant is not nothing. Yet the instant of forgiveness is not utterly disposable or readily available to us, and it inevitably does not remain. There is not even time enough for the "I can" inherent in the act of will to unfold its capacity. Rather, "the grace of forgiveness and of selfless love," Jankélévitch says, "is *granted to us* in an instant and as a disappearing appearance . . . at the same moment it is found and lost again."[132] "I" forgive, but forgiveness is not mine, not my own, nor my possession that I subsequently impart to the other. It is my freedom to will to forgive, to intend to forgive, but it is not by the assertion of the power of my will that I am able to forgive. "Intentional purity is not an adjectival property of the subject," Jankélévitch explains; "it is an event, an occurrence that is the contrary to a thing."[133] Alain Gouhier explicates further that the subject of forgiveness is an "I pure of all egocentricism" because "the pure interiority of love is the source of forgiveness." The most true I, he concludes, is the one who forgives as an act that will never return to it: This "I is love."[134]

But I am not love; I am not pure; I am not absolute. I am a finite being. Consciousness is reflexive, and the will has a direction and therewith duration. It is projective and retentive, inescapably bound to consciousness, self-reflection, and chronology. To say that projective and retentive consciousness haunt both sides of the instant is already to make of the point a peak, to enter into language, commonality, and understandability. The instant, according to Jankélévitch, marks the limit of language, which utilizes the idealizations of being: Language belongs to the interval. His apophatic method is thus not a luxury.

> It is impossible to have a discourse on the ineffable, inexplicable, and indescribable instant that is wholly contained in the pure quoddity of the word *grace*. For grace, which is the spark and fluttering of the eyelids, says nothing, or better yet, says one single word, and this monosyllable of grace seems itself to be in the image of a fine point that is without thickness, just as it is in the image of a punctual instant that is without an interval.[135]

"Almost nothing [*presque rien*]," the instant of intuition, as Jankélévitch suggests, cannot be continued, just as a spark cannot be captured in a bottle. One brushes against the limit of pure love, which lasts but for an instant as a spark that lights up as it goes out and is I-know-not-what. The event, he summarizes, is purely its coming to pass.[136]

The imperative to forgive, like all moral imperatives, according to Jankélévitch, is thus irreal and not relative to our interest but oppositional to the self-concentricity of our ego. He therefore resists what he sees as the common temptation to conflate morality with existence and make of it a catalogue of articles, a codex of prescriptions, or a refinement of societal mores. Jankélévitch's ethics is rather a hyperbolic value-ethics because it requires the orientation of moral action toward the absolute or toward the unconditionality of ideas such as pure love and forgiveness.[137] Morality, for Jankélévitch, thus concerns the human being essentially and wholly, but the human being as human being is committed to or obliged by an absolute to which he or she, as a human being, cannot correspond.[138] It is categorical and a source of continual bad conscience: first, because forgiveness cannot be achieved or accomplished. It does not and cannot exist in the world; second, because the imperative to forgive leads us to aporias within morality, to the "sporadicity" (*sporadisme*) of values, to an insurmountable conflict of duties within a torn sky.[139]

Jankélévitch characterizes human beings as mixed beings, or beings of mixture, belonging to both the interval and the instant. He interprets ambiguous human existence as consisting in being caught between nostalgia and vocation; between the vocation of the instant, which is the doing without being (*faire-sans-être*), and the nostalgia of the interval, which is the complacency of being without doing (*l'être-sans faire*).[140] In morality, humans are called by the absolute to the absolute, which is not reconcilable with human existence or with existence in general. The absolute or unconditional "exists" only as fulguration itself: a disappearing appearance, "a fugitive spark, a spark brévissime."[141] The creature never becomes identical with the absolute; he never completely transcends his finitude. "When he gives or forgives," Jankélévitch writes, "the disinterested human being transcends the naturalness of his passions and the mercenariness of his egoism, but he does not transcend his condition as a finite creature subject to general determinism and to the laws of trophic existence."[142] In other words, there is transcendence and self-transcendence, but it is pointed like an apogee and cannot be made a center. The oscillation of the interval and the instant constitute human temporality. The interval prevents the spark from becoming an eternal truth and the intuition from becoming inexpugnable knowledge. The instant prevents the deep, dogmatic sleep of complacency, intermittently reanimating human beings, reminding them of their relative divinity.[143]

Pure forgiveness, for Jankélévitch, is the limit-concept of human capacity. The limit includes and excludes. It is tangential. He claims that "the limit of human possibilities coincides with the superhuman, with inhumane impossibility."[144] The coincidence with the absolute of the relative, finite, and corrupted is thus an "impossible possibility" or the "possibility-flash [*possibilité-éclair*] of the impossible" given to humans in the suprahuman sublimity of the instant.[145] But only in the instant as the event of tangency with the absolute. Pure forgiveness is consequently never accomplished; it has never been done, nor will it ever be done in the past perfect tense; it does not mark a possession of virtue or serve as a source of good conscience. It is not a perfection that we have become or a habit we have cultivated. The good will is called on to act and not to be its own witness. The ideal quickens in us desire—a desire inflamed by the gift of the instant and the impoverishment of bad conscience, a desire for creation that refuses complacency. In this sense, the idea of forgiveness, although aporetic, is inspiring; or perhaps it is inspiring because it is aporetic.[146] It serves as an ideal limit like "an impossible Fénelonian pure love," but it is an ideal that we can approach only asymptotically.[147] Even if always appearing in its corrupted, conditioned, or approximate forms, the idea of the forgiveness-limit, Jankélévitch insists, "comes back to admitting implicitly the possibility of a quick-as lightning encounter with pure innocence."[148] We (only) "glimpse [*entrevision*]" the absolute in the instant of intuition, Jankélévitch says, and forgiveness is at the limits of human strength: It represents both the highest possibility and the impossibility of passage beyond—impossible possibility in the grace of the instant and at the limits of human strength.

Repentance
Concerning Unconditionality

Our contemporary conception of repentance is inherited from a broad and multifaceted lineage, both theological and philosophical. It is Jewish, Christian, and Islamic and thus Hebrew, Greek, and Arabic, with, as Derrida emphasizes, a strong Christian Latin imprint.[1] The multiplicities of histories and their marks on language can be read from the translations of the word *repentance* itself. The Hebrew word for repentance, *teshuva,* means "to return" and has its Greek cognates in *strephein* and *epistrephein.* The Greek term that is most commonly used in ancient philosophy and in the New Testament to designate repentance, however, is *metanoia,* which means "to change one's mind."

In contrast to its raised significance within a theological setting, repentance has been tendentially dismissed by philosophy because of the prevailing interpretation of it as a feeling, not an act. The Jews who translated the Hebrew Bible into Greek made the choice to use *metanoein* to translate the verb *niham,* "to be sorry, to be moved to pity, have regret," instead of the verb *sub,* "to turn" (from *teshuva*).[2] *Metanoia* and its cognates and relations, like *metameleia,* have often been translated as *regret.* Even today, from the courts to the streets, repentance is often used synonymously with notions like regret or remorse. Many moral theories recognize, however, a connection between emotion and action. The feeling of remorse or compunction, for example, signals the registration of wrongdoing in the conscience, and action, like compensation and dedication to betterment, is moved by this feeling. Frequently, this unity of steps to personal recovery and interpersonal reconciliation is separated into disparate phenomena.

The separation of the feeling of remorse from the action it inspires further implies a separation of temporal vectors: in one direction toward the past, in the other toward the future. Does repentance, then, primarily aim at the past or the future? The Latin root of the English word *repentance*, *repedere*, indicates a future orientation in its meaning to repay, reciprocate, replace, recompense, or make good. In Vladimir Jankélévitch's critical perspective, this understanding of repentance entails the work of future acts that seek to remove the consequences of the offense or the stain of the misdeed. From the interpretation of repentance as directed at the past, two distinct conceptions emerge. Insofar as the past is viewed as having fallen into the category of necessity, it represents the sorrow at having committed an offense that one cannot undo precisely because it is past. This predominant view in the history of philosophy sees the feeling of remorse either as a springboard for future betterment (e.g., Aristotle) or as a sign of impotence, which is, at best, morally ambiguous (e.g., Spinoza and Nietzsche). The other view of repentance regards the past as reparable and open, at least in its meaning, witnessing in the repented misdeed a potential transformation of the entire self.[3]

The question of temporality is thus paramount in a reconstruction of repentance, as is the question of sociality. Is repentance monological as the predominant Greek philosophical conception of *metanoia* maintains? Or is repentance fundamentally dialogical? In a theological framework, repentance does not merely concern the individual moral self; it may involve the intertwinement with others, past and future, but it always requires the response of the other. Repentance is considered the task of the offender within the dialogue of forgiveness. In relation to God, the turn of repentance is always a re-turn because the original, good relation of humans to God established in creation and covenant has been ruptured by the human estrangement from God in sin. Parallel to the relation to God, the repentance of an offense done to another person is conceived as a turn or a return to the offended. As such, repentance may be interpreted as a revisionary practice that repairs damaged or broken relations.[4] This interpersonal act is missing in Greek conceptions of *metanoia* and its heritage at least through Kant, who spoke of repentance as a *revolution* required to reorient one's maxims from "radical evil" to the moral law.[5] The primarily monological or dialogical character of repentance dictates whether it resembles more the quest for self-salvation or a *symbolon* awaiting its complementary piece, the peace of forgiveness.[6]

As revisionary practice, repentance is a phenomenon that gets at the heart of both the Psalmist's and Kant's question: What is the human? (Ps. 8:4).

It is concerned with freedom, memory, and power. Can one liberate oneself from the guilt of the past? Can one, may one, or must one be liberated by an other? In other words, is my redemption in my own hands, or am I delivered over in some way to the other toward whom I am guilty? What are the limits of responsibility for oneself and for the other? Repentance thus treats the Kantian questions about the human, namely, *what ought I do?* especially in the light of what I have done; *what can I know?* especially regarding my intentions toward the other, my motivations for change, and my awareness of the consequences of action; and *for what may I hope?* especially with a view to future relations with self and others.

The questions concerning the temporality and the sociality of repentance coalesce in the question of unconditionality. This question informs the divide between Jankélévitch and Derrida. Jankélévitch believes that nothing is impossible for forgiveness, yet he seems to insist on the precondition of repentance so that forgiveness is not made a "simple buffoonery."[7] In contrast, Derrida maintains that forgiveness is only forgiveness when it is unconditional, without or before repentance. Derrida's critique of Jankélévitch focuses on the latter's supposed reduction of forgiveness to an exchange: The one returns forgiveness for the other's having repented. But it is not the perspectives of Derrida and Jankélévitch alone that diverge on the issue of conditionality or unconditionality. The Abrahamic traditions themselves, which inspire their respective ideas of forgiveness, differ on whether forgiveness first requires repentance. On this point, Judaism, Christianity, and Islam are not pitted against each other. Rather, a conflict wages within these traditions between the logic of conditionality and the logic of unconditionality.

Repentance, therefore, should be regarded both within the context of the monotheistic religious traditions and as a moral philosophical phenomenon. It should be examined both in its relation to forgiveness and on its own accord. I trace a brief philosophical history of repentance in Western thought in order to demonstrate its significance to philosophy, its monological character, and how its meaning has shifted from an act to a feeling. I then explore the issues of freedom, memory, and power through a reading of Levinas's Talmud readings. In the final parts of this chapter, I address the systematic problems of repentance revolving around identity, integrity, and transformation through a discussion of Nicolai Hartmann, Jean-Paul Sartre, and, more extensively, Søren Kierkegaard and Max Scheler.

An important aspect of Scheler's idea of repentance as a "self-healing of the soul" can be found in Derrida, who points out that a forgiveness aimed at the repentant person misses the guilty person, who has already become another. Jankélévitch contradistinctively conceives the repentant person as the guilty person, observing that repentance itself is not redeeming or expiatory. He suggests that liberation from guilt is not aligned with the power of the human will to extricate itself from the guilt that has become integrally a part of the self. To express this phenomenon, he introduces the category of *remorse* as the sign of the irrevocable and as an organ-obstacle—that is, that which can facilitate liberation or impede it. Nonetheless, I believe Jankélévitch and Derrida are closer to each other than is often perceived. Both are concerned with the possibility of repentance making forgiveness into an exchange, a meritorious affair, or an economic activity, and both principally agree that the gratuity of forgiveness precludes conditions, including repentance. Yet neither one markedly decides on the question of conditionality or unconditionality. Instead, both negotiate between the conditional and unconditional and recognize the necessity of negotiating the aporia of the gift of forgiveness between the order of knowledge, acknowledgment, and rationality, on the one hand, and love, charity, and grace, on the other.

Philosophical Conversions

Pierre Hadot has eloquently shown that a philosophical practice of *metanoia* was held to be of utmost significance for the "spiritual exercises" of the Greek schools. Literally meaning a "change of mind," *metanoia* further connotes a "change of heart" or even a "change of being." As an act, this form of "repentance" has its core in a dramatic change or in a turning (*shuv, strephein*) and returning. In Latin, this "turn" is represented by the *conversio*. Therefore, a philosophical conception of repentance has its basis in conversion or in the changing of one's mind, which is essentially a dramatic change in one's way of life. It appears primarily as an imperative to "convert" to a philosophical life, and in this sense, it is the philosophical act par excellence.

Everything depends on this turn for Plato. His "Allegory of the Cave" revolves around the turning of one's head and one's gaze from the shadows of ephemerality to the good sun of the eternal ideas. The change involves a conversion (*metastrophe*) of one's entire being. The philosophical life is contingent on this conversion, enabling and enacting the contemplative life. Since the structure of the polis, for Plato, is isomorphic with that of the individual soul (the polis being the soul writ large; the soul, the polis writ small), the connection of his "Allegory of the Cave" and his idea of the philosopher-king demonstrates that the well-ordered ideal state depends on this fundamental turning.[8] Even the art of education is concerned with how to turn the pupil's eye from the darkness to the light.[9] This revolution first and foremost designates the supremacy of the theoretical position and the conversion from the mundane to the philosophical: being over becoming and the eternal over the temporal.

It may be objected, of course, that the true sage has never had any need of repentance, even or especially when understood as conversion. In the words of Seneca, "The wise man never regrets his actions, or amends what he has done, or alters his plans."[10] As Pierre Hadot has pointed out, however, the sage is to be distinguished from the philosopher as an ideal role model to an apprenticing imitator.[11] The philosopher is a "lover of wisdom" whose love, like an open wound of desire, propels him upward toward the immutability of wisdom, which remains unattained or perhaps even unattainable, at least in its perfection. Seneca, for whom Sextus was a true sage, therefore adds a set of qualifications to his description of the wise man:

> The wise man never changes his plans while the conditions under which he formed them remain the same; therefore, he never feels regret, because at the time nothing better than what he did could have been done, nor could any better decision have been arrived at than that which was made; yet he begins everything with the saving clause, "If nothing shall occur to the contrary." This is the reason why we say that all goes well with him, and that nothing happens contrary to his expectation, because he bears in mind the possibility of something happening to prevent the realization of his projects.[12]

Regret, remorse, and repentance are seen to be a result of contingency. Only in a contingent world and only in a world where beings are free in their action is regret or repentance possible. An essential element of the sage's wisdom is his mindfulness of contingency in his every action. He cannot account for every alternative possibility for how things turn out, but his accounting for the fact that things can and often do turn out otherwise than anticipated is a quality, not a qualification, of his wisdom. When the conditions under which he made his plans change, he, too, may need to change and act otherwise, for the sage is mindful of time.

If the point of philosophical conversion is to change one's mind and therewith to change one's life, there is only one direction in which this change can happen, and there is only one time in which it can occur. Life is lived forward, as Kierkegaard reminds us, and the moment for change is the present. Philosophical conversion is intimately linked to the present and to the possibility of moral improvement, beginning now, and taking hold in the future.

In his *Nicomachean Ethics,* Aristotle states that there is no possibility of improvement where regret is absent. He distinguishes between two kinds of moral corruption: licentiousness and incontinence. A licentious person (*akolastos*) is an intemperate person who pursues excessive pleasures or pleasures excessively, exclusively, and for their own sake. Analogous to a chronic sickness, such a person is "bound to have no regrets, and so is incurable, since someone without regrets is incurable."[13] The incontinent person (*akrates*) is like one who succumbs to periodic sickness: The single act is the weak exception to the health of the overarching life maxim. Whereas the incontinent person momentarily suspends the principle of the good to follow sensual impulses, the licentious person makes of pleasure or enjoyment itself a principle.

In his reflections on the possibility of self-friendship, however, Aristotle concedes that even the wicked can have regrets and therefore can improve morally. The difference consists in the interrelation of the self and temporality. On the one hand, the incontinent person is, so to speak, synchronically at discord with himself. The affect takes effect in disobedience to the lawful principle, but the principle has not disappeared. Rather, divided, the person deems one thing good and desires another. On the other hand, because the licentious person is synchronically undivided (the desire matching the principle), he is diachronically discordant, for the pleasure-principle leads to a distended, distracted self, pursuing at one moment one thing and at the next moment something different. Both the incontinent person and the licentious person, according to Aristotle, are at "variance with themselves," their respective souls are "rent by faction," and they are "laden with regret."

The virtuous person, in contrast, "is at unity with himself, and desires the same things with his whole heart." This self-organizing principle, the principle organizing and harmonizing the parts of the self, is intellectual: Practical reason, *phronēsis*, is bound to or aligned with the virtues, *aretē*.[14] The virtuous person is thus characterized by the unity and integrity of the self, which manifests in self-consistency and consequently in the lack of a need for regret (*metameleia*): "It is always the same thing that is painful or pleasant, not different things at different times. This is because he never regrets [what he has done]."[15] Therefore, what is sometimes translated as *repentance* in Aristotle is more aptly translated as *regret* because it simply signals the discrepancy between the principle and the individual act, between the good and the actual or factual. It marks a morally necessary stage on the path to moral improvement, but it is to be overcome. In the truly virtuous person, like the sage, there is no need of regret.

For those requiring moral improvement, however, the consequences of regret lie in the future. The object of the *prohairesis* (moral choice) is not the past but the future, because the future represents the horizon of possibilities, whereas the past is consigned to necessity and irreversibility.[16] Explaining the primacy of the future for morality, Aristotle writes, "Nothing that is past can be an object of the moral purpose . . . for we deliberate not upon what is past but upon what is future or contingent; but the past cannot be undone." Sealing this point, he quotes the tragic poet Agathon: "For this alone is lacking even to God, to make undone things that have once been done."[17]

With respect to the past, therefore, regret is useless, but with respect to the future, it maintains a useful function in demarcating the discrepancy between ideality and reality. As a signal of this discrepancy arousing conscience, Aristotle's conception of regret is in no way a transformative act. It is not an act of any kind but is rather a moral feeling: what one feels when one is at variance with oneself, whether synchronically or diachronically. This feeling of being rent by discord is precisely the meaning that becomes associated with repentance in later moral philosophies.

Kant, for example, describes the repentant recollection of an offense as "a painful feeling produced by the moral sentiment." Following Aristotle, he deems this feeling "practically void in so far as it cannot serve to undo what has been done." The incapacity of feeling to do anything does not jeopardize its legitimacy, however, because it is the result of the axiological instantiation of the moral law on which time has no effect. As Kant elucidates, "The pain is quite legitimate [*rechtmäßig*], because when the law of our intelligible existence (the moral law) is in question, reason recognizes no distinction of time, and only asks whether the event belongs to me, as my act, and then always morally connects the same feeling with it, whether it has happened just now or long ago."[18] The act of "turning" is converted into a morally legitimate, although practically useless, feeling or pain. For Kant, this pain is passivity; it does not itself compel future action but merely marks the violation of the law.

In contrast, Descartes and Spinoza acknowledge a certain utility in repentance, but they are particularly leery of its rational virtuousness. Although Spinoza dictates that repentance (along with hope, fear, and humility) is to be preferred for the masses to arrogance, the danger of repentance for the weak arises in its tendency to conflate the individual act with regret and self-doubt concerning all action. Because it blurs the distinction between act and actor it potentially leads to resignation. For Descartes and Spinoza, repentance no longer represents the compunction of the moral conscience but is disjoined from both virtue and reason. So although Spinoza allows that it has some practical value for the maintenance of social hierarchy and order, he insists that "repentance is not a virtue, i.e., it does not arise from reason. Rather, he who repents what he did is twice miserable, i.e., impotent."[19] The impotence of the offender is doubled by adding mourning to the error of concupiscence.

In *The Wanderer and His Shadow*, Nietzsche depicts this notion unequivocally: "Never yield to remorse [*Reue*], but at once tell yourself: remorse would simply mean adding to the first act of stupidity a second." Whereas Aristotle recognized the opportunity for moral improvement in the compunction of conscience, Spinoza and Nietzsche focus on repentance as a purely retrospective and therefore useless and irrational occupation. It marks an inability or unwillingness to consign the past to necessity or to forget what one has done. As Nietzsche contends, forgetting the past may be a better precondition for doing good than trying to make good what was wrong or to learn from the bad in order to do good. He ends this aphorism by severing the past from the future: "If we have done harm[,] we should give thought to how we can do good."[20] The past, for him, is disconnected from the future in the moment of forgetting. He advocates the chance of the future.

Uniting these philosophical conceptions of repentance is their common concern with the self's concern with itself. From the act of conversion to a philosophical way of life to the possibility of moral improvement, repentance is represented as a solitary endeavor or a monologue within the interior of the self, which may result in social repercussions. In the wake of Aristotle, repentance begins to be associated with a moral feeling concerning the discrepancy between a wrongful act and the good. Such repentance is understood as moral regret or compunction, the pricks of conscience. Connected with the conscience, the pain of compunction indicates an unwavering, axiological moral judgment that potentially awakens the person to a readjustment of one's moral maxims or to resolution in acting in the future according to a morally good character. Compunction itself does no good; it does not do anything, for it is not an act but a feeling: a painful reminder that we are finite and fallible beings. Insofar as repentance is aligned with compunction and interpreted as directed at the past, however, it is deemed not only practically useless but also vitally laming and potentially morally inhibiting.

Theological Returns: Levinas's Talmud Readings

A different approach to repentance that emphasizes its dynamic and dialogical character is found in the theological traditions. Always in the context of forgiveness, repentance partakes in the give-and-take of petition and response. Responding to a past action, repentance exhibits a dynamic quality that is both social and temporal. The "return" of the repentant one appeals to an embrace by the other. It involves the approach and address of one to the other. Repentance, moreover, entails an accounting—both a reckoning and a kind of narration of what is "mine," including primarily that which I have done and who I have been but also who I promise to be. Repentance, in this context, expresses both the sociality of responsibility and the responsibility of sociality: not just for myself but before the other as judge and witness and to the other in an act of self-opening.

Sociality and temporality constitute the core of the Judaic-Christian understanding of repentance. Its emphasis on relationality is grounded in the relation to God: Humans require repentance because they have strayed from God. Yet it is this presence of God that complicates the sociality of repentance conceived as a direct relation between two persons. Recourse to God, especially if God is portrayed as the only one who can forgive, evokes the question of mediation. The introduction of a third party—whether a judge, a facilitator, another offended, or a witness, all of which God represents—has consequences for social ethics. One of the main consequences pertains to the interpretation of the past. In contrast to the philosophical conceptions of repentance in which the past falls to necessity and is equated with fate, repentance in a religious context considers the possibility of transforming the past, while oscillating between the dual logic of unconditionality and conditionality.

The Coming of the Messiah

Theologians have meditated on the "condition" of repentance for centuries. The doctors of the Talmud have held debates on this subject upholding two or more contentious arguments at the same time, one teacher or school representing one side, and another, another side. Their discourse consists in an exchange of positions and sides. Both sides draw on scripture, which leads to the increase in positions and aspects within a set of related ideas. In its layered richness, scripture does not end the debates but provides the surface of friction that extends and deepens both the understanding of the subject matter and the stakes. This movement or dance of differing theses does not lend itself to the synthesis of reconciliation or a Hegelian *Aufhebung*. In fact, the Talmudic commentaries do not seek an end. As commentaries, they elicit as much interpretation as the text they are interpreting. Tensions circulate in textual and existential inexhaustibility.

In his Talmud lecture "Toward the Other," Levinas emphasizes that, since Maimonides, all that is said of God in Judaism signifies through human praxis. For the Talmud, religious experience is primarily moral experience.²¹ Yet the religious is not reduced here to moral experience in the sense of a humanistic ethics in which humans are not only the only source of justification for ethics but also the sufficient justification for all ethics. This distinction is particularly significant with regard to the question of repentance. Maimonides' codification of Jewish law, the *Mishneh Torah,* contains in its first book a treatise on the Laws of Repentance. As Alan Udoff indicates, there is no corresponding treatise on forgiveness because "repentance essentially treats of man; forgiveness essentially treats of God."²² But even God's forgiveness signifies through the human praxis of repentance. The issue of human agency thus emerges at the heart of theology in the quest for redemption.

Levinas traces the debate concerning the coming of the messiah and whether his coming is conditional or unconditional—that is, whether it hinges on human action, via prayer, the storming of the heavens, zealous revolutions, the establishment of monarchies or theocracies, or, most predominantly, repentance. Either everything is in God's hands and the messiah will come on his own accord at the appointed time, or humans are religiously responsible for taking at least a step toward salvation on their own. On the one hand, as Gershom Scholem explains, the magnitude of the messianic idea "corresponds to the endless powerlessness in Jewish history during all the centuries of exile, when it [the Jewish nation] was unprepared to come forward onto the plane of world history." What he calls the "price of messianism" has historically been the price Jewish people have had to pay for waiting in faith. On the other hand, "Overtones of Messianism have accompanied the modern Jewish readiness for irrevocable action in the concrete realm, when set out on the utopian return to Zion."²³ Such efforts to hasten the end and ignite the kingdom of God, however, have mostly ended in failure or—often and devastatingly—in the tearing open of the abysses of violence. That is why Levinas admonishes, "Patience! It [the fulfillment] is not 'at hand'!"²⁴ But what ought the faithful do besides live in hope, which, as Scholem notes, is always both "grand" and "profoundly unreal"?²⁵

At stake in these debates is the relation of human freedom before God, and God's freedom toward humans. Malachi 3:7A constitutes the fulcrum of the discussion: "Return unto me, and I will return unto you." This verse highlights the reciprocity and equality of God's freedom and human freedom. Levinas teases out a consequence of the freedom posited in this call. He observes that the "and" in this promise reads like a conditional: The coming of the messiah actually depends on humans returning, repenting: *If* we don't return/repent, the messiah will never come. If redemption is contingent on human freedom, the world may remain unredeemed.

Without the unconditional promise that good will ultimately prevail, the world, according to this view, would be given over to itself, to the possibility of immorality within absolute freedom, to the "wicked and atheist belief that it is governed by chance," and perhaps even to the likely "triumph of evil."[26] For this reason, Rabbi Joshua concludes his argument by affirming that the world will be redeemed by a fixed date. Deliverance, he insists, cannot depend on human morality.

One can press the disjunction of the moral state of the world and the coming of redemption in the figure of the messiah to further bounds. The furthest reaches would entail the upheaval of a continuum between morality and salvation, leading to a "lawless heresy" according to which redemption would come through sin.[27] The inversion of the moral order and its concomitant depravity would thus form the condition for the messiah's arrival, or it could also be, in an extreme interpretation, the outward sign of an internally already appropriated redemption. The notion of redemption through sin involves the descent into impurity and the willful taking on of corruption. The latter entails a sovereignty antithetical to mores and laws and invokes the fundamental discrepancy between an inner state and outer action or factual state of the world. In other words, being redeemed would manifest itself through its contrary: corruption. Levinas, adamantly rejects the utter depravity of such a faith. Instead, he interprets the belief in the messiah as symbolizing the belief in the ultimate triumph of good over evil. This belief is sustained solely by the belief that the messiah will come regardless of the human condition and its moral achievements or deficits.[28] Thankfully, faith may sigh, redemption does not depend on the redeeming power of human morality. From this perspective, even though the world may warrant despair without a horizon of hope in humanity, one can positively and absolutely affirm the greatness of God on whom alone redemption depends.

Insofar as human morality does play a significant role in the course of redemption, it may be asked, who is the human subject that carries the burden of liberation or damnation? When one speaks of morality, is every individual in his or her own responsibility intended, or is "human" morality always a certain people's morality (like Israel's), or is it a matter of humanity in its entirety? A trace of an answer may be found in the notion of the *trace* itself. The trace is not only marked by the *Spuren* of Heidegger's *Holzwege*. It is rather as basic as the bread at the Passover feast. A trace of leaven is not neutralized in and by the rest of the ingredients of the dough. Mere particles of it can cause dozens of loaves of bread to rise. But if something "a million times greater" can be so readily affected, the process also may be seen inversely. Commenting on a Talmudic passage requiring a set portion of one's harvest for the priests, the scholars suggest that one grain from the whole harvest suffices, for "one grain redeems the whole heap."[29] In the Babylonian Talmud Tractate Yoma 86A–B, Rabbi Meir goes to further lengths, applying the trace of purification to a singular act of repentance: "Great is repentance, for on account of a single individual who repents, the whole world is forgiven in its entirety."[30] Power and hope are expressed in these elucidations: power, in the capacity and primacy of human singularity; hope, in the sufficiency of one despite the doubts about the many. Interwoven as power and hope, the one—singular and isolated—is bound to the many in a relation of responsibility. In the philosophy of Levinas, it is I who am more responsible than all the others; in the words of the Jankélévitch, the singular act sows a seed of "infinitization."

Motivations for Changing the Past

Hosea, the primary early Bible text on repentance, speaks in the voice of God, "I will heal their turnings. I will love them freely; because my anger has turned away from them" (14:4). For Robert Gibbs the meaning is clear: "God will heal or mend the break initiated by the people. The promise arises because God loves freely; we might say unconditionally."[31] It is, then, the unconditional promise God gave to the people of Israel that allows for their return to God. The wall between God and humans was erected from the human side, but God is true, God's love unconditional. Therefore, it is the promise or the welcome of the offended that engenders both the command to return and the willingness, and thus ability, to repent. In terms of forgiveness, one can say perhaps that it is the preceding forgiveness or promise of forgiving that allows the other to repent, just as the unflinching welcome of a parent paves the way for the return of a prodigal child.

Such a return, however, can be spurred by various motives, and the motive for return makes a big difference, according to the Talmud, for alongside God's great desire for his people God is also judge. When the promise issues the command to return, the prodigal child may fear punishment. In the legal realm, before the law and the court, repentance or a sign of remorse may stem from the fear of penalty, whether prison or fines. Yet a return may equally arise from the love of the one offended or the love of the community that has been severed by the sin that has excluded and isolated the offender. The Talmud ties together the motivation—fear or love—with the order of response: "When those who had turned away turn themselves back, returning to God freely: that is out of love. When the turned away are healed by God while still turned away, they may indeed return, but it happens out of fear, for God reminds them that they were turned away."[32] Although a reminder by the offended other or judge that we should repent frequently leads to the sudden recognition of being in the wrong, it does not quicken love in the offender but fear. Repentance out of love thus implies a self-healing, whereas a return out of fear is a response to the other's initiative.

If repentance motivated by love heals, does repentance motivated by fear still have redeeming qualities? The Babylonian Talmud addresses this issue in Yoma 86, in which the renowned third-century Jewish scholar Resh Lakish both lauds and explicates the greatness of repentance: "Great is repentance: by it intentional sins are made like unintentional errors, as it is said: 'Return, Israel, to THE Lord your God, for you have stumbled in your guilt' [Hos. 14:2]." Sin is intentional, but this verse calls it a "stumbling." Parallel to Aristotle, Resh Lakish differentiates the unintentional from the intentional, calling the former errors and the latter sins.[33] The inadvertent offense is here considered easier to forgive than that which was intentional, for which the suspicion of malice may linger. Ordinarily, a relationship ruptured by an unintentional harm can be readily redressed and mended, for the offense is, for example, set in a broader context of positive associations and experiences that outweigh the negative. In such a situation, the offense is rendered a "slight" because it is a minor interstice in the longer story of community. But forgiveness may seem like a nearly impossible solution to repairing relations in which one has willfully harmed another. Such perpetration can cast its dark shadow across the landscape of the entire relation where there is no broader context of light and positive memory. Upon this backdrop, the radical character of Resh Lakish's contention develops its specific contours. He claims that the intentional sin can be made into an unintentional error through repentance. He explains that "even if I chose to harm another, when I repent I realize that I did not know what I was doing. The effort to return and to readdress the other transforms my past action from a cruel deed into one whose effects I did not understand."[34]

Is it thus once again a question of knowledge and of right knowing, of Greek ignorance, of Jesus' cry from the cross, or Jankélévitch's inversion of Jesus' petition? In a reading of another text, Levinas conjoins responsibility and knowledge and the readiness to forgive. "One can forgive many Germans," Levinas states, "but there are some Germans it is difficult to forgive. It is difficult to forgive Heidegger."[35] It is impossible to judge if someone is fully aware of what they are doing or of what they have done, but Levinas's point can be understood as emphasizing the increased responsibility of those in positions of responsibility, especially public intellectuals. In this case, it follows that Heidegger should have known better. His failure could be described in Arendt's terms as "thoughtlessness." A lack of consciousness is inexcusable; inattentiveness, a source of violence. If aggression is at least in part a lack of attention, as Levinas portrays it in his Talmud reading, one can be accountable and held accountable not only for what one does and leaves undone but also for what one could have known and should have known. In short, an obligation to moral knowledge does indeed obtain.[36]

To some extent, however, we never know exactly what we do. In the same text, "Toward the Other," Levinas asks, "Has anyone, in any case, ever finished asking for forgiveness? Our wrongs appear to us as we humble ourselves. The seeking for forgiveness never comes to an end. Nothing is ever completed."[37] In the acknowledgment of one's own wrongdoing by overcoming one's pride and all of its subtle resistances, the nature of our offense is often first brought to light. The humbling is doubly humbling, as it awakens us to what we have done, to our inner motives, and thus also to our true selves as agents acting in history. Yet if nothing is ever completed, as Levinas insists, even the humbling act of repentance will remain provisional and needy: "Is the offender capable of measuring the extent of his wrongdoing? Do we know the limits of our ill will? And do we therefore truly have the capacity to ask for forgiveness?"[38]

The knowledge at stake is not restricted to the knowledge of the offense and the offender. It is also a matter of self-knowledge and thus of one's own ability to forgive. Remnants of ressentiment may linger, or one may ultimately forgive as much, if not more, for oneself and one's own well-being as for the other. The matter of the purity of heart in the act of forgiveness must always leave us less than assured and reveal us as less than sovereign, for we cannot achieve a full transparency to ourselves; we cannot expose the depths of our inner motives and mine the forces of unconsciousness. The problem is intrinsic, not circumstantial. It is not a question of whether this or that has yet to be brought to light; there is always structurally a deficit, a lacuna. The distinction is thus qualitative, not quantitative.

Resh Lakish takes a different approach to this delicate subject. He substantiates that there are intentional harms and unintentional ones; there is sin, on the one hand, and stumbling or error, on the other hand. Nevertheless, like Socrates, he sees the root of evil intentions in ignorance or error—*shegagah*. Repentance thus entails, for him, insight into the errors of one's ways. Through the act of repentance, that which was done does not reflect what the case is presently or what will be the case in future action. The attitude of the wrongdoer, his estimation of the other, and the relation to him has changed so that, in the light of the new position of the repentant subject and his or her promise of how he or she will be, that which belongs to the past can be seen as a mere mistake. However it achieves this and for whomever it is the case (whether for God, objectively, or merely for the wrongdoer), the power of repentance, according to Resh Lakish, is capable of changing the vision of the past.

Resh Lakish does not halt at the potential reduction of ill will to error, however; he speaks in hyperbole about the potential shift from ill will to *merit*! In addition to his interpretation of the passage from Hosea, Resh Lakish takes up a verse from the prophet Ezekiel to explicate this power: "Great is repentance: by it intentional sins are made like merits, as it is said: 'When the wicked man turns from his wickedness and does what is just and right, then because of them he shall live' (Ezek. 33:19)." Resh Lakish seems to straddle two conflicting interpretations: Repentance turns intentional sins into unintentional sins, and, more provocatively, repentance turns intentional sins into merits. Adding to this dilemma, the message in this verse seems to be successive. The moral person *shall live* (future tense) because of his *turning away* from wickedness (past tense) and *doing* what is just and right (present tense). The moral improvement and newfound righteousness in the self-distancing to the past and self-betterment in the direction of the future would morally suffice. But instead, Lakish stretches the verse, requiring that life come as a reward from having sinned and repented.[39] His interpretation demonstrates the heightened joy of reconciliation after a quarrel and is in line with a deep theological tradition, especially in the Christian heritage, the *felix culpa*, the felicitous sin. The *felix culpa* suggests that it is better to have sinned and repented than to have never sinned at all.[40]

Commenting on Resh Lakish's sayings, Joseph Soloveitchik, a twentieth-century American Orthodox rabbi, Talmudist, and philosopher, focuses on the power of repentance to change the past and the motivation behind the act of repentance. He interprets Resh Lakish's comments that repentance renders intentional sins like unintentional errors as a description of the way repentance annihilates sin. "Repentance erases sin," he claims; "intended sins are accounted as errors, as though they never took place at all. They are wiped away."[41] Logically, if sin is made synonymous with intentionality and repentance transforms what was intentional into something inadvertent, then repentance does away with the event as sin. There is no more guilt, only stumbling. The intentional sin is not merely reduced to something less, qualitatively or otherwise; it is not crossed out in an act of revision, while leaving at least a trace of this previous identity. Instead, according to Soloveitchik's reading, the sin is erased, and repentance itself implicates a radical kind of forgetting that recalls the past in order to destroy it completely.[42]

Soloveitchik then shifts to the second strand of Resh Lakish's proposition in which repentance turns sin into merit. He interprets repentance in this context in a Hegelian fashion as the means by which evil is "elevated."[43] In this form of repentance, there is creative power and the capacity to give life to something new. Inverting the regulative priority of sinlessness that Levinas articulates, it is said in Berakhot 34b that "where penitents stand even the perfectly righteous cannot stand."[44] Soloveitchik describes how Resh Lakish himself embodied this transformative faculty of repentance, which caused him to follow the commandments with more strength and vigor than before he sinned and to study the Torah in a way he had not done beforehand.

Soloveitchik links each of these effects of repentance to the motivation of either fear or love. Repentance out of fear leads to the annihilation of sin, whereas repentance out of love invokes the *Aufhebung* of sin—its simultaneous cancellation and elevation. Evil is thus either "blotted out" or made into good, depending on whether repentance is motivated by fear or love. "Fear of punishment," Gibbs comments, "prompts one to erase the past, but love leads one to bring the past back into a source for new growth."[45] To illustrate this new growth, Soloveitchik selects the image of fire, describing how, in repentance from love, sin fans the fire, exalting the repentant person to heights unreached by the person who has not sinned.[46] Whereas repentance from fear ushers in the possibility of forgetting, repentance from love opens the path to transformed memory: The past is not lost but taken up into the present as its passion. No longer a blank neutrality, the present becomes aflame.[47] Whereas fear wipes the slate clean, love embraces the negativity of the past such that its charge turns positive; it becomes more than before, more than otherwise possible. Its gain is not innocence but the plus of history, sociality, and biography; its logic is not "at the price of" but "on account of," not "despite" but "because."

In My Hands?

The Talmud keeps a close account of the correlation between the constellation of repentance and forgiveness in relation to God and the interpersonal relations implied in the human constellation of social ethics. Its interpreters delimit the distinction between offenses against God and offenses against one's neighbor. This distinction is, however, destabilized by the fact that offenses against the neighbor are mostly, if not always, simultaneously offenses against God. The double command to love God with all one's heart and one's neighbor as oneself permeates both the Old Testament and the New Testament; the two commands are inseparably conjoined. The role God plays in interpersonal forgiveness, therefore, needs to be examined. Furthermore, the social setting of forgiveness requires additional explication of the relation of the individuals involved in repentance and forgiveness to the community at large. The community can be, on the one hand, facilitator, supporter, or endorser of forgiveness. The community can also be, on the other hand, antagonistic to, or at least in dissonance with forgiveness insofar as forgiveness between two persons can jeopardize the duties of equality and reciprocity on which community is based. To forgive the other, in other words, may neglect, oppose, or contradict the duty to all others—that is, the duty of justice.

In relation to God, repentance is said to have the power to "compel" or "force God's hand."[48] How is this compulsion to be interpreted? Ordinarily, compulsion or the forcing of one's hand is conceived as the altering of mind. An action that compels causes a "change of mind" (*metanoia*) or a change of action from that which one would otherwise do. But perhaps this change is only possible because of the nature or disposition of the one who is "compelled." Insofar as repentance is considered compelling of forgiveness, it is the necessary and sufficient condition for forgiveness. It triggers a logic of reciprocity: If you repent, I will forgive (anything and everything). God's graciousness manifests itself, from this perspective, in the promise to forgive, but God's justice maintains the requisite responsibility on the side of the wrongdoer.[49]

One of the most familiar of all rabbinic texts, Mishnah Yoma 8:9, handles precisely this division of transgressions between a human and his companion and transgressions between a human and God. The spatial connotation of the term *transgression* implies relationality as a "between" one and the other, borders, and therefore laws. Levinas begins his 1963 Talmud lecture with a reading of another Mishnah text (Yoma 85a–85b) that establishes this difference and the rules guiding their differences: "The transgressions of man toward God are forgiven him by the Day of Atonement; the transgressions against other people are not forgiven him by the Day of Atonement if he has not first appeased the other person."[50] Levinas acknowledges that, in Judaism, "faults toward one's neighbor are ipso facto offenses toward God."[51] In the Mishnah verse the two are also distinguished.[52] "On the face of it," he explains, "nothing is simpler than this distinction: anything that can harm my neighbor either materially or morally as well as any verbal offense committed against him, constitutes a transgression against man. Transgressions of prohibitions and ritual commandments, idolatry and despair, belong to the realm of wrongs done to the eternal."[53]

What is novel here, as Robert Gibbs explicates, is that the Day of Atonement alone does not and cannot atone for the sins between people. He concludes that "the Mishnah is substantializing a category of interhuman relations (we call it ethics), and separates it from the category of sins against God."[54] Repentance consequently has a different capacity in interhuman relations than it does in the relation between God and humans. Levinas writes:

> My faults toward God are forgiven without my depending on his good will! God is, in a sense, the other, par excellence, the other as other, the absolutely other—and nonetheless my standing with this God depends only on myself. The instrument of forgiveness is in my hands. On the other hand, my neighbor, my brother, man, infinitely less other than the absolutely other, is in a certain way more other than God: to obtain his forgiveness on the Day of Atonement I must first succeed in appeasing him. What if he refuses? As soon as two are involved, everything is in danger. The other can refuse forgiveness and leave me forever unpardoned. This must hide some interesting teachings on the essence of the Divine![55]

Although Levinas interprets offenses against God alone as being solely in one's own hands, the relation to God is not therefore leveled, for it is God who forgives on Yom Kippur, the Day of Atonement. Repentance is "merely" the "instrument" effecting forgiveness. In *The Star of Redemption*, Franz Rosenzweig states that the soul "is freed of its burden at the very moment of daring to assume all of it on its shoulders."[56] The soul's redemption of itself is a prerequisite, but it does not absolve the repentant soul of necessitating forgiveness. Rather, as Gibbs observes, "There is security in relation to God: His provision and promise of forgiveness allows me to return with perfect certainty. Although God is the ABSOLUTELY OTHER, God is not fickle and has bound his freedom in the promise of forgiveness. God's direct intervention breaks through my anxiety, encouraging me to make the return."[57] God's promise ensures that forgiveness will be granted. This promise encourages one to repent and, more specifically, to repent out of love for the one who so lovingly promises to love. In other words, it is God's realization of his word, "I will love them freely."

Whereas God's pardon depends only on me, Levinas claims the other can leave me "forever unpardoned."[58] With the other, insecurity and instability enter the stage. The other offers neither the regularity of the calendar nor the reliability of God. The status of social ethics is thus elevated, since God cannot forgive in the place of the offended neighbor. Levinas captures the poignancy of this thought beautifully when he writes that "God's forgiveness—or the forgiveness of history—cannot be given if the individual has not been honored. God is perhaps nothing but this permanent refusal of a history which would come to terms with our private tears."[59]

In this scene of turns and returns, each agent has his or her own specific task. To the offender falls the task of repentance and to the offended that of forgiveness. The vulnerability exposed in the victim by the wrongdoer is, in the act of repentance, the vulnerability of the accused exposed to and waiting for the victim's response. The power dynamic has shifted from "my" hands to the hands of the other: "Forgiveness depends on him. One finds oneself in his hands."[60] The two performances—repentance and forgiveness—therefore carry with them different risks, and each has its own "utterly unexchangeable role."[61]

If forgiveness in relation to God is in our own hands, the forgiveness regarding human offenses rests in the hands of the other. It, too, is in human hands; there is only the between-us without a God to directly intervene. The unavoidable and appropriate asymmetry inherent in the exposure of delivering oneself over to the other, however, bears the possibility of inverting the power dynamics of the relation to the degree of inviting abuse by the one faced with the choice of forgiving the other. On the one hand, the condition of repentance serves to re-level the playing field, for repentance is an act of humility that humbles the perpetrator. By returning to the offended and supplicating him for forgiveness, the returner demonstrates both acknowledgment of the wrong and the reevaluation of the symbolic message of worth or estimation communicated to the other. On the other hand, the humility demonstrated in repentance may be used to humiliate the offender. Forgiveness, in other words, can be used as an effective, highly charged tool for wielding power in human relations. If the offended one usurps this power as a "right," then he or she can withhold forgiveness in order to wield power over the penitent like the sword of Damocles. It can resemble the sovereignty of deciding over the other's redemption. The impetus of compelling forgiveness is thus all the more understandable, and that is why the teaching of Raba implores, "One forgives all sins to whoever cedes his right."[62]

Because the balance of power potentially shifts from the offender to the offended, limits need to be defined for the cases in which the offended person refuses to be satisfied. The text in the Gemara teaches that "one is freed with respect to [the offended party] if he refuses it three times."[63] The limit may seem fairly arbitrary (the number three arises from the Joseph story and the number of pleas his brothers make of him), but if the imperative to forgive asserts itself from the beginning, then the offended runs the risk of incurring guilt upon himself or herself by not forgiving. Since the repentant person cedes his rights and sets himself at the mercy of the other, the concern is legitimate that the person denying forgiveness does so merely to see the offender humbled and humiliated again and again, perverting forgiveness into a whimsical decree and proclaiming sovereignty at the price of degrading others. Such possible haughtiness can ultimately cause the schema of repentance/forgiveness to be turned around: The offended may need to repent and be forgiven for not forgiving. The imperative of the limit functions to open one's eyes to the other person who has only obligations and no rights.

Levinas nevertheless questions the viability of establishing a strict limit. He relays the rabbinic story of the pious Rab, who offended one of his masters and, after years of returning to him for forgiveness without success, asked, "How many times am I to repeat myself."[64] This story can be seen as the flip side to the disciple Peter's question to his master about how many times he must forgive his brother who sinned against him. Why did Rab entreat Rav Hanina thirteen times, especially if the supposed liberating limit is three? And how could Rav Hanina be so hardened as to not forgive even thirteen years, thirteen petitions, and thirteen Days of Reconciliation later? Levinas mines from the text the limits of consciousness and the lack of attention, but perhaps it is not a matter of reckoning at all. Perhaps the question of limits is dependent on context—who? why? what?—so that the mere fact that there are limits requires constant negotiation of where, when, and how. Limits, in this interpretation, are ultimately not—or not ultimately—a matter of quantification. The task of repentance cannot be fulfilled insofar as it is motivated by the desire for completion, the desire to regain a good conscience, move on, close the chapter and the book, and therefore balance the accounts. Levinas and the Jewish scholars question the equation of morality with the balancing of a checkbook or a zero-sum game. They recognize that we are never without obligations on an even playing field of equal and equally assertable rights. We are instead called to be generously attentive to others and critical of ourselves, and this is work that always remains to be done. As Derrida writes, "How to acquit oneself of forgiveness? And does not forgiveness have to exclude all acquitting, all acquitting of oneself, all acquitting of the other? Forgiving is surely not to call it quits, clear and discharged [*pardonner, ce n'est sûrement pas tenir pour quitte*]."[65]

Becoming Other: The Paradox of Repentance

An aspect of what Derrida calls the unforgivable is the absence of repentance. The unrepented offense is that which needs forgiveness, so when an offender repents, she or he already initiates a process of transformation.

The result, Derrida claims, is that a forgiveness dictated by the logic of conditionality forgives a crime that is not the crime per se and the offender who is no longer herself or himself:

> I forgive regardless of the attitude of the guilty party, even if he [or she] does not ask for forgiveness, even if he [or she] does not repent. I forgive him [or her] *as* someone who is guilty, presently, actually guilty; I forgive him [or her] *insofar as* he [or she] is guilty, or even insofar as he [or she] remains guilty.... If I forgive the fault (the "what") of the one who has repented, or the one who has repented himself [or herself] (the "who"), I forgive something or someone other than the crime or the criminal.[66]

Derrida is not concerned that, without the condition of repentance, the relation to the other may be overlooked. Derrida's concern is twofold. On the one hand, his critique of the precondition of repentance aims at the symmetry of the economic transaction. He reads Jankélévitch as stipulating the condition of repentance. With this condition, the desire to be forgiven must be signified, whether uttered, implied, or given in the wink of an eye. He locates in this signification or "before it"—that is, leading up to it, facilitating it, making it perhaps even necessary—the "expiation, remorse, regret, confession, [and] the mea culpa of the one who can beat his breast." And he equates the act of forgiveness, "in the course of a scene of repentance attesting at once to the consciousness of the fault, the transformation of the guilty, and the at least implicit obligation to do everything to avoid the return of evil," with an economic transaction.[67] On the other hand, he portrays repentance as the potential for self-transformation to the point of alterity. In a vein reminiscent of Rosenzweig, he maintains that it is "*by recognizing his [or her] crime,* [that one] dissociate[s] himself [or herself] from the guilty subject, from the subject having been guilty."[68] Consequently, repentance either makes of forgiveness a matter of merit or renders forgiveness superfluous.

Derrida's portrayal of repentance as self-transformation—or, in the words of Max Scheler, as a self-healing of the soul—implies that to forgive the one who repents is to forgive the repentant one, not the guilty one, which renders forgiveness a mere acknowledgment of what is already done.[69] He argues that forgiveness subsequently loses its ground and raison d'être. But it should be asked, what in Derrida's thinking allows for such a self-transformation beyond the play of identity and alterity in *différance*? And it remains to be seen whether one can, by one's own initiative, become another. If this possibility is assumed, does it follow necessarily that forgiveness misses the point, the offense, and the person? With Rosenzweig, we might ask in what tense is the repentant sinner supposed to describe his state. Should he or she say, "I am a sinner" or "I was a sinner"?[70]

Hartmann, Sartre, and Kierkegaard

The nineteenth-century German moral philosopher Nicolai Hartmann claims that, from a metaphysical perspective, there is no dilemma: The repentant offender is the same person as the one who offended. Hartmann argues that guilt accrued cannot be lost or stripped away by later actions because guilt and the capacity for guilt are constitutive of identity and therefore belong essentially to "me." Responsibility issues forth in taking up and giving account of this self-same identity across time and through subsequent action. Although Hartmann concedes that "forgiveness may very well take from the guilt that special sting of guilt which inheres in the deserved contempt and hostility of the man who has been wronged; and it may give back to the guilty the outward peace which he had spurned," he stoutly affirms that "it can never remove the moral guilt itself."[71] In his view, this moral limitation is absolute, applicable to humans and God alike. He thus protests against a Christian theological notion of divine grace that removes the guilt from the guilty party. Hartmann thus echoes Agathon, as quoted by Aristotle, when he writes that "this alone is lacking even to God, to make undone things that have once been done."[72] Even if possible, Hartmann stresses, the removal of guilt would be morally reprehensible.[73] Following Kant and parallel to Jankélévitch's line of argumentation for imprescriptibility, Hartmann insists that, beyond the fact of what is done, guilt remains as long as the value obtains that condemns the offense. Although he allows that attitudes, comportment, and social relations in general may change and be positively transformed by repentance and forgiveness, he upholds the metaphysical self-sameness of identity, which neither repentance nor forgiveness can alter.

In both his dramatic revision of the Orestes story *The Flies* and his philosophical magnum opus, *Being and Nothingness*, which was published in the same year (1943), Jean-Paul Sartre reframes this indissolubility of identity and moral imputation. Human freedom, he contends with existential vigor, is the source of all values. He consequently dismisses repentance as an unfruitful self-denial. By dissociating myself from my guilt, he argues, I dissociate myself from my past insofar as it belongs to me intrinsically as grounded in my decisions and choices. I must take responsibility for the past; and it should be taken up as my responsibility—that is, understood as, in a sense, chosen. For Sartre, I do not *have* freedom, but rather I *am* my freedom, which manifests itself in actions and decisions.[74] Therefore, I am what I do and have done, and I have to own up to being here and thus and not elsewhere or otherwise. He explains that, "since nothing foreign has decided what we feel, what we live, or what we are . . . everything which happens to me is *mine*."[75] Identity and continuity of the self are thus not vouched for by a metaphysical sameness as in Hartmann and Kant. Instead, they are created through acts of existential responsibility by a self that stands alone, in-itself and for-itself. For such absolute responsibility, Sartre believes, repentance is equivalent to the loss of self. In a tone vacillating between triumphalism and resignation, he suggests that "I must be without remorse or regrets as I am without excuse; for from the instant of my upsurge into being, I carry the weight of the world by myself alone without anything or any person being able to lighten it."[76] In other words, no repentance, no forgiveness is allowed to relieve or help carry the burden on Atlas's shoulders.

For the explication of this view, Sartre was undoubtedly influenced by Søren Kierkegaard. Kierkegaard, however, offers a positive rendering of repentance precisely in the terms of "choosing oneself." In the second part of *Either/Or*, he writes that every person by so willing "can become a paradigmatic human being, not by brushing off his accidental qualities, but by remaining in them and ennobling them. But he ennobles them by choosing them."[77] By taking up what is the case in choosing it, one takes responsibility for it, and this responsibility both ennobles the accidental attribute and makes it a part of one's being. Responsibility thus ennobles contingency by integrating it into identity and thereby essentiality. Judge William, who speaks here representing the ethical point of view over against a young aesthete, explains this intertwinement of responsibility and identity in terms of repentance:

> Not until a person in his choice has taken himself upon himself, has put on himself, has totally interpenetrated himself so that every movement he makes is accompanied by a consciousness of responsibility for himself—not until then has a person chosen himself ethically, not until then has he repented himself, not until then is he concrete, not until then is he in his total isolation in absolute continuity with the actuality to which he belongs.[78]

What he means by becoming concrete through repentance is that the dignity of a human being lies in his capacity "to gain a history." History, for Judge William, is not merely a summary of the things that have taken place; it rather entails the transformation of what happened to me into my personal deed. In short, it transfers the past from necessity to freedom.[79] But as Kierkegaard argues under the pseudonym Johannes Climacus, the past itself is a result of a "freely acting cause," it moves from possibility to actuality and is thus of another modal category than necessity. In other words, it is not only the future that is contingent but also the past.[80]

Kierkegaard has William distinguish carefully between choosing and creating as well as between the absolute and the concrete. Choice, he states, is dialectical. Two pairs of two dialectical movements made simultaneously characterize choosing oneself:

> That which is chosen does not exist and comes into existence through the choice—and that which is chosen exists; otherwise it was not a choice. . . . I do not create myself—I choose myself. . . . . Whereas nature is created from nothing, whereas I myself as immediate personality am created from nothing, I as free spirit . . . am born through my choosing myself.[81]

Freedom, he claims, remains abstract unless it becomes concrete in bodily, social, and cultural reality. According to this ethical viewpoint, though, freedom is not contaminated by these in the encounter; it rather transforms them. As the concrete absolute of freedom, the self chooses itself in its "eternal validity."

This choice is the gathering and binding together of multiplicity within oneself, which yields a single history and a thoroughgoing continuity. Yet Judge William acknowledges that, in delving into what is constitutive of the individual, one is led beyond oneself to the multiplicities of others.

> Now he discovers that the self he chooses has a boundless multiplicity within itself inasmuch as it has a history, a history in which he acknowledges identity with himself. This history is of a different kind, for in this history he stands in relation to other individuals in the race and to the whole race, and this history contains painful things, and yet he is the person he is only through this history. That is why it takes courage to choose oneself, for at the same time as he seems to be isolating himself most radically he is most radically sinking himself into the root by which he is bound up with the whole. . . . He can give up nothing of all this, not the most painful, not the hardest, and yet the expression for this struggle, for this acquiring, is— repentance. He repents himself back into himself, back into the family, back into the race, until he finds himself in God. Only on this condition can he choose himself. And this is the only condition he wants, for only in this way can he choose himself absolutely.[82]

As Levinas argues in his Talmud reading, the most solitary moment is simultaneously and paradoxically the one that leads me toward the other.

The path of repentance leading into oneself leads beyond oneself and opens onto a responsibility for that which one did not do but which constitutes the history composing the person one is. One consequence of this solidarity is the possible acknowledgment that one benefits today from the injustices of yesterday, that one, so to speak, lives off the others.[83] Such acknowledgment carries with it the responsibility of reparations. One still has to pay for the offense, pay what one owes, perhaps even with interest, comparable to the benefit one secretly—or unawares—enjoyed for so long.

Repentance is thus cast as simultaneously what most isolates me and what binds me indissolubly to others and ultimately all others. At the moment that repentance seems most monological—that is, a "purely personal drama" concerning "moral intimacy" and "solitary perfection," as Jankélévitch portrays it—it exposes itself as intimately involving others. Far from curbing freedom or the sense of self, repentance exhibits freedom par excellence. It is, in this view, even the measure of freedom. Not merely am I responsible "from the instant of my upsurge into being," as Sartre suggests, but the "profound meaning of repentance" comes to the fore in the simultaneity of this isolating and binding "because my life does not begin now and with nothing, and if I cannot repent of the past, then freedom is a dream."[84]

Both Kierkegaard and Sartre address the relation of freedom and responsibility for the past. They diametrically differ, though, with regard to the role of repentance in selfhood. Whereas Sartre views repentance as a severance of the self, as the flight from the responsibility of choosing oneself in one's facticity, Kierkegaard interprets it as a gathering of the self or as the self's appropriation of itself. For Sartre, it entails a denial of the self; for Kierkegaard it demonstrates the way to becoming a self.[85] Perhaps no one has addressed this interconnection of responsibility, identity, and repentance more deeply than Max Scheler in his essay "Repentance and Rebirth."

A Self-Healing of the Soul: Max Scheler

Max Scheler's phenomenological analysis of repentance in "Repentance and Rebirth" seeks to examine how far philosophical reflection alone can lead to an elucidation of the idea of repentance.[86] He criticizes the philosophical theories that have almost exclusively reduced repentance to a disharmony of the soul (Aristotle), to a negative and ultimately superfluous act (Kant, Spinoza), or, even worse, to self-deception or sickness (Nietzsche). Although he recognizes the negative and rejecting function of repentance, he emphasizes its positive, liberating, and constructive function. He understands repentance as an act, not a feeling. It is an act of rebirth. In this sense, the title of his essay is misleading, for it is not a matter of repentance *and* rebirth; repentance itself entails a process of rebirth. Like a phoenix, it involves a rebirth arising out of the ashes or, more specifically, out of the guilt and sin that it simultaneously annihilates to ashes, for death and rebirth make up the two sides of repentance. As he writes, "Repentance kills only to create. It annihilates only to rebuild."[87] Biblically, it represents the rebirth of a new Adam from the old Adam and the reception of a new heart. For these reasons, Scheler recognizes in repentance "the most *revolutionary* force in the moral world."[88]

The death and rebirth of repentance demonstrate its dual direction. Along with the theological traditions and against the predominant trend of philosophy, Scheler emphasizes that repentance is essentially directed at the past. Its temporal orientation, in other words, is necessarily retrospective.[89] To those philosophical theorists who call on the individual to change his mind and change his ways in future action according to the Nietzschean motto, "If you have done harm, see how you can do good," Scheler asks whence comes this power to change.[90] These jovial men, he states, fail to tell us "where we may find strength to make those resolutions, still less the strength to carry them out, if repentance has not first liberated the personal self and empowered it to combat the determining force of the past."[91] As in the dilemma exposed by Levinas, the self that is simply resolved to do good resembles Münchhausen's futile attempt to pull himself out of the swamp by his own hair. As the saying goes, the road to hell is paved with good intentions. It is also a direct path to self-contempt. In contrast, the repented guilt, to adopt the image of Soloveitchik, fans the fire of good intentions. Indeed, according to Scheler, it is the fire without which resolutions fall into mere expressions of "words, words, words," as Hamlet would say. Contrary to the interpretations that portray repentance as a life inhibiter solely occupied with the past, Scheler states that it is not the repented guilt but the unrepented guilt that exercises a determining and binding power on the future of life.[92] In other words, resolutions fail without repentance because they are based on the person who is still guilty or morally corrupt. The forgetting of guilt in order to leave it behind equals a self-delusion or repression because guilt remains secretly present in every act and intention of the person.[93] Since it is latently omnipresent and determinative, it grows, like a "rigid chain of effect," like an avalanche.[94] Scheler thus condemns the "flight" from guilt as a form of bad faith: "The more you close your eyes to what should be a subject of repentance, the more tightly you bind on your feet the chains that encumber your progress."[95] It is not a matter of refraining from repentance and willing to become and do better but of repenting and, precisely for this reason, being able to do better.[96] He names this the great paradox of repentance: "It sorrowfully looks back to the past while working mightily and joyfully for the future. Its mental concern [*geistiger Blick*] and its living action are in diametric opposition."[97]

Like Levinas, Scheler contends that the willingness to repent is, therefore, conditioned by humility. It involves an overcoming of the self. Through humility, the urge to repress is lifted and the hardening in pride is disbanded, opening the dynamic of life. As a latent quality of the person, guilt hides itself, continuously dulling a feeling for it or an awareness of it.[98] Although pride and arrogance often disavow the association of oneself with wrongdoing and guilt, the deeper guilt lies, the more it becomes a part of the self.[99] Humility encourages the lowering of consciousness into the dark realm of guilt with its hidden reservoirs in the soul, making one aware of this dark and hidden existence, often for the first time.[100] Humility thus enables the self to see itself as it is, as it has come to be. In this sense, Scheler conceives of repentance in terms of a self-collection or gathering.[101] With the self-lowering of humility, the self becomes increasingly sensitive to its own moral failing. For Scheler, the lives of the saints underline this point: Their feeling of guilt is refined with the objective decrease in their guilt.[102] The fear of repentance is inversely rooted in this refinement or sensitivity to the weight of guilt. As Kierkegaard elucidates, "If one gives it [repentance] a finger it takes the whole hand."[103]

If this is the case, the question again arises whether we are or ever can be finished with repentance. Will we not always be capable of a greater attunement to our wrongdoings and bad intentions? Can we ever gain a full transparency to ourselves such that our darkest recesses are filled with the light of consciousness? In a line extending from Kant and to Levinas and Jankélévitch, Scheler states that repentance is an "abiding necessity."[104] In the act of repentance, the repentant person must quit squinting to witness his or her own goodness. Otherwise, he explains, repentance itself can become the fertile ground for glory and vanity. Instead of repentance serving as the pretext for boasting one's goodness, the repentant person is as if lost in the depths of his guilt.[105]

It is this person lost, however, who rises up all the more regally from dust, as if reborn. Along with the backward glance of gathering and introspection emerges the faculty of regeneration. The arduous mining of the self's guilt is the flip side of its divestment, and the self's identifying itself with its past wrongs is the verso of the rejection and expulsion of this self. In a single dynamic act, Scheler claims, the I attains a qualitatively new level of life and a higher plane of moral ideality as it looks back and down at the old I it has expelled from itself. Memory, he states, is the beginning of freedom from the dark power of remembered being. Memory interrupts the current flowing at the center of the self. It entails, for Scheler, a making conscious of the past. He believes that the distance of consciousness from what it knows is already a step of freedom from that which it objectifies: "History comprehended," he writes, "frees us from the power of the history we live."[106]

The act of repentance achieves this higher plane through the dual charge of its paradoxical dynamic. Although Scheler discerns that whoever cannot repent is not free, he asserts that repentance does not presuppose freedom as the condition for its possibility. Rather, the performance of repentance is the act by which one becomes free from the determinative thrust of the past.[107] This liberation from the determinative forces of the past both orients and strengthens the resolutions and dispositional transformations of the moral self and establishes it on a higher plane. Scheler thus formulates a conception of repentance based on the *felix culpa*. He claims that the rhythm of debt and repentance belongs necessarily to the life of finite and corrupted existence. But repentance elevates the self, ideally and morally, to a plane of existence that would not have been possible without the preceding sin and repentance.[108] Repentance, therefore, does not restore the self to its old self; it advances it. The self has become new, according to Scheler, and more truly—that is, ideally—itself. The backward glance gathers to expunge. It shines the light of consciousness into the darkest recesses of the self in order to integrate and divest.

For Scheler, this double-edged sword of repentance is efficacious only because the past remains unfinished. In contrast to dead nature, human time is divided into present, past, and future. Following Husserl's phenomenology of inner time-consciousness, Scheler states that each moment has in it three extensions: the experienced present, the experienced past, and the future. He concludes:

> There are present to us in the experience of every one of our indivisible, temporal moments of life the structure and idea of the *entirety* of our life and personal selfhood. . . . It is by virtue of this wonderful fact that—perhaps not the material reality—but the *sense* and *worth* of the whole of our life still come, at every moment of our life, within the scope of our freedom of action.[109]

In contrast to a natural causality in which each moment is determined solely by the preceding moment, every single experience may be effective for another later moment. Each moment in a series is determined by the series itself. As long as a person's life-context has not closed, the meaning and the value of experiences of the past remain open. Scheler explains:

> Since the total efficacy of an event is, in the texture of life, bound up with its *full* significance and *final* value, every event of our past remains *indeterminate* in significance and *incomplete* in value until it has yielded *all* its potential effects. Only when seen in the whole context of life, only when we are dead . . . does such an event take on the completed significance and "unalterability" which render it a fact such as past events in nature are from their inception. Before our life comes to an end the whole of the past, at least with respect to its significance, never ceases to present us with the problem of *what we are going to make of it*.[110]

Having entered the temporally extensive category of experience, objective time is robbed of its fatality and finality. The past content of time becomes "ours" and is subordinated to the power of the person. Scheler thus contends that we have the authority to decide in what form and to what degree a particular part of our past affects the meaning of our life.[111]

The meaning and value of past conduct or a past attitude can be set in a new relation to the totality of one's life, giving it a new direction. "Repentance," Scheler concludes, "is equivalent to re-appraising a part of one's past life and shaping it for a mint-new worth and significance."[112] Such a fundamental reappraisal goes deeper than the repenting of an isolated act of misconduct. It goes to the core of one's person. Schopenhauer distinguishes between the repentance of conduct (*Tatreue*) and the repentance of being (*Seinsreue*). Whereas a repentance of conduct exclaims, "Alas! what have I done," the repentance of being cries out, "Alas! what kind of person am I?" While adopting this distinction, Scheler rejects the notion that we can repent our whole being or our entire personhood as an "inner impossibility."[113] At most, he claims, one can repent that, at that time, one was such a person that could do such a thing. The object of repentance is, then, neither merely the individual misdeed nor our "very person in its quintessential being" but the "entire concrete constitution of the I." A misdeed or ill will may very well become "understandable" and even be deemed as having been necessary when one accounts for how the self was constituted at that time. But, according to Scheler and in line with Kierkegaard's Climacus, it was never necessary for us to be the person for whom the act may have been unavoidable. It is not merely a counterfactual reference to contingency in the sense that, hypothetically, we could have willed and acted otherwise; rather, our present level of reflection demonstrates that we concretely could have been other than we were.[114] Scheler portrays the relation of the new self to the old self as a relation of the totality of personhood to one of its concrete successions. The self who has repented of how it was is a qualitatively different self, and the free act of repentance establishes this re-marking of the boundary of the self.[115] Consequently, the act of repentance does not belong to what is expunged from the new constitution of the self. It is not a revisionary act of the new self or of a total self latently existent the whole time. It is neither of the old nor of the new, neither on this side nor on that side. Rather, for Scheler, repentance is the act of rebirth itself.[116]

Whereas guilt breeds guilt and the contagion of evil spreads itself with augmenting strength, repentance is the power of transformation from one type of existence to another. Repentance, according to Scheler, does not aim at the *feeling* of guilt but at guilt as a *quality* of the person. It aims at the renewal of the core of all intentions and action and is capable of completely extinguishing the quality of guilt, not merely of covering it up with other good deeds.[117] It cannot remove, however, the external fact of the committed misdeed or its causal effects. Nor can it remove the evil character manifested in the deed. All of these things, Scheler concedes, remain in the world.[118] As a self-healing of the soul, repentance gives us the chance to relate to ourselves as opposed to being driven by the evil and the guilt that secretly accrue and constitute the self: The I that I was has been rejected, condemned, and banished from my person, and yet it was I before my moral rebirth who did that crime. It is not who I am but who I was—or better, who I have been.[119] In this light, the past misdeed becomes the negative condition without which I would not be who I am. To have become different or otherwise is still to have been. Scheler emphasizes that the significance of acts depends on how we relate to them. The repented sin may fan the fire of moral regeneration, channeling the energy applied to sin and implied by guilt to the doing of good.

As a self-healing of the soul, repentance appears to constitute for Scheler a moral monologue. But in several respects, he intends to highlight its dialogical character. First of all, he insists that repentance is not confined to a process in the individual soul. Solidarity is a key principle for Scheler. On the basis of an Augustinian-spirited, ontologically grounded community of persons, every individual shares responsibility for all events of the moral cosmos. Although Scheler distinguishes this shared responsibility for a "tragic guilt" from the self-incurred guilt for a misdeed, he suggests that every person is implicated in the collective guilt of his or her age and should thus regard this guilt as one's own and repent of it. Consequently,

Scheler witnesses in repentance a revolutionary moral power and a social-historical necessity for overcoming human alienation from self, community, and being.[120] Second, Scheler claims that whoever truly repents will also confess his or her guilt. Jankélévitch's complaint that the petition for forgiveness has remained absent therefore could be seen as a sign that repentance has not taken place: If "they" had repented, "they" would have confessed or requested forgiveness. Third, the religious understanding of forgiveness, which Scheler places in parentheses, sets repentance in the dialogical relation with God.

What remains unequivocally missing from Scheler's account of repentance, however, is the role of the other other, the social-ethical role of the other person, the one offended. In his portrayal, the confession that pours forth out of repentance is not a confession before the person I have offended but only a confession before God, and it does not contain in itself a petition for forgiveness. It is rather, as he writes, "an inward confession of guilt . . . when lips are sealed and we are alone with our soul."[121] Repentance, according to Scheler, thus remains a monological endeavor of a soul bound to others in the solidarity of collective responsibility but alone in its self-healing or alone with God behind the closed doors of the intimacy of the soul.

Jankélévitch's Remorse

Like Scheler, Jankélévitch understands repentance as a monologue. He emphasizes the absolutely solitary nature of this private ordeal of conscience. But since forgiveness involves the relation to the other person that he deems absent in repentance, it transcends moral intimacy toward a social ethics that refuses to circumvent the concrete other. Jankélévitch maintains repentance as prerequisite to forgiveness in order to maintain the primacy of the relation to the other. He therefore contrasts the relational and dialogical nature of forgiveness with the "monologue," "solitary rumination," and "soliloquy" of repentance.[122]

Although Jankélévitch's reflections on repentance demonstrate close parallels to Scheler's, he unmasks the theological framework that underlies Scheler's understanding of repentance. Although Scheler speaks of the person lost and approximating despair, Jankélévitch detects a teleological certainty in his representation of repentance. By ignoring the complexity introduced by the other other that Levinas presses into the aporetic, Scheler privileges the self's relation to God who is willing to forgive, which simultaneously privileges the self's relation to itself. Scheler's essay on repentance and rebirth is indeed a meditation on "the eternal in man."[123] He proposes a regenerating return to the center of all things, a return from alienation to the self as it really, eternally is in the mind of God. Jankélévitch's philosophy of innovation and the sporadic problematizes the intertwined self-certainty of the efficaciousness of repentance and the interiority of the individual God-relation.

Jankélévitch aims his criticism at the Christian, and more precisely Catholic, presuppositions within Scheler's analysis.[124] Scheler places these presuppositions at the margins of his essay. He believes that repentance leads us to the idea of God, from its inception as an accusation of conscience to the grace that releases us from guilt. The structure of repentance, for Scheler, is therefore a structure of self-transcendence: first, in the shift within the self from one level to another but also, and more foundationally, in pointing beyond human power to a divine lawgiver who judges through the law of conscience and who releases us from the consequences of the law.[125] The healing of the soul is contingent on the soul alone, for repentance aims at the suspension and annihilation of guilt itself. "But," Scheler asks, "*who* has taken the guilt from us? Who or what is capable of such a thing?"[126] The morality of repentance leads him into the "invisible sphere" of an infinite judge, infinite charity, and an infinite source of power and life. Scheler concludes that "perfect" repentance is carried by the love of God. Although the human spontaneously performs the act of repentance and gradually feels the effects of forgiveness, he retrospectively begins to see that God gives the power to perform the act of repentance, such that our love for God is simultaneously a response to God's love.[127] Beyond the "purely ethical aspect of repentance," Scheler states that from a religious perspective, this "self-healing of the soul" is "the natural function with which God endowed the soul, in order that the soul might return to him whenever it strayed from him."[128]

Jankélévitch rejects this natural representation of repentance.[129] Repentance can be natural only if it is always possible and always within our power. The tears in human relations are rendered superficial when an unsundered and unsunderable ontological unity between individual, community, and God underlies them. It is precisely these presuppositions of theodicy that trouble Jankélévitch. He observes that when God is present behind the scruples of conscience and when God initiates repentance, then God also guarantees that the suffering of remorse cannot be in vain. The outcome is never in doubt in what he calls the "teleology of repentance."[130] On account of this teleology, Jankélévitch argues, the repentant one is always almost already justified. Even pains become sweet in the light of certain restoration—a light shedding of tears, not of agony or desperation but of amelioration and regeneration. Prevenient grace ensures that healing will come, for repentance itself is a gift from God in human nature that enables human individuals to heal all wounds.[131] Or as the apostle Paul declares, "Godly sorrow is not to be repented of, but worketh repentance unto salvation" (2 Cor. 7:10).

Particularly in his early work *La Mauvaise conscience*, originally written in 1933, Jankélévitch sharply distinguishes between *repentance* and *remorse*, even claiming that they are contradictory. Remorse, for him, constitutes bad conscience. It is the fault and guilt (*faute*) itself. Understood as restating the issue of irrevocability, it is unresolved and unresolvable. There is a reason, Jankélévitch suggests, why there is no verb for remorse. In contrast to the transitive character of the verbal form "to repent," remorse is a state of being, which goes nowhere and leads only to itself due to an impotence to repair.[132] And although Derrida opens the possibility that it is in recognizing one's guilt that one dissociates oneself from oneself as guilty subject, Jankélévitch insists that becoming conscious of guilt does not change the guilt or the guilty subject.[133] Remorse lacks the fruitfulness of repentance; it is passive and sterile—a pure suffering without horizon, taking place in the night and in despair.[134]

Jankélévitch subsequently identifies three main characteristic traits of remorse: its impotence, its inscription into the very being of the person, and its inscription in the order of facticity. By treating remorse in terms of irrevocability, Jankélévitch distinguishes it from *regret*. Adopting Kierkegaard's categories of existence, he classifies regret as an aesthetic phenomenon and remorse as an ethical phenomenon. Regret, he claims, is not essentially different from desire except that it desires something past.[135] It has something of nostalgia, resembling the mere wish to change the past, to have it otherwise, like a vague lamentation for better days (whether they were or not). The misfortune of regret, according to Jankélévitch, consists simply in the impossibility of returning to the past. Time alone is to blame, not the person. The desire of regret seeks to turn back time, but irreversibility impedes any and all such return. As a kind of nostalgic desire, regret creates an illusory image of the past that it cannot revive.

Whereas Jankélévitch associates regret with nostalgia, he associates remorse with tragedy. The tragedy of remorse consists in that I have with my own hands fabricated impossibility. In other words, remorse arises solely in the wake of freedom.[136] It is of the order of ethics because it beckons the notion of having-done. Consequently, the primary sign of remorse is the opposite of regret: Remorse does not desire something irretrievably absent because past but instead desires the dissolution of the past. Whereas regret and memory try to retain the past, remorse would like to resolve it. Whereas the former deal with absences and images, remorse is a presence that obsesses and plagues us without pity.[137] Jankélévitch concedes that bad conscience presupposes memory, but the memory of remorse is not willed; it is "monstrous and passionate and obsessive." In the place of the optative of regret, he substitutes the despair of remorse.[138]

Jankélévitch thus witnesses in remorse a state of being or an ontological condition. Faced with the irreparable, there is only despair and a feeling of impotence, for there is nothing one can do.[139] "This impotence," Jankélévitch writes, "is its proper mark . . . and its signature. But in morality is it not precisely the superfluous that is the necessary? Remorse is the most sterile, the most ineffective of all human sentiments."[140] This sterility, this inability to assert oneself, to do anything about what has been done, is accordingly a passivity and a suffering. It is superfluous, first of all, because it does not stand in adequate relation to the misdeed; it instead primarily refers to the simple fact of having willed the misdeed. In other words, it is excessive. Second, it serves no purpose beyond itself—whether punitive, pedagogical, or juridical.[141] In Levinas's terms, it embodies a "useless suffering."[142] Since something irreparable has come into existence through my fault, this suffering is double: the suffering of guilt and the suffering of suffering—that is, the suffering of my impotence to remove my guilt. Although having its origin in time, the fact of having-done becomes eternal and ineffaceable. It represents what Jankélévitch calls an atemporal semelfactivity.[143]

The object of remorse, Jankélévitch claims, is not an isolated misdeed but the entire being of the self.[144] As a kind of cancerous memory, remorse is not interested in just a portion of our experience but involves the totality of the person and its intimate ipseity.[145] It does not allow for a space between the subject and his fault in which a verb could act to further the distance.[146] Bad conscience consists in the condemnation of oneself—the simultaneity of being judge and judged.[147] Remorse thus concerns the essence of the person, for, on the one hand, inexpiable guilt has become deeply instilled in my ipseity and serves to characterize me.[148] The initiative of liberty creates destiny.[149] On the other hand, it is less the fault itself that appears so heinous in remorse than the profound corruption of the will. Beyond the more well-defined faults, it is one's own display of ill will or even fundamental wickedness that occasions self-reproach.[150] In this regard, Jankélévitch draws on Scheler's distinction between *Tatreue* and *Seinsreue* for his metaphysically rooted distinction between repentance and remorse. But he could equally have Kant's distinction in mind between moral evil and the "endless violations" or "infinite guilt" that arise from it.[151] Whereas repentance concentrates on particular actions, remorse places its accent on the concrete constitution of the whole person.[152] My deed and my intention both become part and parcel of my personal ontology, and they express and reveal something about my person.

The inscription of the having-done or having-willed, however, applies not only to one's personal ontology but to the ontology of history. Jankélévitch's texts often read like open wounds, as if he were offering a haunting reminder or a reminder of what haunts Hegel's dictum that "the wounds of the Spirit heal, and leave no scars behind."[153] According to Jankélévitch, remorse is the literal and real presence of the past, that which has been inscribed into being and history and that which survives.[154] He describes it as a metaphysical feeling inherent in the fault—a sin having become exterior whose whole signification is interior.[155] Jankélévitch stipulates that remorse belongs to the order of fact, however, not to the order of knowledge. The metaphysics of the fault severs the dependency of his metaphysics of facticity from feelings or knowledge. Consequently, he allows that one may suffer remorse precisely by not having suffered.[156] He thus underscores that remorse pertains to the fact of the fault itself, which inscribes itself into the very quality of the person and into the texture of history. Jankélévitch's claim that the Shoah burdens all of modernity like an onerous secret is thus to be read in the light of his metaphysics of irrevocability and ontology of guilt.[157] It is secret like an invisible and latent bad conscience. Or, rather, that is precisely its secret. It haunts and returns like an unexorcisable ghost. In the context of the question of the prescriptibility of crimes against humanity, he writes that

> the advocates of prescription admit among themselves that Auschwitz never existed; they do not speak of it anymore. But every now and then a *secret remorse*, attesting to the indestructibility of the "having-taken-place," reminds them of the point at which this fiction is fragile. The impossibility of destroying has the impotence of man as its verso. Considered from its positive side, it is nothing other than the necessity of the quoddity.[158]

The fact that these atrocities took place is something that cannot be atoned or effaced. Even when we have repaired what is reparable, there remains a "residual impossibility" and an "irreducible surplus," which for Jankélévitch indicates incurable remorse.[159]

Whereas Jankélévitch associates remorse with impotence and residual facticity, he associates repentance with the power to efface and to atone. Repentance initiates the construction of a new life. It is concerned with amending the past, with transformation, compensation, reparation, and consolation. He claims that it is thus in the despair of remorse that we find the hope of repentance.[160] Whereas "all the burn and all that is incurable of remorse lie in the impossibility of integrating that which we cannot, however, renounce," repentance carries the hope of reducing the consequences of what one has done and of making something new and better out of the future.¹⁶¹ Whereas remorse is sterile and deep, repentance puts in the work of redeeming peripheral guilt.¹⁶²

Jankélévitch thus follows the authoritative line of philosophy in assigning repentance to the temporal vector of the future. Jankélévitch's emphasis on the more fundamental category of remorse constitutes, however, a critique of this tradition, which prioritizes the future because it prioritizes human possibility, activity, and sovereignty over impotence, passivity, and suffering. Remorse reminds us of a past that is not allowed to pass; repentance, in contrast, follows the nature of duty: the possibility of making it better.¹⁶³ Repair, he explains, is the specialty of repentance. One repents the *factum*, but remorse despairs over eradicating the *fecisse* (the having-done).¹⁶⁴ Whereas there is nothing to do about the quoddity of remorse, repentance constitutes the opening of human possibility and thus a future.

Jankélévitch's skepticism of repentance is rooted in the proximity of morality and economy. Three quarters of morality, he claims, consists in the dissimulation of the inconsolable hell of conscience and in the distillation of remorse, for he believes there is nothing in the world that frightens us like the "metaphysical terror" of the inexpiable. Religion and morality have thus devised systems for compensating and neutralizing the indestructible and irreparable: the inexpiable.¹⁶⁵ In such preoccupation he discovers what Henri Bergson calls "closed justice," a justice based on geometrical equality, equilibrium, and compensatory exchange—a morality of the marketplace. One buys redemption or merits liberation by exchanging acts of penitence for forgiveness, seeking to add enough pluses to the minus of a misdeed that one comes out even or perhaps even a little ahead. Like Kant, however, Jankélévitch repudiates the idea that one can, through future good conduct, produce a surplus.¹⁶⁶ He demonstrates little sympathy for a morality based on equivalences or checks and balances.¹⁶⁷ Under the aegis of such morality, this type of repentance seeks to annul the past by covering it up or even "digesting" it with good works.¹⁶⁸ Jankélévitch's critique of the teleology of repentance thus simultaneously aims at its optimism, finality, and meritoriousness.¹⁶⁹

Displaying his penchant for allying contraries, though, Jankélévitch says that remorse not only constitutes an obstacle that we cannot overcome and that we seek to evade; it is also an organ for liberation. In other words, he interprets remorse as an organ-obstacle.¹⁷⁰ By embracing despair, accepting impotence, and becoming conscious of sin, remorse may facilitate release, he states. Just as forgiveness cannot have the express intention of saving or converting the guilty person, it cannot be my express will to kill in order to create, as Scheler suggests. This lack of intentionality, rationality, and motivation that characterizes the despair of remorse seems to provide the necessary but insufficient condition for redemption. As Jankélévitch explains:

> Despair would not be despair if it squinted toward redemption of which it is perhaps the forerunner and if it were counting on this forerunner as if on a promise. Nothing prevents grace from possibly redeeming the despair of remorse on the condition that this despair has not expected this grace, and on the condition that this person did not put on the act of remorse wholly on purpose.[171]

This line of thought evokes something akin to Kierkegaard's inverse dialectics.

Jankélévitch touches here on what Luther describes as "anguished conscience" and Kierkegaard, in following Luther, comprehends as "consciousness of sin." Far from procuring redemption, the consciousness of sin is characterized by the impotence of one's own accord to obtain it.[172] In Kierkegaard's inverse dialectics, the consciousness of sin potentially precipitates the continuation and intensification of sin, on the one hand, and figures importantly in the forgiveness of sin, on the other. As Kierkegaard's pseudonym Anti-Climacus suggests, persons aware of their despair are, in an important respect, "dialectically closer . . . to being cured than all those who are not regarded as such and who do not regard themselves as being in despair."[173]

In *Forgiveness*, Jankélévitch extends the despair of remorse to repentance. He writes that "sincere repentance repents in poignant inquietude and in the innocence of despair, without any guarantee of amendment," for repentance "is efficacious only if it gives up hope of its own efficacy."[174] Here, too, the relieving grace in repentance and from repentance comes at the darkest hour, so to speak, *repens*—that is, suddenly, quickly, and unexpectedly. Therefore, the relation between repentance and redemption is "entirely undeliberated and indirect," as is the relation between forgiveness and the transfiguration of the guilty person. Their mutual condition of efficaciousness is "the perfect innocence of the hopeless person. . . . For whoever wants to find salvation will miss it."[175]

Jankélévitch's reflections on this ateleological character of remorse and repentance can be interpreted such that the hopeless abyss of despair *may be* redemptive. He says that "in remorse, the desperate person is himself the guilty person, and this desperate person, if he is sufficiently sincere, spontaneously redeems himself all alone; for despair is already an expiation."[176] He claims, moreover, that there is something purifying about pain, and conversely, that there is no "remission without pain."[177] As Jankélévitch observes, however, there is no automatic transition from suffering to healing, for while "suffering without waiting for anything," the remorse-filled person may passively sink into "the hell of his sterile regrets and of his autoscopic confinement."[178] There are no guarantees, no grounds for optimism, no inclination toward finality.

But what happens in despair that allows for the break of the self with the self? From where does redeeming grace intervene? Or as Kant and Scheler ask, how does one become good if one begins with evil?[179] Along with Kant and Scheler, Jankélévitch responds that what is required is a fundamental change or a conversion—*metastrophe*.[180] This radical "change of heart," for Kant, is revolutionary because it consists precisely in the reversal of the fundamental subjective principle of self-love to the love of the moral law. In opposition to an Aristotelian habitualization in the practice of the good, which he associates with external legality and the possibility of gradual reformation, Kant associates this reversal of the supreme maxim of one's will with a "re-birth" and a "new creation," such that the physically self-same person becomes morally another.[181] Similarly, Jankélévitch opposes the gradual change over time with a "sudden metamorphosis" (*métamorphose subite*) that he connects to the moment of creation—the *fiat*, a "*qualité nouvelle*," a rebirth and a renewal of the soul.[182]

Both Kant and Jankélévitch, moreover, contend that conversion constitutes a decision that is nevertheless inseparable from the intervals that precede and follow it. Kant's idea of revolution circumscribes the range and limits of human power.[183] Such radical revolution, he suggests, cannot be a mere "wish" or a passive awaiting.[184] As an act of freedom in the noumenal realm, the instant of revolution is all-decisive, but it still requires the work of "continual progress" in the "process of becoming dead to the old man."[185] In Kant's terminology, "The man who adopts this purity into his maxim is indeed not yet holy by reason of this act (for there is a great gap between the maxim and the deed)."[186] Similarly, Jankélévitch makes the efficacy of the instant of decision dependent on its being extended beyond the instant and sustained in the interval.[187] As marking a beginning, the conversion, he claims, enables repentance, and repentance gives it materiality. Good works, according to Jankélévitch, are thus not the cause of conversion but its effect, and the inexistent existence of the fiat gains increasing objectivity through repentance.[188] While maintaining the connection of repentance to works, Jankélévitch develops here a correlation of repentance to the more fundamental category of remorse. In contrast to the teleological conception of repentance that he aligns with penitence and that either compels or substitutes for forgiveness, repentance here is understood as the reestablishment of autonomy through the metamorphosis of conversion.

Jankélévitch's idea of conversion, however, differs considerably from Kant's on the question of grace. Conversion, for Jankélévitch, constitutes a "mystery" and a "miracle par excellence," whereas for Kant there is next to the starry heaven above only one miracle or wonder and that is the moral law within.[189] Kant thus suggests we make use of the "wonder" that we find in the moral predisposition in us in order to become better persons.[190] Solely on this basis can we hope that what is not within our power will be supplied through cooperation from above.[191] Kant's moral religion denies the dogmatic assumption that God can make one a better person without, at least, oneself having to become a better person. Moral agents are to proceed as if there were no grace, but so that they do not slacken their effort in a world where happiness and morality are disjoined, they are to act as if there is a God. Kant concludes that, although incomprehensible and useless for both theoretical and practical reason, grace may be rationally hoped for.[192] Grace thus incomprehensibly occurs, for Kant, not in the revolution but in the realization or the accountability of the good. Although the "supersensibly *grounded*" revolution is solely dependent on the free will, grace consists in the fact that, while we are "in the world of sense" always only becoming good (or well-pleasing to God), the person post-revolution is considered in full possession of the good.[193] Whereas the conscience might still condemn what one has done as well as one's myriad of moral shortcomings, it is "grace alone," according to Kant, that decrees that satisfaction of justice is carried out during the change of heart itself.[194]

In contrast, Jankélévitch understands conversion as coinciding with the moment of grace, and he contends that conversion is not solely within our power. In his view, grace does not compensate for human finitude and frailty. Instead, the grace of conversion stems from and arises out of the pure suffering of remorse itself.[195] Far removed from Levinas on this point, Jankélévitch claims that suffering itself may be a form of expiation. "Remorse," he writes, "is the instantaneous, gratuitous, unmerited forgiveness which renders healable our faults and which prepares remission."[196] Jankélévitch's inspiration from the mystics is unmistakable. In order for the first hope to spring up in the night of guilt, "an absolutely contingent transfiguration of the will is required: a grace."[197] The rebirth of conversion is mysteriously given in the fleeting flash of grace.[198]

Acts of repentance thus should be considered responses to the gift of grace. In the interplay of the instant and the interval, the instant of conversion remains dependent on being carried out. It is first with the increasing materiality of repentance, Jankélévitch asserts, that the fault becomes increasingly a strange phenomenon to the subject. The form of repentance that is enabled by conversion integrates the fault in a "totality perpetually enlarged, transformed, deepened."[199] Like Scheler, Jankélévitch is clear that this form of repentance does not annihilate the past but entails its transfiguration, redemption, and healing.[200] He confirms that even repaired faults remain in us, remembered like a kind of "beneficial barbarism," a remembrance of the *felix culpa*.[201] He subsequently deems confession (*l'aveu*) a revelation of what is one's own as no longer one's own. More sign or symptom of deliverance through the conversion and work of repentance, the confession of the mea culpa "means we have escaped from the monstrous loneliness of the bad conscience; we only express things that are no more one with us, that are at a distance from us."[202]

Remorse is thus, for Jankélévitch, an organ-obstacle; on the one hand, it is sterile, useless, a feeling of impotence in the light of irrevocability; on the other hand, it is the greatest virtue of which a guilty subject is capable because it signals the silent great distress of having-done.[203] Grace, he claims, does not arrive to those who merely passively wait, but this grace is not a payment for our efforts, either.[204] The will works to redeem itself in the certainty of the irrevocable: It works despite a lack of hope for self-redemption. It asserts itself without overcoming by itself the suffering and passivity of its own impotence to remove the irrevocable. And although Jankélévitch describes the instant of conversion as a decision to change oneself, the fact of deciding to change and alter one's ways at this moment instead of another is arbitrary.[205] It is equally possible at any moment and equally unlikely. It is a decision that is given, that is graced. According to Jankélévitch, it is in the flash of a moment, when everything seems lost, that everything is gained.

Although the structures of this relieving remorse and forgiveness demonstrate a large degree of similitude, this gracious suffering should not be interpreted as a form of self-forgiveness. It is not an act of the self on the self but a grace received. Nevertheless, it does pose a dilemma for the question of forgiveness. It compels a reformulation of the dilemma portrayed in Derrida's critique of Jankélévitch's purported rationalization of forgiveness. Three possibilities of forgiveness within Jankélévitch's account, therefore, should be more closely examined: (1) the possibility of forgiving the person who has not demonstrated remorse or repented; (2) the possibility of forgiving the person who suffers remorse and repents without the experience of conversion; (3) the possibility of forgiving the remorseful and repentant person who already has distanced himself from the past fault and is morally reborn as another. To each of these possibilities belong questions as to the tasks of each party: Does forgiveness make sense if the one who is to be forgiven does not recognize the need of forgiveness or, exacerbating the problem, if she or he has a good conscience—that is, if she or he is unaware of being guilty or of having done anything wrong? Is it not the obligation of the one to discover and acknowledge his or her guilt, repent because of it, and request forgiveness from the other? Because if the remorseful-repentant person has already become another, is not forgiveness rendered superfluous?

Asymmetrical Reciprocity

The dialogue of forgiveness has two sides, and Jankélévitch maintains that each party has his respective task: "To the criminal belongs desperate remorse, and to the victim belongs forgiveness."[206] The relationship between repentance and forgiveness as well as that between remorse, repentance, and the petition for forgiveness needs to be reevaluated in the light of this division of tasks. Clarification of these relationships reframes the concerns about the conditions for forgiveness and illuminates the question of identity.

The tension of the case in which the offender is nonremorseful and nonrepentant is captured by Kierkegaard's Anti-Climacus. He distinguishes between the "despair not to will to be oneself . . . what one is—a sinner" and the "despair to will to be oneself—a sinner."[207] In the first instance, forgiveness is resisted and deemed unnecessary, perhaps even an effrontery; in the second instance, it is viewed as impossible. As Jankélévitch attests, "If unexpiated crimes are precisely the ones that need to be forgiven, then unrepentant criminals themselves are precisely the ones who have no need of forgiveness."[208] If forgiveness is simply given without a preceding consciousness of sin or the despair of having sinned, then it is made into something done to the offender whether or not she or he recognizes a need for it or wills it. Conversely, because forgiveness involves a dialogue, according to Jankélévitch, the will to forgive may be thwarted by the offender whose heart remains hard or whose neck is stiff. Forgiveness, it follows, is dependent on the consent symbolically offered in the gesture of repentance and subsequent petition for forgiveness. The repentant one desires forgiveness and is open to it. Without the experience and acceptance of the gift of forgiveness, forgiveness cannot take place.[209] In other words, the will of the offender can resist forgiveness despite the will of the one who forgives. From this perspective, forgiveness seems to require at least a consciousness of sin, if not an active will of redemption through repentance.

Unconditional forgiveness that ignores the presupposition of this active will of redemption runs the risk of becoming an "infallible mechanism," or automatic dispensation.

Jankélévitch argues that forgiveness is by no means automatically effectual, and it should not be conceived as circumventing or surpassing the other person. As he explains:

> By no means does forgiveness provoke infallibly and in all cases, as if by automatic release, the conversion of the pardoned, redeemed . . . and miraculously cured criminal. That would be too much to hope for! Because if it were really so, then forgiveness would be a legal, obligatory, and universal institution, and as such the refusal to forgive the crime would be the crime. . . . To be able to save a sinner on a sure bet by forgiving him, and yet to prefer to punish him as likewise he "merits," to be able to save him and to refuse to save him, is indeed a type of spiritual murder.[210]

If forgiveness would simply function like an automaton of liberation, one would be morally required to forgive even before and without repentance. He fears that unconditional forgiveness could become exigible, if not a right of the offender, pure and simple. Although Jankélévitch is not immune to the lures of a conception of forgiveness in terms of magico-metaphysical power, he is concerned here with the one-sidedness of unconditional forgiveness. It is one thing to be judged on how one judges others (Matt. 7:2); it is another to hold the other in one's hand like God.

In this light, the condition of repentance serves to unburden the offended of the illusion of solely deciding the redemption of the offender's soul. The forgiver has neither that power nor that right, and the offender has his or her task to perform. Words of forgiveness may do work, even redemptive work, but they cannot automatically, always, and all by themselves do what they say. Upholding the requirement of repentance preserves the integrity of the other's freedom. Repentance balances the asymmetrical power of forgiveness by both involving the offender and relieving the forgiver. Repentance, on this view, is the sine qua non of forgiveness. It indicates the struggle with oneself and the work on oneself that leads to approaching the offended with the request and plea: Please forgive me! Levinas succinctly outlines these steps in his early essay "Reflections on the Philosophy of Hitlerism": "Remorse—that painful expression of a radical powerlessness to redeem the irreparable—heralds the repentance that generates the pardon that redeems."[211]

Jankélévitch's main concern, however, is for the victim. Psychologically, the one who forgives should perhaps forgive the other in order to free himself of the power the other has over him. In being resentful toward the offending person, the power of the misdeed over the psyche of the offended exacerbates the power the wrongdoer wields over him. Repentance is obviously not required for this form of forgiveness. The offended rids himself of the burden and plague, regaining his autonomy. Although this might be extremely important to do at times to enable action, relations, and so on, such a personal and psychological forgiveness mirrors the one-sidedness of repentance. It is solely one's own well-being that is at stake.

The lowering of the offender in the petition of forgiveness, on the contrary, can empower the victim in his freedom by restoring to him the capacity of decision. Whether or not the offended person forgives and opens up a future of reconciled relations with the offender, the injury harming autonomy and self-worth may be transfigured in the gesture of repentance that restores decision to the offended. This gesture does not annul the harm but negates the symbolic message of the offense, the devaluation of the individual, and it can be offered only by the one who committed the act and sent the message of devaluation or undervaluation in the first place. As we have seen, this reversal opens up the possibility that forgiveness could be withheld and thus become an instrument of vindication and revenge. The mandate of the condition of repentance, however, exhibits the interdependence of the two parties. As Charles Griswold elucidates, "Each party holds the other in its power, in this sense: the offender depends on the victim in order to be forgiven, and the victim depends on the offender in order to forgive."[212] In this paradigm of dyadic forgiveness, the transformations that the offender and victim undergo are "mutually dependent" while remaining "asymmetrical."[213]

By asserting the condition of repentance, Jankélévitch underlines the double sacrifice and risk necessary for the act of forgiveness. "Forgiveness," he writes, "is an adventure not only for the guilty person; the one who forgives exposes himself too to hazards of which every relation with the Other is composed."[214] On the one hand, the perpetrator must overcome herself, her pride and ego to prostrate herself (whether literally or symbolically) before the offended. On the other hand, the offended needs "all of his courage in order to sacrifice not a part of his possessions but his being itself, and even more to brave social taboos, to challenge the duty to punish, and to support himself in so-called moral dilemmas."[215] The offended person's attitude toward the offense must not have changed: Condemnation remains.[216] The one who forgives overcomes his injured ego and the demand for justice inherent in ressentiment. He forgives not out of the generosity of one abundantly wealthy and sovereign; he does not give what he can spare but offers forgiveness in an instant of self-transcendence, which is not a power of the self, as Scheler claims, but a "forgetting of the self [*oubli-de-soi*]."²¹⁷

Both sides, according to Jankélévitch, thus require the task of the offender. The efficacy and morality of forgiveness depend on the freedom and acknowledgment of both parties. Like forgiveness, Jankélévitch observes, repentance "echoes a contingent initiative of freedom."²¹⁸ Linked to freedom, repentance exhibits the moral life and belongs to axiology. He explains:

> Repenting implies a drama and a moral life: a moral life, that is to say, acts of contrition: a moral life, that is to say, burning regret accompanied by the wise proposal to do better in the future by courageously taking on the suffering. The repentant person turns and returns the memory of the misdeed and endeavors to redeem it. The time of repenting, in opposition to the twenty hollow years of the prescription, is thus a meditative and contemplative plenitude. What is operative in repenting is the sincerity of the regret and the intensive ardor of the resolution. Repenting is redemptive because it is, first, an active will of redemption.²¹⁹

In this exceptionally rich description, Jankélévitch incorporates under the heading of repentance both the suffering of remorse and the resolution for the future to redeem the offense. It is incumbent on the offender through the "active will of redemption" not to flee the inexpiable but to humbly remove the obstacles of pride that inhibit the feeling of bad conscience, while eradicating the consequences of the deed through the enacted resolution to do better.

Chronology and nature play no role in the drama Jankélévitch portrays. Merely sitting in the penitentiary does not imply penitence. Merely "doing time" does not pass for moral renewal. "Time without drama," he suggests, does not and cannot suffice "to metamorphose a sinner." "In the time of expiation and penitence," he adds, "it is not the years themselves that redeem the criminal, rather it is the rigor of the expiative and penitential ordeal; it is not the raw duration but the duration of suffering."²²⁰ The task of the offender is thus to will redemption "without looking to economize on the sufferings of remorse or on the sacrifices of repenting and of contrition." Time itself will not do the trick because "time, the primary and natural given of lived experience, is incommensurable with the normative order of value; and value, for its part, is of a wholly other order than time."²²¹

Jankélévitch's failure to distinguish what Karl Jaspers calls moral and metaphysical guilt from criminal and political guilt leads him, however, to contradictions in his principled juxtaposition of axiology and chronology.²²²

Forgiveness, he explains, becomes "nothing more than a bad joke" if one does not "release [the other] from his punishment or from part of his punishment." A sense of urgency to forgiveness thus emerges: "Hurry up and forgive," he advises, "before the debtor is cleared!" In other words, he provokes something like a "statute of limitations" on forgiveness itself, as if there is a moment when it is simply too late to forgive.[223] Forgiveness, he insists, "finds a raison d'être when the moral debtor is still a debtor," even if there remains only an unredeemed portion of the offense.[224] In this passage, he strangely includes the paying of reparations and the mere serving of time in prison in his list of ways that debt is removed and even expiated, while occluding repentance.

Despite the moral or axiological character of repentance, Jankélévitch follows the predominant theological tradition in its belief that repentance is not expiatory. Jankélévitch explicitly states that repentance is "much more a matter of *contrition* than of *expiation*." More specifically, he elucidates that "expiation, it is true, removes the raison d'être of forgiveness: expiation, but not repentance."[225] When he describes how in "courageous repenting" the repentant person gives himself "the penalty of expiation," he should be understood as circumscribing the limits of repentance: The guilty person should hold himself accountable for the having-done and willingly submit himself to the moral ordeal that it entails.[226] Accordingly, his assertions that repentance is not expiatory and that, as a matter of the will and work of the self, it cannot substitute for forgiveness should be taken seriously, even though he does not adequately reflect on the heterogeneity of the legal and the moral spheres, which is the fulcrum of his argument in the essay "Should We Pardon Them?"

A central point of his polemic in this work against the political appropriation of forgiveness and the socially coerced forgiveness he witnessed being overtly and covertly propagated following the Shoah pertains to the silent tranquility of good conscience and the slumber of thoughtlessness.[227] His disgust at the prosperity of the wicked and the guilty is fueled by their lack of apparent sorrow or pain at what happened, which was made all the more poignant by the seeming dismissal of culpability. If the crime committed does not have a negative effect but instead leads to prosperity and good conscience, forgiveness, Jankélévitch concludes, becomes "a sinister joke." It becomes "derisory" and "a farce."[228]

Accordingly, Jankélévitch claims it is despair or "costly heartbreak" that is the true precondition of forgiveness.[229] In his words:

> The criminal's repentance and *in particular his remorse,* by themselves alone, give meaning to forgiveness, just as despair alone gives mean-

ing to grace. What good is grace if the "desperate person" has a good conscience and a good mien? . . . Why would we forgive those who regret their monstrous crimes so little and so seldom?[230]

The precondition for forgiveness that Jankélévitch upholds, therefore, is not necessarily first and foremost the work of repentance per se; the elementary condition is "the distress, the insomnia, and the dereliction of the wrongdoer." Although Jankélévitch makes the important qualification that forgiveness does not necessarily require such feelings, he adds:

> This condition is nevertheless that without which the entire problematic of forgiveness becomes a simple buffoonery. To each person belongs a task: to the criminal belongs desperate remorse, and to the victim belongs forgiveness. . . . [But] before there can even be a question of forgiveness, it is first necessary that the guilty person, instead of protesting, recognize himself as guilty without pleas or mitigating circumstances, and especially without accusing his own victims; not at all! In order for us to forgive, it is first necessary, is it not? That one comes to us to ask for forgiveness. Has one ever asked us for forgiveness?[231]

Even if still possible, a forgiveness without these conditions constitutes, in his eyes, a one-sided forgiveness that precludes conscience and responsibility on the part of the offender.

Jankélévitch's reflections represent the paradigmatic sense of forgiveness as contingent on the precondition that there be a recognition of the fault and concomitant distress. Within Jankélévitch's metaphysics and ontology of the quoddity of evil, however, forgiveness need not be dependent on the perception of remorse. Jankélévitch maintains that the having-done, or, more precisely, having ill-willed, inscribes itself into personal ontology and sociohistorical ontology as a metaphysical fact, and he also describes remorse as being more of the order of the fact of this fact of having-done than of the order of phenomenological consciousness of sin and the perceived pangs of conscience. It follows that forgiveness need not wait for the consciousness of sin and conscious suffering of remorse. The sole precondition is that there is something to forgive. That which is to be forgiven is, therefore, not so much the repentant sinner as the fact that the sinner is a sinner, whether he recognizes himself as such or not. Jankélévitch underscores that, "when even the offender would not be desperate, black shadows would still envelop him, for his dereliction is in a certain way more poignant than that of the repentant person."[232] Therefore, forgiveness by his own account does not have to demand the request for forgiveness, repentance, or remorse, which make forgiveness more understandable but less of a hyperbolical and radical possibility.[233] If evil is the object of forgiveness, then the mere having-done, the mere fact of having ill-willed constitutes the stuff of unconditional forgiveness.

Although the preconditions of remorse, repentance, and request belong to the rationality of forgiveness, the condition of remorse and repentance may still obtain for unconditional forgiveness, though in a different light. In other words, there is a difference between the condition of repentance and the precondition of repentance. The feeling of remorse, the consciousness of sin, and the assumption of responsibility may still be required for forgiveness to be effectual. But unconditional forgiveness may itself be the condition that allows the offender to become conscious of her guilt, to repent, and in repenting to appropriate forgiveness. Repentance may be a response to the responsibility of the one who forgives. As Levinas's lectures and Kierkegaard's and Scheler's interventions reveal, the biblical traditions presuppose God's love as the possible condition for conceiving oneself as a sinner and returning to God. By maintaining the condition of repentance, forgiveness is prevented from falling, on one side or the other, into a monologue of monads, each concerned solely with his or her own redemption. Ultimately, the tear of the offense is social, and the sewing of these wounds equally requires sociality: Each party involved has his or her individual tasks, responsibilities, and concomitant risks.

A more complex situation emerges, however, when it is not first the other who, through forgiveness, "opens a breach through the wall of guilty intimacy . . . [and] breaks the enclosure of remorse" but the conversion in remorse itself.[234] Deliverance, for Jankélévitch, is always a possibility under the sign of the *perhaps*: It may come unexpectedly and unintentionally through suffering and humility or from the response of the other. The suffering of remorse and the subsequent trial of repentance may prove expiatory, and in such cases, he concludes that forgiveness is rendered useless: "The one who expiates obviously does not have need that one forgive him."[235] Jankélévitch thus endorses Derrida's implication that forgiving the one who has already undergone the conversion of remorse and repentance is to miss the point and the person. Jankélévitch draws the parallel to forgiveness by stating that the remorse-repentance complex "implies an arbitrary event that is always synthetic in comparison with the old life."[236] Linked to the event, the conversional act breaks with the old life and initiates a new order.

Jankélévitch's thought simultaneously resists this schema. It too readily precludes the aspect of sociality and overestimates the rebirth of the one whose will has been transformed. The one who willingly appropriates the suffering of remorse and who undergoes a change of heart remains in solitude. It is a "monologue" and a "solitary rumination" that is concerned with "moral intimacy," "solitary perfection," "my own destiny."[237] The repentant person, he observes, works solely "to be reconciled with himself."[238] Even if the offender receives forgiveness as the repentant person repents—"in the night"—Jankélévitch detects in repentance "a type of reassuring finality that forgiveness lacks."[239] The supplementary hazard that forgiveness introduces through the presence of the other and the incertitude of receiving forgiveness from the other obtains even when remorse and repentance do not transform the offender and transfigure the offense. Since the offense is social and involves the other person, "the springtime of the guilty person no longer depends on the guilty person alone."[240] Even if he or she has morally become another, the rebirth requires, in the words of Kant and Saint Paul, the continual shedding of the dead old person and the putting on of the new one (Col. 3:9–10; Eph. 4:22–24). Forgiveness may aim at the having-done, which remains a fact even if transfigured, and at the person who is dying of the despair of having-been. Although this conception incorporates the ontological reality of guilt, it also focuses on the social reality of sin.

Confronted with the paradox of repentance as represented by Derrida, Jankélévitch asks, "Am I really the same person?" He offers a compelling response:

> Memory is nothing other than the moral protest by the human against this ambivalence; it implies a kind of ethical responsibility and simultaneously a moral piety, which obliges me to bind the tangible and corporeal present to past, absent, and invisible things. . . . I am required to assume my past, and to declare it to be my own and to be indestructible despite all opposition.[241]

Although Jankélévitch speaks existentially of unity, responsibility, and identity, his memory is divided. On the one hand, remorse serves as the reminder that I am the same person, but this memory is and is not my own. It is the haunted memory of the irrevocable, the obsession of having-done. I do not will this identity. In fact, in remorse, it is against my will. If anything, I want to be rid of it. I can do nothing with it: Through its inscription into my very being in its entirety, it identifies me. This identity signifies the passivity of the accused, composing the accusative "me." In the words of Rosenzweig, this person at most can say, "I am a sinner."

On the other hand, this memory represents the self instantiated in its autonomy, an ethical memory of consciousness and will that holds itself responsible, despite the tides of time and despite even moral transformation.

In the interpretations of Scheler and Jankélévitch, even after rebirth, the fact of having-done remains; it is its meaning and value that have changed. The "reconciled or repentant consciousness," Jankélévitch explains, "carries, in the form of a scar, the trace of old moral traumatisms."[242] Healing has occurred, as the scars testify, and the same physical person has morally become another, but the I she was is integrated into the I she has become. I separate myself not merely from the isolated offense but from the I who committed it, while appropriating culpability for the person I was having committed it. It was I, she says: "I was a sinner."

Negotiations

Jankélévitch offers intelligible reasons for insisting that forgiveness without at least a consciousness of sin or the despair of remorse relinquishes its meaning, its integrity, and its sense. Although he acknowledges that the one who forgives is not required to demand the precondition of remorse or repentance, he seems to follow the predominant logic of the Abrahamic religions, which embeds repentance in the dialogue of forgiveness, as Derrida argues. His position is highlighted by his adamancy that repentance is not expiatory. Jankélévitch's insistence on the precondition of forgiveness reflects his concern about the justice of forgiveness. By repenting, the other gives me a reason to forgive. An element of the rationality of desert seems to pervade his declared suprarationality of forgiveness, regulating the time and place for forgiveness's exceptionality. In short, the voluntary demand of the precondition of remorse and repentance lessens the paradox and the scandal of forgiveness and tends as Derrida criticizes, to make forgiveness an exchange.

Derrida's critique aims at both meritoriousness and meaning.[243] In his critique of the teleology of repentance, however, Jankélévitch is equally dismissive of the economic rationality behind the idea that repentance makes one deserving of forgiveness or, much less, that it in itself elicits forgiveness. In fact, his critique goes deeper than Derrida's because, though he describes how remorse may be expiatory and transformative, he does not believe that remorse and repentance in themselves are self-transforming, absolving, or expiatory. Here, too, he is in line with the predominant theological traditions: The repentant person is the guilty person, the one in need of forgiveness. Although Derrida contends that forgiveness forgives the person *as* guilty and *insofar* as he or she is guilty, Jankélévitch contends that, outside of exceptional cases of conversion, the repentant person *is* the guilty person.[244] Against Jankélévitch, Kierkegaard, and the majority of those who share this heritage, however, Derrida assumes that the person who recognizes, repents, and requests has become better and somehow other than he or she was before.[245] He thus presumes a sovereignty of self—for what could be more sovereign than a kind of self-redemption—that he seeks to criticize in the act of forgiveness—namely, the assumption that it is a human power, subject to the "I can" of the subject. Ironically, therefore, Derrida's concern that a forgiveness post repentance misses the *what* of the fault and the *who* of the person can be inverted: It is forgiveness of the unrepented offense and the unrepentant person that is perhaps amiss insofar as it aims at a fault that, according to the other, was not committed and at a person who, in his or her own self-understanding, is not guilty.

The question of meaning, according to Derrida, goes to the heart of the matter, to the "at once double and contradictory" injunction of the Abrahamic heritage. He states that, "in order to have its own meaning, pure and unconditional forgiveness must have no 'meaning,' no finality, even no intelligibility."[246] His analysis of the tension at the heart of the heritage is based on the tension of the "in-between" or of the "on the one hand and on the other hand." Although prioritizing the unconditional, Derrida is explicit that it is a matter of negotiation between these irreconcilable but indissociable injunctions: the injunction of "unconditional, gracious, infinite, aneconomic forgiveness" and the injunction of "conditional forgiveness proportionate to the recognition of the fault, to repentance, to the transformation of the sinner who then explicitly asks forgiveness."[247]

This tension reasserts itself with regard to the question of presence. Derrida states that forgiveness must be communicated and be understood and that unconditional forgiveness cannot and must not present itself. On the one hand, knowledge, conscious acceptance, and assignment of culpability are required. On the other hand, forgiveness has to remain incomprehensible, irreducible, unintelligible.[248] He writes it is necessary for forgiveness "to understand, on both sides, the nature of the fault, to know who is guilty of what evil toward whom, etc."[249] Even on this side, as Levinas's commentary points out, we do not grasp the depths of our own guilt, the pureness of our motivation, much less the adequacy of the one's response to the other. From the "logic of the unconscious" to the "work of mourning," much disturbs the light of consciousness, as Derrida attests. As soon as it is a matter of understanding or of agreement, he continues, the "scene of reconciliation has commenced." Like the excuse, reconciliation has its basis in understanding, and Derrida seeks to maintain the heterogeneity of forgiveness to this order, the order of all order. Negotiating between the conditional and the unconditional, Derrida concludes that "forgiveness is thus mad. It must plunge, but lucidly, into the night of the unintelligible."[250]

Jankélévitch's representation of forgiveness also can be read as a negotiation between the unconditional and the conditional. He insists that forgiveness becomes a farce or buffoonery if there is not a recognition of guilt on the part of the offender and in the eyes of the offended. Although his analysis is a celebration of forgiveness, he is also, because of its sublimity, critical of its possible reign.[251] He nevertheless continually emphasizes the unconditionality, gratuity, and suprarationality of forgiveness. As a gift of charity, its aneconomic, supernatural character is precisely what characterizes it. He writes:

> Conditions! What does that mean? Would it be that love has need of kindness in order to love? Would love not love if it did not receive gifts? And, if you please, what is a love that loves "conditionally"? We respond: this is precisely a conditional love, and thus hypothetical and mixed with reservations; and consequently this is not love.[252]

It follows that a forgiveness bound by conditions or based on reasons would not be forgiveness. "Reasons for forgiveness," Jankélévitch explains, "abolish the raison d'être of forgiveness."[253] The "free gesture of pardoning" is, for him, "the whole essence of forgiveness."[254] As if in repetition of Derrida's lucid plunge into the night of the unintelligible, Jankélévitch writes that forgiveness itself is nothing other than "this empty intellection of the incomprehensible."[255] Forgiveness, for Jankélévitch, too, evokes madness.

Paradoxically, if forgiveness is to have a meaning, it must be understandable, calculable, motivated, reasonable—that is, it must be of the order of consciousness and knowledge. Nonetheless, if forgiveness has a meaning, it is that it gives us the unconditional and incomprehensible to think. Absurd and unmotivated forgiveness, for Jankélévitch, is more suprarational than irrational, only because suddenly and spontaneously it offers a glimpse of the absolute in the instant in which the absolute and the singular subject are no longer distinguished.[256] It is not of another order; a part from it is outside order, context, history—and meaning.

Jankélévitch might speak of this lucid blindness, as he does of music, as the "meaning of the meaning."[257] He calls the meaning of the meaning music's "charm." To speak of music's meaning, for Jankélévitch no less than for Nietzsche, is a categorical mistake, "less false than off-key."[258] Music reveals and expresses. Although it is a "vehicle for intellectual activity," it simultaneously "derails it, [it] signifies and disfigures" as an "antipode to any coherent system."[259] Though "volatile and fugitive," its charm is non-discursive and "total."[260] Similarly, the metalogical "essence" of forgiveness, according to Jankélévitch, is that it is an *act*, not some thing or a psychological disposition, not a concept or *noema,* but beyond being (the empirical) and beyond thought (the metaempirical).²⁶¹ Almost-nothing, it is an act of creation, which the categories of discursive thought in the interval are given to think but which they cannot grasp, identify, or instill with meaning. The instant is heterogeneous to the interval but also indissociable. The aestheticism of Jankélévitch's ethics and metaphysics comes to the fore here in the impossible explanation of the ineffable.

Following the publication of "L'Imprescriptible" in the newspaper *Le Monde*, a young German, Wiard Raveling, wrote an open letter to Jankélévitch. Without mentioning the word *forgiveness,* he refers to the haunting nature of remorse:

> I am completely innocent of Nazi crimes; but this does not console me at all. My conscience is not clear, and I feel a mixture of shame, pity, resignation, sadness, incredulity, revolt. I do not sleep well. I often remain awake at night, and I think, and I imagine. I have nightmares that I cannot get rid of.²⁶²

Moved by this letter, Jankélévitch responds that "we have long been waiting for a word, a single word, a word of understanding and sympathy. . . . We have hoped for it, this fraternal word!" He adds, however, "I am too old to inaugurate this new era. . . . But you are young; you do not have the same reasons as I. You do not have this uncrossable barrier to cross."²⁶³

Jonathan Judaken suggests we read Jankélévitch's texts as prayers, "as self-reflexive exercises in order to consider the terms upon which his own forgiveness might come about."²⁶⁴ Although Jankélévitch gratefully acknowledges this expression of remorse from one who did not do what nonetheless plagues him, he deems the chasm to cross uncrossable. He speaks only for himself and admits that he cannot forgive. He has reasons not to cross or sacrifice. He undoubtedly does not feel authorized to forgive in the names of others; perhaps, he feels that the other who demonstrates remorse is not responsible; perhaps his sense of justice, his ressentiment, his desire for expressions of remorse, bad conscience, and repentance all prevent him. Whatever his reasons, he reminds his counterpart of the always open possibility that one might not be able to forgive. It might prove an uncrossable divide, and there may be many reasons or no reason in particular.

The imperative character of forgiveness consists in that it is I who is called upon to make this decision.²⁶⁵ It is I who has to negotiate between the conjunction and collision of values; it is I who has to negotiate between conditional and unconditional forgiveness. One can ask that there be a sign of humanity and of moral community in the demonstration of remorse and repentance, but the other or others cannot demand that one forgive. One need not stipulate the precondition of repentance in order to forgive, but one cannot compel another to forgive. Neither the moral philosopher nor the politician can issue a rule; each individual must negotiate the chasm of this crossing for himself. But this "uncrossable barrier" is exactly that which is to be crossed, if one can—that is, if one wills it and if it comes; if it comes to pass.

8

What Remains

What remains of the offense after forgiveness, and what remains of the past? John Caputo succinctly captures the tension inherent in this question when he asks:

> Does not forgiveness require the remission of the irremissible past? Do we not, in forgiving, reach back into the past in order to remedy what has been done, in order to undo the harm done? . . . Yet the real is irremissible and, much as God would like to help, what is done is done.[1]

One common misconception of forgiveness is that it turns a blind eye to what has happened, ignoring both the offense and its consequences. But forgiveness is too vigilant to be conflated with latent condonations. It is perhaps a different matter, however, if forgiveness disregards what has occurred. Although not denying the occurrence itself, forgiveness, in this sense, liberates offended and offender from the hold of the past on the present for the future. It allows for the agents to act as if that which did occur had not occurred. Could the colloquialism "to forgive and forget" be a viable moral alternative? Although it should be clear that, for Vladimir Jankélévitch, to forget is not to forgive, forgiveness perhaps requires forgetting in order to achieve its intention. Forgetting may prove beneficial, if not ultimately indispensable, to "covering up" or disregarding the offense. It may even be part and parcel of a forgiveness that makes a tabula rasa of the past or at least a tabula rasa of the past offense. Both the metaphor of covering up and that of wiping clean are inspired by biblical accounts of forgiveness. Among the pluralism of complementary and competing metaphors in the Bible, these two mark the line between forgetting and memory and between what Caputo calls virginal time and forgiven time.

Biblical Metaphors

In the last chapter of his book *The Ethics of Memory*, the Israeli philosopher Avishai Margalit acknowledges the deep-rootedness of the notion of forgiveness in religion, specifically in the Jewish and Christian religions. He thus sees the uncovering of these roots as a necessary preliminary step before embarking on conceptual analysis. Although he recognizes this necessity, he insists that his own conception of morality is humanistic, not religious.[2] Accordingly, humans are for him the only source of moral justification but not a sufficient source. Religion demonstrates negatively that we humans lack sufficient sources of justification. So even if we can perhaps justify our beliefs and actions *to* others, we cannot, according to Margalit writing in the vein of Jankélévitch, justify that such and such is the case or that such and such should be done.[3] Margalit thus seeks to demarcate the human sphere from religion by distinguishing between God's forgiveness and human forgiveness within the context of the Bible.

God's forgiveness in the Hebrew Bible is linguistically delimited. The word *salakh*, which primarily means "to wash," is used for God's forgiveness alone. But this distinction itself has been washed away, for, as Margalit observes, this word is also used in Modern Hebrew for one person's forgiving another. The prevalent term in the Hebrew Bible for interpersonal forgiveness, however, is *nasa*, which means "to bear" or "to carry." To forgive, in this sense, means to be willing to carry the sin of the other with the other, perhaps even for the other.[4] The interesting thing about this notion for forgiveness is that it applies to God, humans, and animals. God bears the sins of humans both individually and collectively. As the Psalmist declares: "You have borne the iniquity of my sin" (Psalm 32:5); "You have borne the sin of your people" (85:3). In relation to animals, this understanding refers to the sacrificial practice of substitution and the scapegoat. As it is written in Leviticus: "The goat shall carry all their iniquities upon itself into some barren waste" (16:22). In the same chapter of Leviticus, besides the sacrificed goat and the scapegoat, there is mention of the sacrifice of a ram. This reference to the ram also appears in the sacrificial scene of the binding of Isaac (Gen. 22), where in the place of his son Abraham finds a ram whose horns are tangled in the thicket.

Paul Celan's poem "Grosse, glühende Wölbung [Vast, glowing vault]" binds together the images of the ram, burning, and the carrying of the other.[5] The symbolism of the ram is broad in scope. The ram was sacrificed as a peace offering, an offering of atonement, and as a petition for forgiveness. Moreover, its horns became the instrument prolonging the breath and carrying the voice through the call of the *shofar*, which is sounded in the ritual on the Jewish New Year's Day when the story of the binding of Isaac is read in all the synagogues. "The song of the whorls" also announces the end of Yom Kippur and is thus, as Jacques Derrida observes, "associated, for all the Jews of the world, with confession, with atonement, with forgiveness requested, granted, or refused. To others or to oneself."[6] The *shofar* is, therefore, also associated with the book, the book of accounts and the book of names, the book of life.

In Derrida's reading of this poem of Celan's, he gives particular attention to the last line: "Die Welt ist fort, ich muß dich tragen [the world is gone, I must carry you]." The present tense of the poem ("Die Welt ist fort") makes it undecidable whether it pertains to an essential and permanent truth; that is, that there is no world (anymore), or to a singular isolated event in a history. Moreover, the world can designate the totality of beings or all of the others.[7] It may contain what philosophy since Plato has maintained as the object of philosophy: the view to totality in the theoretical life. "The world is gone" would then perhaps mark the end of the primacy of theoretical philosophy and the emergence of ethics as first philosophy. Without the presence of the world as totality, the primacy of the unmediated relation to the other comes to the fore, designating a responsibility of one for the other, of carrying the other and helping him bear his burden. In proximity to the language of sacrifice, Emmanuel Levinas calls this responsibility *substitution*, a responsibility that is responsible to the point of being responsible for the responsibility of the other. It is expressed in what Levinas understands as the words of responsibility and love par excellence, "Here I am." In the story of the binding of Isaac, Abraham responds first to God's command and then to the halting word of the angel with these words: Here I am. I, alone, here before you in response to you, to your dependence on me, in responsibility for you and to you.

If the world is gone, there is no solid ground, no foundation, no common ground to serve as mediation between the two or between one or both of them and all of the others.[8] Forgiveness, in Jankélévitch's representation, involves this relation of the two persons without possible mediation by a third person or party and without grounds to justify itself. The world of reason does not provide the solid ground that can make forgiveness normative and thus regulated by distinct criteria that determine its morality, amorality, or immorality. Even language as a third and common ground fails in its attempt to describe what forgiveness is; it often fails, too, in its directness, as the medium of communication of forgiveness.

The world being gone, moreover, provides the condition for or is the result of the imperative expressed in the "I must." In the imperative form, the "I must" is directed toward the future. Since pure forgiveness has perhaps never taken place in history, it is, as Jankélévitch states, formulated in the imperative of duty, and duty is always oriented toward the future. If "I must" specifies the very subjection of the ethical subject, he is called to take responsibility for the other by carrying him. "To carry," Derrida observes, "speaks the language of birth," referring in everyday usage to a mother carrying a child.[9] This birth of the other who is carried could thus also indicate the rebirth of the offender who, through forgiveness, is born again, reoriented toward the good that remains to do, having been carried away from the offense or perhaps having the offense itself carried away by the other. But since the pronouns *I* and *you* in the line "I must carry you" are open designations and the *you* regards an open destination, the *carry* can equally be addressed to the dead, "to the survivor or to the specter, in an experience that consists in carrying the other in the self, as one bears mourning—and melancholy,"[10] for the world of the other has ended at her death.

Mourning, according to Freud, is juxtaposed to melancholy, and it entails carrying the other in the self through introjection, interiorization (*Erinnerung*), and idealization. Successful mourning, in his view, consists in the interiorized idealization of the other in the self, which, as Derrida criticizes, "allows us to *forget* that to keep the other within the self, *as oneself*, is already to *forget* the other." The norm of successful mourning makes the other disappear through her integration and appropriation into oneself. Mourning thus becomes synonymous with "the good conscience of amnesia."[11] For this reason, Derrida insists that melancholy is necessary because it "welcomes the failure and the pathology" of mourning's appropriative claim. Melancholy thus marks the experience of carrying oneself toward "the infinite inappropriability of the other, toward the encounter with its absolute transcendence in the very inside of me, that is to say, in me outside of me."[12] This experience also encompasses the abiding tension in the memory of the dead invoked by Jankélévitch: I must act on behalf of those who cannot act themselves. In doing so, I must repel the forces of forgetfulness both outside and within me: the natural deterioration of memory, the sociopolitical compulsion to progress and reconciliation, and my own tendency to interiorize and appropriate. I must speak in the name of those

I cannot speak for. In the struggle for justice, against the wake of Kant's dictum, I must do what I cannot.

The metaphor of carrying, from the scapegoat to mourning and from pregnancy to memory, is one of many biblical metaphors for forgiveness. Echoing the Psalmist, Paul writes that God doesn't "reckon sin" (Rom. 4:8; Ps. 32:1–2). Although debt is incurred, God does not reckon this debt into our life's account. A stronger invocation of this notion is expressed in the Greek word used for forgiveness in the Gospels, *aphienai*, which means to cancel a debt. This term is also compatible with several other metaphors: The canceling of a debt can be interpreted as bearing part of a debt, as ignoring the debt even though it still exists, or as wiping it out completely.[13] God is also said to "cover" sin (Ps. 32:1; Rom. 4:7) and to put wrongdoing "behind His back" (Isa. 38:17). The Psalmist writes that God removes our sin "as far as the east is from the west" (Ps. 103:12). Elsewhere it is written that God "blots out" (Isa. 43:25) and "sweeps away" sins "like mist" (Isa. 44:22) and that God will not remember our sins (Isa. 43:25; Jer. 31:34; Heb. 8:12; 10:17).[14]

Margalit discovers in these metaphors two basic models of sin and forgiveness that still permeate conceptions of morality in the present, including Jankélévitch's: forgiveness as blotting out sin and forgiveness as covering up sin. The two models are distinguished by the role of forgetting. The blotting out of a sin entails forgetting it absolutely, whereas covering it up means disregarding it without forgetting it.[15] Inspired by the biblical narratives, Margalit understands forgiveness as the conscious decision to overcome anger and vengefulness. This decision thus represents a change in attitude and behavior. Margalit realizes, however, that the decision-character in forgiveness marks only the beginning of a process and that forgetting may result from this decision and ultimately complete the process.[16] He thus parallels *forgiveness* with *work* because both denote a process and an achievement. As he explains, "The forgiver makes a conscious decision at least in paradigmatic cases to enter a process whose end-result is forgetting the injury and restoring his relationship with the offender as though the injury had never occurred."[17] Although forgiving represents a voluntary act, forgetting does not. Forgetting, therefore, is not guaranteed and cannot be required. The completion of forgiveness is consequently postponed for as long as the offended retains the wounds from the injury.

The metaphor of covering up, however, suggests that forgiveness is a disregarding of the offense without necessarily forgetting it. To disregard is to not allow the reasons for one's own action and behavior to be based on the injury done. This primary decisional element is then followed by what Margalit calls a "second-order" desire to overcome our first-order resentment and vengefulness.[18] The decision to refrain from adopting reasons that supposedly justify hostile or cold behavior toward the person who caused injury is thus accompanied, like a promise, by the commitment to embark on the long effort of mastering anger and humiliation.[19] Despite the fact that both forgetting and disregarding maintain that only the voluntary and initiatory decision is in our hands, disregarding has the advantage, according to Margalit. Disregarding does not require something, namely forgetting, that we cannot voluntarily do, especially when we recognize that traces of the offense linger both psychologically and ethically. Even though both aim at the ideal end result of the "restoration of the original relationship between the offender and the forgiver," Margalit concedes that this restoration can be ideally achieved only when the forgiver has overcome all of his resentment and desire to avenge the injury.[20] In other words, the line between forgiveness in the sense of covering up or disregarding and forgiveness in the sense of blotting out amounts to the difference between the real and the ideal or between what is humanly achievable and what belongs solely to God. Forgiveness, Margalit writes, "in the perhaps unattainable ideal sense is overcoming all traces and scars of the act to be forgiven. But this is God's blotting-out forgiveness rather than the human covering-up forgiveness."

Since Margalit admits that "total forgiveness entails forgetting," he implies that human forgiveness remains partial or a work in progress more than an accomplishment. He therefore concludes that "the right model" for a humanistic ethics for both psychological and ethical reasons is the covering-up model.[21] Whereas we can and ought to "blot out" the reliving of the emotion through the establishment of a policy of behavior and the concomitant commitment to self-mastery or to letting go, we cannot so easily forget or overcome the repercussions of the injury that affect us probably more than we know. Forgiveness in the sense of disregarding thus chooses and commits to acting as if the injury had never occurred, but it does not and cannot achieve a state in which the offense and its repercussions become naught.

As If . . .

For Jankélévitch, the stain of the misdeed is irreversible and irrevocable. Even if reparations are made and the consequences of the offense are attenuated, effaced, or even rendered positive, the bare fact that the crime was committed remains eternally. One cannot make of the factum an infectum, he claims; one cannot undo the fact that something was done. One will always have to live with the fact that one has done what has been done. The fact that one did what one did, according to Jankélévitch, will live on beyond one's own memory, one's own life, and the memory of others.

Although Jankélévitch emphasizes the irreversible and irrevocable facticity of the misdeed that cuts its trace into eternity, he believes that the past can be modified. Like Margalit, he asserts that the most that can be done is to act *as if* that which was done was not done. This "as if" does not entail a mere nostalgic wish that things were different than what they were and consequently what they are now. It should not be understood as a fiction or a piece of revisionist history that, if told often enough, can convince all others and eventually oneself that it is the truth. If forgiveness can make the past offense as if it did not happen, then it opens a future that is not (negatively) based on the offense. The offense in the past, in other words, is disregarded; it does not dictate one's attitude or behavior toward the offender because one does not attribute the offense to him. Jankélévitch writes that "the forgiven offense resembles, after the fact, a misunderstanding. Forgiveness liberates, liquidates, and liquefies the running water that rancor held prisoner."[22] Having forgiven, one encounters the offender freely, free from ressentiment, rancor, or disdain and encounters others freely, too, for one's comportment is no longer compromised by the past event. Having been forgiven, the offender, too, is free from moral guilt and the stigma of that guilt, and she or he, too, is free for present relations and future encounters unconditioned and unshaded by the having-done of the misdeed. The fact of the offense remains but the meaning of the past is opened by what Paul Ricoeur, in contrast to Margalit, calls the "active forgetting" entailed in "difficult forgiving."[23]

Jankélévitch describes this forgiveness as rejecting reality, not in denying it but in covering it up. He writes:

> Forgiveness does not deny that the misdeed has been effectively committed, but it behaves as if it had not been committed. Forgiveness decides to consider the event as null and as not having come to pass, even though it did, alas! come to pass; and come to pass it did only too much! And in spite of everything, forgiveness decrees generously, heroically, despite the absurdity, and against all evidence, that what took place did not take place.[24]

The ineradicability of the having-done is not merely physical but also logical and moral. Jankélévitch claims it is impossible to undo the past, even for the minor gods of mythology, because they cannot do what cannot be allowed. The gods could not morally undo what a human has done, for that would compromise human freedom and integrity, both for the offender and the offended. This aspect is important to Jankélévitch, but it is the logical impossibility that forms the thrust of his argument.

He regards the undoing of the having-done as a contradiction that is based on co-presence or simultaneity. He writes that "it would be contradictory that the same thing was at the same time done and not done." The logical contradiction is, however, circumvented in succession. Jankélévitch recognizes that "undoing" is always subsequent to having done. The "making good" of an offense, for example, through compensation and reparations, both in the broad and the strict sense, and through a renewed orientation toward the good, can be done after having committed a moral offense. But the facticity of the having-done is just as present now as it was immediately subsequent to the act itself. Since the having-done is irrevocable, indestructible, and ineffaceable, it marks a position *sub specie aeternitatis* that cannot be negated. The logical impossibility, according to Jankélévitch, therefore consists in the impossible coincidence of position and negation. Consequently, he explains, "To claim to make a tabula rasa of what was is very close to being an absurdity. We can *make as if*, but we cannot *make it that*, we can make it as if that which happened did not happen, but not that what happened did not happen."[25]

Jankélévitch presses the idea of forgiveness toward both physical and logical impossibility and establishes the precipitousness and miraculousness of forgiveness in its embrace of absurdity. Even though Jankélévitch does indeed insist that "to claim to make a tabula rasa of what was is very close to being an *absurdity*," he simultaneously contends that "in spite of everything, forgiveness decrees generously, heroically, *despite the absurdity*, and against all evidence, that what took place did not take place."[26] While treating the "as if" in conjunction with "the necessity of the quoddity" inherent in the notion of the imprescriptible, he places pure forgiveness in the context of the logical impossibility of the coincidence of position and negation. In an instant and only for an instant, forgiveness binds position and negation in a unity. As Jankélévitch explains, "In order to unify contradictories, a miracle is necessary. . . . We will have to research whether forgiveness is not just this very sudden miracle, this miraculous coincidence of position and negation."[27] What remains to be seen in this passage serves as a prelude to Jankélévitch's conclusion: "By the grace of forgiveness," he writes, "the thing that had been done has not been done."[28] In the language of Nicholas of Cusa, forgiveness thus implies a *coincidentia oppositorum*.

Coincidentia Oppositorum

Jankélévitch conceives the grace of forgiveness as breaking with the logic of the law of identity. Although he claims it is reasonable and just "to honor the principle of identity," he believes that "it is also just to annihilate that which should not be."[29] Beyond the compensatory character of justice, which seeks to neutralize the asymmetry invoked by the offense and reestablish equilibrium, forgiveness aggravates the asymmetrical direction of the offense and thus "doubles the scandal scandalously." Forgiveness "annuls sin," Jankélévitch writes. It does so "not literally and by inverting the direction of evil through punishment, and by returning violence to the violent person, but rather by inverting and converting at the same time the intentional quality of the act and the direction."[30] He understands the gift of forgiveness as a self-negating gift that has its converse side in the positivity of a new era. The negating character of the gift of forgiveness is such that it does not give any *thing* and at times appears only minimally (as in a kiss or the slightest wink), but it also annuls what has been. In annulling what has been in the interval before its occurrence, it opens up a new interval. Since Jankélévitch establishes the heart of evil in the heart itself, namely, in the will or the intention, and not merely in the act, he makes the even stronger claim that forgiveness has the capacity to annul the intention of the past. Through forgiveness, he suggests, the guilty person becomes innocent. Unaware of itself and its own good, unmotivated and claiming nothing, pure forgiveness itself is this innocence by which the other becomes innocent, just as it is the liberty that liberates the other to liberty.[31] Because pure forgiveness, according to Jankélévitch, is *causa sui* and innocent, it "effaces all, sweeps away all, and forgets all." Because of its aseity and grace, "forgiveness makes a tabula rasa of the past in one blink of an eye," and "the obstacle called the *misdeed* vanishes as if by magic!"[32]

Jankélévitch thus takes seriously the notion of forgetting in the phrase "to forgive and forget." This forgetting is a consequence or, better, a by-product of forgiveness. It belongs part and parcel to the radical act of forgiveness but cannot morally substitute for forgiveness. Forgiveness is thus a kind of radical forgetting that first remembers in order to delete.[33] The depiction of forgiveness as "blotting out" the wrongs of the past demonstrates the intimacy of forgiveness and forgetting. What Margalit qualifies as belonging solely to God, Jankélévitch qualifies as belonging intrinsically to the idea of forgiveness itself. He does not distinguish between God's freedom and human freedom but focuses on the grace of the instantaneous coincidence of the divine and the human. In pure forgiveness, the decision to disregard the offense "does not limit itself to suspending hostilities" but initiates in a conversion of heart a radically and entirely new beginning.[34] "The one who loves," Kierkegaard explains, "forgives in this way: he forgives, he forgets, he blots out the sin, in love he turns toward the one he forgives; but when he turns toward him, he of course cannot see what is lying behind his back." Jankélévitch follows Kierkegaard who concludes that the forgetting involved in forgiveness is "the opposite of creating, since to create is to bring forth from nothing, and to forget is to take back into nothing."[35]

The idea that forgiveness forgets absolutely does not represent the dominant tendency in philosophy about forgiveness. In its theological heritage, however, the intimacy of forgetting and forgiving revolves around the definitive and noneconomic character of forgiveness. The history of philosophy, on the contrary, has variously emphasized consciousness coming to itself with loss, estrangement, or forgetting as the condition for its self-return. Indeed, whether in Plato's doctrine of *anamnesis* or Hegel's fundamental concept of *Erinnerung*, the driving force consists in the dialectic of forgetting and remembering, almost always with the emphasis on the economy of return. Caputo calls this a "Greco-Germanic forgetting," which is a sort of forgetting that "is meant to come back on you, to repeat itself on you eventually, the sort that requires recalling (Heidegger) or interiorizing (Hegel), so that the deeper the forgetting, which is the danger, the more one needs the recalling, which is the saving."[36] In contrast, Jankélévitch claims that what is forgiven is removed, hidden, forgotten. The forgiven and forgotten offense will no more return; the offense will not be accounted to the offender, and no return will be expected of him. In relation to forgiveness, then, forgetting is neither an involuntary process nor an active policy; it is rather the result of the conversion to love in grace that moves toward the other.[37]

Jankélévitch describes the "single, radical, and incomprehensible" movement of forgiveness as occurring "in one fell swoop." Due to the *causa sui* nature of love and forgiveness and the almost-nothing character of intuition, forgiveness "pardons undividedly in a single, indivisible *élan*."[38] It is simple, for it has no contours, no basis for grasping it. Understanding functions alone on the coordinates of the interval and discursive reason. In contrast, pure forgiveness signifies the quoddity, the that-ness, which carries with it the abundance or surplus (*perisson*) of the "I-know-not-what." It is that which the understanding cannot grasp.

Linked to the creative instant, forgiveness is heterogeneous to all duration and degree. The absence of duration and degree mark the absence of every reservation, and, according to Jankélévitch, this is a fundamental quality of forgiveness. It knows no limits; it cannot say, "Up to this point but no further." He suggests that it is an all-or-nothing decision. Therefore, it is foreign to forgiveness to insist, "Only until a certain date or a certain time is this forgiveness valid." He suggests that there are no chronological limitations to forgiveness. Consequently, he claims,

> Forgiveness forgives the misdeed and the wrongdoer globally, and in turn it forgives infinitely more misdeeds than the guilty person has committed.... Not only does forgiveness forgive infinitely more misdeeds than the guilty person committed, but it forgives all of the misdeeds that this guilty person would be able to commit or still will commit.[39]

In relation to the other, the movement of forgiveness is thus one of "infinite totalization." Although Jankélévitch presupposes that "forgiveness is a relation with the agent with regard to an act of this agent," he maintains that it is first and foremost the person who is forgiven. As he explains, "Absolution spreads from the isolated misdeeds to the guilty subject who committed them."[40] Since forgiveness is primarily the forgiveness of the other person, it is the person her*self* who is forgiven. The breaking of the logic of identity through forgiveness thus does not apply only to the act but also to the person. The offender is no longer identical with herself.[41] Levinas recognizes a similar capacity of forgiveness to open up a mode of existence where nothing is irrevocable and the I becomes aware of its indefiniteness in a temporally exposed nonidentical relation to itself. It is not that the being of the offender is separated from her work, as a theological tradition implies, but rather that her being is renewed through self-distance from the person who she was. In other words, forgiveness addresses the naked ipseity or selfhood of the person beyond her being thus and thus and breaks up the ontological categories of the ego.

The instant of decision, Jankélévitch writes, "arbitrarily cuts the temporal constitution" and "is alone definitive."[42] Since forgiveness does not belong to the interval, it is not bound to limitations or restrictions. It is unbounded and boundless, an unreserved overflowing of love. Since this love begins with itself, is *causa sui*, it is not pointedly attached to the specific deed that serves as the organ and obstacle for forgiveness to overcome; it detaches itself from its object and occasion and spreads itself indiscriminately from the agent of the act to the agent to all agents of all times. Ideally, Jankélévitch exclaims, "forgiveness forgives everyone for everything for all times."[43] Unfettered by temporal contours and chronological constraints, forgiveness is thus final, "forgiving the misdeed once and for all and forever." Pure forgiveness, he writes, "forgives one time, and this time is literally one time for all!" In other words, it "is an intention of perpetual peace."[44] Beyond any type of normalization, forgiveness is an exception, testing the impossible as if it would interrupt the continued continuity of historical time.[45]

Within the finitude of time, however, the finality of forgiveness takes on the temporal character of infinity:

> It immensely exceeds all culpability, either actual or to come. Its resources are infinite; infinite is its patience. Nothing discourages its inexhaustible generosity; it would wait without becoming disgusted until the end of time. It would forgive seven-and-seventy times were it necessary. . . . Forgiveness extends unlimited credit to the guilty person. And the perverted man will grow tired of hating and tormenting the generous man sooner than the generous man will grow tired of forgiving the perverted man.[46]

To forgive is thus as infinite as it is repetitive. It aims at the personhood of the other person, and in giving once and finally, it is willing to forgive again and again. It is patient and awaits the new era that it inaugurates but which is not solely dependent on it. Therefore, when Jankélévitch formulates the eschatological conclusion that forgiveness intends perpetual peace, he is aware that this end may not come and that the infinity of forgiveness may be tested until the end of time.

Whereas the idea of forgiveness *purissime* perhaps commands such an eschatological understanding, acts of forgiveness remain constricted to the finite limits of human strength. Jankélévitch realizes that, although the intention of perpetual peace may be inherent in the idea of forgiveness, human forgiveness is much more fragile and fragmented. It is, in short, always finite and impure. It thus suffices, he states, that "the intention of forgiving, at the moment of forgiveness, sincerely and passionately excluded every chronological limitation, just as it suffices that love, even if, in fact, it has to be unfaithful and versatile, wanted to be eternal on the day of the oath."[47] On the one hand, Jankélévitch upholds the notion that forgiveness can found a future and is capable of instituting a new order and expediting healing and renewal, for it "does the work of several generations in one instant."[48] On the other hand, he recognizes that forgiveness does not have the time to be self-assured of its regenerating power. Its goodness is determined by the intention in the instant, but living out this intention is subject to the fallibility and frailty of all finite human endeavors, especially those in relation to others.

According to Jankélévitch, the idea of the power of pure forgiveness, however, carries with it an insurmountable tension abiding in the coincidence of the irrevocability of quoddity and the negation of the mysterious dark fact of having-done. Thus he claims that forgiveness can wash away the stain of the misdeed that cannot be washed away, for, he writes, "Nothing is impossible for all-powerful remission! Forgiveness can in this sense do everything," even remove the irremovable quoddity of the having-done.⁴⁹ This event is what he calls "the miracle" that is necessary to unite contradictories: the simultaneity of the position of the having-done and its negation. Paradoxically, that which cannot be undone is undone in forgiveness, and yet it cannot undo what cannot be undone. This paradox manifests a forgiveness taut between omnipotence and impotence:

> Forgiveness is simultaneously omnipotent and impotent. All of its redeeming and absolving power cannot make it so that the action that occurred did not occur. . . . "Out damned spot!" But the damned spot does not go away. For if the bloodstains of the action done are capable of being washed away, the accursed stain of the having-done is indelible, and no amount of polishing will wash it away. And nevertheless, in another truly pneumatic and incomprehensible sense, it is the very miracle of forgiveness that in a burst of joy annihilates the having-been and the having-done.⁵⁰

The infinite force of forgiveness is stronger than the fact of having-done, but simultaneously the fact of having-done is stronger than forgiveness. Always reciprocally, Jankélévitch adds! Since forgiveness can overcome the very quoddity of the offense, it symbolizes the power of love to conquer evil. Love does triumph over evil; it can triumph over evil, and it will. But, as we have seen, Jankélévitch simultaneously maintains that evil is stronger than love. Evil is thus overcome by forgiveness *and* is stronger than forgiveness. It is the organ facilitating forgiveness *and* its insurmountable obstacle. *And* is the key word in this *coincidentia oppositorum*.⁵¹ Human existence abides in the tension of the conjunction and collision, in knowing and believing the truth of both: that love triumphs over evil and that evil triumphs over love. As Jankélévitch writes, "The human spirit oscillates between these two triumphs that are simultaneously true, yet alternately conceived: for they contradict one another. And the reciprocity of these two contradictories is reciprocal to the point of vertigo. . . . No! there is no last word."⁵²

To forgive, for Jankélévitch, cannot be conceived as an accomplishment. The radical power of absolution Jankélévitch attributes to forgiveness is counterbalanced by his acknowledgment of the radical power of wickedness. Forgiveness and wickedness constitute the polar outposts of human freedom. The resulting unfinality can be understood in three interrelated respects: (1) as the exposure of forgiveness to the response of wickedness; (2) as the metaempirical residue of the struggle between love and evil; and (3) as the resistance of the irrevocable to the power of forgiveness to remove the stain of the past.

First, just as forgiveness is a response to wickedness, wickedness may be the response to forgiveness. The one forgiving always risks ingratitude, or what Jankélévitch calls "grace in reverse, which is wickedness."[53] The chiasmus of forgiveness returning good for evil is potentially responded to by the chiasmus of wickedness returning evil for good. Forgiveness thus opens up the very possibility of wickedness in the renunciation of rights and the acceptance of responsibility for the other. Forgiveness involves an exposure and an opening, and this opening does not and cannot dictate what will come; it cannot guarantee peace.

Second, because forgiveness cannot finally and ultimately triumph over evil there remains "the irreducible residue of an infinite and always unfinished reduction," which Jankélévitch describes as an organ-obstacle. Third, there remains a "remainder" of the irrevocable facticity of the having-done. As Jankélévitch writes in his 1974 book *L'Irréversible et la nostalgie,* the absolving revocation of forgiveness leaves behind an irreducible remnant.[54] This remnant marks that which is unforgivable in principle, he suggests, because it represents the impossibility of utterly undoing the last traces of the past offense. It represents the pinch of impossibility from the dream of absolute annulment or annulling absolution and the flip side of forgiveness, its impotence. What remains from the act of forgiveness, then, is to disregard the offense, to act as if it had not occurred, despite the fact that it did indeed occur. What remains, Paul Ricoeur suggests, is the open wound of mourning for what is done and for the one who has been. In this case, the irrevocable has become the inextinguishable and the immemorial.[55]

Jankélévitch fails on this point, however, to demonstrate the relation between a forgiveness "as if" and a forgiveness locked in the paradox of power between omnipotence and impotence. Overly concerned with the possibility or impossibility of forgiveness to wipe the slate clean in order to initiate what Caputo calls the innocence of "virginal time," Jankélévitch overlooks the gift of time and the chance of forgiven time. He proceeds as if the sole alternative to the logic of identity is magico-metaphysical and ontotheological omnipotence.[56] The remnant that forgiveness leaves behind is not what remains unforgivable; it simply testifies to the radical resilience of the irreparable and irrevocable, which calls into question the capacity of forgiveness to revoke the past. What Jankélévitch portrays as the impotence of forgiveness to revoke the irrevocable opens a path for a forgiveness that modifies the past so that that which should not be has the chance to become otherwise. Beyond the power play of all or nothing, this remainder of past action compels an alternative in which both the transformative capacity of forgiveness and the integrity of the past are respected.

Like Levinas, Bergson, and Kierkegaard, Jankélévitch emphasizes the temporality of creation and the newness of each moment. But whereas Bergson preserves a power of the present over the future and Jankélévitch is mostly concerned with the moral experience of the one who forgives, Levinas and Kierkegaard remind us of the ontological exigency of being forgiven. Levinas especially makes clear against Bergson and Jankélévitch that the newness of the future is not first and foremost a result of the creative work of the subject but the gift of the other across the sea of alterity.

Levinas examines "the paradox of the pardon of fault" in reference to "pardon as constitutive of time itself."[57] He considers pardon "the very work of time," for time is socially constituted in the relation to the other. This work of time makes possible "an absolute youth and recommencement."[58] Forgiveness is thus an act that manifests the gift structure of personal existence. What it gives is an augmented gift of time, a future liberated from the continuity of the burden of guilt and therefore the past.[59] This future is not virginal, however, either as a restoration of "prelapsed innocence" or as an eschatological hope, as Jankélévitch suggests.[60] It is rather the opening of the interval of nonidentity within the forgiven subject that allows for the recommencement of the past that has been repaired, transformed, purified, and resurrected; that is, forgiven. Caputo explains that "by releasing me from my past, the other gives me a new past and hence a future."[61] The reverse is at least equally true. It is from the newness of the future that I gain the past, for the gift of time is from the other, and Levinas defines the future by the other, not the other by the future.[62] In other words, I begin again not from myself, from my own intentional work, or from the horizon of my past. I begin again from the eyes of the other who forgives me.[63]

This gift of time can come only from the other. Jankélévitch writes of the task of memory in terms of remembering, repeating, and resuscitating the past. But the limits of memory coincide with the constraints of immanence. Levinas maintains that the memory of a past event within the modus of self-relation is capable of giving the past a new meaning, but he is also attentive to the latent threat of this work of memory to repeat the mistakes or the terrors of the past. The present moment is infected by the failures of the past that in turn shade the view of the past. A free return to the past is first conceivable within the horizon of liberation engendered by the forgiveness of the other. The past, therefore, may not be resuscitated in decisionistic self-cleansing à la Scheler or especially Heidegger, or in the work of memory as Benjamin and Jankélévitch believe, or in the efforts of repentance as Scheler and Soloveitchik suggest. Although memory and repentance may be capable of mending the represented past and compensating the past with a future, the self who carries out these tasks, even with great integrity, remains too captive to the enclosures of itself, its history, and its fate.[64] Both Jankélévitch and Levinas herald a hope of redemption that will not be found within the silent dialogue of the self with itself. Whereas Jankélévitch concentrates on the intentional and creative act of forgiveness on the part of the one who forgives, Levinas foregrounds the freedom that consists in having one's being forgiven by the alterity of the other.[65] Whereas for Levinas, freedom is received in the welcome of the other, for Jankélévitch the emergence of the new beyond all anticipation constitutes a radical position, and such creation is the obligation of human freedom at the very limits of its possibilities.

Although Jankélévitch prioritizes the act of forgiveness and Levinas prioritizes being forgiven, they are in agreement that there must be a rupture of continuity, and continuity across rupture.[66] Levinas calls this *alteration*; Jankélévitch calls it *oscillation*.[67] But Levinas stresses that, through the purification of the rupture, the one who is forgiven returns to his past and therefore to himself. The paradox of forgiveness, for Levinas, "lies in its retroaction," that is, in its repetition of the past event or in the "reversibility of time" itself. Whereas forgetting, he claims, "nullifies the relations with the past, pardon conserves the past pardoned in the purified present." In this respect, forgiveness "permits the subject who had committed himself in a past instant to be *as though* that instant had not passed on, to be *as though* he had not committed himself." Forgiveness, he summarizes, "acts upon the past, somehow repeats the event, purifying it."[68]

Levinas's interpretation of the effect forgiveness has on the past circumvents the either-or structure that Jankélévitch posits in which either forgiveness miraculously wipes away the past or the incorruptibility of the morally corrupt past resists the power of forgiveness. In Levinas's view, forgiveness is more transformative than omnipotent, and the incorruptibility of the irrevocable is upheld with greater integrity because forgiveness takes up the past in its very reality and facticity and alters it. The pardoned being, Levinas insists, is not the innocent being but the redeemed being, the resurrected being. Forgiveness directly acts on the past and as such is "active in a stronger sense than forgetting, which does not concern the reality of the event forgotten."⁶⁹ The redemptive return to the past from the future is inseparable from the opening toward the future with a resurrected past. The guilty past is thus not simply obliterated, as Jankélévitch idealizes; it is repaired and renewed as the past pardoned. As Alphonso Lingis explicates:

> The future is to come to the whole of one's time; the hope for the future is a hope for what one is and was. It will come then with a retroaction back over the present and the past. It would not only bring it a new meaning. It is I myself, the I that exists now and that existed, that will be, that will begin anew in the time hoped for. Thus the promise of the future is a promise of resurrecting the past, with all its forces, but in such a way that it would begin anew. It is just this that is pardon: redemption of the past itself. . . .
> The sense of the future is not the sense of the recurrence of the now, nor the sense of its continuation, but the sense of another instant, another beginning possible, another chance for the now. It is the sense of the accomplished, the effected, having another chance, a chance to recommence otherwise. This is the sense of time not as a determinate infinity of instants, but rather of the *infinition*, the ever recommencing of the definitive, which would be the inner form of our existence.⁷⁰

In the metaphor of the *felix culpa*, Levinas discerns the mystery of time itself. With reference to the offense, this metaphor stands for a "surplus of happiness" in being forgiven. Jankélévitch also recognizes this "surplus of joy" in having been forgiven, and both philosophers speak of resurrection and resuscitation instead of restoration. But, for Jankélévitch, forgiveness introduces a "wholly new spring," whereas Levinas realizes that the newness of springtime arrives already heavy with all the springtimes past.⁷¹

Jankélévitch's reflections on forgiveness rightfully focus on the rupture of being, but his conception of temporality and its connection with ethics suggests precisely what Levinas outlines. Time, for both Jankélévitch and Levinas, is discontinuous and indefinite. They both emphasize the rupture of the instant and utilize the language of natality. Time adds something new to being, Levinas claims, something absolutely new, but this novelty, in his mind, represents an "ever recommencing alterity of the accomplished."⁷² According to Jankélévitch, what is created in the instant must be maintained in the interval, and although the new birth of the instant of creation contains neither history nor projection, it affects both the before and the after, placing them in relation by means of separation or aeration. Human creation is thus always re-creation; even values and virtues, he claims, have to be re-created through our decisions. Therefore, when Jankélévitch describes how forgiveness effectuates "a wholly new dawn" and a "wholly new spring," he recognizes that forgiveness introduces a "time of *renewal* and of a *second* youth."[73] The commencement of a new age is not the restoration of an older one; it is not a restoration of innocence or of the previous relation. It is always a re-commencement, and, temporally and ethically, the "ever" of this recommencement must be underlined or repeated.

Consequently, the "as if" structure of the past in the wake of forgiveness does not represent merely the decision of the one who forgives to disregard the past offense. It does not simply neutralize its consequences. It is not characterized by a mere behavioral modification toward the offender. If it is the "whole lighting of my relations with the guilty person that is modified" and "the whole orientation of our relations that finds itself inverted, overturned, and overwhelmed" through forgiveness, as Jankélévitch claims, then the newness of the future cannot be completely severed from the past.[74] If the one who forgives undergoes a conversion from resentment to love at the limit of experience, then her gift of love will constitute a gift of time, a liberated and resuscitated historically embedded life. This gift initiates something that is best qualified as forgiven time rather than virginal time. It opens the past for reinterpretation and gives it new meaning by integrating it into the forgiven time of the future. Forgiveness thus marks a new beginning *of* the being one is and the being one has been and a new beginning *for* the being one is and the being one has been. This being and not-being is alterity inscribed into identity.

If forgiven time entails the ever-recommencing alterity of the accomplished, then the risk that forgiven time becomes a state of being is suspended. Jankélévitch makes it clear that we do not and cannot abide in the innocence of the gracious instant of forgiveness. Neither the good nor the evil becomes a state of being or a permanent and stable condition. Rather, the way of life and the way of morality is that of becoming. As long as there remains a remnant to be forgiven, whether it is a practical or a structural remnant, a psychological or metaempirical remnant, forgiveness will not have been done. As a duty, forgiveness will always remain to do.

In his essay "Pardonner?" Jankélévitch claims that forgiveness died in the concentration camps. In an interview roughly twenty years later he was asked about this position. "Who said that?" he inquires. "You," responds the reporter. "Yes," Jankélévitch confesses and adds, "It should not die. Forgiveness cannot die."[75] Without repudiating his prior claim, he offers a word of great hope and faith. Taken together, however, both sides constitute an unsewn tear. Evil will not have had the final word; forgiveness will not have had the final word . . . infinitely. For as long as humans exist, there is no solution to this dilemma and no exit to this sleepless agony.[76] Fortunately and unfortunately, the last word is always the penultimate word. It is our legacy and our responsibility. *Ein ladavar sof,* it will never end.

Notes

Introduction: In the Margins

1. Arnold Davidson, "Introductory Remarks," *Critical Inquiry* 22, no. 3 (1996): 545; and Andrew Kelley, "Translator's Introduction," in Vladimir Jankélévitch, *Forgiveness* (Chicago: University of Chicago Press, 2005), vii.
2. Emmanuel Levinas, "Vladimir Jankélévitch," in *Outside the Subject*, trans. Michael B. Smith (Stanford: Stanford University Press, 1993), 84.
3. Xavier Tilliette, "Une Kitiège de l'âme: L'éthique de Vladimir Jankélévitch," *L'Arc* 75 (1979): 67–68.
4. See Vladimir Jankélévitch, *Music and the Ineffable*, trans. Carolyn Abbate (Princeton: Princeton University Press, 2003). [*La Musique et l'Ineffable* (Paris: Éditions du Seuil, 1961).] This work is the only other book of Jankélévitch's besides *Forgiveness* that has been translated into English. See also Carolyn Abbate's translator's introduction, titled "Jankélévitch's Singularity" (ibid., xiii–xx). Abbate writes that, according to Jankélévitch, "music is no cipher; it is not awaiting the decoder. Musical works do not express emotion or reflect optical phenomena. . . . Music has a power over our bodies and minds wildly disproportionate to its lack of obvious or concrete meaning, as to its slippery aesthetic status." But this does not mean that music in Jankélévitch's interpretation slips into ethereal, transcendent air. As Abbate explains, music rather "is always bound to the 'world down here,' to a human experience of time, to human bodies and human spirituality, to culture and the past." She summarizes Jankélévitch's philosophy in *Music and the Ineffable* as an invitation "to imagine metaphors and analogies that 'explain' music only to dismiss them; to realize that it is in imagining and dismissing, and doing it again, and again that one asymptotically approaches an intimation of something that will elude any and all searchlights" (xiii–xiv).

5. Vladimir Jankélévitch, *Le Je-ne-sais-quoi et le presque-rien* I (Paris: Éditions du Seuil, 1980), 100, 105.

6. Ibid., 110.

7. Cf. Jacques Derrida, "How to Avoid Speaking: Denials," trans. Ken Frieden, in *Derrida and Negative Theology*, ed. Harold Coward and Toby Foshay (Albany: State University of New York Press, 1992), 73–143.

8. Wiard Raveling, "Über Vladimir Jankélévitch," *Sinn und Form* 49, no. 3 (1997): 332.

9. Vladimir Jankélévitch, *Henri Bergson* (1931), republished in 1959 and 1999, 4th ed. (Paris: Presses Universitaires de France, 2008), and *L'Odyssée de la conscience dans la dernière philosophie de Schelling* (1933), 2nd ed. (Paris: Editions L'Hartmattan, 2005).

10. Davidson, "Introductory Remarks," 546.

11. Vladimir Jankélévitch, "Quelle est la valueur de la pensee bergsonienne?" in *Premières et dernières pages* (Paris: Seuil, 1994), 87, translation quoted in Davidson, "Introductory Remarks," 546.

12. Vladimir Jankélévitch, "Do Not Listen to What They Say, Look at What They Do," trans. Ann Hobart, *Critical Inquiry* 22, no. 3 (1996): 349–51.

13. Raveling, "Über Vladimir Jankélévitch," 332.

14. Ibid., 333.

15. He criticized, for example, Maurice Merleau-Ponty, who resided in Jankélévitch's Parisian apartment in his absence, for not doing anything for the Resistance because he was working on his habilitation, and Jean-Paul Sartre, whose plays were performed under the occupation and whose books were approved by the censors, for heralding the imperative of engagement and for compensating for his relatively apolitical stance during the war by advocating the political responsibility of philosophy after the crisis of the war had ended. See "Jankélévitch, La Pensée Éclair," interview with Jean-Pierre Barou and Robert Maggiori, in *Libération*, June 8 and 9, 1985. See also Jürg Altwegg, "Kein Vergessen, kein Verstehen, kein Verzeihen—Vladimir Jankélévitch und die Deutschen," in *Das Verzeihen: Essays zur Moral und Kulturphilosphie*. ed. Ralf Konersmann and trans. Claudia Brede-Konersmann (Frankfurt am Main: Suhrkamp Verlag, 2003), 11–18.

16. Raveling, "Über Vladimir Jankélévitch," 320.

17. Vladimir Jankélévitch and Béatrice Berlowitz, *Quelque part dans l'inachevé* (Paris: Gallimard, 1978), 103–4.

18. Altwegg, "Kein Vergessen," 10.

19. Vladimir Jankélévitch, *Une Vie en toutes lettres*, 339, cited in Andrew Kelley, "Translator's Introduction," in Vladimir Jankélévitch, *Forgiveness* (Chicago: University of Chicago Press, 2005), xii. Obviously, this purging had its limits. For a thinker like Jankélévitch who was sensitive to ghosts or to what comes back (*revenants*), he must have been aware that the siphoning off of all things German was an impossibility for someone as steeped in the language and thought as he was. Xavier Tilliette, a scholar on Schelling and a student and friend of Jankélévitch's, describes, for example, how in his meetings with Jankélévitch over the

years, Schelling was present like a third party—"a discreet, mute, and quasi excluded, almost absent third" (Tilliette, "Une Kitiège de l'âme," 65).

20. Jacques Derrida, "Das Leben, Das Überleben: Vom Ethos des Denkens und von der Chance des Europäischen Erbes," interview with Jean Birnbaum in *Lettre International* 66 (2004). See also Peter Sloterdijk, *Derrida ein Ägypter: Über das Problem der jüdischen Pyramide* (Frankfurt a.M.: Suhrkamp, 2007), 9ff.

21. Raveling, "Über Vladimir Jankélévitch," 320. Jankélévitch concludes that he will pass on his fountain pen to his daughter because one will surely listen to her more than to him.

22. Kelley, "Translator's Introduction," xii.

23. As Bruno Liebrucks writes, "Because the crimes of the twentieth century that cry out to the heavens make even forgiveness appear as more of a scorn to humans than as human, philosophy is placed before the task of *learning to think what forgiveness is*." Cited in Klaus-M. Kodalle, "Die Dimension des Unermesslichen: Aufhebung der vermessenen Moralität," in *Cognitio humana—Dynamik des Wissens und der Werte*: Vorträge und Kolloquien/XVII. Deutscher Kongress für Philosophie, Leipzig, 23–27 September 1996 (Berlin: Akademie Verlag, 1997), 106; emphasis mine.

24. Paul Ricoeur, *Memory, History, Forgetting*, trans. Kathleen Blamey and David Pellauer (Chicago: University of Chicago Press, 2004), 457.

25. See Jean-François Lyotard, "Mainmise," trans. Pascale-Anne Brault and Michael Naas, in *The Hyphen: Between Judaism and Christianity*, ed. Jean-François Lyotard and Eberhard Gruber (New York: Humanity Books, 1999), 11.

26. Vladimir Jankélévitch, "Should We Pardon Them?" trans. Ann Hobart, *Critical Inquiry* 22, no. 3 (1996): 553. In the appropriate references, I have substituted *forgiveness* for the word *pardon* that appears throughout the English translation of this essay because the French word *pardonner* in this context is not a matter of pardon but of forgiveness.

27. Vladimir Jankélévitch, "Difficultés du pardon: Entretien avec le Professeur Jankélévitch," interview with Renée de Tryon-Montalembert in *La Vie spirituelle* 619 (March 1977): 194–95. See also Alain Gouhier, "Le Temps de l'Impardonnable et le Temps du Pardon selon Jankélévitch," in *Le Point Théologique, Forgiveness*, ed. Michel Perrin (Paris: Beauchesnes, 1987), 269–71; and Jacques Derrida, "To Forgive," in *Questioning God*, ed. John Caputo, Mark Dooley, and Michael Scanlon (Bloomington: Indiana University Press, 2001), 29–31.

28. Jankélévitch, "Should We Pardon Them?" 553. The letter Jankélévitch originally wrote appeared in the "Opinion libre" of *Le Monde* on January 3, 1965 (Paris: Publications du Groupe Le Monde), 3; this letter forms the basis of his 1965 essay "L'Imprescriptible," which appeared in the January–February issue of *La Revue Administrative*, no. 103 (Paris: Montchrestien, 1965), 37–42; it took its final form in his small book *Pardonner?* (Paris: Éditions Le Pavillon, 1971), which was posthumously included, along with his 1948 essay "Dans l'honneur et la dignité," in *L'Imprescriptible* (Paris: Éditions du Seuil, 1986), 13–63. In the foreword to the republication of this essay, Jankélévitch writes, "In *Le Pardon*, a

purely philosophical work that I have published elsewhere, the answer to the question, Must we pardon? seems to contradict the one given here."

29. Jankélévitch, "La Pensée Éclair." See also Altwegg, "Kein Vergessen," 16.
30. Jankélévitch, "Should We Pardon Them?" 567.
31. Davidson, "Introductory Remarks," 546–47.
32. Derrida, "To Forgive," 29.
33. Vladimir Jankélévitch, *Forgiveness,* trans. Andrew Kelley (Chicago: University of Chicago Press, 2005), 5.
34. Ibid., 1.
35. Vladimir Jankélévitch, "Le Presque-rien," *Bulletin de la Société française de Philosophie* 48, no. 3 (1954): 65.
36. Jankélévitch, "Should We Pardon Them?" 553. I have modified the translation, replacing *undone* for *sundered.* The original sentence from *L'Imprescriptible* reads as follows: *"Il existe entre l'absolu de la loi d'amour et l'absolu de la liberté méchante une déchirure qui ne peut être entièrement décousue."*
37. Jankélévitch, "Difficultés du pardon," 194–95.

1. First Philosophy

1. See, e.g.,Vladimir Jankélévitch, *Premières et dernières pages* (Paris: Seuil, 1994), 54.
2. Henri Bergson, *L'Intuition philosophique,* in *La pensée et le mouvant: Essais et conférences* (Paris: Alcan, 1934), 119, quoted in Vladimir Jankélévitch, *Philosophie première*, 226–27. "En ce point est quelque chose de simple, d'infiniment simple, de si extraordinairement simple que le philosophe n'a jamais réussi à le dire. Et c'est pourquoi il a parlé tout sa vie."
3. Cf., esp., Martin Heidegger's 1935 Freiburg lecture, first published in 1953, *Einführung in die Metaphysik* (Tübingen: Max Niemeyer Verlag, 1987). [*Introduction to Metaphysics*, trans. Gregory Fried and Richard Polt (New Haven: Yale University Press, 2000).]
4. Lucien Jerphagnon, *Ahnen und Wollen: Vladimir Jankélévitch*, trans. Jürgen Brankel (Vienna: Turia + Kant, 2009), 57–58. Levinas is undoubtedly another thinker who emphasizes the idea of creation. In *Otherwise Than Being,* Levinas similarly writes that Western philosophy is "perhaps reification itself" and that philosophers, from Plato to Aristotle, "have always wished to think of creation in ontological terms, that is, in function of a preexisting and indestructible matter" (*Otherwise Than Being, or Beyond Essence*, trans. Alphonso Lingis [Pittsburgh: Duquesne University Press, 1998], 110). Both Levinas and Jankélévitch examine the absoluteness of creation that precedes the separation into dichotomies, whether active and passive, good and bad, being and nonbeing, and so on. A key difference between them is that whereas Levinas speaks of an "absolute passivity" conjoined to the idea of creation, Jankélévitch speaks of an absolute activity or spontaneity. This difference entails more than a shift in perspective, whether viewed from the perspective of the creator or from the perspective of the created.

5. Vladimir Jankélévitch, *Philosophie première*, 2nd ed. (1953; Paris: Quadridge/Presses Universitaires de France, 1986), 1–2.
6. Cf., e.g., Emmanuel Levinas, *Totality and Infinity: An Essay on Exteriority*, trans. Alphonso Lingis (Pittsburgh: Duquesne University Press, 1969), 33–35, 48–52.
7. Plato, *Republic*, 6.509b, in *The Works of Plato*, trans. Benjamin Jowett. (New York: Tudor, 1936).
8. Ibid., 7.518c, 526e.
9. Ibid., 6.507b.
10. Jankélévitch, *Philosophie première*, 32ff.
11. Ibid., 14–15.
12. Ibid., 17.
13. Plotinus, *The Six Enneads of Plotinus*, trans. Stephen MacKenna and B. S. Page (Charleston, S.C.: Forgotten Books, 2007), V, 3, 11 and 12, 15; V, 4, 2; V, 5, 6; VI, 7, 17 and 24.
14. Jankélévitch, *Philosophie première*, 34. Cf. Plotinus, *Enneads* V, 3, 11; VI, 7, 38; VI, 9, 9.
15. Jankélévitch, *Philosophie première*, 2.
16. Ibid., 155.
17. Ibid., 29, 98.
18. Ibid., 12.
19. Cf. ibid., 5–13.
20. Ibid., 22–23. Cf. also Jerphagnon, *Ahnen und Wollen*, 42.
21. Cf. Immanuel Kant, *Critique of Pure Reason* (*The Cambridge Edition of the Works of Immanuel Kant*), trans. Paul Guyer and Allen W. Wood (Cambridge: Cambridge University Press, 1999), A12. The original German is in *Kant Werke*, vol. 2 (Darmstadt: Wissenschaftliche Buchgesellschaft, 1998).
22. Cf. Jankélévitch, *Philosophie première*, 88–90.
23. Ibid., 97.
24. Ibid., 88
25. Ibid., 98.
26. Vladimir Jankélévitch, *Cours de philosophie morale: Université libre de Bruxelles 1962–1963* (Paris: Éditions du Seuil, 2006), 166.
27. Jankélévitch, *Philosophie première*, 93–94.
28. Ibid., 35–36.
29. Ibid., 41.
30. Gottfried Wilhelm Leibniz, "Principles of Nature and Grace," para. 7 in *Philosophical Works*, 2nd ed., ed. and trans. George Martin Duncan (New Haven: Tuttle, Morehouse, and Taylor, [0]1908).
31. Jankélévitch, *Philosophie première*, 65.
32. Ibid., 95.
33. Ibid., 28–29.
34. Ibid., 98. "Si l'empirie intermittente existe sans consister ni subsister, et si la métempirie essentielle consiste et subsiste sans exister, on pourrait dire que le

métalogique est ce qui fait exister la consistance inexistante de l'essentialité, tout comme le métempirique est la consistance même de l'existence inconsistante; non point que la métempirie *fasse* subsister ou consister quoi que ce soit, au sens créateur du verbe auxiliaire 'Faire', l'essence étant justement éternelle *préexistence inexistante à l'existence*, et de nouveau et toujours préexistence à l'infini, et Déjà-là incréé, intemporel, tout accompli, sans commencement ni fin. . . . Le Tout-autre qui fait exister l'essence subsistante n'existe pas lui-même . . . ni a fortiori ne subsiste. A la letter: ce qui confère l'existence n'existe pas; car si ce qui confère l'existence était lui-même un existant, il supposerait à son tour un autre donneur d'existence. Or, le donneur d'existence fait exister à la fois l'essence, L'être-en-général et les êtres empiriques contingents; il est donc aussi inexistant qu'il est inconsistant et insubsistant."

35. Ibid., 97. *Cela va de soi* is an idiomatic expression that means "it goes without saying." In this context it is the self-evidence of the eternal essences and a priori that Jankélévitch expresses.

36. Ibid., 90.

37. Ibid., 92.

38. Ibid., 89. "Si donc l'ordre 'intelligible' est ce qui fait comprendre et rend significatif le désordre sensible, le surordre inintelligible ne vise pas à faire comprendre l'intelligibilité toute transparente et vraiment maximale des axioms et principes éternels, mais il fonde cette intelligibilité et, la fondant, révèle le nonsense de son sens, la contingence et relativité sa nécessité, la nuit enfin d'où sa lumière est issue."

39. Ibid., 130. "La position pure n'est pas, elle, comme l'est l'identité, un impensable qui rend pensable, un inconnaissable qui fait connaître, un incompréhensible qui fait comprendre: elle est plutôt ce qui ferait paraître absurdes ou du moin gratuits et contingents les principes de la raison; et au lieu que l'identité est le foyer même de l'intelligible et la source immobile de tout mouvement intellectif, la position pure est l'insondable mystère qui rend caduques et précarise les vérities éternelles ainsi que toutes les évidences les plus fermement établies."

40. Ibid., 148.

41. Ibid., 91. "L'homme raisonnable trouve dans son intermediarité de créature tout ce qu'il y a à savoir, et il est conforme à la sagesse métempirique comme au sérieux vital de ne pas chercher au delà; . . . Rien ne manque . . . et pourtant il manque quelque chose,—un quelque chose qui n'est rien. Ce qui manque à cette vérité complète et incomplète? Il manque je ne sais quoi d'inexplicable, d'injustifiable et d'impalpable qui est le principe même de l'inquiétude métaphysique: l'homme métalogicien brûle follement d'achever ce qui se suffit pourtant à soi-même et qui lui paraît, quoi qu'il fasse, inaccompli; aussi ce désir infini de quelque chose d'autre a-t-il quelque parenté tant avec l'Éros profane du *Banquet*, qu'avec L'Éros sacré de Jean de la Croix."

42. Ibid., 105.

43. Jankélévitch, "Le Presque-rien," *Bulletin de la Société française de Philosophie* 3 (1954): 71.

44. Jankélévitch, *Philosophie première*, 179–80.

45. Ibid., 171.

46. Ibid., 219–20. "L'attachement de Platon au monde des 'modèles' prouve qu'il n'est pas d'être selon lui auquel ne préexiste un pre-être, pas de "création", qui ne présuppose préschème, préfigure, prénotion ou préconception. . . . Or, c'est la *Genèse*, non point le *Timée* ni la *Théogonie*, qui commence par le commencement et qui affronte vraiment le mystère d'inchoation! C'est ainsi que le Créateur de la *Genèse* n'extrait pas la lumière réelle de la lumière possible, ne porte pas à l'acte une lumière en puissance, ne rembourre pas des essences préexistantes ni n'etoffe des virtualités déjà données: mais il crée du même coup et dans un seul acte la lumière effective des luminaires et la possibilité de la lumière; dans le même instant, il crée la lumière physique . . . et il invente l'idee même de la lumière. . . . Cette création est position génial et supergéniale, jaillissement thétique, improvisation simultanée de l'effectivité et de la possibilitée de cette effectivité."

47. Ibid., 188.

48. Ibid., 137.

49. Ibid., 147.

50. See, e.g., Jankélévitch, *Philosophie première*, 159, where Jankélévitch criticizes Dionysius Areopagita for hypostasizing. Jankélévitch's critique here should be compared with Derrida's distancing himself from negative theology. But this aspect is beyond the scope of this work. Cf. also Jankélévitch, "Le Presque-rien," 66. Cf. also Jerphagnon, *Ahnen und Wollen*, 44.

51. Jankélévitch, *Philosophie première*, 139.

52. Verena Lemcke, *Der Begriff Verzeihen bei Vladimir Jankélévitch* (Würzburg: Königshausen & Neumann, 2008), 44.

53. Jankélévitch, *Philosophie première*, 182–83.

54. Ibid., 125 and 131. Cf. Plotinus *Enneads* VI, 9, 6; V, 3, 14.

55. Jankélévitch, *Philosophie première* , 129.

56. Plato, *Euthyphro* 10a, 11a, in *The Works of Plato*, trans. Benjamin Jowett (New York: Tudor, 1936).

57. Jankélévitch, *Philosophie première*, 199–200.

58. Ibid., 222.

59. Cf. ibid., 234.

60. Plato, *Timaeus*, 29a, 29e, in *The Works of Plato*, trans. Benjamin Jowett (New York: Tudor, 1936).

61. See Jankélévitch, *Philosophie première*, 229–35.

62. See ibid., 187–93.

63. Cf. Jacques Lacan, who says of love that it gives what one does not have in *Ecrits* (Paris: Le Seuil, 1966), 618, 627, 691. Jankélévitch, too, associates this creation with love, but whereas his account demonstrates an unmistakable character of virility, Lacan's various formulas are organized around the woman, as she is deprived of the phallus. See also Derrida's commentary on the gift of love giving what it does not have in Jacques Derrida, *Given Time: I. Counterfeit Money*, trans. Peggy Kamuf (Chicago: University of Chicago Press, 1992), 2n2.

64. Jeffrey Bloechl, "Forgiveness and Its Limits: An Essay on Vladimir Jankélévitch," in *Vladimir Jankélévitch and the Question of Forgiveness*, ed. Alan Udoff (Lanham, Md.: Lexington Books, 2013), 103.

65. Jankélévitch, *Philosophie première*, 239. Cusa witnesses a godlike endowment in human creative freedom, writing that "the human person is a god, yet not absolutely, because he is human; a human god, then" (*De coniecturis* 2.14, in Cusa, *Opera Omnia*, vol. 3, ed. Josef Koch and Karl Bormann [Hamburg: Meiner Verlag, 1972]).

66. Jankélévitch, *Philosophie première*, 248.

67. Ibid., 237.

68. Ibid., 174. From another perspective but still in the spirit of Jankélévitch, however, the argument could be made that humans are precisely beings of the Sabbath—the Sabbath being the day unfettered by the instrumentality of the workweek, the day for that which is unnecessary, luxurious, nonteleological, and undetermined. It is in this sense of Sabbath that Jankélévitch closes his first philosophy, writing that love is like philosophy, joy, and music: one can live without it . . . but not so well (*Philosophie première*, 266).

69. Jankélévitch, *Premières et dernières pages*, 85; cf. Jerphagnon, *Ahnen und Wollen*, 61.

70. Jankélévitch, *Le Je-ne-sais-quoi et le presque-rien* I, 103.

71. Jankélévitch, *Philosophie première*, 241.

72. Aristotle, *Physics* 1.1–4, trans. P. H. Wicksteed and F. M. Cornford, rev. ed. (Cambridge, Mass.: Harvard University Press, 1986), 4.218a3.

73. Jankélévitch, "Le Presque-rien," 77.

74. Ibid., 66–67.

75. Ibid., 76.

76. Ibid., 72. "'Advenit,' dit-on de quelque chose qui n'est jamais chose, et qui n'est pourtant pas rien puisqu'il advient ou survient." Cf. Jankélévitch, *Philosophie première*, 73–74.

77. Jankélévitch, "Le Presque-rien," 73.

78. Emmanuel Levinas, *Outside the Subject*, trans. Michael B. Smith (Stanford: Stanford University Press, 1993), 86.

79. See Jankélévitch, "Le Presque-rien," 67; see also Vladimir Jankélévitch, *Penser la mort?* (Paris: Liana Levi, 1994), 117–18.

80. Cf. Jerphagnon, *Ahnen und Wollen*, 71.

81. Jankélévitch, "Le Presque-rien," 68–69.

82. Vladimir Jankélévitch, *Forgiveness*, trans. Andrew Kelley (Chicago: University of Chicago Press, 2005), 116.

83. Andrew Kelley, "Translator's Introduction," in *Forgiveness* (Chicago: University of Chicago Press, 2005), xvi.

84. Jankélévitch, *Philosophie première*, 242.

85. Cf. Jankélévitch, "Le Presque-rien," 75; Jankélévitch, *Philosophie première*, 242.

86. Jankélévitch, "Le Presque-rien," 73–75.

87. Jankélévitch, *Philosophie première,* 242. See also 249. Jankélévitch's characterization of the instant and interval as a *mixture* follows Bergson's notion of mixture in *Two Sources of Morality and Religion,* trans. R. Ashley Audra and Cloudesley Brereton (Notre Dame, Ind.: University of Notre Dame Press, 1954). In his analyses of human temporality and specifically in his treatment of intuition and of virtues such as love, charity, courage, and forgiveness, Jankélévitch makes a strict and qualitative distinction between the interval and the instant. Derrida offers a much better representation of how Jankélévitch describes this relation of the unconditional to the conditional. He says that they are heterogeneous and inseparable. Accordingly, the instant is heterogeneous to the interval, but the two are inseparable.

88. Jankélévitch, "Le Presque-rien," 78. "L'intuition est une sagesse de la fracture instantanée, une sagesse naissante-mourante, comme l'étincelle."

89. Cf. Jerphagnon, *Ahnen und Wollen,* 26.

90. Jankélévitch, *Philosophie première,* 172.

91. Ibid., 74. "L'intuition es tune prise de conscience qui est perte de conscience, un éveil qui est évanouissement, un éclair déchirant la nuit; la conscience, dans l'instant même qu'elle s'évanouit, se réveille; dans l'instant où elle meurt, ressuscite. L'instant est une renaissance mourante une mort qui est une vie."

92. Cf., e.g., Vladimir Jankélévitch, *L'Austérité et la Vie morale* (1956), in Vladimir Jankélévitch, *Philosophie morale* (Paris: Flammarion, 1998), 405.

93. Jankélévitch, *Philosophie première,* 175.

94. Ibid., 119.

95. Ibid., 166. "L'homme est le Dieu de l'instant."

96. Ibid., 239–41. Cf. *Le sérieux de l'intention: Traité des vertus,* vol. 1 (Paris: Flammarion, 1989), 245. See also Joëlle Hansel, "*Forgiveness* and 'Should We Pardon Them?' The Pardon and The Imprescriptible," in *Vladimir Jankélévitch and the Question of Forgiveness,* ed. Alan Udoff (Lanham, Md.: Lexington Books, 2013), 114.

97. Jankélévitch, *Philosophie première,* 165.

98. Ibid., 113.

99. Ibid., 165.

100. Ibid., 186.

101. Ibid., 201. "En fait, la loi d'exercice et la loi d'économie, la coutume, l'adaptation, la tradition et l'imitation qui règlent le périodisme de notre vie, la mémoire et l'association qui assimilent le nouveau à l'ancien, la pensée même qui épouse si facilement les rythmes reproductifs de notre naturalité, tout et jusqu'à l'installation spatiale du corps et du sensorium dans l'existence intermédiaire, tout conspire à nous render violent l'effort nécessaire pour coïncider avec le point focal de la position."

102. See Martin Heidegger, *Being and Time,* trans. Joan Stambaugh (Albany: State University of New York Press, 1996), esp. para. 25–27 and 35–38. The German is *Sein und Zeit,* 17th ed. (Tübingen: Max Niemeyer Verlag, 1993).

103. Jankélévitch, *Philosophie première,* 241–42.

104. Ibid., 98.

105. Kelley, "Translator's Introduction," xviii, xv. See also Andrew Kelley, "Jankélévitch and the Metaphysics of Forgiveness," in *Vladimir Jankélévitch and the Question of Forgiveness*, ed. Alan Udoff (Lanham, Md.: Lexington Books, 2013), 27–46, esp. 33–34.

106. Vladimir Jankélévitch and Béatrice Berlowitz, *Quelque part dans l'inachevé* (Paris: Gallimard, 1978), 68.

107. Keiji Nishitani, *Religion and Nothingness*, trans. Jan van Bragt (Berkeley: University of California Press, 1982), 220.

108. Kelley, "Translator's Introduction," xviii.

109. Bergson, *Two Sources of Morality and Religion*, 75.

110. Søren Kierkegaard, Pap. IV A 164/JP 1030, cited in Niels Nymann Ericksen, *Kierkegaard's Category of Repetition: A Reconstruction* (Berlin: Walter de Gruyter, 2000), 11.

111. Bergson, *Two Sources of Morality and Religion*, 79.

112. Vladimir Jankélévitch, *L'Austérité et la vie morale*, in *Philosophie moral* (Paris: Flammarion, 1998), 405.

113. Ibid., 388–89.

114. Ibid., 392.

115. See also Jankélévitch and Berlowitz, *Quelque part dans l'inachevé*, 153.

116. Jankélévitch, *L'Austérité et la vie morale*, 406–7. Cf. 414–15. See also Georg Simmel, *Der Begriff und die Tragödie der Kultur*, in Georg Simmel, *Hauptprobleme der Philosophie, Gesamtausgabe*, vol. 14, ed. Rüdiger Kramme and Otthein Rammstedt (Frankfurt a.M.: Suhrkamp, 1996), 385–416.

117. Cf., e.g., Jacques Derrida, *On Cosmopolitanism and Forgiveness*, trans. Mark Dooley and Michael Hughes (London: Routledge, 2002): "On Cosmopolitanism," 16–17, and esp. "On Forgiveness," 44–45.

118. This incommunicability and unverifiability is one of the discourse-theoretical difficulties of all theories of intuition. Intuition has often been criticized and sometimes dismissed on account of the individual and nonobjective, nonintersubjective character of it.

119. Jankélévitch, *Philosophie première*, 83–87.

120. Jankélévitch, "Le Presque-rien," 79; and Jankélévitch, *Forgiveness*, 117.

121. Kelley, "Translator's Introduction," xvi–ii.

122. Jankélévitch, *Forgiveness*, 117.

123. Jankélévitch, *Philosophie première*, 139.

124. Jankélévitch, *Cours de philosophie morale*, 43.

125. See, for example, the motto of Nietzsche's *Ecce Homo:* How One Becomes What One Is [*Wie man wird, was man ist*], trans. Walter Kaufmann (New York: Random House, 1989). The phrase "become what you are" is originally attested to in the works of the Greek poet Pindar. Nietzsche uses this phrase in several works including *Thus Spoke Zarathustra*, chapter 27, "The Virtuous."

126. Cf. Jankélévitch, *Cours de philosophie morale*, 40 and 54.

127. Immanuel Kant, *Groundwork of the Metaphysic of Morals*, ed. and trans. Allen W. Wood (New Haven: Yale University Press, 2002), 393, 9.

128. Jankélévitch, *Cours de philosophie morale*, 29.
129. Ibid., 46–47.
130. Ibid., 156.
131. Ibid., 60.
132. Ibid., 154. "L'intention implique une organisation morale et un aménagement temporel au-delà du présent mort-né."
133. Ibid., 44.
134. Ibid., 135 and 138.
135. Ibid., 60.
136. Ibid., 146–47.
137. Ibid., 76.
138. Ibid., 94.
139. Jankélévitch, *Cours de philosophie morale*, 95. Jankélévitch cites Fénelon as saying, "It is necessary to love the beloved, not the loving [*Il faut aimer pour l'aimé, non pour l'l'aimer*]," but this statement is his paraphrase of Fénelon, who is quoting Francis de Sales. In *The Maxims of the Saints* (not in *Le Gnostique de saint Clément d'Alexandrie*, as Jankélévitch contends), Fénelon writes, "Love would have us not be virtuous for ourselves and . . . we are never so virtuous as when we are least set on being virtuous. One might say that in this sense the passive and disinterested soul no longer wants love as defined as perfection and as happiness but only that it is what God wants of us. Whence comes Francis de Sale's saying that 'we come back to ourselves loving love instead of loving the Beloved'" (*Fénelon: Selected Writings*, ed. and trans. Chad Helms [Mahwah, N.J.: Paulist Press, 2006], 282 [*Oeuvres*, 2 vols. (Paris: Gallimard, 1983), 1:1079–80]). In book 9, chap. 9, of his *Treatise on the Love of God* [*Traité de l'Amour de Dieu*], Francis de Sales writes, "Instead of loving this holy love because it tends to God who is the beloved, we love it because it proceeds from us who are the lovers. Now who does not see that in so doing we do not seek God, but turn to ourselves, loving the love instead of loving the beloved?" (*En lieu d'aimer ce saint amour parce qu'il tend à Dieu qui est l'aimé, nous l'aimons parce qu'il procède de nous qui sommes les amants. Or, qui ne voit qu'ainsi faisant ce n'est plus Dieu que nous cherchons, ains que nous revenons à nous mêmes, aimant l'amour en lieu d'aimer le Bien-aimé?*) (*Oeuvres* [Paris: Gallimard, 1969], 785). Jankélévitch similarly describes how virtue and love require a forgetting of the self (*oubli de soi*). See, e.g., Vladimir Jankélévitch, *Traité des vertus*, vol. 3: *L'Innocence et la méchanceté* (Paris: Bordas, 1972), 1423.
140. Jankélévitch, *Cours de philosophie morale*, 160.
141. Ibid.
142. See, e.g., ibid., 51.

2. Apophatic Approaches

1. Vladimir Jankélévitch, *Forgiveness* (Chicago: University of Chicago Press, 2005), 4.
2. Ibid., 5.

3. Ibid., 14.

4. Ibid.

5. Friedrich Nietzsche. "On the Uses and Disadvantages of History for Life," in *Untimely Meditations*, ed. Daniel Breazeale, trans. R. J. Hollingdale (Cambridge: Cambridge University Press, 1997), 57–124. *Unzeitgemässe Betrachtungen*, in *Friedrich Nietzsche: Werke in Drei Bänden* (Darmstadt: Wissenschaftliche Buchgesellschaft, 1997), 1:213. Nietzsche claims it is possible (just look at the animals) to live almost without memory, to live even happily; but it is completely impossible to live without forgetting.

6. See Jeffrie Murphy and Jean Hampton, *Forgiveness and Mercy* (Cambridge: Cambridge University Press, 1988), 23.

7. Jankélévitch, *Forgiveness*, 13.

8. Aristotle, *Physics* 4.11–13.

9. Jacob Taubes, *Abendländische Eschatologie* (Bern: Francke, 1947), 13.

10. Jankélévitch, *Forgiveness*, 22.

11. The entire passage from Kierkegaard's journal entry reads: "Philosophy is perfectly right in saying that life must be understood backwards. But then one forgets the other clause—that it must be lived forwards. The more one thinks through this clause, the more one concludes that life in temporality never becomes properly understandable, simply because never at any time does one get the perfect repose to take the stance: backwards." (Pap. IV A 164/JP 1030) cited in Niels Nymann Eriksen, *Kierkegaard's Category of Repetition: A Reconstruction* (Berlin: Walter de Gruyter, 2000), 11.

12. Jankélévitch, *Forgiveness*, 22. By futurism, Jankélévitch understands the belief in the need to look forward: belief in the need to look to the future rather than reflect on the past. This belief contains an optimism that the future promises the fulfillment of personal and social aspirations. Futurition is, then, the process of becoming itself, of time being directed toward the future. Futurism, therefore, is aided by the natural fact of futurition. The belief in the priority of the future, granting it a value greater than the present or past, is a consequence of futurition.

13. Vladimir Jankélévitch, *Penser la mort?* (Paris: Liana Levi, 1994), 27.

14. Jankélévitch, *Forgiveness*, 24.

15. Ibid., 54.

16. Walter Benjamin, The Ninth Thesis of "On the Concept of History," Internet publication at the Trinity and All Saints College website: Faculty of Media, Lloyd Spencer. [*Über den Begriff der Geschichte* in *Werke und Nachlass*, vol. 19, ed. Christoph Gödde and Gérard Raulet (Frankfurt a.M.: Suhrkamp, 2010).]

17. Jankélévitch, *Forgiveness*, 28.

18. Ibid., 29.

19. Ibid., 21.

20. Jacques Derrida, *On Cosmopolitanism and Forgiveness*, trans. Mark Dooley and Michael Hughes (London: Routledge, 2002), 40.

21. Desmond Tutu, *No Future without Forgiveness* (New York: Doubleday, 1999). I do not mean to suggest that this is Bishop Tutu's intention or the aim of

the Truth and Reconciliation Committee in South Africa. Rather, I intend to demonstrate how such invocations of forgiveness on the political scene can be perverted.

22. John Caputo, *Against Ethics: Contributions to a Poetics of Obligation with Constant Reference to Deconstruction* (Bloomington: Indiana University Press, 1993), 111.
23. Jankélévitch, *Forgiveness*, 15.
24. Ibid., 55.
25. Ibid., 37.
26. Ibid., 37.
27. Ibid., 34.
28. Ibid., 37.
29. Ibid., 35.
30. Ibid.
31. Ibid., 27.
32. Ibid., 26.
33. Ibid., 33.
34. Cited in Giorgio Agamben, *The Time That Remains: A Commentary on the Letter to the Romans*, trans. Patricia Dailey (Stanford: Stanford University Press, 2005), 69. Jankélévitch compares time to a drug and to sleep, calling time a "medicina doloris; acting as a sedative and an analgesic, the morphine of time attenuates old pains and makes old sorrows sleep" (*Forgiveness*, 41).
35. Jankélévitch, *Forgiveness*, 49.
36. Ibid., 104
37. Jean Améry, *Jenseits von Schuld und Sühne: Bewältigungsversuche eines Überwältigten* (Stuttgart: Klett-Cotta, 1977), 115.
38. Agamben, *Time That Remains*, 41.
39. Jankélévitch, *Forgiveness*, 36.
40. Jankélévitch plays with the French term *revenants*. As a noun, it means "ghost," and as a gerund, it means "coming back." The ambiguity of the word indicates a return that is other than a Platonic or Hegelian recollection in which the return is appropriation or mastery—knowledge. The return also can be a haunting, "a simulcarum and a phantom of what has come" (*Forgiveness*, 15). This term and its consequences assume an important role in Derrida's works, too.
41. Plato, *Republic* 486a.
42. Seneca, *Letter*, 99, quoted in Pierre Hadot, *Philosophy as a Way of Life*, trans. Michael Chase (Oxford: Blackwell, 1995), 182.
43. Marcus Aurelius, *Meditations*, trans. Martin Hammond (London: Penguin Books, 2006), 5, 23. See also, for example, Book 4, meditation 43: "There is a river of creation, and time is a violent stream. As soon as one thing comes into sight, it is swept past and another is carried down: it too will be taken on its way."
44. Jankélévitch, *Forgiveness*, 17.
45. Ibid., 6.
46. Ibid., 17.

47. Charles Griswold, *Forgiveness: A Philosophical Exploration* (New York: Cambridge University Press, 2007), 7–8.

48. Ibid., 9.

49. Aristotle, *Nicomachean Ethics*, trans. Terence Irwin, 2nd ed. (Indianapolis: Hackett, 1999), 1124b31–1125a5, 8–10. In Plato, this notion is poignantly embodied by Socrates. At his trial in the *Apology*, Socrates asserts the power of virtue and justice over the bare fact of life when he defiantly tells his peers that they can do him no harm. Since he is protected by virtue and lives justly, they do more harm to themselves than to him, even by killing him. "Be sure that if you kill the sort of man I say I am, you will not harm me more than yourselves. Neither Meletus nor Anytus can harm me in any way; he could not harm me, for I do not think it is permitted that a better man be harmed by a worse; certainly he might kill me, or perhaps banish or disfranchise me, which he and maybe others think to be great harm, but I do not think so. I think he is doing himself much greater harm doing what he is doing now, attempting to have a man executed unjustly" (30c7–d6 in *The Works of Plato*).

50. Griswold, *Forgiveness*, 9.

51. Friedrich Nietzsche, *On the Genealogy of Morals*, trans. Walter Kaufmann and R. J. Hollingdale (New York: Random House, 1967), 39. [*Zur Genealogie der Moral*, in *Friedrich Nietzsche: Werke in Drei Bänden* (Darmstadt: Wissenschaftliche Buchgesellschaft, 1997), 2:784.]

52. Jankélévitch, *Forgiveness*, 31. This turning of the cheek must neither be done out of strength nor out of weakness, but out of a weakness/strength—a vulnerability that musters strength despite of (or in light of) injury. Jankélévitch writes, "The only healing that is definitive and complete is the one that the injured person, if he had the strength, would give to himself in a sudden decision taken once and for all" (*Forgiveness*, 36–37). And such an eventful turn, according to Jankélévitch, is at the limit of human strength.

53. Ibid., 6–7.

54. Aristotle, *Nicomachean Ethics* 1124b13–14.

55. See, e.g., Jankélévitch, *Penser la mort?* 27.

56. Jankélévitch, *Forgiveness*, 70.

57. Ibid., 58.

58. Vladimir Jankélévitch, "Should We Pardon Them?" trans. Ann Hobart, *Critical Inquiry* 22, no. 3 (1996): 559.

59. Gottfried Wilhelm Leibniz, *Theodicy*, ed. Austin Farrar, trans. E. M. Huggard (Peterborough, N.H.: Open Court, 1988).

60. G. W. F. Hegel, *Introduction to the Lectures on the Philosophy of World History*, trans. H. B. Nisbet (Cambridge: Cambridge University Press, 1975), 67 and 28.

61. Ibid., 43. Cf. Susan Neiman, *Evil in Modern Thought: An Alternative History of Philosophy* (Princeton: Princeton University Press, 2002), 86–88.

62. Jankélévitch, *Forgiveness*, 70. Cf. Lew Schestow, *Spekulation und Offenbarung: Essays und kritische Betrachtungen*, trans. Hans Ruoff (Hamburg: Heinrich Ellermann, 1963), 434–36.

63. Plato, *Apology* 25b–26d.

64. Plato, *Meno* 77d, in *The Works of Plato*. See the section titled "Freedom and Wickedness" in chapter 5 of this book for further explication of the distinction between sin conceived on the basis of ignorance and the evil of wickedness.

65. Jankélévitch, *Forgiveness*, 59.

66. Ibid., 70.

67. Ibid., 60.

68. Ibid., 61–63.

69. The term "*intus-legere*" forms the Latin root from which "intellect" etymologically stems.

70. Jankélévitch, *Forgiveness*, 63.

71. Ibid., 68.

72. Ibid.

73. Ibid., 69–70.

74. Ibid., 65.

75. Ibid., 93.

76. Ibid.

77. Ibid., 64. For a clarification of wickedness and the sacrifice of forgiveness, see chapter 5 in this book and the section titled "Two Absolutes" in chapter 6.

78. Jankélévitch, *Forgiveness*, 84–85.

79. Griswold, *Forgiveness*, 1.

80. Danièle Aubriot, "Quelques réflexions sur le pardon en Grèce Ancienne," in *Le Pardon: Acts du Colloque organizé par le Centre Histoire des Idées Université de Picardie*, ed. Michel Perrin (Paris: Beauchesne 1987), 26.

81. Plato, *Critias* 106c, in *Works of Plato*.

82. Jacqueline de Romilly, *La douceur dans la pensée grecque* (Paris: Hachette Littérature, 1995). Karin Metzler, *Der griechische Begriff des Verzeihens* (Tübingen: Mohr, 1991), 31–32.

83. Jankélévitch, *Forgiveness*, 81. The gentleness of understanding is manifest in the Stoics and Epicureans as well. In *Encheiridion*, §42, Epictetus, for example, writes, "When someone acts badly toward you or speaks badly of you, remember that he does or says it in the belief that it is appropriate for him to do so. . . . Starting from these considerations you will be gentle with the person who abuses you. For you must say on each occasion, 'That's how it seemed to him.'" *Handbook of Epictetus*, trans. and ed. Nicholas P. White (Indianapolis: Hackett, 1983), 25–26.

84. Aubriot , "Quelques réflexions sur le pardon," 15–17.

85. Aristotle, *Nicomachean Ethics* 1109b30–2. Terence Irwin translates *sungnômê* throughout as *pardon* with one exception, which I address later. Aristotle's association of the question of virtue with the voluntary applies equally to the evaluation of justice, the virtue par excellence. In book 5 Aristotle writes that "an act of injustice and a just act are defined by the voluntary and the involuntary. For when the action is voluntary, the agent is blamed, and thereby also it is an act of injustice" (*Nicomachean Ethics* 1135a20–3).

86. Ibid., 1109b35–1110a1.
87. Ibid., 1110a25–6.
88. Ibid., 1110b19–24.
89. See ibid., 111a3–34. The following discussion refers to Aristotle's explication in this passage.
90. Ibid., 1135b14–19.
91. Ibid., 1110b.
92. Cf. ibid., 111a1–2. In this respect, Aristotle follows Athenian law. Draco's laws from around 621 B.C.E. marked the first written constitution in Athens and first codified the distinction between murder and involuntary homicide. According to Ernst Heitsch, the relatives of one who was killed had the right to extend *aidesis* (another Greek term for forgiveness, reconciliation. or pardon) only in the cases of involuntary homicide (*Aidesis im Attischen Strafrecht* (Mainz: Akademie der Wissenschaften und der Literatur, 1984)). In book 9 of *Laws*, Plato makes this distinction as well. He claims that murderers should be banned for life or subject to death, whereas for involuntary homicide the offender should be banned for one year, after which the family should "forgive" him (Benjamin Jowett translates the cognate of *aidesis* here as "pity") and be reconciled with him (in Jowett, it reads "make peace with him") (864D–866A). Plato's idea of compulsory reconciliation did not reflect the law at that time nor did it apparently have any greater influence on the law afterward.
93. See, e.g., Aristotle, *Nicomachean Ethics* 1113b13–14 and 1114a4–7.
94. Ibid., 1135b20.
95. Ibid., 1135b24–5.
96. Ibid., 1136a2. In the case that anger is in response to a previous act of injustice Aristotle makes the argument that the principle of cause is outside the subject (1135b19). Although he would have to admit that the principle is within the person in the sense outlined above, his reasoning seems to indicate that in this case the person is compelled by reason to be angered. Anger is justly prompted by injustice. In such a case, he contends that the two parties do not dispute about whether the action caused by anger happened or not but about whether it was just, since the anger is in response to apparent injustice (1135b29). See also the section titled "Aristotle's Nemesis," in chapter 4 of this work.
97. Ibid., 1149b21–3. Cf. the section titled "Aristotle's Nemesis" in chapter 4 for an interpretation of Aristotle's link between reason and anger.
98. Ibid., 1149b4–6.
99. Ibid., 1149b7.
100. Ibid., 1148a20.
101. Ibid., 1146a2–5.
102. Ibid., 1150b5–12, 14.
103. Ibid., 1136a5–9.
104. Ibid., 1143a24.
105. Ibid., 1137b14ff.
106. Ibid., 1126a1–3.

107. Cf. Aubriot, "Quelques réflexions sur le pardon," 17–18, 26.

108. Griswold, *Forgiveness,* 5. Griswold takes *sungnômê* as the basis for his own approach to forgiveness. He recognizes that it includes an intuited cluster of concepts such as sympathy, common humanity, understanding the other, and consideration of fallibility (77). Incorporating these ideas in their interrelatedness, he explains that "the facts of our shared interdependence, embodiment, finitude, emotive make-up, subjection to forces beyond our control—in short, facts about our imperfection—allow us commiseration with one another, or at least to imagine the world from the other's point of view." His modern appropriation of the notion of *sungnômê* thus focuses on the notion of sympathy. He follows Adam Smith in this respect, who understands sympathy in its simultaneously cognitive and affective attributes as the capacity to take up the perspective of the other while regarding the limitations of the self in relation to the other (Griswold, *Forgiveness,* 88; see also Adam Smith, *The Theory of Moral Sentiments,* ed. D. D. Raphael and A. L. Macfie [Indianapolis: Liberty Press, 1982], 7.3.1.4). Sympathy, for Griswold, is not, therefore, a substitute for forgiveness. He claims rather that the sympathy implied in understanding is a precondition for forgiveness. He writes, "I want to suggest that recognition of shared humanity by the injured party is a necessary step on the way to forgiveness, though it is not sufficient for it" (79). He concludes that "while forgiveness does require sympathy, being able to grasp the situation and point of view of the other is not a sufficient condition for forgiveness for the compelling reason that having sympathetically entered into the situation and motives of the offender, one may justifiably experience even greater resentment" (79). Although he admits that sympathy is not sufficient for forgiveness, he does maintain it to be a necessary condition. The question remains, however, whether after one has sympathized with the offender and in this process found reason for "greater resentment," one can nonetheless forgive him or her. Griswold seems to indicate that if reason is the basis of resentment, forgiveness in such a case is morally impossible because it is not based on reason. One would not will it, for reason dictates otherwise. His attempt to reduce forgiveness to moral grounds is reflective of his overall approach of examining forgiveness outside of grace and the gift. In general, I believe many of the modern theories of forgiveness are ultimately modern appropriations of *sungnômê* in that they attempt to rationalize and morally justify forgiveness.

For an explicit connection of forgiveness with what can be understood under *sungnômê,* see Klaus-Michael Kodalle, *Verzeihung nach Wendezeiten?: Über Unnachsichtigkeit und misslingende Selbstentschuldigung; Antrittsvorlesung an der Friedrich-Schiller-Universität Jena am 2. Juni 1994* (Jena: Palm und Enke, 1994). Although he has emphasized the more radical character of forgiveness in other works, Kodalle pleads here in the spirit of forgiveness for a culture of *Nachsichtigkeit* (indulgence or leniency) so that those who have committed offenses, especially public officials, may be more apt to accept responsibility and issue an apology. To speak of forgiveness in this case I think unfortunately leads to conceptual confusion.

109. Jankélévitch, *Forgiveness*, 75.
110. Ibid., 71.
111. For Kant's extensive treatment of whether an action is undertaken out of duty or simply in conformity to duty, see the first two paragraphs in the second section of *Groundwork* (406–7) and also his *Religion within the Limits of Reason Alone*, for example, B79. In *Religion*, Kant invokes, exactly for this reason, God as the "Herzensforscher" (the searcher of human hearts).
112. Cf. Jacques Derrida, "Typewriter Ribbon: Limited Ink (2)," in Jacques Derrida, *Without Alibi*, ed. and trans. Peggy Kamuf (Stanford: Stanford University Press, 2002). Derrida distinguishes between the excuse and forgiveness, too. In his reading of Augustine and Jean-Jacques Rousseau, he observes that "both authors of *Confessions* speak the language of excuse more often than that of pardon or forgiveness. Augustine speaks of the inexcusable (*inexcusabilis*), Rousseau of 'excusing himself'" (80). Derrida examines the relation between the event and writing and witnesses "a logic of supplementarity at work between excuse and guilt" in the writing of these *Confessions*. The writing of a confession, he argues, is of the order of the excuse and, more precisely, of the self-excuse. Rousseau, for example, "will have spent his life protesting his innocence and thus excusing himself rather than seeking to be forgiven" (83). Far from effacing guilt, however, this strategy tends to exacerbate it, for "excuses engender and augment the fault.... The more one excuses oneself, the more one admits that one is guilty.... Guilty of excusing oneself." "The written excuse," Derrida concludes, "produces guilt.... It overproduces this shame, it archives it instead of effacing it" (101).
113. Jankélévitch, *Forgiveness*, 80.
114. Ibid., 93.
115. Ibid., 75.
116. Ibid., 81.
117. Ibid., 79.
118. Ibid., 82.
119. Ibid., 152–53.
120. In part 3 of *The Passions of the Soul*, Descartes criticizes a forgiveness that is the result of weakness and egotistical self-love, a critique that Nietzsche adopts and sharpens (*The Passions of the Soul*, trans. Stephen H. Voss (Indianapolis: Hackett, 1989). Under such auspices, one does not essentially and primarily forgive the other for the offense, but rather, as Klaus-Michael Kodalle points out, prophylactically oneself (1997, 113). See also Aurel Kolnai, "Forgiveness," in *Proceedings of the Aristotelian Society* (1974): 91–106.
121. Jankélévitch, *Forgiveness*, 93.
122. Ibid., 75.
123. Ibid., 94.
124. Ibid., 95.
125. Ibid., 96.
126. Ibid., 98–99.
127. Ibid., 98.

128. Augustine, *The Nicene and Post Nicene Fathers,* vol. 8: *St. Augustine: Expositions on the Book of Psalms,* ed. Philip Schaff, trans. A. Cleveland Coxe (Grand Rapids, Mich.: Wm. B. Eerdmans, 1980); Psalm 75:2, p. 350 (trans. slightly modified). [*Enarrationes in Psalmo: 51–100,* in *Aureli Augustini Opera* 10, 2, ed. Eligius Dekkers and Johannes Fraipont (Turnhout: Brepols, 1956); Psalm 74:2, p. 1025: *Quid est enim ipsum ignoscere, nisi non noscere? Quid est non noscere? Non animaduertere.*] I want to thank Theo Kobusch for pointing out to me this Augustine reference. For Augustine, this turning away (*ignoscere*) is always conjoined in God with a recognition (*agnoscere*). In the following verses of the same Psalm interpretation, he writes of the one who confesses in humility, "May He turn away face from thy sins, not turn away from thee: turn away face from that which thou hast wrought, not turn away from that which He hat Himself wrought" (351). This Janus-faced God looks with one side at the sinner/creature and with the other away from the sin.

129. Georg Simmel, *Einleitung in die Moralwissenschaft: Eine Kritik der ethischen Grundbegriffe,* vol. 2, in Georg Simmel, *Gesamtausgabe* (Frankfurt a.M.: Suhrkamp, 1991), 4:224: *"Nicht weil man begreift, sondern trotzdem man nicht begreift, kann man verzeihen."*

130. Jankélévitch, *Forgiveness,* 141–42.

131. Rom. 5:20, emphasis mine.

132. Matt. 5:47.

133. Aubriot, "Quelques réflexions sur le pardon," 18–22; Romilly, *La douceur dans la pensée grecque,* 116–17, 140.

134. Isabella seems to be appealing to the self-reflexive and self-critical understanding (*sungnômê*) of Angelo as she continues, saying, "If he had been as you and you as he, / You would have slipt like him; but he, like you, / Would not have been so stern." She thereby also demonstrates the ambiguity of such an understanding.

135. Immanuel Kant, *Metaphysik der Sitten,* in *Kant Werke,* 6 vols. (Darmstadt: Wissenschaftliche Buchgesellschaft, 1998), 4:A207, B237.

136. Carl Schmitt, *Politische Theologie: Vier Kapitel zur Lehre von der Sou veränität,* 7th ed. (Berlin: Duncker & Humblot, 1996), 13–15.

See also, for example, Walter Benjamin, "Zur Kritik der Gewalt," in *Zur Kritik der Gewalt und andere Aufsätze* (Frankfurt am Main: Suhrkamp, 1965); Giorgio Agamben, *State of Exception,* trans. Kevin Attell (Chicago: University of Chicago Press, 2005); Giorgio Agamben, *Homo sacer: Sovereign Power and Bare Life,* trans. Daniel Heller Roazen (Stanford: Stanford University Press, 1998); Jacques Derrida, *Politics of Friendship,* trans. George Collins (London: Verso, 1997); and Jacques Derrida, *Rogues: Two Essays on Reason,* trans. Pascale-Anne Brault and Michael Naas (Stanford: Stanford University Press, 2005).

137. Jankélévitch, *Forgiveness,* 3.

138. See the section titled "Normative Ideal or Impossibility," in chapter 6 for more on this subject.

139. See also Aubriot, "Quelques réflexions sur le pardon," 19.

140. Jeffrie Murphy and Jean Hampton, *Forgiveness and Mercy* (Cambridge: Cambridge University Press, 1988), 166. See also P. Twambley, "Mercy and Forgiveness," in *Analysis* 36, no. 2 (1976): 84–90.

141. Murphy and Hampton, *Forgiveness and Mercy*, 175.

142. In several respects, Jankélévitch's conception of justice misses this flexibility of justice itself. He argues, for example, that forgiveness is like a "halo" around a strict law (*Forgiveness*, 9; see the section titled "Two Absolutes" in chapter 6 of this work for his conception of the dialectic of love and justice). At the same time, he seems to aim at a more fundamental critique of the intimate association of justice with the law. Something has to move the law beyond its own self-referentiality, whether that be a conception of justice beyond the law or the intervention of something outside of the law, namely love or forgiveness.

143. Murphy and Hampton, *Forgiveness and Mercy*, 171–72.

144. Ibid., 176.

145. See the section titled "The Correlation of Punishment and Forgiveness" in chapter 5 of this work for this relation of punishment and forgiveness. In my reading, Jankélévitch remains bound to the retributive framework in his understanding of forgiveness, at least in his insistence that one is faced with the alternatives of forgiveness or just punishment. I suggest that they may coexist on account of the separation of the moral sphere from the sociopolitical and juridical spheres.

3. The Temporality of Human Existence and Action

1. Aristotle, *Physics* 4.218a3.

2. Vladimir Jankélévitch, *La Mort* (Paris: Flammarion, 1977), 295.

3. Cf. Aristotle, *Physics* 4.223a14–15; Plotinus *Enneads* 3.7, 8 and Augustine's *Confessions,* trans. Henry Chadwick (Oxford: Oxford University Press, 1992), 11.24.

4. Jankélévitch, *La Mort*, 324–25. Within this same context, one could equally claim that life is constituted in the greeting or welcome of that which is to come. Adieu and welcome are of one breath. It is their indissolubility that Jankélévitch ultimately emphasizes, as shall be seen.

5. Ibid., 312.

6. Søren Kierkegaard, *Repetition*, in *Fear and Trembling* and *Repetition*, ed. and trans. Howard Hong and Edna Hong (Princeton: Princeton University Press, 1983), 131, 169–70. Constantius repeats at the beginning of several paragraphs throughout his report on the young man at the center of the book the phrase "time passed." See, for example, 140, 141, 179.

7. Ibid., 275.

8. Jankélévitch, *La Mort*, 290–92.

9. Kierkegaard, *Repetition*, 149.

10. Cf. Aristotle *Metaphysics: Gamma, Delta, Epsilon, Bks. 4–6,* trans. Christopher Kirwan, 2nd ed. (Oxford: Oxford University Press, 1993), 5.1015a. See also Vladimir Jankélévitch, *Forgiveness,* trans. Andrew Kelley (Chicago: University of Chicago Press, 2005), 163.

11. Vladimir Jankélévitch, *L'Irréversible et la Nostalgie* (Paris: Flammarion, 1983), 27. See also Thierry Delooz, "L'Irréversible, L'Irréparable et la 'Futurition' selon Vladimir Jankélévitch," *Bulletin de Littérature Ecclésiastique* 107, no. 2 (2006): 243–46.

12. Jankélévitch, *La Mort*, 296. "En fait l'homme modifie les modes du temps quotidien sans extirper la quoddité ou temporalité de ce temps, sans vaincre, comme eût dit Leibniz, le Styx de l'irréversibilité; notre liberté par rapport au temps est-elle purement 'adjectivale' et pelliculaire."

13. Ibid., 297.

14. Ibid., 297–98.

15. Ibid., 309–10.

16. Ibid., 298. "Le souvenir est certes une façon métaphorique et spectrale de revenir."

17. Françoise Schwab, "Vladimir Jankélévitch: Une âme résistante," *Bulletin de Littérature Ecclésiastique* 107, no. 2 (2006): 214.

18. Jankélévitch, *La Mort*, 308. See also Vladimir Jankélévitch and Béatrice Berlowitz, *Quelque part dans l'inachevé* (Paris: Gallimard, 1978), 113.

19. Vladimir Jankélévitch, *Cours de philosophie morale: Université libre de Bruxelles 1962–1963* (Paris: Éditions du Seuil, 2006), 131.

20. Jankélévitch, *La Mort*, 298–99.

21. Jankélévitch and Berlowitz, *Quelque part dans l'inachevé*, 63–64.

22. Jankélévitch, *Cours de philosophie morale*, 136.

23. Jankélévitch, *La Mort*, 312.

24. Giorgio Agamben, *The Time That Remains: A Commentary on the Letter to the Romans*, trans. Patricia Dailey (Stanford: Stanford University Press, 2005), 77.

25. Jankélévitch, *Cours de philosophie morale*, 171.

26. Ibid., 139.

27. Ibid., 170.

28. Jankélévitch and Berlowitz, *Quelque part dans l'inachevé*, 257.

29. Ibid., 113.

30. Cf. Walter Benjamin, The Ninth Thesis of "On the Concept of History," Internet publication at the Trinity and All Saints College website: Faculty of Media, Lloyd Spencer. [*Über den Begriff der Geschichte* in *Werke und Nachlass*, vol. 19, ed. Christoph Gödde and Gérard Raulet (Frankfurt a.M.: Suhrkamp, 2010).]

31. Cf. Friedrich Nietzsche. "On the Uses and Disadvantages of History for Life," in *Untimely Meditations,* ed. David Breazeale, trans. R. J. Hollingdale (Cambridge: Cambridge University Press, 1997). Nietzsche distuinguishes three kinds of history: monumental, antiquarian, and critical.

32. Cf. Paul Ricoeur, *Memory, History, Forgetting*, trans. Kathleen Blamey and David Pellauer (Chicago: University of Chicago Press, 2004), 486, esp. n. 35.

33. Jankélévitch, *L'Irreversible et la nostalgie*, 275. "Celui qui a été ne peut plus désormais ne pas avoir été: désormais ce fait mystérieux et profondément obscur d'avoir vécu est son viatique pour l'éternité."

34. John Milbank, "Forgiveness and Incarnation," in *Questioning God*, ed. John D. Caputo, Mark Dooley, and Michael J. Scanlon (Bloomington: Indiana University Press, 2001), 99.

35. Vladimir Jankélévitch, "Should We Pardon Them?" trans. Ann Hobart, *Critical Inquiry* 22, no. 3 (1996): 556–57.

36. Jankélévitch, *Forgiveness*, 43.

37. Ibid., 47.

38. Jankélévitch, *La Mort*, 337–38.

39. Ibid., 334.

40. Ibid., 333. "Il n'est pas de désastre humain qui ne puisse être humainement réparé. Tout ce qui a été fait peut être défait. Tout ce qui a été défait peut être refait. Et on peut aussi faire mieux, faire autre chose."

41. Jankélévitch, *Forgiveness*, 45–46. See also Jankélévitch, *La Mort*, 333–35. Jankélévitch concludes the quotation above with the same line as in *Forgiveness*: "Mais le fait-d'avoir-fait, lui, ne peut etre defait. Le fait-d'avoir-fait est rigoureusement indéfaisable!"

Semelfactivity is a term taken from linguistics (*semelfactif*) indicating a verb form of an action that takes place only once (cf. Andrew Kelley, "Translator's Introduction," in Vladimir Jankélévitch, *Forgiveness* [Chicago: University of Chicago Press, 2005], 171). Such word constructions like *semelfactivity* or *hapax* bring out Jankélévitch's emphasis on the interconnectedness of singularity, quoddity, or that-ness (the event-character), freedom/creativity, and inexplicability. In drawing from linguistics, Jankélévitch opens up avenues for examining the intercontextuality of existence.

42. Jankélévitch, *Forgiveness*, 47.

43. Jankélévitch, *La Mort*, 402.

44. Shakespeare, *Macbeth* 3.2 and 5.2. See also John Milton, *Paradise Lost*, 9.

45. Jankélévitch, *La Mort*, 336. This tension between future possibilities and the past is reflected, for Jankélévitch, in repentance, on the one hand, and remorse, on the other hand. See chapter 9 in this book on repentance.

46. This principle of identity stating that two contrasting—if not contradictory—positions (or position and negation) cannot simultaneously be the case will be revisited in the concluding discussion of Jankélévitch's idea of forgiveness.

47. Jankélévitch, *La Mort*, 343.

48. In his response to Walter Benjamin's appraisal of the incompleteness of the past, Horkheimer writes in a letter dated March 16, 1937, "The determination of incompleteness is idealistic if completeness is not comprised within it. Past injustice has occurred and is completed. The slain are actually slain. . . . Perhaps, with regard to incompleteness, there is a difference between the positive and the negative, so that only the injustice, the horror, the suffering of the past are irreparable. The justice practiced, the joys, the works, have a different relation to time, for their positive character is largely negated by the transience of things. This holds first and foremost for individual existence, in which it is not the happiness but

the unhappiness that is sealed by death." ("Die Feststellung der Unabgeschlossenheit ist idealistische, wenn die Abgeschlossenheit nicht in ihr aufgenommen ist. Das vergangene Unrecht ist geschehen und abgeschlossen. Die Erschlagnen sind wirklich erschlagen . . . Vielleicht besteht in Beziehung auf die Unabgeschlossenheit ein Unterschied zwischen dem Positiven und Negativen, so daß nur das Unrecht, der Schrecken, die Schmerzen der Vergangenheit irreparabel sind. Die geübte Gerechtigkeit, die Freuden, die Werke verhalten sich anders zur Zeit, denn ihr positiver Charakter wird durch die Vergänglichkeit weitgehend negiert. Dies gilt zunächst im individuellen Dasein, in welchem nicht das Glück, sondern das Unglück durch den Tod besiegelt wird.")

Benjamin, in contrast, upholds the power of remembrance (*Eingedenken*) to potentially reverse the signs Horkheimer places before the events of the past: "Such mindfulness can make the incomplete (happiness) into something complete, and the complete (suffering) into something incomplete." ("Das Eingedenken kann das Unabgeschlossene [das Glück] zu einem Ab[ge]schlossenen und das Abgeschlossene [das Leid] zu einem Unabgeschlossenen machen.") Walter Benjamin, *The Arcades Project*, trans. Howard Eiland and Kevin McLaughlin (Cambridge, Mass.: Harvard University Press, 1999), 471. [*Gesammelte Werke V*, ed. Rolf Tiedemann and Hermann Schweppenhäuser. (Frankfurt am Main: Suhrkamp, 1991), 589.] See also Robert Gibbs's discussion on this correspondence in *Why Ethics? Signs of Responsibility* (Princeton, N.J.: Princeton University Press, 2000), chap. 16, 339–45.

49. Jankélévitch, *La Mort*, 337. "L'irréparable auquel l'homme se résigne est ce qui, en aucun cas, d'aucune manière, sous aucune forme, à aucun degré, à aucun moment ne peut être réparé."

50. Ibid., 336. "Aucune justice humaine ne peut restituer le passé à personne. Le citoyen dédommagé restera un home éternellement lésé."

51. The legal term of *imprescriptibility* implies what is beyond any statute of limitations. Crimes against humanity were defined in the Charters of the International Military Tribunal at Nuremberg and later Tokyo from August 8, 1945, to January 12, 1946. Certain revisions of the concept were undertaken by the United Nations in 1948. The Convention on Imprescriptibility of Crimes of War and Against Humanity and the Council of Europe's treaty on the Non-Applicability of Statutory Limitations to Crimes against Humanity and War Crimes, adopted in January 1974, accorded the concepts of crimes against humanity and imprescriptibility the seal of international law. After public debate, the concepts of crimes against humanity and their imprescriptibility were integrated into French law on December 26, 1964. (See also Ricoeur's *Memory, History, Forgetting*, 472–73, esp. n. 18, and the introduction to *Questioning God*, 17n5).

52. Jankélévitch, *Forgiveness*, 48–49.

53. Ricoeur, *Memory, History, Forgetting*, 471–73.

54. Ibid., 472.

55. Jankélévitch, "Should We Pardon Them?" 566.

56. Jean Améry, *Jenseits von Schuld und Sühne: Bewältigungsversuche eines Überwältigten* (Stuttgart: Klett-Cotta, 1977), 115.
57. Jankélévitch, "Should We Pardon Them?" 566.
58. Ibid., 569.
59. Jacques Derrida, *On Cosmopolitanism and Forgiveness*, trans. Mark Dooley and Michael Hughes (London: [0]Routledge, 2002), 45.
60. Ibid., 53.

4. Translating Resentment

1. Vladimir Jankélévitch, *Forgiveness*, trans. Andrew Kelley (Chicago: University of Chicago Press, 2005), 84, 86.
2. See, e.g., Ronald de Sousa, *The Rationality of Emotion* (Cambridge, Mass.: MIT Press, 1987), and Martha Nussbaum, *Upheavals of Thought: The Intelligence of Emotions* (Cambridge: Cambridge University Press, 2001).
3. P. F. Strawson, "Freedom and Resentment," in *Proceedings of the British Academy* 1962 (London: Oxford University Press, 1963), 190–92, reprinted in *Freedom and Resentment and Other Essays* (London: Methuen, 1974).
4. Jeffrie Murphy, *Getting Even: Forgiveness and Its Limits* (Oxford: Oxford University Press, 2003), 20.
5. See Émile Benveniste's article "Gift and Exchange in the Indo-European Vocabulary," in *The Logic of the Gift: Toward an Ethic of Generosity*, ed. Alan Schrift (New York: Routledge, 1997), 34–35. Benveniste demonstrates the ambivalence of the root *nemo*, which means both to give and to take.
6. Aristotle, *Nicomachean Ethics* 2.8. The discussion here involves this passage and book 2, chap. 9 of the *Rhetoric*, trans. W. Rhys Roberts (Mineola, N.Y.: Dover Thrift Editions, 2004).
7. Aristotle, *Rhetoric* 2.9.
8. Ibid. Aristotle defines *envy* in the next chapter of his *Rhetoric* (2.10) as pain at the sight of good fortune falling upon one's equals. By "equals" Aristotle means equals in birth, relationship, age, disposition, distinction, or wealth.
9. Ibid., 2.8.1386b.
10. Ibid., 2.9.1387a. If one is not in rightful possession of goods due to rightful birth, the secondary goods of social establishment, tradition, or history bestow a sense of properness to these properties. Because, Aristotle believes, "what is long established seems akin to what exists by nature; and therefore we feel more indignation at those possessing a given good if they have as a matter of fact only just got it and the prosperity it brings with it" (ibid).
11. See also Gayne Nerney, "Aristotle and Aquinas on Indignation: From Nemesis to Theodicy," in *Faith and Philosophy* 8, no. 1 (1991): 81–95. Nerney states that "to commend the passion of indignation implies a commendation of temporal goods, e.g., health, wealth, and honor, the perception of the unmerited possession of which is the *causa sine qua non* of undergoing this emotional reaction" (83).
12. See also Vladimir Jankélévitch, *Cours de philosophie morale: Université libre de Bruxelles 1962–1963* (Paris: Éditions du Seuil, 2006), 15–16.

13. Aristotle, *Rhetoric* 2.8.1386a.
14. Ibid., 2.6.1385a.
15. Ibid.
16. Cf. ibid., 2.8.1386b.
17. Tragedy, Aristotle writes in his *Poetics*, "is presented in a dramatic, not narrative form, and achieves, through the representation of pitiable and fearful incidents, the catharsis of such pitiable and fearful incidents" (Aristotle, *Poetics*, trans. S. H. Butler [Mineola, N.Y.: Dover Thrift Editions, 1997], 6.4–11).
18. Aristotle, *Rhetoric* 2.8.1386a. In contrast, friendship for Aristotle consists in wishing for the friend what one believes to be good things, not for one's own sake but for his.
19. Cf. Jean Hampton in Jeffrie Murphy and Jean Hampton, *Forgiveness and Mercy*. (Cambridge: Cambridge University Press, 1988), 54–60; Charles Griswold, *Forgiveness: A Philosophical Exploration* (New York: Cambridge University Press, 2007), 26, 43–47; Strawson, "Freedom and Resentment," 14–15.
20. Aristotle, *Nicomachean Ethics* 1125bff.
21. Murphy, *Getting Even*, 104. See also Bishop Butler, Sermon 8: "And after an injury is done and there is a necessity that the offender should be brought to justice; the cool consideration of reason . . . might indeed be sufficient to procure laws to be enacted, and sentence passed: but is it that cool reflection in the injured person, which, for the most part, brings the offender to justice? Or is it not resentment and indignation against the injury and the author of it? I am afraid there is no doubt which is commonly the case. This, however, is to be considered as a good effect, notwithstanding it were much to be wished, that men would act from a better principle, reason and cool reflection" (Joseph Butler, *Fifteen Sermons Preached at the Rolls Chapel 1827* (Milton Keynes, UK: Dodo Press), 68).
22. Butler, *Fifteen Sermons*, 63.
23. Ibid., 70.
24. Ibid., 64–66. Although he does not differentiate between resentment and indignation, Butler does recognize a discrepancy between the view of the person immediately injured and that of a third party or society as a whole, conceding that it is inscribed in the very constitution of our nature to have a greater sensibility to, and be more deeply interested in what concerns ourselves (66).
25. Ibid., 69, 64.
26. Ibid., 73.
27. Ibid., 74.
28. Murphy and Hampton, *Forgiveness and Mercy*, 15. See also Murphy, *Getting Even*. Murphy names Butler's *Sermons* as "one of the works that have particularly influenced my thinking" (*Getting Even*, 120), and, to a large degree, he bases his reflections concerning the retributive emotions and forgiveness on Butler. Of course, Murphy does not have to have read Butler correctly to have gained insight into the subject (cf. Griswold, *Forgiveness*, 20). Moreover, his misreading appears to be standard fare. Cf. Hampton in her book with Murphy, *Forgiveness and Mercy*, 35; and M. R. Holmgren, "Forgiveness and the Intrinsic Value of Persons,"

American Philosophical Quarterly 30, no. 4 (1993): 341–52, and Trudy Govier, *Forgiveness and Revenge* (New York: Routledge, 2002), esp. 42–61, who states that "to forgive is to overcome resentment and anger in the wake of an offense, and to reframe the offender as a person capable of doing better in the future" (59). In his essay, "Freedom and Resentment," Strawson seems to imply such an understanding without, however, attributing it directly to Butler: "To ask to be forgiven is in part to acknowledge that the attitude displayed in our actions was such as might properly be resented and in part to repudiate that attitude for the future (or at least for the immediate future); and to forgive is to accept the repudiation and to forswear the resentment" (6). For further critical appraisals of Murphy, see Herbert Morris, "Murphy on Forgiveness," in *Criminal Justice Ethics* 7, no. 2 (1988): 15–19, and Marilyn McCord Adams, "Forgiveness: A Christian Model," in *Faith and Philosophy* 8, no. 3 (July 1991): 277–304.

29. Butler explains the coexistence of love and resentment exemplarily in capital punishment. The guilt or demerit that is rightfully resented does not dispense with the obligation of benevolence. Nonetheless "public execution" is justified in his eyes according to consequentialist, utilitarian considerations: If the life an offender is "inconsistent with the quiet and happiness of the world" (76), the good of the greater social body outweighs the obligation to the individual.

30. This respect resembles what Kant calls a practical love as opposed to pathological love. This duty to love knows no limits. No injury or crime, according to Butler, dispenses with or supersedes the duty of love and good will. Cf. Butler, *Fifteen Sermons*, 76.

31. Cf. René Girard, *Violence and the Sacred* (Baltimore: Johns Hopkins University Press, 1979), esp. chap. 1, "Sacrifice," 1–38, for the relation of violence and contagion. An interesting aspect of Girard's reflections is the suspension of social, hierarchical, conceptual distinctions in the contagion of violence. This notion applies equally to Aristotle and Butler. In Aristotle, the class distinctions and the very place of aristocracy and its morality are jeopardized. Butler's qualified defense of resentment reaches a point where resentment no longer can be separated from revenge and malice—a distinction on which its value as a qualified good or a beneficial violence depends. Moreover, the integrity of the social body, with its regulations and order, is a major focal point of his sermons, as the use of bodily metaphors attests.

32. Butler, *Fifteen Sermons*, 78. This movement raises the question whether it is the act or the person who is resented. For this question, cf. Murphy and Hampton, *Forgiveness and Mercy*, and Griswold, *Forgiveness*. Jean Hampton argues that whereas hatred aims at a person, "The object of resentment is an action. When resentment is directed at a person, it is in response to what he did, not who or what he is" (60). In contrast, Charles Griswold claims that we resent not the action but the actor if the link between the action and the actor is close enough (25).

33. Emphasis mine.

34. Butler, *Fifteen Sermons*, 72.

35. Ibid., 72–73.

36. Ibid., 77.

37. Judith Butler, *Giving an Account of Oneself* (New York: Fordham University Press, 2005), 101.

38. Although Bishop Butler tends to group "hatred, malice, and revenge" together and use them synonymously, Griswold identifies an important distinction between hate and the retributive character of the other two and resentment. "Retribution does not necessarily follow from hatred, as it so naturally does from resentment. Misanthropes may hate humankind, but without believing they've been injured by them" (Butler, *Fifteen Sermons*, 25).

39. Ibid., 74. Adam Smith recognizes a gap between appropriate resentment and revenge. He writes that the object which resentment "is chiefly intent upon, is not so much to make our enemy feel pain in his turn, as to make him conscious that he feels it upon account of his past conduct, to make him repent of that conduct, and to make him sensible, that the person whom he injured did not deserve to be treated in that manner." The pain therefore should not be sequential and renewed but simply uncovered. Like Butler, Smith assumes in Socratic fashion that the offender's pain is inherent in the injury itself; self-censorship or self-condemnation are merely awakened by the other. Like Butler, too, Smith suspects the root of wrongdoing is to be found in "absurd self-love" (*The Theory of Moral Sentiments*, ed. D. D. Raphael and A. L. Macfie [Indianapolis: Liberty Press, 1982], II.iii.I.5). See also Griswold, *Forgiveness*, 28.

40. Griswold, *Forgiveness*, 30.

41. Butler, *Fifteen Sermons*, 55.

42. See Jankélévitch, *Forgiveness*, 163.

43. Butler, *Fifteen Sermons*, 69.

44. Ibid., 74; emphasis mine.

45. See Jacques Derrida, "Plato's Pharmacy," in idem., *Dissemination*, trans. Barbara Johnson (Chicago: University of Chicago Press, 1981). See also Marcel Mauss, "Gift, Gift," trans. Koen Decoster, in *The Logic of the Gift: Toward an Ethic of Generosity*, ed. Alan D. Schrift (New York: Routledge, 1997), 28–32.

46. This difference between appropriate self-love and bloated self-love plays a crucial role in Bishop Butler's explication of forgiveness. The offense against me should compel reflection on my own sins, and Butler argues that I should be willing to forgive the other based on our common humanity, our common need for God's forgiveness, and the fact the perpetration of moral injury hurts one's own soul (*Fifteen Sermons*, 79). Moreover, Butler believes most offenses have their source in "inadvertency" and "misunderstanding" primarily due to an inflated self-love. Such self-love prevents us from seeing things "as they are in themselves" (78).

47. Ibid., 68.

48. Walter Kaufmann, *Nietzsche: Philosopher, Psychologist, Antichrist* (New York: Random House, 1968), 371.

49. Richard Bernstein, *Radical Evil: A Philosophical Interrogation* (Cambridge: Polity, 2007), 129.

50. Cf. Kaufmann, *Nietzsche*, 367. This theme of distraction extends from Augustine to Heidegger. Augustine's describes the temptations of the world that distract the mind from itself and its contemplation and yearning for God. Indicatively, the first step Augustine recommends in overcoming such distractions is the return to oneself, and it is in oneself that God is to be found. For Heidegger in the wake of both Augustine and Nietzsche, these temptations are transposed into the fall to the world, the notion of "das Man" (the they), and inauthentic existence. The structural analogy has its obvious limits. Augustine, of course, does not consider neighborly love a distraction, and his theology asserts that the disquieted mind will find its rest in the eschaton with God. Cf., e.g., Jean Grodin, *Von Heidegger zu Gadamer: Unterwegs zur Hermeneutik* (Darmstadt: Wissenschaftliche Buchgesellschaft, 2001), 73–74.

51. Zarathustra tells his disciples: "Go ahead and love your neighbors as you love yourselves—but first be the kind of people *who love themselves*" (3.5). Friedrich Nietzsche, *Thus Spoke Zarathrustra: A Book for All and None*, trans. Adrian Del Caro; ed. Adrian Del Caro and Robert B. Pippin (Cambridge: Cambridge University Press 2006), 137.

52. Nietzsche, *Zarathustra*, 2.13.92.

53. The opposition of the terms *Hellene* and *Nazarene* originates with Heinrich Heine. Thomas Mann points out the relevance of this distinction in anticipating Nietzsche's conception of *ressentiment*. In book 1 of *Heinrich Heine über Ludewig Börne*, Heine writes, "I say Nazarene to use neither the expression 'Jewish' nor 'Christian,' although both expressions are synonymous for me and are used by me not to designate a faith but a character . . . as opposed to 'Hellenes,' with which word I also do not designate a particular people but a bent of the spirit and a way of looking at things. . . . All men are either Jews or Hellenes—men with ascetic, picture-hating drives that crave spiritualization, or men with a life-loving [*lebensheiteren*] . . . and realistic character. Thus there have been Hellenes in German ministers' families and Jews who were born in Athens" (cited in Kaufmann, *Nietzsche*, 376–77).

54. Friedrich Nietzsche, *On the Genealogy of Morals*, trans. Walter Kaufmann and R. J. Hollingdale (New York: Random House, 1989), essay 1, sec. 10, pp. 36–37.

55. Cf. Rüdiger Safranski, *Nietzsche: Biographie seines Denkens* (Frankfurt a.M.: Fischer Taschenbuch Verlag, 2002), 313–14.

56. Friedrich Nietzsche, *Beyond Good and Evil: Prelude to a Philosophy of the Future*, trans. Judith Norman (Cambridge: Cambridge University Press, 2002), part 6, aphorism 212, p. 106. See also Kaufmann, *Nietzsche*, 371.

57. Nietzsche, *Genealogy*, essay 1, sec. 14, p. 47.

58. Ibid., 1.14.47, and 1.10.37.

59. Ibid., 2.16.84–85.

60. Ibid., 1.13.46.

61. Nietzsche, *Zarathustra*, 1.19.50–51.

62. Nietzsche, *Genealogy* 1.10.39.
63. Ibid., 1.11.42–43.
64. Ibid., 1.16.52–53.
65. The two works of Martin Luther that espouse the doctrine of the universal priesthood, otherwise known as "the priesthood of all believers," are *To the Christian Nobility of the German Nation* and *Babylonian Captivity of the Church*, both from 1520. Cf. also Jacob Taubes who meditates on the Greek term *pan* (all) in Paul's letters and its threatening character within the subversive love of Christianity to Roman right and power. *The Political Theology of Paul* (Stanford,: Stanford University Press, 2003).

See also Karl Löwith, *Von Hegel zu Nietzsche: Der revolutionäre Bruch im Denken des neunzehnten Jahrhunderts* (Stuttgart: W. Kohlhammer Verlag, 1953), 281. Cf. Kierkegaard's linking of *ressentiment* and leveling (*Nivelliering*) in *Two Ages: The Age of Revolution and the Present Age: A Literary Review*, trans. Howard Hong and Edna Hong (Princeton: Princeton University Press, 1978). Kierkegaard's understanding of *ressentiment* as a leveling closely resembles Nietzsche's transvaluation of values. Kierkegaard writes: "Characterless *envy* does not understand that excellence is excellence, does not understand that it is itself a negative acknowledgement of excellence but wants to degrade it, minimize it, until it actually is no longer excellence" (83–84). Although Howard and Edna Hong translate the Danish word *misundelse* in the customary way as *envy*, Alexander Dru (in his translation of *The Present Age* ([London: Collins Fontana Library, 1962], 56) translates the term as *ressentiment*, undoubtedly with Nietzsche in mind.

See also Max Scheler's examination of the political ramifications of the association of *ressentiment* and leveling. He claims that, whereas revenge is a matter between persons of a relatively equal standing and the exercise of revenge can serve to reestablish the feeling of self-value, *ressentiment* frequently arises proportionately to the *difference* between the political-constitutional or ethical standing of a group and their factual power. Modern Western societies, Scheler concludes, provide the most fertile ground for the formation of *ressentiment*. Although they uphold a formal equality of political and social rights, they simultaneously demonstrate great differences in practicable power, factual possession, and education. In short, one could say that the sociological root of *ressentiment*, according to Scheler, can be found in a lack of substantial, not merely formal, social and political recognition and equality (Max Scheler, *Ressentiment*, trans. Louis A. Coser (Milwaukee: Marquette University Press, 2007), 29 [*Das Ressentiment im Aufbau der Moralen* (Frankfurt a.M.: Klostermann, 1978), 9].

66. Nietzsche, *Genealogy*, 2.16.85.
67. Ibid., *Genealogy*, 1.12.44.
68. Ibid., 1.11.43.
69. Bernstein, *Radical Evil*, 121.
70. Nietzsche, *Genealogy* 2.16.85.
71. Ibid., 2.19.88.

72. Ibid., 3.28.162.

73. Ibid., 2.24.95.

74. Ibid., 3.28.162–63. Cf. ibid., 3.1.97. Cf. Bernstein, who argues that "the most fundamental battle at the heart of the *Genealogy* is not between the good/bad ethic and the good/evil morality. It is Nietzsche's strenuous war against the nihilism of the 'last man.'" (*Radical Evil,* 122).

75. Nietzsche, *Genealogy,* 1.12.44. For Nietzsche, Napoleon is the historical embodiment of this synthesis of the inhuman and superhuman (*Genealogy* 1.16.54).

76. The figure of Dionysus so important to Nietzsche exemplifies this synthesis. For example, in his reading of Euripides' tragedy *The Bacchae,* René Girard captures its dual edge in his examination of how "the Dionysiac elimination of distinctions rapidly degenerates into a particularly virulent form of violent nondifferentiation." He traces the loss of the distinction between man and beast, on the one hand, as well as "the seemingly indelible distinction between man and god," on the other hand. Dionysus himself appears in a shroud of shuddering ambivalence. He is, on the one hand, the Dionysus of the Maenads who represents "the defender of divine and human laws, the jealous guardian of legality"; on the other hand, he functions as "the subversive *agent-provocateur* of the tragedy whose outbreak spells the disintegration of social institutions and the collapse of the cultural order" (Girard, 126ff.).

77. Nietzsche, *Genealogy* 2.24.96.

78. Ibid., 2.24.95.

79. Ibid., 2.24.96.

80. Scheler, *Ressentiment,* 21 [*Das Ressentiment,* 2]. First the pages from the English translation are given and then the pages of the German original.

81. Scheler, *Ressentiment,* 25; 4.

82. Ibid., 25; 5.

83. Ibid., 42; 25.

84. Ibid., 27; 7.

85. Ibid., 43; 26.

86. Ibid., 34; 15.

87. Ibid., 45; 29. Scheler assumes a universal "apriori hierarchy of value modalities" that precedes all representation and is prior to knowledge. These values do not exist outside of the world, however, but are material a priori—that is, they are emotively experienced as attached to an object, a value-bearer. Although objects may change value and different objects will have different values depending on time and culture, Scheler asserts the a priori universality of binary modalities expressed as positive values and negative disvalues and hierarchically arranged from the lower to the higher: values of utility and disvalues of the useless; the sensual values of the agreeable or pleasurable and the disvalues of the disagreeable or painful; values of the vital and noble and the disvalue of the vulgar; spiritual values and disvalues of the beautiful and ugly, right and wrong, and truth and falsehood; and values of the Holy and disvalues of the Unholy. See Max Scheler,

Formalism in Ethics and Non-Formal Ethics of Values, trans. M. Frings and R. Funk (Evanston, Ill.: Northwestern University Press, 1973), 104–10.

88. Scheler, *Ressentiment*, 46; 30.

89. Ibid., 45; 29.

90. Ibid., 23; 3.

91. See Plato, *Symposium* 204a–206a. Cf. Plato, *Euthyphro* 10aff.

92. Scheler, *Ressentiment*, 56–58; 37–39. See also Scheler's essay "Love and Knowledge," in *On Feeling, Knowing, and Valuing: Selected Writings*, ed. Harold J. Bershady (Chicago: University of Chicago Press, 1992), 147–66.

93. Scheler, *Ressentiment*, 59; 41.

94. Ibid., 64; 47.

95. Ibid., 61; 43–44.

96. Ibid., 60; 42–43.

97. Ibid., 67; 51.

98. Ibid., 62; 45.

99. Ibid., 58; 39

100. Ibid., 62; 45.

101. Ibid., 69; 52–53.

102. Ibid., 64–65; 47–48.

103. Ibid., 66; 49–50. Scheler interprets Jesus' interest in the poor, sick, wretched, and oppressed to mean that "the highest and ultimate *personality values* are declared to be *independent* of contrasts like rich and poor, healthy and sick, etc." He also sees Christian freedom as a positive asceticism, which consists in the act of freely renouncing positive goods. He thus approvingly quotes John Henry Newman's definition of "genuine" asceticism—"to admire the earthly things by renouncing them"—and suggests reading Nietzsche's essay "What Is the Meaning of Ascetic Ideals?" in the light of Newman's definition in order to highlight Nietzsche's misunderstanding (see Scheler, *Ressentiment*, 70n25; 54n1).

104. Scheler, *Ressentiment*, 75; 59.

105. Ibid., 72–73; 55–57.

106. Ibid., 73; 57.

107. Ibid., 74; 58. Scheler's logic holding simultaneously the acceptance of combat by all means and spiritual community, the latter having only the effect on the former of living enmity to the worldly and necessary, is reminiscent of Joseph Butler's line of argumentation regarding a love congruent with capital punishment. The accordance between Scheler and Butler on this point reveals the depth of the two-worlds theory in Christian conceptions of love.

108. Carl Schmitt, *The Concept of the Political*, trans. George Schwab (New Brunswick, N.J.: Rutgers University Press, 1976), 28–29. [*Der Begriff des Politischen*, 7th ed. (Berlin: Duncker & Humblot, 1996), 29–30.] See also Jacques Derrida, *Politics of Friendship*, trans. George Collins (London: Verso, 1997), 83–89, esp. 88–89.

109. Scheler, *Ressentiment*, 62; 45.

110. Ibid., 58; 39.

111. See, e.g., ibid. 60–61, 64; 43–44, 47.

112. Ibid., 58, esp. n. 8; 40 n. 1.

113. Jankélévitch, *Forgiveness*, 95.

114. For Améry's understanding of *ressentiment,* see Thomas Brudholm, *Resentment's Virtue: Jean Améry and the Refusal to Forgive* (Philadelphia: Temple University Press, 2008); see also Stephan Steiner, "Erinnern und Leben: Versuch zum Ort des Erinnerns bei Jean Améry," in *Kritik aus Passion: Studien zu Jean Améry,* ed. Matthias Bormuth and Susan Nurmi-Schomers (Göttingen: Wallstein Verlag, 2005).

115. Cf. Jean Améry, *Jenseits von Schuld und Sühne: Bewältigungsversuche eines Überwältigten* (Stuttgart: Klett-Cotta, 1977), 111.

116. Jankélévitch, *Forgiveness*, 53.

117. Ibid., 49.

118. See ibid., 33, 49. Jankélévitch acknowledges a forgiveness that stems from *ressentiment.* "Here is the impalpable *ressentiment* that men in general call forgiveness. . . . Offended people sometimes resign themselves to undertaking neighborly relations with their former hangmen in spite of terrible memories; these people accept it, they hold out a hand of pacifist coexistence to the hangmen, but not without repugnance. But the heart, as we say, 'is not there'!" (*Forgiveness*, 33). Such resigned "forgiveness" lacks the "*élan* of joy"; it is without heart, the heart of forgiveness.

119. Cf. also David Augsburger, *Helping People Forgive* (Louisville, Ky.: Westminster John Knox Press, 1996). Augsburger makes the distinction between "rage-based resentment" and "reality-based resentment." Rage-based resentment is that felt by those whose conception of themselves is grandiose, perfectionist, and based on unrealistic self-esteem. Reality-based resentment refers to the feeling appropriate to a wrong on the basis of a proper sense of one's moral worth and moral agency.

120. Martha Nussbaum, *The Therapy of Desire* (Princeton, N.J.: Princeton University Press, 1996), 403.

121. Ibid., 416.

122. Elie Wiesel, *From the Kingdom of Memory: Reminiscences* (New York: Schocken Books, 1990), 160. Améry, example, "The world that forgives and forgets has condemned me, not those who murdered and allowed the murders to take place" (*Jenseits von Schuld und Sühne,* 120).

123. Vladimir Jankélévitch, "Should We Pardon Them?" trans. Ann Hobart, *Critical Inquiry* 22, no. 3 (1996): 562.

124. Ibid., 572. In a similar vein and tone of protest, Améry writes in 1976: "What happened, happened. But that it happened is not so easy to accept. I rebel: against my past, against history, against a present that puts the incomprehensible on ice and thereby falsifies it. Nothing has scarred, and what perhaps in 1964 was about to heal breaks open again as an infected wound. Emotions? If you want to call it that. Where is it written that Enlightenment has to be emotionless? The

opposite seems to me to be true. Enlightenment can only do justice to its task when it goes to work with passion" (*Jenseits von Schuld und Sühne,* 14). ("Was geschah, geschah. Aber daß es geschah, ist so einfach nicht hinzunhemen. Ich rebelliere: gegen meine Vergangenheit, gegen die Geschichte, gegen eine Gegenwart, die das Unbegreifliche geschichtlich einfrieren läßt und es damit auf empörende Weise verfälscht. Nichts ist vernarbt, und was vielleicht 964 schon im Begriffe stand zu heilen, das bricht als infizierte Wunde wieder auf. Emotionen? Meinetwegen. Wo steht geschrieben, daß Aufklärung emotionslos zu sein hat? Das Gegenteil scheint mir wahr zu sein. Aufklärung kann ihrer Aufgabe nur dann gerecht werden, wenn sie sich mit Leidenschaft ans Werk macht." —trans. A.L.)

125. Jankélévitch, *Forgiveness,* 51.
126. Jankélévitch, "Should We Pardon Them?" 281.
127. Jankélévitch, *Forgiveness,* 54.
128. Ibid., 53.
129. Ibid., 53, 55.
130. Françoise Schwab, "Vladimir Jankélévitch: une âme résistante," *Bulletin de Littérature Ecclésiastique* 107, no. 2 (2006): 213.
131. Cf., e.g., Wiesel, *From the Kingdom of Memory,* 188.
132. Jankélévitch, "Should We Pardon Them?" 572.
133. Jankélévitch, *Forgiveness,* 130.
134. Améry, *Jenseits von Schuld und Sühne,* 115, 124.
135. Ibid., 111.
136. Jankélévitch, *Forgiveness,* 103.
137. Ibid., 52.
138. Ibid.
139. Ibid., 51.
140. Vladimir Jankélévitch and Béatrice Berlowitz, *Quelque part dans l'inachevé* (Paris: Gallimard, 1978), 149.
141. Jankélévitch, *Forgiveness,* 54.
142. Ibid., 55. See also Jankélévitch and Berlowitz, *Quelque part dans l'inachevé,* 65–66.
143. Jankélévitch, *Forgiveness,* 53.
144. *Haecceity* is a term coined by Duns Scotus and taken up by other medieval philosophers in the debate over universals between nominalism and realism. From the Latin, it literally means "thisness," as opposed to a quiddity, *hypokeimenon,* or essence. Scotus uses *haecceity* to indicate the nonqualitative property responsible for individuation. It aims at the individualizing differences of a particularity that distinguish it from a genus, species, or universal. For example, the person Socrates represents a haecceity or individuality to be distinguished from a numerical unity subsumable under the concepts *human* or *man.* See Duns Scotus, *Ordinatio* II, d.3, p.1, q.2, n.48 and II, d.3, p.1, q.4, n.76, in *Opera Omnia,* ed. Carolus Balić, José Rodríguez Carballo, and Barnaba Hechich, vol. 7 (Vatican City: Vatican Polyglot Press, 1973). Both Scotus and Jankélévitch undertake the difficult task

of expressing indivisible singularity. Although Jankélévitch often seems to use *haecceity* and *ipseity* almost interchangeably, he distinguishes ipseity not only from quiddity but also from haecceity in his essay "De l'ipséité,"in *Premières et dernières pages* (Paris: Seuil, 1994), 196. Ipseity, or selfhood, connotes for him the simple *fact that* this person is this person and is thus closely related to his notion of quoddity ("thatness").

145. Jankélévitch, *Forgiveness*, 4.

146. Søren Kierkegaard, *Works of Love*, ed. and trans. Howard V. Hong and Edna H. Hong (Princeton, N.J.: Princeton University Press, 1995), 352. Kierkegaard understands this duty of remembrance as a duty to love, because the love expressed in the recollection of the dead is the hallmark of selfless and free love precisely because it cannot be reciprocated (349–51).

147. Jankélévitch, *Forgiveness*, 55.

148. Ibid., 44.

149. Ibid., 50.

150. Ibid., 49.

151. Ibid., 11.

152. Vladimir Jankélévitch, *Philosophie premiére: Introduction à une Philosophie du "Presque,"* 2nd ed. (Paris: Quadrige/Presses Univeristaires de France, 1986), 51.

153. Jankélévitch, "De l'ipséité," esp. 196.

154. Jankélévitch, *Forgiveness*, 47, 55.

155. Ibid., 49–50.

156. Ibid., 50.

157. Schwab, "Vladimir Jankélévitch," 217.

158. Jankélévitch and Berlowitz, *Quelque part dans l'inachevé*, 94.

159. Jankélévitch, *Forgiveness*, 102.

160. Ibid., 25.

161. Wiesel, *From the Kingdom of Memory*, 248.

162. Jankélévitch, "Should We Pardon Them?" 572.

163. Wiesel writes, "Memory restores absence to presence and the dead to the living. Does it also involve pain? I welcome it. I think of the children—walking slowly, almost peacefully, toward the flames—and I am almost grateful for the pain that links me to them" (*From the Kingdom of Memory*, 200). See also 187.

164. Jankélévitch and Berlowitz, *Quelque part dans l'inachevé*, 67. Another example of this type of solidarity in Jankélévitch's circle of influence is Henri Bergson. Due to Bergson's near cult status between the wars, the Vichy regime intended to exempt him from the brunt of its anti-Semitic laws. Instead of accepting this exemption and his exceptional status, Bergson, eighty-one years old and seriously ill, rose from his sickbed to sign the registry for Jews at the end of 1940. Later, in his will, he explained this action: "My reflections have led me closer and closer to Catholicism, in which I see the complete fulfillment of Judaism. I would have become a convert, had I not foreseen for years a formidable wave of anti-

Semitism about to break upon the world. I wanted to remain among those who tomorrow were to be persecuted." Cited in Daniel Boorstin, *The Seekers: The Story of Man's Continuing Quest to Understand His World* (New York: Random House, 1998), 293. Bergson died just a few months later in January 1941.

165. Nietzsche, *Genealogy*, 2.1.58.

166. From a theological perspective, God is often invoked as the absolute witness with an unfaltering and absolute memory. Wiesel, too, writes that "only God and God alone can and must remember everything all the time" (*From the Kingdom of Memory*, 243). In his *Der letzte Gottesbeweis*, Robert Spaemann offers grammatical proof of the existence of God from the futurum exactum (otherwise known as the completed future, future II: e.g., will have been, will have lived). The present, he argues, remains true as the past of the future. He writes, "If a present reality will at some time not have been, then it is not real. Whoever abolishes the futurum exactum abolishes the present" (*Der letzte Gottesbeweis* [Munich: Pattloch Verlag, 2007], 23). For Spaemann, however, it is not being remembered that is significant but being known, and God, as absolute consciousness, ensures that the presently known will have been known. Jankélévitch, in his mystical agnosticism, does not, however, take recourse to God as the absolute witness. Whether God does take on this role is not irrelevant, but at the same time, the fact that nothing and nobody eludes his thought, love, and memory—to draw upon Augustine's Trinitarian model—does not absolve human beings from their responsibility and duty.

167. Emmanuel Levinas, *Time and the Other*, trans. Richard Cohen (Pittsburgh: Duquesne University Press, 1987), 112.

168. Giorgio Agamben, *The Time That Remains: A Commentary on the Letter to the Romans*, trans. Patricia Dailey (Stanford: Stanford University Press, 2005), 39.

169. Ibid., 40.

170. Jankélévitch, *Forgiveness*, 130.

171. Ibid., 103.

172. Ibid., 21.

173. Nussbaum, *Upheavals of Thought*, 19–21.

174. Jankélévitch, *Forgiveness*, 19.

175. In a letter (211, Para. 11) Augustine wrote: "With love for the persons and hatred of their vices." *Letters 211–270, 1–29*, in *The Works of Saint Augustine*, vol. 2, no. 4, ed. Boniface Ramsey, trans. Roland Teske (New York: New City Press, 2005), 25.

176. Trudy Govier, *Forgiveness and Revenge* (London: Routledge, 2002), 132.

177. Desmond Tutu, "It is the deed that is evil, not the doer," *Cape Times*, April 17, 1997, cited in Govier, *Forgiveness and Revenge*, 110.

178. Immanuel Kant, *Religion within the Limits of Reason Alone*, trans. Theodore M. Greene and Hoyt H. Hudson, (New York: Harper and Row, 1960) [*Kant Werke*, vol. 4 (Darmstadt: Wissenschaftliche Buchgesellschaft, 1998)], B33; 30 and B19; 23. Page numbers refer first to the academic pagination and second to the page number(s) in the English edition.

179. Ibid., B18–20; 22–23.
180. Ibid., B33–34; 31.
181. Immanuel Kant, *Groundwork for the Metaphysics of Morals*, ed. and trans. Allen W. Wood (New Haven: Yale University Press, 2002) [*Kant Werke*, vol. 4 (Darmstadt: Wissenschaftliche Buchgesellschaft, 1998)], 454–55; 70–71. Page numbers refer first to the academic pagination and second to the page number(s) in the English edition.
182. Kant, *Religion*, B 44; 36.
183. Govier, *Forgiveness and Revenge*, 112.
184. Even the expressions of putting wrongs in the past and letting bygones be bygones need not be incompatible with acknowledgment. As Govier explains, "It does not mean denying what I did or deceiving myself into thinking I had good excuses, that nobody suffered after all, or that it was not really wrong. What it does mean is firmly resisting any idea that I am *captured* by this past, that what I did in the past fixes my character and exhaustively defines what sort of person I am, so as to fully determine my present and future" (ibid., 133).
185. The role of *ressentiment* in Jean Améry's thinking takes on a similar tone. Invoking the irreversibility of the past and the irrevocability of the having-done, Améry says that *ressentiment* is haunted by a double impossibility: the impossibility of returning to what has already been experienced and the impossible rescindment of what happened— impossible reversibility and impossible revocation. For Améry, the returning of the offender to the offense and to the offended may produce the moral turning around of time or the moralization of history. He suggests that such a return conceivably could achieve the revolution, the turning around that didn't happen during the twelve years of Hitler's regime (*Jenseits von Schuld und Sühne*, 116, 125). Both Jankélévitch and Améry observe that the internal revolution never seemed to happen. Rather, external forces overthrew the regime, and the march forward through the Marshall Plan and reconstruction began immediately thereafter. The self-exertion and self-expansion never seemed to be called into question but instead was perpetuated in self-pity and self-excuse.
186. Améry, *Jenseits von Schuld und Sühne*, 113. "Meine Ressentiments aber sind da, damit das Verbrechen moralische Realität werde für den Verbrecher, damit er hineingerissen sei in die Wahrheit seiner Untat."
187. Cf. Murphy and Hampton, *Forgiveness and Mercy*, 60.
188. Cf. Jankélévitch, "Should We Pardon Them?" 565. Jankélévitch is particularly critical of the German philosophers and moralists (if there are any, he half-appropriately adds) too occupied with Dasein and Existentialism to unreservedly repudiate the acts and the regime of National Socialism (see ibid., 568). He is equally critical of the overwhelming majority of French intellectuals who were silent, inactive, or acquiescent to the Nazi reign and the Vichy regime.
189. Ibid., 567. Cf. ibid., 565, and Jankélévitch, *Forgiveness*, 157.

190. Jankélévitch, "Should We Pardon Them?" 566.
191. See, e.g., ibid., 556.
192. Jankélévitch, *Forgiveness*, 157. See also "Should We Pardon Them?" 567.
193. Jacques Derrida, "To Forgive," in *Questioning God*, ed. John D. Caputo, Mark Dooley, and Michael J. Scanlon (Bloomington: Indiana University Press, 2001), 28–29. See also Jankélévitch, "Should We Pardon Them?" 564–65 for Jankélévitch's partial justification of the aggregation under the "name" Germans.
194. See, e.g., Jankélévitch, "Should We Pardon Them?" 558, 565.
195. Jankélévitch, *Forgiveness*, 157; Jankélévitch, "Should We Pardon Them?" 567.
196. See, e.g., Nietzsche, *Genealogy* 3.4.123–24. Ironically, Nietzsche also invokes in this passage the image of rabid dogs for his exhortation of the Aryan moralists of his day.
197. Strawson, "Freedom and Resentment," 207.
198. Jankélévitch, *Cours de philosophie morale*, 53–54.

5. The Inexcusable and the Unforgivable

1. Vladimir Jankélévitch, "Difficultés du pardon: Entretien avec le Professeur Jankélévitch," interview with Renée de Tryon-Montalembert in *La Vie spirituelle* 619 (March 1977): 194–95
2. Vladimir Jankélévitch, "Should We Pardon Them?" trans. Ann Hobart, *Critical Inquiry* 22, no. 3 (1996): 555.
3. Cf. Plato, *Meno* 77b–78b.
4. Hannah Arendt makes this point poignantly manifest in her study of Eichmann. Cf. *Eichmann in Jerusalem: A Report on the Banality of Evil* (New York: Penguin Books, 1994).
5. Plato, *Gorgias* 467c–468e.
6. Plato, *Protagoras* 358c. In his later dialogue *The Sophist*, Plato seems to maintain a different position, one that includes the possibility of wickedness. He identifies two kinds of ills in the soul, ignorance and wickedness (Jewett translates the Greek word for the latter, *ponēria*, as *vice* because it entails only "cowardice, licentiousness, and injustice"). In an analogy to bodily ills, Plato associates the former with ugliness or deformity and the latter with sickness. Here, too, Plato says that no soul is willingly ignorant and that ignorance occurs precisely when the soul aims for the truth but due to an aberration of the mind misses its mark. The understanding, in other words, errs or is perverted. In contrast, the sickness of soul that is wickedness is due to a discord ("discord and disease are the same"). People in "poor or bad condition" suffer from a discord or dissension within their souls between beliefs and desires, anger and pleasures, reason and pains. Corresponding to this division of ills are two purifying acts to deal with them: Just as gymnastics is the purifying act of dealing with ugliness and medicine is the remedy for sickness, instruction or teaching (*didaskalikē*) is the purifying act of

ignorance and correction (*kolastikē*) is the remedy for wickedness. Whereas Nicholas White translates *kolastikē* as *correction*, Jewett translates it as *chastisement*; Schleiermacher, in the German translation, uses the word *Rechtsverwaltung*, which means the administration of law. Indeed, the Greek word *kolasis* includes the meanings of chastisement, penalization, and punishment. Plato would thus seem to be arguing for the practice of punishment as the appropriate purifying response to wickedness, as he does in *Gorgias* 472c–474c.

7. This explanatory or, at least, reflective capacity of dualistic doctrines outlives in various forms the existence of these religions. See, for example, Pierre Bayle's essay "Manicheans," in his *Historical and Critical Dictionary*, trans. Richard Popkin (New York: Bobbs-Merrill, 1965), esp. 144–47. Bayle's book was one of the most read works of the eighteenth century and had a profound influence on Enlightenment thinkers. For the historical trajectory of this work, see Susan Neiman, *Evil in Modern Thought: An Alternative History of Philosophy* (Princeton, N.J.: Princeton University Press, 2002), esp. chap. 2. For central passages in Augustine's many early writings against Manichaeism, see *Ce moribus ecclesiae catholicae et de moribus manichaeorum* in *Opera/Augustinus*, vol. 25, ed. Johannes Brachtendorf (Paderborn: Schöningh, 2004), esp. book 2; *Confessions*, 7.11, 17–16, 22; and *City of God*, trans. Marcus Dods (New York: Modern Library, 2000), 11.7–23 and 12.1–5.

8. Augustine, *The Enchiridion*, trans. J. F. Shaw, http://www.leaderu.com/cyber/books/augenchiridion/enchiridiontoc.html, chaps. 10–17, here chap. 11.

9. Thomas Aquinas, *Summa contra gentiles*, 3.7.2, trans. Vernon J. Bourke (New York: Doubleday, 1955–57).

10. Aquinas, *Summa contra gentiles*, 3.11.4. Cf. Augustine, *The Enchiridion*, chap. 13.

11. Aquinas, *Summa theologiae*, 1.5.3.

12. Gottfried Wilhelm Leibniz, *Theodicy: Essays on the Goodness of God, the Freedom of Man, and the Origin of Evil*, ed. Austin Farrer, trans. E. M. Huggard (La Salle, Ill.: Open Court, 1951), §21, 136 and §31, 142.

13. John Milbank, "Forgiveness and Incarnation," in *Questioning God*, ed. John D. Caputo, Mark Dooley, and Michael J. Scanlon (Bloomington: Indiana University Press, 2001), 92–128. Cf. John Milbank, *Being Reconciled: Ontology and Pardon* (London: Routledge, 2003), esp. chap. 1, "Evil: Darkness and Silence," 1–25. See also John Milbank, "The Ethics of Honor and the Possibility of Promise," in *Vladimir Jankélévitch and the Question of Forgiveness*, ed. Alan Udoff (Lanham, Md.: Lexington Books, 2013). 161–90.

14. Milbank, "Forgiveness and Incarnation," 102.

15. Ibid.

16. Ibid., 103.

17. Ibid., 102.

18. Immanuel Kant, *Religion within the Limits of Reason Alone*, trans. Theodore M. Greene and Hoyt H. Hudson (New York: Harper and Row, 1960) [*Kant Werke*, vol. 4 (Darmstadt: Wissenschaftliche Buchgesellschaft, 1998)], B27–28;

27–28. Page numbers refer first to the academic pagination and second to the pages in the English edition.

19. Ibid., B8; 17

20. See Augustine, *On the Free Choice of the Will*, in *On the Free Choice of the Will, On Grace and Free Choice, and Other Writings*, ed. and trans. Peter King (Cambridge: Cambridge University Press, 2010).

21. Augustine, *Confessions*, 2.14.

22. Immanuel Kant, *Groundwork for the Metaphysics of Morals*, ed. and trans. Allen W. Wood (New Haven: Yale University Press, 2002) [*Kant Werke,* vol. 4 (Darmstadt: Wissenschaftliche Buchgesellschaft, 1998)], 393; 9.

23. Cf. Neiman, *Evil in Modern Thought*, 76–81.

24. Kant, *Religion,* B26–27; 27.

25. Ibid., B26; 26.

26. John Silber, "The Ethical Significance of Kant's *Religion*," in Immanuel Kant, *Religion within the Limits of Reason Alone*, trans. Theodore M. Greene and Hoyt H. Hudson (New York: Harper & Row, 1960), xc.

27. Kant, *Religion,* B8; 17, and B209; 129. See also Kant's *Groundwork,* 458–60; 74–76; and the section "Of the Deduction of the Fundamental Principles of Pure Practical Reason," in *Critique of Practical Reason*, trans. Thomas Kingsmill Abott (Mineola, N.Y.: Dover, 2004), for Kant's explication of how "speculative freedom" must remain undetermined and how the practical freedom through the moral law cannot be proven or shown. Theoretical knowledge, according to Kant, cannot a priori know or prove practical freedom, but it is compelled to posit the possibility of freedom as a complement to the requirements of theoretical reason. See also Kant's representation and resolution of the Third Antinomy in his *Critique of Pure Reason* in *The Cambridge Edition of the Works of Immanuel Kant*, trans. Paul Guyer and Allen W. Wood (Cambridge: Cambridge University Press, 1999). For a detailed analysis of these topics, see Reiner Wimmer, *Kants kritische Religionsphilosophie* (Berlin: Walter de Gruyter, 1990), 134. See also chapter 5, "Bedingunglose Schuldvergebung?" in Reiner Wimmer, *Religionsphilosophische Studien in lebenspraktischer Absicht* (Freiburg: Academic Press Fribourg, 2005), 103–22, for an in-depth and multifaceted discussion involving Kant, Jankélévitch, and Derrida on the question concerning the morality of unconditional forgiveness.

28. Richard Bernstein, *Radical Evil: A Philosophical Interrogation* (Cambridge, UK: Polity Press, 2007), 45.

29. Kant, *Religion,* B43; 36.

30. Ibid., B40; 34.

31. Ibid., B50–51; 40.

32. Ibid., B37; 32.

33. Bernstein, *Radical Evil,* 39.

34. Ibid., 41.

35. Vladimir Jankélévitch, *Forgiveness*, trans. Andrew Kelley (Chicago: University of Chicago Press, 2005) 158.

36. Ibid., 67.

37. Jean-Luc Nancy, *The Experience of Freedom*, trans. Bridget McDonald (Stanford: Stanford University Press, 1993), 126.

38. Ibid., 124–25.

39. Jankélévitch, *Forgiveness*, 162; emphasis mine.

40. Vladimir Jankélévitch, *Penser la mort?* (Paris: Liana Levi, 1994), 38.

41. Jankélévitch, *Forgiveness*, 162. Cf. also Vladimir Jankélévitch, *Cours de philosophie morale: Université libre de Bruxelles 1962–1963* (Paris: Éditions du Seuil, 2006), 110–14.

42. Vladimir Jankélévitch, "Orkan der Gewalt," trans. Ulrich Kunzmann, *Sinn und Form* 53, no. 6 (2001): 729. See also Vladimir Jankélévitch, *Le Pur et l'impur* (Paris: Flammarion, 1960), 182–205, esp. 184–88.

43. Emmanuel Levinas, "Transcendence and Evil," in *The Phenomenology of Man and of the Human Condition: Individualisation of Nature and the Human Being*, ed. Anna-Teresa Tymieniecka, trans. Alphonso Lingis (Dordrecht, Holland: D. Reidel, 1983), 153–65, 158.

44. Levinas's description of evil strikingly parallels his critique of totality and the appropriation of the other by the same. As Bernstein observes, the transcendence of evil ruptures totality just as the infinity of the other does (Bernstein, *Radical Evil*, 175). For Jankélévitch, it is also the excess of forgiveness that parallels this excess of evil.

45. Jean Nabert, *Essai sur le Mal* (Paris: PUF, 1955).

46. Paul Ricoeur, *Memory, History, Forgetting*, trans. Kathleen Blamey and David Pellauer (Chicago: University of Chicago Press, 2004), 463–64.

47. Jankélévitch, "Should We Pardon Them?" 558, 561–62.

48. Jean Nabert, *Essai sur le mal*, cited in Ricoeur, *Memory, History, Forgetting*, 464.

49. Ricoeur, *Memory, History, Forgetting?* 464. See also Jean Améry's *Jenseits von Schuld und Sühne: Bewältigungsversuche eines Überwältigten* (Stuttgart: Klett-Cotta, 1977).

50. Jankélévitch, "Should We Pardon Them?" 554, 558, 561–62.

51. Bernstein, *Radical Evil*, 212.

52. Emmanuel Levinas, *Totality and Infinity: An Essay on Exteriority*, trans. Alphonso Lingis (Pittsburgh: Duquesne University Press, 1969), 198.

53. Jankélévitch, "Orkan der Gewalt," 735. See also Jankélévitch, *Cours de philosophie morale*, 118.

54. Hannah Arendt, *Hannah Arendt/Karl Jaspers. Correspondence 1926–1969*, ed. Lotte Kohler and Hans Saner, trans. Robert Kimber and Rita Kimber (New York: Harcourt, 1992), 166. [*Hannah Arendt/Karl Jaspers. Briefwechsel 1926–1969*, ed. Lotte Köhler and Hans Saner (Munich: Piper, 1985), 202.] See also Bernstein, *Radical Evil*, 206–7.

55. Hannah Arendt, "Some Questions of Moral Philosophy," in *Responsibility and Judgment*, ed. Jerome Kohn (New York: Schocken Books, 2003), 54–55. See

also Arendt's *Denktagebuch,* vol. 1, ed. Ursula Ludz (Munich: Piper, 2002), 7; and *Hannah Arendt/Karl Jaspers, Correspondence,* 54 [*Briefwechsel,* 90].

56. Jankélévitch, "Should We Pardon Them?" 555.

57. Ibid., 556.

58. Cf. Emil Fackenheim, *God's Presence in History: Jewish Affirmations and Philosophical Reflections after Auschwitz* (New York: New York University Press, 1970). Fackenheim similarily claims that, although "whole peoples have been killed for 'rational' (however terrifying) ends such as power, territory, wealth . . . . the Nazi murder . . . was annihilation for the sake of annihilation, murder for the sake of murder, evil for the sake of evil" (69–70). Cf. also Emmanuel Levinas, "Useless Suffering," in *The Provocation of Levinas: Rethinking the Other,* ed. Robert Bernasconi and David Wood (New York: Routledge, 2002), 156–67, esp. 162ff.

59. Jankélévitch, "Should We Pardon Them?" 555, 561.

60. In several passages, Jankélévitch refers to the crimes of Auschwitz and to its perpetrators in terms of sadism. See, e.g., Jankélévitch, "Should We Pardon Them?" 555, 558, and 563. These allusions do not mean that wickedness is reducible to a philosophical account of sadism, but the conjunction is nonetheless meaningful. Jankélévitch is not the only thinker to invoke this association. Jean Améry similarly links his experience of torture with sadism, and contrary to Hannah Arendt, he claims National Socialism in its entirety is formed much more by sadism than by totalitarianism (66). Walter Benjamin summarily declares that one must always go back to Sade in order to "explain" the evil of wickedness (*Charles Baudelaire: A Lyric Poet in the Era of High Capitalism,* trans. Harry Zohn [London: Verso, 1973], cited in Derrida, *Given Time: I. Counterfeit Money,* 165n31).

61. Maurice Blanchot, "Sade," in *The Marquis de Sade,* ed. and trans. Richard Seaver and Austryn Wainhouse (New York: Grove Press, 1965), 54–55.

62. Following Georges Bataille's analysis of sadism, Jean Améry discovers in torture this same radical negation of the other and the rejection of both the social principle and the principle of reality. For Améry it involves the annihilation of the world as the world of commonality and community. The torturer and murderer in genocide, he writes, want "to annihilate this world and in the negation of his fellow human he wants to make real his own total sovereignty. He is lord over body and soul, life and death." This exercise of arbitrary power, he contends, leads to "the total eversion of the social world in which we can only live if we vouchsafe the life of our fellow humans, bridle our desire to extend our selves, [and] allay their suffering" (*Jenseits von Schuld und Sühne,* 66).

63. Hannah Arendt, *The Origins of Totalitarianism* (New York: Harcourt, 1973), 296. As Bernstein elucidates, "It is because of the threat of superfluousness that Arendt insists that the most fundamental right is 'the right to have rights,' the right to belong to a community that protects one's rights—a community in which one can exercise these rights" (*Radical Evil,* 209).

64. Arendt, *Origins,* 451.

65. Ibid., 452.

66. Neiman, *Evil in Modern Thought*, 190.

67. Ibid., 274. The term *Muselmann* or *Musselmann* refers to those concentration camp prisoners who, because of starvation and exhaustion, had become living corpses. In the chapter "The Drowned and the Saved," Primo Levi writes, "The word 'Muselmann,' I do not know why, was used by the old ones of the camp to describe the weak, the inept, those doomed to selection" (Primo Levi, *Survival in Auschwitz*, trans. Stuart Woolf [New York: Touchstone, 1996], 88). See also Giorgio Agamben, *Remnants of Auschwitz: The Witness and the Archive*, trans. Daniel Heller-Roazen (New York: Zone Books, 2002), chap. 2: "The Muselmann," 41–86. The *Sonderkommando* of Auschwitz-Birkenau was a work unit composed of Jewish prisoners who were forced to make preparations for the murder of the deported, to recover any valuables from the corpses, and to dispose of the bodies in the crematoriums.

68. Augustine, *City of God*, bk. 12, chap. 20, 405.

69. Arendt, *Origins*, 479.

70. Ibid., 438.

71. See also the next section of chapter 5, "The Correlation of Punishment and Forgiveness."

72. Arendt, *Human Condition*, 8.

73. Ibid.

74. Arendt, *Origins*, 438.

75. Ibid.; *Human Condition*, 7; and *Hannah Arendt/Karl Jaspers: Correspondence*, 69 [*Briefwechsel*, 106]. One important difference arises regarding plurality in the work of Arendt, Jankélévitch, and Levinas. Whereas Arendt connects singularity to the plurality requisite for politics, Jankélévitch and Levinas claim that ethics, unlike politics, recognizes the singularity or otherness of the other. Cf. Bernstein, *Radical Evil*, 267n18.

76. See Bernstein, *Radical Evil*, 165.

77. *Hannah Arendt/Karl Jaspers: Correspondence*, 423 [*Briefwechsel*, 459].

78. Jankélévitch, "Should We Pardon Them?" 555.

79. Drawing on Jankélévitch's talks titled "Ressembler ou dissembler" and "Le judaïsme, problème intérieur" at the *Colloques des intellectuels juifs de langue française*, Jonathan Judaken states that, according to Jankélévitch, Jews embody the "principle of alterity"; they embody a "torn being." Jankélévitch, he writes "insists that Jews are, or ought to be the opening to alterity for others, an invitation to transcending their being themselves. Jews are movement, an opening in the economy of being." Jonathan Judaken, "Vladimir Jankélévitch at the *Colloques des intellectuels juifs de langue française*," in *Vladimir Jankélévitch and the Question of Forgiveness*, ed. Alan Udoff (Lanham, Md.: Lexington Books, 2013), 12.

80. Jankélévitch, "Should We Pardon Them?" 555–56.

81. Max Horkheimer and Theodor Adorno, *Dialectic of Enlightenment: Philosophical Fragments*, ed. Guenzlin Schmid Noerr, trans. Edmund Jephcott (Stanford: Stanford University Press, 2007), 92.

82. *Hannah Arendt/Karl Jaspers: Correspondence*, 62 [*Briefwechsel*, 99].
83. See Arendt, *Eichmann*, 277. Cf. Neiman, *Evil in Modern Thought*, chap. 4, 267–80, esp. 271–73.
84. Ibid., 287.
85. Arendt, "Eichmann in Jerusalem: An Exchange of Letters between Gershom Scholem and Hannah Arendt," *Encounter* 22 (January 1964): 51–56, cited in Bernstein, *Radical Evil*, 218. See also Neiman, *Evil in Modern Thought*, 301.
86. Bernstein, *Radical Evil*, 216–24.
87. Ibid., 218.
88. Neiman, *Evil in Modern Thought*, 303.
89. Ibid., 273.
90. Bernstein, *Radical Evil*, 220–24.
91. Arendt, *Eichmann*, 49. See also Arendt, *Responsibility and Judgment*, 100–101.
92. Neiman, *Evil in Modern Thought*, 272. See also Bernstein, *Radical Evil*, 221.
93. Gregory of Nyssa, *De virginitate* 12, 20–21, in *Opera* VIII/I, ed. Werner Jaeger (Leiden: Brill, 1952), 298.
94. Kant, *Critique of Practical Reason*, 2 [*Kritik der praktischen Vernunft*, A5].
95. Jankélévitch, *Forgiveness*, 45.
96. Levinas, "Transcendence and Evil," 59–60.
97. Améry, *Jenseits von Schuld und Sühne*, 14.
98. Jankélévitch, "Should We Pardon Them?" 558.
99. Emmanuel Levinas, *Otherwise Than Being, or Beyond Essence*, trans. Alphonso Lingis (Pittsburgh: Duquesne University Press, 1998), 159.
100. Ibid., 117.
101. Levinas, "Transcendence and Evil," 163–64.
102. Bernstein, *Radical Evil*, 178–79.
103. Levinas, *Totality and Infinity*, 88.
104. Levinas, "Transcendence and Evil," 163–64. See also Levinas's usage of *elevation* in *Otherwise Than Being*, 125–26.
105. Emmanuel Levinas, *Entre Nous*, trans. Michael B. Smith and Barbara Harshav (New York: Columbia University Press, 1998), 92. See also Levinas, *Totality and Infinity*, 75.
106. Bernstein, *Radical Evil*, 178.
107. Levinas, "Transcendence and Evil," 164.
108. Levinas, *Otherwise Than Being*, 109.
109. Levinas, *Entre Nous*, 92.
110. Levinas, *Otherwise Than Being*, 75.
111. The relation of radical good and radical evil to the law they surpass has, for Jankélévitch, four interrelated frameworks: (1) rationality, (2) language, (3) ethics, and (4) temporality. This relation reveals the proximity of Jankélévitch and Levinas. Demonstrating his indebtedness to Bergson, Levinas calls the structure constituting itself in repetition "alteration: recuperation and rupture, knowing and sociality" ("Transcendence and Evil," 164). Jankélévitch calls it *oscillation*.

(1) This oscillation takes place between rationality and that which transcends it. As Levinas explains, "The knowledge of the world, thematization, does not give up its efforts. It tries to reduce the disturbance of the Same by the Other, and succeeds. It reestablishes the order troubled by Evil and by the Other, through the history in which it accepts to enter" ("Transcendence and Evil," 164).

(2) The difficult language of Jankélévitch and Levinas reflects their respective attempts to signify a transcendence that cannot be known and a singularity that cannot be expressed in the universality and ontology of language (cf. Derrida, "Violence and Metaphysics: An Essay on the Thought of Emmanuel Levinas," in Jacques Derrida, *Writing and Difference*, trans. Alan Bass [Chicago: University of Chicago Press, 1978], 79–153). Levinas renders this tension as the heterogeneity and inseparability of the *saying* and the *said*. Jankélévitch approaches the transcendence of the radical good via negativa and is aware of the manner in which discourse appropriates that which exceeds it, whether forgiveness or evil. Both claim that philosophy has the task of conceiving the "ambivalence" between order, the law, and the same, on the one hand, and singularity, the event, and the other, on the other hand (*Otherwise Than Being*, 162).

(3) In the ethical sphere, this oscillation determines, for Levinas, the rupture of the other and the imminent introduction of the third party, the other(s) of the other. But oscillation also applies to evil. Evil is that which goes beyond moral norms and codes of laws. Aristotle understands that some acts, like bestiality, are inexcusable, but he does not know of a crime that defies all social and legal norms. Arendt, Jankélévitch, and Levinas each interpret the radical evil of the twentieth century as surpassing all norms, but the laws and norms, like the law of imprescriptibility, for example, extend in inscribing the event into history.

(4) Jankélévitch describes time as the oscillation of the instant and the interval. The instant, he suggests, is absorbed in the being of the interval. Levinas, too, defines time in terms of the failed reconciliation between rupture and recuperation. He writes that this lack of a synthesis "would define time itself, time in its enigmatic diachrony.... It would signify the ambiguity of an incessant adjournment" ("Transcendence and Evil," 164).

112. Levinas, "Transcendence and Evil," 164.

113. Cf. Arendt, *Denktagebuch*, 181.

114. In aphorism 68 of *The Wanderer and His Shadow*, Nietzsche, too, implies a correlation between the capacity to forgive and the capacity to punish. He writes that "if the ill-doers did know what they did [which he believes "always remains at least questionable"]—we would have a right to forgive them only if we had a right to accuse and to punish them." In contrast to Jankélévitch and Arendt, however, Nietzsche claims that "we do not have" such a right (Friedrich Nietzsche, *Human, All Too Human: A Book for Free Spirits*, trans. R. J. Hollingdale [Cambridge: Cambridge University Press, 1996], 327).

115. Jankélévitch, *Forgiveness*, 10.

116. Ibid., 153.

117. Ibid., 78.

118. Ibid., 119.
119. Ibid., 126.
120. Ibid., 142.
121. Luke 6:29.
122. Jankélévitch, *Forgiveness*, 142.
123. Ibid., 153.
124. Arendt, *Human Condition*, 240.
125. Ibid., 241.
126. Jankélévitch, "Should We Pardon Them?" 556, 563.
127. Alain Gouhier, "Le Temps de l'Impardonnable et le Temps du Pardon selon Jankélévitch," in *Le Point Théologique, Forgiveness*, ed. Michel Perrin (Paris: Beauchesnes, 1987), 275.
128. Jankélévitch, "Should We Pardon Them?" 558.
129. Jacques Derrida, *On Cosmopolitanism and Forgiveness*, trans. Mark Dooley and Michael Hughes (London: [0]Routledge, 2002), 36. Cf. Jacques Derrida, "To Forgive," in *Questioning God*, ed. John D. Caputo, Mark Dooley, and Michael J. Scanlon (Bloomington: Indiana University Press, 2001), 34.
130. Derrida, *On Cosmopolitanism and Forgiveness*, 37.
131. Jankélévitch, *Forgiveness*, 49; emphasis mine.
132. Ibid., 45.
133. Jankélévitch's portrayal of penal action should be considered carefully. With regard to "venial" offenses, he depicts penal action as at best a "beneficial approximation" whose liquidation of the offense "passes" for expiation. It should be asked, therefore, whether penal action in general, that is, for both "venial" and "capital" offenses, serves merely as the approximation of expiation.
134. Jankélévitch, *Forgiveness*, 48.
135. Derrida, "To Forgive," 31.
136. Ibid., 32.
137. Jankélévitch, "Should We Pardon Them?" 567. I have substituted *forgiveness* for the word *pardoning* in this quotation from the English translation.
138. Cf. Matthew 12:31–32; Luke 12:10; Mark 3:29.
139. See, e.g., Jankélévitch, "Should We Pardon Them?" 569.
140. Cf., e.g., Xavier Tilliette, "Une Kitiège de l'âme: L'éthique de Vladimir Jankélévitch," *L'Arc* 75 (1979): 71; and Wiard Raveling, "Über Vladimir Jankélévitch," *Sinn und Form* 49, no. 3 (1997): 333–34, for positions that recognize that forgiveness according to Jankélévitch aims at the unforgivable. See also Jan-Heiner Tuck, "Unforgiveable Forgiveness? Jankélévitch, Derrida and a Hope against All Hope," trans. David C. Schindler, in *International Catholic Review Communio* 31 (2004): 522–39.
141. Vladimir Jankélévitch and Béatrice Berlowitz, *Quelque part dans l'inachevé* (Paris: Gallimard, 1978), 125.
142. Jankélévitch, *Forgiveness*, 109.
143. Ibid., 156.
144. Jankélévitch and Berlowitz, *Quelque part dans l'inachevé*, 125.

145. Ibid., 129. "Le pardon aux bourreaux nazis relèverait de cette tangence surnaturelle puisqu'il s'agit de pardonner à ceux qui n'ont jamais demandé pardon, qui ne comprennent même pas le sens de ce mot et n'ont jamais regretté leurs abominables forfaits Car telle est l'epreuve la plus difficile de toutes . . . Que dis-je? L'impossibilité par excellence: pardoner à la méchanceté absolue." Cf. Jankélévitch, *Forgiveness*, 97 and Tilliette, "Une Kitiège de l'âme," 71. As Tilliete comments, "The paradox of forgiveness is also the impossibility of forgiveness [*Le paradoxe du pardon est aussi l'impossible du pardon*]."

146. Jankélévitch, *Forgiveness*, 61.

147. Ibid., 106 and 158. Cf. Jacques Derrida, *Given Time: I. Counterfeit Money*, trans. Peggy Kamuf (Chicago: University of Chicago Press, 1992), 165n31.

148. Derrida, *On Cosmopolitanism and Forgiveness*, 32.

149. Cf. Jankélévitch and Berlowitz, *Quelque part dans l'inachevé*, 125.

150. Derrida, "To Forgive," 28.

151. Jankélévitch, *Forgiveness*, 156.

152. Ibid., 158.

153. Ibid., 93. Verena Lemcke (*Der Begriff Verzeihen bei Vladimir Jankélévitch*, [Würzburg: Königshausen and Neumann: 2008]). argues, for this reason that, while Jankélévitch asserts that forgiveness forgives the unforgivable, she interprets him as introducing a conceptual break in the concept of *forgiveness* with the "ontological evil" and "metaphysical crime" of Auschwitz. For Jankélévitch, however, there is nothing that cannot potentially be forgiven; there is no act that we are not called upon to forgive. Jankélévitch does allow, though, that evil overcomes forgiveness and that, owing to the metaphysical abomination of wicked crimes, we may not be able to or willing to forgive. Lemcke, therefore, underestimates the oscillation inherent in the organ-obstacle of evil as well as the oscillation between the duties to love and to justice.

154. Jankélévitch, *Forgiveness*, 71.

155. Ibid., 72. The motif of teaching is itself Greco-Christian: Plato teaches the mistrust of appearances; Origen makes teaching and providence the pillars of his theology (a connection inherent in Peter's speech directed toward the *felix culpa* of the Jews, the sin that leads to joy, for it is according to God's plan—a theological complexity we can presently ignore); and Lessing and the Enlightenment attempt to instruct the people in using their own reason.

156. Jeffrie Murphy and Jean Hampton, *Forgiveness and Mercy* (Cambridge: Cambridge University Press, 1988), 20.

157. Arendt, *Human Condition*, 238.

158. Ibid., 240, see also ibid., n. 78.

159. Jankélévitch, *Forgiveness*, 72.

160. Ibid., 73.

161. Ibid.

162. Jankélévitch, "Should We Pardon Them?" 564.

163. Jankélévitch, *Forgiveness*, 67 and 160.

164. Ibid., 160.

165. Ibid., 161. Jankélévitch's treatment of lying in *Du Mensonge* (in *Philosophie morale* [Paris: Flammarion, 1998]) demonstrates the significance in his thinking of this willingness to self-critically appraise one's own responsibility for the fault of the other. Setting aside the classical imputation of guilt, he argues that both sides carry responsibility for the lie. Consequently, he claims that the key to deciphering a lie is not intellectual insight but the capacity for empathy. Through empathy we may overcome our unwillingness to understand the other, our rivalry, our coldness, or our lack of interest, which contributed to the lie. He concludes that only generosity, love, and compassion will help convert the liar to the truth: "The fundamental cause of the lie is the lack of generosity, and only generosity, because it is the source of restored existence, will make us innocent and transparent like on the first day of the world" (240). ("La cause fondamentale du mensonge est le manque de générosité, et la générosité seule, parce qu'elle est la source de l'existence retrouvée, nous fera innocents et transparents comme au premier matin du monde.")

166. Jankélévitch, "Should We Pardon Them?" 563.

167. Jankélévitch, *Forgiveness*, 162.

168. Ibid.

169. Ibid., 160.

170. Ibid.

171. Ibid., 162.

172. Ibid., 158.

173. Jankélévitch and Berlowitz, *Quelque part dans l'inachevé,* 129.

174. Jankélévitch, *Forgiveness*, 164.

175. Cf. Lucien Jerphagnon, *Ahnen und Wollen: Vladimir Jankélévitch*, trans. Jürgen Brankel (Vienna: Turia + Kant, 2009), 84.

176. Jankélévitch, *Forgiveness*, 162. Cf. Jacques Derrida, *Without Alibi*, ed. and trans. Peggy Kamuf (Stanford: Stanford University Press, 2002). In his reading of Paul de Man's reading of Rousseau's *Confessions* and *Reveries*, Derrida focuses on the last word that becomes the next to last word. Of de Man's analysis, he writes that "it mobilizes what seems necessary in order to explain the history and the mechanism that transforms the last into the next to last, the motor that regresses from the final to the penultimate." Like Jankélévitch, Derrida suggests that both the eschatological dimension and the deferred end or penultimate character constitute forgiveness. He explains that forgiveness or pardon is "always proposed in the figure, so to speak, of the 'last word.' A pardon not granted with the assurance, the promise, or, in any case, the meaning of a last word or an end of history . . . would that still be a pardon? . . . *I forgive you* has the structure of the last word, hence its apocalyptic and millenarian aura; hence the sign it makes in the direction of the end of time and the end of history" (100).

177. Ibid., 158.

178. Ibid., 164–65.

179. G. W. F. Hegel, *Lectures on the Philosophy of Religion*, trans. R. F. Brown, P. C. Hodgson, and J. M. Stewart (Berkeley: University of California Press,

1988), 478–79. Hegel writes, "Insofar as evil does emerge among human beings when they do evil, at the same time it is present as something null, over which spirit has power: spirit has the power to undo evil. . . . Thus evil is known as something that has been overcome in and of itself, having no power of its own."

180. Jankélévitch, *Forgiveness*, 164.

181. The phrase "it is never finished" also evokes Jesus' final words according to the Gospel of John (and only in this Gospel). From the cross, Jesus says, "It is finished, bowed his head and gave up his spirit" (19:30). The sentence is ambiguous, but it appears to refer to finishing the work of the one who sent him (John 4:34) and to the cup that his father has given him to drink (John 18:11), namely his path to the cross. "It is never finished," therefore, can be viewed as an eschatological reservation. Human forgiveness can never be finished; human responsibility is infinite. An end is perhaps something only God can bring.

6. Love and Justice

1. Vladimir Jankélévitch takes up this conflict in his last book, *Le Paradoxe de la morale* (Paris: Éditions du Seuil, 1981).

2. Vladimir Jankélévitch, *Forgiveness*, trans. Andrew Kelley (Chicago: University of Chicago Press, 2005), 163.

3. Ibid., 162.

4. Andrew Kelley, "Translator's Introduction," to *Forgiveness*, by Vladimir Jankélévitch, (Chicago: University of Chicago Press, 2005), xxvi.

5. Cf. Vladimir Jankélévitch and Béatrice Berlowitz, *Quelque part dans l'inachevé* (Paris: Gallimard, 1978), 119, 151. See also *Le Paradoxe de la morale*, 153. See also Joëlle Hansen, "*Forgiveness* and 'Should We Pardon Them?'" in *Vladimir Jankélévitch and the Question of Forgiveness*, ed. Alan Udoff (Lanham, Md.: Lexington Books, 2013), 114–15.

6. Vladimir Jankélévitch, *Penser la mort?* (Paris: Liana Levi, 1994), 123–26.

7. Jankélévitch, *Forgiveness*, 163.

8. Cf. Vladimir Jankélévitch, *Traité des vertus*, vol. 2: *Les Vertus et l'amour* (Paris: Flammarion, 1986), 142–45. In his foreword to Stéphane Mosès's *System und Offenbarung*, Levinas alludes to the proximity of his notion of *responsibility* to Rosenzweig's *love*. *System und Offenbarung: Die Philosophie Franz Rosenzweigs*, foreword by Emmanuel Levinas, trans. Rainer Rochlitz (Paderbon: Wilhelm Fink Verlag, 1985), 10–18.

9. Emmanuel Levinas, *Otherwise Than Being or Beyond Essence*, trans. Alphonso Lingis (Pittsburgh: Duquesne University Press, 1998), 157.

10. Jacques Derrida, *Adieu: To Emmanuel Levinas*, trans. Psacale-Anne Brault and Michael Naas (Stanford: Stanford University Press, 1997), 33.

11. Emmanuel Levinas, *Nine Talmudic Readings*, trans. Annette Aronowicz (Bloomington: Indiana University Press, 1990), 100.

12. Paul Ricoeur, *Liebe und Gerechtigkeit: Amor et Justice* (Tübingen: J. C. B. Mohr [Paul Siebeck], 1990), 52.

13. Jacques Derrida, *On Cosmopolitanism and Forgiveness*, trans. Mark Dooley and Michael Hughes (London: [0]Routledge, 2002), 42.

14. Jacques Derrida and Elisabeth Roudinesco, *For What Tomorrow . . . A Dialogue*, trans. Jeff Fort (Stanford: Stanford University Press, 2004), 162.

15. Jacques Derrida, "To Forgive," in *Questioning God*, ed. John D. Caputo, Mark Dooley, and Michael J. Scanlon (Bloomington: Indiana University Press, 2001), 25.

16. Jankélévitch, *Forgiveness*, 127.

17. Kelley, "Translator's Introduction," xxii–iii.

18. Cf. Aristotle, *Nicomachean Ethics*, bk. 5. Aristotle's conservative association of justice with the existing law is demonstrated in chapter 1 of book 5 in which he writes, "Since, as we saw, the lawless person is unjust and the lawful person is just, it clearly follows that whatever is lawful is in some way just; for the provisions of legislative science are lawful, and we say that each of them is just. In every matter that they deal with, the laws aim either at the common benefit of all, or at the benefit of those in control, whose control rests on virtue or on some other such basis. And so in one way what we call just is whatever produces and maintains happiness and its parts for a political community" (1129b12–19). Cf. chap. 2 of this work. This idea is not unique to Aristotle; it is represented also by Plato, Kant, and Hegel, for example.

19. See Vladimir Jankélévitch, *Philosophie premiére: Introduction à une Philosophie du "Presque."* 2nd ed. (Paris: Quadrige/Presses Univeristaires de France, 1986). 181.

20. Ibid., 236. "L'Être est cette décision décidée, refroidie, déposée."

21. Ibid.

22. Cf. Vladimir Jankélévitch, *Le Pur et l'impur* (Paris: Flammarion, 1960), 306; see also Lucien Jerphagnon, *Ahnen und Wollen: Vladimir Jankélévitch*, trans. Jürgen Brankel (Vienna: Turia + Kant, 2009), 86ff.

23. Walter Benjamin, *Zur Kritik der Gewalt und andere Aufsätze* (Frankfurt a.M.: Suhrkamp, 1965); English translation by Edmund Jephcott in Walter Benjamin, *Reflections: Essays, Aphorisms, Autobiographical Writings*, ed. Peter Demetz (New York: Schocken, 1986).

24. Derrida discusses Benjamin's thesis extensively in "Force of Law: The 'Mystical Foundation of Authority,'" in *Acts of Religion*, ed. Gil Anidjar (New York: Routledge, 2002), 269. For an in-depth discussion of the relation between Benjamin and Derrida, see Matthias Fritsch's study, *The Promise of Memory: History and Politics in Marx, Benjamin, and Derrida* (Albany: State University of New York Press, 2005).

25. Jankélévitch, *Les Vertus et l'amour*, 141–42.

26. Ibid., 140. Cf. Levinas's interpretation of the commandment "thou shall not kill," which increases in its imperative to "you shall not let me die (alone)." According to Jankélévitch, the infinitude of love and charity is limited only by death, and death, as is the case for Levinas as well, is always first and foremost the death of the other. He writes, for example, "L'amant attendra donc son aimee, s'il le faut, jusqu'a la fin des siecles. L'amour aime jusqua en mourir, usque ad

mortem, et la mort est donc son ultime et seule limite [142; The lover will attend his beloved, if necessary, until the end of the ages. Love loves until death, usque ad mortem, and death is therefore its ultimate and only limit.]"

27. Ibid., 139–40. "Ce qui suffit est insuffisant; juste assez, ce n'est pas assez, c'est trop peu. . . . Car le surplus, pour cette arithmétique paradoxale, est justement le strict nécessaire!"

28. Ibid., 142–45.

29. Ibid., 143. "Les personnes en effect se comparent non par leur ipséité, qui est incomparable, mais par leur dentition, leurs talents ou l'angle de leur nez."

30. Ibid., 144.

31. Cf. ibid., 57–59.

32. Aristotle, *Nicomachean Ethics* 5.6.5.1134a35.

33. Jankélévitch, *Forgiveness*, 68–69.

34. Jankélévitch, *Les Vertus et l'amour*, 144.

35. Ibid., 145.

36. Ibid., 139.

37. Jankélévitch, *Forgiveness*, 9.

38. Ibid.

39. Ibid.

40. Ibid.

41. Paul Ricoeur, *Amor et justice: Liebe und Gerechtigkeit* (Tübingen: J. C. B. Mohr Paul Siebeck), 1990). 64.

42. Jankélévitch, *Forgiveness*, 9.

43. Jankélévitch and Berlowitz, *Quelque part dans l'inachevé*, 124: "L'amour n'est-il pas plus vrai que la vérité et plus juste que la justice?"

44. Jankélévitch, *Forgiveness*, 139–40. Cf. Luke 6:27–35; Matt. 5:43–47.

45. Cf. Ricoeur, *Amour et justice*, 58.

46. Jankélévitch, *Forgiveness*, 141.

47. Jankélévitch, *Les Vertus et l'amour*, 140.

48. Ibid., 143. "L'amour lui-même qui est le Bien."

49. Ibid., 147.

50. Ibid., 138.

51. Ibid., 137.

52. Ibid., 136.

53. Cf. Immanuel Kant, *Groundwork for the Metaphysics of Morals*, ed. and trans. Allen W. Wood (New Haven: Yale University Press, 2002). 15.

54. Cf., e.g., Jankélévitch, *Les Vertus et l'amour*, 142.

55. Ibid., 137.

56. Ibid., 136.

57. Jankélévitch, *Forgiveness*, 37, 154; cf. also Jankélévitch, *Les Vertus et l'amour*, 136–37.

58. Jankélévitch, *Les Vertus et l'amour*, 146.

59. Jankélévitch, *Forgiveness*, 117.

60. Jankélévitch, *Philosophie premiére*, e.g., 249.

61. Vladimir Jankélévitch, "Le Presque-rien," *Bulletin de la Société française de Philosophie* 48, no. 3 (1954): 75.

62. Jankélévitch, *Forgiveness*, 114–15.

63. Jacques Derrida, *Given Time: I. Counterfeit Money*, trans. Peggy Kamuf (Chicago: University of Chicago Press, 1992), 14.

64. Jankélévitch and Berlowitz, *Quelque part dans l'inachevé*, 69–70.

65. Jankélévitch, *Forgiveness*, 115.

66. Ibid.

67. Derrida, *Given Time*, 16–17.

68. Jankélévitch, *Forgiveness*, 114–15.

69. Jacques Derrida, "Hostipitality," in *Acts of Religion*, ed. Gil Anidjar (New York: Routledge, 2002), 398. In his critique of Marcel Mauss's analysis of the gift, Derrida discovers the same aporia of the gift. He writes, "The simple identification of the gift seems to destroy it. . . . *At the limit, the gift as gift* ought *not appear as gift*: *either to the donee or to the donor*. It cannot be gift as gift except by not being present as gift. Neither to the 'one' nor to the 'other'" (*Given Time*, esp. chap. 1, here 14). It is also in this passage that Derrida offers his critique of *gratitude* as a form of acknowledgment of having receiving the gift.

70. J. L. Austin, "Performative-Constative," in *The Philosophy of Language*, ed. J. R. Searle (Oxford: Oxford University Press, 1977), 13, cited in Joram Graf Haber, *Forgiveness: A Philosophical Study* (Lanham, Md.: Rowman and Littlefield, 1991), 40.

71. Cf. Haber, *Forgiveness*, 52.

72. J. L. Austin, *How to Do Things with Words* (Cambridge, Mass.: Harvard University Press, 1962), 16.

73. Ibid. See also Haber, *Forgiveness*, 40–44.

74. Thomas Macho, "Fragment über die Verzeihung," in *Zeitmitschrift* (Düsseldorf: Bollmann, 1988), 142.

75. Jankélévitch, *Forgiveness*, 118. Cf. Macho, "Fragment über die Verzeihung," 141–42. The appropriateness of a gesture also applies to remorse and repentance. Jankélévitch mentions with appreciation and respect, for example, the gesture of Germany's Chancellor Willy Brandt, who fell to his knees on December 7, 1970, before the memorial to the insurrection of the Jews in the Warsaw ghetto ("Should We Pardon Them?" trans. Ann Hobart, *Critical Inquiry* 22, no. 3 [1996]: 565). For more on Brandt's gesture in relation to forgiveness, see Verena Lemcke, *Der Begriff Verzeihen bei Vladimir Jankélévitch* (Würzburg: Königshausen and Neumann, 2008), who dedicates the last chapter of her book to this topic.

76. Derrida, too, vacillates on the question concerning the priority of forgiveness and the gift. In "To Forgive," for example, he writes, that, although the gift and forgiveness both share the aporetic structure of impossibility, of having to appear and not to appear, of being binding and beyond binds, bonds, and bounds, "we must ask ourselves, breaking the symmetry or the analogy between gift and forgiveness, if the urgency of an im-possible forgiveness is not first what the enduring and non-conscious experience of the im-possible gives to be forgiven, as if

forgiveness, far from being a modification or a secondary complication or a complication that arises out of the gift, were in truth its first and final truth. Forgiveness as the impossible truth of the impossible gift. Before the gift, forgiveness" (48). But in *Given Time* he speaks of an "absolute forgetting" as a condition of a gift-event and a condition for the advent of a gift and claims that this forgetting absolves and "unbinds absolutely and infinitely more than excuse, forgiveness, or acquittal" (16).

77. Cf. Derrida, "To Forgive," 31.

78. Jankélévitch, *Forgiveness,* 56.

79. Ibid., 128. For an intensive discussion of the relation of the gift and sacrifice, see Jacques Derrida, *The Gift of Death,* trans. David Wills (Chicago: University of Chicago Press, 1995).

For Aristotle's understanding of the gift, see, for example, *Topoi/Topics* (125a.18). Aristotle does think of the gift in asymmetrical terms. He defines *dōrea* as a *dosis anapodotos,* a gift that does not require a return gift. The distinction Jankélévitch makes still obtains, but it cannot simply entail the nonrequirement of a return gift.

80. In his philological-linguistic essay "Gift and Exchange in the Indo-European Vocabulary" from 1948–49, Émile Benveniste shows that, in most of the Indo-European languages, "to give" is expressed by a verb from the root "dō" (*The Logic of the Gift: Toward an Ethic of Generosity,* ed. Alan Schrift [New York: Routledge, 1997]). And "dō" can mean both to take and to give. This root thus manifests an exceptional ambiguity. The terms *to give* and *to take,* according to Benveniste, express notions that "were organically linked by their polarity and which were susceptible of the same expression" (34). He claims that these terms first became antithetical and conceptually differentiated in the course of time through a process of reduction and separation and in a movement from ambivalence or polyvalence to equivalence.

81. Vladimir Jankélévitch, "Do Not Listen to What They Say, Look at What They Do," trans. Ann Hobart, *Critical Inquiry* 22, no. 3 (1996): 551.

82. Cf. Jankélévitch and Berlowitz, *Quelque part dans l'inachevé,* 74.

83. Cf. Jerphagnon, *Ahnen und Wollen,* 79.

84. Jankélévitch and Berlowitz, *Quelque part dans l'inachevé,* 126.

85. Paul Ricoeur, *Memory, History, Forgetting,* trans. Kathleen Blamey and David Pellauer (Chicago: University of Chicago Press, 2004), 482.

86. This spectral compulsion or spiritual power has the name *hau* in Maori culture. The sociologist and anthropologist Marcel Mauss calls *hau* "one of the key ideas of Maori law" (15). "The word *hau,*" he explains, "designates, as does the Latin *spiritus,* both the wind and the soul—more precisely, at least in certain cases, the soul and the power in inanimate and vegetal things" (114). The good that is received inextricably possesses both the *hau* of the thing itself and the *hau* of the giver of the gift, and, according to Mauss, this double-spiritedness imposes an obligation on the beneficiary: "What imposes obligation in the present received and exchanged, is the fact that the thing received is not inactive. Even

when it has been abandoned by the giver, it still possesses something of him. Through it the giver has a hold over the beneficiary" (Marcel Mauss, *The Gift* [*Essai sur le don*], trans. W. D. Halls [Abingdon, UK: Routledge, 2002], 15). See also Jacques Derrida, *Given Time*, esp. 40.

87. Lucius Annaeus Seneca, *De Beneficiis*. in *L. Annaei Senecae Opera*, ed. Carolus Rudolphus Fickert (Lipsiae: Sumptibus Librariae Weidmannianae, 1843) [*On Benefits*, trans. Aubrey Stewart, at http://ancienthistory.about.com/library/bl/bl_text_seneca_benefits_i.htm.], 2.10: "Haec enim beneficii inter duos lex est: alter statim obliuisci debet dati, alter accepti numquam" (42). Cf. ibid., 1.4, where Seneca speaks of laying down "a rule of life" for this "chief bond of human society." Humans, Seneca writes in close correspondence to the studies of Marcel Mauss, "must be taught to be willing to give, willing to receive, willing to return; and to place before themselves the high aim, not merely of equalling, but even of surpassing those to whom they are indebted, both in good offices and in good feeling" (15).

88. J. E. Erdmann, "Vom Vergessen," in *Ernste Spiele: Vortraege* (Berlin, 1875), 323–45, quoted in Klaus-Michael Kodalle, "Diesseits der Logik des Moralismus: Vom 'Geist' der Verzeihung bei Kierkegaard, Nietzsche-Scheler, Dostojewski und Camus," in *Kierkegaard Revisited* (Berlin: Walter de Gruyter, 1997), 395–97.

89. Kodalle, "Diesseits der Logik des Moralismus," 396.

90. Ibid., 396–97. "Wo aber wirklich die eben geforderte Begegnung der ungleich Bennanten Statt findet, wo der Eine spricht: das du mir dies vergeben und vergessen hast, will ich dir ewig gedenken, und den Anderen zu immer neuem Vergeben bringt, dass der Freund oder Geliebte dessen noch gedenkt, was er selbst längst vergessen hat, da entzündet sich an dem Vergessen das Gedenken, am Gedenken das Vergessen, und man macht die Erfahrung, dass auch im Verkehr der Menschen es Augenblicke giebt, wo das Sich-vergeben-lassen (das Absoluiertwerden) der höchste Genuss, und so die eigene Verschuldung zum Mittel der süßesten, heiligsten Lust wird" (344).

91. Jankélévitch, *Forgiveness*, 127.

92. Luke 15; see also Matt. 18:12–14.

93. Luke 7:36–43.

94. Jankélévitch, *Forgiveness*, 149–50.

95. Ibid., 143.

96. Friedrich Nietzsche, *Human, All Too Human*, trans. R. J. Hollingdale (Cambridge: Cambridge University Press, 1996), vol. 1, sec. 2, para. 44, p. 36. [*Menschliches, Allzumenschliches*, bd. 1, 44 in *Friedrich Nietzsche Werke* I (Darmstadt: Wissenschaftliche Buchgesellschaft, 1997), 482.] See also Derrida, *Given Time*, 13–14.

97. Jankélévitch, *Forgiveness*, 142.

98. Ibid.

99. Seneca, *De Beneficiis* 1.5: "Nec aurum nec argentum nec quicquam eorum quae promaximis accipiuntur beneficium est, sed ipsa tribuentis uoluntas" (17).

100. Cf. Jankélévitch, *Forgiveness*, 128.

101. Ibid., 113–14.
102. Ibid., 108.
103. Ibid., 136–37.
104. Ibid., 107.
105. Ibid., 144.
106. Ibid., 133.
107. Ibid., 131.
108. Ibid., 131.
109. Ibid., 132–33.
110. Arendt, *The Human Condition* (Chicago: University of Chicago Press, 1989), 242.
111. Derrida, *Given Time*, 163.
112. Cf. Plato, *Phaedrus* 255A–256A. For Plato, this back and forth mirroring of love is that of *philia* (friendship), not *eros*.
113. Jankélévitch and Berlowitz, *Quelque part dans l'inachevé*, 127ff.
114. Theodor W. Adorno, *Minima Moralia: Reflexionen aus dem beschädigten Leben* (Frankfurt a.M.: Suhrkamp, 2001), 104, 308–9.
115. Jankélévitch and Berlowitz, *Quelque part dans l'inachevé*, 132–33. "Et pourquoi l'amour gratuit ne serait-il pas réchauffé, exalté, illuminé par la mutualité, dès l'instant qu'il n'a pas expressément revendiqué cette mutualité comme un salaire? Cette oscillation entre les deux pôles de l'amour mutuel et de l'amour immutuel, chacun de nous la sent dans son coeur; mais cela ne signifie pas qu'il faille absolument choisir entre l'un et l'autre amour, celui qui nous retient dans le silence sans promesse et dans l'attente sans récompense, et celui qui nous fait rire et chanter d'amour: l'amour n'a pas la prétention d'être cohérent, la cohérence n'a pas plus de sens en amour qu'en musique! L'amour lui-même est déchiré, aussi la logique passionnelle s'accommode-t-elle de l'ambivalence. Que dis-je? La contradiction est plus souvent un aliment paradoxal de l'amour qu'un empêchement d'aimer. . . . Car ces deux faces de l'amour entre lesquelles nous ne cessions d'hésiter sont comme systole et diastole; c'est leur alternance qui règle la pulsation vitale, et c'est de leur rythme que bat notre coeur."
116. Seneca, *De Beneficiis* 2.17: "Optimus ille qui dedit facile numquam exiget: reddi gausius est bona fide quid praestitisset oblitus qui accipientis animo receipt" (52).
117. Jankélévitch, *Philosophie premiére*, 266. See also Françoise Schwab, "Vladimir Jankélévitch: Une âme résistante," *Bulletin de Littérature Ecclésiastique* 107, no. 2 (2006):214–15.
118. Jankélévitch and Berlowitz, *Quelque part dans l'inachevé*, 115. Cf. ibid., 151–42. Like Hermann Cohen, Franz Rosenzweig, and Emmanuel Levinas, Jankélévitch believes the singularity of Jewish existence reveals something fundamental and universal about human existence. He recognizes in Jewish existence a privileged position of bearing witness to this inherent tension in the human condition. "Without doubt," he says, "Jewish existence is in its own way a privileged witness to the insoluble: intrinsically torn and incapable of deciding with

an unequivocal decision the dilemma of assimilation and difference, it simultaneously wills contradictories. . . . In its being itself it testifies to the wound that will never heal and to the impossible synthesis [Sans doute l'existence juive est-elle à sa manière le témoin privilégié de l'insoluble; intrinsèquement déchirée, et en premier lieu incapable de trancher par un choix univoque l'insoluble dilemma de l'assimilation et de la différence, elle veut a la fois les contradictoires. . . . Elle témoigne dans son être même de la blessure jamais cicatrisée et de l'impossible synthèse]." Jankélévitch and Berlowitz, *Quelque part dans l'inachevé,* 131.

119. William Shakespeare, *Hamlet,* 1.v. Derrida opens his *Specters of Marx* with this statement from Hamlet, and that whole work can be read as a meditation on a time out of joint and its repercussions for justice (*Specters of Marx: The State of the Debt, the Work of Mourning, and the New International,* trans. Peggy Kamuf (New York: Routledge, 1994).

120. Jankélévitch, *Forgiveness,* 2.

121. Ibid.

122. Ibid.

123. Ibid.

124. Ibid., 3.

125. Ibid., 115–16.

126. Cf., e.g., Jankélévitch and Berlowitz, *Quelque part dans l'inachevé,* 69–70.

127. Jankélévitch, *Philosophie premiére,* 118.

128. Cf. Lemcke, *Der Begriff Verzeihen,* 68–71, and Jerphagnon, *Ahnen und Wollen,* 116.

129. Jankélévitch, *Philosophie premiére,* 118. "Après l'épuration graduelle, voice la purification gracieuse, qui est la seule vraie catharsis et la seul conversion effective de toute l'âme. Cette catharsis est l'intuition."

130. Jankélévitch, *Forgiveness,* 116.

131. Vladimir Jankélévitch, "Difficultés du pardon: Entretien avec le Professeur Jankélévitch," *La Vie spirituelle* 619 (March 1977): 188–89.

132. Jankélévitch, *Forgiveness,* 4; emphasis mine.

133. Jankélévitch, *Le Pur et l'impur,* 275: "La pureté intentionnelle n'est pas une propriété adjectivale du sujet, c'est un événement, une occurrence qui est le contraire d'une chose."

134. Alain Gouhier, "Le Temps de l'impardonnable et le temps du pardon selon Jankélévitch," in *Le Point Theologique, Forgiveness,* ed. Michel Perrin (Paris: Beauchesnes, 1987), 275.

135. Jankélévitch, *Forgiveness,* 117–18.

136. Ibid., 116.

137. Lemcke, *Der Begriff Verzeihen,* 76.

138. Ibid., 72; cf. also Jankélévitch and Berlowitz, *Quelque part dans l'inachevé,* 69.

139. Jankélévitch, *Le Paradoxe de la morale,* 153. See also Hansen, "*Forgiveness* and 'Should We Pardon Them?'" 115.

140. Jankélévitch, *Philosophie premiére*, 245.

141. Jankélévitch, *Forgiveness*, 116.

142. Vladimir Jankélévitch, *Philosophie premiére*, 247: "L'homme désintéressé transcende, quand il donne ou pardonne, la naturalité de ses passions et la mercenarité de son égoïsm,—mais sa condition de créature finie soumise au déterminisme général et aux lois de l'existence trophique, il ne la transcende pas!"

143. Ibid., 244.

144. Jankélévitch, *Forgiveness*, 3–4.

145. Jankélévitch, *Philosophie premiére*, 260–61.

146. Cf. Jacques Derrida, *Given Time*, 29: "Finally if the gift is another name of the impossible, we still think it, we name it, we desire it. We intend it. And this *even if* or *because* or *to the extent that* we *never* encounter it, we never know it, we never verify it, we never experience it in its present existence or in its phenomenon."

147. Jankélévitch, *Forgiveness*, 3.

148. Ibid., 116.

7. Repentance: Concerning Unconditionality

1. Jacques Derrida, for example, *For What Tomorrow . . . A Dialogue* (with Elisabeth Roudinesco), trans. Jeff Fort (Stanford: Stanford University Press, 2004).160–61.

2. Edith Humphrey, "And I Shall Heal Them: Repentance, Turning, and Penitence in the Johannine Writings," in *Repentance in Christian Theology*, ed. Mark Boda and Gordon Smith (Collegeville, Minn.: Liturgical Press, 2006), 109.

3. In the correspondence between Walter Benjamin and Max Horkheimer, the question is addressed whether this view is essentially and necessarily theological. Benjamin distinguishes between *science* and *remembering* (*Eingedenken*) and attributes to the latter a responsibility for righting the injustices of the past. "In remembering," he writes, "we make an experience that forbids us from conceiving history principally atheologically, as much as we are not allowed to write in immediate theological concepts." Walter Benjamin, *The Arcades Project*, trans. Howard Eiland and Kevin McLaughlin (Cambridge, Mass.: Belknap Press of Harvard University Press, 1999), 471. [*Gesammelte Werke*, ed. Rolf Tiedemann and Hermann Schweppenhäuser (Frankfurt am Main: Suhrkamp, 1991) 5:589.] Cf. the section titled "Irrevocability," in chapter 3 of this book.

4. Robert Gibbs, *Why Ethics? Signs of Responsibility* (Princeton, N.J.: Princeton University Press, 2000), 307.

5. See Immanuel Kant, *Religion within the Limits of Reason Alone*, trans. Theodore M. Greene and Hoyt H. Hudson (New York: Harper and Row, 1960) [*Kant Werke*, vol. 4 (Darmstadt: Wissenschaftliche Buchgesellschaft, 1998)], A50–52; 697–99. Page numbers refer first to the academic pagination and second to the pages in the English edition.

6. A *symbolon* was the qualification marker used for entrance into games, legal proceedings, and people's assemblies in Greece. It was also used as a residence

permit for foreigners. In Rome, such markers were called *tesserae*. In the private sphere, the *symbolon* was a sign of friendship. A ceramic ring was broken in half and carried by the separate parties, who would recognize each other by fitting together the two pieces.

7. Vladimir Jankélévitch, *Forgiveness*, trans. Andrew Kelley (Chicago: University of Chicago Press, 2005), 157.

8. Plato, *Republic* 2.368c–369a and 4.435a–b.

9. Ibid., 7, esp. 518c.

10. Seneca, *On Benefits* IV, chap. 34. Cf. *Epictetus*, Discourses II, 22, 35 (*Epictetus, The Discourses as reported by Arrian, the Manual, and the Fragments*, with English trans. W. A. Oldfather, 2 vols. [1928; London: William Heinemann 1928]) and Albert Esser, *Das Phänomen Reue: Versuch einer Erhellung ihres Selbstverständnisses* (Cologne: Hegner, 1963), 19. This prejudice follows the logic of Esser's thesis that the Greeks have no conception of repentance. I am arguing, on the contrary, that their conception is a different one, which is informative for an understanding of repentance that is beyond the purely psychological or theological interpretations and that revives a philosophical topic that has been unjustly buried, largely as a result of these dominant interpretations. This dual ground, furthermore, opens the path for revisiting the theological and philosophical practices of moral life in their common roots, growth, as well as in their distinctive understandings and practices.

11. Pierre Hadot, *Philosophy as a Way of Life*, trans. Michael Chase (Oxford: Blackwell, 1995), 261.

12. Seneca, *On Benefits* IV, chap. 34.

13. Aristotle, *Nicomachean Ethics* 7.7.1150a22. The following passages come from this book and book 9, chap. 4. Throughout his 1908 translation, however, W. D. Ross uses the word *repentance* instead of *regret*.

14. Ursula Wolf, *Aristoteles "Nikomachische Ethik"* (Darmstadt: Wissenschaftliche Buchgesellschaft, 2002), 180–81.

15. Aristotle, *Nicomachean Ethics* 1166a27–29.

16. Esser, *Das Phänomen Reue*, 26.

17. Aristotle, *Nicomachean Ethics* 1139b10–11, Ross's translation. Irwin translates this sentence as "Of this alone even a god is deprived—to make what is all done to have never happened."]

18. Immanuel Kant, *Critique of Practical Reason*, trans. Thomas Kingsmill Abott (Mineola, N.Y.: Dover, 2004), A177. [*Kant Werke*, (Darmstadt: Wissenschaftliche Buchgesellschaft, 1998) 4:A177.]

19. Baruch Spinoza, *Ethics: Treatise on the Emendation of the Intellect and Selected Letters,* ed. Seymour Feldman, trans. Samuel Shirley (Indianapolis: Hackett 1992), part 4, proposition 54, p. 184.

20. Nietzsche, *The Wanderer and His Shadow,* 323 in *Human, All Too Human: A Book for Free Spirits*, trans. R. J. Hollingdale (Cambridge: Cambridge University Press, 1996) 2.2.390. Nicolai Hartmann echoes this tone with Luther-like vigor: "Sei schuldig, soviel du willst, nur sorge, dass das Gute geschehe [Be guilty

as much as you want to, just take care that the good occurs]" (Nicolai Hartmann, *Ethik*, 4th ed. [Berlin: Walter de Gruyter, 1962], 820, author's trans.).

21. Emmanuel Levinas, *Nine Talmudic Readings*, trans. Annette Aronowicz (Bloomington: Indiana University Press, 1990), 14–55.

22. Alan Udoff, "'After Such Knowledge, What Forgiveness?' On Jankélévitch and the Question of Repentance," in *Vladimir Jankélévitch and the Question of Forgiveness*, ed. Alan Udoff (Lanham, Md.: Lexington Books, 2013), 205. Elaborating on this point, Udoff adds that "the Jewish tradition enumerates in the Torah 613 commandments. There is no imperative to forgive. That which it enjoins is repentance" (202).

23. Gershom Scholem, *The Messianic Idea in Judaism and Other Essays on Jewish Spirituality*, trans. Michael Myer (New York: Schocken Books, 1971), 35.

24. Emmanuel Levinas, *Difficult Freedom: Essays on Judaism*, trans. Seán Hand (Baltimore: Johns Hopkins University Press, 1990), 227. His reading regards pages 97b and 98a of Tractate Sanhedrin.

25. Scholem, *Messianic Idea in Judaism*, 35.

26. Levinas, *Difficult Freedom*, 77.

27. See Gershom Scholem's essay "Redemption through Sin" in *Messianic Idea in Judaism*, 78–141), in which he analyzes the Sabbatai Zevi movement beginning in the late seventeenth century and interprets Christianity in this light.

28. Levinas, *Difficult Freedom*, 77.

29. Joseph Dov Soloveitchik, *On Repentance: The Thought and Oral Discourses of Rabbi Joseph Dov Soloveitchik*, ed. Pinchas H. Peli (Lanham, Md: Rowman and Littlefield, 1996), 274–76. See also Edith Wyschogrod, "Repentance and Forgiveness: The Undoing of Time," *International Journal for Philosophy of Religion* 60, no. 1–3 (2006): 166.

30. Quoted in Jacob Neusner, "Repentance in Judaism," in *Repentance: A Comparative Perspective*, ed. Amitai Etzioni and David E. Carney (Lanham, Md.: Rowman and Littlefield, 1997), 60–75; here, 67.

31. Gibbs, *Why Ethics?* 310.

32. Ibid., 313.

33. Cf. Aristotle's distinction between voluntary and involuntary action. See the section titled "*Sungnômê* (Understanding)" in chapter 2 of this work.

34. Gibbs, *Why Ethics?* 314.

35. Levinas, *Nine Talmudic Readings*, 25.

36. Cf. Deut. 15:9: "Beware that there be not a thought in thy wicked heart." Levinas's usage of the term *attention* can be seen as a translation the Delphic dictum to "know thyself." He calls for continuous vigilance and presence of mind. In this manner, his usage demonstrates parallels to and decisive differences from the traditional usage, the ethical significance of which is primarily attached to a vision without the blurs of passion aimed at a sense of self-mastery. *Attention* (*prosoche*) is, for example, the fundamental Stoic spiritual attitude (cf. Hadot, *Philosophy as a Way of Life*, 84–87, 130–33). In the later monastic practices, it indicated the setting right of the human's being in the world, which foremost

concerned the right relation to God. Simone Weil elaborates on this Stoic-monastic practice while separating attention from the will, making it the heart of her spiritual ethics by focusing on the perception of things and behaviors of others without impetuousness, envy, prejudice, and neurosis. For her, it is the "letting be" of things in order to see them clearly, not, as the apostle Paul writes of present human experience, "through a glass dimly." See Simone Weil, *Gravity and Grace*, trans. Emma Crawford and Mario von der Ruhr (London: Routledge, 2002), 116–22.

37. Levinas, *Nine Talmudic Readings*, 24.

38. Ibid., 25. In aphorism 68 of *The Wanderer and His Shadow*, "Whether we are able to forgive?" Nietzsche takes quite a different stance: "How *can* we forgive them at all, if they know not what they do? One has nothing whatever *to* forgive.—But does a man ever know *completely* what he does? And if this must always remain at least questionable, then men never do have anything to forgive one another and pardoning is to the most rational man a thing impossible. Finally, if the ill-doers did know what they did—we would have a right to forgive them only if we had a right to accuse and to punish them. But this we do not have" (*Human, All Too Human*, 327).

39. Gibbs, *Why Ethics?* 315.

40. Levinas recognizes that the *felix culpa* exposes a slippery slope, for the greater estimation of the repentant sinner over the nonsinner is susceptible to perversion. Wrongdoing could be conceived as a condition for greater happiness or even salvation. It would be a means, necessary but not sufficient, of getting there. Levinas protests, however, that "no repentant sinner can have access to the place of the just, who have never sinned. It is better not to sin than to be granted forgiveness. This is the first and necessary truth, without which the door is opened to every perversion" (*Nine Talmudic Readings*, 24). The supremacy of the principle "not to sin" holds a regulative function so that one does not sin *in order to* attain greater joy. But factually, the supremacy of repentance accentuates the task of human existence and agency in relation to God. We are called to return (cf. Gibbs, *Why Ethics?* 310) because as the Psalmist (Psalm 143) writes, "in thy sight shall no man living be justified."

Moreover, Levinas sees in the shift from intentional sin to an unintentional one a trace of the humanization of the justice system. As soon as an offense has been committed, the nature of justice, he comments, consists in putting a stop to the chain reaction of violence that ensues. "Humanity is born in man," he writes, "to the extent that he manages to reduce a mortal offence to the level of a civil lawsuit, to the extent that punishing becomes a question of *putting right what can be put right* and *re-educating the wicked*." It is in the name of humanity that the felony is downgraded to a misdemeanor punishable by fine, that the transference of money replaces and abolishes capital punishment. He concludes that "justice without passion is not the only thing man must possess. He must also have justice without killing" (*Difficult Freedom*, 147). This path of humanizing justice is obviously subject to abuse, and it has its limits. He recognizes that even a kinder, bloodless justice reinscribes a justice of the strong and rich, opening unto a world in which "outrage and fracture take on a market value and are given a price." In short, Levinas witnesses in this evolution of justice the potential rebuttal of all justice. He consequently suggests that it is a matter of balancing the spirit of kindness with the strictness of the letter of "an eye for an eye."

41. Soloveitchik, *On Repentance*, 256.

42. Gibbs, *Why Ethics?* 340.

43. See the chapter "Blotting Out Sin or Elevating Sin," in Soloveitchik, *On Repentance*, 228–65.

44. Quoted in Wyschogrod, "Undoing of Time," 159.

45. Gibbs, *Why Ethics?* 341. For a discussion of Levinas's representation of the *felix culpa* in the light of forgiveness, see the section titled "*Coincidentia Oppositorum*" in chapter 8 of this book.

46. Soloveitchik, *On Repentance*, 256.

47. Gibbs does not hesitate to call these two sides *forgetting* and *forgiveness*, respectively. Repentance out of love, however, is not the same as being forgiven. It is either repentance itself which, according to this Talmud reading, achieves this transformation, or it is the forgiveness received from God as a response to repentance from love that occasions this transformation.

48. For the former, see Neusner, "Repentance in Judaism," 68; for the later, see Gibbs, *Why Ethics?* 310.

49. Entailed in this line of interpretation is the notion of *intercession*. In the Book of Exodus (chap. 32), there appears a rare mentioning of God repenting (or turning). This Exodus story, the history of the golden calf, paradigmatically fleshes out the connection of repentance and forgiveness to memory and forgetting as well as the intricacies of the dynamics between God, the other, and others. I can merely touch on the complexities:

The Lord tells Moses that he is weary of the "stiff-necked" people of Israel, a people who do not have the flexibility of turning (their heads, their minds, or their lives) and requests of Moses to "let me alone" (for destruction requires solitude) so that his "wrath may wax hot" against and ultimately "consume" his people. This wrath is not directed at Moses, however. Rather, the Lord promises to make of Moses a "great nation." But Moses reminds him who the nation is—both created and chosen—by recalling him to the covenant made with Abraham, Isaac, and Jacob. The "great nation" is thus perhaps not so "great" but rather is composed of many stiff-necked and short-sighted people. It is nonetheless the nation of the covenant, the people he delivered from Egypt.

Even though "the Lord *repented* of the *evil* [not necessarily *justice*] he thought to do unto his people," Moses is the one whose anger waxes hot upon his return to the people from the mount, for they have built an idol, a golden calf, which they worship as their deliverer. After witnessing their idolatry subsequent to his intercession on their behalf, Moses does not command repentance or seek forgiveness. Instead, fratricide and filicide ensue. God commands that those who are on the side of the Lord, the Levites, go "from gate to gate throughout the camp, and slay every man his brother, and every man his companion, and every man his neighbor . . . even every man upon his son, and upon his brother." It is first after this civil bloodshed that Moses tells the people that he will go to the Lord, and "*perhaps I* can make atonement for *your* sin."

Intercession is thus possible but is never a sure thing. Sacrifice—even or especially of blood, fraternal blood—may not ever appease. It all depends on Moses, this "I" who, for whatever reason (as the one of whom God wants to make a great nation, the one he spares, the one who hasn't turned away but is loose-necked and ready to be turned toward him), can *perhaps* make atonement for that which you, not I, have done. As if intercession was not bold enough, he offers himself as a sacrifice. "Please forgive their sin," he pleads after acknowledging the wrong the others had done, "but if not, then *blot me out* of the book you have written." Subsequent to the petition follows the substitution on the condition the petition of forgiveness fails. Moses demands his *absence* from the *presence* of life in the book. The book is the book of life, and to "blot out" what is already written is to render the pages of life empty and bare. It is to wipe the slate clean; it is to make of it, in the language of the book, a tabula rasa. From Soloveitchik to Jankélévitch, forgiveness is often interpreted as a blotting out—a blotting out of the past offense as if it never were, as if it never occurred. But Moses, again commanding God, lays down an ultimatum for what gets removed from the book of life: either blot out the sin (if indeed that is what forgiveness does) or blot out my name as substitute and sacrifice (or at least my name, too, in solidarity with the name or those names of my people, as Paul will later write to the Romans). God's response, however, is to reject the either-or of Moses' alternative: "Whosoever has sinned against me, *him* will I blot out of my book." There will be no substitution or acceptance of sacrifice. The one cannot take the place of the other. Rather, it is the life of the sinner that is required: Either the sin or the sinner is blotted out, not the interceder, the ram, the lamb, or the advocate. Whereas intercession on behalf of other is possible, substitution and sacrifice are not.

50. From Tractate Yoma, pp. 85a–86b. Neusner's text reads: "For transgressions done between man and the Omnipresent, the Day of Atonement atones. For transgressions between man and man, the day of Atonement atones, only if the man will regain the good will of his friend" ("Repentance in Judaism," 65).

51. Levinas, *Nine Talmudic Readings*, 16.

52. In Jankélévitch's nontheological treatise, the difference is organized as the offense against individuals and the offense against values. The latter manifests in the former. The conjunction of value and the other person parallels the conjunction of God and neighbor. But not all offenses against individuals are simultaneously offenses against values. Notably, both here and for Jankélévitch, the metaphysical juxtaposition of time and eternity forms the background.

53. Levinas, *Nine Talmudic Readings*, 16.

54. Robert Gibbs, "Returning/Forgiving," in *Questioning God*, ed. John D. Caputo, Mark Dooley, and Michael J. Scanlon (Bloomington: Indiana University Press, 2001), 78.

55. Levinas, *Nine Talmudic Readings*, 16.

56. Franz Rosenzweig, *The Star of Redemption*, trans. Barbara E. Galli (Madison: University of Wisconsin Press, 2005), 195. [*Der Stern der Erlösung*, (Frankfurt a.M.: Suhrkamp, 1988), 200–201.]

57. Gibbs, "Returning/Forgiving," 78–79.

58. In contrast, the Jewish theologian Jacob Neusner advocates a theological ethics in which repentance not only "compels" God but also, and equally, compels the offended neighbor. For Neusner, it is unequivocally necessary that repentance precede forgiveness. Unconditioned forgiveness is thus not imitative of divinity but is a violation of justice. He grounds his reflections in a passage from Leviticus, "You shall not bear a grudge nor pursue a dispute beyond reason, nor hate your brother in your heart, but you shall love your neighbor as yourself (19:18)" ("Repentance in Judaism," 61). Although he acknowledges that repentance has social-ethical implications, Neusner writes that repentance primarily "defines a stage in the relationship of Man and God, inclusive of repentance to one's fellow for sin against him or her" (62). The duty to forgive the one who fulfills his duty to repent is thus a religious duty. Therefore, Neusner casts the refusal of forgiveness as "un-Judaic" and consequently as "immoral," regardless of grounds. Whereas a "natural Jew," he suggests, might waver on forgiving a repentant offender, the "supernatural Jew" must forgive, for this action is both what God does and what God commands his people to do (73). Between the natural and the supernatural Jew, it is Judaism itself, he concludes, that is at stake because reconciliation is possible only on a religious basis.

59. Levinas, *Nine Talmudic Readings*, 20.

60. Ibid., 19. See also Gibbs, "Returning/Forgiving," 83.

61. Gibbs, "Returning/Forgiving," 82.

62. Levinas, *Nine Talmudic Readings*, 24.

63. Ibid., 21. Again the question of the subject rears its head. Who frees the repentant offender? In a return to normalcy, contrary to imprescriptibility, is the validity of having offended in itself terminated on the condition of repentance? Or does God then say enough is enough, initiating release?

64. Levinas, *Nine Talmudic Readings*, 24.

65. Jacques Derrida, "Hostipitality" in his *Acts of Religion*, ed. Gil Anidjar (New York: Routledge, 2002), 381.

66. Derrida, *For What Tomorrow*, 161. Cf. also Jacques Derrida, *On Cosmopolitanism and Forgiveness*, trans. Mark Dooley and Michael Hughes (London: [0]Routledge, 2002), 35 and 39.

67. Derrida, *On Cosmopolitanism and Forgiveness*, 34

68. Jankélévitch, *Forgiveness*, 35; emphasis mine.

69. Cf. Aurel Kolnai, "Forgiveness," in *Proceedings of the Aristotelian Society*, 74 (1974): 91–106. Kolnai frames this dilemma as "the logical paradox of forgiveness" in which repentance renders forgiveness either unjustified or pointless (98–99).

70. Rosenzweig, *Star of Redemption*, 194. [*Der Stern der Erlösung*, 200.] See also Gibbs, *Why Ethics?* 334.

71. Hartmann, *Ethik*, 818.

72. Aristotle, *Nicomachean Ethics* 6.2.1139b10–11.

73. Hartmann, *Ethik*, 819. Cf. Kant, *Critique of Practical Reason*, A177. Miroslav Volf quotes the first passage from Hartmann and is in agreement with him that, as a moral act, forgiveness concerns only the conduct toward the guilty. The moral incapacity to remove the guilt of another, he argues, however, applies only to human forgiveness. "Only divine forgiveness," he writes, "actually removes guilt. . . . As a result of human forgiveness, the guilty is treated as if he or she were not guilty. But unless forgiven by God, he or she remains guilty, human forgiveness notwithstanding" ("Forgiveness, Reconciliation, and Justice: A Christian Contribution to a More Peaceful Social Environment," in *Forgiveness and Reconciliation: Religion, Public Policy, and Conflict Transformation*, ed. Raymond G. Helmick, SJ, and Rodney l. Petersen [Philadelphia: Templeton Foundation Press, 2001], 45n30).

74. Esser, *Das Phänomen Reue*, 42–43.

75. Jean-Paul Sartre, *Being and Nothingness: A Phenomenological Essay on Ontology*, trans. Hazel Barnes (New York: Washington Square Press, 1992), 708.

76. Ibid., 710.

77. Søren Kierkegaard, *Either/Or*, ed. and trans. Howard Hong and Edna Hong (Princeton, N.J.: Princeton University Press, 1990), 2:262.

78. Ibid., 248.

79. Ibid., 250.

80. In *Philosophical Fragments*, Kierkegaard's pseudonym Johannes Climacus challenges Hegel's famous Owl of Minerva regarding the necessity of the past. Although he concedes that "what has happened has happened and cannot be undone, thus it cannot be changed," he argues in a double dialectic that the past in having come into existence moved from possibility to actuality, and the fact of coming into existence through a "freely acting cause" "demonstrates that it is not necessary . . . because the necessary *is*." So although the true significance of events may become visible only in hindsight, if the past were necessary, he claims, "it would follow that the future would also be necessary," and freedom and the contingency of history would be an illusion. Yet it is another, higher change that interests Climacus even more, the dialectical change of repentance, "which wants to nullify an actuality" (Søren *Kierkegaard, Philosophical Fragments*, ed. and trans. Howard Hong and Edna Hong [Princeton, N.J.: Princeton University Press, 1985], 74–75). See also Merold Westphal, *Becoming a Self: A Reading of Kierkegaard's Concluding Unscientific Postscript* (West Lafayette, Ind.: Purdue University Press, 1995).

81. Ibid., 215–16.

82. *Either/Or* 2:216.

83. See, for example, the discussion initiated by a question from Francis Schüssler-Fiorenza in the "Roundtable Discussion with Jacques Derrida," in *Questioning God*, 62–64. Schüssler-Fiorenza is particularly interested in the connection between collective guilt and collective repentance. For a more thorough

handling of this difficult subject matter, see Karl Jaspers's *The Question of German Guilt,* trans. E. B. Ashton (New York: Fordham University Press, 2000).

84. *Either/Or* 2:239.

85. This debate on the role of repentance and responsibility has been reevaluated in recent literature in terms of rationality, agency, and selfhood. Cf., for example, Bernard Williams, *Moral Luck* (Cambridge: Cambridge University Press, 1981), Although Bernard Williams, like Aristotle and Sartre, shapes his argument in terms of regret, he understands regret as structurally parallel to how I am approaching repentance here. Regret, he says, intrinsically belongs to the concept of rationality. Like Arendt, he is basically concerned with unintentional aspects of human action, but he makes the strong claim that, as rational subjects, we cannot detach ourselves from these aspects and still retain our identity and character as agents (29). Rüdiger Bittner rightly dismisses the stronger possible interpretation of Williams's claim that the agent ceases to be an agent if he does not repent or feel regret for past actions ("Is It Reasonable to Regret Things One Did?" *Journal of Philosophy* 89, no. 5 [1992]: 262–73). Instead, the agent demonstrates himself to be without character. As Bittner writes, "He lacks character the way a person does who, on encountering any sort of resistance, abandons people and projects to which he was committed: the person without regret abandons his deeds" (269). Such a person would symbolically proceed to execute the self-dismemberment that Jesus suggests, cutting off the hand or the foot that causes one to sin (Matt. 5:30; 18:8; and Mark 9:45). Like Kierkegaard and Sartre, Williams focuses on the instantiation and preservation of the integrity and identity of the self, which he sees jeopardized by the one who does not regret but instead ignores past wrongs in order to move on.

86. Max Scheler, "Repentance and Rebirth," in *Person and Self-Value: Three Essays,* trans. M. S. Frings (Boston: Martinus Nijhoff, 1987), 122. ["Reue und Wiedergeburt," in *Vom Ewigen im Menschen* (Bern: Francke Verlag, 1954), 57. In the following, the original German text and page numbers will be listed after those of the English translation.

87. Scheler, "Repentance and Rebirth," 114; "Reue und Wiedergeburt," 50.

88. Ibid., 113; 49.

89. Cf., e.g., ibid., 90, 99, 108, 109; 29, 37, 45, 46. Cf. Meir Dan-Cohen, "Revising the Past: On the Metaphysics of Repentance, Forgiveness, and Pardon," in *Forgiveness, Mercy, and Clemency,* ed. Austin Sarat and Nasser Hussain (Stanford: Stanford University Press, 2007), 117–37. Dan-Cohen makes the moral philosophical case for this temporal orientation toward the past; in contrast to conceptions of repentance oriented toward the present (e.g., Jeffrie Murphy) and toward the future (e.g., Norvin Richards) (Dan-Cohen, "Revising the Past," 118).

90. Nietzsche, *Wanderer and His Shadow,* 323, 390; and Hartmann, *Ethik,* 820.

91. Scheler, "Repentance and Rebirth," 98; "Reue und Wiedergeburt," 36.

92. Ibid., 97; 36.

93. Ibid., 112; 49.

94. Ibid., 97; 36.
95. Ibid., 97–98; 36.
96. Ibid., 114; 50.
97. Ibid., 113; 49.
98. Ibid., 112; 48.
99. Ibid., 100; 38.
100. Ibid., 114–15; 51.
101. Ibid., 106; 43.
102. Ibid., 112; 48.

103. Søren Kierkegaard, *Stages on Life's Way: Studies by Various Persons*, ed. and trans. Howard Hong and Edna Hong (Princeton, N.J.: Princeton University Press, 1988), 477.

104. Scheler, "Repentance and Rebirth," 121; "Reue und Wiedergeburt," 57. On several occasions, Scheler does speak, however, of a perfect or completed repentance (cf. 104, 113, 119, 123; 42, 49, 54, 58).

105. Ibid., 114; 50.
106. Ibid., 96; 35.
107. Ibid., 97; 36.
108. Ibid., 122; 57.
109. Ibid., 94; 33.

110. Beyond the individual person, this indeterminacy of meaning and unfinished value apply equally to the life of a species or world history. According to Scheler, the same principle is in effect: Since the past is unfinished it remains redeemable (ibid., 95; 34).

111. Ibid., 95; 34.
112. Ibid., 97; 35.
113. Ibid., 101–2; 40.
114. Ibid., 102–3; 40–41.

115. Cf. Peter Spader, *Scheler's Ethical Personalism: Its Logic, Development and Promise* (New York: Fordham University Press, 2002), 234–36; and Dan-Cohen, "Revising the Past," 136n28.

116. Scheler, "Repentance and Rebirth," 104–5; "Reue und Wiedergeburt," 42.

117. Scheler therefore asserts that every repentance of an act is not immediately concerned with the act but with the person's having become guilty through the act (112; 49). Similarly, Jankélévitch states that forgiveness moves from the act to the person and that it is fundamentally the person who is forgiven for the act.

118. Ibid., 113; 49.
119. Ibid., 94; 33.
120. Ibid., 115–16; 50–52. Scheler's focus on spiritual renewal and the vast capacity of a change of consciousness is expressed in the idea that the entire moral world from the past to the future could be radically different if I alone were different (115; 51). Cf. Graham J. McAleer, "New Spartans: Jankélévitch, Scheler,

and Tolkien on Vanity," in *Vladimir Jankélévitch and the Question of Forgiveness*, ed. Alan Udoff (Lanham, Md.: Lexington Books, 2013), 129–41; esp. 134.

121. Scheler, "Repentance and Rebirth," 119; "Reue und Wiedergeburt," 55.

122. Jankélévitch, *Forgiveness,* 121, 151.

123. *On the Eternal in Man* (*Vom Ewigen im Menschen*) is the title of Scheler's book in which his essay on repentance first appeared.

124. Although Scheler intends to examine how far a purely moral interpretation of repentance extends, he admits that it assumes its full meaning "within the universal framework of metaphysics and religion" ("Repentance and Rebirth," 118; "Reue und Wiedergeburt," 54). He finds the deepest conception of the meaning and worth of repentance in Christianity and, more specifically, in the Catholic Church (122; 57).

125. Ibid., 89–90, 119; 29, 55ff.

126. Ibid., 119; 55.

127. Ibid., 123–24; 58–59.

128. Ibid., 94; 33.

129. Cf. McAleer, "New Spartans," 136.

130. Vladimir Jankélévitch, *La Mauvaise conscience,* in *Philosophie morale* (Paris: Flammarion, 1998), 119.

131. Ibid., 119–21.

132. Ibid., 118. "Il n'y a pas de verbe pour le rmords, parce qu'au remords nulle fonction ne correspond: on 'a' simplement du remords, on vit nez à nez avec son remords, c'est-à-dire avec sa faute, c'est-à-dire avec soi-même. . . . Le remords, en tant qu'il n'about it qu'à soi, apparaît comme entièrement insoluble."

133. Ibid., 117–18.

134. Jankélévitch, *Forgiveness,* 151.

135. Jankélévitch, *La Mauvaise conscience,* 79. Jankélévitch points out that the Greek word *pothos* designates both regret and desire.

136. Ibid., 80.

137. Ibid.

138. Ibid., 81.

139. Vladimir Jankélévitch, "Should We Pardon Them?" trans. Ann Hobart, *Critical Inquiry* 22, no. 3 (1996): 558.

140. Jankélévitch, *La Mauvaise conscience,* 82. "Cette impuissance est sa marque propere et . . . sa signature. Mais en morale n'est-ce pas justement le superflu qui est le nécessaire? Le remords est le plus stérile, le plus inefficace, de tous les sentiments humains."

141. Ibid., 127. In this context, Jankélévitch even claims that remorse is unjust and irrational, but he qualifies this assertion, stating that it entails a supernatural justice. Although remorse is never unmerited, he insists, it is disproportionate to the act itself because it is not the act for which one feels remorse but one's wickedness in general (ibid., 169).

142. Levinas, "Useless Suffering," in *The Provocation of Levinas: Rethinking the Other*, ed. Robert Bernasconi and David Wood, trans. Richard Cohen (New

York: Routledge, 2002). Levinas, too, speaks of a "pure suffering," which is "intrinsically meaningless and condemned to itself without exit" (158), a suffering that is "essentially gratuitous and absurd" (161). For Levinas, however, "the very phenomenon of suffering in its uselessness is, in principle[,] the pain of the Other" (163), while one's own suffering signifies the ethical possibility of meaning. As Levinas explains, "A radical difference develops between *suffering in the Other*, which for *me* is unpardonable and solicits me and calls me, and suffering *in me* . . . whose constitutional or congenital uselessness can take on a meaning . . . in becoming a suffering for the suffering—be it inexorable—of someone else" (159).

143. Jankélévitch, *La Mauvaise conscience,* 118. Cf. Jankélévitch, *Forgiveness,* 45.

144. Jankélévitch, *La Mauvaise conscience,* 84, 116.

145. Ibid., 81.

146. Ibid., 118.

147. Ibid., 84.

148. Ibid., 123.

149. Jankélévitch, *Forgiveness,* 45.

150. Jankélévitch, *La Mauvaise conscience,* 171. Jankélévitch depicts this wickedness as being at the same time free and necessary: free because free acts or decisions alone provoke remorse and necessary because, through our free acts, we have created in ourselves a malice that we no longer govern.

151. Kant, *Religion,* B96; 66.

152. Jankélévitch, *La Mauvaise conscience,* 169–70, 125.

153. G. W. F. Hegel, *Phenomenology of Mind,* trans. J. B. Baillie (Mineola, N.Y.: Dover, 2003), 393. [*Phänomenologie des Geistes* (Frankfurt a.M.: Suhrkamp, 1988), 407, §669.]

154. Jankélévitch, *La Mauvaise conscience,* 84.

155. Vladimir Jankélévitch, *Cours de philosophie morale: Université libre de Bruxelles 1962–1963* (Paris: Éditions du Seuil, 2006), 176; Jankélévitch, *La Mauvaise conscience,* 82.

156. Jankélévitch, *La Mauvaise conscience,* 84.

157. Vladimir Jankélévitch and Béatrice Berlowitz, *Quelque part dans l'inachevé* (Paris: Gallimard, 1978), 66.

158. Jankélévitch, *Forgiveness,* 48; emphasis mine.

159. Vladimir Jankélévitch, *La Mort* (Paris: Flammarion, 1977), 337.

160. Jankélévitch, *Cours de philosophie morale,* 176.

161. Jankélévitch, *Forgiveness,* 47.

162. Jankélévitch, *La Mauvaise conscience,* 123.

163. Jankélévitch, *Cours de philosophie morale,* 176.

164. Jankélévitch, *La Mort,* 337.

165. Jankélévitch, *La Mauvaise conscience,* 122.

166. Kant, *Religion,* B94–95; 66.

167. Cf., e.g., Jankélévitch, *La Mauvaise conscience,* 123.

168. Ibid., 163.

169. Ibid., 119.

170. I want to thank Andrew Kelley for pointing out to me the organ-obstacle character of remorse.

171. Jankélévitch, *Forgiveness,* 120–21.

172. Sylvia Walsh, *Living Christianly: Kierkegaard's Dialectic of Christian Existence* (University Park: Pennsylvania State University Press, 2005), 40.

173. Søren Kierkegaard, *Sickness unto Death: A Christian Psychological Exposition for Upbuilding and Awakening,* ed. and trans. Howard V. Hong and Edna H. Hong (Princeton, N.J.: Princeton University Press, 1983), 26.

174. Jankélévitch, *Forgiveness,* 151. Cf., e.g., Jankélévitch, *La Mauvaise conscience,* 119.

175. Jankélévitch, *Forgiveness,* 121.

176. Ibid.

177. Ibid., 41.

178. Ibid., 121–22.

179. Cf., e.g., Kant, *Religion,* B50–51; 43.

180. Jankélévitch, *La Mauvaise conscience,* 151.

181. Kant, *Religion,* B99; 68.

182. Jankélévitch, *La Mauvaise conscience,* 154.

183. John Silber argues that Kant recognizes the incompatibility of forgiveness and freedom but does not resolve the antimony, vacillating instead between freedom, power, and personal responsibility, on the one hand, and grace and forgiveness, on the other hand: "His absolute conception of freedom precludes the need for grace . . . [and] the purity of the moral law precludes the granting of grace. . . . [because] if the individual has done all that he can, he does not need grace. And if he has not, even Kant agrees he should not get it. . . . In order to make sense of the idea of personal responsibility, Kant argued that freedom is absolute. Yet by holding that man's responsibility is absolute, he condemned man to an insufferable burden of guilt" (Silber, "The Ethical Significance of Kant's *Religion,* in Immanuel Kant, *Religion within the Limits of Reason Alone,* trans. Theodore M. Greene and Hoyt H. Hudson [New York: Harper & Row, 1960], 132–33).

184. Kant, *Religion,* B62–63; 47–49.

185. Ibid., B56, 43; B99, 69.

186. Ibid., 42.

187. Jankélévitch, *La Mauvaise conscience,* 159.

188. Ibid., 153, 160–61.

189. Ibid., 151: "une transfiguration absolument contingente de la volonté: une 'grâce.'"

190. Kant, *Religion,* B58; 44, and B79; 57.

191. Ibid., B62; 47.

192. Ibid., B64; 49.

193. Ibid., B99; 69.

194. Ibid., B98–99; 67, and B102; 70.

195. Jankélévitch, *La Mauvaise conscience*, 151: "Cette grâce est la pure douleur du remords."

196. Ibid., 158: "Le remords est le pardon instantané, gratuit, immérité, qui rend guérissables nos fautes et qui prépare la remission."

197. Ibid., 151: "Pour que dans cette nuit obscure la première espérance puisse jaillir, il faut une transfiguration absolument contingente de la volonté: une 'grâce.'"

198. Cf. ibid., 163.

199. Ibid., 164: "Le repentir es l'intégration de notre faute dans une totalité perpétuellement élargie, transformée, approfondie." For both, repentance involves the annihilation of guilt but not of the deed or the past itself.

200. Cf. McAleer, "New Spartans," 134–35. McAleer understandably identifies Jankélévitch with the idea of irrevocability and juxtaposes it to Scheler's belief in the reparability of the past. This distinction, for him, determines "the distinction between an act being redeemable and an act forgivable" (132).

201. Jankélévitch, *La Mauvaise conscience*, 164.

202. Ibid., 162. Cf. Catherine Chalier, "The Great Distress," in *Vladimir Jankélévitch and the Question of Forgiveness*, ed. Alan Udoff (Lanham, Md.: Lexington Books, 2013), 76.

203. Jankélévitch, *La Mauvaise conscience*, 172.

204. Ibid., 159.

205. Ibid., 153.

206. Jankélévitch, *Forgiveness*, 157.

207. Kierkegaard, *Sickness unto Death*, 113.

208. Jankélévitch, *Forgiveness*, 158.

209. Joachim Kopper, "Kants synthetisch-praktischer Satz a priori und Jankélévitch's Verständnis der Vergebung," *Kant-Studien* 61 (1970): 247.

210. Jankélévitch, *Forgiveness*, 110–11.

211. Emmanuel Levinas, "Reflections on the Philosophy of Hitlerism," trans. Sean Hand, *Critical Inquiry* 17, no. 1 (1990): 65.

212. Charles Griswold, *Forgiveness: A Philosophical Exploration* (New York: Cambridge University Press, 2007), 49.

213. Ibid., 47.

214. Jankélévitch, *Forgiveness*, 151–52.

215. Ibid., 128.

216. Ibid., 152–53.

217. Vladimir Jankélévitch, *Traité des vertus*, vol. 3: *L'innocence et la méchanceté* (Paris: Bordas, 1972), 1423. Significantly, Jankélévitch states that "*all* virtues, in the measure in which they proceed from an intention without pretension or arrogance, are, thus, modalities of the forgetting of oneself" (emphasis mine). (Toutes les vertus, dans la mesure où elles procèdent d'une intention sans prétention ni arrogance, sont ainsi des modalités de l'oubli-de-soi.) See also Andrew Kelley, "Jankélévitch and the Metaphysics of Forgiveness," in *Vladimir Jankélévitch and the Question of Forgiveness*, ed. Alan Udoff (Lanham, Md.: Lexington Books, 2013), 35.

218. Jankélévitch, *Forgiveness*, 124.
219. Ibid., 39. Jankélévitch's reference to "twenty years" is recurring and refers to the time from the Shoah to the time of writing.
220. Ibid.
221. Ibid., 47.
222. Karl Jaspers, *The Question of German Guilt*, trans. E. B. Ashton (New York: Fordham University Press, 2000), 25–26. Originally published as *Die Schuldfrage* (Heidelberg: Lamber Schneider, 1946).
223. Ethan Kleinberg, "To Atone and to Forgive: Jaspers, Jankélévitch/Derrida, and the Possibility of Forgiveness," in *Vladimir Jankélévitch and the Question of Forgiveness*, ed. Alan Udoff (Lanham, Md.: Lexington Books, 2013), 147.
224. Jankélévitch, *Forgiveness*, 10.
225. Ibid., 151, 158.
226. Ibid., 41.
227. Cf. Jankélévitch, "Should We Pardon Them?" e.g., 572.
228. Jankélévitch, *Forgiveness*, 157–58.
229. Ibid., 41.
230. Ibid., 157; emphasis mine.
231. Ibid., 124.
232. Ibid., 151.
233. Vladimir Jankélévitch, *Philosophie premiére: Introduction à une Philosophie du "Presque,"* 2nd ed. (Paris: Quadrige/Presses Univeristaires de France, 1986), 63.
234. Jankélévitch, *Forgiveness*, 121–22.
235. Ibid., 39.
236. Ibid., 148.
237. Ibid., 151. Cf. 121.
238. Ibid., 124.
239. Ibid., 151.
240. Ibid.
241. Jankélévitch, *Quelque part dans l'inachevé*, 65. "La mémoire n'est rien d'autre que la protestation morale de l'homme contre cette ambiguïté; elle implique une sorte de responsabilité éthique, et comme une piété morale qui m'oblige à lier le présent tangible et charnel aux choses révolues, absentes et invisibles. . . . Je suis mis en demeure d'assumer mon passé, de le déclarer mien et indestructible envers et contre tous."
242. Jankélévitch, *Forgiveness*, 27.
243. Cf. Derrida's critique of Jankélévitch's insistence on the "meaning" of forgiveness in *On Cosmopolitanism and Forgiveness*, 36.
244. Cf. Derrida, *On Cosmopolitanism and Forgiveness*, 34.
245. Cf., e.g., Kierkegaard's *Upbuilding Discourses in Various Spirits*, ed. and trans. Howard V. Hong and Edna H. Hong (Princeton, N.J.: Princeton University Press, 2009), 17–18.

246. Derrida, *On Cosmopolitanism and Forgiveness*, 45.
247. Ibid., 34–35.
248. Cf. Derrida, "Hostipitality," 398.
249. Derrida, *On Cosmopolitanism and Forgiveness*, 48.
250. Ibid., 49.
251. Cf. Levinas, "A Religion for Adults," in *Difficult Freedom*, 20.
252. Jankélévitch, *Forgiveness*, 124.
253. Ibid., 107.
254. Ibid., 151.
255. Ibid., 160.
256. For Jankélévitch's references to forgiveness as absurdity, see *Forgiveness*, 98, 127, 133. Chapter 3 of *Forgiveness*, in which Jankélévitch details the difference between the inexcusable and the unforgivable, is entitled "Mad Forgiveness: 'Acumen Veniae.'"
257. Cf., e.g., Vladimir Jankélévitch, *Music and the Ineffable*, trans. Carolyn Abbate (Princeton, N.J.: Princeton University Press, 2003), 71–73.
258. Susan Neiman, *Evil in Modern Thought: An Alternative History of Philosophy* (Princeton, N.J.: Princeton University Press, 2002), 225.
259. Jankélévitch, *Music and the Ineffable*, 148, 18.
260. Ibid., 46, 53.
261. Jankélévitch, *Philosophie premiére*, 102.
262. Wiard Raveling, "Lettres pour un pardon," *Magazine Littéraire* 333 (1995): 53. Translations from Jacques Derrida, "To Forgive," in *Questioning God*, ed. John D. Caputo, Mark Dooley, and Michael J. Scanlon (Bloomington: Indiana University Press, 2001), 38–40.
263. Raveling, "Lettres pour un pardon," 57: Letter from July 5, 1980, from Jankélévitch to Raveling.
264. Jonathan Judaken, "Vladimir Jankélévitch at the Colloques des intellectuels juifs de langue française," in *Vladimir Jankélévitch and the Question of Forgiveness*, ed. Alan Udoff (Lanham, Md.: Lexington Books, 2013), 18.
265. Cf. Robert Bernasconi, "Travelling Light: The Conditions of Unconditional Forgiveness in Levinas and Jankélévitch," in *Vladimir Jankélévitch and the Question of Forgiveness*, ed. Alan Udoff (Lanham, Md.: Lexington Books, 2013), 87.

8. What Remains

1. John Caputo, *The Weakness of God: A Theology of the Event* (Bloomington: Indiana University Press, 2006), 185. In chapters 9 and 10, Caputo offers an insightful discussion of the constellation of problems that I address in this chapter.
2. Avishai Margalit, *The Ethics of Memory* (Cambridge, Mass.: Harvard University Press, 2002), 183.
3. Ibid., 184.
4. Ibid., 185–86.

5. "Grosse, glühende, wölbung / mit dem sich/hinaus- und hinweg / wühlenden Schwarzgestirn-Schwarm: / der verkieselten Stirn eines Widders / brenn ich dies Bild ein, zwischen / die Hörner, darin, / im Gesang der Windungen, das / Mark der geronnenen/Herzmeere schwillt. / Wo gegen rennt er nicht an? / Die Welt ist fort, ich muß dich tragen." ("Vast, glowing vault / with the swarm of / black stars pushing them- / selves out and away: / onto a ram's silicified forehead / I brand this image, between / the horns, in which, / in the song of the whorls, the / marrow of melted / heart-oceans swells. In- / to what / does he not charge? / The world is gone, I must carry you.") This English translation is by Michael Hamburger, quoted in Jacques Derrida, "Rams: Uninterrupted Dialogue—Between Two Infinities, the Poem," in *Sovereignties in Question: The Poetics of Paul Celan*, ed. Thomas Dutoit and Outi Pasanen (New York: Fordham University Press, 2005), 141.

6. Derrida, "Rams," 156.

7. Ibid., 160.

8. Ibid., 158.

9. Ibid., 159. Cf. Levinas's use of the metaphor of maternity in conjunction with substitution in *Otherwise Than Being, or Beyond Essence*, trans. Alphonso Lingis (Pittsburgh: Duquesne University Press, 1998), 75–76.

10. Ibid.

11. Ibid., 160.

12. Ibid., 161.

13. Margalit, *Ethics of Memory*, 191.

14. For this list, I have followed Miroslav Volf, *Free of Charge: Giving and Forgiving in a Culture Stripped of Grace* (Grand Rapids, MI: Zondervan, 2005), 142–43. For an excellent theological treatise on forgiveness and its cultural and social implications see also Volf's book *Exclusion and Embrace: A Theological Exploration of Identity, Otherness, and Reconciliation* (Nashville: Abingdon Press, 1996).

15. Margalit, *Ethics of Memory*, 188–89.

16. Ibid., 193.

17. Ibid., 205.

18. Ibid., 209.

19. Ibid., 202, 204.

20. Ibid., 205–6. Cf. 196–97. Margalit's repeated emphasis on the restorative aim of forgiveness follows the biblical scheme of the relation between God and his people. It also represents for him the difference between forgiveness and gift giving. On the one hand, he portrays the duties involved in forgiveness as similar to the duties involved in exchanging gifts. In an interesting turn of giver and receiver, he compares the obligation to forgive with the obligation to accept a gift, writing that "rejecting a sincere plea for forgiveness is like rejecting a gift," which one should not do "unless there is good reason to reject it" (196). On the other hand, he argues that, whereas the practice of gift exchange following Marcel Mauss is intended "to form or strengthen social ties," forgiveness seeks to restore a rela-

tion to its previous state (195–96). In Margalit's view, the gift is thus both initiatory and progressive, while forgiveness is restorative.

21. Ibid., 208.

22. Vladimir Jankélévitch, *Forgiveness*, trans. Andrew Kelley (Chicago: University of Chicago Press, 2005), 150–51.

23. Paul Ricoeur, *Memory, History, Forgetting*, trans. Kathleen Blamey and David Pellauer (Chicago: University of Chicago Press, 2004), 457–59.

24. Jankélévitch, *Forgiveness*, 98.

25. Ibid., 48.

26. Ibid.; emphasis added. Cf. Vladimir Jankélévitch and Béatrice Berlowitz, *Quelque part dans l'inachevé* (Paris: Gallimard, 1978), 91–92.

27. Jankélévitch, *Forgiveness*, 48.

28. Ibid., 164.

29. Ibid., 142. Jankélévitch's argument is similar to a line of argumentation of Christian nominalists, such as Peter Damian (1007–1072), in the early medieval debates over God's power in the world. As Caputo summarizes, "God has the power to annul the past just so long as that would be *good*" (*Weakness of God*, 187).

30. Jankélévitch, *Forgiveness*, 142, 153.

31. Ibid., 145.

32. Ibid., 153.

33. Robert Gibbs, *Why Ethics? Signs of Responsibility* (Princeton, N.J.: Princeton University Press, 2000), 340.

34. Jankélévitch, *Forgiveness*, 154.

35. Søren Kierkegaard, *Works of Love*, ed. and trans. Howard V. Hong and Edna H. Hong (Princeton, N.J.: Princeton University Press, 1995), 296

36. John Caputo, *Against Ethics: Contributions to a Poetics of Obligation with Constant Reference to Deconstruction* (Bloomington: Indiana University Press, 1993), 111.

37. See, e.g., Jankélévitch, *Forgiveness*, 152.

38. Ibid., 153.

39. Ibid., 154.

40. Ibid., 152.

41. Emmanuel Levinas, *Existence and Existents* (Pittsburgh: Duquesne University Press, 1978), 85–86; 91. For a commentary on this topic in Levinas, see Klaus-M. Koldalle, "Lévinas' Beitrag zu einer philosophischen Theorie der Verzeihung," in *Gottesgabe: Vom Geben und Nehmen im Kontext gelebter Religion*, ed. Michael Biehl and Amélé Adamavi-Aho Ekué (Frankfurt a.M.: Lembeck, 2005), 323–46, esp. 332–34. Robert Spaemann also highlights how forgiveness provides a requisite break with identity in *Glück und Wohlwollen: Versuch über Ethik* (Stuttgart: Klett-Cotta 1989), 239–54, esp. 241–46. Cf. also Knut Berner, "Vergessen—Verzeihen—Eingedenken: Das Gedächtnis als Thema theologischer Anthropologie," *Berliner Theologische Zeitschrift* 23, no. 1 (2006): esp. 40–41.

42. Jankélévitch, *Forgiveness*, 154.

43. Ibid., 157.
44. Ibid., 154.
45. Jacques Derrida, *On Cosmopolitanism and Forgiveness*, trans. Mark Dooley and Michael Hughes (London: Routledge, 2002), 32.
46. Jankélévitch, *Forgiveness*, 152–53.
47. Ibid., 155.
48. Ibid.
49. Ibid., 156. Cf. Jankélévitch and Berlowitz, *Quelque part dans l'inachevé*, 125.
50. Jankélévitch, *Forgiveness*, 164.
51. Ibid. See also Nicholas of Cusa's *On Learned Ignorance. Nicholas of Cusa on Learned Ignorance: A Translation and an Appraisal of De Docta Ignorantia*, trans. Jasper Hopkins (Minneapolis: A. J. Banning Press, 1985).
52. Jankélévitch, *Forgiveness*, 163.
53. Ibid., 142.
54. Vladimir Jankélévitch, *L'Irréversible et la nostalgie* (Paris: Flammarion, 1983), 237–39. See also Vladimir Jankélévitch, *La Mort* (Paris: Flammarion, 1977), 337.
55. Ricoeur, *Memory, History, Forgetting*, 486, esp. 602n35.
56. Caputo, *Weakness of God*, 183.
57. Emmanuel Levinas, *Totality and Infinity: An Essay on Exteriority*, trans. Alphonso Lingis (Pittsburgh: Duquesne University Press, 1969), 283.
58. Ibid., 284.
59. See Kodalle, "Levinas' Beitrag zu einer philosophischen Theorie der Verzeihung," 334–35.
60. Jankélévitch, *Forgiveness*, 149.
61. Caputo, *Weakness of God*, 231. Cf. Spaemann, *Glück und Wohlwollen*, esp. 242–45.
62. See, e.g., Emmanuel Levinas, *Time and the Other*, trans. Richard A. Cohen (Pittsburgh: Duquesne University Press, 1987), 82.
63. Gibbs, *Why Ethics?* 350.
64. Cf. ibid., and Kodalle, "Levinas' Beitrag zu einer philosophischen Theorie der Verzeihung," 332–33. For a more thorough analysis of the ethical task of historians, see Edith Wyschogrod, *An Ethics of Remembering: History, Heterology, and the Nameless Others* (Chicago: University of Chicago Press, 1998).
65. Levinas, *Existence and Existents*, 97.
66. Levinas, *Totality and Inifinity*, 284. See also idem, "Transcendence and Evil," in *The Phenomenology of Man and of the Human Condition*, Analecta Husserliana, 14, ed. A.-T. Tymieniecka, trans.Alphonso Lingis (Dordrecht: D. Reidel, 1983), 164.
67. Levinas, "Transcendence and Evil," 164. See also, e.g., *Otherwise Than Being*, 126.
68. Levinas, *Totality and Infinity*, 283; emphasis added.
69. Ibid., 282–83.

70. Alphonso Lingis, "Translator's Introduction," in *Existence and Existents*, 25–26.

71. Jankélévitch, *Forgiveness*, 150; Levinas, *Totality and Infinity*, 283.

72. Levinas, *Totality and Infinity*, 283.

73. Jankélévitch, *Forgiveness*, 150; emphasis added.

74. Ibid., 152.

75. Vladimir Jankélévitch, "Jankélévitch, la pensée éclair," interview with Jean-Pierre Barou and Robert Maggiori, *Libération*, June 8 and 9, 1985: *"Je pense à cette phrase grave et terrible: Le pardon est mort dans les camps de la mort."* V.J.: Qui a dit cela? *Vous.* V.J.: Oui . . . Il ne devrait pas mourir. Le pardon ne peut pas mourir.

76. Cf. Jankélévitch and Berlowitz, *Quelque part dans l'inachevé*, 126.

Bibliography

Works by Vladimir Jankélévitch

Jankélévitch, Vladimir. *L'Austérité et la vie morale*. In *Philosophie morale*, 375–582. Paris: Flammarion, 1998.

———. *Cours de philosophie morale: Université libre de Bruxelles 1962–1963*. Paris: Éditions du Seuil, 2006.

———. "Difficultés du pardon: Entretien avec le Professeur Jankélévitch." Interview with Renée de Tryon-Montalembert. *La Vie spirituelle* 619 (March 1977): 180–99.

———. "Do Not Listen to What They Say, Look at What They Do." Translated by Ann Hobart. *Critical Inquiry* 22, no. 3 (1996): 349–51. ["N'écoutez pas ce qui'ils disent, regardez ce qui'ils font." In *Premières et dernières pages*, 82–84. Paris: Seuil, 1994.]

———. *Forgiveness*. Translated by Andrew Kelley. Chicago: University of Chicago Press, 2005. [*Le Pardon*. In *Philosophie morale*, 993–1149. Paris: Flammarion, 1998.]

———. *Henri Bergson*. 1931. Republished in 1959 and 1999. 4th ed. Paris: Presses Universitaires de France, 2008.

———. *L'Irréversible et la nostalgie*. Paris: Flammarion, 1983.

———. *Le Je-ne-sais-quoi et le Presque-rien* I. Paris: Éditions du Seuil, 1980.

———. "Jankélévitch, la pensée éclair." Interview with Jean-Pierre Barou and Robert Maggiori. *Libération*, June 8 and 9, 1985.

———. *La Mauvaise conscience*. In *Philosophie morale*, 32–202. Paris: Flammarion, 1998.

———. *La Mort*. Paris: Flammarion, 1977.

———. *Du Mensonge*. In *Philosophie morale*, 203–88. Paris: Flammarion, 1998.

———. *Music and the Ineffable*. Translated by Carolyn Abbate. Princeton: Princeton University Press, 2003. [*La Musique et l'Ineffable*. Paris: Éditions du Seuil, 1961.]

———. *L'Odyssée de la conscience dans la dernière philosophie de Schelling*. 1933. 2nd ed. Paris: Editions L'Hartmattan, 2005.

———. "Orkan der Gewalt." Translated by Ulrich Kunzmann. *Sinn und Form* 53 (2001): 725–41.

———. *Le Paradoxe de la morale*. Paris: Éditions du Seuil, 1981.

———. *Penser la mort?* Paris: Liana Levi, 1994.

———. *Philosophie premiére: Introduction à une philosophie du "presque."* 2nd ed. Paris: Quadrige/Presses Univeritaires de France, 1986.

———. *Premières et dernières pages*. Paris: Seuil, 1994.

———. "Le Presque-rien." *Bulletin de la Société française de Philosophie* 48, no. 3 (1954): 65–95.

———. *Le Pur et l'impur*. Paris: Flammarion, 1960.

———. *Quelque Part dans l'inachevé* (with Béatrice Berlowitz). Paris: Gallimard, 1978.

———. "Should We Pardon Them?" Translated by Ann Hobart. *Critical Inquiry* 22, no. 3 (1996): 552–72. ["Pardonner?" In *L'Iimprescriptible*. Paris: Éditions du Seuil, 1986.]

———. *Traité des vertus*, vol. 2: *Les Vertus et l'amour*. Paris: Flammarion, 1986.

———. *Traité des vertus*, vol. 3: *L'Innocence et la méchanceté*. Paris: Bordas, 1972.

Other Works

Adorno, Theodor W. *Minima Moralia: Reflexionen aus dem beschädigten Leben*. Frankfurt a.M.: Suhrkamp, 2001.

Agamben, Giorgio. *Homo Sacer: Sovereign Power and Bare Life*. Translated by Daniel Heller Roazen. Stanford: Stanford University Press, 1998.

———. *Remnants of Auschwitz: The Witness and the Archive*. Translated by Daniel Heller-Roazen. New York: Zone Books, 2002.

———. *State of Exception*. Translated by Kevin Attell. Chicago: University of Chicago Press, 2005.

———. *The Time That Remains: A Commentary on the Letter to the Romans*. Translated by Patricia Dailey. Stanford: Stanford University Press, 2005.

Altwegg, Jürg. "Kein Vergessen, kein Verstehen, kein Verzeihen—Vladimir Jankélévitch und die Deutschen." In *Das Verzeihen: Essays zur Moral und Kulturphilosphie*, edited by Ralf Konersmann and translated by Claudia Brede-Konersmann. Frankfurt am Main: Suhrkamp Verlag, 2003.

Améry, Jean. *Jenseits von Schuld und Sühne: Bewältigungsversuche eines Überwältigten*. Stuttgart: Klett-Cotta, 1977.

Aquinas, Thomas. *Summa contra gentiles*. Translated by Vernon J. Bourke. New York: Doubleday Edition, 1955–57.

Arendt, Hannah. *Denktagebuch*. Vol. 1. Edited by Ursula Ludz. Munich: Piper, 2002.

———. *Eichmann in Jerusalem: A Report on the Banality of Evil*. New York: Penguin Books, 1994.

———. *Hannah Arendt/Karl Jaspers. Briefwechsel 1926–1969*. Edited by Lotte Köhler and Hans Saner. Munich: Piper, 1985.

———. *Hannah Arendt/Karl Jaspers: Correspondence 1926–1969*. Edited by Lotte Kohler and Hans Saner. Translated by Robert Kimber and Rita Kimber. New York: Harcourt, 1992.

———. *The Human Condition*. Chicago: University of Chicago Press, 1989.

———. *The Origins of Totalitarianism*. New York: Harcourt, 1973.

———. *Responsibility and Judgment*. Edited by Jerome Kohn. New York: Schocken Books, 2003.

Aristotle. *Metaphysics: Gamma, Delta, Epsilon, Bks. 4–6*. 2nd ed. Translated by Christopher Kirwan. Oxford: Oxford University Press, 1993.

———. *Nicomachean Ethics*. 2nd ed. Translated by Terence Irwin. Indianapolis: Hackett, 1999.

———. *Physics*. Vol. 1, bks.1–4. Rev. ed. Translated by P. H. Wicksteed and F. M. Cornford. Cambridge, Mass.: Harvard University Press, 1986.

———. *Poetics*. Translated by S. H. Butler. Mineola, N.Y.: Dover, 1997.

———. *Rhetoric*. Translated by W. Rhys Roberts. Mineola, N.Y.: Dover, 2004.

Aubriot, Danièle. "Quelques Réflexions sur le pardon en Grèce Ancienne." In *Le Pardon: Acts du Colloque organizé par le Centre Histoire des Idées Université de Picardie*, edited by Michel Perrin, 11–27. Paris: Beauchesne 1987.

Augsburger, David. *Helping People Forgive*. Louisville, Ky.: Westminster John Knox Press, 1996.

Augustine. *Ce moribus ecclesiae catholicae et de moribus manichaeorum*. In *Opera/Augustinus*, vol. 25. Edited by Johannes Brachtendorf. Paderborn: Schöningh, 2004.

———. *The City of God*. Translated by Marcus Dods. New York: Modern Library, 2000.

———. *Confessions*. Translated by Henry Chadwick. Oxford: Oxford University Press, 1992.

———. *The Enchiridion*. Translated by J. F. Shaw, http://www.leaderu.com/cyber/books/augenchiridion/enchiridiontoc.html.

———. *The Nicene and Post Nicene Fathers*, vol. 8: *St. Augustine: Expositions on the Book of Psalms*. Edited by Philip Schaff. Translated by A. Cleveland Coxe. Grand Rapids, Mich.: Wm. B. Eerdmans, 1980. [*Enarrationes in Psalmo: 51–100* in *Aureli Augustini Opera* 10, 2. Edited by Eligius Dekkers and Johannes Fraipont. Turnhout: Brepols, 1956.]

———. *On the Free Choice of the Will, On Grace and Free Choice, and Other Writings*. Edited and translated by Peter King. Cambridge: Cambridge University Press, 2010.

Aurelius, Marcus. *Meditations*. Translated by Martin Hammond. London: Penguin Books, 2006.

Austin, J. L. *How to Do Things with Words.* Cambridge, Mass.: Harvard University Press, 1962.

———. "Performative-Constative." In *The Philosophy of Language*, edited by J. R. Searle. Oxford: Oxford University Press, 1977.

Benjamin, Walter. *The Arcades Project.* Translated by Howard Eiland and Kevin McLaughlin. Cambridge, Mass.: Belknap Press of Harvard University Press, 1999. [*Gesammelte Werke*, vol. 5: *Das Passagenwerk.* Edited by Rolf Tiedemann and Hermann Schweppenhäuser. Frankfurt am Main: Suhrkamp, 1991.]

———. *Charles Baudelaire: A Lyric Poet in the Era of High Capitalism.* Translated by Harry Zohn. London: Verso, 1973.

———. "On the Concept of History." Internet publication at the Trinity and All Saints College website: Faculty of Media, Lloyd Spencer. [*Über den Begriff der Geschichte*, in *Werke und Nachlass*, vol. 19. Edited by Christoph Gödde and Gérard Raulet. Frankfurt a. M.: Suhrkamp, 2010.]

———. *Zur Kritik der Gewalt und andere Aufsätze.* Frankfurt am Main: Suhrkamp, 1965. ["Critique of Violence." In *Reflections: Essays, Aphorisms, Autobiographical Writings*, edited by Peter Demetz. New York: Schocken, 1986.]

Benveniste, Émile. "Gift and Exchange in the Indo-European Vocabulary." In *The Logic of the Gift: Toward an Ethic of Generosity*, edited by Alan Schrift, 33–42. New York: Routledge, 1997.

Bergson, Henri. *The Two Sources of Morality and Religion.* Translated by R. Ashley Audra and Cloudesley Brereton. Notre Dame, Ind.: University of Notre Dame Press, 1954.

Bernasconi, Robert. "Travelling Light: The Conditions of Unconditional Forgiveness in Levinas and Jankélévitch." In *Vladimir Jankélévitch and the Question of Forgiveness*, edited by Alan Udoff, 85–96. Lanham, Md.: Lexington Books, 2013.

Berner, Knut. "Vergessen—Verzeihen—Eingedenken: Das Gedächtnis als Thema theologischer Anthropologie." *Berliner Theologische Zeitschrift* (*BThZ*) 23, no. 1 (2006): 26–42.

Bernstein, Richard. *Radical Evil: A Philosophical Interrogation.* Cambridge, UK: Polity Press, 2007.

Bittner, Rüdiger. "Is It Reasonable to Regret Things One Did?" *Journal of Philosophy* 89, no. 5 (1992): 262–73.

Blanchot, Maurice. "Sade." In *The Marquis de Sade*, edited and translated by Richard Seaver and Austryn Wainhouse, 37–72. New York: Grove Press, 1965.

Bloechl, Jeffrey. "Forgiveness and Its Limits: An Essay on Vladimir Jankélévitch." In *Vladimir Jankélévitch and the Question of Forgiveness*, edited by Alan Udoff, 97–110. Lanham, Md.: Lexington Books, 2013.

Boorstin, Daniel. *The Seekers: The Story of Man's Continuing Quest to Understand His World.* New York: Random House, 1998.

Brudholm, Thomas. *Resentment's Virtue: Jean Améry and the Refusal to Forgive.* Philadelphia: Temple University Press, 2008.

Butler, Joseph. *Fifteen Sermons Preached at the Rolls Chapel 1827.* Milton Keynes, UK: Dodo Press.
Butler, Judith. *Giving an Account of Oneself.* New York: Fordham University Press, 2005.
Caputo, John. *Against Ethics: Contributions to a Poetics of Obligation with Constant Reference to Deconstruction.* Bloomington: Indiana University Press, 1993.
———. *The Weakness of God: A Theology of the Event.* Bloomington: Indiana University Press, 2006.
Chalier, Catherine. "The Great Distress." In *Vladimir Jankélévitch and the Question of Forgiveness*, edited by Alan Udoff. Lanham, Md.: Lexington Books, 2013.
Dan-Cohen, Meir. "Revising the Past: On the Metaphysics of Repentance, Forgiveness, and Pardon." In *Forgiveness, Mercy, and Clemency*, edited by Austin Sarat and Nasser Hussain, 117–37. Stanford: Stanford University Press, 2007.
Davidson, Arnold. "Introductory Remarks." *Critical Inquiry* 22, no. 3 (1996): 545–48.
Delooz, Thierry. "L'Irréversible, l'irréparable et la 'futurition' selon Vladimir Jankélévitch." *Bulletin de Littérature Ecclésiastique* 107, no. 2 (2006): 243–46.
Derrida, Jacques. *Adieu: To Emmanuel Levinas.* Translated by Pascale-Anne Brault and Michael Naas. Stanford: Stanford University Press, 1997.
———. *Dissemination.* Translated by Barbara Johnson. Chicago: University of Chicago Press, 1981.
———. "Force of Law: The 'Mystical Foundation of Authority.'" In *Acts of Religion*, edited by Gil Anidjar, 230–98. New York: Routledge, 2002.
———. *For What Tomorrow . . . A Dialogue* (with Elisabeth Roudinesco). Translated by Jeff Fort. Stanford: Stanford University Press, 2004.
———. *The Gift of Death.* Translated by David Wills. Chicago: University of Chicago Press, 1995.
———. *Given Time: I. Counterfeit Money.* Translated by Peggy Kamuf. Chicago: University of Chicago Press, 1992.
———. "Hostipitality." In *Acts of Religion*, edited by Gil Anidjar, 358–420. New York: Routledge, 2002.
———. "How to Avoid Speaking: Denials." Translated by Ken Frieden. In *Derrida and Negative Theology*, edited by Harold Coward and Toby Foshay, 73–143. Albany: State University of New York Press, 1992.
———. "Das Leben, das Überleben: Vom Ethos des Denkens und von der Chance des Europäischen Erbes." Interview with Jean Birnbaum. *Lettre International* 66, no. 3 (2004).
———. *On Cosmopolitanism and Forgiveness.* Translated by Mark Dooley and Michael Hughes. London: Routledge, 2002.
———. "On Forgiveness: A Roundtable Discussion with Jacques Derrida, moderated by Richard Kearney." In *Questioning God*, edited by John D. Caputo,

Mark Dooley, and Michael J. Scanlon. Bloomington: Indiana University Press, 2001.

———. *Politics of Friendship*. Translated by George Collins. London: Verso, 1997.

———. "Rams: Uninterrupted Dialogue—Between Two Infinities, the Poem." Translated by Thomas Dutoit and Philippe Romanski. In *Sovereignties in Question: The Poetics of Paul Celan*, edited by Thomas Dutoit and Outi Pasanen, 135–63. New York: Fordham University Press 2005.

———. *Rogues: Two Essays on Reason*. Translated by Pascale-Anne Brault and Michael Naas. Stanford: Stanford University Press, 2005.

———. *Specters of Marx: The State of the Debt, the Work of Mourning, and the New International*. Translated by Peggy Kamuf. New York: Routledge, 1994.

———. "To Forgive." In *Questioning God*, edited by John D. Caputo, Mark Dooley, and Michael J. Scanlon. Bloomington: Indiana University Press, 2001.

———. "Violence and Metaphysics: An Essay on the Thought of Emmanuel Levinas." In *Writing and Difference*, translated by Alan Bass, 79–153. Chicago: University of Chicago Press, 1978.

———. *Without Alibi*. Edited and translated by Peggy Kamuf. Stanford: Stanford University Press, 2002.

Descartes, René. *The Passions of the Soul*. Translated by Stephen H. Voss. Indianapolis: Hackett, 1989.

De Sousa, Ronald. *The Rationality of Emotion*. Boston: MIT Press, 1987.

Epictetus. *Epictetus, The Discourses as Reported by Arrian, the Manual, and the Fragments*, 2 vols. 2nd ed. Translated by W. A. Oldfather. London: William Heinemann, 1959.

———. *Handbook of Epictetus*. Translated and edited by Nicholas P. White. Indianapolis: Hackett, 1983.

Erdmann, J. E. "Vom Vergessen." In *Ernste Spiele: Vortraege*, 323–45. Berlin, 1875.

Eriksen, Niels Nymann. *Kierkegaard's Category of Repetition: A Reconstruction*. Berlin: Walter de Gruyter, 2000.

Esser, Albert. *Das Phänomen Reue: Versuch einer Erhellung ihres Selbstverständnisses*. Cologne: Hegner, 1963.

Fackenheim, Emil. *God's Presence in History: Jewish Affirmations and Philosophical Reflections after Auschwitz*. New York: New York University Press, 1970.

Fénelon, François de Salignac de la Mothe. *Fénelon: Selected Writings*. Edited and translated by Chad Helms. Mahwah, N.J.: Paulist Press, 2006.

———. *Oeuvres*, 2 vols. Paris: Gallimard, 1983.

Fritsch, Matthias. *The Promise of Memory: History and Politics in Marx, Benjamin, and Derrida*. Albany: State University of New York Press, 2005.

Gibbs, Robert. "Returning/Forgiving." In *Questioning God*, edited by John D. Caputo, Mark Dooley, and Michael J. Scanlon, 73–91. Bloomington: Indiana University Press, 2001.

———. *Why Ethics? Signs of Responsibility*. Princeton, N.J.: Princeton University Press, 2000.

Girard, René. *Violence and the Sacred*. Translated by Patrick Gregory. Baltimore: Johns Hopkins University Press, 1979.

Goethe, Johann Wolfgang von. "An Grafen Paar." In *Goethes Sämtliche Werke*, vol. 3. Stuttgart: Cottasche Jubiläumsausgabe, 1902.

Gouhier, Alain. "Le Temps de l'impardonnable et le temps du pardon selon Jankélévitch." In *Le Point theologique, Forgiveness*, edited by Michel Perrin, 269–82. Paris: Beauchesnes, 1987.

Govier, Trudy. *Forgiveness and Revenge*. London: Routledge, 2002.

Gregory of Nyssa. *De virginitate*. In *Opera* VIII/I. Edited by Werner Jaeger. Leiden: Brill, 1952.

Griswold, Charles. *Forgiveness: A Philosophical Exploration*. New York: Cambridge University Press, 2007.

Grodin, Jean. *Von Heidegger zu Gadamer: Unterwegs zur Hermeneutik*. Darmstadt: Wissenschaftliche Buchgesellschaft, 2001.

Haber, Joram Graf. *Forgiveness: A Philosophical Study*. Lanham, Md.: Rowman and Littlefield, 1991.

Hadot, Pierre. *Philosophy as a Way of Life*. Translated by Michael Chase. Oxford: Blackwell, 1995.

Hansel, Joëlle. "*Forgiveness* and 'Should We Pardon Them?' The Pardon and The Imprescriptible." In *Vladimir Jankélévitch and the Question of Forgiveness*, edited by Alan Udoff, 111–25. Lanham, Md.: Lexington Books, 2013.

Hartmann, Nicolai. *Ethik*. 4th ed. Berlin: Walter de Gruyter, 1962.

Hegel, G. W. F. *Introduction to the Lectures on the Philosophy of World History*. Translated by H. B. Nisbet. Cambridge: Cambridge University Press, 1975.

———. *Lectures on the Philosophy of Religion*. Translated by R. F. Brown, P. C. Hodgson, and J. M. Stewart. Berkeley: University of California Press, 1988.

———. *Phenomenology of Mind*. Translated by J. B. Baillie. Mineola, N.Y.: Dover, 2003. [*Phänomenologie des Geistes*. Frankfurt a.M.: Suhrkamp, 1988.]

Heidegger, Martin. *Being and Time*. Translated by Joan Stambaugh. Albany: State University of New York Press, 1996. [*Sein und Zeit*, 17th ed. Tübingen: Max Niemeyer Verlag, 1993.]

———. *Introduction to Metaphysics*. Translated by Gregory Fried and Richard Polt. New Haven: Yale University Press, 2000. [*Einführung in die Metaphysik*. Tübingen: Max Niemeyer Verlag, 1987.]

Heitsch, Ernst. *Aidesis im Attischen Strafrecht*. Mainz: Akademie der Wissenschaften und der Literatur, 1984.

Holmgren, M. R. "Forgiveness and the Intrinsic Value of Persons." *American Philosophical Quarterly* 30, no. 4 (1993): 341–52.

Horkheimer, Max, and Theodor Adorno. *Dialectic of Enlightenment: Philosophical Fragments*. Edited by Guenzlin Schmid Noerr. Translated by Edmund Jephcott. Stanford: Stanford University Press, 2007.

Humphrey, Edith. "And I Shall Heal Them: Repentance, Turning, and Penitence in the Johannine Writings." In *Repentance in Christian Theology*, edited by Mark Boda and Gordon Smith. Collegeville, Minn.: Liturgical Press, 2006.

Jaspers, Karl. *The Question of German Guilt*. Translated by E. B. Ashton. New York: Fordham University Press, 2000.

Jerphagnon, Lucien. *Ahnen und Wollen: Vladimir Jankélévitch*. Translated by Jürgen Brankel. Vienna: Turia + Kant, 2009.

Judaken, Jonathan. "Vladimir Jankélévitch at the *Colloques des intellectuels juifs de langue française*." In *Vladimir Jankélévitch and the Question of Forgiveness*, edited by Alan Udoff, 3–26. Lanham, Md.: Lexington Books, 2013.

Kant, Immanuel. *Critique of Practical Reason*. Translated by Thomas Kingsmill Abbott. Mineola, N.Y.: Dover, 2004.

———. *Critique of Pure Reason*. In *The Cambridge Edition of the Works of Immanuel Kant,* translated by Paul Guyer and Allen W. Wood. Cambridge: Cambridge University Press, 1999.

———. *Groundwork for the Metaphysics of Morals*. Edited and translated by Allen W. Wood. New Haven: Yale University Press, 2002.

———. *Kant Werke*. 6 vols. Darmstadt: Wissenschaftliche Buchgesellschaft, 1998.

———. *Religion within the Limits of Reason Alone*. Translated by Theodore M. Greene and Hoyt H. Hudson. New York: Harper and Row, 1960.

Kaufmann, Walter. *Nietzsche: Philosopher, Psychologist, Antichrist*. New York: Random House, 1968.

Kelley, Andrew. "Jankélévitch and the Metaphysics of Forgiveness." In *Vladimir Jankélévitch and the Question of Forgiveness,* edited by Alan Udoff, 27–46. Lanham, Md.: Lexington Books, 2013.

———. "Translator's Introduction." In *Forgiveness*, 7–27. Chicago: University of Chicago Press, 2005.

Kierkegaard, Søren. *Either/Or II*. Edited and translated by Howard Hong and Edna Hong. Princeton, N.J.: Princeton University Press, 1990.

———. *Fear and Trembling* and *Repetition*. Edited and translated by Howard V. Hong and Edna H. Hong. Princeton, N.J.: Princeton University Press, 1983.

———. *Philosophical Fragments*. Edited and translated by Howard V. Hong and Edna H. Hong. Princeton, N.J.: Princeton University Press, 1985.

———. *The Present Age*. Translated by Alexander Dru. London: Collins Fontana Library, 1962.

———. *Sickness unto Death: A Christian Psychological Exposition for Upbuilding and Awakening*. Edited and translated by Howard V. Hong and Edna H. Hong. Princeton, N.J.: Princeton University Press, 1983.

———. *Stages on Life's Way: Studies by Various Persons*. Edited and translated by Howard Hong and Edna Hong. Princeton, N.J.: Princeton University Press, 1988.

———. *Two Ages: The Age of Revolution and The Present Age. A Literary Review*. Edited by and translated by Howard V. Hong and Edna H. Hong. Princeton, N.J.: Princeton University Press, 1978.

———. *Upbuilding Discourses in Various Spirits.* Edited and translated by Howard V. Hong and Edna H. Hong. Princeton, N.J.: Princeton University Press, 2009.

———. *Works of Love.* Edited and translated by Howard V. Hong and Edna H. Hong. Princeton, N.J.: Princeton University Press, 1995.

Kleinberg, Ethan. "To Atone and to Forgive: Jaspers, Jankélévitch/Derrida, and the Possibility of Forgiveness." In *Vladimir Jankélévitch and the Question of Forgiveness*, edited by Alan Udoff, 143–58. Lanham, Md.: Lexington Books, 2013.

Kodalle, Klaus-Michael. "Die Dimension des Unermesslichen: Aufhebung der vermessenen Moralität." In *Cognitio humana—Dynamik des Wissens und der Werte*, 106–30. Vorträge und Kolloquien/XVII. Deutscher Kongress für Philosophie, Leipzig, 23–27. September 1996. Edited by Christoph Hubig. Berlin: Akad. Verl., 1997.

———. "Diesseits der Logik des Moralismus: Vom 'Geist' der Verzeihung bei Kierkegaard, Nietzsche-Scheler, Dostojewski und Camus." In *Kierkegaard Revisited*, 387–409. Berlin: Walter de Gruyter, 1997.

———. "Lévinas' Beitrag zu einer philosophischen Theorie der Verzeihung." In *Gottesgabe: Vom Geben und Nehmen im Kontext gelebter Religion*, edited by Michael Biehl and Amélé Adamavi-Aho Ekué, 323–46. Frankfurt a.M.: Lembeck, 2005.

Kolnai, Aurel. "Forgiveness." In *Proceedings of the Aristotelian Society* (1974): 91–106.

Kopper, Joachim. "Kants synthetisch-praktischer Satz a priori und Jankélévitchs Verständnis der Vergebung." *Kant-Studien* 61 (1970): 238–47.

Lacan, Jacques. *Ecrits.* Paris: Le Seuil, 1966.

Leibniz, Gottfried Wilhelm. "Principles of Nature and Grace." 2nd ed. In *Philosophical Works*. Edited and translated by George Martin Duncan. New Haven: Tuttle, Morehouse, and Taylor, 1908.

———. *Theodicy.* Edited by Austin Farrar. Translated by E. M. Huggard. La Salle, Ill.: Open Court, 1988.

Lemcke, Verena. *Der Begriff Verzeihen bei Vladimir Jankélévitch.* Würzburg: Königshausen and Neumann, 2008.

Levi, Primo. *Survival in Auschwitz.* Translated by Stuart Woolf. New York: Touchstone, 1996.

Levinas, Emmanuel. *Difficult Freedom: Essays on Judaism.* Translated by Seán Hand. Baltimore: Johns Hopkins University Press, 1990.

———. *Entre Nous.* Translated by Michael B. Smith and Barbara Harshav. New York: Columbia University Press, 1998.

———. *Existence and Existents.* Translated by Alphonso Lingis. Pittsburgh: Duquesne University Press, 1978.

———. *Nine Talmudic Readings.* Translated by Annette Aronowicz. Bloomington: Indiana University Press, 1990.

———. *Otherwise Than Being, or Beyond Essence.* Translated by Alphonso Lingis. Pittsburgh: Duquesne University Press, 1998.

———. *Outside the Subject*. Translated by Michael B. Smith. Stanford: Stanford University Press, 1993.

———. "Reflections on the Philosophy of Hitlerism." Translated by Sean Hand. *Critical Inquiry* 17, no. 1 (1990): 62–71.

———. *Time and the Other*. Translated by Richard A. Cohen. Pittsburgh: Duquesne University Press, 1987.

———. *Totality and Infinity: An Essay on Exteriority*. Translated by Alphonso Lingis. Pittsburgh: Duquesne University Press, 1969.

———. "Transcendence and Evil." In *The Phenomenology of Man and of the Human Condition*. Analecta Husserliana, 14. Edited by A.-T. Tymieniecka. Translated by Alphonso Lingis. Dordrecht: D. Reidel, 1983.

———. "Useless Suffering." In *The Provocation of Levinas: Rethinking the Other*, edited by Robert Bernasconi and David Wood, translated by Richard Cohen, 156–67. New York: Routledge, 2002.

———. "Vorwort." In Stephane Moses, *System und Offenbarung: Die Philosophie Franz Rosenzweigs*, translated by Rainer Rochlitz, 10–18. Paderborn: Wilhelm Fink Verlag, 1985.

Lingis, Alphonso. "Translator's Introduction." In Emmanuel Levinas, *Existence and Existents*, xvii–xxvi. Pittsburgh: Duquesne University Press, 1978.

Löwith, Karl. *Von Hegel zu Nietzsche: Der revolutionäre Bruch im Denken des neunzehnten Jahrhunderts*. Stuttgart: Kohlhammer Verlag, 1953.

Luther, Martin. *Martin Luthers Werke: Kritische Gesamtausgabe*. Weimar: H. Böhlau, 1883–.

Lyotard, Jean-François. "Mainmise." Translated by Pascale-Anne Brault and Michael Naas. In *The Hyphen: Between Judaism and Christianity*, edited by Jean-François Lyotard and Eberhard Gruber. New York: Humanity Books, 1999.

Macho, Thomas. "Fragment über die Verzeihung." In *Zeitmitschrift*, 135–45. Düsseldorf: Bollmann, 1988.

Margalit, Avishai. *The Ethics of Memory*. Cambridge, Mass.: Harvard University Press, 2002.

Mauss, Marcel. *The Gift [Essai sur le don]*. Translated by W. D. Halls. Abingdon, UK: Routledge, 2002.

———. "Gift, Gift." Translated by Koen Decoster. In *The Logic of the Gift: Toward an Ethic of Generosity*, edited by Alan D. Schrift, 28–32. New York: Routledge, 1997.

McAleer, Graham J. "New Spartans: Jankélévitch, Scheler, and Tolkien on Vanity." In *Vladimir Jankélévitch and the Question of Forgiveness*, edited by Alan Udoff, 129–41. Lanham, Md.: Lexington Books, 2013.

McCord Adams, Marilyn. "Forgiveness: A Christian Model." *Faith and Philosophy* 8, no. 3 (July 1991): 277–304.

Metzler, Karin. *Der griechische Begriff des Verzeihens*. Tübingen: Mohr, 1991.

Milbank, John. *Being Reconciled: Ontology and Pardon*. London: Routledge, 2003.

———. "The Ethics of Honor and the Possibility of Promise." In *Vladimir Jankélévitch and the Question of Forgiveness*, edited by Alan Udoff, 161–90. Lanham, Md.: Lexington Books, 2013.

———. "Forgiveness and Incarnation." In *Questioning God*. edited by John D. Caputo, Mark Dooley, and Michael J. Scanlon, 92–128. Bloomington: Indiana University Press, 2001.

Milton, John. *Paradise Lost*. Edited by John Leonard. London: Penguin Classics, 2003.

Morris, Herbert. "Murphy on Forgiveness." *Criminal Justice Ethics* 7, no. 2 (1988): 15–19.

Murphy, Jeffrie, and Jean Hampton. *Forgiveness and Mercy*. Cambridge: Cambridge University Press, 1988.

———. "Forgiveness and Resentment." *Midwest Studies in Philosophy* 7, no. 1 (1982): 503–16.

———. *Getting Even: Forgiveness and Its Limits*. Oxford: Oxford University Press, 2003.

Nabert, Jean. *Essai sur le mal*. Paris: PUF, 1955.

Nancy, Jean-Luc. *The Experience of Freedom*. Translated by Bridget McDonald. Stanford: Stanford University Press, 1993.

Neiman, Susan. *Evil in Modern Thought: An Alternative History of Philosophy*. Princeton, N.J.: Princeton University Press, 2002.

Nerney, Gayne. "Aristotle and Aquinas on Indignation: From Nemesis to Theodicy." *Faith and Philosophy* 8, no. 1 (1991): 81–95.

Neusner, Jacob. "Repentance in Judaism." In *Repentance: A Comparative Perspective*, edited by Amitai Etzioni and David E. Carney. Lanham, Md.: Rowman and Littlefield, 1997.

Nicholas of Cusa. *De coniecturis*. In *Opera Omnia*, vol. 3. Edited by Josef Koch and Karl Bormann. Hamburg: Meiner Verlag, 1972.

———. *Nicholas of Cusa on Learned Ignorance: A Translation and an Appraisal of De Docta Ignorantia*. Translated by Jasper Hopkins. Minneapolis: A. J. Banning Press, 1985.

Nietzsche, Friedrich. *Beyond Good and Evil: Prelude to a Philosophy of the Future*. Translated by Judith Norman. Cambridge: Cambridge University Press, 2002.

———. *Ecce Homo*. Translated by Walter Kaufmann. New York: Random House, 1989.

———. *Friedrich Nietzsche: Werke in drei Bänden*. Darmstadt: Wissenschaftliche Buchgesellschaft, 1997.

———. *Human, All Too Human: A Book for Free Spirits*. Translated by R. J. Hollingdale. Cambridge: Cambridge University Press, 1996.

———. *On the Genealogy of Morals*. Translated by Walter Kaufmann and R. J. Hollingdale. New York: Random House, 1989.

———. "On the Uses and Disadvantages of History for Life." In *Untimely Meditations*, edited by Daniel Breazeale, translated by R. J. Hollingdale, 57–124. Cambridge: Cambridge University Press, 1997.

———. *Thus Spoke Zarathustra: A Book for All and None.* Translated by Adrian Del Caro and Robert B. Pippin. Cambridge: Cambridge University Press, 2006.

Nishitani, Keiji. *Religion and Nothingness.* Translated by Jan van Bragt. Berkeley: University of California Press, 1982.

Nussbaum, Martha. *The Therapy of Desire.* Princeton, N.J.: Princeton University Press, 1996.

———. *Upheavals of Thought: The Intelligence of Emotions.* Cambridge: Cambridge University Press, 2001.

Plato. *Sämtliche Werke.* 3 vols., Berlin Edition. Edited by Erich Loewenthal. Heidelberg: Lambert Schneider, 1982.

———. *The Works of Plato.* Translated by Benjamin Jowett. New York: Tudor, 1936.

Plotinus. *The Six Enneads of Plotinus.* Translated by Stephen MacKenna and B. S. Page. Charleston, S.C.: Forgotten Books, 2007.

Raveling, Wiard. "Lettres pour un pardon." *Magazine Littéraire* 333 (June 1995): 52–58.

———. "Über Vladimir Jankélévitch." *Sinn und Form* 49, no. 3 (1997): 328–38.

Ricoeur, Paul. *Amor et justice: Liebe und Gerechtigkeit.* Tübingen: J. C. B. Mohr (Paul Siebeck), 1990.

———. *Memory, History, Forgetting.* Translated by Kathleen Blamey and David Pellauer. Chicago: University of Chicago Press, 2004.

Romilly, Jacqueline de. *La Douceur dans la pensée grecque.* Paris: Hachette Littérature, 1995.

Rosenzweig, Franz. *The Star of Redemption.* Translated by Barbara E. Galli. Madison: University of Wisconsin Press, 2005. [*Der Stern der Erlösung.* Frankfurt a.M.: Suhrkamp, 1988.]

Safranski, Rüdiger. *Nietzsche: Biographie seines Denkens.* Frankfurt a.M.: Fischer Taschenbuch Verlag, 2002.

Sales, Saint François de. *Oeuvres.* Paris: Gallimard, 1969.

Sartre, Jean-Paul. *Being and Nothingness: A Phenomenological Essay on Ontology.* Translated by Hazel Barnes. New York: Washington Square Press, 1992.

Scheler, Max. *Formalism in Ethics and Non-Formal Ethics of Values.* Translated by M. Frings and R. Funk. Evanston, Ill.: Northwestern University Press, 1973.

———. "Love and Knowledge." In *On Feeling, Knowing, and Valuing: Selected Writings,* edited by Harold J. Bershady, 147–66. Chicago: University of Chicago Press, 1992.

———. "Repentance and Rebirth." In *Person and Self-Value: Three Essays.* Translated by M. S. Frings. Boston: Martinus Nijhoff, 1987. ["Reue und Wiedergeburt." In *Vom Ewigen im Menschen.* Bern: Francke Verlag, 1954.]

———. *Das Ressentiment im Aufbau der Moralen.* Frankfurt a.M.: Klostermann, 1978. [*Ressentiment.* Milwaukee: Marquette University Press, 2007.]

Schestow, Lew. *Spekulation und Offenbarung: Essays und kritische Betrachtungen.* Translated by Hans Ruoff. Hamburg: Heinrich Ellermann, 1963.
Schmitt, Carl. *Der Begriff des Politischen.* 7th ed. Berlin: Duncker & Humblot, 2002.
———. *Politische Theologie: Vier Kapitel zur Lehre von der Souveränität.* 7th ed. Berlin: Duncker & Humblot, 1996.
Scholem, Gershom. *The Messianic Idea in Judaism and Other Essays on Jewish Spirituality.* Translated by Michael Myer. New York: Schocken Books, 1971.
Schwab, Françoise. Foreword to Vladimir Jankélévitch, *Kann man den Tod denken?* Vienna: Turia + Kant, 2003.
———. "Vladimir Jankélévitch: Une âme résistante." *Bulletin de Littérature Ecclésiastique* 107, no. 2 (2006): 213–23.
Scotus, Duns. *Ordinatio.* In *Opera Omnia,* vol. 7. Edited by Carolus Balić, José Rodríguez Carballo, and Barnaba Hechich. Vatican City: Vatican Polyglot Press, 1973.
Seneca, Lucius Anneaus. *De Beneficiis.* In *L. Annaei Senecae Opera,* edited by Carolus Rudolphus Fickert. Lipsiae: Sumptibus Librariae Weidmannianae, 1843. [*On Benefits.* Translated by Aubrey Stewart, http://ancienthistory.about.com/library/bl/bl_text_seneca_benefits_i.htm.]
Shakespeare, William. *The Complete Works of Shakespeare.* 4th ed. Edited by David Bevington. New York: HarperCollins, 1992.
Silber, John. "The Ethical Significance of Kant's *Religion.*" In Immanuel Kant, *Religion within the Limits of Reason Alone,* translated by Theodore M. Greene and Hoyt H. Hudson, lxxix–cxxxv. New York: Harper & Row, 1960.
Simmel, Georg. *Der Begriff und die Tragödie der Kultur.* In *Gesamtausgabe,* vol. 14. Edited by Rüdiger Kramme and Otthein Rammstedt. Frankfurt a.M.: Suhrkamp, 1996.
———. *Einleitung in die Moralwissenschaft: Eine Kritik der ethischen Grundbegriffe,* vol. 2. In *Gesamtausgabe,* vol. 4. Edited by Otthein Rammstedt. Frankfurt a.M.: Suhrkamp, 1991.
Sloterdijk, Peter. *Derrida ein Ägypter: Über das Problem der jüdischen Pyramide.* Frankfurt a.M.: Suhrkamp, 2007.
Smith, Adam. *The Theory of Moral Sentiments.* Edited by D. D. Raphael and A. L. Macfie. Indianapolis: Liberty Press, 1982.
Soloveitchik, Joseph Dov. *On Repentance: The Thought and Oral Discourses of Rabbi Joseph Dov Soloveitchik.* Edited by Pinchas H. Peli. Lanham, Md: Rowman and Littlefield, 1996.
Spader, Peter. *Scheler's Ethical Personalism: Its Logic, Development, and Promise.* New York: Fordham University Press, 2002.
Spaemann, Robert. *Glück und Wohlwollen: Versuch über Ethik.* Stuttgart: Klett-Cotta, 1989.
———. *Der letzte Gottesbeweis.* Munich: Pattloch Verlag, 2007.

Spinoza, Baruch. *Ethics: Treatise on the Emendation of the Intellect and Selected Letters.* Edited by Seymour Feldman and translated by Samuel Shirley. Indianapolis: Hackett, 1992.

Steiner, Stephan. "Erinnern und Leben: Versuch zum Ort des Erinnerns bei Jean Améry." In *Kritik aus Passion: Studien zu Jean Améry*, edited by Matthias Bormuth and Susan Nurmi-Schomers. Göttingen: Wallstein Verlag, 2005.

Strawson, P. F. "Freedom and Resentment." In *Proceedings of the British Academy* 1962. London: Oxford University Press, 1963. Reprinted in *Freedom and Resentment and Other Essays*. London: Methuen, 1974.

Taubes, Jacob. *Abendländische Eschatologie*. Bern: Francke, 1947.

———. *The Political Theology of Paul*. Stanford: Stanford University Press, 2003.

Tilliette, Xavier. "Une Kitiège de l'âme: L'éthique de Vladimir Jankélévitch." *L'Arc* 75 (1979): 65–73.

Tück, Jan-Heiner. "Das Unverzeihbare verzeihen? Jankélévitch, Derrida und die Hoffnung wider alle Hoffnung." *Internationale Katholische Zeitschrift Communio* 33 (2004): 174–88. ["Unforgivable Forgiveness? Jankélévitch, Derrida and a Hope against All Hope." Translated by David C. Schindler. *International Catholic Review Communio* 31 (2004): 522–39.]

Tutu, Desmond. *No Future without Forgiveness*. New York: Doubleday, 1999.

Twambley, P. "Mercy and Forgiveness." *Analysis* 36, no. 2 (1976): 84–90.

Udoff, Alan. "'After Such Knowledge, What Forgiveness?' On Jankélévitch and the Question of Repentance." In *Vladimir Jankélévitch and the Question of Forgiveness*, edited by Alan Udoff, 191–217. Lanham, Md.: Lexington Books, 2013.

Volf, Miroslav. *Exclusion and Embrace: A Theological Exploration of Identity, Otherness, and Reconciliation*. Nashville, Tenn.: Abingdon Press, 1996.

———. "Forgiveness, Reconciliation, and Justice: A Christian Contribution to a More Peaceful Social Environment." In *Forgiveness and Reconciliation: Religion, Public Policy, and Conflict Transformation*, edited by Raymond G. Helmick, S.J., and Rodney L. Petersen. Philadelphia: Templeton Foundation Press, 2001.

———. *Free of Charge: Giving and Forgiving in a Culture Stripped of Grace*. Grand Rapids, Mich.: Zondervan, 2005.

Walsh, Sylvia. *Living Christianly: Kierkegaard's Dialectic of Christian Existence*. University Park: Pennsylvania State University Press, 2005.

Weil, Simone. *Gravity and Grace*. Translated by Emma Crawford and Mario von der Ruhr. London: Routledge, 2002.

Westphal, Merold. *Becoming a Self: A Reading of Kierkegaard's Concluding Unscientific Postscript*. West Lafayette, Ind.: Purdue University Press, 1995.

Wiesel, Elie. *From the Kingdom of Memory: Reminiscences*. New York: Schocken Books, 1990.

Williams, Bernard. *Moral Luck*. Cambridge: Cambridge University Press, 1981.

Wimmer, Reiner. *Kants kritische Religionsphilosophie*. Berlin: Walter de Gruyter, 1990.

———. *Religionsphilosophische Studien in lebenspraktischer Absicht*. Freiburg: Academic Press Fribourg, 2005.

Wolf, Ursula. *Aristoteles "Nikomachische Ethik."* Darmstadt: Wissenschaftliche Buchgesellschaft, 2002.

Wyschogrod, Edith. *An Ethics of Remembering: History, Heterology, and the Nameless Others*. Chicago: University of Chicago Press, 1998.

———. "Repentance and Forgiveness: The Undoing of Time." *International Journal for Philosophy of Religion* 60, nos. 1–3 (December 2006): 157–68.

Index

absurdity, 69, 90, 160, 163–64, 198–99, 267–68, 351n256
Adorno, Theodor W., 151, 200
Agamben, Giorgio, 128
almost nothing, 3, 12, 30–31, 37, 44, 205. See also *presque rien*
alterity, 26, 54, 58, 181, 228, 275–78, 322n79
Améry, Jean, 119, 122, 132–33, 153, 312nn114,122,124, 316nn185–86, 321nn60,62
amnesia, 91, 121, 164, 264
amnesty, 48, 70, 91, 121, 164, 174–75
apathy, 51–52
aphienai, 165, 265
apophatic method, 10, 45, 49, 71, 91, 205
aporia, 21; of forgiveness, 163, 188, 211; of the gift, 331n69; of morality, 11, 206
Aquinas, Thomas, 138–40
Arendt, Hannah, 146–59, 165, 175, 188, 199, 221, 317n4, 321nn60,63, 322n77, 324nn111,114, 344n85
Aristotle, 13, 27–29, 46, 53–55, 60–66, 74, 78, 80, 86, 94–97, 102, 104, 107, 113, 177–78, 181, 192, 209, 212–15, 220, 229, 232, 284n4, 295n85,

296nn92,96–97, 304nn8,10, 305nn17–18, 324n111, 329n18, 332n79, 338n33, 344n85
aseity: of forgiveness, 68, 269; of freedom, 145, 166; of love, 118, 185, 199
asymmetry: of forgiveness, 59, 269; of freedom, 87; of the gift, 193; between good and evil, 88, 157, 170–71; relation between reciprocity and, 201; of responsibility, 173
ataraxia, 51–52, 59
atonement, 156, 263; Day of, 224–25, 341n50. *See also* Yom Kippur
Aubriot, Danièle, 60, 70
Augustine, 17, 41, 69, 78, 82, 116, 138–43, 149, 152–53, 298n112, 299n128, 308n50, 315n175, 318n7
Aurelius, Marcus, 52, 293n43
Auschwitz, 8–9, 159, 161, 170, 321–22, 326, 358, 362, 365
Austin, J. L., 189–91
autonomy, 142, 154, 246, 250, 255

benevolence, 97–99, 101, 103, 185, 196–97, 306n29
Benjamin, Walter, 83, 292, 299, 301, 303, 329, 336

373

Benveniste, Émile, 304n5, 332n80
Bergson, Henri, 4, 6, 12, 28, 31, 34–38, 46, 179, 186–87, 243, 275, 289n87, 214–15n164, 323n111
Bernstein, Robert, 102, 142–43, 146, 151, 155, 310n74, 320n44, 321n63
Blanchot, Maurice, 148
Butler, Joseph, 9, 97–102, 117, 120, 130, 305nn21,24, 306nn28–31, 307nn38–39,46, 311n107

Caputo, John, 3, 48, 261–62, 270, 274–75, 351n1, 353n29
Celan, Paul, 263
charity, 3, 26, 35, 37, 44, 203, 329n26; forgiveness and, 59, 120, 211, 258; justice and, 176, 180, 182, 196; repentance and, 239; spontaneous, 44, 49, 59, 68, 186–87, 289n87
charm, 3, 258
circumstances, mitigating, 56, 61, 66, 68, 133, 162, 253
clemency, 54
coincidentia oppositorum, 28, 268, 273
compassion, 60, 73–76, 98, 101, 103, 154, 327n165
complacency, 27, 187, 206–7; of being, 28, 34, 206; of good conscience, 183, 187, 193
conditio humana, 194, 202
conscience, 5, 208, 214–15, 238, 284n91; bad, 6, 35, 105, 107, 109, 206–7, 240–42, 247, 251, 259; daimonic, 14; God and the law of, 239; good, 27, 88–89, 178, 183, 193, 227, 248, 252–53, 264; ressentiment and, 122, 126
contagion, 134, 185; of evil, 237; of resentment, 100–1, 105, 110–11; of violence, 94, 99, 306n31
creation: act of, 19, 21–24, 32, 178–79, 259; gift of, 25; God's, 23, 26, 139–41, 177, 209; difference between God's, and human, 26–27, 31–32, 178–79, 182; human, as re-creation, 13, 22, 26–27, 32–34, 179, 186, 192, 278; idea of, 12–13, 284n4; instant of, 10, 28, 186, 201, 207, 275–77; love

and, 24–25, 113, 186, 201, 287n63; philosophy of, 13; in Plato's *Timaeus*, 19, 23, 25, 60; repentance as a new, 245; wholly other order of, 16, 18–19, 21, 204
crimes: against humanity, 5, 77, 90, 133, 146, 149–51, 160, 166, 172, 242, 303; inexpiable, 90, 147, 160, 162, 243; war, 303

Davidson, Arnold, 3–4, 9
decay, 44–46, 49, 51–52, 55, 84
Derrida, Jacques, 7, 9, 32, 38, 40, 48, 91–92, 119, 134, 156, 159–63, 170, 173–77, 179, 186–89, 191, 199, 210–11, 227–28, 240, 247, 254–58, 263–64, 287nn50,63, 289n87, 293n40, 298n112, 327n176, 331nn69,76, 335n119, 336n146
Descartes, René, 214, 298n120
despair, 47, 87, 135, 218, 224, 238; forgiveness as tangency with, 162; irreversibility and, 79; irrevocability and, 85; memory and, 127; remorse and, 240–45, 248, 252, 255–56
dignity: human, 54, 120, 122, 125–26, 146, 148, 230; inherent to persons, 53; justice and, 125; of the sovereign, 70
Dionysus, 310n76; Dionysian, 185
discursive reason, 23, 34, 270
dissonance, 11, 173, 202, 224
duration, 28, 30–31, 38, 57, 81, 187, 197, 203; degree and, of resentment, 98; forgiveness as heterogeneous to degree and, 270; of justice, 122–23, 126; of suffering, 251
duty: to forgive, 165, 176, 202, 342n58; of justice, 172, 175–76, 224; to love, 99, 172–75, 197, 306n30, 314n146; to punish, 192, 250; to remember, 125–27

economy, 33, 70, 145, 154, 170, 183, 243; of being, 322; closed, of the status quo, 183; exchange and, 195; forgiveness as economic transaction, 228; justice and, 180; of law, 183; rationality and, 70, 256; of reason and

morality, 145; of returns, 170, 270; of symmetrical relations, 154
effectivity, 3, 13, 19, 23–25, 59, 127
élan, 37–38, 44–45, 59, 177, 270, 312
envy, 94–95, 97, 108, 110, 115, 304, 309, 339
epekeina, 14, 16, 18
Epictetus, 52, 295n83
Erdmann, J. E., 194
essence, 13, 286n34, 313n144; creation and, 22–25, 31, 178; of the Divine, 225; event of forgiveness and, 3, 28–29, 258; evil and, 138, 140, 145; existence and, 18–20, 84, 112; of the human, 27, 137, 146–47, 166, 172, 241; of love, 113; of morality, 40, 115; of ressentiment, 103; temporality and, 30, 78. See also *epekeina*
Esser, Albert, 337n10
evil: banality of, 151–52; demiurge of, 152; freedom and, 10, 87, 103, 131, 137–55, 160, 162, 269, 321nn58,60; beyond good and, 109; ignorance and, 137–38, 221, 295n64, 299n128; justice and love as responses to, 172–75, 185; limits of reason and, 184; metaphysical negation of, 56–57, 328n179; personifcation of, 23; punishment and, 157, 175, 269; ontological, 326n153; organ-obstacle of, 164, 168–71; power of forgiveness and power of, 11, 163–69, 254, 273–74, 279, 320n44, 324n111; radical, 135–36, 140–43, 146–47, 152, 158–59, 163, 167, 209, 323n111; relation between good and, 29, 66, 88, 102, 104, 106, 108, 154, 197, 278, 310n74; repentance and, 218, 223, 228, 237, 241, 245, 253, 257; retributive emotions and, 94, 98–101; separation of, deed and doer, 130, 215nn175,177. See also *privatio boni*; wickedness
excess, 14, 25, 178; of evil, 145–47, 149, 153, 155, 163, 184; of forgiveness, 69–70, 163, 170, 176, 180, 184, 320n44; of history, 45; of power, 106;

of remorse, 241; of retributive emotions, 94, 101
excuse, 10, 55–68, 136, 162, 164–68, 182, 199, 230, 257, 298, 332; intellective, 56–58; partitive, 56, 66; self-, 298n112, 316n185; total, 56, 66, 68
Existentialism, 316n188; existentialistic spiritualism, 4
existentialists, 7
expiation, 156, 160, 228, 244, 246, 251–52, 325; the inexpiable, 161, 243, 251

faith, 71, 108, 115, 122, 141, 165, 198, 217, 218, 233, 278, 308
felix culpa, 195, 222, 235, 247, 277, 326n155, 339n40, 340n45
Fénelon, François, 6, 42, 193, 207, 291n139
fidelity, 6–7, 35, 47, 81, 83, 90, 121–29, 135, 199
forbearance, 60, 75–76
forgetting: of creatureliness, 141; difference between disregarding an offense and, 262, 265–67, 269–70, 276; difference between forgiving and, 46, 48–51, 261, 269; futurition and, 47–48, 120–21, 125, 129, 292n5; having-been, having-done, and, 55, 84, 89, 91, 93; as a precondition for good, 215; repentance and, 222–23, 233, 340nn47,49; self-, 42, 184, 188, 193–95, 251, 291n139
forgiveness: absurdity of, 163, 198, 268, 351n256; aneconomic, 257; apocryphal, 10; conditional, 9, 257; death of, 161–62, 278; eschatology and, 170, 327n176, 328n181; exceptionality of, 11, 69, 174, 191, 256, 272, 300n142; pure, 9–10, 44, 52, 58, 163, 174, 182, 187–88, 202–4, 264, 268–70, 272; simili-, 10, 45, 58, 163, 199; super-, suprarrationality of, 10, 14, 55, 119, 197–98, 256, 258; unconditional, 9, 162, 186, 249, 254, 257, 259, 319n27; unconditionality of, 206, 258

Index ■ 375

free will, 77, 142–44, 152, 246
Freud, Sigmund, 6, 50, 105, 187, 264
futurition, 45, 47–48, 80–81, 83, 121, 126, 128–29, 292

Genesis, the Book of, 23, 25, 139, 141, 287n46
Gibbs, Robert, 219, 223–25, 340n47
gift: ambiguity of, 94, 105; aporia of, 211, 331n69, 336n146; of creation, 22, 25; difference between forgiveness and, 192, 197, 269, 331–32n76, 352–53n20; gratitude and, 195–96; gratuity of, 44, 49, 52, 55, 57–59, 73–74, 76, 182, 196, 297n108, 332n79; of the instant, 207; justice and, 156, 178, 183; memory and, 194–95; relation to the other and, 59, 71, 76, 118, 156, 275, 332n86; repentance, grace, and, 239, 246, 248; resentment as, of God, 101; time and, 139, 274–75, 278; unconditional, 186–89, 192–93, 258
Girard, René, 306n31, 310n76
Goethe, Johann Wolfgang von, 80
Gouhier, Alain, 159, 162, 205
Govier, Trudy, 130–33, 306n28, 316n184
grace, 24, 37, 59, 71, 156, 172, 179, 186, 191, 196, 199, 202, 211, 244–47, 270, 274, 348n183; act of, 73–74; of forgiveness, 184, 205, 268–69, 297n108; infinite, 170; instant of, 32, 178, 184, 207; justice and, 177; of love, 178; 182, 185; order of, 26, 65, 70, 118, 176–77, 183; poetic, 2; reduction of, to the law, 182; right to, 198; triple, of making-be without being, 25–26; spark of, 3
Gracián, Baltasar, 6
gratitude, 11, 47, 188–89, 194–97
Gregory of Nyssa, 152
Griswold, Charles, 53, 59, 101, 250, 297n108, 306n32, 307n38
guilt: collective, 237, 343–44n83; confession of, 159, 238; consciousness of, 240, 248, 254, 257–58; excuse and, 298n112; forgiveness and, 194, 198, 226; history and, 45; liberation from, 210–11, 239, 246, 267, 272, 275, 343n73, 349n199; lying and, 327n165; moral and metaphysical, distinguished from criminal and political, 175, 251–55; ontological and peripheral, 242–43; responsibility, intentionality, and, 151, 222, 233, 348n183; self, identity, and, 211, 228–29, 234, 237, 240–41, 256–57

Hadot, Pierre, 52, 211–12
haecceity, 54, 124, 313–14n144
Hampton, Jean, 305n28, 306n32
hapax, 54, 79, 84, 124, 126, 302n41
Hartmann, Nicolai, 210, 229–30, 337n20, 343n73
having-been, 83–84, 86, 126–27, 255, 273
having-done, 83–89, 125–27, 130, 132, 139, 160–61, 240–43, 247, 252–56, 267–68, 273–74, 316n185. *See also* irrevocability
Heidegger, Martin, 6, 12–13, 15, 18, 34, 154, 218, 220, 270, 276, 308n50
Heine, Heinrich, 106, 308n53
Heraclitus, 79
heteronomy, 128, 142, 154
hope, 7, 41, 48, 88, 214, 217, 219, 249; despair and, 47, 87, 135, 162, 218, 244, 247; eschatological, 39, 275; Kant's rational, 210, 246; nostalgia and, 82; redemption and, 276–78; repentance and, 242; returns and, 105, 184
Horkheimer, Max, 88, 151, 302–3n48, 336n3
human nature, 138, 167. *See also conditio humana*
human rights, 127, 173
Husserl, Edmund, 41, 187, 235
hypokeimenon, 313. *See also* substance

identity, 21, 32, 83, 150, 210, 222, 230–32, 255, 344n85; with the absolute, 4; break with, 353n41; law of, 269; logic of, 271, 274; moral imputation and, 229; non-, 275; play of alterity and, 228, 278; of position

and conversion, 33; principle of, 16, 24, 88, 269, 302n46; question of, 248
I-know-not-what, 3, 21–22, 29, 39, 78, 144, 201, 205
imperative, 211, 227, 264, 329n26; double, of love and justice, 10, 172–73, 176; to forgive, 183, 205–6, 226–27, 259, 338n22; indicative contrasted with, 40–42, 83, 202; to love, 11, 172, 183
impossibility, 77, 88, 128, 153, 236, 282n19; of definition and circumscription, 24, 147; of forgiveness, 162, 174, 206–7, 274, 326n145, 331n76; of immobility, 80; logical, of the coincidence of position and negation, 268; of memory, 81–82; of repetition, 79; of returning to the past, 85, 240, 316n184; of undoing the past, 161, 242, 274, 316n184
impotence, 103–5, 109, 112, 116, 171, 209, 240, 302n45; of evil, 169; of forgiveness, 169, 273–74; human, 77, 161, 195; of memory, 84; power and, 87; of the offender, 215; of remorse, 240–44, 247
imprescriptibility, 5, 90, 160–61, 229, 268, 342n63; law of, 77, 89, 92, 303n51
impurity, 10, 142, 156, 192–93, 218
indignation, 69, 104, 107, 126–27, 129, 135, 304nn10,11, 305n21; envy, distinguished from, 95; Nemesis, the personification of, 94; pity, distinguished from, 94–96; resentment, distinguished from, 96–97, 305n24
inexcusable: acts, 8, 64–65; confession and the, 298n112; crimes, 146, 156, 163; forgiveness and the, 55, 67–68, 136, 162–63, 168, 170, 176, 198; lack of consciousness and the, 221; understanding and the, 55, 59, 136, 155, 162, 166, 176; the unforgivable and the, 159, 162–70, 351n256; wickedness and the, 55, 155, 163, 168. *See also* unforgivable

infinity, 200, 272, 277; bad, 14; of the crime of Auschwitz, 159–60; of forgiveness, 163, 272; of good will, 197; of history, 52; of human responsibility, 170; of the other, 42, 155; of wickedness, 162
innocence, 24, 67–68, 105, 143, 166, 198, 204, 207, 223, 269, 298n112; of creation, 37; of despair, 244; of the instant, 129, 187, 278; restoration of, 275, 278; of virginal time, 274
instant: almost-nothing character of, 10, 18, 22, 28–29, 32, 37, 186, 191, 205; of creation, 10, 23, 28, 30, 57, 87, 178, 201, 270, 277; of decision, 33, 40, 57, 71, 166–67, 203, 245–47, 271; of forgiveness, 39, 49, 52, 71, 191–93, 197–98, 202–7, 258, 268–70, 272, 278, 324n111; of giving, 196; intuition and, 4, 18, 22, 30–35, 37–38, 197, 204–7; joy and, 195; love and, 42, 118, 182–84, 186, 188, 201; relation between interval and, 3, 28, 30, 32, 35, 37–39, 177–79, 184, 186–88, 193, 198, 201, 205–6, 245–47, 259, 289n87
intellection, 13, 15, 17, 22, 42, 59, 181, 258
intentional acts: distinguished from unintentional acts, 62, 220–22
intentionality, 3, 41, 128, 153, 177, 185, 222, 243
interval. *See* instant
intuition, 4, 15, 17–22, 28–38, 57, 201, 289nn87–88, 290n118; instant of, 22, 31–35, 37–38, 197, 205, 207; tangent of, 166, 204
ipseity: divine, 24; evil and, 148, 150; forgiveness and, 137, 271; gratitude and, 196; of the individual, 27, 119, 124–26, 313–14n144; love and, 155; 180; remorse and, 241
irreversibility, 46, 77–82, 85, 88, 91, 214, 316n185
irrevocability, 77, 84–91, 126, 132, 240, 247, 273, 316n185, 349n200. *See also* having-done

Jaspers, Karl, 146, 150–51, 251
je-ne-sais-quoi. *See* I-know-not-what

Jerphagnon, Lucien, 13
Jesus, 54, 85, 114, 116–18, 159, 164–65, 195, 220, 311n103, 328n181, 344n85
Judaken, Jonathan, 259, 322n79
justice: atemporality of, 92, 125; claim of, as precondition for forgiveness, 129, 132; closed, 243; as decency (*epieikeia*), 64–65, 72; distributive, 26, 122–23, 157–58, 177–78, 184; fidelity and, 35, 121–29; forgiveness as opposed to, 67, 157–58, 171, 176, 224; interval and, 35, 177–79, 182–86; moral dilemma between love and, 10–11, 155, 171–76, 202; passions and, 93, 97, 313n124; peace and, 158, 177, 185–86; reason and, 55, 58–59, 65, 68, 112, 120, 172, 180–84; revenge and, 106, 115, 120; retributive, 73, 75–76, 146, 173, 300n145; talion, 183, 339–40n40

Kant, Immanuel, 16–18, 40, 43, 66, 70, 123–24, 131, 133, 135, 141–45, 147, 151–53, 155, 158, 167, 177, 185, 187, 203, 209, 214, 229–30, 232, 234, 241, 243, 245–46, 255, 265, 298n111, 306n30, 319n27, 329n18, 348n183
Kelley, Andrew, 172, 176, 348n170
Kierkegaard, Søren, 4, 34, 37, 46, 79–80, 125, 183, 198, 210, 212, 229–32, 234, 244, 248, 254, 256, 270, 275, 292n11, 300n6, 309n65, 314n146, 343n80, 344n85
Kodalle, Klaus-Michael, 194, 297n108, 298n120

law: anti-Semitic, 314n164; Athenian, 296n92; of being, 154, 206; of benevolence, 98; of conscience, 239; cosmic, of compensation, 94; criminal, and civil, 73–74, 76; force of, 123, 182; forgiveness and, 182–83, 186, 300n142; of freedom, 142; God's, 143, Jewish, 217; of love, 11, 180; of prescription, 91; rule of, 11, 70–71, 74; suspension of, 90. *See also* moral law
Leibniz, Gottfried Wilhelm, 18–19, 29, 56, 80, 139, 202, 301n12

Lemcke, Verena, 162, 326n153
Levi, Primo, 9, 322n66
Levinas, Emmanuel, 2, 14, 128, 145–46, 150, 153–55, 173–74, 184, 210, 215–27, 231, 233–34, 238, 241, 246, 249, 254, 257, 263, 275–77, 284n4, 320n44, 322n75, 323–24n111, 328n8, 329n26, 334n118, 338n36, 339–40n40, 340n45, 347n142, 352n9, 353n41
Liebrucks, Bruno, 283n23
Lingis, Alphonso, 277
love: absurdity of, 199; asymmetrical, 174; ecstatic, 200; hyperbolic, 11, 173, 178; pure, 14, 186, 188, 199–200, 205–7; self-, 24, 58, 67, 97, 101, 103, 142, 143, 144, 181, 298, 307nn39,46; unconditional, 11, 42, 162; unconditonality of, 105, 206; unmerited, 184, 199; unmotivated, 184
Luther, Martin, 107, 244, 309n65, 337n20

Macho, Thomas, 191
malevolence, 145, 151, 153, 158–59, 162, 165
malice, 95, 98–101, 110, 138, 151–52, 220, 306n31, 307n38, 347n150
Margalit, Avishai, 262, 266–67, 269, 352–53n20
martyrdom, 124, 148
Marxists, 7
Mauss, Marcel, 194, 331n69, 332n86, 333n87, 352n20
megalopsychia, 54, 59–60
melancholy, 264
memory, 8, 33, 109, 210, 220, 262, 265; Augustine's account of, 82, 139; of the dead, 124, 264, 314n163; as a duty, 84, 124, 126; of God, 140–41, 315n166; irrevocability and, 86–87, 161, 267; limits of, 83, 128, 275–76; loss of, 46, 49–50, 264; as a precondition for forgiveness, 54, 129, 192; relation of gift to, 193–95; remorse and, 240–41; repentance and, 223, 251, 255, 276, 340n49; repetition

and, 82–84, 275; resentment and, 51, 55, 120, 124; traumatic, 127; of the will, 127
mercy, 70–76, 139, 226
Messiah, 113, 216
metaempirical, 13, 15–17, 19–21, 31, 38, 44, 91, 158, 178, 259, 274, 278
metalogical, 15–16, 19, 21–22, 44, 258
metanoia, 208–9, 211, 224. *See also* repentance
metaphysics, 12–14, 18, 24, 26, 39–40, 242, 253, 346
Metzler, Karin, 60
Milbank, John, 139–41
Mishnah, 224–25
modernity, 202; Christianity and, 115; critique of, 107; Shoah as burden of, 242
moral law, 17, 131, 142–43, 152–53, 155, 209, 214, 245–46, 319n27, 348n183
moral monsters, 129–31, 135, 151
mourning, 46, 49, 215, 264–65, 274; work of, 91, 257
Murphy, Jeffrie, 73–74, 94, 97–98, 165, 305–6n28, 344n89
mysticism, 4
mystics, 4, 15, 24, 30, 36, 193, 246

Nabert, Jean, 145–46
Nancy, Jean-Luc, 144
National Socialism, 316n188, 321n60
Neiman, Susan, 149, 152
Neoplatonism, 15–16, 19, 31
Nicholas of Cusa, 26, 28, 268, 288
Nietzsche, Friedrich, 6, 40, 45, 49, 54, 97, 102–12, 114–17, 119–20, 127, 130, 134, 187, 196, 209, 215, 232–33, 258, 290n125, 292n5, 298n120, 301n31, 308nn50–53, 309n65, 310nn74–76, 311n103, 317n196, 324n114, 339n38
Nishitani, Keiji, 35
nostalgia, 27, 81–82, 88, 206, 240
Nussbaum, Martha, 120–21, 129

omnipotence, 11, 147–48, 169, 273–74
ontology, 12, 28–29, 154, 241–42, 253, 324

organ-obstacle, 164, 168, 211, 243, 247, 274, 326n153
oscillation, 164, 276, 324n111, 326n153, 334n115; between asymmetrical love and reciprocal love, 200–2; between excuse and evil, 168; between forgiveness and evil, 169, 202; of the instant and the interval, 206; between love and evil, 168–71; in mind and values, 164; of two truths, 202
ousia, 13, 28, 78

paradox: of atemporal semelfactivity, 86; of creation, 21, 25–26, 28, 32; of fidelity, 83; of forgiveness, 8, 11, 28, 163, 170, 176, 202, 256, 258, 273–76, 326n145, 342n69; of a gift, 25–26, 192; of morality, 7, 171, 173–76; of repentance, 227, 231, 234–35, 255
pardon, 60–65, 70–73, 159, 283n26, 295n85, 296n92
Pascal, Blaise, 25, 32, 198
Paul, the apostle, 70, 101, 170, 198, 240, 255, 265, 309n65, 339n36, 341n49
perissos, 70, 179, 183, 196, 270
perpetual peace, 177, 185, 272
philauty, 58, 181
pity, 167, 208, 259; *aidesis*, 296n92; compassion and, 98, 101, 103, 154; forgiveness, distinguished from, 76; in Greek drama, 60; indignation, distinguished from, 94–96; justice and, 74–75; pardon and, 61, 67, 154; remorse and, 240; self-, 316n185
Plato, 5, 14–15, 19, 23–24, 27, 29, 32, 34, 51, 57, 60, 82, 112–13, 137–38, 173, 202, 211, 263, 270, 284n4, 287n46, 293n40, 294n49, 296n92, 317–18n6, 326n155, 329n18, 334n112
pleonexy, 157
Plotinus, 3, 15, 17, 24, 31, 34, 78
presque rien, 31, 44, 205. *See also* almost nothing
privatio boni, 137–41, 152
prohairesis, 64, 213
providence, 56, 118, 326n155
psychology, 66, 102

punishment, 61, 70, 72–73, 76, 91, 110, 115, 145, 156–60, 163, 175, 177, 219, 223, 252, 269, 300n145, 318n6; capital, 99, 306n29, 311n107, 339n40
purity, 10, 17, 186–87, 199, 202, 204–5, 221, 245, 348

quiddity, 29, 145, 313–14
quoddity, 3, 302n41; evil and, 144–45, 153, 166, 253; forgiveness and, 270; freedom and, 144, 166; grace and, 205; having-been and, 84, 314n144; irrevocability and, 67, 80, 88–90, 161, 242, 268, 273; quiddity, distinguished from, 18, 29; remorse and, 243

radical evil, 140, 143, 146–47, 151, 153, 167, 324n111
rancor, 15, 46–49, 58, 93, 120, 125–27, 129–30, 267
rationality, 13, 93, 142, 344n85; emotions and, 93–94; excuse and, 55, 68; of forgiveness, 254; irrationality and, 14, 23, 198; remorse, the lack of, 244; superrationality and, 14, 55, 70, 119, 197, 211, 256; transcendence and, 323–24n111
Raveling, Wiard, 5, 7, 259, 283n21, 325n140
reciprocity, 170, 176, 191, 199; asymmetrical, 248, 250; between giving and receiving, 193; between God's freedom and human freedom, 217; justice and, 11, 55, 59, 178, 184; law of, 58, 181; logic of, 174, 224; love and, 155, 200–1, 273
reconciliation, 10, 121, 170, 174, 257, 264, 296n92, 324n111, 342; apostles of, 122; *Aufhebung* of, 170; Days of, 227; between God and humans, 76; Hegelian, 46; interpersonal, 209; joy of, 222; political therapy of, 92; scene of, 257; sign of, 1; strategic, 121; synthesis of, 216; Truth and, Committee, 293n21
redemption, 88, 115, 210, 217, 225–26, 243, 247, 254, 276–77; active will of, 249, 251; of God, 141, 218; remorse, as condition for, 244, 248, 251; self-, 9, 210, 217, 225, 247, 257
regret, 47, 62–63, 212–15, 228, 230, 245, 337n13, 344n85, 346n135; nostalgia and, 82, 85, 240; as a precondition for forgiveness, 251, 253; remorse, distinguished from, 208, 240–41
remorse, 47, 131–32, 172, 212, 215, 230, 346n141, 347n150, 348n170; absence of, 9, 159, 162, 248, 252–53; despair of, 243–44, 255; fear of penalty and, 219; feeling of, 208–9, 239, 252–54; irrevocability and, 240–43, 249; organ-obstacle of, 247; as a precondition for forgiveness, 133, 228, 248, 251–56; prescription, as a replacement for, 91; redemption and, 244–47, 251, 254; regret, distinguished from, 208, 240–41; repentance, distinguished from, 211, 239–45, 302n45
repentance: as a condition for forgiveness, 9, 133, 159, 210–11, 216–17, 226, 238, 248–50, 252–42, 256, 259–60; fear, as the motivation for, contrasted with love, as the motivation for, 219–20, 222–23, 340n47; toward God, distinguished from, toward persons, 225–26, 238, 340n49, 342n58; identity and, 210, 229–32, 236–37, 255–57; monologue of, 215, 237–38, 255; paradox of, 227, 231, 234–35, 255; rationality and, 214, 256, 344n85; remorse, distinguished from, 211, 239–45, 302n45; ressentiment, as precipatating, 132; sociality of, 209–10, 215–16, 224, 232, 238, 255, 342n58; substitutes for, 91; task of, 209, 226–27, 251, 253, 338n22, 339n40; teleology of, 239, 243, 256
repetition, 3, 32; Kierkegaard and, 46, 79–80; memory and, 82–83, 85, 276; temporal dialectic of, 81, 177, 186, 323–24n111
resentment. *See* indignation; ressentiment
ressentiment: action and, 123, 126–27, 182; duty of, 93, 123–28;

equivocalness of, 129–30, 132–34, 166; forgiveness, out of, 312n118; indignation and, 126–27, 129; irrevocability and, 122, 127–28, 316n185; justice and, 93, 120–22, 124, 126, 129, 132, 135, 175, 250, 259; leveling and, 107, 209n65; memory and, 120, 122, 124, 126–29; morality and, 102–8, 112, 120, 124; as a prerequisite of forgiveness, 120, 129; psychology and, 106, 110–11, 120, 126; remnant of, in forgiveness, 188, 221, 267; values and, 103–4, 111–15, 120

restoration, 88, 239, 266, 275, 277–78
resurrection, 31, 83, 275–77
resuscitation, 68, 83, 85, 275–78
retribution, 44, 76, 94, 116, 157–58, 160, 175
retributive emotions, 93–94, 102, 305n28
revenants, 282n19, 293n40
Ricoeur, Paul, 7–8, 91, 145, 183, 193, 267, 274
Romilly, Jacqueline de, 60
Rosenzweig, Franz, 225, 228, 255, 328n8, 334n118
Rousseau, Jean-Jacques, 43, 107, 298n112, 327n176

sacrifice, 37, 193, 259, 341n49; of an absolute, 172; of Christ, 185; forgiveness and, 59, 116, 192, 250, 295n77; gift and, 192, 332n79; of justice, 173, 176; love and, 14, 41, 173; of repentance, 251; of revenge, 116; Socrates', 14
Sade, Marquis de, 148–49, 321n60
Sales, François de, 42, 291n139
Sartre, Jean-Paul, 115, 210, 229–30, 232, 282n15, 344n85
scapegoat, 262, 265
Scheler, Max, 9, 109–20, 127, 130, 210, 228, 232–41, 243, 245, 247, 251, 254, 256, 276, 309n65, 310n87, 311nn103,107, 345nn104,110,117,120, 346n124, 349n200
Schelling, F. W. J., 4, 6, 17–18, 31, 144, 185, 282–83n19

Schmitt, Carl, 71, 117
Scholem, Gershom, 151, 217, 338n27
Schopenhauer, Arthur, 18, 236
Schwab, Françoise, 81, 127
semelfactivity, 86, 241, 302n41
Seneca, Lucius Anneaus, 52, 194, 196, 212, 333n87
Shakespeare, William, 70, 72–73
Shoah, 8, 50, 121, 150, 158–60, 173, 242, 252, 350n219. *See also* Auschwitz
Silber, John, 142, 348n183
Simmel, Georg, 32, 37, 69
singularity, 29–30, 79, 82, 302n41, 314n144, 322n75, 324n111; of each human individual, 125–26, 146, 149–50, 180, 219; of Jewish existence, 334n118; of love, 112; of the Shoah, 159
Socrates, 14, 17, 24, 29, 43, 57, 60, 104, 137, 138, 221, 294n49, 313n144
Soloveitchik, Joseph Dov, 222–23, 233, 276, 341n49
Spinoza, Baruch, 56, 111, 209, 214, 215, 232
statutory limits, 5–6, 9, 77, 90
Stoics, 46, 52, 194, 295n83, 338–39n36
Strawson, P. F., 135, 306n28
substance, 13, 28, 78, 138, 140. *See also hypokeimenon*
substitution, 154–55, 262–63, 341n49, 352n9
sungnômê, 55, 59–65, 295n85, 297n108, 299n134

Talmud, 10, 210, 215–16, 219–24, 231, 340n47
tangency, 3, 31–32, 38–39, 162, 204, 207
teleology, 113, 239, 243, 256
teshuva, 208
theodicy, 56, 97, 101, 152, 154, 239
transcendence, 3, 31, 77, 108, 163, 170, 324n111; evil and, 145, 155, 320n44; of forgiveness, 171, 197; radical, 14–18, 80, 264; self-, 27, 32, 154, 206, 239, 250. *See also epekeina*
Tutu, Desmond, 130–33, 292n21, 315n177

Udoff, Alan, 217, 338n22
unconditionality, 186–87, 192, 211; logic of, 119, 210, 216; of love, 105, 206
unforgivable: acts, 8, 140, 156, 160; Auschwitz and the, 8, 159, 161, 326n153; crimes against humanity and the, 149; the inexcusable, distinguished from the, 55, 136, 159, 162–68, 170; persons, 8, 132–33; in principle, distinguished from, in practice, 136, 156, 159, 170, 274; punishment and the, 158, 160; radical evil and the, 140, 159; remnant of the, 227; repentance and the, 227
unintentional offenses, 62, 220–22, 339n40, 344n85
universality, 16, 42, 147, 149, 310n87; of human value, 54; justice and, 11, 174, 176; of language, 324n111; law of 58, 65

value: act-, 114–15, 118–19, 199; atemporality of, 29, 84, 90, 125–26, 251; creation and, 20, 24, 278; dissonance of, 173, 202, 259; fidelity to, 93, 124–25, 128; freedom, as source of, 229; hierarchy of, 111–12, 114, 118–19, 152, 199; offenses against, distinguished from personal offenses, 160, 175, 341n52; persons and, 54, 79, 85, 124–25, 127; reason and, 5, 17; ressentiment and, 97, 103, 106, 120–22, 129; transvaluation of, 108, 112, 309n65
via negativa, 4, 10, 45, 324. *See also* apophatic method

vice, 62–64, 74, 98, 100, 138, 146, 152, 315n175, 317n6
virtue, 98, 122, 138, 207, 289n87, 291n139, 349n217; in Aristotle, 53, 61, 64, 178, 213, 295n85, 329n18; creation and, 278; exclusion of forgiveness from, 53; of giving, 194; of humility, 193; of impotence, 103–4; of the instant and the interval, 35, 37, 123; justice and, 92, 123, 294n49; of mercy, 73–74; of pity and indignation, 95–96; of remorse, 247; repentance and, 214; royal, of pardon, 70

wholly other, 2, 13–16, 18–20, 22–24, 35, 38–39, 182, 204, 251
wickedness, 63, 98, 134, 165, 169, 179, 197, 199, 222, 241, 295n64, 317–18n6, 321n60; absolute, 162–63; belief in, 11, 137, 144, 153, 166–67; diabolical, 133; freedom and, 10, 135, 137, 144, 153, 166–67, 347n150; gratuitous, 144–45, 147, 151, 167; the inexcusable and, 55, 155, 163, 168; in Kant, 142–43, 155; misfortune and, 167–68; negation of, 56; ontological, 147–48; the organ-obstacle and, 164, 166–69, 176, 202, 273–74; remorse and, 346n141; understanding and, 55, 136, 145, 155
Wiesel, Elie, 120–21, 127, 314n163, 315n166

Yom Kippur, 225, 263

Perspectives in Continental Philosophy
John D. Caputo, series editor

John D. Caputo, ed., *Deconstruction in a Nutshell: A Conversation with Jacques Derrida.*

Michael Strawser, *Both/And: Reading Kierkegaard—From Irony to Edification.*

Michael D. Barber, *Ethical Hermeneutics: Rationality in Enrique Dussel's Philosophy of Liberation.*

James H. Olthuis, ed., *Knowing Other-wise: Philosophy at the Threshold of Spirituality.*

James Swindal, *Reflection Revisited: Jürgen Habermas's Discursive Theory of Truth.*

Richard Kearney, *Poetics of Imagining: Modern and Postmodern.* Second edition.

Thomas W. Busch, *Circulating Being: From Embodiment to Incorporation—Essays on Late Existentialism.*

Edith Wyschogrod, *Emmanuel Levinas: The Problem of Ethical Metaphysics.* Second edition.

Francis J. Ambrosio, ed., *The Question of Christian Philosophy Today.*

Jeffrey Bloechl, ed., *The Face of the Other and the Trace of God: Essays on the Philosophy of Emmanuel Levinas.*

Ilse N. Bulhof and Laurens ten Kate, eds., *Flight of the Gods: Philosophical Perspectives on Negative Theology.*

Trish Glazebrook, *Heidegger's Philosophy of Science.*

Kevin Hart, *The Trespass of the Sign: Deconstruction, Theology, and Philosophy.*

Mark C. Taylor, *Journeys to Selfhood: Hegel and Kierkegaard.* Second edition.

Dominique Janicaud, Jean-François Courtine, Jean-Louis Chrétien, Michel Henry, Jean-Luc Marion, and Paul Ricoeur, *Phenomenology and the "Theological Turn": The French Debate.*

Karl Jaspers, *The Question of German Guilt*. Introduction by Joseph W. Koterski, S.J.

Jean-Luc Marion, *The Idol and Distance: Five Studies*. Translated with an introduction by Thomas A. Carlson.

Jeffrey Dudiak, *The Intrigue of Ethics: A Reading of the Idea of Discourse in the Thought of Emmanuel Levinas*.

Robyn Horner, *Rethinking God as Gift: Marion, Derrida, and the Limits of Phenomenology*.

Mark Dooley, *The Politics of Exodus: Søren Kierkegaard's Ethics of Responsibility*.

Merold Westphal, *Overcoming Onto-Theology: Toward a Postmodern Christian Faith*.

Edith Wyschogrod, Jean-Joseph Goux, and Eric Boynton, eds., *The Enigma of Gift and Sacrifice*.

Stanislas Breton, *The Word and the Cross*. Translated with an introduction by Jacquelyn Porter.

Jean-Luc Marion, *Prolegomena to Charity*. Translated by Stephen E. Lewis.

Peter H. Spader, *Scheler's Ethical Personalism: Its Logic, Development, and Promise*.

Jean-Louis Chrétien, *The Unforgettable and the Unhoped For*. Translated by Jeffrey Bloechl.

Don Cupitt, *Is Nothing Sacred? The Non-Realist Philosophy of Religion: Selected Essays*.

Jean-Luc Marion, *In Excess: Studies of Saturated Phenomena*. Translated by Robyn Horner and Vincent Berraud.

Phillip Goodchild, *Rethinking Philosophy of Religion: Approaches from Continental Philosophy*.

William J. Richardson, S.J., *Heidegger: Through Phenomenology to Thought*.

Jeffrey Andrew Barash, *Martin Heidegger and the Problem of Historical Meaning*.

Jean-Louis Chrétien, *Hand to Hand: Listening to the Work of Art*. Translated by Stephen E. Lewis.

Jean-Louis Chrétien, *The Call and the Response*. Translated with an introduction by Anne Davenport.

D. C. Schindler, *Han Urs von Balthasar and the Dramatic Structure of Truth: A Philosophical Investigation*.

Julian Wolfreys, ed., *Thinking Difference: Critics in Conversation*.

Allen Scult, *Being Jewish/Reading Heidegger: An Ontological Encounter*.

Richard Kearney, *Debates in Continental Philosophy: Conversations with Contemporary Thinkers*.

Jennifer Anna Gosetti-Ferencei, *Heidegger, Hölderlin, and the Subject of Poetic Language: Toward a New Poetics of Dasein*.

Jolita Pons, *Stealing a Gift: Kierkegaard's Pseudonyms and the Bible*.

Jean-Yves Lacoste, *Experience and the Absolute: Disputed Questions on the Humanity of Man*. Translated by Mark Raftery-Skehan.

Charles P. Bigger, *Between* Chora *and the Good: Metaphor's Metaphysical Neighborhood.*

Dominique Janicaud, *Phenomenology "Wide Open": After the French Debate.* Translated by Charles N. Cabral.

Ian Leask and Eoin Cassidy, eds., *Givenness and God: Questions of Jean-Luc Marion.*

Jacques Derrida, *Sovereignties in Question: The Poetics of Paul Celan.* Edited by Thomas Dutoit and Outi Pasanen.

William Desmond, *Is There a Sabbath for Thought? Between Religion and Philosophy.*

Bruce Ellis Benson and Norman Wirzba, eds., *The Phenomenology of Prayer.*

S. Clark Buckner and Matthew Statler, eds., *Styles of Piety: Practicing Philosophy after the Death of God.*

Kevin Hart and Barbara Wall, eds., *The Experience of God: A Postmodern Response.*

John Panteleimon Manoussakis, *After God: Richard Kearney and the Religious Turn in Continental Philosophy.*

John Martis, *Philippe Lacoue-Labarthe: Representation and the Loss of the Subject.*

Jean-Luc Nancy, *The Ground of the Image.*

Edith Wyschogrod, *Crossover Queries: Dwelling with Negatives, Embodying Philosophy's Others.*

Gerald Bruns, *On the Anarchy of Poetry and Philosophy: A Guide for the Unruly.*

Brian Treanor, *Aspects of Alterity: Levinas, Marcel, and the Contemporary Debate.*

Simon Morgan Wortham, *Counter-Institutions: Jacques Derrida and the Question of the University.*

Leonard Lawlor, *The Implications of Immanence: Toward a New Concept of Life.*

Clayton Crockett, *Interstices of the Sublime: Theology and Psychoanalytic Theory.*

Bettina Bergo, Joseph Cohen, and Raphael Zagury-Orly, eds., *Judeities: Questions for Jacques Derrida.* Translated by Bettina Bergo and Michael B. Smith.

Jean-Luc Marion, *On the Ego and on God: Further Cartesian Questions.* Translated by Christina M. Gschwandtner.

Jean-Luc Nancy, *Philosophical Chronicles.* Translated by Franson Manjali.

Jean-Luc Nancy, *Dis-Enclosure: The Deconstruction of Christianity.* Translated by Bettina Bergo, Gabriel Malenfant, and Michael B. Smith.

Andrea Hurst, *Derrida Vis-à-vis Lacan: Interweaving Deconstruction and Psychoanalysis.*

Jean-Luc Nancy, *Noli me tangere: On the Raising of the Body.* Translated by Sarah Clift, Pascale-Anne Brault, and Michael Naas.

Jacques Derrida, *The Animal That Therefore I Am.* Edited by Marie-Louise Mallet, translated by David Wills.

Jean-Luc Marion, *The Visible and the Revealed.* Translated by Christina M. Gschwandtner and others.

Michel Henry, *Material Phenomenology.* Translated by Scott Davidson.

Jean-Luc Nancy, *Corpus.* Translated by Richard A. Rand.

Joshua Kates, *Fielding Derrida.*

Michael Naas, *Derrida From Now On.*

Shannon Sullivan and Dennis J. Schmidt, eds., *Difficulties of Ethical Life.*

Catherine Malabou, *What Should We Do with Our Brain?* Translated by Sebastian Rand, Introduction by Marc Jeannerod.

Claude Romano, *Event and World.* Translated by Shane Mackinlay.

Vanessa Lemm, *Nietzsche's Animal Philosophy: Culture, Politics, and the Animality of the Human Being.*

B. Keith Putt, ed., *Gazing Through a Prism Darkly: Reflections on Merold Westphal's Hermeneutical Epistemology.*

Eric Boynton and Martin Kavka, eds., *Saintly Influence: Edith Wyschogrod and the Possibilities of Philosophy of Religion.*

Shane Mackinlay, *Interpreting Excess: Jean-Luc Marion, Saturated Phenomena, and Hermeneutics.*

Kevin Hart and Michael A. Signer, eds., *The Exorbitant: Emmanuel Levinas Between Jews and Christians.*

Bruce Ellis Benson and Norman Wirzba, eds., *Words of Life: New Theological Turns in French Phenomenology.*

William Robert, *Trials: Of Antigone and Jesus.*

Brian Treanor and Henry Isaac Venema, eds., *A Passion for the Possible: Thinking with Paul Ricoeur.*

Kas Saghafi, *Apparitions—Of Derrida's Other.*

Nick Mansfield, *The God Who Deconstructs Himself: Sovereignty and Subjectivity Between Freud, Bataille, and Derrida.*

Don Ihde, *Heidegger's Technologies: Postphenomenological Perspectives.*

Suzi Adams, *Castoriadis's Ontology: Being and Creation.*

Richard Kearney and Kascha Semonovitch, eds., *Phenomenologies of the Stranger: Between Hostility and Hospitality.*

Michael Naas, *Miracle and Machine: Jacques Derrida and the Two Sources of Religion, Science, and the Media.*

Alena Alexandrova, Ignaas Devisch, Laurens ten Kate, and Aukje van Rooden, *Re-treating Religion: Deconstructing Christianity with Jean-Luc Nancy.* Preamble by Jean-Luc Nancy.

Emmanuel Falque, *The Metamorphosis of Finitude: An Essay on Birth and Resurrection.* Translated by George Hughes.

Scott M. Campbell, *The Early Heidegger's Philosophy of Life: Facticity, Being, and Language.*

Françoise Dastur, *How Are We to Confront Death? An Introduction to Philosophy.* Translated by Robert Vallier. Foreword by David Farrell Krell.

Christina M. Gschwandtner, *Postmodern Apologetics? Arguments for God in Contemporary Philosophy.*

Ben Morgan, *On Becoming God: Late Medieval Mysticism and the Modern Western Self.*

Neal DeRoo, *Futurity in Phenomenology: Promise and Method in Husserl, Levinas, and Derrida.*

Sarah LaChance Adams and Caroline R. Lundquist, eds., *Coming to Life: Philosophies of Pregnancy, Childbirth, and Mothering.*

Thomas Claviez, ed., *The Conditions of Hospitality: Ethics, Politics, and Aesthetics on the Threshold of the Possible.*

Roland Faber and Jeremy Fackenthal, eds., *Theopoetic Folds: Philosophizing Multifariousness.*

Jean-Luc Marion, *The Essential Writings.* Edited by Kevin Hart.

Adam S. Miller, *Speculative Grace: Bruno Latour and Object-Oriented Theology.* Foreword by Levi R. Bryant.

Jean-Luc Nancy, *Corpus II: Writings on Sexuality.*

David Nowell Smith, *Sounding/Silence: Martin Heidegger at the Limits of Poetics.*

Gregory C. Stallings, Manuel Asensi, and Carl Good, eds., *Material Spirit: Religion and Literature Intranscendent.*

Claude Romano, *Event and Time.* Translated by Stephen E. Lewis.

Frank Chouraqui, *Ambiguity and the Absolute: Nietzsche and Merleau-Ponty on the Question of Truth.*

Noëlle Vahanian, *The Rebellious No: Variations on a Secular Theology of Language.*

Michael Naas, *The End of the World and Other Teachable Moments: Jacques Derrida's Final Seminar.*

Jean-Louis Chrétien, *Under the Gaze of the Bible.* Translated by John Marson Dunaway.

Edward Baring and Peter E. Gordon, eds., *The Trace of God: Derrida and Religion.*

Vanessa Lemm, ed., *Nietzsche and the Becoming of Life.*

Aaron T. Looney, *Vladimir Jankélévitch: The Time of Forgiveness.*